Marius Petipa

М. И. ПЕТИПА.

М. РЕТІРА.

Marius Petipa

The Emperor's Ballet Master

NADINE MEISNER

OXFORD
UNIVERSITY PRESS

OXFORD
UNIVERSITY PRESS

Oxford University Press is a department of the University of Oxford. It furthers
the University's objective of excellence in research, scholarship, and education
by publishing worldwide. Oxford is a registered trade mark of Oxford University
Press in the UK and certain other countries.

Published in the United States of America by Oxford University Press
198 Madison Avenue, New York, NY 10016, United States of America.

Library of Congress Cataloging-in-Publication Data
Names: Meisner, Nadine, author.
Title: Marius Petipa : the emperor's ballet master / Nadine Meisner.
Description: New York : Oxford University Press, [2019] |
Includes bibliographical references and index.
Identifiers: LCCN 2018027086 (print) | LCCN 2018053235 (ebook) |
ISBN 9780190659301 (updf) | ISBN 9780190659318 (epub) |
ISBN 9780190659325 (oso) | ISBN 9780190659295 (cloth : alk. paper)
Subjects: LCSH: Petipa, Marius, 1818–1910. |
Choreographers—France—Biography. | Ballet dancers—France—Biography. |
Choreographers—Russia (Federation)—Biography. |
Ballet dancers—Russia (Federation)—Biography.
Classification: LCC GV1785.P42 (ebook) |
LCC GV1785.P42 M45 2019 (print) | DDC 792.8/2092 [B] —dc23
LC record available at https://lccn.loc.gov/2018027086

1 3 5 7 9 8 6 4 2

Printed by Sheridan Books, Inc., United States of America

For the absent, always present
mon papa, oncle *Jacques, Nicholas, John*

For the absent, always present
mon papa, oncle *Jacques, Nicholas, John*

Contents

Acknowledgements

MANY PEOPLE—FRIENDS, acquaintances, even strangers—have amazed me by their generosity and I don't know how best to list them. The only thing I do know is that I should begin with the Moscow dance historian Elizabeth Souritz, who too many years ago opened doors and initiated me into the dusty but addictive mysteries of Russian archives. She has supported and guided me and I owe her a lot.

My other thanks, in no particular order, go to: Anthony Cross and Simon Franklin in the Slavonic Studies Section at the University of Cambridge who didn't know what to make of me, but stood by me through thick and thin; Alexander Etkind, Masha Sutton, David Secher, Murray Frame, Lucia Ruprecht, Philip Bullock, and the balletomane-classicists Paul Cartledge and Fiona McIntosh. There are those who helped as international couriers and book-finders (Zhenia Shoenberg, Vera Rennie, and Sveta Dikaanidas), as translators from Spanish and German (Kathy Elgin, Heather Jones, Pam Wilkinson, and Jo Smith), as resourceful fixers (Jon Gray, editor of the *Dancing Times*, and Lena Kamenskaya), as encouragers and readers (Jenny Gilbert, Rosamund Bartlett, David Jays, Ann Nugent, Thomas Tuohy, Stefanie Fischer, the late Judith Percival, and Inès and Jean Zenati). I am also grateful to the following: Jane Pritchard for supplying me with information about the ballet master Joseph Hansen and more; Doug Fullington for his close knowledge of Petipa's choreography; Yelena Demikovsky for helping with some of the more perplexing phrases of Russian; Robert Greskovic and Alastair Macaulay; Jean-Philippe Van Aelbrouck who with spontaneous magnanimity handed me a memory-stick containing his conference paper about Petipa's family; Barry Wordsworth for trying to inculcate some musical understanding into my brain; Elena Goodwin; and the wonderful Galya Scott, who by coincidence knew Petipa's granddaughter Xenia and who spent countless hours proofreading the Cyrillic parts of this book.

There are many people to thank in St Petersburg and Moscow. In St Petersburg they include: the dance critic Igor Stupnikov; the director of the Mariinsky Theatre's Music Library Maria Shcherbakova; Irina Boglacheva who made my life immeasurably easier through her practical help as well as through her scholarly books;

Olga Pantaleeva; Lidia Ader; and Makbal Musina, dogged archive detective *extra-ordinaire*. The staff of the St Petersburg State Museum of Theatrical and Musical Art (GMTMI) have been wonderful: the director Natalia Metelitsa and her assistant Alexandra Shtarkman, the chief curator Tatiana Vlasova together with many other curators, so keen to share their enthusiasm, among them Sergei Laletin and especially Elena Fedosova, possessor of great ballet knowledge and insight. In Moscow, I will not forget the late Inessa Preobrazhenskaya in the manuscript department of the Bakshrushin State Theatre Museum (GTsTM); and I extend my thanks also to Xenia Iakovleva of the Russian State Archives of Literature and Art (RGALI), and Andrei Galkin.

In France, I received help from Élisabeth Guillaume, curator at the Archives de Nantes, Frédéric Laux at the Archives Bordeaux Métropole, Agnès Vatican at the Archives départementales de la Gironde, and the staff at the Bibliothèque municipale de Bordeaux.

In New York, I need to thank Lynn Garafola and Elizabeth Kendall. Laura Quinton did much archival research on Jean Petipa's New York season and unearthed important newspaper coverage. She worked in the New York Public Library for the Performing Arts, the New-York Historical Society, the Harvard Theatre Collection, and the Library of Congress, helped by expert archivists. I am additionally indebted to Lynn Garafola's immense scholarship in compiling a Petipa genealogy and list of Petipa's works, originally published in her edition of Petipa's diaries. These are indispensable aids which I have gratefully reproduced with slight modifications in this book. My OUP editor Norm Hirschy and his assistant Lauralee Yeary also have my sincere thanks, as does the project manager Rajesh Kathamuthu.

The financial help from the British Association of Slavic and East European Studies (BASEES) was a real boost, as was a fellowship from the Likhachev Foundation. The fellowship enabled me to spend an exhaustingly fruitful ten days in St Petersburg, buoyed by the dynamism and resourcefulness of Elena Vitenberg and Anna Shulgat.

Finally, I would like to salute the late, great Ivor Guest, explorer of the virgin territories of ballet history. His many books have accompanied me down the years and his erudition, made graceful by a compulsively readable style, has been a model to aspire to.

Style Notes

TRANSLITERATION IS A field littered with treacherous potholes and the glaring chasms of inconsistency. After much dithering, with the more general reader in mind, I have opted to retain the familiar flawed spellings for well-known names, with occasional deviations. For other Russian names and words, I have used a watered down (and unsystematic) version of the Library of Congress system; but for titles and words contained within brackets or in the endnotes and the bibliography, I have followed the full system fairly strictly, with an apostrophe for the Cyrillic soft sign, but without other diacritics.

For quotations translated in the text, the originals are reproduced in the endnotes, with modernized Cyrillic spelling.

The familiar titles of ballets are preferred (*La Bayadère* rather than *Baiaderka*), while less familiar titles, when needed, are translated into English. In contrast, book and newspaper titles remain in transliterated Russian. But please do not panic. English translations are provided in the bibliography.

For dates of events in Russia (but not elsewhere), I have kept to the Julian calendar used before 1918; this was eleven days behind the Western calendar in the eighteenth century, twelve days in the nineteenth, and thirteen days in the twentieth. I have, however, excluded the standard patronymic in Russian names, except for the Petipa family genealogy in the appendices.

National or folk dance on the ballet stage is often called character dance and I use the terms interchangeably. A character dancer can also denote a dancer performing character roles where there is emphasis on personality and mime.

The Spanish quotes were translated by Kathy Elgin, Heather Jones, and Jo Smith. All other translations are my own, except where stated.

Overture

On 24 May 1847, I reached St Petersburg by ship, and since that
time have been employed by the Imperial Theatre. Sixty years of
service in one place, in one institution, is quite rare, and a des-
tiny not granted to many mortals.[1]

MARIUS PETIPA'S DESTINY, it is true, was exceptional, even if he was only one
of many French artists and other foreigners who flocked to Russia because their
services were in high demand. For more than a century and a half, Russia had
been turning its gaze to the West, seeking to acquire the cultural apparatus that
would help transform it into a modern world power. When Petipa arrived in St
Petersburg he had the promise of a contract and the hope that he would make a
career, if not a fortune, although foreign dancers were rewarded with higher pay
than native Russians. He was twenty-nine, not so young for a dancer. In his suitcase were three scarves, packed by his anxious mother. 'She was,' he wrote, 'very
disturbed about the fate of my nose, which would have to bear the onslaught of
frosts so severe that even the bears could hardly stand them.'[2]

He arrived, however, in spring sunshine, not on 24 May, but six days later. (It
was his contract which was pre-dated 24 May and, in his elderly mind, Petipa conflated the two.)[3] The ship, Le Tage, which had travelled for ten days from Le Havre,
had anchored at Kronstadt, St Petersburg's main seaport, and a ferry took the
passengers the thirty kilometres to the customs house on Gagarin, now Kutuzova,
Quay (*naberezhnaia Kutuzova*). The journey had been pleasant, marked by the
happy acquaintance of Léontine Volnys, a reputable French actress accompanied
by her cheerful aunt who was doubling as her dresser.[4] At the customs house,
Petipa, feeling the heat, took off his hat and put it on a bench, before hurrying
to open his luggage and that of Madame Volnys who had asked him to help. 'We
will not examine the belongings of artists who have been invited to Russia for the
first time,' the customs officer said. (This was in marked contrast to the series of
interrogations endured by the French travel writer the Marquis de Custine eight
years earlier.)[5] Petipa, delighted, bowed and reached out for his hat—only to find it
gone. He turned this into a joke in his memoirs: 'Apparently it had tempted some

admirer of foreign things, who was happy to seize the opportunity to acquire it, not only without paying any duty, but absolutely free.'[6]

This contretemps was soon overtaken by bewilderment when the travellers exited the customs house. They had taken the precaution of asking the ship's captain to recommend a hotel—the Hotel Klee on Mikhailovsky Street (*Mikhailovskaia ulitsa*), the site of today's Grand Hotel Europa—and now they needed transport. The city's *drozhkis*, however, were more like backless benches on wheels.[7] (Petipa describes them as *guitars*.)[8] Madame Volnys was rather alarmed, unable to imagine how to sit, until one of the drivers demonstrated how men sit astride and women side-saddle. Petipa, always gallant, helped Madame Volnys on to one *drozhki* and placed her aunt and himself on another, securing the aunt, who was very large, by holding her round the waist. The pair made a comical picture, especially as Petipa had tied a kerchief round his bare head against the sun. As they made their way the short distance along Nevsky Prospect, Madame Volnys was overcome by giggles, which soon spread to her companions and even, it seems, to passers-by.

Such was the joyous entry into the city 'which', Petipa writes, 'was to prove so hospitable to me'.[9] The next day, dressed in white tie and tails, he hurried to the directorate of Imperial Theatres, just a few hundred yards away. He had been invited to St Petersburg at the suggestion of the company's chief ballet master, Antoine Titus Dauchy, known simply as Titus, to replace the French dancer Émile Gredelue who after ten years in Russia had returned home.[10] In the event he saw Titus's superior, the director of Imperial Theatres, Alexander Gedeonov, and signed a standard contract, dated 24 May 1847, as a *premier danseur* and mime. It was designated for one year, with a two-year renewal option if agreed by the directorate.[11]

Petipa would remain in Russia up to his death sixty-three years later. During that time he became the century's greatest choreographer, recognized as a genius by his adopted country. His achievement owed as much to tirelessly industrious ambition as to his genes and background. (His father Jean was a prominent ballet master.) But he was also the right person in the right place, implanted in a cultural setting where artistic imaginations, under the emperor's often generous gaze, were more indulged than elsewhere.

He died in Gurzuf, near Yalta, on 1 July 1910, a victim of pneumonia, brought on by chronic bronchitis. Three days later the following appeared in *Peterburgskaia gazeta*:

> **YALTA, 3 July (by telegraph). His Majesty's soloist Marius Ivanovich Petipa has passed away in Gurzuf. The body will be taken to St Petersburg for burial.**

So goes to his grave Marius Ivanovich Petipa. With just reason, he could have said: 'Russian Ballet—is me.' He gave it all his strength, creativity, artistic talent. For sixty years he ceaselessly choreographed and staged ballet after ballet, he nurtured Russian dancers who perfected themselves and flourished under the guidance of this true choreographer.[12]

As an established dance historian and critic, the bulletin's writer Alexander Pleshcheev had known Petipa well. Given Petipa's French origins, it was a neat turn of phrase to write 'Russian Ballet—is me', echoing Louis XIV's apocryphal dictum 'L'État—c'est moi'. Louis XIV, himself a dancer, had founded French ballet with the Académie royale de danse. Petipa did not found anything, but it is largely thanks to him that an existing company and school became the greatest in the world. As tends to happen with long careers, though, he outlived his time. In his final years he became an embittered old man, a relic, put out to pasture by the promoters of a modernist age, although he retained his title as first ballet master to the end. Since his death, however, he has become the world's most performed choreographer. On any day *Swan Lake* (Lebedinoe ozero) and *The Sleeping Beauty* (Spiashchaia krasavitsa), to scores by Petr Tchaikovsky, are playing somewhere on stage or screen, while others—*La Bayadère* (Baiaderka), *Don Quixote*, the 'Grand Pas from *Paquita*'—although lesser known, have become popular constituents of many ballet repertoires.

The longevity of his tenure and quantity of his output remain unsurpassed by anyone except his twentieth-century successor George Balanchine. In his career with the St Petersburg Imperial Ballet, he served four emperors, was chief ballet master for forty-one years, created more than fifty original ballets, staged versions of nineteen other ballets, and made dances for thirty-seven operas.[13] Among the extant ballets, *La Bayadère* is considered to contain unparalleled, groundbreaking choreography. He built a repertoire, developed a style (albeit under certain pressures), and shaped a company of dancers which would exert an enormous influence on ballet everywhere. When his pupil Anna Pavlova appeared in London days after his death, the London *Times* wrote:

> Nothing like it has been seen before in the London of our time. There was, to be sure, the delightful Genée, with her gaiety and brilliance, and there was the seductive posturing of Isadora Duncan and Maud Allan.[14] But Pavlova and the Russian dancers of the present moment [...] have given us Londoners something really new: an extraordinary technical accomplishment, an unfailing sense of rhythm, an unerring feeling for the elegant in fantasy, and what Hazlitt would have called a 'gusto', a passionate enjoyment. The dancing of Anna Pavlova is a thing of perfect beauty. This is no case of Mr Pepys and his 'best legs that ever I saw'. In the presence of art of this stamp one's pleasure is purely aesthetic. Indeed, the sex-element (though of course necessarily somewhere in the subconscious) counts for

very little: for a man the dancing of M. Mordkin is *almost* as pleasure-giving as that of Mlle. Pavlova. The combination of the two, above all in their bacchanalian dance, is an even choicer thing than their *pas seuls*. Quite as much of a novelty to Londoners is the dancing of the troupe. The freedom and swing of their limbs in the mazurka almost lures you from your seat to 'shake a leg' with them; but you sit quite still while they are alternately quickening up and slowing down in the *tempo rubato* of the 'Rhapsodie hongroise', seeing clearly that here is something you couldn't do to save your life. This is a very different thing from the ballet to which Londoners used once upon a time to be mercilessly subjected—rank after rank and file after file of honest bread-winners from Camberwell and Peckham Rye with the dogged perseverance of a company of Boy Scouts. When people tell you, as they sometimes will, that ballet dancing is a bore, you recognize the trail of the honest British bread-winners.[15]

o o o o o

AS A REVERED public figure, Petipa's activities, awards, and illnesses were chronicled by the Russian press. Yet his name was not so well known elsewhere, even in his native country. There, his elder brother Lucien, star of the Paris Opera and Albrecht at the 1841 premiere of the iconic *Giselle*, was more famous. The reason for Marius's relative obscurity has to be the unequal traffic of dance between East and West. While foreign dancers, teachers, and ballet masters streamed into Russia, their Russian counterparts only occasionally made the reverse journey. This was unsurprising in the eighteenth century when ballet was a new import into Russia. Moreover an art form takes time to become fully implanted, and nineteenth-century Russia continued to rely on foreigners. Ballets created in Paris were quickly transferred to Russian stages; but ballets created in Russia were mostly the work of foreigners and remained in Russia.

What foreign ballet masters and teachers could do, however, was mould performers; and by the beginning of the nineteenth century, Russia had some strong dancers of its own. Even so they seldom travelled abroad. True, from the 1840s to the 1860s a handful of Russian ballerinas did appear in foreign capitals: the 'Russian Taglionis' Tatiana Smirnova, Elena Andreianova, and, from Moscow, Ekaterina Sankovskaya; also, Nadezhda Bogdanova and Marfa Muraveva. Many of their Paris performances were documented by the reviews of the poet and writer Théophile Gautier.[16] The half-French St Petersburg ballerina Zinaida (Zina) Richard moved to the Paris Opera in 1857, and, being not only extremely pretty but technically strong, danced leading roles there.[17] She guested in London at Covent Garden the following year and in 1861 married the Paris Opera's *premier danseur* Louis Mérante. (He became first ballet master and wears a stylish white suit in

Degas's 1872 painting *Le Foyer de la danse à l'Opéra*.) In 1861, 1862, and 1863 Petipa arranged for his first wife, Mariia Surovshchikova-Petipa, to appear in Paris at the Opera, in Riga, and in Berlin. For the first Paris performances he and his brother Lucien adapted a one-act ballet he had choreographed two years earlier in St Petersburg—*The Parisian Market* (Parizhskii rynok) which was renamed *Le Marché des Innocents*, after a well-known market in central Paris. Premiered on 29 May 1861, with Surovshchikova-Petipa in the central role she had created in St Petersburg, this became the first Russian ballet to be exported to the Paris Opera stage.[18]

By the end of the nineteenth century, occasional groups from the St Petersburg company were winning much applause in Central European cities, Monte Carlo, and Paris. But essentially it was the Paris launch of Sergei Diaghilev's Ballets Russes in 1909 that woke Western audiences to Russian ballet. The dancers included Vaslav Nijinsky, Anna Pavlova, Tamara Karsavina, and Adolph Bolm, and it was clear that the Russians had now far outstripped the foreigners who had been their teachers and models.

The artistic explosion that was the Ballet Russes' first season notwithstanding, Petipa's death a year later went unnoticed outside Russia. There was a flurry of tributes in Russian newspapers, but nothing in the London *Times*. The Paris *Figaro* reported the death on 16 July of the Swiss painter Albert Anker, but failed to notice a fellow countryman.

o o o o o

PETIPA WAS THE creator of a distinct pre-revolutionary repertoire that shaped twentieth-century ballet not only in Russia, but across the world. Inside Russia he was the father of a style that was preserved and developed by the Soviet regime—an unlikely alliance given ballet's close imperial associations. Yet, although there were occasional ideological skirmishes and casualties on the way, Petipa's classical ballet emerged as a triumphant survivor. Not only that, it became the supreme emblem of Soviet culture from 1956 onwards, able to vault over linguistic boundaries and be paraded in the West as an emblem of national artistic excellence.

Outside Russia, Petipa's legacy would also have far-reaching repercussions. As a representative of the old artistic order, he was fair game for the new generation at the turn of the century; as the target for rebellion, his impact on the reformist aesthetic of the Ballets Russes was therefore indirect. But he also directly fathered the company: he had shaped and inspired many of its dance artists; some of his choreography—notwithstanding its *ancien régime* focus—was included in the repertoire. Without the traditions and training of the St Petersburg school and company, this expatriate company, which only ever performed outside Russia, could never have been launched.

The Ballets Russes created shock waves that even now are still apparent. Its first Paris season shattered the etiolated image that Western ballet had acquired in the second half of the nineteenth century. From its twenty-year existence emerged several pioneers.[19] One of these was Marie Rambert, the founder of Britain's first ballet company, named after her.[20] Another was Ninette de Valois, whose own company, the Vic-Wells Ballet, would become the Royal Ballet.[21] She imported Petipa's ballets, and his versions of existing ballets, to form the foundation stones of her company's repertoire where they remain to this day. A third pioneer was Balanchine, the co-founder of New York City Ballet, who in so many ways was the spiritual son of Petipa. He took Petipa's style and transmuted it into the signature classicism of twentieth-century American ballet; and although Petipa never fully discarded narrative, Balanchine took Petipa's emphasis on exquisitely wrought passages of choreography, able to stand as a self-sufficient poetic language, to its logical extension of plotlessness.

○ ○ ○ ○ ○

IN 1896, GIORGIO Saracco staged the Petipa-Tchaikovsky *Sleeping Beauty* (1890) at La Scala, Milan, and in subsequent decades there appeared other stagings, in other locations, of Petipa's ballets and productions, often in abbreviated form. But it took a while for his ballets to become widely popular in the West. In 1921 the Ballets Russes premiered their notoriously luxurious version of *The Sleeping Beauty*, renamed *The Sleeping Princess*, which put the company heavily into debt, and in 1932 Ninette de Valois, with the former *régisseur* of the St Petersburg company Nikolai Sergeyev, mounted the first lakeside scene of *Swan Lake* for the Vic-Wells Ballet, presenting the full ballet in 1934.[22] Now Petipa's work is everywhere, yet most of his ballets are actually missing. The performances so widely spread on today's stages represent only a fraction of his oeuvre.

The inescapable fact, well known to regular ballet-goers, is that ballet before the twentieth century was an ephemeral art. Unlike opera, there was no written text to lean on and attempts to devise a notation system made little headway until the 1890s. Given there was no film or video either, the only method of conservation was person-to-person transmission, fallible, unreliable, short-term. The consequence is that the large body of work by the nineteenth-century's most eminent choreographers—among them, Charles-Louis Didelot, Jules Perrot, Marius Petipa, all Frenchmen who worked for substantial periods in Russia—is mostly lost.[23]

Being the oldest, the biggest victim is Didelot, Russia's first great ballet master (he worked in St Petersburg in 1801–1811 and 1816–1833). All his ballets have evaporated despite his talent, his fame—in London, especially, as well as in St Petersburg—and the poet Alexander Pushkin's famous description of him as 'crowned with glory'.[24] Perrot has suffered a similar fate, although at least some of his choreography does remain in modern productions of *Giselle* and *Esmeralda*, an issue to be discussed later. Petipa, being the youngest, has the greatest number of surviving ballets, but they are in more or less altered form, even in recent attempts to reconstruct more authentic versions. The roots of this gradual distortion lie not just in the Chinese Whispers frailty of transmission, but, just as crucial, in dance's unique reliance on the human body. Choreography needs a dancer's body to come to life, but each body is different, better or less able to perform movements created on someone else. As a result ballets (before the stricter ownership rules of the twentieth century) have had to endure subsequent 'improvers', wanting to simplify, complicate, or just embellish. Moreover, even when a text remains untouched, the manner of performance will change over time with fashion. We will never truly, completely, know how Petipa's ballets looked.

If there have been recent attempts to reconstruct more authentic versions, this is because Petipa does have one advantage: towards the end of his life, twenty-one of his ballets and productions, plus individual dances from ballets and operas, were notated using a new system developed by a young dancer in the St Petersburg company, Vladimir Stepanov. The notations, now preserved in the Harvard Theatre Collection, were written down by the *régisseur* Sergeyev and his two assistants and vary considerably in detail, none being truly comprehensive and some being no more than *aides-mémoires*. But when Sergeyev left Russia in 1918 and took these notations with him, they became important reference points for his work staging ballets in the West, notably the Ballets Russes *Sleeping Princess* and Ninette de Valois's productions for the Vic-Wells Ballet.[25] Today therefore they have become valuable sources for reconstructions by producers such as the late Sergei Vikharev and Alexei Ratmansky.[26]

Petipa has another advantage over his predecessors, which is an abundance of photographs and sketches. There are drawings for set and costume designs; there are photographs of ballets on stage and the performers in them, although most of the close-ups of the latter are studio poses, not action shots. There are also many photographs of Petipa himself and his family.

Contemporary written records of Petipa's work also provide useful information. Dance had a moderately consistent presence in the Russian press, and in the earlier part of Petipa's career articles appeared at fairly regular intervals, penned in St Petersburg by reviewers such as Rafail Zotov, Fedor Koni, and Mavrikii Rappaport.[27] Coverage increased as the century advanced, the extra column space being a reflection of the growing popularity of theatre-going.[28] Among the writers at this later stage were Konstantin Skalkovsky, Nikolai Bezobrazov, and Alexander Pleshcheev.[29] On 2 December 1896 the first interview with Petipa appeared in *Peterburgskaia gazeta*. This and subsequent interviews are remarkable for their direct questions and equally direct answers and form a contrast with the rather woolly reviews of performances. It is not that reviewers lacked knowledge or interest; on the contrary, they were ballet specialists who pursued their work with dedication and passion. Supported by their editors, they were even known to review a ballet several times, so as to focus on different angles; when the score was by a concert-hall composer they sometimes shared the reviewing with a music critic. The problem rather is one of convention, frustrating to a present-day dance historian. Reviews might give priority to an over-detailed description of plot, or spend precious lines enumerating the gifts offered to the performers. Although opinions about policies, say, are expressed trenchantly, any analysis of choreography or performance tends to be couched in imprecise and formulaic language. Perhaps most frustrating is the focus on the ballerina, reflecting her primacy during much of the nineteenth century. The men get barely a mention, even hugely popular and respected performers such as Pavel Gerdt, whose career spanned sixty-two years.

More revealing are the books that were published during Petipa's lifetime, although, regrettably, in Russia as elsewhere dance historiography arrived late on the scene. It was only in 1882 that Konstantin Skalkovsky (as *Baletoman*) wrote Russian ballet's first history, *Balet: Ego istoriia i mesto v riadu iziashchnykh iskusstv*, following this (under his real name) with *V teatral'nom mire: Nabliudeniia, vospominaniia, i rassuzhdeniia* (1899). Both books provide evaluations of ballets, ballerinas, and dance issues of the day written in Skalkovsky's often droll, vivid style. Pleshcheev's *Nash balet* (1896) is a heavyweight, factually informative chronicle. Also invaluable is the Yearbook of the Imperial Theatres, *Ezhegodnik imperatorskikh teatrov*, launched in 1890, which provides an exhaustive annual audit of repertoire and staff, as well as descriptive overviews and articles, up to its demise in 1915.

Other written sources present a real mixed bag. Petipa's daughter Vera drafted an unpublished and undated memoir, *Moia sem'ia: Petipa v zhizni i iskusstve*, which, although just thirty-three pages long, does offer illuminating details about family life.[30] Petipa himself was an unstoppable note taker: he sketched out his choreographic ideas and floor plans; he set down details of dances, librettos, designs, and dancers; he wrote constant reminders to himself. However, these papers are more useful as pointers to the practicalities of ballet production, even if they do provide a wonderful insight into the meticulous way Petipa worked.[31] Other personal documents are in short supply. There are letters, but not vast bundles. Petipa, it seems, routinely kept a diary, but only a couple of notebooks survive, published in various forms, the fullest being an English translation edited, with an invaluable preface, by Lynn Garafola and a recent French volume edited by Pascale Melani.[32] The notebooks start on New Year's Day 1903 and, with interruptions for the summers of 1903 and 1905, run up to 31 December 1905; they then pick up again in mid-March 1907, when Petipa left St Petersburg for Gurzuf, and end on 14 July. The loss of other probable notebooks is particularly frustrating since even these few offer tantalizing glimpses. Although the entries are brief, they indicate the timing of certain events and provide direct access into both family life and Petipa's mind; the entries for 1903 and 1904 show him still working, still coaching, despite the active hostility of the new director of Imperial Theatres, Vladimir Teliakovsky, and make clear, as Garafola says, Petipa's 'formative influence on dancers of the early Diaghilev period'.[33]

Then there is Petipa's autobiography, *Memuary Mariusa Petipa, solista ego imperatorskogo velichestva i baletmeistera imperatorskikh teatrov*, which could have been so much more. It was published in 1906 when he was eighty-eight and is not only remarkably short, but distorted by a failing memory, so that the chronology is erratic and the facts approximate, to put it mildly.[34] The Russian translation of the original French flattens Petipa's style; the text is tainted by the anxious, defensive egocentricity of a formerly powerful man who feels that he has been shunted into a siding. His last performed ballet, *The Magic Mirror* (Volshebnoe zerkalo), premiered on 9 February 1903, had been a catastrophic failure; his arch-enemy Teliakovsky had then effectively manoeuvred him out of the theatre. Distraught by what was happening to him, obsessed by the need to demonstrate his worth, Petipa's state of mind skews and mangles the last chapters of his book. Indeed, he explicitly states that he was spurred to start writing in order to launch a counterattack against Teliakovsky.[35] The pseudonymous reviewer Nikolai Negorev rightly judged the book a missed opportunity: 'A person who has served in Russia for sixty years, could have talked a great deal about the conditions of theatre work. But unfortunately the actual memoirs of Petipa occupy only one third of the book; two thirds consists of rebukes towards the present director of the Imperial Theatres, V. A. Teliakovsky, who has cruelly wounded the venerable ballet master.'[36] (Actually, Negorev exaggerates: the proportion is the other way round, with one-third devoted to settling scores.)

Offsetting this disappointment are the memoirs of people who worked with Petipa: most notably, the ballerina Ekaterina Vazem, whose detailed recollections, dating from the early 1870s, go further back than anybody else's; Alexander Shiriaev, assistant to Petipa, who provides much information about how Petipa worked; and Teliakovsky who, in his memoirs and diaries, documents the turbulent politics of life in the theatre and outside it, including the events surrounding the 1905 uprising and march on the Winter Palace.[37] Other memoirs, such as those by the ballerina Matilda Kshesinskaya, offer brief but sometimes telling glimpses.[38] And finally there are the Imperial Theatres' official dossiers in St Petersburg about Petipa's employment: a repository of contracts, letters, and memos with complaints, requests, proposals, and details of travel.[39]

At the end of 1896 Petipa's imminent half-century of service prompted profiles in a number of publications, followed by another batch for his sixty years, including one by Alexander Pleshcheev, published both as a separate booklet and in the May 1907 edition of *Istoricheskii vestnik*. The two decades after Petipa's death saw a trio of brief monographs, centenary tributes by Denis Leshkov, M. Iakovlev, and by I. Ivanov and K. Ivanov.[40] The journalist and librettist Sergei Khudekov, a former collaborator of Petipa, wrote his four-volume *Istoriia tantsev* which was published in 1913–1918 and contains, in the final volume, important sections about Petipa's work.[41] However, it was not until 1971 that the first substantial monograph on Petipa appeared: *Marius Petipa. Materialy, vospominaniia, stat'i*, edited by Anna Nekhendzi. This is a collection of testimonies, analytical essays, and archival materials, including a partial re-translation of Petipa's memoirs, the first published extracts (in Russian) of Petipa's surviving diaries, and an abridgement of Vera Petipa's unpublished memoir, listed above. Then came another long gap, before the publication in 2006 of *Baletmeister Marius Petipa. Stat'i, issledovaniia, razmyshleniia*, edited by Olga Fedorchenko; most of the essays in this important collection focus on individual ballets, a few others, on individual persons. But we had to wait until 2015 for the first single-author biography, Marina Ilicheva's *Neizvestnyj Petipa*, a welcome arrival—except that it covers only the first fifty years of Petipa's life. (Perhaps another volume is in the pipeline.)

In the West the literature is no more plentiful, although, in addition to Garafola's version of the diaries, Petipa's memoirs were published in English as *Russian Ballet Master: The Memoirs of Marius Petipa* (1956), edited by Lillian Moore.[42] There is a 1975 German edition of Nekhendzi's crucial 1971 collection of source materials and essays, and a 1990 abridged French version.[43] And there are translated extracts from Russian Petipa literature, including some of the books mentioned above, published in English-language specialist journals.[44] English speakers also owe a colossal debt to the musicologist Roland John Wiley, whose *Tchaikovsky's Ballets: Swan Lake, Sleeping Beauty, Nutcracker* and *Life and Ballets of Lev Ivanov* (Petipa's deputy) are essential and pioneering contributions. Equally indispensable are the source materials collected by Wiley with annotations in *A Century of Russian Ballet: Documents and Eye Witness Accounts, 1810–1910*.

Two substantial publications have arrived in this century. Laura Hormigón's Spanish-language *Marius Petipa in Spain 1844–1847* not only reproduces some of the materials (including the memoirs) in *Marius Petipa: Materialy, vospominaniia, stat'i*, but also publishes the results of her scrupulous searches in French and Spanish archives, all of which illuminate hitherto unknown details of Petipa's life before Russia. A French book, *De la France à la Russie, Marius Petipa*, edited by Pascale Melani, brings together the wide-ranging proceedings of a conference dedicated to Petipa, held in Bordeaux (where he once worked) in 2015.

Finally, in this the bicentenary of Petipa's birth, has come news of two other new Russian publications: Iulia Iakovleva's *Sozdateli i zriteli. Russkie balety epokhi shedevrov*, which surveys Petipa's work in a wider context of Russian ballet and its public; and *Balety M. I. Petipa v Moskve*, edited by Iurii Burlaka and Marina Leonova, which examines Petipa's contributions to the Moscow stage. I discovered these books too late to read them, but I have included them in the bibliography for other researchers and readers. I was, though, able to read another last-minute arrival, *Marius Petipa. 'Memuary' i dokumenty*, which is an annotated edition of Petipa's memoirs reproducing both the published 1906 Russian-language version and the surviving pages of the French manuscript. The editor Sergei Konaev's exhaustive commentary has enabled me to make a number of important modifications to my text, for which I am immeasurably grateful.

◦ ◦ ◦ ◦ ◦

TO MY KNOWLEDGE no full-length biographical study has yet been published and this book is an attempt to fill the lacuna.[45] There are, however, many things it does not do. It does not even try to examine all of Petipa's works, given their unnerving quantity, and it ignores his dances for opera. Nor does it attempt to offer a forensic, scientific analysis of Petipa's aesthetics or compositional procedures; and it most certainly steers clear of musico-choreographical analysis—well outside this writer's scope. It does not direct a piercing, X-ray gaze on Tchaikovsky's ballets either, since that has already been done by more competent specialists.

Rather, this study chooses to focus on other works, especially if they are accompanied by ample archival material. It proposes an overview, touching down on certain topics for more detail. It aims to place Petipa in his context, describing the times he lived in and the people and places around him, although, alas, it neglects Moscow, just as the directorate of Imperial Theatres neglected Moscow throughout the nineteenth century. It is intended to serve as a general introduction, able to serve as a stepping stone for further research, and it is in this spirit that the endnotes, especially, have been conceived, as signposts pointing to further ways ahead.

The structure of this book is not entirely chronological. There are flashbacks covering Petipa's life before Russia and his father Jean's career (chapters 2 and 4) and fast-forwards in the sections dealing with aesthetic issues, to summon future ballets as illustrations. This will not, I hope, be disorienting for the reader, but will read as smoothly and naturally as intended.

I

Prologue

To win applause for a dance, in St Petersburg, is not easy.
Russians are great ballet connoisseurs and the glare of their
opera glasses is fearsome.[1]

The St Petersburg Stage

When Petipa arrived in St Petersburg, Nicholas I was emperor, serfdom had not been abolished, and Italian opera was all the craze. The Imperial Italian Opera received substantial financing from the court and, when in 1843 it moved into the *Bolshoi* (Big) Theatre, it joined the ballet and displaced the German and Russian opera companies. (Both were eventually banished to Moscow.) With its glitter of celebrities—Giovanni Battista Rubini, Pauline Viardot, Antonio Tamburini—it often trumped ballet in the public's enthusiasm.[2]

Even so, the ballet company had an important following, led by the emperor himself, and was by any measure an ensemble of outstanding quality. It was not so different from the company which made a huge impression on Gautier when he made his seven-month trip in 1858 and on his return wrote *Voyage en Russie*. Not everything pleased Gautier in St Petersburg, however. He thought the city's monumental classical facades looked out of place and unhappy: they were Grecian edifices longing for their native sun and shivering under the snow. He would have preferred less derivative architectures more closely linked to their Russian setting and climate. But about everything else he was volubly enthusiastic. The Bolshoi had a colossal grandeur rivalling La Scala; the immense square in front of the theatre provided easy access for all the coaches; the glass-fronted vestibules at the front formed a barrier against the freezing outside air to keep the auditorium beautifully warm; and veteran soldiers in uniform waited for you at the entrance to take your coats, furs, and galoshes, and returned them without ever mixing their owners up. Equally impressive was the audience, the men wearing the obligatory white tie and tails or military dress, the women with elegant *décolletées* and bare arms. The stalls (*parterre*) were divided down the centre by a wide aisle and bordered by a circular one: this was a practical arrangement, adopted by other European capitals except Paris, allowing you to reach your seat with minimum inconvenience to others. However, where in most theatres the royal box was usually positioned close to the stage, here it was directly opposite, its high opening cutting in half not one but two levels of seating. Sculpted above it, in full heraldic glory, was the imperial double-headed eagle, surrounded by exuberant decorative flourishes, the gilded curlicues catching the glow of the chandeliers in a thousand twinkling pinpoints.[3] 'A profusion of velvet, gold, light, what more do you need?'[4]

One surprise was that the stalls were the preferred place for persons (usually men) of distinction, not the boxes (apart from the imperial box, of course), although these might well be occupied by the wives and families of the same persons of distinction. The stalls were divided into a hierarchical seating plan that was tacitly agreed and rigidly observed: in the first three rows, only ministers, the highest-ranking officers, ambassadors, and perhaps a famous titled foreigner were allowed; in the fourth, the palette broadened to include bankers, certain civil servants, foreigners, artists; a merchant would not dare to venture further up than the fifth or sixth. This classification, Gautier concluded, must have seemed normal in Russia where Peter the Great's Table of Ranks effectively divided educated society into fourteen distinct categories. The ballerina Ekaterina Vazem, who created roles in many of Petipa's ballets, painted a later picture of the Bolshoi audience in the 1860s–1870s:

> The auditorium at the Bolshoi Theatre had a very dressed-up appearance and created an extremely animated picture. Although the Italian opera was at that time considered the most fashionable theatre for gatherings of the *beau monde*, and as a group ballet spectators outwardly seemed as if humbler than the 'Italians', the ballet auditorium, even so, yielded little to the 'Italians', especially at benefit performances. The first row of the *parterre* was chiefly occupied by Guards officers—cavalry and horse-guards—who placed their copper helmets or white caps in front of them on the barrier separating the seats from the orchestra. In their midst civilians stood out like dark patches. [...]
>
> Foreign diplomats often came to the ballet. Especially zealous in their ballet visits were the Spanish envoy, the Marques de Campo Sagrado, and his Italian counterpart, Count Greppi. The first stood out by an uncommon corpulence. He did not fit into a theatre seat and they always placed a small sofa equivalent to two seats in the front row for him. Conversely, Greppi was very thin and during their conversations together they made a very comical picture.
>
> Besides the aristocrats a significant part of the ballet public consisted of the well-off bourgeoisie—railway chiefs, factory owners, directors of banks and public companies, tax collectors. The male section usually showed little of note in its external appearance, but the ladies stood out greatly with

the splendour of their outfits and valuable jewellery. Not for nothing in the old days the *bel-étage* [grand tier or dress circle] of the Bolshoi Theatre was called 'the diamond row', where they liked to sit in state, especially at benefit evenings and other exceptional performances.[5]

The Bolshoi's stage had sophisticated machinery, allowing the speedy transfer of the latest ballets shown in Western Europe. Gautier refers to how 'the flights through the air, the disappearances, the transformations, the play of electric light and all the technical devices demanded by a complicated mise en scène are mobilized with the most assured promptness.'[6] Other writers besides Gautier remarked on the Bolshoi's lavish production values, although it must be noted that the theatre's machinists were aided by the stage's enormous depth, which added a dramatic perspective.[7] *Sankt-Peterburgskie vedomosti* describes how, when Joseph Mazilier's *Le Corsaire* was imported from Paris in 1858, the machinists, headed by Andrei Roller, met the challenge of its signature shipwreck scene with alacrity.[8] 'The battling of the ship with the waves, the rending of the sails, the collapse of the masts with sailors on the rigging and finally the sinking of the ship beneath the stormy waters inspired real fear in the audience. Roller surpassed himself and everyone who had seen the ballet in Paris awarded him the palm over the machinists of the Paris Opera. Extraordinarily effective also in this scene was the lightning that flashed through the clouds, blazing up and illuminating the whole stage.'[9]

Ballet performances at the Bolshoi took place three times a week and were not only spectacular, they were lengthier and more elaborate than in the West. From 1850 onwards ballets occupied a full evening rather than being bolted to an opera or play, as was still the case in Paris up to 1861.[10] 'As the dancing has to make up the whole programme,' Gautier writes, 'ballets have a more elaborate structure than on our stage: they run for up to four or five acts, with many scenes and scenery changes, or else they give two ballets in the same evening.'[11]

Finally, there were the dancers. There were the foreign celebrities, of course, who, like their operatic counterparts, were persuaded—albeit often a little late in their careers—to make the long journey. 'By dint of roubles and a warm welcome, the illusory fear of a loss of voice or of rheumatisms was vanquished. No throat, no knee has suffered in this land of snow where you see the cold without feeling it.'[12] The year (1858) that Gautier was in Russia the Italian virtuosa of the Paris Opera Ballet Amalia Ferraris made her Russian debut in a new lengthened version of Jules Perrot's *Éoline, ou la Dryade*. But Gautier was also attentive to the St Petersburg dancers: 'Their dance school produces remarkable soloists and a corps de ballet which has no equal for its unison, precision and rapidly evolving patterns. It is a pleasure to see such straight lines, such clear-cut groups which dissolve exactly at the required moment to reform in another shape; all those small feet which touch down in perfect time, all those choreographed battalions which are never ruffled or muddled in their manoeuvres!'[13] The impression made on Gautier would have been all the stronger in comparison with Paris's own ensemble dancers, men and women, who (along with the opera chorus) had earlier provoked the *Journal des théâtres* to exclaim: 'It is incredible that such inadequacy should be displayed before an élite public on the world's leading stage.'[14] But then the Petersburg dancers received four hundred roubles a month, approximately equivalent to one thousand six hundred francs, way out of the league of a Paris dancer. As Gautier remarked tartly in *La Presse*: 'It is not when you earn sixty francs a month that you can devote much time to dance.'[15]

According to figures for 1857–1858, the St Petersburg ballet received the largest subsidy (193,448 roubles), more than the French drama company (179,150 roubles) and the Italian opera (123,448 roubles). It staged sixty-five new ballets and acquisitions from 1855 to 1881, an annual average of two-and-a-half company premieres, all created by foreigners. There are no figures for the size of the company during the same period—or at least none that could be found. Later, when statistics for the ballet personnel were published in the newly founded *Yearbook of Imperial Theatres*, the first volume showed that dancers for the 1890–1891 season numbered 143 female dancers and 69 male: a total of 212, almost one-third bigger than today's Paris Opera Ballet (146) and two-and-a-half times as big as the Royal Ballet (86).[16]

At the time of Gautier's visit, Perrot had been in St Petersburg some seven years, replacing his elderly French compatriot Titus as first ballet master. He had arrived as the best—and best paid—choreographer of his generation, the unattributed co-creator of *Giselle* whose libretto was part-written by his friend, Gautier. But Perrot had not much longer to go before being also replaced by another famous Frenchman, Arthur Saint-Léon, in 1860. He, in turn, would be replaced by Petipa nine years later. Being French, but not an international celebrity, Petipa only half-matched the pattern. Humbler foreigners like him were attracted to the St Petersburg Imperial Theatres by their reputation for offering conditions (including preferential pay) that equalled or surpassed the best anywhere. The Bolshoi's chief machinist-designer Andrei (Andreas) Roller, for example, was German. The ballet's staff composer was an Italian, Cesare Pugni, appointed in 1851, because Perrot wanted his longtime collaborator at his side.[17] Male dancers, victims of the growing feminization of ballet in Western Europe, to the point that women *en travesti* sometimes played male parts, came to Russia for the opportunities that were lacking elsewhere.[18]

The line of foreign ballet masters and dancers, mainly Italian and French, which Petipa followed was a long one, stretching back to the eighteenth century. Foreigners were deemed indispensable, the possessors of superior expertise, since ballet—like opera and drama—was a Western import, developed in the eighteenth and nineteenth centuries when Russian culture, for the most part, looked to Western fashions and models.

The Founding of Russian Ballet

The urge to emulate the West was the legacy of Peter the Great (1682–1725), the Westernizer who had forced men to shave their beards and bring their women out of seclusion into the wider world. He had imposed his vast programme of reforms even if it meant hauling his country by the scruff of the neck and clambering over the corpses of the thousands who perished in the building of his Western-style capital St Petersburg.[19]

Ballet came much later to Russia than the rest of Europe. Elsewhere, ballet and opera (the two were originally merged) had their roots in the court spectacles of the Renaissance. These began in Italy, but soon appeared in France, and in them dance was mixed with singing, declamation, and impressive decorative effects. In Russia, the year 1738 is generally taken to mark the beginning of ballet; it is the date when Empress Anna Ioannovna agreed to the foundation of a school. She had been petitioned by Jean-Baptiste Landé, a French dancing master who arrived at the tail end of a stream of foreign dancing masters employed to teach the European social dances imposed on a reluctant gentry by Peter the Great. Early ballet was not so different from social dancing and Landé became director of the school whose first pupils, history says, were the children of palace servants, handpicked by the empress herself.

The school provided the material for a group of trained dancers, performing on an ad hoc basis at court, as part of evenings with opera or drama. Foreign and Russian troupes not only continued to appear at court, but also outside it, in privately owned theatres, accessible to the general public and organized, for the most part, by foreigners. To manage the court theatre activities Catherine the Great founded in 1766 the directorate of Imperial Theatres, the administrative structure which would employ Petipa in the next century.[20] She also had the enormous 2,000-seat Stone (*Kamennyi*) Theatre erected in 1783, the directorate of Imperial Theatre's first permanent public theatre building for drama, opera, and ballet.[21] This was the theatre described by Gautier, also known by his time as the Bolshoi because it had been rebuilt on several occasions and made even bigger. The immense square on which it stood had six pavilions where bonfires were lit to warm the coachmen waiting long hours in the bitter cold.[22] Already then, as now, this location was called Theatre Square (*Teatral'naia ploshchad'*), but today the site of the Bolshoi is occupied by the Rimsky-Korsakov State Conservatoire, opposite the Mariinsky Theatre which was built in 1860.

When Petipa arrived the Imperial Theatres' domain in St Petersburg encompassed ballet, opera, several orchestras, French and German theatre, Russian theatre, and the school which had grown to include drama, music, and singing divisions. Ballet pupils were accepted between the ages of nine and twelve. Those who, with time, were deemed unpromising were returned to their parents if they were not older than thirteen; the older ones were directed towards the other divisions, or crafts such as costume-making or backstage work such as prompter or machinist. In this way students, who had spent all their formative years training in the performing arts, were sure of employment on graduation. (Down the decades, however, this utopian system changed.)[23]

For the companies there were several state theatres, in addition to the Bolshoi, the biggest and most important.[24] There was the Alexandrinsky, designed by the Italian architect Carlo Rossi and opened in 1832 on the site of the wooden Maly or Small Theatre, which had been acquired by the state at the beginning of the century but couldn't cope with the rapidly growing numbers of theatregoers. The Alexandrinsky became the home of the Russian drama company, so that by 1836 the Bolshoi's stage was reserved for opera and ballet alone. Another theatre was the Mikhailovsky, finished in 1833 and located not far away from the Alexandrinsky, on the other side of Nevsky Prospect.[25] The Mikhailovsky staged performances by St Petersburg's French drama company (which, like its Russian counterpart, had previously used the Bolshoi), as well as plays and operettas in German, and concert performances, which sometimes included ballet. There was also the Theatre-Circus, built in 1849 opposite the Bolshoi, not only for circus shows, but drama, opera, and occasionally ballet; when it burnt down in 1859, it was this site that became the location for the Mariinsky. Another theatre, the 800-seat theatre on Kamenny Island (*Kamennoostrovskii teatr*), opened in 1827 and was used in the summer when the city-centre theatres were closed. Its stage was big enough for opera and ballet as well as drama and had a rear wall which, thanks to a sliding mechanism, could be opened to reveal a picturesque backdrop of real parkland.[26]

These then were the state theatres, but there were also private theatres, usually used when the nobility and gentry abandoned the summer heat of the city for the surrounding countryside. The Krasnoselsky theatre, in the village of Krasnoe Selo, presented informal seasons of dance, comic plays, and vaudeville from 1851 to 1916 and was administered by the military; its audience was mostly Guards officers posted for summer manoeuvres nearby, as well as members of the imperial family. Performers loved the relaxed atmosphere; it was like a picnic outing. Before a railway was built, they were transported to the village in large imperial carriages and after a convivial lunch spent the pre-performance afternoons boating on the lake or fishing or going round the encampment in troikas.[27] Early in her career, Matilda Kshesinskaya performed a summer season there; the tsar's brother Grand Duke Vladimir Alexandrovich attended rehearsals and would sit in her dressing-room, gossiping and regretting he was no longer young. Her most assiduous admirer, though, was Tsarevich Nicholas, whose mistress she famously became.[28] Besides Krasnoselsky, there was also the open-air theatre at the Peterhof summer palace and the Chinese Theatre at the Tsarskoe Selo imperial estate. The latter, so-called because of its Chinoiserie decorations, was built by Catherine the Great and rarely used after her death, until Nicholas II came to the throne. The city's Winter Palace also had a theatre founded by Catherine, the Hermitage Theatre, but by Petipa's time it was only rarely used. However, in 1900, it was luxuriously restored and reopened, providing a stage for Petipa's last works. It is still used today and as such is St Petersburg's oldest theatre.[29]

The independent city theatres which had existed from the eighteenth century had, like the Maly Theatre, been gradually absorbed. State intervention, driven by the belief that theatre activity not only represented enlightened sophistication but had a role as a 'school for morals', meant that by 1827 there were no private theatres in St Petersburg. In Moscow the picture was more complicated, but by 1843 the directorate had finally gained complete control of theatrical activity in both capitals.[30] The provinces escaped the imperial grip, however, and the number of regional theatres grew appreciably after Alexander I's accession in 1801. Between 1813 and 1825 there were at least fifteen large permanent regional theatres (six of which were linked to serf companies).[31] Theatre censorship intensified: in 1828 a new regulation required the infamous Third Section (Nicholas I's secret police) to vet works intended for performance, as well as reviews for *Severnaia pchela* before publication.[32]

Obviously, the school, known today as the Vaganova Academy (*Akademiia russkogo baleta imeni A. Ia. Vaganovoi*), was an important component of the Imperial Theatres. In 1836, it moved to its present location at 2 Architect Rossi Street (*ulitsa Zodchego Rossi*). The street, formerly known as Theatre Street, is also famous for a harmony that comes from Rossi's decision to make it as wide as the buildings are high, so that if you were to cut a transversal section you would see a perfect square. He also decorated the ochre-coloured classical fa-cades with white columns, matching his design for the Alexandrinsky Theatre standing across one end of the street. In the early 1960s the old choreographer Fedor Lopukhov, bumping into the writer Solomon Volkov in Nevsky Prospect, claimed that those columns start to dance when you walked down the street. He was hurrying back to his small apartment in the ballet school building and, while Volkov accompanied him, also described, more realistically, how Rossi (Theatre) Street basically consisted of just two huge buildings. In the building occupied by the school on one side had also been the offices of the directorate of Imperial Theatres; in the building opposite were the Ministries of Internal Affairs and National Education.[33] Today, the St Petersburg State Museum of Theatrical and Musical Art (*Sankt-Peterburgskii gosudarstvennyi muzei teatral'nogo i muzykal'nogo iskusstva*) has taken over the offices of the directorate, its entrance situated round the corner in Ostrovsky Square (*ploshchad' Ostrovskogo*) where the Alexandrinsky is located.

Despite its late start, the ballet company developed fast and by the 1760s included at least thirty Russian-born dancers. A succession of reputed, innovatory foreign ballet masters introduced the new *ballet d'action*, where movement and narrative were fused together to produce an autonomous, dramatic entity, although it continued to share the programme with plays or operas. The first of these ballet masters was an Austrian, Franz Hilverding, who worked in St Petersburg from 1759 to 1764; his ballets, mostly pastorales, achieved particular success at court, the Russian dancers appearing alongside his own foreign performers.[34] Then came Hilverding's Italian disciple Gaspero Angiolini, who worked in St Petersburg and Moscow (with interruptions) between 1762 and 1786.[35] Angiolini was in turn succeeded by the French dancer Charles Le Picq.[36] He staged the ballets of another famous proponent of the *ballet d'action*, Jean-Georges Noverre.[37] Noverre never visited Russia, but Le Picq made him widely known. At the Russian premiere of Noverre's *Médée et Jason* in 1789, 'all Petersburg craved to see it' and hundreds of people, not possessing tickets, were turned away.[38]

Although largely Western in its repertoire, ballet had less difficulty winning an audience than imported drama because it did not rely on foreign texts and appealed to the eye with its visual luxury and beauty and surprises. A satirical journal in Catherine II's time criticized theatregoers for the fact that 'posing as connoisseurs of plays and acting, they conduct themselves noisily and improperly during a performance, and silence and calm is restored among them only during the ballet.'[39]

The pattern started by Landé, of a foreign ballet master using native dancers, would endure in the imperial ballet to the end of the nineteenth century—and be epitomized by Petipa and the Russian ballerina Maria Surovshchikova-Petipa, his muse and first wife. It was a question of pragmatism, since it is easier to train good dancers than produce good ballet masters. The court purse spared no effort to attract the biggest international names, offering conditions, as already seen, that enabled the most ambitious artistic visions. Even so, some nuances need to be added to the general picture. For a start, a proportion of foreigners also existed among the dancing rank and file. They received higher salaries than their Russian counterparts, but at least they operated as useful exemplars. There were also a few Russian ballet masters in the early days. Ivan Valberkh (1766–1819), a graduate of the St Petersburg Theatre School, became the company's first Russian ballet master and was appointed to lead the company and school in 1794, although he was soon supplanted by foreigners, notably Didelot in 1801, a superior talent by far. Valberkh, however, did continue to mount ballets and had a lasting impact as a gifted teacher. Later came another Russian, Didelot's pupil, Adam Glushkovsky

(1793–1870), who in 1812 was put in charge of the Moscow company and remained in that capacity for twenty-seven years.

But it was thanks to its foreigners and to imperial largesse that ballet in Russia was able to keep abreast of the latest European trends right from the start. So when in Paris in the early 1830s the Italian ballet master Filippo Taglioni and his ballerina-daughter Marie helped shape the aesthetic of an era that became known as the Romantic Ballet, this new genre reached Russia just a few years later. Further down the line, in the last decades of the century, Italian dancers would once again inject a new excitement in performance and Petipa would exploit this.[40]

National Consciousness

The secular arts in Russia, developing later than in Western Europe, took time to shake off the styles and narratives of their Western models. Sweeping generalisation might therefore claim that ballet, when Petipa arrived, had retained most—or all—of its Western identity; and ballets reflecting Russian civilization were rare specimens, even among works created on home ground. However, as often happens, the closer picture is more complicated.

Decades before Petipa's arrival, ballet, like drama and opera, *did* show glimmers of a national consciousness; the glimmers were there as early as the eighteenth century. Perhaps they were most evident in drama: Denis Fonvizin's 1782 comedy *The Minor* (Nedorosl') was the first play to hold a mirror to Russian society, breaking with imported European drama, as well as with the style of Alexander Sumarokov, nicknamed The Northern Corneille, who modelled his plays on the French classics.[41] Comic opera, which arrived in Russia in the 1770s and quickly became popular, also attracted Russian composers whose simple protagonists provided congruous contexts for folk (national) dance and folk music. Folk dance meanwhile had long been showcased at court and the early foreign ballet masters, spotting its potential, sometimes incorporated it into their staged spectacles. Angiolini, Noverre's Italian rival, for instance, collated old Russian dances for a ballet in 1767 set to Russian folk music.[42] As the century reached its end, so this awakening of national consciousness gained speed. It was given political impetus by the French Revolution and the tsarist government's fear of anything similar coming to Russia. But national consciousness was also the culmination of earlier literary undercurrents, accompanying the decline of classicism and the advent of sentimentalism and early romanticism, which turned away from distant history or myth towards more humble, more rooted, more modern subjects. In other words the universal themes and lofty, internationalized protagonists of classicism were superseded by the local people of sentimentalism.[43]

So, rather than being against the odds, Valberkh's emergence could be seen as part of the trend. He created pieces that reflected the new didactic sentimentalism, pieces such as *Clara, or the Resort to Virtue* (Klara, ili Obrashchenie k dobrodeteli, 1806) and *The Triumph of Evgenia's Love* (Torzhestvo liubvi Evgenii, 1807), alternatively called *Evgenia, or the Secret Marriage* (Evgenia, ili Tainyi brak). Unlike, say, Noverre's Medea, his protagonists were often people of unexceptional social standing, presented as edifying examples in melodramatic plots. On the other hand, he did also make ballets about foreign historical personages, although they were accompanied by the twist of moral enlightenment—hence, *Henry IV, or the Reward of Virtue* (Genrikh IV, ili Nagrada dobrodeteli, 1816). For *The New Werther* (Novyi Verter, 1799), he turned to Goethe, but reworked his source by depicting events in contemporary Moscow (which made quite a splash with his audience) and presenting characters in modern street clothes, the men dressed in frock coats.[44]

National consciousness exploded into patriotism with Napoleon's expansionism in the first decade of the century, his Russian defeat in 1812, and forced abdication in 1814 at the hands of the Allies in Paris. A surge of patriotic plays appeared and the French drama companies of St Petersburg and Moscow were dissolved in 1812. (But they returned after hostilities.) Opera went down the same nationalistic route, with, for example, Caterino Cavos's popular *Ivan Susanin* in 1815, about the peasant Ivan Susanin who sacrificed his life to save Mikhail, the first Romanov tsar, from Polish invaders.[45] Valberkh matched this with a stream of Russo-military ballets and became the choreographer of the hour, firing up his audiences. The titles say it all: *The New Heroine, or the Woman Cossack* (Novaia geroinia, ili Zhenshchina-kazak, 1810); *Russia's Victory, or the Russians in Paris* (Torzhestvo Rossii, ili Russkie v Parizhe, 1814); *A Festival in the Allied Armies Camp at Montmartre* (Prazdnik v stane soiusnykh armii pri Monmartre, 1814). When in *The Home Guard, or the Love of the Fatherland* (Opolchenie, ili Liubov' k otechestvu, 1812) the protagonists were seen to donate their belongings to the national cause, one spectator got so carried away he threw his wallet at the stage, shouting 'and take my last seventy-five roubles!'[46] These patriotic ballets were often co-choreographed with the dancer Auguste Poirot, known simply as Auguste, a French dancer who had embraced Russia as his home. Auguste was a famous proponent of Russian folk dance, an important figure in its transformation into a theatrical form.[47]

Being an obviously plausible language for the simple individuals of pre-romantic and romantic narratives, folk dance became an important component in ballets not only in Russia but elsewhere in Europe. In Russia, though, because folk dance, along with its music and song, was receiving the additional boost of patriotism, it became an immensely popular feature of theatrical life, staged as part of an opera or play or simply as a single spectacle. This was particularly the case in Moscow: in his memoirs the ballet master Glushkovsky remembered how in Moscow 'ballets in the French manner were little performed in those days, but instead, there were mostly Russian *divertissements*'.[48] Isaac Ablets, a pupil of

Valberkh, quickly became known for these *divertissements*. Between 1813 and 1815 his compositions were performed almost nightly in Moscow, some also staged in St Petersburg, their swagger toned down and shapes elaborated to match Petersburg tastes. His biggest success was *Semik, or the Fair at the Maria Woods* (Semik, ili Gulian'e v Mar'inoi roshche), created in Moscow in 1815. Glushkovsky describes how the professional dancers had prepared for a performance of *Semik* in honour of King Frederick William of Prussia. 'Many sought out gypsies and paid them a lot of money just to imitate their manner in folk dance.'[49]

In the realm of classical ballet or 'ballets in the French manner', the 1820s also saw choreographers turning to Russian literary sources (effectively, Pushkin) and history. In Moscow, Glushkovsky's 1821 dance version of *Ruslan and Liudmila* was the first instance of a ballet based on national literature; the same choreographer's 1831 *The Black Shawl, or Infidelity Punished* (Chernaia shal', ili Nakazannaia nevernost'), was inspired by the poem *The Black Shawl* (Chernaia shal'). Didelot himself used a Pushkin poem, *The Prisoner of the Caucasus* (Kavkazskii plennik), for a ballet of the same title, created in 1823 and set to a score by Cavos. Three years later he started work with the same composer on a ballet based on Russian history. Scheduled for the opening of the new Alexandrinsky Theatre, this was *Sumbeka, or The Subjugation of the Kazan Kingdom* (Sumbeka, ili Pokorenie Kazanskogo tsarstva), about Ivan the Terrible's overthrow of the Kazan Mongols in 1552. Didelot, however, never finished the ballet. He was ignominiously forced out of his position in 1831, ending a career in Russia that had lasted twenty-five years. The ballet would be finished in 1832 by another Frenchman called Alexis Blache, son of the famous ballet master, Jean-Baptiste Blache.[50]

It wasn't only the era of Didelot which came to an end, it was also the era of enlightened debate. Among the intelligentsia, theatre had become a focal point for concerns about national identity. Writers like the vaudeville specialist Prince Alexander Shakhovskoi increasingly demanded and tried to write works which reflected native life, in opposition to the foreign, especially the French, plays favoured by the *beau monde* and the Imperial Theatres.[51] Nicholas I, succeeding his brother Alexander I in 1825, slammed the door on these aspirations. In the year of his accession, he crushed the uprising of the army officers who became known as the Decembrists. Some were executed, others were condemned to hard labour; the poet Pushkin, although not directly implicated, was exiled. They had been liberals in the spirit of the Enlightenment and French Revolution; many had served in the 1812 war and, as part of the occupying forces in Paris, had seen the fruits of French political reform.[52] Their brutal defeat inaugurated a thirty-year period of repression, paranoia, and surveillance. 'Absolute power,' Custine wrote, 'becomes all the more chilling when it is afraid.'[53] Under Nicholas the directorate of Imperial Theatres asserted its near-monopoly and established magnificent new theatre buildings: these were the years that saw the opening of the Alexandrinsky, the Mikhailovsky, and the theatre school's new home in Rossi (Theatre) Street. But artistic independence was stifled and Western influences filled the repertoires.

There were, as always, exceptions. In opera, Mikhail Glinka's *A Life for the Tsar* (Zhizn' za tsaria) is generally considered the first true Russian opera, although, as already seen, there were several earlier works that laid the ground, including Cavos's version (*Ivan Susanin*) of the same patriotic story. Glinka's opera was premiered in 1836, followed by his *Ruslan and Liudmilla* in 1842. But after that, during the next two decades, Russian composers wrote little of importance, while the St Petersburg Italian opera was built into one of the most important opera companies in Europe. In drama, a subgenre of plays about the Russian merchant classes did appear in the 1830s, but vaudevilles and melodramas fashioned from foreign models continued to dominate.[54] The great Russian dramatist Alexander Ostrovsky, founder of realism in his portrayals of everyday Russian life, completed his first play in 1849, but it was banned, he was put under police surveillance, and it wasn't until 1853 that he had a play performed in public.[55] Similarly, Alexander Griboedov's *Woe from Wit* (Gore ot uma), a verse comedy satirizing Moscow society in general and gallomania in particular, became, in Frame's words, 'the most notorious forbidden play of Nicolaevan Russia'.[56] Although bowdlerized versions were occasionally performed, the complete play had to wait until 1895. And even if Nikolai Gogol did—eventually—succeed in persuading Nicholas to approve his play *The Government Inspector* (Revizor) in 1836, it was for the most part in vain that he exclaimed in the same year: 'For heaven's sake, give us Russian characters, give us ourselves, our own scoundrels and cranks! [...] We are grown so indifferent from watching insipid French plays that now we are afraid to look at ourselves.'[57] The Mikhailovsky, which housed the French drama company, was the most socially prestigious of Russia's theatres. The Italian opera may have been the most popular, but French drama attracted the *crème de la crème* of Petersburg society. Frame is surely right to argue that the enduring fascination of the Petersburg establishment for French theatre epitomized its enduring alienation from ordinary Russians; and this in turn gave a political colouring to the calls for a more Russian repertoire, implying criticism of the establishment.[58]

This re-Westernization could be seen as a contradiction for a political regime which in 1833 published its ideological tripartite mantra of so-called Official Nationality: Orthodoxy (*pravoslavie*), or the adherence to the official Church and its moral role; Autocracy (*samoderzhavie*), or the affirmation of the sovereign's absolute power; and Nationality (*narodnost'*), or the proclamation of Russianness, which made the Russian people mighty and dedicated supporters of the sovereign's dynasty and government.[59] Nevertheless, the re-Westernization of the arts in general and the homeless fate of St Petersburg's Russian opera in particular suggests a conscious policy to compete with Western Europe on its own terms.

After Didelot, the possibility of a truly Russian ballet was nipped in the bud and the company stagnated for almost twenty years. Even so, great prestige was ascribed to the St Petersburg ballet, prominently positioned in the imperial field of vision. And what mattered most to imperial taste was spectacle: big crowd scenes, lavish decor, elaborate scenic effects, or ballerinas who stood out by virtue of glittering display.

Hostile press articles, though, marked the post-Didelot period. In 1834, one critic wrote:

> As for our ballets, it is better not to speak of them. . . . They are feet without a head, language without speech, gestures without understanding. For them it suffices to have five thousand yards of silver lace, five hundred candles, fifty dressmakers, five scenic painters and their success will be brilliant and sure.[60]

The critic had in mind the two Frenchmen, Alexis Blache and Titus, first and second ballet masters, who replaced Didelot. Both had little originality and their emphasis on spectacle led to the temporary decline of choreography. Blache's first ballet, *Don Juan, or the Defeated Atheist* (Don Zhuan, ili Porazhennyi bezbozhnik, 1832), elicited great advance interest—and great disappointment. Reviews remarked on the colourless choreography. No better was the ballet started by Didelot, *Sumbeka* (also in 1832), despite its luxurious scale, nationalistic theme, and battle scenes.

When Blache left in 1836, Titus became first ballet master, remaining seventeen years until Jules Perrot's arrival. Soviet historians point to the puny choreography of his dances for the first productions of Glinka's *A Life for the Tsar* and *Ruslan and Liudmilla*. His own productions were also flops: for instance, *The Swiss Milkmaid* or *La Laitière suisse* (Shveitsarskaia molochnitsa, 1832), based on Filippo Taglioni's dramatically skimpy ballet of the same name, created in Vienna in 1821 and reworked for Paris in 1832 as *Nathalie, or the Swiss Milkmaid*. Titus first produced his own version in Paris, then in Berlin, where he was ballet master, before bringing it to St Petersburg as his opening salute.[61] 'In the first act they dance, mill about, run around, and abduct the milkmaid, while in the second act they marry her, run around, mill about, and dance,' *Severnaia pchela* wrote. Nothing could save *The Swiss Milkmaid*, not even the new costumes and decor, and at the end, 'spectators parted from it exactly as they might part from a person who tires you with endless chatter.'[62]

Even so, it was under Titus's watch that the emblematic works of the Romantic Ballet came to Russia. Modestly scaled and succinct, often dealing with simple, day-to-day people, while also unveiling a hidden supernatural world, the Romantic style ran counter to the big spectacles of the St Petersburg repertoire. It had taken Paris by storm in the 1830s, launched by Filippo Taglioni's 'Ballet of the Nuns' which appeared in Meyerbeer's opera *Robert le Diable* in 1831. The ghostly nuns who are summoned from their graves at night prefigured the nocturnal *wilis* of *Giselle* a decade later and the assorted sprites of other ballets. The same choreographer's *La Sylphide* in 1832 confirmed the transformation of the old classical ballet into what seemed a sensationally new language of poetic transfiguration, moulded on his daughter Marie. Taglioni exploited Marie's strong point work and eerie stamina (achieved through hours of unremitting training) to produce images of drifting ethereality, tracing contours that were soft, delicate, and apparently effortless.[63] This was the Taglioni embodiment of the Romantic style, an idealized otherworldly vision, but there were other versions. Fanny Elssler, an Austrian, was the antithesis of Taglioni, a mesmerizing creature of carnal passions and drama. Gautier famously contrasted the two ballerinas with the epithets of 'Christian' for Taglioni and 'pagan' for Elssler.[64]

Titus brought the Romantic Ballet to Russia by staging his versions, freely copied from the successes on the Paris stage. In 1835, he mounted his production of Taglioni's *La Sylphide* and in 1836 the same choreographer's *The Rebellion in the Seraglio* or *La Révolte au sérail* (Vosstanie v serale). Then, he invited Marie Taglioni. The Blache and Titus regimes had used many foreign dancers, but Taglioni was the first major dance celebrity to appear since the glamorous French virtuoso Louis Duport in Didelot's day. She made her St Petersburg debut, aged thirty-four, in 1837 and appeared there for five subsequent seasons. Her arrival restored to the stage the expressive artistry that had been neglected since Didelot's time. Her style stimulated and inspired her Russian rivals; her performances always created a stir with the public. But by 1842 her success had declined, partly because her father's ballets were inferior to her talent.

The Romantic Ballet in Russia was also represented by Titus's 1842 version of *Giselle*, a year after its Paris world premiere. Elena Andreianova, leading ballerina of the St Petersburg company, was the first Russian Giselle. Later, in 1850, after replacing Titus as first ballet master, Jules Perrot, the ballet's original co-choreographer, mounted his superior version with Carlotta Grisi who had created the titular role in Paris.[65]

When Perrot first arrived in 1848 rehearsals were already under way for his ballet *Esmeralda*, created in London four years earlier and based on Victor Hugo's *Notre Dame de Paris*. The Russian premiere was scheduled for 20 December, with Gautier's pagan ballerina Fanny Elssler in the title role. To make sure the ballet would be ready in time Elssler had started work, assisted by a capable French dancer, who had come to Russia the previous year and whose name was Marius Petipa.

The arrival of Perrot and Petipa would mark the end of ballet's post-Didelot decline, but both were also clearly part of the re-Westernization process. Of course, ballet has always been an international art, its prominent creators and interpreters moving from capital to capital; however, the theatre world which Petipa entered contained little that was Russian, apart from its rank-and-file personnel. The repertoire was foreign, the celebrities were foreign, the creative staff was foreign. Not only that, but among educated and aristocratic theatregoers French was still widely spoken. In fact, before the Napoleonic invasion, aristocratic families preferred French as the superior language, the mark of civilization. So for Petipa, within the theatre walls, it was a home from home.

Serfdom

Further afield, however, Russia was an alien place, un-Westernized, primitive. When Petipa arrived, serfdom still existed, although the question of its morality was very much in the air and its abolition in 1861 was one of the first important reforms by Nicholas's son Alexander II.[66] In the previous century there had been a vogue for landlords to create their own private serf theatres. The first were established in Moscow and St Petersburg in the late 1760s and 1770s before gradually spreading to the provinces. Besides attesting to the equation of wealth, power, and servitude, serf companies confirmed the growing prestige of theatre in Russian society.[67] They reached their zenith in the eighteenth century's last decade when rich nobles were made even richer by gifts of lands and peasants, distributed on a grand scale by Catherine the Great to consolidate their support.

Serf theatres are estimated to have reached a total of 173 by the early nineteenth century, the majority located in urban areas, principally Moscow and its environs. Generally they were small theatres for special events, such as holidays, and for the private enjoyment of the owner and his guests. Some, though, occasionally with encouragement from the imperial government, had a philanthropic purpose and were open to the public, for free or just a small charge.[68] As such, these open theatres, when located in the provinces, often provided the only access to a play or opera; and when serf companies were dissolved, as happened in the nineteenth century, their theatres were sometimes donated to the local administration for continued use.

In this way, serf companies moulded the public's taste for the performing arts and some of them attained high artistic standards. Arguably the best was the troupe founded early on by the fabulously rich Sheremetev family, owners of some 210,000 serfs and two million acres. There are records for 116 productions, of which seventy-three were operas, twenty-five were comedies, and eighteen were ballets.[69] Among the 115 performers in 1789 were twenty-six dancers.[70] Their eight theatres included two on the family estates of Ostankino and Kuskovo near Moscow and spared nothing in technological sophistication. The theatre at Kuskovo was so successful that the English entrepreneur Michael Maddox, possessor of the Moscow public theatre monopoly, complained it was robbing him of an audience.[71]

Overall, comic operas, folk-dance *divertissements*, and ballets predominated in serf-repertoires.[72] The Soviet dance historian Vera Krasovskaya proposes several reasons for the popularity of ballet and folk dance. For instance, the large resources demanded by dance—an orchestra, a corps de ballet, soloists—allowed grandees to flaunt their wealth. Equally, a serf was more naturally disposed to learning stage dance than mastering the lines of some foreign play in translation. After all, folk dance was very much part of country life and before too long, a serf dancer could also shape his or her skills to a balletic vocabulary which was not so different, at that time, from social dance.[73]

The ballet masters tended to be serfs themselves. Even Count Nikolai Sheremetev (1751–1809), who on occasion employed famous foreign ballet masters, relied on serf teachers and ballet masters at other times. These were, consequently, the first Russian ballet masters, preceding Valberkh at the Imperial Theatres. Most serf-artists had to lead a cruelly incongruous double life: they appeared on stage as princes, princesses, shepherds, and shepherdesses, but by day they continued as labourers, cooks, footmen, and housemaids, indistinguishable from other serfs except for kid gloves which protected their hands and broad hats which preserved their faces from sunburn and hid the paper curlers in their hair.[74] Some owners treated their artists with extreme brutality, the women being particularly vulnerable, since they also had to suffer sexual exploitation. One story says that a Iusupov prince, at performances in his Moscow theatre, used to force the corps de ballet to remove their clothes at a given signal.[75] But a few owners were enlightened, such as the Sheremetevs who provided salaries and allowances, as well as compassion and respect. Nikolai Sheremetev, who succeeded his father Petr as Russia's wealthiest man, even married one of his opera singers, Praskovia Kovaleva-Zhemchugova, behaviour that was regarded as social treason by many of his class.[76] Very occasionally, having become stage celebrities, serfs were able to buy themselves out of bondage, as illustrated by Mikhail Shchepkin, the greatest Russian actor of the nineteenth century, who began as a child serf-actor.[77]

By the mid-1820s, many serf theatres had disappeared, their decline dating from 1797 when Paul I introduced measures restricting their activities. It was not unusual for their owners, striving to recoup the money they had so extravagantly spent, to transfer or sell as many performers as possible to commercial or imperial theatres. Valberkh, in 1800, was despatched to the town of Shklov to collect fourteen dancers from the heirs of Count S. G. Zorich, a favourite of Catherine the Great; they were destined for the St Petersburg ballet where they remained as the serfs of their original owners. There were other bulk transactions: in 1805, for example, one serf-owner took his whole ballet company to St Petersburg and sold it to an impresario; another, in 1806, sold his large company, which included thirty-six dancers, to the Imperial Theatres in Moscow.[78]

The Other Capital

Petipa must have been aware of the existence of serfs early on, albeit by his time only free citizens were accepted into the school and company. He must also have heard about the serf companies which existed just a few decades before his arrival. It is tempting to think that he was shocked, given the empathetic spirit revealed in his diaries, and perhaps it is indicative that he noted the anniversary of the 'emancipation of the Russian people' in his diary on 19 February 1905.

If serfdom was an alien truth to a newcomer like him, the St Petersburg ballet's cocooned and international world must by contrast have felt reassuringly familiar, as must the city's Westernized architecture. During the first four months of his arrival, with time on his hands because it was the company's long summer break, he acquainted himself with the city. He writes that he visited the Hermitage museum (housed in extensions of the Winter Palace) and the different islands of the city, after morning ballet practice at the theatre school.[79]

Moscow, however, was something else, more deeply Russian, more oriental, an ancient citadel (*kreml'*) that had grown piecemeal, with little streets running in all directions and byzantine churches on every corner. An estimated three-quarters of Moscow, though, had burnt down in the fire that accompanied Napoleon's invasion in 1812. By Petipa's time many of the wooden buildings had been replaced with stone ones so that elegant, colonnaded classical mansions stood next to tiny yellow-painted wooden houses. There were also the new Boulevard and Garden Rings (*Bul'varnoe kol'tso* and *Sadovoe kol'tso*), broad European-style concentric avenues which traced the lines of the old city ramparts and cut across the ancient winding lanes.[80]

No longer needed by Elssler for the rehearsals of *Esmeralda*, Petipa was sent to the ballet company in Moscow towards the end of 1848, together with his father Jean, who by then had followed his son to Russia. The Moscow ballet and opera were now under the control of the Imperial Theatres and the Petipas' instructions were to mount two ballets, premiered in St Petersburg the previous year: Mazilier's *Paquita*; and *The Devil in Love* (Le Diable amoureux) under its Russian title *Satanilla, or Love and Hell* (Satanilla, ili Liubov' i ad).[81] The Petipas must have seen how different things were in Moscow. They would have noticed that the company was smaller, its surroundings less opulent. Right from the beginning, Moscow was disadvantaged: figures published by Frame show that in 1809 the St Petersburg company had almost three times the budget of the Moscow company (85,620 roubles compared with 32,093) and the St Petersburg theatre school three times that of its Moscow counterpart (49,956 roubles, compared with 16,660).[82]

Like much else in Moscow, the ballet company was closer to the spirit of pre-Petrine Russia. One reason is that the Moscow audience was different. In Moscow lived the old ancestral nobility and rich merchants; in St Petersburg, the court and high-ranking officials. Moscow was the centre of business and commerce; St Petersburg, the centre of banking and imperial power, its streets colonized by military uniforms. As a result, Moscow might have been richer, but St Petersburg was grander, and although in the last decades of the century Moscow shed its image as a cultural backwater, some of its provincial features were slow to disappear. Vladimir Teliakovsky, who in 1901 moved from Moscow to St Petersburg to become the new director of the Imperial Theatres, saw what Gautier and Vazem saw in St Petersburg's audiences and explains how a Moscow visitor, taking his seat for a performance, would be amazed:

> This is not as in Moscow, where the public is dressed in little shawls and jackets. Here everyone is in tails, officers with spurs and elaborate moustaches, the women with snowy white décolletés—diamonds, perfume, lace. ... Here even without the ballet there is something to look at. The royal box is not empty, as it usually is in Moscow. Everybody is in their place. [...] everybody knows everybody, everybody bows to each other, everybody belongs. And the ushers are so polite and so well-dressed—in Moscow the livery often sits on them like sacks, but here it is as if it is made to measure.[83]

The Moscow audience not only looked different, its tastes were different too. It was inclined to favour ballet with a strong narrative, mime scenes, folk and comic dances.[84] In St Petersburg, rich spectacle and elegance were pivotal elements. Allied to these dissimilarities was the fact that ballet in Moscow not only started later, but differently. In St Petersburg ballet started as a court entertainment, in Moscow early companies were largely private enterprises. The first, launched in 1759 and bringing together singers, dancers and actors, was the creation of an Italian, Giovanni Locatelli, who, fired by the success of his opera-buffa troupe in St Petersburg, opened his own theatre in Moscow—and soon went bankrupt. More durable was the company launched in 1776 by Michael Maddox, an English maverick who had started as a tightrope-walking entertainer and along the way had taught mathematics and physics to Catherine the Great's son, the future Paul I.[85] It is this company that marks the beginning of the ballet and opera of the Bolshoi Theatre. Maddox started in partnership with the Moscow prosecutor Prince Petr Urusov who had been granted an exclusive permit for theatrical presentations by the city's governor-general.[86] Urusov eventually ceded the privilege to Maddox and on 30 December 1780 Maddox opened a home for his company, the specially built 1,500-seat theatre, the Petrovsky, Moscow's only public theatre. Maddox presented seasons of what appear to have been mixed programmes of ballet, drama, and opera, rather like music hall or vaudeville. Many of the supporting dancers came from Moscow's Imperial Foundling Home, which had an in-house theatre for amateur performances and a succession of foreign ballet masters who taught the pupils dancing. For the Petrovsky's opening, sixteen orphanage pupils took part in the programme's allegorical ballet-pantomime *The Bewitched School* (L'École enchantée).[87] A few years later, Maddox took fifty dancers (and twenty-four actors and thirty musicians) from the orphanage into his company.[88]

The beginnings of the Moscow ballet coincided with the vogue for Russian-style comic opera and with the new literary currents of sentimentalism and early-romanticism which inspired Valberkh's ballets in St Petersburg. In the same way, the ballets presented by Maddox often focused on ordinary citizens and peasants. Ballets such as *Village Festivities* (Derevenskii prazdnik, 1786) and *The Deceived Miller* (Obmanutyi mel'nik, 1793) attracted spectators of all social classes. However, Maddox was steeped in debt and in 1786 his venture was taken over by the government agency that had provided many of his loans. He remained, though, responsible for daily operations until a calamitous finale in 1805, when fire burnt the Petrovsky down.[89]

At this point Tsar Paul II intervened. It was decided to establish the directorate of Imperial Theatres in Moscow and the following year (1806) the company was taken under the directorate's jurisdiction. In 1822 came a hiatus: the city's governor-general took over responsibility for theatre administration until 1843 when the directorate of Imperial Theatres resumed control. From then on the manager of the Moscow office reported to the director in St Petersburg.

For twenty years after the fire, Maddox's former company led a semi-nomadic existence. In 1825 it finally took up residence in the custom-built New Bolshoi Petrovsky, not far from the old Petrovsky and next door to the Maly, recently completed for the city's drama company.[90] But once again fire, the hazard of all pre-twentieth-century theatres, struck the new Bolshoi in 1853, leaving only the outer walls. The reconstruction took just three years, pushed through for the coronation celebrations of Alexander II. The architecture by Alberto Cavos (son of the composer) enlarged the previous building, creating an auditorium of 2,150 seats. This is the theatre that remains today, although the hurried work contributed to the problems that necessitated the theatre's protracted, much publicized closure and refurbishment early this century.

By contrast, the Imperial Ballet of St Petersburg was, most of the time, the reflection of a city which had not, in the Moscow manner, grown organically over the centuries, but was artificially created, its symmetries and palaces modelled on Western capitals, its focus on the imperial machinery. The courtiers and senior civil servants who lived there were often foreign or had foreign sympathies. The sovereigns also tended to have a Western outlook. Catherine the Great, who was born a minor German princess, might have displayed a very public love for Russian folk culture, but she was Western by upbringing and inclination. Nicholas

I was married to Princess Charlotte of Prussia and had a strong attachment to his new family—King Frederick William III was his father-in-law and Frederick William IV his brother-in-law. This Prussian link seems to have exercised a profound influence on him personally, which inevitably became extended to cultural and political life in general.[91]

Serving the Tsar

The Moscow ballet, then, was closer to the 'real' Russia, but the St Petersburg ballet was the more significant because it had a symbolic, politicized identity. It was not so much Russian Ballet as the Ballet of Russia. If the city of St Petersburg was an image of a Westernizing and Westernized Russian autocracy, then so, on a more modest scale, was the ballet company.

The historian Richard S. Wortman has argued that the foreign character of the Russian monarchy was no accident. From the fifteenth to the late nineteenth centuries the monarchy deliberately withdrew from the rest of society in order to mythologize itself and thereby assert its ascendance. 'By appearing like foreigners, the monarch and the elite affirmed the permanence and inevitability of their domination of subject populations, both Russian and other nationalities,' Wortman writes. 'Peter the Great made Europe the referent of foreignness and superiority, and taught his servitors to act like Europeans.'[92]

Peter the Great's successors continued to promulgate the benefits of Western civilization in an enormous variety of forms and one of these was, of course, ballet. By its creation as a court company and by its physical proximity, the Petersburg ballet was an extension of the monarchy, brought out for state visits, weddings, and coronations. The Petersburg ballet was not therefore representative of everyday Russia. It was a reflection of Russian absolutism, a showcase for the allegorical enactment of imperial rituals and themes; it was a mirror of the splendour and civilizing destiny of the sovereign. At their most idealistic, the despots of the Enlightenment saw the stage as a powerful didactic instrument, igniting moral self-improvement among their subjects: when in 1768 Catherine II agreed to undergo the then new procedure of a smallpox vaccination, Angiolini staged an allegorical ballet, *Prejudice Conquered* (Pobezhdennyi predrassudok) to celebrate the event. The stage was also the predictable arena for adulation during Elizabeth's coronation festivities in 1742, as shown by just the titles of Landé's ballets. One of them, for example, was called *The Happiness of the Nations at the Appearance of Astrea on the Russian Horizon and the Restoration of the Golden Age* (Radost' narodov po povodu poiavleniia Astrei na russkom gorizonte i vosstanovleniia zolotogo vremeni). This practice would be revived a hundred and forty years later, with Petipa's *Night and Day* (Noch' i den'), which showed night banished by a new dawn, for Alexander III's coronation. (Night, presumably, was a metaphor not for

Alexander II's reign, but for the anguish following his assassination.) Meanwhile, Glinka's opera *A Life for the Tsar* had long served as a hymn for imperial absolutism, opening the theatre season each year, as well as fulfilling its patriotic duty on other important occasions, such as coronations.

Like all state companies, the ballet was subject to imperial tastes and intervention, the emperors and the nobility often involving themselves personally in the ballet's business. Nicholas I had an eye for pretty ballerinas: one such was Varvara Volkova in the early 1830s, but she was in love with a wealthy landowner and declined Nicholas's repeated offers.[93] He also made a habit of attending rehearsals and busying himself with details, as happened during Titus's preparations for his production of Taglioni's *The Rebellion in the Seraglio*. The ballet's subject—a rebellious harem which forms an Amazonian battalion—greatly appealed to the emperor, as remembered by the actor of the Alexandrinsky Theatre Fedor Burdin:

> The sovereign interested himself greatly in the production of the ballet *The Rebellion in the Seraglio*, where women had to perform various military manoeuvres. Reliable non-commissioned officers from the Guards were sent to instruct them in all the various moves. At first the female dancers were interested, but then they got bored and became lazy. Hearing about this, the Sovereign arrived at a rehearsal and sternly announced to the theatre amazons that 'If they didn't perform as required he would order them to stand outside with their rifles and in their dancing shoes for two hours in the freezing cold.' One should have seen with what ardour the frightened skirt-wearing recruits set to work.[94]

Petipa records a similar incident in his memoirs, when Nicholas arrived unexpectedly for a rehearsal of Perrot's ballet *Catarina*, revived for the imperial stage in 1849.[95] Perrot had strained his foot and had asked Petipa to rehearse Elssler and the corps de ballet in the ballet's 'Pas stratégique' in which the dancers had to manipulate rifles. 'We [...] were immediately interrupted by the voice of His Majesty, speaking to the dancers: "You are holding your rifles, incorrectly, Mesdames! I will show you how the rifles should be handled." ' Directed by the emperor, Elssler and the other dancers followed his movements, until he was satisfied. News of this spread like wildfire and ensured that the *pas* was encored at the first performance.[96]

By character rigid and austere, Nicholas was above all an army man who only truly relaxed at ballet performances.[97] No doubt he found the alliance of feminine charm and regimented precision irresistible. Apparently, he never missed a single performance of *The Rebellion in the Seraglio* where he could appreciate the ballet regiment, armed, in the words of *Severnaia pchela*'s reviewer, 'with the white weapons of full shoulders and rounded little arms'.[98] In childhood, soldiers and military games were the endless passion of his younger brother Michael and himself. Fear was part of the equation. Whenever he built a summer house for his governess out of chairs, toys, whatever was at hand, he never forgot to fortify it with a gun for protection. As emperor, he staked all on making the entire land an impregnable fortress and his passion for regimentation and regulation underpinned government policy.[99] He was an expert in such things as the field manual, drill, and playing the drum. His greatest attachment was to the minutiae: attending as often as he could military parades and exercises, he was especially concerned about the physical appearance of his troops, the buttons, ribbons, and colours of their uniforms.[100]

Battle scenes were a popular feature of plays, operas, and ballets and were, it seems, a response to imperial military taste. However, in the discipline and visual geometries of ballet, Nicholas must have found a particularly kindred spirit. The strict tempi, the unison, the elaborate stage formations: all these had an obvious connection with the parade ground. Imperial interest accentuated these elements in ballets in general and Petipa's ballets in particular.[101]

The inevitable constraints brought by the proximity of the imperial presence were balanced by considerable advantages. As an emblem of Russian autocracy, the St Petersburg ballet had the highest visibility and most money, while throughout the nineteenth century the Moscow company was starved. For St Petersburg, only the best talent was chosen; for Moscow, it was the second-best, although the career of Ekaterina Sankovskaya, Russia's Taglioni, shone brightly. (Taglioni never appeared on the Moscow stage.)[102] True, productions might be transferred from one city to the other, as might certain dancers for guest appearances. Occasionally the transfer of dancers was more permanent, often to fill gaps. But ballet-master staff positions in Moscow were positions of lesser prestige.

It was always the St Petersburg ballet which was considered the repository of the highest excellence, even in the twentieth century, although the Soviets did try to redress the balance.[103] In nineteenth-century St Petersburg they had Didelot, Perrot, Saint-Léon, Petipa. In Moscow, apart from brief tours of duty by the great Italian teacher Carlo Blasis (1861–1863, 1866), they had semi-forgotten first ballet masters: Wenzel Reisinger, Joseph Hansen, Alexei Bogdanov, Jose Mendez—or none at all. Located far from the direct imperial gaze, Moscow's ballet enjoyed the only asset of neglect, which was greater autonomy.

Standing six feet three inches tall, severe and erect, Nicholas I was an imposing and handsome figure. People who met him were invariably impressed. He was, according to different accounts, Apollo, Jupiter, Mars, a terrestrial divinity. Pushkin compared him to Moses; a Polish enemy recorded how he was overcome by his stunning majesty and couldn't meet the imperial gaze.[104] Even Custine wrote about his noble features and Grecian profile.[105]

The close interaction between the monarch and the Imperial Theatres was reinforced by the fact that the Imperial Theatres budget came directly from the court.

The buildings themselves were named after members of the imperial family: the Alexandrinsky, after Nicholas I's wife; the Mikhailovsky, after Nicholas's brother; the opera house that was opened after Nicholas's death, the Mariinsky, after Alexander II's wife.[106]

The emperor's regular visits to the theatre meant that everyone was on the alert for signs of his approval or otherwise, since the fate of a production or a performer depended on him. 'It was enough for the tsar to say a good word about the latter and their future career could be considered secure,' writes Vazem. 'It is no surprise that the adroit, obsequious Frenchman Petipa was always looking for approval from the members of the imperial family, vigilantly monitoring the impression created by his ballets.'[107] Putting aside her personal dislike of Petipa, evident in many pages of her memoirs, he probably *was* anxious and deferential, given the status quo.

The successive emperors treated company members as their extended family, as almost their personal responsibility. In this way, serfdom imprinted itself on the collective mind, even after it was abolished. About Nicholas I the character dancer Timofei Stukolkin wrote in his memoirs: '[He] showed us so much kindness, he loved us and treated us like his own children.'[108] The heady mix of an emperor's powerful status and his proximity inspired a real devotion which was extended to other members of his family, even from foreigners like Petipa. In his diaries, Petipa noted the birthdays of the empress and 'dear Emperor Nicholas II', as well as the anniversary of the death of Alexander III, and recorded buying a portrait of Grand Duke Michael.[109] Artists saw themselves as special servants, elevated by their physical closeness to the emperor and graded medals were awarded to outstanding artists.[110] Petipa clearly considered they had great prestige since he lists his awards in the preface to his memoirs.[111] It was also commonplace for the emperor's regular attendances at the ballet to include not only conversations with the artists during the intervals, but gifts of jewellery and similar items for an artist's benefit performance or other special occasion.[112]

The conditions under which Petipa worked were among the best available anywhere. Yet just as without this favourable context Petipa would not have achieved the same success, so without Petipa the Petersburg ballet would not have achieved the same excellence. The interaction between Petipa and the Imperial Ballet of St Petersburg was therefore pivotal, its importance accentuated towards the end of the century by the decline of ballet in Western Europe. By the end of the century it remained largely unseen outside Russia, but it had become Europe's leading company.

2

The Travelling Dancer

After having received an abundance of applause in Seville, the delicate Guy-Stéphan and Mr Petipa have moved on to Cadiz where they arrived on the third of this month and on the fifth they will give their first performance in the main theatre of this city, where undoubtedly they will achieve the same success as in Seville.[1]

Marius Petipa, Aged Twenty-nine

According to his contemporaries, Petipa was a gifted raconteur, a dapper dresser, and an indefatigable worker who hated holidays.[2] The passport issued to him in 1844 in Bordeaux says that he measured 1.68m (slightly above the French average for the time) and had brown hair and eyes; he remained slim, erect, and carefully groomed right to the end of his life.[3] Matilda Kshesinskaya, who graduated into the St Petersburg company in 1890, remembers: 'He usually arrived at the theatre whistling, wrapped in a check plaid.'[4] Although he never fully mastered the Russian language, he grew to love his adopted country, where he eventually became a Russian citizen and which he 'learned to love with all my heart and with all my soul'.[5]

He had come to Russia as an energetic and ambitious twenty-nine-year old, his international reputation as a choreographer inexistant, although he certainly did have some choreographic experience, and had already described himself on his Bordeaux passport as 'artist choreographer and librettist' (*artiste chorégraphe et libretor*). As a dancer, on the other hand, he appears to have had considerable success during two-and-a-half years spent in Spain. The day after his arrival in St Petersburg he had dressed in white tie and tails to report to the offices of the directorate, apparently unaware that the company had started its long summer vacation. He knew about Russia's reputation as a richly rewarding destination, but his reception by the director of the Imperial Theatres Alexander Gedeonov outstripped expectations.

I was immediately invited into the office of His Excellency, who greeted me in a very friendly manner.

'When would you like for me to make my début?'

'*Allez vous promener*,' replied the director.[6]

'What, Your Excellency?—but you were kind enough to engage me ...'

'I know, but surely it doesn't disturb you to have four more months of freedom?'

'Four months?' I asked, fearfully.

'Nearly that.'

'But indeed, Your Excellency, in these months also, one must live.'

'And live well. You will be paid your full salary. And if you need money immediately, you may draw an advance.'

'I would be grateful for an advance, Your Excellency.'

'Is 200 roubles enough?'[7]

'More than enough.'

'Then present this paper at the office of the Imperial Theatre, and you will get 200 roubles.'

I was bursting with gratitude, and on leaving the director, gave thanks to heaven, which had sent me such good fortune. What luck! I said to myself, yes, this is simply the promised land. To receive four months salary for doing nothing, and to obtain an immediate advance of 200 roubles—what a contrast to the administration at Nantes, where they had refused to pay me when I broke my leg while in service.

Beside myself with excitement, I shared my happiness with my mother immediately, sending her 100 roubles.[8]

The standard one-year contract he signed as *premier danseur* and mime ran from 24 May 1847 and included an option for a further two years, if agreed by the directorate. His annual payment was 10,000 francs, supplemented by the proceeds of one half-benefit performance.[9] His contract does not note his date of birth; later in the 1860s, when renewing his passport on two occasions, he knocked off seven years, claiming to be born in 1825. Later still, he settled on 1822 as his 'chosen' year of birth, so that after his death tributes were published in 1922 in celebration of the presumed centenary of his birth.[10]

At a guess, the 'improved' age was not an outlandish tactic at a time when personal data were less easily verifiable. It was especially understandable for a twenty-nine-year-old still trying to clamber upwards in a profession demanding youth. He had already subtracted a year for the passport issued to him in 1844 in Bordeaux—and that was considerably less than his father Jean who removed twelve years for his own passport to Madrid (via Marseilles) soon after.[11] Marius's progress had not been as smooth as that of his extremely handsome brother Lucien, his elder by three years. The two boys were moulded professionally by their father who had spent a large part of his career in Brussels, building up the company at the Théâtre de la Monnaie. Later, from 1835 to 1839 Jean was the ballet master at the Grand-Théâtre in Bordeaux and it was at this point that Marius, a formerly reluctant ballet student, started to commit himself fully to his dance training and 'to examine the theory of *pas* [dances]'.[12]

The Glamorous Lucien Petipa

During this time, Lucien was displaying his refined classical technique and skilful mime on the Bordeaux stage. In 1836 he performed the lead mime role of Oswald opposite a guest celebrity, Fanny Elssler, in his father's production of Taglioni's *Nathalie, or the Swiss Milkmaid*.[13] (Jean had first staged the ballet as *The Swiss Milkmaid* in 1824 during his term as ballet master in Brussels.)[14] It was maybe Elssler who, recognizing Lucien's talent, recommended him to the Paris Opera.[15] Either way, Lucien made his Paris Opera debut, dancing James in Taglioni's *La Sylphide* on 10 June 1839, opposite Elssler. This production, staged with care the previous year, deviated from the original in only one respect: James's second-act pas de deux with the titular sylphide was replaced by a duo for two sylphides, performed by Fanny and Therese Elssler, Fanny's sister who profited by Fanny's fame. For Lucien's debut, however, the sisters adapted this into a pas de trois: a gracious concession that was fully vindicated by Lucien's performance. His pleasing appearance, grace, and easy elevation immediately won over both the public and management, and he was forthwith engaged.[16] He seems to have been a perfect all-rounder, admired for his 'intelligent and passionate' mime, his 'bold and supple dancing which has contributed for a large part to the success of modern ballets'.[17] He had charm, he was 'always elegant, graceful and refined', he was the skilful and chivalrous partner of the century's greatest ballerinas.[18] Soon he was 'without equal the hero and the prince loved in all the ballets' of the Paris Opera.[19] It was Lucien who created the role of Albrecht in *Giselle*, partnering Carlotta Grisi—and conquering her heart offstage as well as on. He became Grisi's regular partner and enjoyed great success on visits to London, appearing with Grisi and two other ballerinas, Adèle Dumilâtre and the part-Irish, part-Flemish Adeline Plunkett. He also partnered the great Marie Taglioni for her final performances in her signature ballet *La Sylphide* in 1844. 'Petipa, by the expressiveness and warmth of his acting, by the energy of his dance, showed himself worthy of such a partner,' Gautier reported in *La Presse*, adding, 'even though male dancers are completely out of fashion, he was applauded on several occasions.'[20] A couple of years later, reviewing Jean Coralli's *La Péri*, created with Grisi and Petipa, Gautier also wrote:

> And here, as on so many other occasions, we must pay tribute to Petipa. How devoted and attentive he is to his ballerina, and how well he supports

her! He does not seek to attract attention to himself. And in spite of the sometimes unjust disfavour in which male dancers are held today, he is completely accepted by the public, for he does not put on the artificial graces and the revolting mincing manner that have turned the public against male dancing. A very intelligent mime, he always holds the stage and never overlooks the smallest detail. His success was therefore complete, and he can lay claim to a fair share of the applause that was produced by that admirable pas de deux.[21]

The 'admirable pas de deux' was a high point of the ballet, full of spectacular holds and a perilous leap, loudly cheered every evening, in which Grisi seemed to fly into Petipa's arms.

A group photograph of Lucien with his mother, Marius, and his sister Victorine shows an elegantly slender young man with a fine-drawn, regular-featured face. Later on, no longer playing romantic heroes, he became slightly less slender. In 1855 he launched himself as a choreographer with a *divertissement* for Verdi's *The Sicilian Vespers* (Les Vêpres siciliennes) and in 1860 succeeded Joseph Mazilier as the Paris company's first ballet master. As such it was he who gave the moving address at the funeral of Emma Livry, the tragic young ballerina who died after her costume caught fire.[22] And it was he who choreographed the Venusberg scene's bacchanal for the notorious French production of Wagner's *Tannhäuser* in 1861, withdrawn after just three performances. About his first full ballet *Sacountala* (1858), Gautier, who was its librettist, praised him for showing grace, originality, and freshness, and for possessing 'a feeling for plastic form in groups and an ease in handling masses'.[23] (These would also be salient qualities in Marius's work.) However, the fact that he created only three more ballets suggests that, even if they were accomplished, they were probably not outstanding. The composer Albert Vizentini was unimpressed by the way he discharged his duties in rehearsals, 'inoffensive, addressing everybody as *tu*', and compared him unfavourably to previous ballet masters.[24]

In November 1868 the Opera's management forced him to retire after he fell ill—he may have suffered a hunting accident in the summer.[25] His wife Angélique's letter pleading for a further two months for recuperation ('to tell him at this moment that his post is lost would *kill* him') fell on deaf ears.[26] Eventually, though, he briefly held the post of director of the dance conservatoire in Brussels (1872–1873), where his father had also been director and where he gave his first performances as a child.[27] In 1881 he began teaching at the Paris Opera in charge of a newly launched mime class.[28] In addition he gave private lessons in ballroom dancing and deportment for children, among them the future Napoleon III.[29] His choreographic swan song at the Paris Opera was *Namouna* in 1882, but that, together with all his other compositions, has disappeared. He died suddenly, aged eighty-three, on 7 July 1898 at his home in Versailles and today his name has all but faded from the collective memory.[30]

New York! New York?

Although Marius is now the best-known Petipa, he did not find the same rapid recognition as Lucien. He achieved brief success in Spain, but did not follow his brother to Paris Opera, the best ballet stage in the world. It was with his arrival in Russia that his position was elevated to international standing. In Russia, he then had to bide his time before finding the chance to prove himself as a choreographer. Although he staged a small number of character dances for opera early on, he was already in his late thirties when he started creating his own ballets.

Lillian Moore, basing herself on Petipa's memoirs, but slightly shifting his chronology, dates his adult professional performing debut as being in 1838, before his engagement in Nantes. The performance was, allegedly, at the Comédie-Française in Paris, at a benefit for the great tragedienne Mlle Rachel in which he danced with Carlotta Grisi. No trace, though, has been found. Instead, thanks to a programme advertised in *Le Coureur des spectacles*, the Soviet dance writer Iurii Slonimsky was able to establish that Lucien and Marius Petipa, along with Grisi, took part in a benefit on 27 October 1842 for Lucinde Paradol, retired actress of the Comédie-Française, by which time Marius had already spent three seasons as a *premier danseur* in Nantes. (They gave a performance of Molière's *comédie-ballet Le Bourgeois gentilhomme*.)[31]

There now follows even bigger confusion in the Petipa story. In 1839, just three months after Lucien's debut at the Paris Opera, Jean Petipa, who was no longer employed in Bordeaux, accepted a tantalizing new opportunity to work in New York and, according to Marius's memoirs, brought Marius into the equation. A ballerina, Éléonore Lecomte, who was putting together a company, invited Jean as ballet master. She had danced in London, in Russia (probably), and at the Paris Opera; she had been *première danseuse* at the Théâtre de la Monnaie when Jean was in charge.[32] Now, with her husband Jean Lecomte, a retired tenor, as her manager, she had already danced in the United States for two seasons. The audiences had been so receptive, she decided to bring over a group of European dancers. Among them were: Pauline Desjardins, who would later tour the United States with Fanny Elssler; Mme Lecomte's brother Jules Martin, a *premier danseur*; Kaiffer, another *premier danseur*; and a German eccentric dancer and mime called Klishnig. There was also a corps de ballet.[33]

Records show that on 29 August 1839 Jean Petipa took a ferry from Boulogne to London. From England, it is probable that on 2 September, along with Éléonore Lecomte's husband, he set sail to New York on the new *British Queen*, the largest passenger ship in the world.[34] The crossing took nineteen days, and Jean would have arrived just as Paul Taglioni (brother of Marie) and his wife Amalia Galster were finishing a popular four-month tour.

The Lecomte company was no gimcrack venture. It had been hired by the actor-manager James W. Wallack who, with his backers, had for two years successfully leased the National Theatre, located on the corner of Leonard and Church Streets, close to West Broadway. His repertory company was one of the finest ever gathered in the United States, headed that summer by the great American tragedian Edwin Forrest, and the ballet was scheduled to appear alongside this company.[35] However, on 23 September, the same day that Charles Kean, son of the famous Edmund Kean, was due to appear as Richard III, a fire broke out in the theatre. The conflagration was so devastating, it destroyed not only the theatre but three churches and several houses.[36] Wallack's losses were spectacular; even so, he managed to find a temporary home, a 1,200-seat theatre on Broadway adjoining Niblo's Garden, and on 1 October, less than a week after the fire, the National Theatre opened there.[37] The ballet's own opening on 29 October was part of a programme also containing a drama and a farce. They staged *La Tarentule*, a two-act ballet by Jean Coralli, premiered at the Paris Opera only a few months earlier.[38] The cast was led by Lecomte, Martin, his wife Égerie, and, in the comic mime role of Dr Omeopatico, Jean Petipa. An enthusiastic review appeared in the *Spirit of the Times*, praising Madame Lecomte as 'an acknowledged artiste' who was particularly effective in the scene where she was afflicted by the tarantula's bite and whose dancing still had 'that wonderful rapidity and finish' which had impressed before. Pauline Desjardins had a 'very pretty, pleasing face, and dances with a light, airy step', Jules Martin's mime was admirable, but about the other men—as too often happened—the reviewer declined 'to judge upon first sight'.[39]

La Tarentule was performed three more times; then on 4 November, sharing the bill with Edwin Forrest, Jean Petipa mounted *Jocko, the Ape of Brazil* (Jocko, ou le singe du Brésil), about an ape who saves his captor's child from drowning. Created in 1825 by Frédéric Blache (brother of the St Petersburg ballet master Alexis Blache) at Paris's Théâtre de la Porte-Saint-Martin, the ballet's sentimental story had immediately conquered the audience's heart and it was widely shown elsewhere, including Brussels, where it was staged by Jean Petipa in 1826. (A year later the nine-year-old Marius appeared as the child saved by the ape.)[40] In New York, Klishnig played the ape and made such a strong impression that he later toured the United States, starring in his own productions. According to the poster Jean Petipa seems to have played Pedro, the 'factotum' of Don Fernandez (Kaiffer), a Brazilian planter who was presumably the ape's captor. (The names did not match those of Blache's ballet.)[41]

Despite the combined attractions of foreign dancers and eminent actors, Wallack was losing money. On 12 November he withdrew the ballet company and on 18 November closed the theatre, having lost five thousand dollars. Some newspapers blamed the theatre's location and the difficult times.[42] The Lecomtes, however, promptly found another venue, the Bowery Theatre, where the company opened on 18 November with *Jocko*.[43] On 21 November they presented Jean's third production, *Marco Bomba, or the Bragging Sergeant*, a one-act burlesque about a boisterous band of Galician village boys, who, urged on by their sweethearts, assume all manner of physical infirmities to escape conscription when Sergeant Marco Bomba arrives. The ballet had been premiered at the Théâtre de la Renaissance in Paris on 23 August (*Marco Bomba, ou Le Sergent fanfaron*), just days before Jean's departure to New York. Jean knew the choreographer Jean Ragaine, since he had been one of his *premier danseurs* at the Monnaie.[44] The libretto's rollicking premise, with its open invitation to knockabout comedy, meant that when Jean returned to the Monnaie in 1841 and mounted *Marco Bomba* two years later, he produced a hit. (In 1854, the same ballet appeared on the St Petersburg stage, in a mise en scène by Perrot for Marius Petipa's benefit performance, with Perrot, Petipa, and a polished dancer called Christian Johansson enjoying themselves enormously.)[45]

At the Bowery, however, it was given only three times and didn't prevent the company collapsing into financial failure. Deciding to leave not with a whimper but a defiant flourish, they gave their farewell on 23 November with *Marco Bomba* and a special 'Grand Carnival Ball'.[46] Marius in his memoirs accuses Éléonore Lecomte's husband of being a 'swindler-impresario' who robbed them of the box-office receipts. He writes that this, together with an epidemic of yellow fever, prompted his father to book their return to Europe on the first available passage. He adds that 'the enterprise ended in a most shameful bankruptcy, and the company who worked there full time didn't receive a cent.'[47]

In fact the company continued performing well into the following year, appearing in Mobile, New Orleans, St Louis, and Boston. (Éléonore Lecomte and Jules Martin eventually settled as ballet teachers in Philadelphia.)[48] Also in fact, contrary to Marius's claim, he himself never took part in the American season. His name is nowhere to be found in passenger records or advertisements. Even more decisive is Sergei Konaev's incontrovertible evidence in his new edition of Petipa's memoirs: theatre listings in the local newspapers *Le Breton* and *Vert-Vert* show that during the whole of the American tour, Petipa was busy performing on the stage of the Grand-Théâtre of Nantes. For example, as advertised in *Le Breton* of 22 October, just one week before the New York opening, he was dancing a pas de quatre that same day in the one-act *The Six* Ingénus, *or the Family of Innocents* (Les Six Ingénus, ou la Famille des innocents); and again, as advertised by *Le Breton* of 30 November, he was dancing a pas de deux that same day with the *première danseuse* Armande Ferdinand in a *divertissement*, *Spanish Rosita* (Rosita l'espagnole).[49] What to make of this? The most charitable interpretation is that, remembering his father's stories, Petipa in his old man's mind had actually convinced himself that he too had been there.

Nantes

Petipa's first employment, at the age of twenty-one, was at the Grand-Théâtre of Nantes. His name appears in the company lists as *premier danseur* for three seasons: 1839–1840, 1840–1841, and 1841–1842.[50] The season started in May and he joined the small company when the ballet master was Étienne-Hughes Laurençon, another dancer who had served in Brussels under Jean Petipa.[51] Petipa claims he choreographed three complete ballets in Nantes, as well as dances for operas; he also says he received an author's fee for each performance, which 'flattered my ego, and I decided to devote myself to this speciality'.[52] The ballets he names—*The Master's Prerogative* (Le Droit du Seigneur); *The Gypsy Girl* (La Petite Bohémienne); *The Wedding Celebration in Nantes* (La Noce à Nantes)—have not been found. But *Le Breton* does record the following ballet as part of a double bill:

> Grand-Theatre—Today Thursday, 16 July 1840, at six o'clock. 1. *Don Juan of Austria*, comedy in five acts, by M. Casimir Delavigne; 2. *The Scatterbrain, or the Love Affair*, ballet in two scenes, by M. Marius Petipa.

Given the date it seems likely that this represents his very first professional ballet; Petipa's choreographic ambitions therefore existed right from the start. There are also traces of dances he created for himself and the two sisters in the company, Armande and Thérèse Ferdinand: among them, a pas de trois in the opera *La Favorite* (25 April 1841), 'A New Tyrolean' (*Une Nouvelle Tyrolienne*, 9 December 1841), and a Saxon dance in the style of a *cracovienne* (14 March 1842).[53]

His name often appears as a performer; he was, with Laurençon, the company's only *premier danseur* (Laurençon was a *premier danseur* in the *comique* genre).[54] He is not singled out for specific description, but on 4 October 1840 *Vert-Vert* wrote enthusiastically about the company in general, praising the precision, lightness, and wonderful grace with which it performed Spanish, Russian, Styrian, and Tyrolean dances and calling for its members to be allowed less cramped working conditions.[55]

On the subject of working conditions, Petipa writes in his memoirs that in his second season he broke his leg on stage. During the six weeks of recovery he discovered 'how the majority of impresarios treat the actors whom they exploit'. Although his injury had been sustained while performing, he learnt that, without performances, his salary would be withheld. So he found a ruse, devising a Spanish *pas* in which he played the castanets while another dancer performed the steps. With this, the management found itself legally obliged to pay his salary.[56] In his exhaustive researches in Nantes, Konaev has not been able to find anything to corroborate the castanet-playing strategy, but the absence of Petipa's name on the theatre bills during February and March 1840 suggests that he did indeed sustain an injury.[57]

Meanwhile, Jean Petipa returned to Brussels in September 1841 for another two seasons. And at some point Petipa spent two months in the Paris classes of the elderly Auguste Vestris, who had been the greatest male dancer of his generation and was now an important teacher. In his memoirs Petipa gives the timing as preceding his employment in Bordeaux, in which case it would have been not long before Vestris's death aged eighty-two in 1842.

Bordeaux

Petipa arrived at the Grand-Théâtre de Bordeaux on 1 May 1843, back to the city where he had spent four years before joining the Nantes company. Six months before his return, a new general director and former actor, Auguste Devéria, had signed an agreement for a three-year lease on Bordeaux's theatres, chief among which was the Grand-Théâtre. Built in 1780, its elegant colonnaded stone architecture survives to this day and still houses a ballet company and a wooden auditorium, now restored with the original royal colours of blue, white, and gold. Petipa calls it a 'luxurious theatre' in a 'wonderful city', and both epithets remain accurate.[58] In Petipa's time the inside of the theatre had gas lighting and the outside was illuminated during performances. There was heating during the winter, while in hot weather the foyer and entrances were sprinkled with water.[59] The theatre's performance history is distinguished: Jean Dauberval was ballet master from 1785 to 1790 and it was on this stage in 1789 that he created his famous ballet *La Fille mal gardée* under its original name, *Le Ballet de la paille, ou Il n'est qu'un pas du mal au bien*.[60] When Petipa arrived, though, the Grand-Théâtre was in dire financial straits and the press was complaining of declining standards, a monotonous repertoire, and crumbling stage designs. The new appointee, Devéria, was the latest in a long succession of speedily bankrupted directors. He had won an increased subsidy and much hope was pinned on his plans to expand the number of performers and attract bigger audiences.[61]

It was customary in municipal theatres for artists engaged by the director to be confronted with a further hurdle—the public's response. At Nantes, for example, with each new season, artists seeking entry or promotion also depended on the audience's cheers or jeers over the course of three performances.[62] Bordeaux followed the same practice and for the third performance, according to Petipa, he was one of five aspirants, among whom were a tenor and an actress of the *soubrette* genre. There was a *commissaire*, who was a member of the police, to oversee the nerve-wracking proceedings.[63]

In reality Petipa's ordeal was even more complicated and precarious than he lets on. For his first performance on 13 May 1843, he was ambitiously announced as 'first dancer in all styles' (*premier danseur en tous genres*) and appeared not in any old *divertissement* but as Albrecht in *Giselle*, partnering the popular *première danseuse* Élisa Bellon who was returning to Bordeaux after a year at the Paris Opera. Maybe Devéria was hoping the pairing would stir the Bordeaux masses—and, in the event, it did: where Petipa was concerned it provoked a great deal of hissing as well as applause. The police report, describing the event, was not optimistic: 'Petipa [...] will not achieve the success he was, it is said, counting on.'[64] The press reviews were mixed. The arts weekly *La Sylphide* on 18 May 1843 described him as 'young, with a good physique, light and with good schooling, but a bit rigid and inexpert [...] work will make him acquire what he needs'.[65] Another publication, *L'Indicateur*, reported 'M. Petipas [sic] is a very young dancer who shows excellent abilities; his dancing is rather weak, it is true, but his bearing is good; he mimes and gestures well.'[66] Other reviewers, though, were less forgiving.

This over-challenged debut poses the question of who thought of it in the first place. Maybe Lucien or Jean Petipa pulled strings; maybe Devéria, talent-scouting in Paris, saw Marius in the Lucinde Paradol benefit and was impressed; or maybe, as Sergei Konaev suggests, it was Élisa Bellon who, having danced *Giselle* in Paris and getting to know Marius there, wanted him as her partner. Natalie Morel Borotra, quoting Pierre Lacotte's claim that Marius, helped by Lucien, notated *Giselle* in great detail when he first saw the ballet in 1842, also wonders whether Marius might have participated in the ballet's staging on the Bordeaux stage. Either way, the resulting state of affairs seems to have prompted Petipa's superiors to pressure him to accept a demotion.[67] His second appearance on 22 May was as an understudy for the *premier danseur* Charles Albert (son of the reputable ballet master 'Albert') in a pas de deux with Joséphine Delestre, a *deuxième danseuse* (second-rank dancer).[68] But that was not enough to mollify the writers of *La Sylphide* and *L'Indicateur* who judged his performance heavy and listless. A further downgrading was needed, and this was made public. The local theatre periodical *L'Homme gris* reported that Petipa had definitively renounced his *premier danseur* ambition; the *Mémorial bordelais* commented 'after M. Marius Petipas [sic] made it known that he would accept a more modest rank than the one he was initially pursuing, his future, rather dark at first, has brightened a little.'[69]

His third appearance was before a tumultuous audience, which rejected the debuts of two singers, amid hostilities between the different factions. He was about to go the same way, and at some point a spectator threw a scrap of paper on stage with the scrawled message 'no more Petipa', adding the humiliating phrase 'at any price'.[70] But the *régisseur* appeared, to emphasize to the audience that Petipa was a candidate for the replacement of M. Honoré, a *troisième danseur* (third-rank dancer) who took *deuxième danseur* roles when needed.[71] In the end he was accepted into the company with the rank of *deuxième danseur*, as indicated by a letter he wrote to the press 'to reassure those who might object to me, believing I am claiming a *premier* position, when I am limiting myself to *deuxième danseur*'.[72]

Devéria's ballet company was led by the ballet master Alexis Blache, the same Blache who had been in St Petersburg. The top rank of the performing hierarchy was occupied by two married couples: Albert and Bellon; Lucien Clair and his wife, the second pair being *demi-caractère* dancers. The corps de ballet of thirty-two was equally divided between men and women; above them was a total of about fifteen *troisième* and *deuxième danseurs* and mimes. There was even a ballet school attached to the company. Meanwhile, the orchestra under Louis Costard de Mézeray (who would become one of France's most eminent conductors) had fifty-one musicians.[73]

After such a bad start, things could only improve for Petipa. He was kept busy partnering *deuxièmes danseuses* such as Delestre and Célina Moulinié. He appeared with Moulinié in the familiar *El Marcobomba* (spelt here as one word), dancing a pretty pas de deux 'whose execution', according to *L'Homme gris*, 'showed a progress which the public was able to appreciate'.[74] Other reviews make encouraging comments. On 14 March 1844 *La Sylphide* reported: 'M. Petipa enjoys greater favour from the public every day.'[75] Between May 1843 and June 1844, besides Albrecht in *Giselle*, he had roles in other popular ballets: *The Village Sleepwalker* (La Somnambule villageoise); *The Millers* (Les Meuniers) by Jean-Baptiste Blache (eminent father of Alexis and Frédéric); *La Sylphide; La Fille mal gardée* (which he had also danced in Nantes). He was Osvald in *Nathalie, or the Swiss Milkmaid*; he danced in Auber's opera-ballet *Le Dieu et la bayadère* (The God and the Bayadère). He appeared in character dances, often with Moulinié: mazurkas and other Central European numbers, but especially Spanish dances—the *cachucha, bolera, jota aragonesa*—which were especially popular with Bordeaux's Iberian community.[76] For the new season, the company list published on 30 April 1844 shows him as aiming for *deuxième danseur, premier* when needed (*premier au besoin*): a modest promotion which seems to have been jeopardized by the audience's reception on 3 May—another rowdy gladiatorial occasion, where opposing spectators tried to drown each other out. The atmosphere seems to have unnerved Petipa and, appearing with Delestre in Donizetti's *La Favorite*, he made the mistake of acknowledging applause that was meant for her. This, as described by the police report, lost him any shred of favour he might have had with the subscribers, although the rest of the audience seemed more benevolent.[77] However, he was accepted by the management, according to *L'Indicateur* (5 May) and *La Sylphide* (9 May), the latter describing him as tireless and well-schooled, and adding a week later that 'M. Petipa is well thought of and deserves it.'[78] In his memoirs Petipa claims to have choreographed four ballets, but no mention of them has yet been found.[79]

After only eleven months, he was forced to join the stream of dancers leaving Bordeaux. On 22 March 1844, Devéria informed the city authorities that he had a deficit of more than 60,000 francs; on 13 May 1844, his enterprise was declared bankrupt; and on 15 June Petipa's departure was reported in the press.[80] His passport had already been issued on 12 June for travel to Madrid via Bayonne, to join the Teatro del Circo.

Spain

The Teatro del Circo had reopened as a theatre in 1842 and was the city's fashionable 1,600-seat home of opera and ballet.[81] It had an orchestra of 116 players, a ballet school, and even a shuttle—special carriages transporting spectators to performances from various points in the city. The theatre's director José, Marques de Salamanca, wanted to show the best of opera and ballet and was in the process of repopulating the ballet company. He engaged the ballet master Jean-Baptiste Barrez from the Paris Opera; among the dancers, the most famous was Marie Guy-Stéphan, a refined classicist as well as a talented performer of character dances, who had appeared with much success in London, Milan, and Paris. It was possibly Barrez, since he had coached Lucien Petipa at the Paris Opera, who thought of inviting Marius. Or maybe the idea came from Guy-Stéphan, who needed a partner. She knew the Petipa family: she had been engaged as a *première danseuse* in Bordeaux when Jean Petipa was ballet master.[82]

Either way, Petipa was brought to Madrid to be Guy-Stéphan's partner in the fashionable ballets of the day. His appearances were tracked by numerous reviews, although he was more often mentioned in the shadow of the ballerina. His debut with *Giselle* on 24 June 1844 'was received with general applause' and showed that 'his dance schooling, like his mime, was very good'.[83] Among the other ballets he subsequently performed were: Albert's *The Beautiful Maid of Ghent* (La Jolie Fille de Gand, renamed La Hermosa Beatriz o el sueño), where he danced a polka and an *allemande* with Guy-Stéphan; Coralli's *La Tarentule*, in which he appeared as the male lead Luis; and Joseph Mazilier's *The Devil in Love* (El Diablo Enamorado), in which he was also cast as the male lead Frédéric.[84] As the months passed, so the reviews of Petipa gained in enthusiasm and detail. He was 'from the modern school, bringing together good taste and decent execution'. Dancing in *La Péri*, he was superior to the other men, Mr Ferranti and Mr Gontie, which 'made us regret how short was the part he played'. In *The Devil in Love* 'he performed the part of Count Frédéric with great skill and understanding.'[85] When the company was again reorganized for the 1845–1846 season, all the existing dancers were removed 'with only the inimitable Guy-Stéphan and Mr Petipa staying for the next year'.[86] The new dancers included Petipa's Bordeaux stage partner Joséphine Delestre and Frédéric Montessu, who had also worked in Bordeaux.[87] For the *Crónica de*

Madrid Montessu turned out to be the city's best male dancer, with high, confident, and effortless jumps, whereas Petipa, in 'classical (*heroic*) dance is no better than average, but in the character or ballroom dances he is excellent' and 'his acting is natural and realistic'.[88]

From *deuxième danseur* in Bordeaux to the partner of Madrid's *prima ballerina assoluta* was quite a promotion, even if the Teatro del Circo was not one of Europe's premier stages. The reviews are almost unanimous concerning the enormous popularity not only of Guy-Stéphan but of Petipa: they encored their dances to tumultuous applause; they were 'the lovely and nimble Guy-Stéphan and the energetic and intelligent Petipa' who 'will no doubt receive as much applause as always'.[89] As would be the case in Russia, Petipa seems to have been a good partner, a gifted actor, and a particularly effective character dancer. Perhaps his lesser talent in classical dance is the reason why Frédéric Montessu and Pierre Massot head the male dancers in the company's hierarchy, published on 25 March 1845, with Petipa listed directly below them.[90] In the spring of 1846, as described in his memoirs, he and Guy-Stéphan were invited by Fernando Millet, impresario of the Teatro Principal of Seville, to tour Andalusia with Millet's ballet company.[91] They started in Seville on 21 April and went on to visit seven other cities, among them Cádiz, Málaga, and Granada, performing changing programmes of extracts from the Madrid repertoire. In Seville, for example, their programme included a pas de deux from *Ondine*, a polka, and a *jaleo de Jerez*. Elsewhere they also showed extracts from *Esmeralda*, the pas de deux from Perrot's divertissement *L'Aurore* (Dawn), and a tambourine dance (*Paso de la Pandereta*).[92] (About *Ondine* and *Esmeralda*, see below.) In Sanlúcar de Barrameda their visit coincided with an annual festival and Petipa, wearing a Spanish costume and feeling 'just like a Spaniard', joined in the dancing in the torchlit streets, accompanied by students playing guitars. In Granada, the last city, they appeared without the Seville company and were directly employed by the Teatro Comico, giving five performances between 16 and 21 July. Later, in Russia, Petipa would make ample use of his firsthand experience of Spanish dance, most obviously in *Don Quixote* in 1869. Once again, though, there is no trace of the ballets claimed by him as his own creations in Madrid, which doesn't mean they didn't exist. Some of them may have been ad hoc *divertissements* for special occasions or for the Andalusian tour.[93]

In 1845, presumably at his son's recommendation, Jean Petipa became ballet master of the Circo company, replacing Barrez.[94] That same year (26 December), for a corps de ballet benefit performance, he created *The Milliners of Paris* (Las Modistas de París) which didn't survive its first performance.[95] He also staged two recent Perrot ballets: *Esmeralda* (18 November), in which Jean played Quasimodo and Marius danced a 'Waltz of Madness' with Guy-Stéphan's Esmeralda; and, before that, *Ondine* (30 July), in which Guy-Stéphan was the titular water nymph and Marius, the fisherman bewitched by her. In the second act of *Ondine*, one reviewer stated: 'Mr Petipa understood perfectly the character of the dance he performed and it is unnecessary to say that he was peerless.'[96] It was also *Ondine* that provoked an incident amusingly described in Petipa's memoirs.[97] The narrative required Petipa to give Guy-Stéphan a kiss, but this contravened strict Spanish proprieties and at a later performance the chief of police forbade the kiss, ruining the *pas*. It was later reinstated, Salamanca having explained its importance to the authorities, which allowed *El Globo* to report: 'At the moment of the kiss, the audience applauded the kisser, the kissed, and also the official who allowed the innocent and contentious kiss.'[98]

Ondine and *Esmeralda* won enthusiastic notices, as did Jean Petipa's own three-act composition on 3 March the following year, *Farfarella, or the Daughter of Hell* (Farfarella o la Hija del Infierno), which featured Marius in the central part of Pablo, a painter. No expense was spared for the designs and costumes. Reviewers were particularly taken by the *redowa*, a Bohemian polka made hugely popular by the stars of the Romantic Ballet and here performed by Guy-Stéphan *en travesti*; they also liked the 'Mirror Dance' in which Guy-Stéphan seemed to be dancing in front of a mirror, actually a gauze with another dancer behind, matching her moves exactly.[99]

The careers of both Petipas were going so well. Marius was now a celebrity, he and Guy-Stéphan mentioned in the same breath as Carlotta Grisi, Perrot, and Vestris. They were credited with giving 'life again' to the Circo after their return from Andalucia.[100] Jean was preparing another original ballet, *Sorrowful Alba Flor* (Alba Flor la pesarosa). But then Marius got himself into a major scrape and Jean can't have been too pleased.

At this point, once again, the story as told by Marius is chronologically tangled. He describes a duel with the first secretary of the French embassy, the 'Marquis X', who had challenged him after discovering that he was making nocturnal visits to the house of a Spanish noblewoman. The marquis, who was romantically linked with this woman, had jumped to the wrong conclusion that Petipa was a rival, when in fact Petipa was conducting a secret love affair with the woman's daughter.[101] The following morning at dawn, having hurriedly found a compatriot, a former tradesman from Bordeaux, to act as his second, Petipa appeared at the agreed location where the marquis was already trying out his pistols.

> 'Permit us to do the same,' says my modest witness, who was present at a duel for the first time. When I shot, he quietly observed:
> 'I see, with pleasure, that you shot without a miss, as before.'
> I was astonished at the ingenuity of this simple plebeian, who instinctively knew that to frighten my opponent, and deprive him of the necessary coolness of mind, meant to give me a better chance of a fortunate (for me) outcome of the duel.[102]

Petipa's account goes on to state that the marquis's second, the duke d'Alba, then approached him with an offer of 10,000 francs in exchange for his immediate departure from Madrid. Petipa refused, so the men took up their positions. The marquis had first go, and missed; Petipa managed to shoot him in the jaw and 'the story of the duel flew round the whole city'.[103] Soon he was being questioned by the police and on advice denied everything, duels being, of course, illegal. However, the French embassy was also stirring things up and it was becoming clear that he needed to leave Madrid immediately to avoid further investigation.

Recent research, however, by Laura Hormigón and Sergei Konaev, not only un-covers the possible identity of Petipa's opponent (after fruitless attempts by other dance historians), but dates the duel much earlier. This would have occurred not long after Petipa's arrival in Madrid and not later than the middle of September 1844, because it was reported in a semi-accurate bulletin in a German newspaper, *Augsburger Tagblatt*, on 23 September 1844. A detailed article then appeared in another German publication, *Der Bayerische Eilbote*, on 4 October 1844. It an-nounced that a duel between the French count de Gabriac and the dancer Petipa had provoked much talk in Madrid. The count, who had earlier been attached to the French embassy in Copenhagen, had arrived in Madrid the year before, as the companion and ardent admirer of the Spanish 'marquise de V'.[104] The article then describes how the twenty-five-year-old daughter of the marquise had started dance lessons with Petipa and a romance had developed. When the marquise found out, she banished Petipa from her house and even offered him a significant sum of money in exchange for his departure from Madrid. Petipa, however, became all the more determined not to give up his paramour, following which the count de Gabriac threatened to give him a thrashing. In response, Petipa challenged him to a duel. After taking the requisite twenty steps away from each other, the count was the first to shoot, but his pistol misfired. Petipa suggested he try again, but while the count was loading his pistol, Petipa exploited the moment to take leisurely aim and shattered the left side of his opponent's jaw. The bullet also penetrated the count's neck, but fortunately a skilful surgeon managed to pull it out. After just a few days, Petipa appeared again on stage.

Evidently this account puts Petipa in a highly unflattering light; one can only hope that either there are journalistic distortions or that, in the anxious drama of the moment, there was a misunderstanding about whose turn it was to shoot. Either way, Petipa in his memoirs seems to have conflated two separate inci-dents: the duel was much too early to be, as he claims, the direct cause of his departure in January 1847 (unless the police was pursuing him retrospectively). The German article might also explain why the Spanish press gossip in 1847 did not mention a duel in connection with his disappearance and the conse-quent cancellation of the performance of *The Devil in Love* on 11 January. Instead it alluded to a romantic scandal. Laura Hormigón's unrelenting research has revealed that Petipa's sweetheart was most probably Carmen Mendoza y Castro, the twenty-three-year-old daughter of Maria de la Concepción, marquesa de Villagarcia.[105] One of Hormigon's sources is a letter dated 23 January 1847 from the French writer Prosper Merimée to the condesa (countess) de Montijo (mother of the future empress Eugénie): 'I thought that M. Petitpas [sic] was after the marquesa de Villagarcia herself and not her daughter. But they say that he's a man without prejudices who eats the mature fruit first and the green fruit later.'[106]

All this suggests that the passion between Carmen and Petipa did not die after the duel, rather it continued and the pair decided to elope. (Under Spanish law Carmen was still underage.) The newspapers were full of oblique references and jocular innuendos. El Heraldo was the first, writing of 'the disappearance of one of the most elegant young ladies of the court' which 'has coincided with the sudden disappearance of a prominent person currently attracting attention at one of Madrid's major theatres.'[107] La Opinion added: 'if the family of this bewitched but interesting young lady intend to track down the kidnapper, they should not over-look the fact that [...] this person's most remarkable quality is a truly amazing lightness of foot.'[108] El Español and La Opinion both offered the further detail that Carmen went out to Mass and did not return.[109] Juan Valera, in a letter to his father, had a slightly different version:

> The most notable event occupying gossipmongers these days is the elope-ment of the dancer Petipa with the daughter of the marquesa de V. They say that this smitten girl disappeared from her house at dinner time, leaving a letter for her mother in which she explained the reasons which pushed her to take such an exceptional course of action; she cited the excessive burden of the intense love she felt for the aerial and vaporous lover with whom she has eloped.[110]

La Opinion reported that the 'runaway lovers have been discovered and caught', five days after the disappearance.[111] El Clamor Publico provided a pun and a prediction: 'This act of seduction is a petit-pas (small step) to a marriage of conscience.'[112] The French newspaper La Presse seemed to confirm the attempt to save the young girl's honour (here called Carmen de Medina and given her mother's title):

> French theatre artists find success in more than one genre abroad; for here comes, in Madrid, the announcement of the marriage of Monsieur Marius Petipa, first soloist at the Teatro del Circo, and brother of Lucien Petipa, our French dancer, with Mademoiselle Carmen de Medina, marchioness of Villagarcia.[113]

However, instead of getting married and rehearsing his father's new *Sorrowful Alba Flor*, premiered on 3 March 1847, in which Jean appeared as an old gypsy, Julion, Marius was in France with Carmen. This is confirmed by another letter, from the first secretary of the Spanish embassy in France, Domingo de Aguilera y Contreras, marqués de Banalúa, written on 27 January 1847 to the French minister of the interior Charles-Marie-Tanneguy Duchâtel. The letter records the disappearance of Carmen on 10 January

> without the consent of her parents to follow Mr Petipas [*sic*], dancer, to France. I am appealing to the goodwill of Your Excellency to request that he give the orders necessary to ensure that Miss Mendoza y Castro be carefully sought out and committed to a suitable place until her parents can send someone to bring her back.
>
> According to the information received, Mr Petipas is travelling under an assumed name and must have left Bayonne on the fourteenth of this month for Paris, where on the twenty-third he was apparently seen on the platform for the train from Rouen.[114]

In her recent research, Hormigón has discovered that from Paris, Petipa and Carmen went to Le Havre, and then on to England where they stayed to the end of February. On their return to France, they hid in a village near Rouen until they were discovered by the police who arrested Carmen on 13 March 1847, in keeping with the request of the Spanish authorities.[115]

So Petipa had abandoned a successful Spanish career for nothing. He was now alone, probably depressed, penniless (the elopement was an expensive venture), and in Paris. He must have discarded his incognito status, since he claims he danced a pas de quatre, with his brother Lucien and Fanny and Therese Elssler, for Therese's farewell benefit at the Opera, although this does not tally with the known dates of the sisters' last performance together (30 January 1840) and Therese's retirement in 1850.[116] More reliable is the next statement that he received a letter from 'the old ballet master Titus', inviting him to St Petersburg, to replace Émile Gredelue, 'a very talented artist' who was returning to France. For Marius, clearly in need of an opportunity at this juncture, the letter must have been hugely welcome.

There are various theories explaining how he received such a letter. 'Svoï' (One of Us) in *Birzhevye vedomosti* writes that Lucien was invited but turned the invitation down. Lucien was now established as the Paris Opera's leading male dancer, performing on the world's most important ballet stage, and would have had no reason to take up permanent employment in Russia. Equally plausible is Pleshcheev's account that Lucien, following Titus's visit to Paris to see *Giselle*, had then written to Titus recommending his younger brother.[117] Whatever the truth, the fact is that Marius, Lucien, and Jean were always helping each other in the effort to find work. A career in the theatre was precarious and peripatetic, especially for those outside the big national opera houses. True, there were theatrical agencies, including one in Paris with close ties to St Petersburg.[118] But, like today, nothing was more effective than personal contacts. And just as Jean helped his sons find employment, so Marius, it seems, helped his father, securing an invitation for him to work not only in Spain, but also, as will be seen, in Russia.

3

Russian Debut

*Petipa-son [...] made his debut in Paquita and danced the 'Pas
de folie' with Andreianova, in which he displayed much art.¹*

First Steps

Petipa's debut was scheduled for 26 September 1847, in the Russian premiere
of Mazilier's *Paquita* (to a score by Deldevez), a ballet that would occupy an important place in Petipa's creative career. The evening was a benefit for the company member, Pierre Frédéric Malavergne, known simply as Frédéric, and Petipa
would be partnering the principal ballerina Elena Andreianova who was making
her return to the Russian stage after a season in Paris. When *Paquita* was created
at the Paris Opera on 1 April 1846 with Carlotta Grisi and Lucien Petipa it had a
tremendous success, despite certain narrative absurdities, and repeated this success later in London (again with Grisi).² Set in Napoleonic Spain, in the province
of Saragossa, it is the story of how Lucien d'Hervilly (in a dashing hussar's uniform) wins the heart of a gypsy girl called Paquita, despite the machinations of
Don Luis de Mendoza, the anti-French Spanish governor of the province, and his
unlikely accomplice the brutal gypsy leader Inigo. The two villains, for their separate reasons, want Lucien dead, but fail in their attempt. The final twist of the
dénouement comes with Paquita's discovery that instead of being a gypsy she is
in fact the kidnapped child of Lucien's uncle who, with his wife, was murdered by
bandits. She is therefore Lucien's first cousin, blue-blooded enough to marry him
(without worrying about genetic proximity) and provide a happy ending.

Lucien d'Hervilly was largely a mime role; that, along with the ballet's Spanish
gypsy dances, meant Petipa was breathing the kind of air he knew well. Presumably
it was during rehearsals that his usefulness became apparent, so that on the poster
he is named as co-producer with Frédéric, who had already staged Coralli's *La Péri*
in 1844.³ The dance historian Marina Ilicheva further proposes the theory that it
was in fact Frédéric who first thought of transferring *Paquita* to St Petersburg.
He had been dismissed by Gedeonov and was kicking his heels in Paris while
Andreianova was there. Her enthusiasm for Mazilier's new ballet suggested to
him that here was an opportunity for his reinstatement and Andreianova, for

her part, had no difficulty persuading Gedeonov that *Paquita*, staged by Frédéric, should be her next big moment. As a result, Frédéric returned to St Petersburg as ballet master, mime artist, and teacher at the school.[4]

That Petipa, in replacing Andreianova's regular partner Gredelue, should be assigned the role of Lucien d'Hervilly seems to have been agreed before his departure from Paris. Gedeonov had by mid-June 1846 already invited Frédéric back into the company, and records show that Petipa arrived in St Petersburg with a specially made hussar's costume. (See later in this chapter.) His Russian debut was, according to his memoirs, watched by Nicholas I and earned him the imperial gift of a ruby and diamond ring. He also won the phrase 'a most excellent acquisition for our troupe' from Rafail Zotov, reviewer of *Severnaia pchela*. Zotov, however, reserved more expansive judgement for later: 'He danced in the "pas de folie" and the *jaleo*, which is to say two character dances. His lightness and vigour were astonishing, but we await his future debuts in dances of a noble and serious genre before giving a detailed assessment.'[5]

Gedeonov appears to have been sufficiently impressed by Petipa's work in staging *Paquita* to be open to further suggestions. Perhaps it was Petipa who suggested Mazilier's *The Devil in Love*, remembering its success when he danced it in Madrid. It was a ballet that combined two attractive possibilities: it would provide him with a leading role; and he could propose that his father help with the staging which, if Jean were to come, might offer the prospect of well-paid permanent employment.[6]

Jean Petipa arrived in St Petersburg on the boat *Amsterdam* on 12 October 1847 and signed a three-year contract with the Imperial Theatres as a teacher of the school's senior boys.[7] Shortly after Jean's arrival, Marius made his Russian debut in two other roles, originally created in Paris by his brother Lucien: Ahmet in *La Péri* (26 October) and Albrecht in *Giselle* (23 November), partnering Andreianova for both. Meanwhile Jean must have set to work fairly quickly because *The Devil in Love* or *Satanilla*, to give the Russian title, was premiered for Andreianova's benefit performance on 10 February 1848.[8] The ballet, devised in collaboration with *Giselle*'s co-librettist Jules Henri Vernoy de Saint-Georges, was created at the Paris Opera in 1840, with Pauline Leroux in the central role of Urielle, a demon who falls in love with Frédéric, the young man whose soul she has been ordered to lure to the service of her master Beelzebub. Marius was Frédéric, renamed Fabio in St Petersburg, Andreianova was Satanilla (Urielle), and Fabio's tutor Hortensius was Jean. The posters advertised a 'big pantomime ballet' in three acts and seven scenes, produced by 'Petipa 1 [Jean] and Petipa 2 [Marius]', with all the dances newly created by them.[9] The critic Fedor Koni called the ballet 'a genuine triumph' in which, as in *Giselle*, everything—the staging, the designs, the story—came together in perfect synthesis. The dancers rose to the occasion. Andreianova was

'more than superb' with the speed and lightness of her movement and the animation and expressiveness of her acting. About the two Petipas, Koni wrote:

> It is almost possible to wager that in Paris's 'Grand Opera' it [the ballet] has
> never been played with such splendour and magical charm. [...]
>
> Mr Petipa-son performs the role of Count Fabio with animation. In this
> artist is one priceless quality: he strives to project ballet characters simply
> and naturally. [...] Petipa's face is expressive, and with his facial expres-
> sions he adds to what is implied by his movements.
>
> The role of Hortensius, the count's mentor, is filled by Mr Petipa-father.
> In him we see an adroit and experienced artist, a noble actor, not allowing
> himself anything superfluous for the amusement of the ignorant, but
> knowing how to be entertaining without farce, with only delicate irony and
> naturalness.[10]

In fact *Paquita* and *Satanilla* were a blast of oxygen in the St Petersburg ballet.
The company, since Didelot's exit, had been stagnating choreographically. This
had been counterbalanced, starting in 1837, by the visits of Marie Taglioni, who
had been an inspiration to the gifted Andreianova and her contemporary Tatiana
Smirnova. But in 1842, after Taglioni's final departure, the ballet slumped again.
It was in order to find a remedy that the directorate sent Titus to Paris to study
Giselle, for transfer to the St Petersburg stage; Paris's potent new ballet, it was
felt, would allow Russian ballerinas to shine and bring back audiences. The St
Petersburg premiere of *Giselle* on 18 December 1842 gave Andreianova her first
major part, and by all accounts she had full measure of its contrasting demands.
'This delightful dancer,' wrote Zotov, 'was complete consolation for the absence
of Taglioni.'[11] She also danced the ballet's Moscow premiere the following year.

Even so, *Giselle* did not dispel all the problems enveloping the St Petersburg
ballet. Reviewing the premiere (19 January 1847) of Titus's fantastical ballet *The
Talisman*, his last in Russia, Zotov surveyed the situation since Taglioni's departure. Other dancers had plenty of talent, he wrote, but the fickle audience
had nonetheless switched their allegiance to the Italian opera. All attempts
to please them, such as inviting the Danish ballerina Lucile Grahn, had failed.
Meanwhile, the company's most promising talents had been forced to find appreciation abroad: Smirnova appeared in Paris and Brussels in 1844; Andreianova in
Hamburg, Paris, Milan, and London from 1844 to 1852. 'We have delightful female dancers, skilful male dancers, an amazing corps de ballet,' lamented Zotov,
'we have a nursery blossoming daily with the rarest talents: we just lack a desire among the public to look at them. The only means of stimulating this desire
would be, perhaps, the creation of new, engaging ballets; but for this a new Didelot

is needed, a new Prometheus, a new choreographer *extraordinaire*, and at present, it seems, there is no such person in the whole of Europe.'[12]

For this reason, the two ballets staged by the Petipas had a pivotal effect, even if Mazilier was not in the same league as Didelot (or Prometheus). 'Overall,' wrote *Literaturnaia gazeta*, 'the year 1847 could go down in theatre chronicles as the year of the renaissance of ballet, demonstrated by the new success of the two ballets *Paquita* and *Satanilla* and the shared eagerness of the public for this genre of presentation.'[13]

The Elssler-Perrot Pas de Deux

Actually, the new Didelot *did* exist but had yet to come to Russia. He was Jules Perrot and his ballets in Vienna, Milan, and especially London, at His Majesty's Theatre, had marked him out as a remarkable talent. Initially, he had found fame as a prodigiously virtuosic dancer. According to the choreographer August Bournonville, who had known him as a fellow-student of Auguste Vestris, Perrot had been trained by Vestris to avoid 'picturesque poses', because of his alleged ugliness, but instead to 'jump about from place to place, turn and move around' so that the public never had time to observe him closely. His aerial plasticity became '*le genre de Perrot*, that is, Zephyr with the wings of a bat, a divinity belonging not to mythology, but to cabalism, a restless creature of indescribable lightness and suppleness with an almost phosphorescent brilliance! He truly created an epoch at the time when the diabolic was the predominant element on the French stage. He became the ideal of male dancing.'[14] Engaged as a dancer at the Paris Opera, his dancing proved to be the match of Marie Taglioni when he appeared with her in the 1831 revival of Didelot's *Zéphire et Flore* and drew the greater applause— 'a circumstance which,' Charles Maurice wrote, 'many people observed.'[15] Soon after, he signed a fresh one-year contract which confirmed his status as the Paris Opera's top male dancer by giving him a salary of 10,000 francs plus *feux* of 30 francs (bonus payments for each performance). This was four times what the Paris Opera had been paying him before and more than double what Joseph Mazilier was getting (4,500 francs).[16] On a later occasion, when Perrot partnered Taglioni in a pas de deux at the premiere of her father's *The Rebellion in the Seraglio* (1834) and Perrot bounded and skimmed with easy weightlessness, Taglioni flew into a rage at the end of the performance. 'It is too bad,' she cried to Dr Véron, director of the Paris Opera, 'that a male dancer should obtain more applause than I. It is monstrous!'[17] Even so, Taglioni did not nurse this particular grudge. They would dance together again in London and Paris to huge applause.

Perrot's career as a great mime and choreographer followed a few years later. Romantically linked to Carlotta Grisi, he had discovered her in Naples in 1836 as a fresh, gifted sixteen-year old, hesitating between opera (she was from a family of celebrated singers) and ballet. He became her teacher, mentor, and lover, and in 1837 they had a daughter. It was for Grisi that Perrot started choreographing, culminating in *Giselle* in 1841, which he co-created with Jean Coralli, then the Paris Opera's first ballet master. Although not acknowledged on any of the posters or on the printed programme, it is generally accepted that Perrot was responsible for the dances of Grisi's Giselle. The perfect integration of dance and drama established *Giselle* as the emblematic ballet of the Romantic period and laid the way for Perrot's future ballets.

Perrot's name had already reached the ears of Gedeonov who, desperately seeking a choreographer to replace Titus, had contacted him. But lost letters, Perrot's clashing commitments, and his ambitious demands as ballet's highest-paid man had foiled the negotiations.[18] In the end, it was Fanny Elssler, the interpreter of many of Perrot's ballets, who engineered his invitation to St Petersburg. She had long yearned to crown her career with a Russian triumph, as her rival Marie Taglioni had done. According to Perrot's biographer Ivor Guest, Elssler and Perrot had probably discussed St Petersburg while working in Milan and agreed that together they would make a choreographer-dancer tandem too alluring for the Russians to resist. However, when it came to the crunch Gedeonov was reluctant to invite either of them. Concerning Elssler, he had been advised by the London-based Russian diplomat baron (later count) Brunnov, who was a knowledgeable ballet subscriber, that she was well past her best. Concerning Perrot, he had again been warned by Brunnov that Perrot, to produce his best work, would require an international ballerina. Consequently, approaches were made to Grisi but she was not available.

Gedeonov then became embroiled in the manoeuvrings of Perrot and Elssler to force his hand. There are several conflicting accounts of how Elssler signed a contract with the St Petersburg ballet, but most say that she appealed over Gedeonov's head to Emperor Nicholas and she arrived unannounced in St Petersburg on 8 September 1848.[19] By order of the emperor, Gedeonov was moreover forced to instruct the Russian Consul-General in Paris to negotiate a formal contract with Perrot.[20] Meanwhile Elssler made her Russian debut in Titus's production of *Giselle* on 10 October. She was partnered by Petipa, but, just as when he had partnered Andreianova in the same ballet, reviewers failed to mention him. Elssler, being both a ballerina and a new celebrity, commanded complete attention, although reactions were mixed. She had chosen a role that was, in the supernatural second act, against type and against her age. (She was thirty-eight.) Besides paying homage to her justified fame for the passion and fire of her national dances, Pleshcheev, writing in retrospect, summed up the consensus. If people were disappointed by her second act, which required a spectral weightlessness, they were electrified by the heartbreaking directness with which she conveyed the very human tragedy of the first act. The difference between her and Taglioni, he wrote, echoing Gautier's polarity of Christian (Taglioni) and pagan (Elssler), was that of the sky and the earth. Taglioni personified the aerial creatures of poetic fantasy, Elssler gave shape to earthbound images taken from life. In pure technique she yielded to Taglioni; but as an actress she had 'betwitching beauty' and 'a fullness of intellect', with a face that 'communicated without words the innermost secrets of her soul and heart to the spectator, it forced him to feel joy and suffering with the artist'.[21]

For her next role, she herself staged *A Painter's Delirium* or *Le Délire d'un peintre* (Mechta khudozhnika), a *divertissement* Perrot had created for both of them in London in 1843. She added her celebrated Spanish dance, the *cachucha*, and chose Petipa as her partner. She also danced Lise in *La Fille mal gardée*. During all this, she was directing the rehearsals of Perrot's *Esmeralda*; although Grisi had created the titular role in London in 1844, Elssler had danced it in Perrot's Milan staging the same year. In St Petersburg, the ballet was scheduled for her benefit on 21 December 1848 and, pending Perrot's arrival, to make sure the ballet would be ready in time, she had, as seen earlier, already started work, with Marius Petipa as her assistant.[22]

As usual, the rehearsals were conducted at the Theatre School, a practice that provided a bridge between inspirational professionals and eager pupils allowed to watch. (The premises, though, were cramped and in 1891 a rehearsal hall was built a few yards away, in the courtyard of the directorate's offices. With a raked floor replicating the stage, this was able to accommodate almost 300 people, big enough for the full company and any student onlookers.)[23] Perrot himself finally arrived on 7 December.[24] Small, with a broad nose and prominent eyes, he was generally well liked by the pupils and dancers and, despite his looks, was nick-named Iulii Ivanovich the Handsome.[25] However, when he appeared for his first rehearsal of *Esmeralda*, he created a rebarbative impression by making a fuss at seeing the corps de ballet dancers in long skirts. 'I can't see their legs,' he complained. 'Why are they not in ballet dress?' He insisted they wear at least tunics, despite protestations from the *régisseur* Ivan Marcel that the corps de ballet did not have practice clothes because they didn't do daily class. But it became clear that Perrot would not budge: a new expenditure therefore had to be made in the corps de ballet budget and for the next rehearsal everyone arrived in short dresses.[26]

Elssler received many accolades for *Esmeralda*, appearing alongside Perrot (as Gringoire), Smirnova (Fleur de Lys), and the wonderful veteran, Nikolai Golts (Frollo), who, now approaching fifty, had been an outstanding dancer during the Didelot years and had become a compelling mime artist. Titus exclaimed that he had never seen such a glorious trio on stage. Frédéric was cast as Phoebus (re-named Feb in Russian), a non-dancing role that Petipa took over for later perform-ances with Elssler.[27] Quasimodo was a small part, played by Golts's contemporary Petr Didier. As well as the superlative performances, it was the ballet itself that impressed. The designs vividly evoked old Paris, Notre Dame depicted against the night sky and the Seine glinting with reflected lights. Perrot's staging, with its interesting use of the corps de ballet, vividly individualized characters, powerful emotional realism, and fast-moving, suspenseful narrative, showed indisputably that here was the master-choreographer the company needed.[28]

Elena Andreianova, Ballerina

Before Perrot's arrival, Petipa and his father were sent to the Moscow company, to mount *Satanilla* and *Paquita*. Andreianova also went, despatched by Gedeonov for private reasons. Already while still at the theatre school she was, despite her plain features, romantically linked to Gedeonov, who had become a widower.[29] Gedeonov, now in his sixties, did not have good looks on his side either, but his power was a heady attractant to the shrewd and ambitious young dancer.[30] Avdotia Panaeva, in her memoirs, remembers how she once saw Gedeonov and Andreianova talking at one end of the school's long dormitory; Panaeva, hidden from view at the other end, could hear Andreianova sometimes shouting at him and once even laying into him with her dance shoe. 'Her boldness surprised me, but at the same time it was nice to see how "the menace" of all the artists meekly obeyed her orders.'[31] He arranged that Andreianova's meals be served separately with expensive wine and to pre-empt gossip had also arranged the same privilege for her fellow-student Tatiana Smirnova. But word was out all the same. Although she was supremely talented, worked hard, and deserved her roles, when she graduated into the company in 1838, she soon had enemies among the supporters of rival ballerinas. They hissed and booed her; they protested when ballets, such as *La Péri*, *Paquita*, and *Satanilla*, were mounted for her.[32] Her unpopularity was further fanned by the premiere of *Paquita* when Smirnova appeared on stage with a black ribbon round her neck. The rumour machine alleged that Smirnova's mother had died on that same day, but when Smirnova asked to be excluded from the performance, Andreianova had ensured permission be refused.[33]

The desire to protect Andreianova had been another motive behind Gedeonov's reluctance to welcome Elssler to Russia, but with Elssler now a *fait accompli*, he judged it safer to move Andreianova away from the competition. However, once in Moscow, Andreianova found that she had jumped from the proverbial pan into the fire, her arrival considered an affront to Moscow's own enormously popular Ekaterina Sankovskaya. Appearing first in *Giselle*, on 22 October 1848, she received a cordial enough reception, but gradually hostility mounted. On 5 December, during the first act of *Paquita* a very dead black cat was hurled on to the stage, with an inscription 'to the *première danseuse étoile*' attached to its tail, and hit Frédéric Montessu—Petipa's colleague from Bordeaux and Madrid days—on the head, just as he had finished dancing the *saltarello* with Andreianova. Cursing, Montessu picked up the animal and lobbed it into the wings. But Andreianova, shaken, left the stage and refused to continue. Meanwhile, a large part of the audience had risen to their feet and were shouting their support of Andreianova, the men waving their hats, the women, their handkerchiefs. Eventually, reassured by the audience's encouragement, she continued the performance, to colossal applause.[34]

At Andreianova's request Petipa wrote a letter to Gedeonov the next day, describing what had happened—with much emphasis on the audience's and company's support for Andreianova.[35] The malefactor was Pavel Bulgakov, son of the director of the postal service, who paid a tradesman to throw the cat. Bulgakov was in fact the ringleader of fans not of Sankovskaya, but Yrca Matthias, a Franco-Hungarian dancer, who had also been deprived of roles by Andreianova.[36] As punishment he was exiled in the Caucasus for several years.[37]

Being aware of Andreianova's special status, everybody in the theatre, especially the administrative staff, approached her with careful courtesy. But Panaeva's memoirs credit her with loyalty to her contemporaries: she never 'told on' the rule-breaking antics of her school friends or abused her implicit power with company colleagues.[38] Petipa on the other hand sketches an unflattering portrait when, still in Moscow, he finds her 'storming with rage' after a performance of *Satanilla* because he had danced a pas de deux with Matthias who received a huge ovation. Although Andreianova had accepted Petipa's invitation to take the main role (it was his benefit performance), she was feeling too tired to perform the pas de deux, so Matthias had been substituted.[39]

Back in St Petersburg, Andreianova had no alternative but to resume performances in parallel with Elssler and, later, Carlotta Grisi, and she danced in several Perrot ballets. In 1850 she lost the favour of Gedeonov, who fell for Mila Deschamps (known professionally as Mila), a French operetta star and actress appearing at the Mikhailovsky Theatre.[40] In the summer of 1852, she danced in London; later, in St Petersburg, for her benefit performance on 22 February 1853, the company revived Didelot's *Hungarian Hut, or the Famous Exiles* (Vengerskaia khizhina, ili Znamenitye izgnanniki). The following season (1853–1854) she managed, with some difficulty, to persuade the directorate to allow her, with Frédéric, to tour the Russian provinces—Odessa, Kharkov, Voronezh, and elsewhere—with a small group of Moscow dancers. It was an unprecedented venture, during which she herself choreographed *The Fountain of Bakhchisarai* (Bakhchisaraiskii fontan), based on Pushkin's poem, making her one of the rare women choreographers of the nineteenth century. Ill-health forced her to retire; she left Russia and, aged just thirty-eight, died in Paris in 1857, where she is buried in Père Lachaise.[41]

The Perrot Years

Elssler stayed two-and-a-half years in Russia and, in defiance of the directorate's grudging welcome, she, like Perrot, was long remembered with great affection.

From her first appearances 'everything went crescendo', and any tickets remaining after the subscription sales were seized from the box office 'by assault'.[42] Her art of characterization, especially of earthly heroines, fused perfectly with Perrot's gift for creating powerfully narrative choreography, the movement permeated with dramatic significance.[43] 'Here we saw not just a lovely dancer, but also a sublime artist,' Zotov wrote. 'Her dances by themselves [...] revealed a new genre in this art. Up to now we required only graceful poses, supple movements, lightness, speed, strength: here we saw *acting* in the dances. Every movement spoke to the mind and the heart; every moment expressed a feeling; every look fitted the development of the narrative. It was a new, enchanting revelation in the field of dance.'[44]

Esmeralda was followed on 16 February 1849 by Perrot's 1846 *Catarina, ou la Fille du bandit* (Katarina, doch' razboinika) for Perrot's own benefit.[45] Elssler played Catarina (a role created by Lucile Grahn), who on her father's death has become the leader of a gang of bandits, and Perrot returned to his original role as Diavolino, her lieutenant. Cast as the romantic hero, the artist Salvator Rosa, was the Swedish dancer Christian Johansson who, just one year older than Petipa, had arrived in St Petersburg in 1841. He was not an expressive mime artist. Rather, he was a supremely elegant dancer. His classical precision, lightness, and elegance— he had studied with Bournonville in Copenhagen—made him an outstanding exemplar of the French-Danish school of male dance, uncluttered by virtuoso tricks. By 1857, though, he was displaying a more spectacular side: 'Johansson amazed everyone with his pirouettes,' wrote the chronicler Alexander Volf. 'After his debuts at the time of Taglioni, he has quickly perfected himself and become the public's supreme favourite.'[46] Later, he would become Russia's greatest teacher, revered in his work of perfecting the most luminous talents for Petipa's ballets.

Caterina again proved that Perrot's work represented the pinnacle of the Romantic Ballet. His choreography was remarkable not only because of the internal expressiveness of the dance sequences, but also because of the dynamic and compelling use of ensembles. That, and the emphasis on vivid, interesting drama, made everything look refreshingly different to what had been on the menu post-Didelot, when extravagant visual ostentation was accompanied by groups in monotonous unison postures and soloists performing a jumble of jumps and pirouettes.[47] 'Perrot has not spared the corps de ballet,' observed the *Sanktpeterburgskiye vedomosti*. 'He is continually giving them work to do. Dramatic situations lead into balletic and, if I may use the word, transcendental *pas* by the soloists, general evolutions by the corps de ballet, and character dances by the principals. Go to the ballet this winter, and see what I mean.'[48]

The directorate had by then opened negotiations for Perrot's services as first ballet master, dancer, and mime and secured his signature on 7 January 1849 for a standard one-year contract, starting mid-October.[49] In the event, contractual obligations in Paris forced him to delay his journey to St Petersburg by over a month, during which time the Russian debuts of the Italian opera stars Mario and Giulia Grisi (relatives of Carlotta) had proved irresistible to *le tout Pétersbourg* and ballet sales slumped again, despite Elssler's presence.

At Perrot's return Petipa asked him to assist with his benefit, scheduled for 4 December. Elssler had agreed to take part and Jean Petipa, aided by Marius, was preparing *Nathalie, or the Swiss Milkmaid*, except the heroine was now called Lida (Lida, shveitsarskaia molochnitsa). It was probably Elssler's urging or at least her presence which prompted this choice since not only had Elssler often performed the ballet, but Jean had staged it for her in Brussels and Bordeaux.[50] It was, though, a poor decision, made worse by the hurried preparations. The ballet had a meagre plot which needed youthful freshness and naivety. This was more than the mature Elssler could muster and it survived only for two performances. Fedor Koni called it 'an extremely weak and very unsuccessfully warmed-up antiquity'. Not even the wonderful *scène dansante* added by Perrot, who also played the country boy Fritz, could save a ballet that was, like much of Filippo Taglioni's oeuvre, 'meagre in content' and 'pitiful in invention'.[51] However, Ivor Guest's description of one of Perrot's inserted dances, in which Fritz teasingly entices Elssler's milkmaid with a basket of cherries, suggests that Petipa later recycled it as the 'Pas de cerises' for his early ballet, *The Parisian Market*.[52]

Perrot worked for a total of twelve years in Russia and staged eighteen ballets, often with Petipa as both his assistant and peerless interpreter of leading roles. Over this long period Perrot's example became an important formative influence on Petipa and a creative friendship was formed. Although this ended with a widely publicized court battle over copyright (about which more later), Petipa never lost his high esteem for Perrot.

Perrot's first production as chief balletmaster on 12 February 1850 had been premiered in Paris the previous year as *The Fairies' Goddaughter* (La Filleule des fées). In Russia the title was changed to *The Foster-Child of the Fairies* (Pitomitsa fei) because Gedeonov had raised an objection about the mix of folklore and Christianity: 'It might seem odd,' he had said, 'that fairies are able to be god-mothers.' Elssler danced the role created by Grisi and, to match the opulent production values of the Paris version, electric lighting was used on the Russian stage for the first time, to sensational effect.[53]

In the autumn of 1850, Carlotta Grisi was engaged instead of Fanny Elssler, who made her farewell with a series of winter performances in Moscow. Baron Brunnov in London had been right in forecasting that Perrot would require foreign celebrities to dance his work—or, to put it another way, ballerinas whose talents were familiar to him.

That same year, in July, Perrot's long-standing collaborator Cesare Pugni was engaged as ballet composer, a position that would require not just composing complete scores, but arranging existing ones with additions or cuts. Gedeonov had met him in London and negotiated his salary at 12,000 francs for one year. But Pugni didn't have the cash to arrange his journey, so a few days before his departure he managed to get an advance and travelling expenses via Baron Brunnov.[54] He had, it would seem, a chaotic family life; somehow he could never make ends meet, a problem that would last to the end of his days. (Simon Morrison writes that he was an alcohol and gambling addict.)[55] Despite an industry that resulted in nearly 300 ballet scores, he would sometimes ask Petipa and others for financial help. His death in 1869 left his family in such desperate poverty the Imperial Theatres organized a benefit for them.[56]

Carlotta Grisi made her Russian debut on 8 October 1850 as Giselle, dancing opposite Johansson, in the ballet made for and inspired by her in Paris. In putting together the production, Perrot was helped by Petipa. Although Petipa worked to Perrot's indications, he also introduced independent touches in the second-act dances of the *wilis*. His revival of *Giselle* in 1884 would further elaborate these dances so that while the first act remained much as Coralli-Perrot made it, the second act was considerably enlarged, and it is this sensitive staging which has become the standard version for many companies today.

Other ballets danced by Grisi in Russia included Mazilier's *Le Diable à quatre* (literally, The Devil Four Ways), renamed *The Wilful Wife* (Svoenravnaia zhena) and mounted by Perrot for her and Andreianova on 14 November 1850.[57] She also danced in the premiere of Perrot's *The Naiad and the Fisherman* (Naiada i rybak) on 30 January 1851, a lengthened reworking (to meet the Russian demand for full-evening ballets) of *Ondine, ou la Naïade*, created with Fanny Cerrito in London in 1843. As well as Grisi (the Naiad) and Perrot (Matteo, a fisherman), the cast featured Andreianova (Matteo's abandoned fiancée) with Johansson and Petipa as two young fishermen. Each of the men was given a variation, and Petipa's was performed to a cornet solo.[58]

For unclear reasons, the negotiations for the renewal of Perrot's contract for the 1851–1852 season faltered.[59] Consequently, at the last minute, the directorate invited Mazilier who hurriedly made his way, leaving Arthur Saint-Léon to finish the ballet *Vert-Vert* he was preparing for the Paris Opera. To St Petersburg, Mazilier brought another staging of *The Wilful Wife* as well as Albert's *The Beautiful Maid of Ghent* (Flamandskaia krasavitsa), both in October, followed by *Vert-Vert* in January. None of these, however, suggested he was in Perrot's league, 'despite his noisy Paris reputation'.[60]

The following season Perrot was back in charge, reunited with Grisi and Pugni. Among his projects was *The War of the Women, or the Amazons of the Ninth Century* (Voina zhenshchin, ili Amazonki deviatogo veka). The scenario, partly inspired by Lope de Vega's *Fuenteovejuna* and originally given the French title *Wlastha, ou la Guerre des servantes* (Vlastha, or the War of the Servants), had been entangled with the censor, who objected to the subversive aspects of Perrot's scenario. Perhaps it was one thing for women to overcome oppression, as in Taglioni's *The Rebellion in the Seraglio*, but in Perrot's proposal they actually stripped the tyrannical duke of his estate. The ballet that finally emerged on 11 November 1852 told a modified story preserving the aristocratic status quo. The villain was now a usurper who had deposed the duke of Bohemia and whose overthrow restored the duke of Bohemia's heir to his duchy. *The War of the Women* gave Petipa his first created Perrot role and marked the start of a series of complex characters portrayed by him to great effect.[61]

Petipa, Premier Danseur *and Mime*

Petipa's performing career in Russia lasted twenty-two years, ending in 1869. As the partner of some of the century's greatest ballerinas, he had started, from the moment of his arrival, with Andreianova and Elssler, and continued with Grisi, Fanny Cerrito, and Amalia Ferraris. Christian Johansson also partnered these ballerinas, but Perrot preferred Petipa for his dramatic expressiveness and discreetly prioritized him.[62] However, it had taken some time to win Perrot round. For the earlier performances of some of his ballets, such as *Catarina* and *The Foster-child of the fairies*, Perrot had chosen Frédéric or Johansson. There may have been personal reasons for this. Marius was the brother of Lucien who had eventually replaced Perrot as the Paris Opera's leading dancer, perhaps because he had more pleasing looks. But, even more woundingly, Lucien had also caused the collapse of Perrot and Grisi's relationship, after winning Grisi's heart during rehearsals of *Giselle*.[63]

Journalistic descriptions of Petipa's dancing are rare, and of his classical dancing even rarer. As already noted, reviews tended to focus on the ballerina, either staying completely silent about her partner, or offering only glimpses. 'A young, rather agile dancer' is a miserly morsel from Fedor Koni about Petipa in *Satanilla*.[64] A little more informative is *Sovremennik*, referring to Petipa's finale with Grisi in *The Wilful Wife*: he performed 'to perfection' a 'ravishing and extremely difficult pas de deux' which prompted 'a unanimous enthusiasm'.[65]

Reviews of Petipa's character dancing, including those before his arrival in Russia, are slightly less meagre and leave the cumulative impression that he was better as a character dancer than a classical one. True, as late as 29 October 1857 he chose, for his benefit performance, to appear as James opposite Nadezhda Bogdanova in a revival of Taglioni's *La Sylphide*; but it is probable that he performed predominantly as a mime and partnering support. It is also true that he was Albrecht in *Giselle* where classical dancing in the second act has an important narrative relevance; but exactly what he danced and how remains unexplained by reviewers. Perhaps it is significant that Albrecht was the first role he stopped dancing, yielding it to Johansson, an experienced Albrecht, in 1856.[66]

The ballerina Ekaterina Vazem confirms Petipa's relative weakness as a classical dancer, although she must have been relying more on hearsay, since she only saw Petipa at the tail end of his performing career. (She was born in 1848, the year after his arrival.) Her memoirs, notable for their forensically cool observations and her personal dislike of Petipa, give a damning verdict: 'He was indifferent in classical dances, at any rate he looked very unattractive. His feet did not suit classical dance, lacking an arch and moving with big flat steps.'[67]

His gifts as a performer of character dances, however, were undisputed. 'He was,' Vazem writes, 'superb in character dances, showy, exciting, filled with temperament and emotion. He was especially successful in Spanish dances, which he had studied thoroughly in his youth while working in the theatres of Spain.'[68] In the second performance of *The Naiad and the Fisherman* he performed a *manola* with Grisi, a dance 'which was the same as the one he danced with Marie Guy-Stéphan in Madrid'.[69]

Most of all, though, he was an outstanding mime artist, blazing out emotional truths and vicissitudes with a clarity and conviction that remained in the mind's eye of all who saw him. Vazem pays vivid tribute:

> The crowning glory of Petipa's art as a ballet artist was his mime. Here he was really beyond the highest praise. His dark, burning eyes, his face mirroring a whole range of experience and mood, his broad, clear, convincing gestures and a most profound identification with his role and the character of the person portrayed, verging on a veritable reincarnation, placed Petipa, as a 'silent actor' on a pinnacle, which only a very few of his colleagues attained. His acting could, without overstating the case, excite and shake his audience.[70]

He had a broad palette. He was, for example: Lucien (*Paquita*), Achmet (*La Péri*), Fabio (*Satanilla*), Conrad (*Le Corsaire*), and, in two of his own ballets, Gautier (*The Blue Dahlia*) and Lord Wilson-Taor (*The Pharaoh's Daughter*). It was, though, in Perrot's ballets that he found his most substantial, most psychologically complex roles. For his debut in *Esmeralda* in January 1850, Olga Fedorchenko surmises that Petipa drew on his own enthusiasm for pretty women and his French sense of gallantry to give the handsome, alluring, but unfaithful Phoebus an added sensual abandon and emotional delicacy.[71] Sadly reviewers did not leave any comments, but legend says he earned from Elssler the compliment that 'he was the best of all the Phoebuses she had danced with.'[72] As Mitsislas, the usurper of the Bohemian dukedom, in *The War of the Women*, he was, according to the libretto, anything but a two-dimensional villain. One side of him was the brutal warrior and abductor of women, implacable in battle, merciless in his will. The other was a version of Don Juan, a seducer who, once he had seized his prey, stalked it with an irresistible, courtly charm and a genuine sincerity. In the narrative's ending not only is Mitsislas defeated by the heroine (Grisi) and her fiancé the legitimate duke (Johansson) but, in an echo of Don Juan's final scene with the statue of the Commendatore, Mitsislas's vengeful mistress (Andreianova) invokes the help of the statue of the former duke of Bohemia which drags Mitsislas deep underground.[73]

With the title role of Faust, created by Perrot in Milan in 1848 and considerably revised for St Petersburg on 2 February 1854, Petipa was assigned the most vivid and multifarious of Perrot's characters. Mephistopheles was played by Perrot and Marguerite, by Gabriele Yella, a Viennese dancer of some obscurity, imported when Grisi left Russia. All the roles are of a colossal complexity, requiring transformations from the real to the supernatural. Faust begins as a decrepit old man, then changes into a virile youth burning with passion; he is desperately in love with Marguerite, but brings horror and death into her life. As Fedorchenko points out, the one stable trait of his character is a preternatural sensibility, defining him as a quintessential romantic hero. The language of the printed libretto communicates this particularity: 'Faust [...] shakes at this vision'; 'Faust cannot overcome his emotions'; 'Faust trembles and looks at Marguerite with emotion, he quivers at her slightest movement.'[74] A photograph of Petipa as Faust, his head thrown back and hand to his brow (sadly not reproduced in this book), clearly evokes a being who operates at a higher pitch of intensity.[75]

As well as mime, the role of Faust demanded a considerable quantity of dancing, more than for any other of Perrot's heroes. Perrot also made much use of the company's younger talent, male as well as female. The elaborate set-piece of 'The Seven Deadly Sins', which was considered the highlight of the ballet, contained a succession of enticing solos. Anna Prikhunova as Luxury, who entered wearing a magnificent costume and bearing a dove in her hands, impressed particularly with her delicate technical fluency and elegant mime. The ball scene similarly featured six brilliant variations, set into the action like precious stones, among which was one for Petipa and Johansson each, with Johansson, the perfect classicist who played Marguerite's fiancé Valentin, given pride of place. Another of these variations, a mazurka, belonged to a young dancer, still at the theatre school, who was cast as Martha, Marguerite's friend.[76] She was Maria Surovshchikova, her charm and talent attracting the rhapsodic praise of Sankt-Peterburgskie vedomosti— 'Miss Surovshchikova presents the brightest hope as dancer and mime. [...] Nature has given her everything necessary to become an outstanding dancer and we don't doubt that she will fulfill her vocation.'[77] She also attracted the attention of Petipa, who would soon marry her.

Produced with lavish designs and scrupulous attention to detail, Faust stayed in the repertoire for more than twenty years. That first season 'it completely sold out, rousing unanimous accolades' and Perrot 'emerged as victor in a difficult battle with this colossal subject. Apart from a few weaknesses [...] and one slightly long scene, the whole ballet is wonderfully put together, and its success was completely deserved.'[78] Incredibly, reviewers offer few words about the titular part. However, I. and K. Ivanov, in their short monograph on Petipa, draw upon the recollections of those who had seen Petipa play Faust:

> Petipa tried to give [the role] a dimension closer in spirit to Goethe's verses. His interpretation of Faust differed significantly from that of other artists. In the first act there appeared before the audience a shy, timid young man who did not yet understand all the power of the feeling which had come alive in him for the first time; in the following scene (the garden) this timid feeling grew into a passionate love in which was evident only carnal impulse, eclipsing the platonic ideology of love. After this compelling scene, the pitch of Marius Petipa's acting did not diminish, but actually grew in intensity, and his suffering, his remorse (the scene in the prison) awakened a feeling of profound sympathy and pity.[79]

On 9 January 1858, Petipa was also the first Russian Conrad, in Perrot's staging of Mazilier's 1856 ballet *Le Corsaire*, distantly inspired by Byron's poem of the same name. He appeared opposite Ekaterina Friedberg as Medora, a part-Russian who had finished her training in London, and whose talents would prove too uneventful for a long-term engagement. Conrad was not a dancing role, but the heroic dimension, the vigour, ardour, and Byronic romance of Petipa's portrayal filled the stage. Vazem, a later Medora, leaves another vignette (and in passing mentions some of his other roles):

> I remember him in the roles of Faust in Perrot's ballet of that name and Lord Wilson-Taor in *The Pharaoh's Daughter* and I myself danced with him in *Le Corsaire* in the spring of 1868, the first season, that is, of my employment. That evening Petipa was making his last appearance on stage. His creation of the character of Conrad, leader of the corsairs, was quite unforgettable: his every movement indicated that he was accustomed to rule and command. At the same time, one was conscious of his colossal mastery of the use of gesture, executed with utter assurance. He never employed meaningless flourishes of the arms, which time and again I have had to observe from other interpreters of the role of Conrad. One could learn from his acting, but not by slavish imitation, since this artist put too much of his creative self into the role. In the courtship scene in the grotto, Petipa became very carried away. During his declaration of love to Medora his whole body was shuddering and, convulsively embracing her, he was whispering: 'Je t'aime, je t'aime.' ... I was then a very young girl, and shocked

by this naturalistic acting. At rehearsals, when he was demonstrating a scene, Petipa would habitually act out all the parts and here his mime was always very expressive.[80]

The last remark is elaborated by Nikolai Legat, who joined the company in 1888:

> The most fascinating moments of all were those when Petipa composed his mimic scenes. Showing each participant in turn he would get quite carried away by the parts, and the whole hall would sit with bated breath, following the extraordinary expressive mimicry of this artistic giant. When the scene was set there would be a terrific outburst of applause, but Petipa paid little attention. He would return quietly to his seat, smiling and licking his lips in a characteristic gesture [way], lighting a cigarette, and sitting silent for a time. Then the whole scene would be repeated while Petipa put the finishing touches to the actions of the individual artistes.[81]

Although Vazem was mistaken about the date, Petipa did choose the role of Conrad for his farewell as performer on 8 May 1869 on the occasion of Pugni's benefit performance.[82] Conrad was close to his heart: he had created the role in its first Russian staging and he would keep the ballet sedulously in the company's repertoire throughout his career, restaging it four times. Perrot had allowed him to choreograph a new dance for two slaves, the 'Pas d'esclaves', for the 1858 production, when a new talent, Marfa Muraveva, took over the role of Medora from Ekaterina Friedberg.[83] On 24 January 1863, he revived the ballet with the addition of a small *travesti* solo, 'Le Petit Corsaire', for Surovshchikova-Petipa, to the delight of her many fans.[84] On 25 January 1868, following the example of the 'Pas des fleurs' introduced into the Paris production a year earlier, he included a substantial *divertissement*, 'The Animated Garden', usually known as 'Le Jardin animé' and set to the same music by Delibes. This remains an impressive piece of dance classicism to this day, the garland-carrying dancers arranged in borders and clusters. Finally, on 13 January 1899 he inserted a pas de deux for the Italian ballerina Pierina Legnani for which Riccardo Drigo composed a waltz and adagio.[85] This was not, however, today's famous 'Corsaire pas de deux', added in 1915 and choreographed by Samuil Andrianov as, originally, a pas de trois for Medora (Karsavina), Conrad (Andrianov), and another male dancer (Mikhail Obukhov). It was Agripinna Vaganova who changed this pas de trois into the bravura pas de deux we know today.[86]

The Crimean War

The popularity of *Faust* apart, the ballet box office, in keeping with most of Europe, was again battling the lure of Italian opera. Feeling that the Russian public's enthusiasm towards her had cooled, Grisi decided not to return for the following 1853–1854 season.[87] It must have been a blow to Perrot's morale. Unlike Elssler, she was still in her prime (thirty-one) when she had arrived in Russia three years before. Théophile Gautier, who remained hopelessly in love with her all his life, wrote that her qualities placed her between Elssler and Taglioni.[88] The stylistic duality of *Giselle* is surely testimony that she possessed both the penetrating human truth of Elssler and the chaste aeriality of Taglioni. More than that, she had a point technique that went beyond Taglioni's evanescent balances; she turned on point, she ran on point, she even jumped on point, Italian feats that were beyond homegrown Paris dancers, their training still frozen in the old French school.[89] But in 1853 she left Russia and appeared the same year in Warsaw, dancing three of Perrot's unforgettable heroines—Giselle, Esmeralda, Catarina. These were her last performances. With Grisi gone Perrot lost his remaining muse and would never find another again.[90]

To make matters worse, the directorate now decided not to engage guest ballerinas of similar status. This resulted in several less-established visitors, although one of these, Gabriele Yella, had enthused Perrot enough for him to cast her as Marguerite in the Russian premiere of *Faust*. Another problem was the rumble of hostilities between Russia and the Turkish Empire, which escalated into fighting in October 1853. In March 1854 France and England sided with Turkey, and the Crimean War was under way. The mood was sombre, the theatres were half-empty, and it was known in court circles that Tsar Nicholas was sick with worry, grieving for the soldiers who were giving up their lives. One year later, on 2 March, he was dead, personally shattered by the defeats of his beloved army.[91] His had been a repressive regime. He had clung with a desperate determination to the old ways, freezing Russia in all spheres of life, including the arts. The old ways meant that theatres were continually facing West, towards foreign talents and foreign themes, their backs turned against their own culture.

The Crimean War halted travel between Russia and France, complicating access to guest ballerinas. This, together with a general atmosphere of patriotism, had the effect of encouraging home-grown ballet talent. Perrot now focused his gaze all the more on a cluster of promising young ballerinas. As already seen, they included Maria Surovoshchikova and Anna Prikhunova, who appeared in *Faust*; there was also Zina Richard and, later, the very gifted ballerina called Marfa Muraveva. Already reviewers had been comparing the St Petersburg company favourably to other companies and now spectators had the chance to see this more clearly. Thanks to Perrot's strong repertoire and an ensemble of dancers as good as those in Western Europe, the public were receiving the message that Russia's ballet did not need outsiders. It offered them a few crumbs of pride in a period of military catastrophe and political sorrow.[92]

In contradiction to this tendency, the 1855–1856 season saw the arrival of an Italian, Fanny Cerrito, another Perrot ballerina, although like Elssler she was coming to Russia at the sunset of her career.[93] She made her debut on 8 November 1855 at the premiere of Perrot's new and ambitious four-act *Armida*, based on Tasso's epic poem *Jerusalem Delivered*. The ballet received mixed reviews and for Cerrito it was not the most flattering showcase, for she was outshone by Muraveva, a mere pupil, whose technique, already at 'a remarkable degree of development', was all too evident in the role of Cupid.[94] With the end of the war on 30 March 1856, she also had the bad luck soon to be challenged by the arrival of a Russian, Nadezhda Bogdanova, a peripatetic dancer trained by her father, who at the start of the hostilities had been appearing as guest at the Paris Opera. Trapped in France, in difficult conditions, Bogdanova could now return to Russia, where her well-publicized ordeal ensured that her performances in *Giselle* and other ballets were greeted with great emotional fervour and mountains of bouquets, even though most people had not even heard of her.[95] The patriotic welcome rather outstripped her talent, but delighted the box office, giving another boost to native Russian ballet, although the directorate's interest in her dwindled after a few years.

By 1858, the busy traffic of invited ballerinas had resumed as normal. Ekaterina Friedberg had achieved popularity on the London stage after being sifted out of the St Petersburg school and finishing her training abroad. But, returning to St Petersburg to dance *La Sylphide* and become Russia's first Medora, her height drew more attention than anything else and the public did not like her.[96] Then came the Italian virtuosa Amalia Ferraris, star of the Paris Opera, who made her Russian debut in the premiere of Perrot's *Éoline, ou la Dryade* (16 November 1858), first created in London and now much expanded for the Russian stage. This was the ballet, with Ferraris dancing, that Théophile Gautier saw on his Russian journey, when the ballet company so impressed him.

Éoline, ou la Dryade was Perrot's last ballet in Russia. He now had a Russian wife, Capitolina Samovskaya, apparently unconnected with the theatre, and two young daughters. He might have imagined settling in St Petersburg for good. But an injured leg, increasingly fraught relations with Gedeonov, and finally Gedeonov's replacement by Andrei Saburov in 1858 spelt the end of his life in Russia.

The Directorate of the Imperial Theatres

Gedeonov himself had already been somewhat sidelined by the appointment of Pavel Fedorov in 1853 as director of the Imperial Theatre School and head of the repertoire division of the Imperial Theatres. The author of vaudevilles, Fedorov was on home turf and on friendly terms with Gedeonov's superior, the minister of the Court, Count Vladimir Adlerberg. He communicated with Adlerberg directly over Gedeonov's head and did the same with Gedeonov's successors. This meant that Gedeonov signed the memos and contracts, but in real terms it was often Fedorov who made the decisions about repertoire, benefits, artists' debuts, and salaries. He hosted large Saturday-evening gatherings for invited artists and staff to eat and play lotto in his state apartment above the directorate offices. He was responsible for many necessary theatre and school reforms during his twenty-six years of service and always treated artists with respect—except that he disliked Marius Petipa.[97] This put spokes in Petipa's wheels and encouraged the machinations of the dancer and ungifted choreographer Alexei Bogdanov, who saw himself as Petipa's rival.[98] When Fedorov died in 1879, his responsibilities were split between two individuals: Nikolai Lukashevich was put in charge of the repertoire division; Alexander Frolov was appointed director of the Theatre School and in 1882 was also put in charge of the ballet company.[99] Frolov, like many high functionaries, had been a professional soldier (a colonel). He imposed a pseudo-military regime at the school, requiring the boys to do drills and adopt a military comportment.[100] Meanwhile, further down the ballet hierarchy was the *régisseur* (Ivan Marcel during Gedeonov's time). As company manager, the *régisseur* was responsible for all communication between the directorate and the dancers, for scheduling rehearsals, for discipline, and for the accounts.[101]

After distinguished service in the Horse Guards, Gedeonov had begun his civil career in Moscow, where he worked in the Armoury Museum before becoming director of Moscow's Italian opera. The gutter press alleged that he owed his progress to his beautiful wife. In 1833 he was appointed as director of the Imperial Theatres in St Petersburg and was, according to the memoirs of the actor Petr Karatygin, a welcome contrast to his predecessor, the lofty, inaccessible prince Gagarin. It was Gedeonov who initiated and oversaw the relocation in 1836 of the theatre school, the directorate offices, the music office, and wardrobe to Theatre (Rossi) Street. At the end of the 1830s he would forever earn the gratitude of long-serving theatre artists for successfully campaigning to have them considered as members of the intelligentsia, eligible for certain civil privileges.[102] Less impressive was his financial inconsistency. He had successfully pushed for a substantially bigger budget but always showed a deficit at the end of each financial year. He would spend a profligate 10,000 roubles without any visible benefits, and then refuse a few hundred to meet real necessities.[103] Maybe it was this that pushed him from office because it can't have been his firm support of the imperial cultural autocracy. This political conservatism was evidenced by the proceedings of a committee which the minister Adlerberg had set up in 1856 to find ways of reducing the deficits. While one or more members of the committee had argued for a liberalized structure which, as in most European countries, would give substantial place to private theatres, Gedeonov had voiced his opposition. He had emphasized the need to keep the tightly controlling status quo where the morality expressed on theatre stages was in keeping with the aims of the government. And since this was also the view of Adlerberg and the new emperor Alexander II, the monopoly continued as before.[104]

But if Gedeonov was a hardline conservative, he was also personally benign. Petipa gives an affectionate description of his character, echoing other accounts: 'Gedeonov was an extremely kind man, but affected an air of severity; we nicknamed him the "grumbler-benefactor".'[105] He describes an evening at Mlle Mila's house after a performance during which Petipa had angered Gedeonov with what Gedeonov considered indecorous poses. Forced to play a game of chess with Gedeonov, he deliberately lost to put him in a better mood.[106] This chimes with the detailed portrait painted by Karatygin of a complex character, woven out of contradictions. Wilful to the point of childishness, he was an inveterate card player who always had to win. Ridiculously indulgent towards some, towards others he could be unreasonably harsh. His contrariness was so well known that employees would sometimes cunningly exploit it, such as the actor who, very keen to accept an invitation from the Moscow troupe but needing Gedeonov's go-ahead, came to Gedeonov with a long face and the news that—alas!—Moscow was insisting on his transfer. 'So you don't want to go?' asked Gedeonov. 'No, Your Excellency,' was the answer. 'Well, you will go; we don't have any need of you here.'[107]

Towards the female pupils of the theatre school, Gedeonov was a genuine father, the concerned guardian of an enclosed, segregated world that was raging with teenage hormones. This world was irresistible to the equally ardent young men on the outside, junior hussars circling around like wasps. 'Silly girl', he would say to an enamoured pupil, planning to marry after graduation. 'Well, he has nothing, apart from debts and gold braid; he'll ditch you after a month. Spit on him!'[108] Karatygin remembers how, while visiting Gedeonov's sons to play billiards, Gedeonov arrived fuming from a performance, because he had spotted an older pupil, Pimenova, throwing a smile 'without ceremony' from the stage not at 'a respectable person' but at 'X.X. who hasn't a farthing to his name'.[109]

He seems to have adopted the same paternalistic attitude towards the young Petipa, as suggested by an extended rigmarole when Petipa got himself in debt. He had arrived for the first time in Russia with a new pair of silk trousers from a tailor, M. Milon, plus costumes from the Paris Opera's costumier M. Nonnon. (The latter's bill specifies a green velvet doublet with white satin shirt for *Giselle* and a hussar's jacket and trousers, presumably for *Paquita*.) Citing the 'colossal amounts' he had to repay for his departure from Spain (almost certainly true), he had promised both suppliers to pay them in September. But letter after letter shows him pushing back the deadlines, until a year later Milon threatened to take action. 'I was very surprised to read that you were proposing to write to the general [Gedeonov], my director, to ask for the sum I owe you,' Petipa answered. 'I believe that if you do this, the general will tear up your letter and that he himself does not have the power to hold back my pay and also that I know him to be too kindly to ever do this.'[110] A further two years on, Milon *did* write to Gedeonov, as did Nonnon, enclosing their bills plus (in Milon's case) interest for three years. Since it was not unusual for artists to supply their own costumes, it begs the question of why Petipa did not follow the established procedure of claiming reimbursement from the directorate.[111] Perhaps he simply did not know he should do this. Either way, it would seem that the costumier Nonnon was paid. Perhaps also the directorate came to an agreement with Petipa to dock the money from his salary for Milon's trousers. They certainly did this for further debts incurred with a Moscow tailor not long after and the jeweller Fabergé in 1853.[112]

During his sixty years in Russia, Petipa would see many ministers and directors come and go, as well as four emperors. He served under Nicholas I, Alexander II, Alexander III, and Nicholas II. Directly below the emperor, head of the Imperial Theatres, was the minister of the Imperial Court, whose ministry, founded in 1826, held the Imperial Theatres' purse strings. There was a succession of five ministers during Petipa's time: Prince Petr Volkonsky (brother-in-law of the famous Decembrist Prince Sergei Volkonsky), Count Vladimir Adlerberg, Count Alexander Adlerberg (Vladimir's son), Count Illarion Vorontsov-Dashkov, and Baron Vladimir Fredericks.[113] Under the minister of the Imperial Court was the director of the Imperial Theatres, whose remit was the administration of the Imperial Theatres of St Petersburg and usually Moscow as well. Petipa worked for eight such directors. First, Alexander Gedeonov, then the following: Andrei Saburov, Count Alexander Borkh, Stepan Gedeonov (son of Alexander), Baron Karl Kister, Ivan Vsevolozhsky, Prince Sergei Volkonsky (grandson of the Decembrist), and finally Vladimir Teliakovsky. (For dates, see the Chain of Command appendix.) Working relationships were obviously crucial, since it was to the director that the first ballet master had to turn for approval of planned ballets and changes in personnel. Conversely the director would often initiate ballet projects and appointments and would act as the conduit for imperial wishes.[114] However, the bureaucratic hierarchy was extensive and, as seen earlier, the influential position held by Pavel Fedorov meant that the picture in practice could be more complicated.

On his retirement Gedeonov left for Paris, where he died in 1867. His successor Andrei Saburov 'did not know his business at all, and fulfilled his obligations very carelessly'.[115] When in Moscow, he would spend his nights playing cards in the English Club, cards being his only common ground with Gedeonov. Narrow-minded, ungracious, and short-tempered, he preferred to leave the daily business of management to his assistant.[116] He had taken against Perrot from the start, showed little tolerance for his absences, and, given that Perrot had earlier failed to initiate the renewal of his contract, was able, on 1 December 1860, to terminate his services.[117]

Saburov had already taken the precaution the previous year of drawing up a contract with Arthur Saint-Léon, to run from 1 September 1859 to 27 May 1860, officially as ballet master in Moscow, but with the stated requirement to stage ballets in both capitals. Saint-Léon's common-law wife, the dancer Louise Fleury, signed the contact on his behalf in Paris on 2 July 1859.[118] On 13 September 1859, Saint-Léon premiered his staging of Mazilier's *Jovita* in Saint Petersburg, with a new guest ballerina, Carolina Rosati, who had created the title role in Paris six years earlier. The new power structure was now taking shape. Although three years younger than Petipa, Saint-Léon was a ballet master of international repute; he had spent 1850 to 1853 as the Paris Opera's first ballet master and he had already been introduced to St Petersburg audiences through two productions staged by Perrot—*La Vivandière* or *The Sutler* (Markitantka) in 1855 and *La Fille de marbre* or *The Girl of Marble* (Mramornaia krasavitsa) in 1856, both with their original ballerina, Cerrito. If Petipa had harboured secret ambitions to succeed Perrot he must also have known that he lacked the choreographic back-catalogue expected for such a distinguished appointment.

Perrot would have a huge influence on Petipa's own creativity. Petipa was able to watch the master at close quarters and admired him right to the end of his own life. He ensured that Perrot's most impressive ballets—*Catarina, Faust, The Naiad and the Fisherman, Esmeralda, Giselle*—were preserved for many years and if *Esmeralda* and *Giselle* survive to this day, it is entirely thanks to Petipa and the Imperial Ballet. They kept these works alive while the rest of Europe allowed Perrot's ballets to fall into oblivion. Sensitive to changing fashions and the individual demands of performers, Petipa made alterations, especially additions, but he always strove as far as possible to leave the original choreography intact.

4

Looking Back, Moving Forward

*For three years now I have been of great service to the admin-
istration of the Imperial Theatres as a creator of ballets and
divertissements, without ever receiving any reward or compensation for all the efforts and tiring exertions I put myself through.
[...] I have the honour to bring again to the attention of Your
Excellency that I am employed only as premier danseur, mime,
and dance teacher at the School of the Imperial Theatres. I am
therefore approaching Your Excellency with a request for a recompense for all my efforts in fulfilling the work of ballet master.[1]*

Endings and Beginnings

The year before the end of the Crimean War, Jean Petipa died. Perrot, as first
ballet master, fellow-expatriate, and friend, gave the address at his graveside in the
Volkovo Lutheran Cemetery (*Volkovskoe liuteranskoe kladbishche*), the resting place
for faiths other than the Russian Orthodox Church.[2] Marius's younger brother
Jean Claude Tonnerre (also known as Jean) would later be buried there, as would
Marius's daughter Evgenia (Eugénie)—and Marius himself, initially. Although
close to the city centre, the Volkovo Lutheran Cemetery is somewhat overgrown
today and Jean Claude Tonnerre's tombstone no longer exists. Jean's, however,
is an imposing block of granite with a cross on top and a simple inscription in
French: 'Here lies/A much-loved father/Jean Antoine Petipa/Died on 16 Jul 1855
at the age of sixty-eight.'[3]

As well as being a ballet master and mime artist, Jean was remembered
with affection as a teacher, when he took charge of the senior boys' class at the
Theatre School. The younger boys were taught by Alexander Pimenov, a martinet
who shouted and hit them with a stick. (One day he actually caused an injury,
so that first the stick disappeared, then the man himself.) Jean Petipa, according
to a former student, Alexander Sokolov, produced a sharp contrast: 'Of medium
height, agile, vivacious, with gentle and elegant manners, kind to the point of
self-effacement, he was worshipped by the pupils.'[4] Another former pupil of the

school, Anna Natarova, assesses his importance: 'With Petipa a new school of dance was introduced, and attention was paid to mime. Petipa *père* was a very fine actor-mime.'[5]

Jean was part of a fresh cohort of teachers which pulled the school out of the slump in which it had languished for too long. Marius seems to have been one of these from the start, even though he was not designated as a teacher by his contract. Daria Richard (Zina's mother) was another, joining in 1848, the same time as Eugène Huguet, a Frenchman, employed by the Imperial Theatres as a *premier danseur*. He taught a class that was exclusively for the best girls, those destined to be soloists, among whom was Marfa Muraveva.[6]

Assuming he attended the single performance, Jean lived to see what is probably Marius's earliest stand-alone composition in Russia, an uncredited *divertissement* of Spanish dances. Called *The Star of Granada* (Zvezda Granady), it featured Maria Surovshchikova and formed the finale of a benefit performance for the French actress Mila at the Mikhailovsky Theatre on 22 January 1855. It was not the first time Surovshchikova had performed Spanish dances under Petipa's guidance: already, for Petipa's benefit in 1853, she had danced a *gallegada* with Petipa, Perrot, and Anna Prikhunova.[7] However, according to the reviewer Fedor Koni, *The Star of Granada* divided opinion: some were unquestioningly delighted; others thought that she danced too authentically, as would 'the people on the streets of Grenada, Seville, and Madrid', without taking care to show 'that French grace which the St Petersburg public had come to expect in ballets'.[8] It would seem that Marius had indeed observed folk dancers closely during his time in Spain. St Petersburgers evidently expected a 'ballet-ization' of folk dance, a subject this study will return to.

Jean also lived to see his son's marriage. Marius had Perrot to thank for bringing Maria Surovshchikova to his notice: it was Perrot who, as a teacher of the school's senior girls, had chosen the best pupil to play Martha, a new *ingenue* role he was creating for his Russian staging of *Faust*. Petipa was the company's leading male dancer, the stage partner of the top ballerinas of the day; he was also thirty-six-years old, slim and pleasant-looking, much-travelled, glamorously French, and with an eye for a pretty girl. Drawn to the enchanting student, who was exactly half his age, he would find pretexts to stay on at the school, and everyone saw how he would kiss her hands. She must have been impressed by him on many levels. Being a boarder, there was no way she would be allowed to meet him on the outside; but flirting in the school, at least in this case, was tolerated, the staff turning a blind eye.[9]

Surovshchikova was one of seven girls who graduated in March 1854, the only one to be accepted into the company directly as a soloist, starting 3 April with a yearly salary of 500 roubles. According to the rules, she would have to serve ten years in the company, counting from when she turned sixteen in 1852. The couple now being free to marry, on 15 May 1854 Petipa applied for permission to do this without relinquishing his French citizenship. To support the request, Perrot and Jean Petipa provided written testimonials that Petipa was a bachelor, which he was; it would probably have been irrelevant for them to mention that he had a seven-year-old son, Marius, born in St Petersburg from a relationship with Marie-Thérèse Bourdenne, a milliner who died in 1855.[10] Although a special dispensation allowed him to retain his French citizenship, he, a Roman Catholic, had to undertake to raise all future children in the Russian Orthodox faith. He also had to provide a written assurance that he would observe a rule of ten years' service in parallel with his wife.[11] Conversely, marriage to Marius meant that Maria would receive French citizenship, as would any children.[12]

The marriage certificate is dated 28 June 1854, but the religious ceremony took place on 4 July, first in the Trinity Church (*Troitskaia tserkov*), which was linked to the Imperial Theatres, then in the Roman Catholic Church of St Catherine (*Sviataia Ekaterina*) on Nevsky Prospect.[13] Those present included Jean Petipa, Maria's mother, Agrippina (*née* Belavina), and Agrippina's own new husband Mikhail Bekker, a former dancer with the Imperial Ballet and now a teacher at the theatre school. Under normal times, this being the summer vacation, the spouses would have visited Marius's family in Paris, but the Crimean War had closed the borders.[14]

Jean Petipa, Paterfamilias

Perhaps it was only appropriate that Jean Petipa, who had travelled so widely for work, should be buried far from home. In life, he had been a ballet master of international repute and the attentive father of six children, three of whom—Lucien, Marius, Victorine—became successful theatre artists.

Little is known about his origins. Being singularly appropriate, the name Petipa, a homonym of *petit pas* (small step), might seem to be a stage name. But variously spelt—Petipa, Petipas, Petitpas—it does crop up nationally and, additionally, in the annals of the Paris Opera. A singer-actress Mademoiselle Petitpas, the daughter of a locksmith, charmed audiences before an early death in 1739 and, more recently, Jean Petitpas sang in *Tristan and Isolde* from 1949 to 1951.[15] Neither, however, seems to have been related to Marius's family.

Jean Antoine Nicolas Petipa, Marius's father, was, according to one source, the child of a shoemaker.[16] Jean François Petipa and his wife Marie Suzanne Le Beau had three children, of whom Jean was the eldest, born in Paris on 16 February 1787. He was a pupil at the ballet school of the Paris Opera and, aged eight, appeared among the zephyrs and cupids in a revival of *Psyché*, a ballet by Pierre Gardel. In 1799 his father Citizen Petipa ('*le Citoyen* Petitpas [*sic*]') wrote to the '*Citoyen Ministre*' of the Interior asking that Jean be accorded leave for one year to appear with other companies and thereby earn the extra money needed by the struggling family. (It is not known if the petition was successful.)[17]

Later, Jean joined a touring troupe headed by Filippo Taglioni. In 1810 this settled in Kassel, the capital of Westphalia, before being dispersed by the rumblings of Napoleon's Russian campaign two years later. The 1813–1814 season found Jean with the Lyons ballet; then he was in Hamburg, with the Théâtre-Français, a small troupe founded by Crown Prince Charles of Sweden. The Théâtre-Français appeared in Brussels for six weeks from 15 September 1814. The repertoire was extensive and all but one of the ballets were staged by Jean, among them Pierre Gardel's *La Dansomanie* and *Psyché*, renamed *Psyché et l'Amour*. After Brussels, the company appeared in Ghent for a few performances and then moved to Paris, becoming part of the Théâtre de la Porte-Saint-Martin which, after a seven-year closure, had reopened on 26 December 1814 under the Bourbon Restoration.[18] Jean, a *premier danseur* in the ballet company, staged two mime presentations (*pantomimes*) in 1815. He also met a young actress there, Victorine Morel or Maurel, whose stage name Grassau (also that of her sister Lucile, another actress) was her mother's maiden name. Some sources say she was born in Lyons around 1794, others in the former French colony of Saint-Domingue (now Haiti). They married on 20 April 1815 at the Saint-Laurent church in the tenth *arrondissement* and that autumn left for Marseilles, where both spouses had found employment: Jean as *premier danseur* of the 'serious and *demi-caractère* genre' and the twenty-one-year-old Victorine, now using the name Petipa, as an actress specializing in 'very young leads, romantic characters'.[19] The ballet company, led by the ballet master Monsieur Roger, had eleven dancers, more or less equally divided between men and women; the drama company had about twenty-four actors.[20] The Marseilles opera house, built in 1787, was the second biggest regional theatre after Bordeaux. It survives to this day, although a fire destroyed much of the interior in 1919 and it was rebuilt using the original external walls and colonnade. The Petipas' first child Joseph Lucien (born 22 December 1815) was followed by Élisabeth Marianne (18 December 1816).

Monsieur Roger was soon replaced by Jean as ballet master. In 1817 he staged a well-received version of Jean-Baptiste Blache's *The Birth of Venus and Love* (La Naissance de Vénus et de l'amour); and it was during a rehearsal of this ballet on 11 March 1818 that Victor Marius Alphonse Petipa was born.[21] He arrived, with characteristic morning punctuality at nine o'clock, in the Petipa home at 6 rue Dumarsais, a narrow street just a few minutes from the opera house.[22]

And so from the start Jean seems to have been a leader, with singular energy and ambition, and a prolific creative drive. Despite three very young children, he accepted an invitation from the ballet master Eugène Hus to move as *premier danseur* to Brussels. Hus had revived the city's ballet company and was in need of further recruits; moreover, Victorine could also find employment there, playing young leads or 'ingenuous' characters (*jeunes premières, ingenuités*).[23] In April 1819, the Petipas left Marseilles in a specially hired coach, since rail travel had yet to be commercialized, and arrived after several days. Among the other newcomers were: Marie Lesueur (*première danseuse*), also newly arrived from Marseilles, and Jean-Baptiste Desplaces (*deuxième danseur*), from the Théâtre de la Porte-Saint-Martin.[24] As shown by the *Almanach royal* of 1820, the ballet had six other soloists and a corps de ballet of eight men and ten women.[25] Together with Lesueur and Desplaces, Jean made his Brussels debut on 20 May 1819 in Hus's staging of a three-act *ballet-pantomime* by Jean-Baptiste Blache, *Almaviva et Rosine*. Five days later, the new Théâtre-Royal de Bruxelles (also called the Théâtre de La Monnaie) was opened on the Place de La Monnaie, where it still stands today.[26] The inaugurating performance, *The Cairo Caravan* (La Caravane du Caire), an opera by André Grétry, finished with a *divertissement* choreographed by Jean, now named first ballet master to replace Hus who was cutting back his theatre duties, although still performing mime or father roles. The following morning the newspaper *L'Oracle* reported that the dances had delighted the audience with their charm.[27]

From then on, as ballet master, the hard-working Jean was responsible for the staging of a large quantity of ballets. His first complete creation for Brussels, just four months after his arrival, was the one-act *The Fair, or the Village Fête* (La Kermesse, ou la Fête villageoise) on 1 September 1819. It was, according to the Belgian dance historian Jean-Philippe Van Aelbrouck, a flop, but that didn't deter him.[28] Other ballets and dances for opera-ballets followed in quick succession, both original creations and stagings of existing works. Among these were: *Les Bayadères* (1820), a three-act opera-ballet by Charles-Simon Catel created in 1810 with choreography by Pierre Gardel; *The Swiss Milkmaid* (1824), after Titus's version; Jean's two-act composition *Frisac, or the Double Wedding* (Frisac, ou la Double Noce, 1825), a shortened version of which would be staged by Marius in St Petersburg; and Jean's *The Small Danaïdes* [butterflies], *or Ninety-Nine Victims* (Les Petites Danaïdes, ou Quatre-vingt-dix-neuf victimes, 1828), based on a vaudeville entertainment at the Théâtre de la Porte-Saint-Martin. He also produced Frédéric Blache's *Jocko ou le Singe du Brésil* (1826), the ballet which would feature in his New York season; and *The Sleeping Beauty* (La Belle au bois dormant), a *ballet-pantomime-féerie* in four acts, with a libretto by Eugène Scribe, music by Ferdinand Hérold, and choreography by Jean Aumer, premiered at the Paris Opera on 27 April 1829 and staged by Jean in Brussels on 31 August the same year.[29] By the end of the 1820s the repertoire had twenty-eight ballets, half by Jean Petipa either fully or partially. The creation and maintenance of such a repertoire demanded great knowledge, experience, and work. Of the ballets created by other choreographers, some were probably left largely unchanged, others might be substantially revised, possibly with different music.[30] He would have to have done all this from memory, aided by notes, in the same way that Titus brought *Giselle* from Paris to St Petersburg.

Opinions about Jean were mostly positive. The *Almanach des spectacles pour l'an 1822* referred to 'M. Petipa, a nimble and graceful dancer, whom we have seen at the Théâtre de la Porte-Saint-Martin: he directs the ballet with much good taste and intelligence.'[31] Reviewing *Cinderella* on 16 May 1824 the *Almanach théâtral* wrote: '*Cinderella*, the ballet, was a real pleasure, and although it is often shown, it is always given the same reception. M. Petipa, whose zeal and talent are tireless, has staged this work with all the taste and freshness we could wish for.'[32] When age encouraged him to give up dancing roles, his talent as a mime was singled out.[33] He seems to have set his aims high as a ballet master: his efforts to drive up standards and maintain a large repertoire, together with the calibre of the leading ballerina Mlle Lesueur, all this elevated the company's standing. Even the sometimes caustic writer of *L'Aristarque des spectacles* claimed that 'our ballet is, indisputably, the best of any town of France,' although he accepted he should exclude the Paris Opera company, 'the finest there is in European dance.'[34] (Brussels at that time was claimed by the French and the Dutch.) The same writer, while on an earlier occasion critical of both the corps de ballet and Jean's choreography, described the company in September 1824 as 'well structured, well organized, well run, and it performs without interruption; everybody makes progress; and from the lowest corps de ballet member who earns only thirty francs a month, right up to the principals who earn fifty francs a day, everyone seeks to be noticed by their talent and zeal.'[35] The Théâtre de la Monnaie was therefore considered a flourishing centre of the performing arts, an important destination for guest celebrities, among them, the great dancer Auguste Vestris, the French tenor Adolphe Nourrit, and François-Joseph Talma, the most famous French tragic actor of his time.[36] A friend of Napoleon Bonaparte and the painter Jacques-Louis David, Talma was also, according to Marius's memoirs, godfather to Lucien.[37] At his death in 1826 the Monnaie staged a *Hommage à la mémoire de Talma*, a composite of dialogue, music, and dances, with Jean responsible for the dances and *tableaux emblématiques*.

This then was Marius's upbringing: his parents' friends were actors, dancers, singers; his father had a long experience of the ballet repertoire, its performers, its teaching. From Jean, Marius acquired the genes and examples of hard work and ambition that would shape his own life.

Meanwhile the family was expanding: Jean Claude Tonnerre was born on 24 May 1820; Aimée Victorine Anne (known as Victorine) on 10 July 1824; and Adélaïde Antoinette on 18 January 1826.[38] Victorine, Jean's wife, decided to retire from the stage after the 1822–1823 season, to dedicate herself to raising the family, although Jean's salary as ballet master was modest for a large family.[39]

(Marius, like many men of his time, would live out a similarly onerous pater-familias responsibility.)

Eugène Hus, who had re-established the Brussels ballet, also founded the city's Conservatoire de Danse in 1817. His pupils regularly performed small ballets choreographed by him at the Théâtre du Parc. In 1823, aged sixty-five, he died; legend says that with his last breath he cried out, 'Who will replace me?'[40]

The answer was Jean. After the inevitable disarray, Jean reorganized and re-located the school. With the consent of the *Commission royale des théâtres*, he drew up a schedule of regulations, prescribing the maximum number of pupils (twenty-four), their age (six to twelve), and an annual examination, with prizes for encouragement.[41] Among the pupils were Lucien and Marius, aged eleven and eight.[42] Performing was certainly a dynastic skill, handed down by parents to pro-vide children with a means of employment, but Marius was a reluctant pupil:

> At seven, I started instruction in the art of dancing, in the class of my father, who broke many bows on my hands in order to acquaint me with the mysteries of choreography. Such pedagogical means were necessary, because in my childhood I did not feel the smallest inclination to this branch of art. To the young thinker, it seemed unworthy for me to fuss in all sorts of graceful poses.[43]

In addition to dancing, Marius went to the music conservatoire where he studied the *solfège* (music theory) and the violin. One of his fellow pupils was the violin prodigy Henri Vieuxtemps who, from 1846 to 1851, played solo violin with the Bolshoi orchestra in St Petersburg. In his memoirs Petipa calls the school the *Fétis Conservatoire*, but in fact François-Joseph Fétis, Belgian composer and musicologist, only took charge in 1833. Not long after his arrival, Fétis wrote a damning report, which stated that the standard was so poor he doubted most of the pupils could read music.[44] When Marius returned to the conservatoire in December 1832, after the Belgian Revolution had driven the Petipa family away for almost two years, he joined the violin class of François Schubert.[45] (Not *the* Franz Schubert.) Marius's beginnings in music seem even less promising than his beginnings in dance. In the register of exam results of June 1835 appears the following disappointing verdict: 'Petitpas [*sic*] Marius, born in Marseilles, fifteen and a half [*sic*], entered December 1832. No talent, kept on for special reasons.'[46]

Notwithstanding Marius's reluctance, four of the Petipa children performed at the Monnaie. Marius writes that it was his adored mother who gradually per-suaded him to obey his father's wish.[47] Lucien's first appearance was on 25 March 1821, playing a child, Castagnet, in Gardel's *La Dansomanie*, staged by Jean. From then on he regularly appeared on stage. On 31 August 1829, for example, he was a page in Aumer's *Sleeping Beauty*, with Marius as a dwarf and their sister Victorine

as a village child. Van Aelbrouck's year-by-year compilation of performances suggests that from the start Lucien was the most adept, appearing far more often than
Marius, and even more so than Victorine or Jean (Claude Tonnerre).[48]

Marius made his stage debut on 19 March 1823 (that is, shortly after his fifth
birthday), as a small cupid (*petit Amour*), in the company's premiere of Gardel's
Psyché et l'Amour, the same ballet in which his father had appeared as a child.
Lucien, also on stage, played another cupid and later acted as the model for the
cupid in Jacques-Louis David's imposing painting *Mars Disarmed by Venus* (Mars
désarmé par Vénus), in which Mlle Lesueur was the model for Venus.[49] In his
memoirs Petipa remembers appearing in *La Dansomanie* aged nine; the date, in
fact, was 25 August 1826, when he was eight. He then refers to being dressed 'in
the costume of a Savoyard, with a monkey in my arms'.[50] His text seems to link
this role with *La Dansomanie* when actually it belongs in *Jocko, or the Ape of Brazil*.
He made his debut in *Jocko* on 11 July 1827 and this marked a new level of performance, since he had the ballet's second most important dancing role.[51] A month
earlier (9 June 1827), he had appeared in a school performance (at the Théâtre du
Parc) of Jean-Baptiste Blache's *The Millers*. About it, *L'Aristarque des spectacles* wrote
that Marius Petipa, 'the character dancer (*danseur comique*)' distinguished himself
'by his imperturbable aplomb, unusual for his age'.[52]

In 1825, according to the *Almanach royal*, the corps de ballet consisted of sixteen couples and fourteen children. There were nine featured men, including
Jean Petipa and Benoni (real name Pierre Bertaud) as *premiers danseurs*, and
Lucien, listed as official holder of the roles of cupids. There were eight featured
women, among them Lesueur, *première danseuse*, and *la petite* Chodoir, performer
of children's roles.[53] (The previous year it was *la petite* Chodoir who played cupids.)[54] In 1826 Mlle Lesueur retired. Not long before, she had fallen seriously
ill, keeping her off stage for six weeks. Returning for a performance of *The Swiss
Milkmaid*, she had been greeted by hissing from cynics who believed she had been
malingering. (The turbulence of nineteenth-century audiences has already been
noted.) Very troubled, she walked to the front of the stage, and said: '*Messieurs,
I have only two months left for performing, let me finish this ballet.*' Murmurs
of approval and clapping followed her words.[55] Her departure would leave a hole;
although Antoinette-Désirée Leroux (probable sister of the famous Paris Opera
dancer Pauline Leroux) shone among several new *premières danseuses*, she didn't
have the potent presence and virtuosic technique that had made Mlle Lesueur the
cynosure of Belgian ballet.[56]

In 1828 the Monnaie was rocked by scandal. The *danseur comique* Etienne-
Hughes Laurençon, who had joined the company five years earlier, was arrested
on six counts of theft. The complainants were his fellow-dancers. Among them
were the spouses Étienne and Julie Leblond: Laurençon, presumably in a desperate financial situation, stole their monthly salary from Julie Leblond's reticule

during rehearsals. At the trial for this particular theft, he was sentenced to one year of prison but after appeal was released. The case provoked much public interest and when he reappeared on stage soon after, he was met with such noisy protest that the police removed all the spectators and issued a ban on his future perform- ances. Laurençon's crimes did not hinder his longer-term prospects, however. He was soon engaged as *premier danseur comique* at Paris's Théâtre de la Porte-Saint- Martin and, as mentioned in chapter 2, from 1838 to 1840 was ballet master and dancer at Nantes while Marius was there.[57]

Of greater historical significance was the performance of Daniel Auber's opera *La Muette de Portici* (The Dumb Girl of Portici) at the Monnaie on 25 August 1830, to honour the birthday of William of Orange, king of the Netherlands. (Belgium had become part of the Netherlands.) Although *The Dumb Girl of Portici* had been performed before at the Monnaie, it was an inflammatory choice in the context of political discontent among the largely Catholic and French-speaking inhabit- ants of Brussels.[58] The opera tells the story of the seventeenth-century Neapolitan uprising against Spanish rule, triggered by the fisherman Masaniello whose mute sister, Fenella, has been seduced by the Spanish viceroy's son Alphonse.[59] The performance of such a story that particular evening famously sparked the riots that marked the start of the Belgian Revolution and the establishment of the Kingdom of Belgium. When the French tenor Jean-François Lafeuillade, as Masaniello, sang the rousing 'Amour sacré de la patrie' ('Sacred Love of the Fatherland'), he was encored by an audience full of students and neo-liberals. When he then cried 'To arms!' they erupted in similar cries. History does not re- cord whether Lafeuillade, as claimed by Petipa, dashed out into the street in full costume, where a crowd of revolutionaries was waiting for him.[60] But the fired- up audience did rush out on to the square, wrecking and looting and drawing in parts of a crowd which had gathered to watch fireworks and were disappointed when these did not materialize.[61]

The Belgian Revolution was bad news for the Petipa family, since it caused the theatres to be closed. 'It was not easy to feed the family, being deprived of the main source of income,' writes Petipa; 'often we lacked the bare necessities, because my father had to be satisfied with the small amount received from two boarding schools where he taught social dance. My brother Lucien and I helped our father by copying out music for Prince Trezine, a passionate lover of waltzes and quadrilles, which he himself composed in incredible quantity. But neither our earnings nor father's income was enough for more than a meagre existence.'[62] Necessity being the mother of risk, Jean, after much anguished hesitation, decided to rent the theatre in Antwerp, where the French forces had assembled to support the Belgians against the Dutch. The entire company consisted of the Petipa family (parents and three children), supplemented by locals hired and trained as super- numeraries. The ballet was Blache's much-liked two-act *The Millers*.

The Petipas pasted posters round the town and, because the theatre had no lamps, they improvised with tallow candles, jammed into potatoes which were glued to the floor. These worked well until the finale, an energetic galop, caused the potatoes to roll into the performing space, provoking much 'jolly laughter' and applause among French officers in the auditorium, and fortunately no fire. Petipa writes: 'Returning to the hotel after the performance, we, the younger generation, were still laughing, but our father and mother had no heart for laughter, crushed by the miserable receipts.'[63]

The following morning Jean and his wife deliberated over whether to risk a second performance and wondered how they would pay the hotel and coach. Meanwhile, the children had gone outside. There, rolling up in the hotel driveway, was a carriage, arriving for a change of horses, and out of it stepped the actor Talma. Being a family friend and hearing of their desperate plight, he gave the children three gold *louis* with the words 'tell your father and mother that in two months I will visit them in Brussels,' then hurried off in his carriage.[64] The elderly Petipa tells this anecdote in vivid detail, but it is problematic, to say the least, since Talma was long dead by this time. Either Petipa is misremembering the identity of the stranger or, as Lillian Moore suggests in her editorial note, recalling an earlier incident when Talma did come to their aid.[65]

The Revolution officially ended on 17 July 1831 with the coronation of Leopold I as first king of the Belgians. The theatres had already reopened and on 4 January 1831 Jean staged *23, 24, 25, et 26 Septembre*, in memory of the four days when savage fighting stained the streets of Brussels with blood.[66] The new political constitution initiated a reform of the artistic institutions and a lengthy period of instability for the ballet. Jean, identified with the old Orange regime, was forced out of his post and, taking his family, went in search for work. With his distinguished record and contacts, he was able to move profitably from town to town. He staged ballets in Anvers and Lyons; he worked as a ballet master in Marseilles again, then Bordeaux. The end of 1832 marked the Petipas' return to Brussels, with Jean back at the Monnaie for the 1833–1834 season (the seasons started in April or May) where he was joint ballet master with Victor-Claude Bartholomin, the acting ballet master during Jean's absence.[67] Jean stayed two seasons, then left with his family for Bordeaux on 22 April 1835 where he was engaged as ballet master and Lucien as *premier danseur*.[68] There followed for the Brussels ballet company a period of change and uncertainty, with a succession of ballet masters or none at all.

Jean—alone this time—returned to Brussels in 1841, after New York. He stayed three seasons, before joining Marius in Spain. During those seasons he mounted the ballets he had shown in New York: *La Tarentule* and *Marco Bomba*.[69] In the early summer of 1843, Fanny Elssler delighted the Brussels audience in ballets such as *Giselle*, *La Tarentule*, and *The Swiss Milkmaid*. Her final performance was a packed benefit for the blind and incurable. The auditorium, lit with candles, looked magnificent and at the end of the performance a deputation of elderly beneficiaries was introduced to the ballerina. She, moved to tears and unable to think of anything to say, kissed them all instead. On leaving the theatre her modest carriage was pulled by young admirers to cries of 'long live Elssler!'[70]

Although Lucien did return to Brussels for the 1872–1873 season, Jean never went back. But when in 1855 the Monnaie went up in flames, he and Marius joined Perrot, Gedeonov, and others at the Imperial Theatres in contributing to a collection of 1,000 francs, sent, as stated in the accompanying letter, 'for the most needy victims of the fire at the Théâtre Royal de la Monnaie. ... this beautiful theatre which today is no more than a pile of ashes.'[71]

Victorine returned to Brussels, not as a dancer, but a notable soprano, to sing the role of Fidès in Meyerbeer's *Le Prophète* in 1850.[72] Auditioning in Liège five years earlier, she had gone through the same brutal trial-by-audience process as Marius in Bordeaux. She was then aged twenty-one. Her third debut provoked such violent whistling that the in-house police lowered the curtain and emptied the auditorium; however, her opponents being more relentless than numerous, the unanimous applause from the boxes won her the engagement.[73] She also appeared in Montpellier, where she was 'the pretty *prima* donna, the audience's favourite child, captivating them with the suppleness and exquisite delicacy of her singing'.[74] She went on to become a *première chanteuse* at the Paris Opera.[75] She married Josua Mendès de Léon, scion of a prominent Dutch Jewish family: *L'Argus* referred to her as Mme Léon Petipa on 7 July 1850, and she is buried as such in the Cimetière de Courbevoie in the Paris suburbs. However, a birth certificate records that in 1861 Victorine gave birth in Tournai to Eugénie Champenois, the father being a musician, Joseph Eugène Champenois, a reflection, perhaps, of the difficulty of divorce.[76]

With Josua Mendès de Léon, Victorine had a son Jacob Joseph Victor (born 1846) and he, in turn, had many children, among them Berthe, a soprano at the Paris Opera. Berthe's sisters, Jeanne and Lucienne (also a singer), were twins who corresponded with Petipa and are mentioned in his diaries. Petipa refers to Jeanne as his godchild and to 'my niece [Lucienne] Mendès, who is engaged as a singer in Saigon'.[77]

In her final years Victorine lived in a retirement home for singers and actors in the Paris suburb of Auteuil.[78] Marius's youngest daughter Vera recalls visiting Victorine there on trips to Paris and meeting her son and his children. He was not a theatre artist; he had only a modest income, so they were badly off. Vera had pleasant memories of Victorine: 'Aunt Victorine was a wonderful old lady, reminiscent of my father, thin, erect and very agile. I marvelled at her speed and lightness, as, heels tapping, she clambered up the stairs of a double-decker omnibus which filled my much younger mother with alarm.' In contrast Lucien seemed severe and haughty and she was afraid of him and his wife. Her parents had given her flowers to present to both Lucien's wife and Victorine, but she offered them all to Victorine, since the other woman seemed so inaccessible.[79] Victorine was especially close to Marius: as his diaries make clear, they corresponded with a touching frequency and he regularly sent her money from St Petersburg. Her death came on 25 January 1905, an event poignantly recorded in Petipa's diary: 'This evening my dear Victorine died.'[80]

Of the other Petipa siblings, little is known. Élisabeth married Henri-Eugène Zagolini (known as Groslambert) in the 6th *arrondissement* of Paris on 9 July 1842.[81] As yet no trace has been found of Adélaïde, apart from her birth certificate.[82] Although the eight-year-old Jean Claude Tonnerre appeared with the Brussels ballet during 1830 and 1831, he later became an actor, employed in Paris, Anvers, and elsewhere. Ivor Guest has found gossip in the *Coureur des spectacles* about an incident when a furious Lola Montez violently attacked him in a ballet class. Their idyll was apparently short-lived. When he announced his intention to leave her, she told him that her ring contained a deadly poison that would kill them both. One day, having managed to get hold of the ring, inside which was a grey powder, he sent the powder to a chemist for analysis and was relieved to be told that it was nothing more than ash.[83]

Later, he moved to St Petersburg. A street directory for 1867–1868 shows he lived at 20 Bolshaya Morskaya Street and had a glove shop on the corner of Nevsky and Vladimirsky Prospects, as well as a hairdressing salon on Bolshaya Morskaya.[84] He died on 1 July 1873. Petipa's diary entry for 24 December 1903 records that that he laid flowers on the graves of his daughter 'Génie' (Evgenia), his father, and brother Jean in the Volkov cemetery.[85]

Teacher at the School of the Imperial Theatres

On 6 September 1855, two months after his father's death, Petipa was appointed to take over the senior boys' class with a salary of 80 roubles.[86] Presumably he also sometimes taught the girls, since Alexandra Kemmerer, who graduated in 1862, left the following memories:

> He was a real terror to us. An outstanding ballet master and great expert in his subject, he did not hesitate to be irascible, outspoken, and sometimes impossibly harsh. The smallest mistake or lack of understanding from a pupil would cause him to boil over. We were all afraid of him, like fire, although behind his back we also sniggered, because he spoke Russian badly and it would come out in a very funny way.[87]

Petipa's merciless treatment of pupils or even company members is recorded in several accounts. He had been trained by his own father who, according to his daughter Vera, did not tolerate argumentative children. 'Grandfather used to say, when you grow up and are yourself a teacher, then you can speak, but for now learn, listen and be quiet.'[88] Maybe this glimpse of Jean contradicts Alexander Sokolov's image of a gentle and kindly teacher at the beginning of this chapter—or maybe not. Either way, his son Marius's short fuse certainly differed from the kindly and consequently popular approach used by Frédéric, who taught the senior girls.

For I. and K. Ivanov, Petipa as teacher and coach was only demanding the perfectionism he demanded of himself: 'he well knew from his own life experience that in art, as in every task, it is necessary to work, work and work.'[89] These were also harsher times and the revered Johansson, who spoke a similarly broken Russian intermingled with French, didn't mince his words either, although they had a benign edge. His class for company soloists (*classe de perfectionnement*) in the 1890s–1900s could be a chamber of insults: the future ballerina Olga Preobrazhenskaya was 'a hunchbacked devil'; Karsavina, 'weak-minded' and a 'cow on the [*sic*] ice'.[90]

Johansson became an official teacher at the school in 1863, after Petipa was promoted to second ballet master and asked that his school duties be transferred to Johansson. It seems, though, that Petipa continued teaching occasional classes and in 1885 he took over the senior girls' class. After just a year, however, he asked to stop and Ekaterina Vazem replaced him. In 1887 he started to teach mime, which hitherto had not been given a special class.[91] Alexander Shiriaev, a virtuosic demi-caractère dancer who became Petipa's assistant and also happened to be Pugni's grandson, was a pupil during the 1880s and initially disliked Petipa's methods:

> I did not like the method of teaching in this class. Petipa insisted that the pupils copy exactly all the inflections of his face, all his gestures. And it was only a few years later after finishing school that I assessed the worth of Petipa's school of mime. In the role of Quasimodo in *Esmeralda* or the pasha in *Le Corsaire*—wherever, Petipa with his lessons prepared the ground for the creation of these roles.[92]

The Ballet Master's First Muse

Maria Surovshchikova-Petipa was the first famous ballerina to be shaped by Petipa's teaching. She was his muse; he was her route to prominence. Although she had been the most promising pupil of her year, her strengths lay more in charm, plastique, and expressiveness, and Petipa set about perfecting those qualities.[93] He had a raked floor, mirror, and barre installed in their home and coached her, accompanying her on the violin. In the tradition of Auguste Vestris, he would emphasize that the first obligation of a ballerina was to captivate her audience.

With his guidance she became famous for the eloquence of her mime and the harmony of her poses, inspired by the classical sculpture and painting Petipa studied.[94] The roles he made for her exploited those qualities, while concealing her technical weaknesses.[95]

The photographs don't all do justice to the beauty and charm she was famed for, but the earliest show an elfin grace, a delicate body, and a pretty, calm-browed face. Her point work was feeble, even though Vazem says she was the first Russian ballerina to reinforce the toe-ends of her shoes by doubling them with those of other shoes.[96] But thanks to Petipa's efforts, she bewitched the public, or as Khudekov writes, 'she did not astound anyone with her dances, but enchanted everyone immediately.'[97]

On 2 February 1854, when Perrot's production of *Faust* was premiered in the presence of the imperial family, Surovshchikova made a sweet and poetic impression as Marta, the heroine Marguerite's friend, and received a gift of diamond earrings from Nicholas I.[98] She then appeared in Petipa's *Star of Granada* and a series of secondary roles: for example, in Perrot's new heroic-fantastic *Armida* (1855), which marked Fanny Cerrito's Russian debut and gave Petipa another substantial role as the hero Rinaldo, Maria was the chief nymph who assumes human form, to trick the minstrel, Gianneo (Perrot), and dance with him.[99]

With the end of the Crimean War the Petipas visited Paris in May–June 1856. Maria met her new relatives, including Lucien, who showed her round the Paris Opera.[100] On their return to St Petersburg, they were part of the ballet contingent which went to Moscow for the festivities surrounding Alexander II's coronation on 26 August. A railway now linked the two cities, so everybody could travel in comfort: Perrot, Johansson, Frédéric, the future ballet master Lev Ivanov, Golts, the Petipas. The Petersburg dancers joined their Moscow counterparts for a run of performances. The Petipas took part in an opera and ballet evening, performing one act from Perrot's *Gazelda, or the Gypsy* (Gazelda, ili Tsygane); they did not, however, appear in the glittering gala, for which Cerrito danced Saint-Léon's *La Vivandière*, accompanied by Perrot, Frédéric, and Johansson. At the end, the new tsar presented Perrot with a gold snuff box, inlaid with a miniature by the Rococo artist François Boucher and inscribed 'To the great little Perrot' (*Au grand petit Perrot*).[101]

Maria Petipa's career progressed as did her popularity. She began dancing the lead roles in *The Wilful Wife, La Vivandière, The Naiad and the Fisherman*, and *Esmeralda*.[102] She may also have appeared in a new one-act dance scene, *The Rose, the Violet, and the Butterfly* (Rosa, fialka, i babochka) in 1857. Petipa claims it as his own in his memoirs, but confusion abounds, apart from the composer's identity—the dilettante Petr, duke of Oldenburg, who had written the music for Petipa's 'Slave Dance' ('*Pas d'esclaves*') in *Le Corsaire*.[103] Irina Boglacheva says the dance scene was performed at the Bolshoi on 8 October, as part of a mixed programme for the *régisseur* Marcel's benefit; its staging and libretto were by Perrot, and the dancers were Liubov Radina, Nadezhda Amosova, and Muraveva. Denis Leshkov names Petipa as the creator and Maria as a performer, and describes the location as Oldenburg's residence in Tsarskoe Selo, either in the summer or on 8 October. Konstantin Skalkovsky refers to a big *divertissement* by Petipa, *The Butterfly, the Rose, and the Violet (Motylek, roza i fialka)*, that was shown at Peterhof on 8 December.[104]

One thing is certain: if Maria did perform on 8 October, then she would have had to restrict herself to careful poses, because she gave birth to a daughter, Marie, on 17 October.[105]

Author or not of *The Rose, the Violet, and the Butterfly*, Petipa was now devoting much energy to choreography. In his early Russian years, it had been a case of collaborative effort, with Frédéric for *Paquita* and his father for *Satanilla*, or the occasional requirement to compose dances for operas. (His first opera composition on 7 January 1849 was a polka in Act II of Friedrich von Flotow's *Alessandro Stradella*.)[106] But now he had won Perrot's confidence in his ballet-master abilities and he had a muse whose special qualities he had perfected. Maria's growing success had a double benefit. If she had the advantage of a husband who could help her gain the attention she craved, then so also her presence, in these days of ballerina-worship, could give extra cachet to Petipa's compositions. To add to this, with Andrei Saburov's appointment as director in May 1858, it was becoming clear that Perrot's days were limited. Although Petipa certainly sympathized with his friend's plight—his memoirs paint a vivid picture of Saburov's high-handed treatment of Perrot—it is likely that he saw an opening for his ambitions and understood that this meant seeking every opportunity to draw attention to himself and his wife.[107]

Some months on, Petipa was hard at work on the creation of his first full ballet, the comic two-act *A Marriage during the Regency* (Brak vo vremena regentstva). Meanwhile, on 4 November 1858 Maria Petipa appeared in *Éoline, ou la Dryade*, Perrot's last ballet in Russia. Although the Paris star Amalia Ferraris had the title role, Maria did not escape the connoisseur's eye of Gautier, who was in the audience: 'As for Madame Petipa [...] she is fine-drawn, pretty, light, and worthy of belonging to this family of distinguished choreographers.'[108]

A Marriage during the Regency was premiered at Petipa's benefit on 18 December 1958. Pugni wrote the music and Petipa the scenario about a prince (played by himself) who conceals his real identity in order to ensure that the young woman he proposes to, Nathalie (Anna Prikhunova), loves him sincerely for himself.[109] The cast included Maria Petipa and Marfa Muraveva as Nathalie's sisters, the popular character dancer Timofei Stukolkin as a caricatural dancing master called Sylph, and Lev Ivanov as a marquis. The ballet obtained Petipa's first substantial reviews as choreographer. The device of concealed identities was familiar, not to say clichéd, and the press judged Petipa's treatment to be weak.[110] That apart, they made enthusiastic and prescient comments about his choreographic abilities. 'He has known how to compose a dance for each of the four ballerinas that corresponds to the nature of their talent and shows it to its best advantage,' wrote *Muzykal'nyi i teatral'nyi vestnik*.[111] The point was echoed by the *Sankt-Peterburgskie vedomosti*: 'He has composed some delightful *pas* [...] which were especially remarkable for the fact that they suited the temperaments of each of the dancers. [...] This demonstrates in the young choreographer a considerable discernment, a knowledge of the task, and an ability to use what he has to hand.'[112] The ballet continued into the following year and, on 23 October, it had the first of three showings in Moscow, mounted by the French ballet master Théodore Chion (known as just Théodore) for his wife Thérèse Théodore's benefit performance.[113] In St Petersburg it was revived on 19 April 1870 with Ivanov as the prince. Reviewing the revival, *Golos* judged it to be more an extended *divertissement*, made up of classical and character dances, 'than a ballet in a real sense, since it has almost no narrative'.[114] Another performance on 21 May was given as part of the benefit programme for the destitute family of the recently deceased Pugni.

Petipa's industriousness continued. He choreographed dances for the three-act *Sleepwalker Bride* (Nevesta-Lunatik), premiered at the benefit on 29 January 1859 for Ekaterina Friedberg, who was now back in St Petersburg. The ballet was based on Jean Aumer's 1827 *La Somnambule* with music by Ferdinand Hérold and a libretto by Eugène Scribe, which Friedberg had already performed in Paris. Perrot being ill, the Petersburg staging fell to Friedberg, helped by Petipa. The poster mistakenly attributed the choreography to Alexei Bogdanov, but in any case the ballet, which prioritized mime, turned out to be supremely tedious, the only successful components being a pas de deux for Friedberg and Petipa and 'The Four Cantons' ('Les Quatre Cantons') for Friedberg, Prikhunova, Muraveva, and Maria Petipa.[115] Next came the Italian celebrity Amalia Ferraris's benefit on 12 February for which Petipa partnered Ferraris in his *Venetian Carnaval* (Venetsianskii karnaval), a big and effective (but uncredited) pas de deux, to a score by Pugni on a theme by Paganini.[116] For Pleshcheev, writing many years later, it was 'a masterpiece [...] a breath of something new, poetic, graceful' and it would often be revived.[117] And now it was Maria Petipa's turn for her benefit on 23 April 1859 which Petipa planned as a showcase for his choreography. As well as *A Marriage during the Regency*, the programme included the second act of *Le Corsaire* with his 'Pas d'esclaves' and the talented Praskovia Lebedeva, straight out of Moscow's theatre school as Medora. To finish, came a new comic one-act ballet, *The Parisian Market*.

The narrative was adapted from a French *comédie-vaudeville* by Emmanuel Théaulon, shown at the Mikhailovsky, with the whimsical title *The Countess of the Wine Barrel, or the Two Cousins* (La Comtesse du tonneau, ou les Deux Cousines). Charming or naive or just plain silly, the ballet was more a pretext for the dances to Pugni's music. Simon (Petipa), a fruit trader, has a stall in the marketplace and he loves Lizetta (Maria Petipa), a needlewoman who mends and darns (*shtopal'shchitsa*). Lizetta is so poor she can't afford a proper stall and has to improvise with a large wine barrel and an umbrella. Simon, as he himself explains in a mimed monologue, is also poor, too poor to marry Lizetta. But this notwithstanding he tries to entice her with a basket of his best cherries, in the hope of snatching a kiss with each cherry: 'Especially successful,' the critic Mavrikii Rappaport wrote, 'is the "Pas de cerises", in which Miss Petipa again captivates us.'[118] A troupe of commedia dell'arte players enters the marketplace and there follows a performance within a performance.[119] Next, a foppish, ridiculous marquis de Maigrelet (French for 'skinny'; played by Stukolkin) enters and, immediately captivated by Lizetta, asks her to darn a hole in his stocking; a group of fishmongers breaks into a fight which turns into an ensemble dance, described by *Sankt-Peterburgskie vedomosti* as reminiscent of the cancan, much in vogue at the time; and suddenly almost at the end another character appears—Georgetta, who is not only Lizetta's cousin, but also the marquis's mistress.[120] By spectacular mistiming, the marquis (who had earlier left the stage) also enters, bearing a bouquet of flowers which he presents to Lizetta—and then, in an attempt to save the situation, to another street trader. But it's too late: Georgetta is furious. All is soon resolved, however, when Lizetta, who just happens to have a casket full of incriminating letters belonging to Georgetta, threatens to show them. Georgetta changes tone and persuades Lizetta to give her the casket in exchange for a purse of gold. So all is happily resolved, since nothing now hinders the marriage of Simon and Lizetta. This is the cue for a *divertissement*, starting with a 'Valse parisienne' for the happy couple, followed by a finale in which Petipa demonstrated 'his skill in moving rather significant massed corps de ballet groups'.[121]

Maria Petipa's performance was unanimously praised, *Sankt-Peterburgskie vedomosti* singling out her character dances 'which it would be difficult to dance better than her'.[122] Petipa was also applauded for his 'undoubted choreographic abilities'.[123] But the ballet was weak, although Rappaport congratulated Petipa for mounting it in such a short space of time and managing to do a great deal with very little.[124] For all its failings, *The Parisian Market* would be the means by which Petipa's choreography first came to the attention of audiences outside Russia and his wife would achieve international fame.

On 30 August 1859 Maria opened the new season with the demanding title role of Perrot's *Catarina*. Dancing opposite her husband who had taken over Perrot's role as Diavolino, Catarina's lieutenant, she had all the necessary grace, but, to modern minds, the fact that she attempted the role at all is astonishing. If the dates are correct, she was by then once again heavily pregnant. It's no surprise therefore that she was found wanting in technique to match the fast tempo of the complicated variations; and these were, surely, also simplified.[125]

On 19 September Maria gave birth to her second child, Jean. By then Perrot's fate was well and truly sealed. Saint-Léon had arrived and staged *Jovita* on 13 September and just over a year later his appointment as Perrot's successor was made official. For the Petipas, there would have been some compensation for disappointment had his tenure ushered in a host of new roles for them, but these did not materialize. There were, though, exceptions. Maria Petipa, for example, scored a success in a featured part in Saint-Léon's *Pâquerette* (Pakeretta), staged on 26 January 1860 for the Italian ballerina Carolina Rosati. (The original production had featured Cerrito.) And a year later, on 1 February 1861, she succeeded Muraveva in Saint-Léon's *Saltarello, or the Passion for Dance* (Sal'tarello, ili strast' k tantsam) dancing opposite Saint-Léon's Saltarello. Besides dancing and choreographing, the multitalented Saint-Léon had composed the music, written the libretto (as he did for most of his ballets), and, as a concert-standard violinist in the showy style of Paganini, played the violin on stage.[126]

The Petipas were busy with other projects, other roles. On 8 November 1859 Petipa as Conrad partnered Rosati who had created the role of Medora at *Le Corsaire*'s Paris premiere. A few weeks later (29 November), Maria Petipa made her debut in the title role of the complete *Gazelda*—previously she had danced only parts of Perrot's ballet. On 12 April 1860 for her benefit performance came a revival of *Marco Bomba*, with Alexei Bogdanov and Lev Ivanov, and, most important, the premiere of her husband's next ballet, *The Blue Dahlia* (Golubaia georgina), a two-act fantasy (music by Pugni), agreed by the directorate on the condition that, like *A Marriage during the Regency*, it did not cost any money.[127]

The ballet is interesting from several points of view.[128] Petipa's scenario, his third, is the first not to be a light-hearted comedy. A variant of the Pygmalion story, its principal characters are a young gardener, Gautier (Petipa), and a blue dahlia (Maria Petipa), his great botanical achievement, blue being an impossible colour for dahlias. The gardener's name, perhaps, is a reference to Théophile Gautier, famous not only for his literary output but for his open adoration, as a ballet critic, of various ballerinas. The young gardener is obsessed with the blue dahlia, which he hopes will allow him to win an upcoming flower competition. (Marina Ilicheva also sees this as an allegory for the Petipa's own attitude to his wife.) But his tending of the dahlia goes beyond a gardener's mere zeal. He is a true romantic hero, so entranced by his flower that his passion becomes a lover's ardour and he neglects his fiancée Cecile (Anna Kosheva). In one scene, Cecile is so incensed that she runs into the garden to pluck the blue dahlia, but is prevented by Gautier. Not even the intervention of Gautier's mother Susanna can bring him to reason.

By choosing to personify flowers, Petipa was, like Saint-Léon who did the same, tapping into a fashion. It is perhaps surprising to learn that the enthusiasm for fresh flowers, one of the decorative elements of the Romantic movement, arrived in Russia only in the 1840s. Before it was not customary even to give performers bouquets. But this changed to the extent that by November 1848 at the Mikhailovsky an entertainment, *The Love of Roses, or the May Beetle and the Butterfly* (Liubov' rozy, ili Maiskii zhuk i babochka), depicted a succession of kingdoms—first flowers in which 'floral-performers' danced and sang, then butterflies, and finally vegetables.[129]

The Blue Dahlia has a subplot featuring a barber, Beausoleil, played to great effect by Stukolkin. Although Beausoleil (Beautiful Sun) is a comic character, there is also irony in his name. He is hopelessly in love with Cecile and she flirts with him, in an attempt to arouse Gautier's jealousy; but, when she ultimately rejects him, he tries to hang himself from a tree. The branch breaks, and Beausoleil survives, but the episode reportedly brought the audience to tears.[130]

The arrival of the mayor and the local landowner marks the beginning of the competition, which is translated into dance terms by a big *divertissement*. This includes a pas de deux, 'The Garland of Flowers' ('*La Guirlande de fleurs*'), for Lev Ivanov and Vera Liadova, a variation for Maria Petipa, 'The Magical Dahlia' ('*La Dahlia fantastique*'), and a concluding Hungarian dance ('*Pas de caractère hongrois*'). The Hungarian component is justified by the story's Hungarian setting, although in the mysterious logic of ballet all the characters have French names. Gautier wins the competition and takes the prize of a purse of gold, but just as he prepares to gather up his flowers, the mayor tells him they no longer belong to him. In despair, Gautier flings the money at the mayor's feet and, rushing towards the blue dahlia, breaks its stem into pieces. Out of his mind with grief, now all alone, he falls to the ground, the flower withering in his hands. All his attempts to revive it fail, its petals fall, and its spirit is carried away to the skies.

The Blue Dahlia was the start of an attention to flowers—and insects—that would run through Petipa's oeuvre right to the end. Baskets of flowers, garlands, bouquets, and single blooms were used as props to adorn his choreography, most famously in *The Sleeping Beauty*'s 'Rose adagio'. They were also animated, transformed into dancing groups and solos, as in *Le Corsaire*'s 'Jardin animé' and in Petipa's final (but unperformed) ballet *The Romance of the Rosebud and the Butterfly* (Roman butony rosy i babochki). The aesthetic of the Romantic Ballet was drawing to an end; but it is clear that in *The Blue Dahlia* Petipa used its tropes to create a poetic dimension. In this and subsequent ballets, he refreshed the emblems of the Romantic Ballet; the sylphs and dryads would reappear, often as the inhabitants of visions and dreams. Or at other times they were replaced: the Blue Dahlia, unattainable and idealized, was the sylph of the old Romantic Ballet.

Although Stukolkin later considered *The Blue Dahlia* to be without any remarkable qualities, Rappaport's review recorded not only 'creativity and an abundance of invention' but also observed that in this ballet 'prevails a poetic content'.[131] *Severnaia pchela* noted echoes of Taglioni's *Sylphide*, where the titular heroine dies because of a mortal's love, but praised 'both the creative talent and the imagination of the young choreographer' and a composition in which 'dances and groupings stand out with a freshness of invention, a gracefulness, and diversity. The flowers, and in particular, the animated dahlia, play a major role in the ballet. For her, the ballet master has devised new *pas, attitudes,* and poses, which beg for an artist's pencil.'[132]

Paris

On 26 April 1860 Petipa received permission to go to France for four weeks to see his dying mother.[133] The following year he and Maria decided they should perform abroad, to add lustre to their status. They were undoubtedly conscious that February 1862 would mark the completion of Maria Petipa's obligatory ten-year service and the necessity of negotiating a new contact. Their request for a paid four-month leave during the summer vacation was accepted on 28 February 1861.[134]

Petipa claims that first, in March, they went to Riga, where they gave eight performances, then they went to Berlin; however, Sergei Konaev, in his new edition of the memoirs, shows that Riga and Berlin happened much later, in 1863.[135] Instead, the couple went straight to Paris, where, according to Petipa's unreliable account, for their petition to secure performances at the Opera, they enlisted the support of a minister, the duke de Morny, who had a Russian wife. Although the Opera's director Alphonse Royer was not overly enthusiastic, the result was permission for six performances, starting 29 May 1861; this was later extended to eighteen, ending on 16 August.[136]

The Opera, whose official name was in perpetual modification, was now called the *Théâtre Impérial de l'Opéra* and still in the rue Le Peletier, not far from today's Palais Garnier. Built in 1821 and known informally as the *Opéra* or *Salle Le Peletier*, it saw the birth of many of the century's grand operas, as well as *La Sylphide, Giselle, Paquita, Le Corsaire,* and *Coppélia.* It was technologically advanced for its time, with, from 1822, gas lighting; it also had a moveable stage and orchestra pit, allowing the auditorium to be transformed into an enormous hall.

For this, Europe's premier opera house, the Petipas were anxiously assiduous in their efforts to make a big impression. They had decided to bring the one-act *Parisian Market,* but, worried that it might fall short of the sophisticated audience's expectations, Petipa had sought out the librettist René Lordereau, recommended by his brother Lucien, who was by then the company's first ballet master. Lordereau advised Petipa on how best to cultivate the French critics (PR departments belonged to the future); he wrote draft letters for him to influential persons; and he devised a few adaptations to Petipa's libretto. The title was changed to *Le Marché des Innocents;* the setting was updated from the reign of Louis XV to the Directory; Lizetta was renamed Gloriette; and the ridiculous Marquis de Maigrelet became

Lindor, an *incroyable*.[137] Lucien also worked on the ballet, although what he choreographed is unclear; however, the contribution was deemed significant enough for him to be credited as co-author and to receive royalty payments, equal to those of Marius. (Later, in 1872, Lucien mounted the ballet in Brussels.)[138]

The Petipas' energetic self-promotion clearly bore fruit because in the audience on 29 May were Napoleon III and the empress Eugénie; on stage Louis Mérante replaced Petipa as Simon; and on the same programme was Verdi's *Il Trovatore*. Reviewers noted Maria Petipa's grace, acting talent, and what they considered her Slav qualities, all highlighted by her husband's choreography. She was a character dancer rather than a classicist, her vivacious spontaneity and naturalness contributing to the impression that she danced as inspiration moved her.[139]

No fee had been arranged for Maria.[140] That, and the enthusiastic reception for her debut, prompted the Opera's directorate, very exceptionally, to offer her a benefit performance on 6 August 1861, the glitter of the audience rivalling that of the stage. Not only were Napoleon and Eugénie there (again), but also the king of Sweden, Ivan Turgenev, Gedeonov who was now living in Paris, and other lofty personages. The singers Enrico Tamberlik and Pauline Viardot, muse of Turgenev, took part in the mixed programme, as did Louis Mérante and his new wife Zina Richard. Maria Petipa was a big hit in a 'new *pas*', unfamiliar to the Paris audience, called 'Cosmopolite', added, for the special occasion, to the end of *Le Marché des Innocents*.[141]

One reviewer judged that the sole worth of *Le Marché des Innocents* rested with Maria Petipa and that her departure would leave long regrets among the Parisian public. Perhaps he was wrong to minimize the ballet's merits, since it would receive many performances in the ten years following its premiere. His overheated description of Maria, focusing on her appearance, gives some idea of the sexual allure that were among her principal assets. 'Madame Petipa is the model of all that is pretty, sweet. [...] Her slightly upturned nose, her white teeth between pink lips give her face something strange, wild, tartar, added to which is hair of reddish brown with waves that refract, here and there, flashes of fire. [...] You have no idea of the passion of her dancing.'[142] Maria Petipa was photographed by Nadar; she was portrayed in lithographs and engravings; she was the subject of two monographs by Louis Lemercier de Neuville and Pierre Fiorentino.[143]

Le Marché des Innocents and 'Cosmopolite' were both triggers for legal conflict, however. On 28 May 1861, when the Paris premiere of *Le Marché des Innocents* was advertised, René Lordereau took out a lawsuit on the same day against Petipa and Alphonse Royer for the failure to acknowledge his collaboration. Petipa, who had apparently paid Lordereau 175 francs for his work, had already warned him that Royer had removed his name because he didn't want (presumably for financial reasons) to submit a new author to the minister for just a one-act ballet. The judgement the following day found against the plaintiff on the grounds that, although he may well have helped in a way deserving the remuneration he had received, the ballet was already in existence so that his contribution was not substantial enough to qualify as collaboration.[144]

The second lawsuit was more damaging, as well as being probably the first over copyright in ballet. Although the legal case was complex, the circumstances leading up to it were straightforward. For the prestigious benefit performance, the Petipas wanted to include the 'Cosmopolitana' pas from Perrot's Gazelda, an audience-winning solo composed of a succession of different national dances (hence its name). It had become one of Maria Petipa's signature numbers in St Petersburg and she clearly felt it would be a fitting showcase. And so Petipa went to his old friend Perrot and asked him. Perrot, however, was on bad terms with the Paris Opera and refused. Upset, perhaps also feeling disbelief, Petipa went ahead anyway. He modified the title to 'Cosmopolite', but used the same Pugni accompaniment and choreography that was remarkably similar. Hearing of this, Perrot demanded that the dance be withdrawn from the benefit performance, but the Opera refused; not only that, the pas was repeated on three occasions after the benefit.[145]

At the trial on 11 July the following year, the prosecution argued that the plaintiff, a choreographer who had achieved fame on the greatest stages of Europe, had no need of money, but was defending the principle of ownership and, with Saint-Léon's testimony, asserted that the two variations were identical.[146] Petipa, represented by the Opera's eminent lawyer Maître Chaix d'Est-Ange, opposed several arguments which not only outlined the complexities that surround copyright even today, but also highlighted the free-for-all that was ballet in the nineteenth century when ballet masters staged and modified each other's work with only a relaxed concern for ownership. One argument evoked the difficulty of even defining the composition of a dance, when this was so dependent on its performer. Another argument pointed to the inalterable fact that Perrot's dance was actually made up of folk dances long known and performed before.[147]

In the end the court found for Perrot: folk dances were maybe common property, but the way Perrot presented, linked, and set them to his chosen music belonged to him; moreover, Petipa had aggravated his action by passing off the dance as his own. (He falsely claims in his memoirs that he did not.)[148] The sum set for damages, however, was not the 10,000 francs claimed by Perrot, but three hundred. (Petipa mistakenly remembers the sum as five francs.) It must have seemed even more derisory considering that records show the benefit earned 16,075 francs, more than three times the average for performances at the Paris Opera. So Petipa's claim in his memoirs of 18,000 francs was not far off.[149]

The trial seems to have done no harm to Petipa. On the principle that bad publicity is better than no publicity, it may even, as he says in his memoirs, have helped to promote the Petipa name.[150] Either way, the couple's Paris triumph of

1861 earned them the offer of a two-month season in May the next year. On that trip, as well as appearing in *Le Marché des Innocents*, Maria Petipa made her debut in *Le Diable à quatre*, sharing the stage with Zina Richard (now Mérante) and Lucien Petipa. A mazurka was inserted, Maria partnered by the Polish specialist Felix Kshesinsky (father of Matilda Kshesinskaya) who had been brought specially from St Petersburg. Performed with a verve and skill that was new to Paris, it made a huge impression.[151]

Maria's final performance was on 9 August, at which she danced a pas de deux, *The Jewess* (La Juive), created for her by Lucien Petipa.[152]

Success! The Pharaoh's Daughter

The conquest of Paris on the Petipas' first visit had the desired effect when they returned to St Petersburg. At the end of 1861 the directorate offered Maria a contract with highly favourable terms: an increase in her annual pay to 5,000 roubles with a four-month summer break for foreign touring.

That same year she added to her repertoire with revivals by her husband of Perrot's *Eoline* and *Faust*. She was especially impressive as *Faust*'s Marguerite, displaying real dramatic power in the scene of Marguerite's mental collapse, and prompted the poet Dmitrii Minaev to dedicate a poem to her, describing her as 'the star of Russian ballerinas'.[153] She also danced as Terpsichore in *Euterpe and Terpsichore* (Evterpe i Terpsikhora), staged on 15 November at Tsarksoe Selo by Petipa and the duke of Oldenburg, with a young opera singer Zhosefina Mikhailovskaya playing Euterpe, the muse of music and lyric poetry. This animated tableau or, in Oldenburg's locution, *ballad*, was one of several composed by Oldenburg as private entertainments combining song and dance. (When Petipa claimed authorship of the 1857 *The Rose, the Violet, and the Butterfly*, he must have had one of these entertainments in mind.) Ekaterina Vazem took part in several as a student and remembered how in *Euterpe and Terpsichore* she threw a succession of floral wreaths to the floor and stepped in the middle of each, matching the sung words about Terpsichore who 'flies, soars playfully through the flowers'.[154] (Stepping into floral wreaths was a popular conceit: it was used by Perrot for *Faust*'s Marguerite, as a photograph of Maria Petipa shows, and again by Petipa, for Medora in *Le Corsaire*'s 'Jardin animé'.)[155]

Petipa was by now already aged forty-four and, like his wife, determined to advance his career. Having secured the agreement of Carolina Rosati, he successfully petitioned Saburov to allow him to create a big ballet for the ballerina's contractual benefit performance. Rosati, much admired at the Paris Opera, was thirty-three when she arrived in Russia and it was perhaps an exaggeration to describe her as far from her first youth (Petipa) or faded (Khudekov). About her talent, Petipa dismisses her laconically with the comment that her Russian debut in *Jovita* 'had

no success at all'.[156] Khudekov provides more detail: she lacked lightness of movement, she had gained weight, 'and barely lifted herself from the floor, performing
only very short variations, with which she could not satisfy lovers of the art'.[157] She
was however a first-class actress, consequently doing best in drama-led ballets,
and had some success in character dance, even dancing a cancan in Saint-Léon's
Graziella, complete with twitching skirts. But the public was not convinced: ticket
sales for her appearances in the same choreographer's *Pâquerette* and *Marikita—
The Pearl of Seville* (Marikita—Sevil'skaia zhemchuzhina) were poor. Despite this
she spent three years in Russia, the reason, Khudekov concluding, not her talent,
but 'unseen support from an influential hand'.[158]

According to Petipa, the influential hand was Saburov's.[159] Given that Saburov
had agreed to a big ballet choreographed by Petipa for Rosati, Petipa returned to
Paris in November to work with the prolific dramatist and librettist Saint-Georges,
already known in Russia through *Satanilla* and *Giselle*.[160] They took Gautier's 1857
The Story of the Mummy (Le Roman de la momie) as their starting point; the setting of Ancient Egypt was novel for ballet, whose extra-European locations were
the harems of Turkey and temples of India.[161] But they were also tapping into a
widespread interest in Egypt, triggered by archaeological excavations and the construction of the Suez Canal, started in 1859. After three weeks, Petipa returned to
Petersburg, stopping off in Berlin, where he viewed the city's Egyptian antiquities.

Once back in St Petersburg, however, he found the situation changed. The pot-
bellied, wig-wearing Saburov had, after bestowing special favours on Rosati, fallen
out with her.[162] For several months Petipa waited, and Rosati waited, for the order
to proceed with rehearsals. Finally, Rosati became convinced that Saburov was
deliberately forgetting her benefit. (Around that time, there were also attempts
to reduce the Imperial Theatres' deficit.)[163] Mindful that the end of the 1861–1862
season and termination of her contract were just a few months off, she asked
Petipa to come with her to speak to Saburov. The encounter in Saburov's office
becomes one of Petipa's amusing anecdotes, in which Saburov's green dressing
gown, which he habitually wore to receive 'all the artists, men, and women', becomes the pivotal player. At first Saburov replies that the ballet is no longer possible
because of a lack of time and money, but Rosati will be liberally recompensed for
her financial loss. Rosati is outraged and an argument ensues, until Saburov irrit-
ably places a foot on a chair and the dressing gown falls open revealing he is naked
underneath. The embarrassment prompts Saburov to pause and, turning towards
Petipa, to ask: 'M. Petipa, can you stage this ballet in six weeks?' After some hesitation, Petipa commits himself to producing the three acts and seven scenes with
prologue and epilogue in a near-impossible six weeks.[164] The schedule of two rehearsals a day tested even Pugni's customary speed in composition.

The libretto mixes two time dimensions: the present, as represented by
Lord Wilson (played by Petipa), an English explorer, with his servant John Bull

(Stukolkin); and the ancient past, as represented by a pharaoh and his daughter Aspichia (or Aspicia).[165] The setting of the prologue (designed by Herman Wagner) is the Sahara desert: a long road winds back to mountains on the horizon; the sky is full of stars.[166] A caravan of Armenian merchants, complete with camels and slaves, gradually appears and sets up camp for the evening by palm trees and water. Next arrive two other travellers, Lord Wilson and an exhausted but comical John Bull, who ask the merchants if they can join them. The merchants invite them to eat while bayadères who are accompanying the merchants enter-tain them with dances. A dust storm is gathering, however. There are terrifying peals of thunder, the sky lights up, waves of sand appear on the horizon, and a turbulent wind blows away the merchants' tent and bends and uproots the palm trees. (All this was wonderfully accomplished by the theatre's apparatus and al-most frightened the spectators out of their seats.) The travellers take shelter in the pyramid nearby. The scene changes to the pyramid's interior (designed by Andrei Roller): inside is a statue of the pharaoh and, placed in a richly decorated niche, a mummy (Aspichia), flanked by other mummies around the walls.[167] Lord Wilson smokes opium and like everyone else falls into a deep sleep. A bright ray of light illuminates the face of Aspichia's mummy and the beautiful princess comes to life, as do the other mummies. Aspichia notices the sleeping Englishman and lays a hand on his heart, but soon everything disappears in thick clouds, in the middle of which appear the bright letters: 'A Dream from the Past' ('*Son iz minuvshego*'), which is the cue for the story proper to begin.

The curtain lifts to reveal a glade, with a charming little hut covered in flowers and a bridge in the distance.[168] The horns and trumpets of the pharaoh's hunting party sound. Aspichia appears with her companions and there follows, in audience-pleasing women-warrior tradition, a dance for huntresses ('Grand Pas des chasseresses') led by Aspichia and her favourite slave Ramzeia (the popular Liubov Radina). While the ladies take a graceful rest a monkey appears among the branches, played by a pupil, Alexander Shtikhling, who wakes everybody and provides an amusing interlude that always delighted the audience. Ballet lore says that it so pleased the little George Balanchine, he announced to his parents: 'I want to be the same monkey!'[169]

Meanwhile, time-travelling in his dream, Lord Wilson has become an ancient Egyptian, Taor, accompanied by his servant, Pasifont, the former John Bull. (Taor, a quintessential hero, fearless, honourable, passionate, was perfectly portrayed by Petipa.) Entering the scene, he meets Aspichia again and as he lays a hand on her heart, the music reprises the moment when she had made the same gesture in the pyramid. The romantic spell is broken, however, by the appearance of another wild animal, a lion. In the ensuing disarray, Taor suddenly sees Aspichia running across the bridge with the lion bounding after her; he seizes a bow and kills the lion. He then turns to the aid of Aspichia who has fainted and, just as he is holding her, the stern pharaoh (tall, imposing Nikolai Golts) enters. When Aspichia explains that Taor saved her life, the pharaoh's anger at the presumptuous posture of such a lowly individual turns to gratitude and he invites Taor to his palace.

The second scene (designed by Roller) is set in a magnificent hall, opening out on to a garden.[170] Around the walls are caryatids holding torches; at the back is a big rostrum with the pharaoh's throne. Taor is with Aspichia; he refuses all the gifts she offers, telling her he only wants her love. Now comes the pharaoh and his entourage—grandees, soldiers, slaves—entering in a procession. A fanfare announces the arrival of the Nubian king (Kshesinsky) with his own splendid suite, to ask for Aspichia's hand in marriage. The pharaoh seems favourable to this alliance and Taor, alarmed, surreptitiously draws his dagger, until Aspichia calms him, assuring him the marriage will never take place. The pharaoh then commands that the festivities, in honour of his daughter's rescue, should start.

A typical Petipa-esque *grand pas d'action* (group and solo dances mixed with action) follows, during which Aspichia, Taor, and Ramzeia plot an escape. Fedor Lopukhov, who remembered the ballet's 1898 revival, describes the dancing as a pure-dance pas de cinq for one unnamed male character (Johansson) with Aspichia, Ramzeia, and two female friends. (Taor is present, but doesn't take part.) For Lopukhov, the single male presence was a tricky gender ratio for any choreographer to attempt. And yet it stood out as 'a peerless diamond', a masterpiece with a sonata structure and an unrivalled originality that emerged from the absence of other men. The introduction, rather than containing conventional partnering, was built out of ensemble patterns; the middle section was an elaboration with broader movement and variations; and this was followed by a final coda. The variations were predominantly solos, but at times the dancers joined up in pairs. Lopukhov remembered some of the steps as being *glissés* into *arabesque, glissés* with turns, turning *emboîtés, sauts de basque*, and big, backward-leaning *cabrioles*. Many critics heaped praise on Johansson for his classical perfection in a solo that began with unusual *écarté* poses. It is also likely that Rosati danced what was listed on the premiere's poster as the 'Variation orientale'. Lopukhov recalled this as having 'pseudo-Persian' movements performed with a dagger and a shawl; but because it clashed with the strict classicism of the rest of the grand pas, he mistakenly assumed it had been composed for the revival at the insistence of the new Aspichia, Matilda Kshesinskaya.[171]

The act closes with a 'Grand Ballabile des caryatides animées': one of Petipa's large-scale ensembles, which all the reviewers mentioned and Rappaport in *Syn otechestva* singled out as particularly effective.[172] Three soloists—Maria Sokolova, Anna Kosheva, the final-year student Alexandra Kemmerer—were accompanied by thirty-six corps de ballet men and women, and the same number of children, adding up to a total of seventy-five dancers, not counting various supernumeraries.[173] The dancers, representing caryatids, carried baskets of flowers on their heads; at the end, according to the libretto, children appeared out of the baskets (presumably no longer balanced on heads). For the three soloists, Petipa composed variations that vividly exploited their individual qualities. Kosheva, who excelled in rapid turns, span like a whirlwind along the footlights so that it seemed she might fly into the orchestra.[174] Airy Maria Sokolova's solo was remembered by reviewers even decades later, the critic of *Peterburgskaia gazeta* lamenting her *entrechats six-royal* at another, earlier (1885) revival.[175] But the dancing in the narrative serves as a decoy. The lovers, helped by their faithful servants, flee the palace. The pharaoh, discovering their absence, orders a chase and the Nubian king also sets out in pursuit.

The second act opens in a fisherman's cottage on the bank of the Nile.[176] The fisherman (Lev Ivanov) and his wife (Kemmerer) are in the midst of festivities, as ballet characters tend to be. They perform an 'Egyptian Fishermen's Dance' ('*Danse des pêcheurs égyptiens*') with twelve other dancers. Just before or during another dance, a 'Pas fellah', a knock at the door announces the fugitives, dressed as simple peasants.[177] The travellers are received with kindness, their hunger is satisfied, and, when the lively dancing resumes, they join in. Night comes, the fishermen prepare to go fishing and, to repay their hospitality, Taor offers to help. Aspichia remains alone. A stranger breaks into the darkened house, lit only by a single lamp and the reflection of the moon. He turns out to be the Nubian king. To escape, Aspichia jumps out of the window into the depths of the Nile; in horror, the Nubian king lets out a wild cry, at which his retainers drag him away from the window. Just seconds later Taor returns and together with his servant is arrested by the king.

Next comes the scene of an underwater kingdom, essentially a supernatural fantasy within the big dream that is the ballet.[178] The effect of Aspichia, slowly sinking from the water's surface, high above, down to the riverbed, as replicated by Pierre Lacotte's re-creation in 2000, is magical.[179] She reaches the bottom where the majestic, grey-bearded Nile (Frédéric) sits on his jasper throne in a grotto made of coral and glittering stalactites. He is holding a golden trident and is surrounded by water sprites and various deities. To welcome the daughter of the pharaoh, rivers appear and perform a 'Grand Pas of Rivers, Streams, and Sources' ('*Grand Pas des fleuves, ruisseaux, et sources*'), an ambitious *divertissement*, not detailed in the libretto. However, as described by reviewers and the performance poster, a succession of soloists each performed a variation with national-dance motifs representing their respective rivers: the Tiber, in the style of a tarantella, Maria Sokolova praised for her light, clear jumps; the Huang-he or Yellow River with Anna Kosheva as 'an adorable Chinese girl'; the Rhine (Elizaveta Nikitina), based on the turning, steady steps of the Austrian *Länder*; the Thames (Maria Efremova), a pizzicato dance; the Guadalquivir (Vera Lapshina), echoing a *bolero*.[180] The Neva (the senior pupil Matilda Madaeva) was particularly appreciated, beginning with plangent moves that accelerated into the rhythms of a *trepak* for the finale.[181]

Because Aspichia is worried about Taor, the Nile now conjures up Taor's image and there follows a sequence (Pas de vision) in which Aspichia, framed by naiads, undines, and various small rivers, tries to reach him but fails, obstructed by the animated sprites around her. (Petipa would use a similar tactic in *The Sleeping Beauty*'s vision scene, where the Lilac Fairy stands between Prince Désiré and Aurora.) Aspichia then asks to return to land and is transported back to the surface in a mother-of-pearl shell, pushed upwards by a column of water.

The final act returns the action to the palace, where preparations are under way for Taor's execution using a venomous snake.[182] In the nick of time Aspichia returns, carried high on the shoulders of a joyous crowd of young people. She mimes a detailed account of what has happened and blames the Nubian king for her jump into the Nile. The pharoah orders the Nubian king to leave but does not yield to Aspichia's pleas for Taor's life. In terrible anguish Aspichia tries to thrust her arm into the basket with the snake. Her frightened father stops her and, touched by the depth of her feeling, forgives Taor who falls at Aspichia's feet and is declared her husband by the pharaoh. Rosati apparently carried off this long scene superbly and it became one of the ballet's signature episodes, a measure of a ballerina's dramatic skills.[183] There follows a celebratory 'Pas de crotales' (small cymbals attached to the elbows and hands), featuring the lead characters, seven pairs of soloists, and a large corps de ballet. Finally comes an apotheosis. Clouds descend and when they disperse the interior of the pyramid reappears, only this time the top opens, revealing a tableau of Osiris and Isis in the sky, surrounded by other Egyptian deities, while below are the mummified Pharaoh and Aspichia as before, along with the awakening travellers.

Mixing richly exotic design, spectacle, drama, comedy, and romance, the ballet was a medley of genres that entertained, charmed, and gripped its audience. Although Petipa would always go to much trouble to research national dances, the historical and cultural inaccuracies were probably blatant—but then this was the language of ballet, in itself unreal, and audiences did not worry too much. Pugni's music, in Rappaport's opinion, had effective instrumentation, but would have benefitted from a more Eastern colouration and languor, as well as more vigour where appropriate.[184] Roller and Wagner deployed their spectacular theatrical im-aginations and machinery, as a result of which Roller was named a member of the Academy of Arts.[185] Like Rappaport, the reviewer of *Sankt-Peterburgskie vedomosti* had reservations about the length: 'to sit through nearly five hours [...] even with lions and monkeys, is slightly wearisome' and that 'with a few cuts the sumptuous and costly staging will give more pleasure'.[186]

This notwithstanding, *The Pharaoh's Daughter*, premiered on 18 January 1862, was by most accounts a winner. 'Your work is an enormous artistic success,' Rosati wrote to Saint-Georges, 'and an enormous box-office success. People fight for tickets three days in advance.'[187] In Petipa's achievement Rappaport saw 'the assurance of an artist's hand, knowledge [and] good taste combined with grace'. Then he adds: 'It is evident that he belongs to the school of Perrot, that, in his staging of the new ballet, he was under Perrot's influence, although in his groupings and dances there is much originality and character.'[188] Years later, in his history of dance, Khudekov would repeat the same observation: 'In it [*The Pharaoh's Daughter*] was the undoubted influence of his predecessor Perrot. Boldly, but without, of course, being aware of it, he followed the direction set by Perrot's works. Strong dramatic scenes with absolutely clear, vivid action, illustrated by expressive, meaningful dances, made the ballet so interesting that, in spite of its length (from 7 o'clock to midnight), the audience stayed in the auditorium right to the end.'[189]

Remarkably, *The Pharaoh's Daughter* already contained all the strategies that Petipa would use for his large-scale ballets: the alternation of dramatic scenes and dance; the reliance on *divertissements* which often include character dances and appear during celebrations of some kind; a vision or dream scene tending to interrupt the narrative line; a procession, usually preceding a celebration and serving to display the ballet's protagonists, together with picturesque costumes and accessories; and big ensemble dancing for the finale, followed by an apotheosis. Although there are exceptions, Petipa would seldom deviate from this formula.

According to Stukolkin, Rosati gave generous assistance to Petipa and the other artists during rehearsals.[190] She also won the audience's approval, the ballet's substantial dramatic scenes allowing her to display the outstanding expressive power on which her reputation was built. 'She performed [...] with great animation,' Khudekov writes, 'bringing to the fore the mimetic dimension of her talent.'[191] She appeared in the ballet seven times before leaving Russia and retiring from the stage.[192]

Maria Petipa inherited the role on 9 October of the same year and 'created such a furore that the ballet ran for twenty-seven performances in succession during the winter [and] the theatre was always full'.[193] For Khudekov the role became Maria Petipa's crowning achievement, no one after her had such a tumultuous triumph. The appearance of her graceful silhouette in the pyramid as she came to life, 'her astonishment at the sight of the sleeping, handsome man—all this produced endless applause'.[194] Even better, she won in the 'Pas de sabre' (another name, it would appear, for the 'Variation orientale') a greater success than any other ballerina so that 'a loud roar rose up' when she finished and 'the public was choked with delight'.[195] Petipa mounted the ballet in Moscow on 17 November 1864 with Praskovia Lebedeva in the title role and the ballet remained a firm favourite in both cities. Ballerinas such as Vazem, Matilda Kshesinskaya, and Anna Pavlova were always keen to dance it, knowing it would guarantee them full houses. It was last performed in April 1928.[196]

Following this victory, Petipa wrote a letter on 28 February 1862, asking for recognition of his unremunerated choreographic work. He was accordingly promised a promotion when the new contract was due in May 1863, with increased pay. This made him second ballet master, Saint-Léon's deputy, with a salary which, adding together his pay for teaching, performing, and ballet-master duties, totalled 7,000 roubles.[197]

5

Ballet Wars Real and Imagined

The arrival of Saint-Léon in Russia in 1859 somewhat changed Petipa's situation. The new leader of the Petersburg ballet, constantly on the road and staging work in Petersburg, Moscow, and other cities in Europe, looked favourably on the ballet-master experience of the young stage producer, especially as he did not consider him a rival in any way, and could not do without an assistant.[1]

Arthur Saint-Léon

When Petipa signed his new contract in 1863 and became officially second ballet master, his duties required him, like Saint-Léon, to mount ballets not only in St Petersburg, but also in Moscow. The obligation towards Moscow reflected the fact that the company had had no contractually designated first ballet master since 1846. It relied on local or visiting staff, such as the company's leading dancer Sergei Sokolov and the Italian teacher Carlo Blasis in the 1860s, or on St Petersburg's ballet masters—Perrot, Petipa father and son, Saint-Léon. Frédéric staged some fifteen ballets in Moscow, including new ones, and was eventually transferred from St Petersburg to Moscow but never appointed first ballet master.[2] In Saint-Léon's case, this meant responsibilities towards not two stages, but four, since from 1863 onwards he was also mounting ballets at the Paris Opera and, with Émile Gredelue's in situ help, at the Théâtre-Italien.

Composer, violinist, the inventor of a system of dance notation (*la sténographie*), dancer, and choreographer, Saint-Léon was prodigiously gifted and productive from an early age. The son of Léon Michel, dancer and fencing master (*maître d'escrime*) at the Paris Opera, Arthur (born in 1821) spent his childhood in Stuttgart where his father (who called himself Michel Saint-Léon) was dancing master at the Court of Württemburg. Arthur's first public appearance was in 1834 as a thirteen-year-old solo violinist at the Königlicher Redouten-Saal in Stuttgart. (Throughout his life he would be held in considerable esteem as a musician.) The following year in Munich he made his debut as a dancer, billed as a pupil of his father. When in 1836 the family returned to Paris he attended the classes of the former *premier danseur* Albert, now a progressive teacher of the highest order, instrumental in the virtuosic evolution of ballet technique.[3]

In 1843 he was engaged as principal dancer at Her Majesty's Theatre in London and made an immediate impact. 'Whirled about as a hurricane, he stops as firm as a rock,' exclaimed *The Times*. 'Saint-Léon is a phenomenon.'[4] It was in his first London season that Saint-Léon became the regular partner of Fanny Cerrito, one of the legendary stars of the Romantic Ballet, whose fame rivalled that of Taglioni and Essler. He also became her partner off-stage and they were married on 17 April 1845.

After appearing in London for four years, they signed contracts with the Paris Opera in 1847, Saint-Léon arriving as both a dancer and choreographer. The ballets he created—*La Fille de marbre*, for example, *La Vivandière*, *Le Violon du Diable*, *Pâquerette*—were vehicles for Cerrito and often reworkings of choreography made by him elsewhere. (Reworkings were a constant feature of his repertoire.) These Paris versions established his reputation as a choreographer, although he was still a remarkable dancer, even if some defects were becoming more noticeable, such as a certain vulgarity in his technical displays.[5]

Saint-Léon and Cerrito separated in 1851, and in December 1852 Saint-Léon's contract with the Paris Opera ended. In 1854, after working at the Théâtre-Lyrique in Paris, he took up an appointment at the São Carlos theatre in Lisbon, accompanied by several dancers from the Théâtre-Lyrique, including Louise Fleury, the new companion of his private life, who would accompany him to Russia. Saint-Léon's two Lisbon years were fruitful: as well as staging new ballets he was appointed a professor of the Conservatoire and awarded the Cross of the Order of Christ. However, in February 1856 he also ended up in jail. The theatre, in dire financial straits, failed to pay the salaries due to him and the dancers, and they went on strike. The uproar that ensued resulted in his arrest and he was only released after the intervention of the French government.[6]

Despite all this, Lisbon made fresh overtures to Saint-Léon to renew his contract, but nothing came of it. Instead, after an arduous but highly successful eighteen-month tour of Central European theatres with Louise Fleury, Saint-Léon accepted his prize appointment in St Petersburg. He and Fleury had been travelling with costumes for a small repertory of easily staged ballets and, as is evident in his letter to his agent Charles Formelle, had been hoping to extend the tour to Warsaw, Bucharest, Odessa, and Moscow, but had dismissed the idea of St Petersburg, knowing Perrot to be there.[7]

This then was the much-travelled, remarkably active, and experienced thirty-eight-year-old ballet master appointed by Saburov in 1859—three years younger than Petipa but with much more to his name.

Petipists vs Muravevists

Saint-Léon's basic brief in St Petersburg and Moscow was quite simple: to create profitably popular ballets for the day's leading (and often foreign) ballerinas. His first assignment *Jovita, or the Mexican Robbers* (Jovita, ili Meksikanskie razboiniki), a reworking of Mazilier's 1853 *Jovita, ou les Boucaniers*, was also Rosati's Russian debut. It was a flop. Rosati was tepidly received; but maybe also the public, accustomed to Perrot's meaty dramas, were disconcerted by Saint-Léon's lighter manner. Either way, the lack of enthusiasm continued and by 14 February 1862, Saburov was blaming the ballerinas, not the ballets, in a report to Vladimir Adlerberg, the minister of the Imperial Court. In this, he noted a decline in public interest in both Bogdanova and Rosati and proposed, for the following 1862–1863 season, not to engage foreign ballerinas, but to rely on the rising Russian stars Maria Petipa and Marfa Muraveva. This, together with a salary increase for both dancers, was approved by Alexander II and marked the beginning of a newly *Russianized* ballet.[8]

This was to be one of Saburov's final measures. On 16 April 1862 he went abroad and in his absence was sacked. The reason was not so much his extravagant management of theatre funds, as a major scandal, involving the female section of the theatre school, in which he—aged sixty-five, wig, and pot belly notwithstanding—was implicated.[9] His successor, Count Alexander Borkh, a former diplomat, was, unlike Saburov, courteous and active, although in his decisions he tended to be swayed by his moods.[10] Being extremely wealthy, as well as married to a major landowner, he accepted a yearly salary of 6,800 roubles—less than Petipa. One account says he was inefficient in his duties; yet when he crossed swords with Vladimir Adlerberg, artists in Moscow and St Petersburg wrote to him, begging him not to resign. It would be his death which removed him, in 1867.[11]

Maria Petipa's junior by two years, Marfa Muraveva seemed to have the edge from the start. The directorate had always treated her with solicitude: although she could have graduated from the school in 1857, she was kept back another year to further hone her talent: moreover, in the spring of 1859, she was sent abroad with the Moscow dancer Praskovia Lebedeva for a four-month rest, chaperoned by a widow who had been selected for her impeccable moral qualities.[12] Looking at the photographs of Muraveva's gaunt face, it is easy to imagine her as vulnerable to the obsessive perfectionism that is a hazard of ballet training. She was far from pretty, with thin arms, strongly muscled legs, and a long nose like 'the beak of a bird frightened off its branch'.[13] Yet by dint of relentless work and aptitude she transformed herself into a beacon for Russian ballet. During the 1860–1861 and 1861–1862 seasons she swapped places with Lebedeva and danced at the Moscow Bolshoi. She could have fallen foul of the audience, always alert to outsiders and their smallest failings. But she won over Carlo Blasis, ballet master in Moscow at that time. He admired the classical purity and legibility of her outlines, the way she glided fleetingly along the ground, scattering 'diamond sparks'. She was essentially what the nineteenth century called a *terre-à-terre* dancer, focusing on a grounded footwork that was musical, precise, effortlessly mapping the most delicate lace. But she was also able, when she chose, to escape into the air with a peerless lightness.[14]

It was not, therefore, just looks that differentiated Muraveva from Maria Petipa. Where Maria Petipa relied on the beautiful vivid imagery of her shapes, the heart-touching eloquence of her mime, and the panache of her character dances, Muraveva dazzled by the classical perfection of her technique, so that as soon as she began to dance the audience forgot about her plain looks and was instantly electrified. She had what Maria Petipa lacked: she had, in the words of Théophile Gautier, pointed feet 'driven into the ground like arrows' and strong legs 'with nerves of steel that she can flex and soften'.[15] For Khudekov, 'Muraveva delighted the whole auditorium with her technically perfect dances, but charmed no one,' whereas 'Maria Petipa [...] so captivated the public that her wonderful image was imprinted on the spectator's imagination for a long time.'[16]

In the Petersburg autumn of 1862, while Maria Petipa was creating her furore in the *Pharaoh's Daughter*, Muraveva's debut in *Giselle* conquered spectators and contradicted the notion that she lacked dramatic depth. On 6 December she also created the title role in Saint-Léon's *The Orphan Theolinda, or the Sprite of the Valley* (Sirota Teolinda, ili Dukh doliny), a revised version of the same choreographer's 1853 *The Sprite of the Valley* (Le Lutin de la vallée). It was Saint-Léon's best ballet in Russia so far, with striking designs and an attractive score by Pugni. But it was Muraveva who won the most rhapsodic plaudits, for her dancing and for an interpretation, which were, in the words of *Sovremennoe slovo*, beyond praise.[17]

The Pharoah's Daughter and *Theolinda* launched the so-called rivalry between Maria Petipa and Muraveva. It was most probably a rivalry manufactured by the audience, facilitated by the ballerinas' stylistic opposites and stoked by their obsessional fans. From that time on, two camps were established: the 'Petipists', as they were called, and the 'Muravevists'. They furiously opposed each other, championing the qualities of their respective ballerinas and on one occasion at least coming to blows.[18] The two groups epitomized a fundamental dichotomy that continues to this day: the Petipists were essentially supporters of dramatic ballet and expressive movement; the Muravevists ultimately believed in the supremacy of the language of classical dance. The Muravevists accused the Petipists of a weak understanding of choreographic art in their prioritization of feeling and theatricality; the Petipists condemned the transformation of ballet into empty technique.

These ideological battles were conducted before a backcloth of demographic and economic expansion in both capitals. The 1860s were the decade of Alexander II's Great Reforms, a reaction to Russia's humiliating defeat in the Crimean War. These included the emancipation of the serfs in 1861. Moscow's traditional status as the centre of commerce was reinforced by the construction of a national railway network; the city's population spurted, adding 238,000 individuals between 1864 and 1871, when in the previous thirty-four years it had only grown by 60,000.[19] St Petersburg, the centre of government and finance, of majestic architecture and military order, echoed these developments. Estate owners, their pockets filled with the financial compensation received after their serfs were liberated, arrived determined to enjoy themselves. Industry and trade burgeoned, company offices and banks filling the city-centre streets. 'In town there was a lot of "mad money",' writes Vazem, 'and this was reflected in all the facets of social life and, of course, in the theatre.'[20]

The 1862–1863 and 1863–1864 seasons buzzed with excitement over Russian, not foreign, ballerinas. In this era of the idealized ballerina, young and not so young worshippers, mostly male, proclaimed their adoration with gifts of flowers and jewellery, and with extravagant gestures, as already seen when Elssler's retinue of fanatics drew her carriage through the streets of Brussels. The craze was adopted in Russia with extra vigour. In Moscow the dead cat hurled on to the stage in protest against Andreianova was its darker variant. In St Petersburg fans toasted Muraveva's debut in *Theolinda* with champagne drunk from the shoes she had used, an echo of the legend which said that a group of Taglioni's admirers cooked and ate a pair of her shoes.[21] Maria Petipa's followers tended to sit in the stalls and included the ballet critic and eminent mineralogist Alexander Ushakov, who wrote copiously about her, and the future German chancellor Otto von Bismarck, then ambassador to St Petersburg.[22] Muraveva's most fervent fans sat in a box whose subscribers were members of the Yacht Club; the box was nicknamed 'infernal', after the Paris Opera's *loges infernales*, so called because of their hot-blooded occupants. The St Petersburg *loge infernale* was lined with bright red damask, its glare reflecting on the occupants, as if they were in Hell.[23] They did not, it must be said, meet the standards of Gautier's 'perfect gentleman' who 'does not applaud with his white gloves raised above his head, like the *beaux* of the *loges infernales*' and 'does not throw a garland at the singer in vogue, because anything which attracts the attention of a large number of assembled people is in bad taste'.[24] The Petipists and Muravevists applauded deafeningly, drummed their feet, shouted out the name of their idol. The opposition between the two camps reached ridiculous proportions of one-upmanship: if Muraveva received five bouquets and two baskets of flowers after one performance, then Maria Petipa's fans made sure she received seven bouquets and three baskets; if the two ballerinas appeared during the same evening, then, when the applause for Muraveva lasted five minutes, the Petipists made sure to applaud longer for their heroine, Ushakov and others checking with their watches to be sure, so they could boast that the audience preferred Maria Petipa.[25]

The balletomanes, including members of the imperial family, also directed their fanatical attentions towards other dancers. Alexander II, a lover of women and assiduous ballet-goer, may well have had mistresses in the company. His brothers, Nicholas and Constantine, definitely did. Nicholas's mistress, Ekaterina Chislova, was a *coryphée* (below soloist rank) of little talent, but lived in great style; Constantine's mistress, Anna Kuznetsova, had good looks which were not matched by her dance technique either, but she was effective in mime roles.[26] Other dancers with influential protectors profited in the perpetual scramble for important roles, so that Saint-Léon could write that Matilda Madaeva's performance as the Tsar-Maiden in *The Little Humpbacked Horse, or the Tsar-Maiden* (Konek-Gorbunok, ili Tsar'-devitsa) made him feel sick—'but she is protected by the minister, damn it!'[27]

Muraveva in Paris

Petipa responded to the success of *Theolinda* with a new production of *Le Corsaire* on 23 January 1863. Maria Petipa was the heroine Medora and she danced her new solo, 'Le Petit Corsaire', which was Medora's attempt to raise Conrad's spirits. The choreography was simple, but Maria created a charming picture, with her winning smile and a pirate's costume that followed the Paris fashion for ballerinas *en travesti*. Her mime explained that the little pirate was brave and ready for anything, even if he was very young, and the dance concluded with her shouting, 'On board!' through a megaphone.[28]

Over in the Muraveva camp, their ballerina was now believed to have international potential. She needed to be seen abroad, especially at the Paris Opera which, Khudekov joked, 'dispensed diplomas of "Magnitude, First Class" to its stars'.[29] Perhaps it was Eugène Huguet, Muraveva's former teacher at the theatre school, who first wrote about her to Émile Perrin, the new director of the Paris Opera, since he kept Perrin informed during the subsequent negotiations.[30] Either way, Muraveva was invited to perform at the Paris Opera in 1863. The news of her easily won invitation shook Maria Petipa, who had had to devote much effort into acquiring her first invitation. She had been hoping for a third Paris season and it would seem that she now tried to get Muraveva disinvited. She and her husband even enlisted the help of the French ambassador, Baron de Talleyrand, who telegraphed Perrin, suggesting Maria Petipa instead of Muraveva. Count Borkh, fearing the inevitable big hole should Muraveva decide to stay in Paris as Zina Richard had done, also tried to dissuade Muraveva. The invitation, though, had been made at the highest levels and the minister Count Vladimir Adlerberg had given his consent. This, together with the emperor's personal blessing, ensured Muraveva's trip to Paris, accompanied by Saint-Léon.[31]

Muraveva was the third Russian-trained ballerina to appear in Paris in the space of just six years. The direction of traffic between East and West was still heavily weighted towards Russia as the destination, but this was a sudden spurt from the opposite side. The fact is, there was a crisis at the Paris Opera. All the big stars—Elssler, Ferraris, Grisi, Cerrito—had retired. There was nobody of the same calibre to fill the space, although Gautier claimed that the Paris Opera had several dancers just as good as the exotic and expensive Russian celebrities; but they suffered from being familiar to audiences since childhood so that 'the growth of a small shrub under our very noses passes almost unnoticed'.[32] Whatever the reality, Paris remained the world capital of dance, it had several theatres showing ballet, audiences were hungry for the next ballerina-sensation, and the most prestigious theatre was the Paris Opera.[33] Perrin wanted Muraveva to make her debut on 6 May in *Giselle*, the Paris Opera's iconic ballet, although it had not been performed for six years. Rehearsals were conducted by Lucien Petipa and, as preparation, Muraveva asked to be coached by Perrot himself.[34] Partnered by Louis Mérante, her first performance was watched, as had been Maria Petipa's, by the emperor Napoleon and empress Eugénie. Two months later, on 6 July, came another role, with Saint-Léon's *Diavolina*, a specially created, rather hurried confection based on his earlier *Graziella* and *Pâquerette*. Despite this, Muraveva's performances in both ballets were received with tremendous enthusiasm; some journalists, having got wind of the Petipa-Muraveva rivalry, pronounced Muraveva to be supreme.[35]

Meanwhile Maria Petipa had been offered a contract by the Opéra-Comique to appear in a new opera-ballet with a libretto by Saint-Georges, but nothing came of it, although the Petipas did arrive in Paris later and attended the performance on 10 July of Muraveva in *Diavolina*.[36] Before that, they were in Riga and Berlin, on the tour that Petipa misdates in his memoirs.[37] In Riga, from 2 to 11 March they performed national dances, the 'Pas de cerises' from *The Parisian Market* or *Le Marché des Innocents*, and extracts from *Le Corsaire*. They then stayed on in Riga, because Maria had injured herself falling from a coach, before opening in Berlin on 20 April. (Judging by Petipa's previous form in Paris for self-promotion, it seems perfectly plausible that he did, as he claims, gain help from the aristocrat-composer Oldenburg, who pulled strings to make the Berlin appearances possible.) They chose to show *The Parisian Market*, as part of a double bill with a comic opera and with, presumably, reinforcements from the Berlin ballet. There were further performances on 23, 27, and 30 April. Maria had great success as Gloriette; King William I himself came on stage on 30 April and yielded to Maria's plea that she be allowed more performances and other roles. The result was two more performances of *The Parisian Market* (2 and 4 May) and two performances of *The Wilful Wife* (Le Diable à quatre, 7 and 9 May). She was much fêted in the latter and during one evening provoked a great deal of admiring brouhaha when the ribbons of one shoe came undone and she continued dancing with the shoe in her hand.[38] For Muraveva, the following year (1864) was a rerun of the previous Paris negotiations: convinced of her talent, Perrin again invited her; Count Borkh was less than enthusiastic but was eventually forced to face up to the inevitable. She was scheduled to reprise *Giselle* and appear in a new Saint-Léon ballet, *Néméa, or Love Avenged* (Néméa, ou l'Amour vengé), a version, shortened for Paris tastes, of *The Flame of Love, or the Salamander* (Plamen' liubvi, ili Salamandra) created in Moscow in November 1863. This was Saint-Léon's first collaboration with Ludwig Minkus and the following February it was transferred to St Petersburg with modifications, Muraveva in the lead, and the title *Fiametta, or the Triumph of Love* (Fiametta, ili Torzhestvo liubvi).[39] Borkh, for his part, was sensitive to Muraveva's ten-year obligation which was drawing to an end and anxious that she sign a new contract for three seasons before her departure. With her signature duly inscribed, Muraveva became the highest-paid Russian ballerina of her time, earning 12,000 roubles a year. She left for France in March, where, repeating her previous success, she was contracted for a third visit, in 1865; however, when the time came, her fragile health would make this impossible.[40]

The Beauty of Lebanon

In the spring of 1863, the directorate asked Petipa to prepare a new big ballet, but the premiere was postponed. First Maria Petipa injured her leg, then she came down with a cold, then it was time for the vacation and Maria's appearances abroad.

As a result, *The Beauty of Lebanon, or the Mountain Spirit* (Livanskaia krasavitsa, ili gornyi dukh) was premiered only on 12 December for Maria's benefit performance. Before curtain-up, her fellow-dancers filled her dressing room with flowers and brought her a laurel wreath dedicated in verse to 'the pride of our ballet' who 'with each new dance has aroused general delight'.[41] Set in the forested and mountainous backbone of today's modern Lebanon, the libretto, spread over three acts, a prologue, and apotheosis, was a collaboration between Petipa and the critic Mavrikii Rappaport, a fervent Maria Petipa supporter. It was apparently the result of much research and, in the cave scene of the final act, drew upon the knowledge of another Petipist, Nikolai Koksharov, professor of mineralogy at the Institute of Mining, to include a *divertissement* of minerals—diamond, alexandrite, iron, cinnabar, gold, and silver. Underpinning the action is the war between the Christian Maronites and the Muslim Druzes. Mirana (Maria Petipa), a Maronite, is the focus of the ballet; according to the published libretto, she combines Christian modesty with Eastern passion and moves under the green branches of the countryside as lightly as a gazelle, without creasing the grass underfoot.[42] She and Esmar (Johannson), a Druze, love each other but obstacles, of course, lie in their way. First and most obvious, is the religious conflict; then there is the Druze leader Beshir (Stukolkin) who, in a narrative twist, captures Mirana for himself; and then there are the machinations of the evil mountain spirit (Marius Petipa) called Lebanon (*Livan*). Although the collision of the real world with the supernatural is a defining characteristic of the Romantic Ballet, here, on paper at least, the mix seems jarring, Christian imagery jostling with fairy-tale elements. (There are unintentional echoes even of *Snow White*, when Mirana is immured in a rock in Lebanon's cave and gnomes appear as his servants.) Mirana's salvation comes when the patron saint of the Maronites carries her to an enchanted garden filled with birds of paradise. The final apotheosis shows Mirana, transformed into a dove, flying in the blue sky towards what the libretto calls the guardian spirit of the land, and below them appear Esmar and the Maronite clan, victorious over the Druze.[43]

In the run-up to *The Beauty of Lebanon*, the directorate had behaved like modern-day Hollywood moguls, reacting to the unexpected success of *The Pharaoh's Daughter* by throwing great quantities of money at Petipa's new project. They spent 40,000 roubles on it, the equivalent of a month's box-office takings for all the St Petersburg theatres combined. This expenditure was cited in a satirical poem, written anonymously, although rumour attributed it to the actor and memorialist Petr Karatygin. It started with the lines: 'Forty thousand! Forty thousand!/Cost our new ballet! They should flog the ballet master, so that he remembers for forty years!'[44]

The ballet provoked a mixed response at best. The Petipists in the audience were delirious with joy, their standing ovations continuing until the auditorium lights were extinguished.[45] Pugni's music was well received. The admittedly biased Rappaport called him 'the master of his art' in *Syn otechestva* and said that his music was full of fresh melodies and interesting instrumentation.[46] He also said that Petipa had embroidered rich patterns on to the drama's canvas, including character dances, in which 'he excels, always trying faithfully to capture the local colour'.[47] The first act featured a dance for Lebanese highlanders, Matilda Madaeva and Felix Kshesinsky making a particularly vivid impression; the second act included a dance for whirling dervishes ('*Pas de derviches tourneurs*'). Among the classical dances was a variation for Johannson (by now, aged forty-six) called the 'Beating Heart' ('*Le Battement de coeur*'), its movement and music like the palpitations of a tremulous lover.[48] Some of the supporting dancers were widely praised: Maria Sokolova, for the perfection of her classical technique; Alexandra Kemmerer, full of promise as a virtuoso; and finally Anna Kosheva, always with her distinctive attack and daring, breakneck speed.[49]

But Petipa—in what would be a lifelong weakness of excessive zeal—overdid the number of variations, especially in the final act's *divertissement* of minerals. The ballet in general was suffocated by *longueurs*. The worst culprit, though, was the scenario. Not only were some of its entanglements hard to follow, but it contained too many absurdities, or, as *Golos* said, 'it is hard to imagine anything more ridiculous than the story of the ballet *The Beauty of Lebanon*.'[50]

All the reviewers agreed that the ballet's high point was 'La Charmeuse', a graceful Eastern dance for Maria Petipa, performed in the second-act scene where she finds herself a captive in Beshir's harem. The choreography traced plangent movements that obeyed the cantilena of the solo violin of the 'Polish Paganini' Henryk Wieniawski.[51] Once again, Rappaport was in raptures, deeming it impossible 'to convey the voluptuous expressiveness of her face'.[52] The solo, as always, was carefully tailored to Maria's strengths and contained few technical difficulties. She belonged to the old school, Rappaport wrote approvingly, in contrast to today, where all manner of tricks, acrobatics, and loud effect was the popular style.[53]

Always bringing, in Khudekov's later words, 'the public to a state of frenzied ecstasy', 'La Charmeuse' became one of Maria Petipa's signature dances.[54] It was a big hit again when Petipa revived the ballet the following year on 20 December 1864, with important revisions (as was his custom) and the addition of a pas de deux for Maria and Johansson taken from Le Corsaire. (This last was technically challenging, but Maria was on good form, executing two pirouettes on point before falling into Johansson's arms 'without any loss of grace, plastique, or expressiveness'.)[55]

The summer of 1864 saw the Petipas in Paris, as well as Muraveva, engaged for her second season. Maria Petipa, who had been suffering from an unnamed illness before the summer break, received treatment from the best Paris doctors. She was offered a contract at the Théâtre-Italien on very favourable terms for three full years, but declined, explaining she would miss her audience and colleagues in St Petersburg; she also declined invitations from Berlin, Vienna, and Madrid apparently because of her ill-health. (She would, however, appear again on the Berlin stage the following summer of 1865, after turning down an invitation from New York, which offered a tempting 17,000 dollars or some 25,000 roubles, for just two months.)[56] Returning home at the end of August, she was met by fans at the Tsarskoe Selo railway station and told them she was fully recovered. However, she did not immediately appear on stage; instead, she was replaced in The Pharaoh's Daughter by the soloist Alexandra Kemmerer. She finally returned to The Pharaoh's Daughter on 11 October, watched not only by Muraveva, but also Praskovia Lebedeva and many other dancers from the Moscow company since they were due to premiere the ballet on 17 November. While Petipa was in Moscow to mount it, Lev Ivanov took over the role of Taor-Lord Wilson, as well as the title role of Perrot's Faust.[57]

Alliance or Feud?

Because Saint-Léon favoured Muraveva for his ballets and Petipa, his wife, the assumption was often made—by Khudekov, for example—that the so-called rivalry between the ballerinas mirrored the state of affairs between the two ballet masters.[58]

When on 3 December 1864 Saint-Léon created *The Little Humpbacked Horse*, based on Ershov's popular Russian fairy tale of the same title, and when Muraveva created a sensation in it with her *kamarinskaia* folk-dance solo, accompanied, as for 'La Charmeuse', by Henryk Wieniawski's solo violin, it seemed that this could not go unanswered by the Petipas. At the premiere of *The Little Humpbacked Horse*, Muraveva had had to repeat her solo several times. As Khudekov remembered it, Wieniawski produced as big an effect as the dancers. 'He would shake his long black hair and somehow, from the top, would strike his whole bow down the strings to play the mazurka at a fast tempo. In his hands the violin became a living being.' Muraveva claimed that, dancing to this violin, she would lose herself and that she owed her success exclusively to Wieniawski, but this, Khudekov says, would be considerably to undervalue her performance:

> Hardly touching the boards, the famous Muraveva floated along the stage [...] then quickly going up on point, in an instant she halted, froze ... only to make a transition first to the quiet tempo of the *kamarinskaia*, and then, all crescendo, speeding up the tempo, she finished the dance with the broad sweep of an arm and a low Russian bow from the waist.[59]

The Petipas gave their ostensible answer on 31 January 1865 at Maria's benefit performance. The programme's predictable extracts—such as 'La Charmeuse'—brought the usual delighted response from the audience. But then came a surprise: Maria Petipa entered the stage wearing an enigmatic smile, and male clothes—the boots, baggy trousers, and shirt of a *muzhik*. Moving her arms in wide sweeps, her dance started with a smooth singing cadence, then gradually shifted into a vibrant, wholehearted folk dance with the tempo of a *trepak*. The audience literally went into a frenzy; the shouting was deafening.

Actually, this 'Little Muzhik' (*Muzhichok*) number was a version *en travesti* of the Neva variation from the rivers' section in *The Pharoah's Daughter*. But performed in this way, the impact was intensified, as explained (with some poetic licence) by the journalist V. P. Burenin: 'during "The Little Muzhik" a thousand patriotic hearts beat so loudly that, I swear, it muffled the orchestra.'[60] The choreographer, in another journalist's judgement, had 'thoroughly learnt all the nuances, not of theatrical, but actual, Russian folk dance'.[61] This was later confirmed in a poem, 'Ballet', by a famous writer and champion of the poor, Nikolai Nekrasov, which was published in the February 1866 issue of the magazine *Sovremennik*: 'Everything [...] was true: on the hat, flowers,/a Russian boldness in each sweeping gesture/You are not an artist—you are a magician!/We never saw such/A likeness: a real Russian lad!' But elsewhere in the poem, he satirizes the privileged audience and deplores the tasteless clash of worlds; the muzhik, with his real poverty and misfortunes, should not be paraded in this rarefied, glittering setting. He exhorts Maria Petipa to choose other roles: 'You are sweet, you are as light as air,/so dance *The Maid of the Danube* but leave the muzhik alone!'[62]

Despite the Little Muzhik, the rivalry between Saint-Léon and Petipa did not run deep. True, Petipa was ambitious; true also, Saint-Léon, for all his international experience, was having difficulty adapting to Russian requirements and tastes. But Petipa has left no trace of hostility towards Saint-Léon.[63] The same goes for Saint-Léon, whose correspondence contains only a few remarks about Petipa, and none of them personally disparaging, even if he didn't rate his wife as a dancer. 'Mme Petipa is very good in it [*The Wallachian Bride, or the Golden Braid*] as a danseuse plastique but as for technique—*nichego* [nothing].'[64] There is even fellow-feeling for Petipa about the stresses of their work: 'I am up to the eyes, and Petipa too.'[65] And when in 1866 the director Count Borkh wants to find a ballet master able to transfer Petersburg ballets to the Moscow stage, Saint-Léon recommends not Petipa, to be rid of him, but Théodore (Théodore Chion), ballet master at Paris's Théâtre-Lyrique who had produced a quantity of ballets in Moscow between 1850 and 1861.[66] Although Théodore was apparently willing to take up the offer, nothing came of it and Petipa's name, as shall be seen later, was briefly and unsuccessfully mooted by the directorate. In 1869, there was renewed talk, it seems, of transferring Petipa to Moscow since Saint-Léon, in a letter dated 29 November 1869, was clearly perturbed:

> I have decided not to prolong my engagement, which ends next season. [...] M. Guedeonov wants me to remain here for the whole year except for two months' holiday, leaving me with all the work in Petersburg. M. Petipa would stay in Moscow. Good God, I will not stand for that![67]

Iurii Bakhrushin's thinking, quoted at the beginning of this chapter, seems correct. Saint-Léon would not have viewed Petipa as a rival; on the contrary, constantly on the go, he would have welcomed Petipa's help in shouldering his heavy responsibilities.

Narratives and Nationalism

The focus on Russian ballerinas, largely triggered by the Crimean War, had produced a Russian ballet revival, not seen since the Napoleonic War, even if there had been pauses with the engagements of Fanny Cerrito (1855–1858) and Amalia Ferraris (1858–1859). As if to reinforce this, Russo-Polish relations took a dramatic turn when a Polish insurrection flared up in January 1863 and lasted to May of the following year. In this climate the creation, not long after, of Saint-Léon's *The Little Humpbacked Horse*, the first-ever ballet based on a Russian fairy tale, could only be seen as patriotic, and even more so after the assassination attempt on Alexander II on 4 April 1866.

Russian patriotism, though, had never been on Saint-Léon's mind, or on Pugni's, the ballet's composer. It was, according to Khudekov, the Muravevists of the *loge infernale* who conceived the idea of creating a fairy-tale vehicle for Muraveva and targeted Petr Ershov's verse-story. It took a lot of persuading to win Saint-Léon round. Eventually, Saint-Léon may have shrewdly calculated that the *loge infernale* regulars, having initiated the venture, would do their utmost to support it, and a success would obviously strengthen his position as ballet master, which was by no means secure, given his previous failures.

The ballet found favour with the audience—especially children—but not with many reviewers. They called it a *balagan* (fairground entertainment) not a ballet. It was also full of absurdities and mismatching cultural references: failings which bore Saint-Léon's mark. (His cavalier approach, according to Khudekov, boiled down to the following thought process: 'If a mazurka crosses one's mind in a ballet which involves red Indians, put it in!')[68] The ballet's main focus was Foolish Ivanushka and his horse, so that in fact Muraveva had little to do as the Tsar-Maiden. Her only real opportunity to shine was the *kamarinskaia* and a classical variation in the final act. Foolish Ivanushka had been assigned to Stukolkin, the company's best comedian, but he injured his leg and was replaced by Nikolai Troitsky, an artist at the beginning of his career. Troitsky's knockabout comedy was dull, but because he performed at the premiere he kept the role for all subsequent performances. Considerably more vivid was Madaeva in the first-act Russian dance, in which 'she glided exactly like a swan, waving a handkerchief' and 'enchanted everyone with her wonderful, alluring smile'.[69] The big *divertissement* of the final act was a showcase for the dances of the Russian Empire's different nationalities—Ukrainian, Lettish, Cossack, Caucasian—and was the idea, again, of a *loge infernale* balletomane.

The native—or pseudo-native—subject matter was probably part of the reason for the ballet's box-office success and long life in the repertoire; it was restaged by Petipa in 1895 and, although much changed, is still performed today. But when on 26 September 1867 Saint-Léon returned to the same easy formula with *The Golden Fish* (Zolotaia rybka), based on Puskhin's *The Tale of the Fisherman and the Fish* (Skazka o rybake i rybke), he created a flop destined for oblivion, despite the luxurious designs.[70] It had been ill-fated from the start. Saint-Léon's relationship with the Muscovite ballerina Lebedeva, who was again working in St Petersburg, seems to have been mutually uncomfortable: 'Lebedeva is going to kill my new ballet which I am beginning without any enthusiasm,' Saint-Léon wrote to Nuitter.[71] Lebedeva then suffered a serious eye injury, the ballet had to be postponed, and soon after she announced her retirement, delaying the premiere again. (Her re-placement in the role was an Italian visitor, Guglielmina Salvioni, who aroused little excitement.)

Ballet has always been international in its subject matter and Petipa ranged as widely as Saint-Léon for his material, beyond borders and continents. True pupils of the Romantic Ballet, they both laid much value on national dance, which added the spice of exoticism in their creations and reflected the humble status of at least some of their characters. But a Russophilia urging them, foreigners, to showcase Russian culture was not on their agenda; nor does it seem to have been a par-ticular preoccupation of most of their audience.

And yet, the new climate after Nicholas I's death encouraged native artists and subject matter. The flowering of great novels—*War and Peace* was published in 1869—was paralleled by the dramatic repertoire of Alexander Ostrovsky, whose vast body of plays portrayed the different social classes of Russia. The surge of na-tionalist composers was marked by the formation in 1856 of the group known as The Mighty Handful (*Moguchaia kuchka*), whose members were Milii Balakirev, César Cui, Modest Mussorgsky, Nikolai Rimsky-Korsakov, and Alexander Borodin. Their aim was to continue what Glinka had started and produce a Russian style of music, separate from Western influences and European conservatoire training. The Russian Opera, ousted from the Petersburg Bolshoi Theatre by the Italians, returned to the city in 1860, to the new Mariinsky Theatre. To Italian operas were gradually added Russian ones, joining Glinka's *A Life for the Tsar* and *Ruslan and Liudmila*. Rimsky-Korsakov's *The Maid of Pskov* (Pskovitianka) was premiered at the Mariinsky in 1873, as was Mussorgsky's *Boris Godunov* a year later; even Tchaikovsky with his European-influenced training was composing operas with Russian themes, such as *The Guardsman* (Oprichnik), premiered at the Bolshoi, St Petersburg, in 1874 and *Eugene Onegin*, premiered at the Moscow Conservatoire in 1879.

Meanwhile, Petipa's choice of subject matter was remarkable, throughout his career, for being almost exclusively foreign. He looked far beyond the Russian Empire to India, Spain, Ancient Rome, the Arctic Circle, Franco-Germanic fairy stories, unspecified fantasy lands, and France. True, *Roxana, the Beauty of Montenegro* (Roksana, krasa Chernogorii, 1878), a patriotic response to the Russo-Turkish War of 1877–1878, and *The Daughter of the Snows* (Doch' snegov, 1879), in-spired by the *Snow Maiden* (Snegurochka) folk tale, were closer to home ethnically, as was the Slav legend-making of *Mlada* (1879); equally, *The Magic Mirror* used the *Snow White* story told by both Pushkin and the Brothers Grimm. But these were the exceptions.

Occasionally ballets contained a topicality, like *Roxana, The Pharaoh's Daughter*, and *La Bayadère*, the setting of the latter being partly inspired, it is thought, by Edward, prince of Wales's widely reported and photographed

1875–1876 tour of India. But topicality is a separate question; and Petipa's neglect of Russian fairy tales and epics was sharply criticized by Khudekov, who
reports an occasion, during Ivan Vsevolozhsky's directorship, when Petipa
agreed to a libretto featuring the well-known characters of Ivan Tsarevich and
Vasilisa the Wise. Vsevolozhsky approved it, the designs were ordered, all was
signed and agreed—and then Drigo, the ballet's director of music, declined to
compose the score because he was unfamiliar with Russian motifs. Of course,
it would have been possible to find a replacement, but Petipa did not pursue
this option, openly admitting he was relieved. In his opinion, he said, it was
impossible to create anything new after Saint-Léon's *Little Humpbacked Horse*;
all the *trepaks* and Russian dances had already been choreographed. 'We leave,'
Khudekov writes, 'the validity of these conclusions on the conscience of the
ballet master who has served on the Russian stage for more than sixty years,
without once deploying his creative powers in the broad sphere of the Russian
fairytale world.'[72]

Some reviewers of *The Sleeping Beauty*, premiered on 3 January 1890, criticized
the French setting for a fairy tale which, they argued, by its very essence should
have no specific nationality. With each of the subsequent ballets, *Cinderella* and
Bluebeard, based, like *The Sleeping Beauty*, on Charles Perrault's fairy tales, came
further complaints about the absence of Russian sources. 'Why so persistently
thrust a hand in the one and same foreign pocket,' lamented 'Svoi' in his review of
Bluebeard, 'when in our own [pocket] there languishes perfectly good material.'[73]
While decrying the 'false patriotism' of such attacks, the music critic and friend
of Tchaikovsky, Herman Laroche, in his own review of *The Sleeping Beauty* noted
the French nationality not only of Petipa, but of his predecessors, resulting in
a company that was imbued with French tradition.[74] He might have added that
the ballet's allusions to the Sun King's France were partly determined by the fact
that Perrault lived in the reign of Louis XIV.[75] He might also have added that the
ballet's ultimate message can be read as a celebration of order and autocracy, and
that, although located in the France of Louis XIV, the story is by extension a salute
to the Russian imperial status quo.[76]

That subtext cannot have escaped reviewers, although they didn't mention
it. Nor did they, Laroche excepted, write about the ballet's other underlying
layers (to be examined in chapter 9). Instead they chose to take it at face value,
as many of the audience did, just as they did with Petipa's other ballets. And
those ballets, viewed in that way, were exactly what the imperial court and gentry
wanted: escapism into a fantasy that would allow them to forget uncomfortable
reality. In this they were no different to ballet audiences all over Europe. But in
consequence ballet was, in Alexander Benois's words, 'considered unworthy of
the attention of serious people' and the tsar's government was reproached for
patronising it.[77]

The End of the Ballerina War

Muraveva's performance in *The Little Humpbacked Horse* on 8 February 1865 was to be her last appearance on stage, because she fell ill. Nadezhda Bogdanova was invited to Paris, to replace her, but failed to impress Perrin and danced just one performance.[78] When at the start of the 1865–1866 season, it became clear that Muraveva could not return, her roles were taken over by Lebedeva who was again transferred from Moscow to fill the gap. Muraveva had married in 1865 and had hoped, with her husband's support, to recover from her illness, but this was not to be. Her career had been a comet, shining fast and intensely bright, for just seven years. She died in 1879, aged forty, giving birth to a daughter who did not survive either.[79]

The 'ballerina war' had lasted little more than two years, but such intense froth and heat would have had to burn itself out anyway. Without the rivalry, the agitation around Maria Petipa soon calmed down. For Nikolai Golts's benefit on 4 November 1865 she appeared in *The Travelling Dancer* (Puteshestvuiushchaia tantsovshchitsa), a one-act 'episode' staged by her husband to Pugni's music. The central role suited her, but although it was transferred to Moscow in 1868, it was a slight piece, its theme and possibly some of its dances taken from Paul Taglioni's 1849 *The Prima Ballerina, or the Ambush* (La Prima Ballerine, ou l'Embuscade). Meanwhile, Saint-Léon was lamenting the loss of Muraveva and Maria Petipa's terminally declining technique. 'Mme Petipa is losing her strength from day to day,' he wrote to Perrin, and this was leaving the company 'without a *première danseuse*.'[80]

On 20 January 1866 came Petipa's second premiere of the season, the three-act *Florida*.[81] He had been forced to ditch his preparations for a more elaborate ballet, *The Alpine Queen* (Alpiiskaia tsaritsa), because of the expense surrounding the staging of Meyerbeer's opera *L'Africaine*, and consequently had to extemporize. Less a ballet than, as Rappaport wrote, a protracted *divertissement*, it consisted of new and recycled dance numbers and mime scenes, held together by a slender dramatic thread, although it did have the distinction of using electric lighting in the final act.[82] Florida (Maria Petipa), the daughter of a ballet master, organizes a dance performance to raise money for flood victims. At the same time, she hopes that she can charm the proud family of her beloved sea captain Count Ernest (Lev Ivanov) into accepting her as a suitable bride, so that the final act is a celebration of their wedding, with the corps de ballet performing a fantastical, unbridled 'Phrygian grand pas', wearing red Phrygian bonnets and waving red and white scarves. The ballet was another showcase for Maria, but there was scope for others. Two students, for example, performed a scene from Perrot's *Faust*; Madaeva, with the young Pavel Gerdt in his first featured role, danced 'The Crown of Roses' ('*La Couronne de roses*'), which was probably a classical dance in a village setting; Maria reprised 'The Little Muzhik', which prompted Nekrasov, who was at the *Florida* premiere, to write his poem 'Ballet'; she even performed a mime scene inspired by the great French actress Mlle Rachel. Most reviewers agreed that many of the dances in themselves were attractive, but the ballet as a whole suffered from an 'embarrassment of riches', resembling 'an album in which Miss Petipa appears in the most varied manifestations', and the lack of narrative content built 'a certain weariness in the spectator'.[83] Quite what a Phrygian dance was doing in the mix is unclear.

Not long after, on 6 February 1866, when Maria Petipa took part in a mixed bill, performing her role in *The Travelling Dancer*, the public made it clear that they preferred Lebedeva in the second act of Saint-Léon's *Fiametta*.[84] Maria Petipa probably faced the harsh truth that this was a turning point in her career. In April the directorate invited the Italian dancer Claudina Cucchi to dance in the revivals of two Perrot ballets, *Catarina, the Bandit's Daughter* and *Esmeralda*. Petipa added a new pas de deux for Cucchi of such originality in *Esmeralda* that it was long remembered as the 'pas Cucchi'.[85] The monopoly of Russian ballerinas was at an end in St Petersburg. The revival of a Russian ballet, stimulated by political events, burgeoning home talent, and maybe even *The Little Humpbacked Horse*, had lasted just a decade, reaching its peak with the excitement around Maria Petipa and Muraveva. Now, the ballet company needed to excite the public again.

The ban on foreign guests had ended slightly earlier in Moscow with the appearance on 15 November 1865 of a twenty-year-old German ballerina, Adèle Grantzow (*Grantsova* to the Russians). Saint-Léon had spotted her prodigious airborne technique in Hanover. It was possibly with his financial help that she went to Paris, to complete her training with his old friend Madame Dominique, leading teacher at the Paris Opera Ballet's school. He must have monitored her progress closely, to recommend her for the important post of principal ballerina in Moscow, despite the fact that she had never danced a complete ballet.[86] She arrived in Moscow, the city's first foreign guest dancer in twelve years, to be launched at a single bound as 'a true prima ballerina in a country which may be the dirtiest but where the pay is really good'. She had 'suffered from the climate, fleas, lice, bugs, the food, the air'. She had to overcome 'memories of Muraveva and Lebedeva and the handicap of nationality, stronger here than in Petersburg'.[87] Yet despite these obstacles, her debut, dancing in *Fiametta*, exceeded Saint-Léon's wildest hopes. He had never seen such a talent, so complete and varied, allied to a charming appearance. People, he wrote to Perrin, were comparing her to Elssler:

Yes, but Elssler never had her suppleness or her ballon, and she has in addition amazing pointes, tacqueté, batterie, an expressiveness in her miming and her dancing worthy of a great artist, and a confidence as if she had played in grand ballets for twenty years. In the fourth act she was as light, delicate, and vigorous as in the first.

Her most enthusiastic admirers accompanied her to her hotel, behind her carriage, applauding. Four performances have been sold out from today, and to complete these antics the *régisseur* has recorded thirty-three curtain calls. Her success has therefore been complete. God knows what these crazy people are going to think up, but what has really touched me is to find such a rare intelligence and such a perfect talent.

If I were you, I would hurry and let Paris see her in all her freshness. She would be suitable to play in the whole of Muraveva's repertoire.[88]

Before appearing in Paris, however, Saint-Léon's protégée made a triumphant St Petersburg debut in *Giselle* on 13 December 1866. Petipa would also cast her in his ballets and in *Le Corsaire*, choreographing the famous 'Jardin animé' scene for her in 1868, which she had also performed in Paris, in Mazilier's version, the previous year. Reminiscing much later in a newspaper interview, Petipa would call her the greatest ballerina he had ever seen.[89] But bad luck dogged her life. Although Saint-Léon initially had her in mind for his new *Coppélia* (1870) in Paris, she fell ill, so that the ballet went to the young Giuseppina Bozzacchi. In 1877, aged just thirty-two, Grantzow died as a result of gross medical negligence: 'The poor girl died so prematurely, from some pimple,' as Petipa remembered. 'They operated unsuccessfully, the consequence of which was the development of an infection of the blood.' This then necessitated the amputation of a leg but she died anyway.[90]

A Marriage at War

On 18 October 1866, Petipa revived *Satanilla* (or *The Devil in Love*), not for his wife, but for Lebedeva. A month later (18 November), as part of the celebrations for the engagement of the tsarevich (the future Alexander III) and Princess Dagmar of Denmark (the future empress Maria Fedorovna), he staged a choreographic 'miniature', *Titania*, at the palace of Princess Elena Pavlovna. *Titania* may represent the first ballet setting of Mendelssohn's incidental music, composed in 1843 for a court production in Potsdam of Shakespeare's *A Midsummer Night's Dream*, and it begs the question of how the choice of music came about.[91] Maria Petipa was Titania, Marius, Oberon, and the subject matter must have been painful for them, since their own marriage was now in crisis. Unsurprisingly, performances were flat. *Titania* was to be Petipa's last ballet for his wife: in all he had created two big ballets for her and five small ones, as well as concert numbers and dance scenes.[92] She had been his first significant pupil and he had moulded and maximized her talent. Several writers suggest that her technical limitations were now holding back his choreographic ambitions, but there was surely nothing to stop him using other more suitable dancers.[93]

On 13 November, five days before *Titania* and two days after the premiere of Saint-Léon's *The Wallachian Bride* in which Maria danced the titular role, occurred an incident which marked a turning point in the Petipa marriage. Maria subsequently went to stay with her mother and lodged a formal complaint to the procurator of the Saint Petersburg district court on 18 February 1867:

Complaint

In the duration of my ten-year married life literally not one week has passed when my husband has not subjected me to severe assaults, leaving consequences for my already weak health.

From my side there has not been the slightest reason for such treatment by my husband. Knowing his character to be irascible and jealous to the point of fury, I would carefully avoid anything that might arouse in him not only a feeling of jealousy, but even anger, understanding that under the influence of these feelings a person, forgetting about the consequences, becomes capable of committing criminal acts. With this aim I turned away from any acquaintance, not only with individuals not having anything in common with me through my kind of work, but even with theatre artists; I would keep silent before him when, backstage, he tore apart the bouquets brought to me by the public, accompanying this with outbursts, which don't bear repeating in writing; never did I contradict him over any serious issues if I noticed that he was not in a good mood; in short—I did not consider doing anything other than to calm his suspicions, in which I supposed was rooted the reason for his cruelty towards me. But it was all in vain! His treatment of me grew more cruel day by day, the physical abuse was repeated more and more often and with even more violence than before. In this way my situation was unbearable, but out of my feelings as a wife and mother I was hesitant to use the power of the Law for mediation between me and my husband, and perhaps would not have turned to the Law, if it were not for an incident on 13 November which broke the limit of my endurance. On this day, when I was returning from the theatre in a carriage with my maid, my husband, having caught up with the carriage, stopped it, dragged my servant out of it, sat in her place, seized me by the throat and began to throttle me and spit in my face. I was not able to bear this latest insult and, with the resolve to find protection in the Law from my cruel husband, quickly left him and moved in with my mother, with whom I am now living. During three months I tried to make my husband change his attitude and treatment of me, if not for me, then for our children, on whose upbringing the antics of such a father cannot but have a disastrous effect; but having ascertained that it was not possible to act upon him in a civilized way, through persuasion, I am turning to Your Worship with a complaint against my husband, asking for a formal investigation into his actions.

Fearing to weary your attention with a catalogue of each of my husband's actions—since they, recurring without interruption in the course of ten years, form too long a list and do not stand out from one another in character—I consider it enough only to say what precisely they consisted of. Wishing to get even with me for whatever misdeed created by his imagination, he would seize me by the hand, drag me into the bedroom, lock it, and start to hit me, in the majority of cases to the point that I would fall unconscious, and it was in this state that the serving girls, Elena Sokolova, Olga Andreeva, and the laundress Solomonida Smirnova, would find me when they entered the bedroom after my husband had left. Later my husband stopped being inhibited by the presence of the children and the maid and assaulted me in their presence, which the aforementioned laundress Solomonida Smirnova can confirm.

About the incident on 13 November last year the following persons can corroborate the facts: the serving girl Sofia Lindshtrem, the coachman Ivan Averin, and the civil servant Apolon Afanasevich Grinev, who was drawn to the incident by my cries in the carriage.

Apart from the witnesses indicated by me, I consider it relevant to men- tion two other persons who, while visiting our home, several times had to restrain my husband from hitting me. This was Ivan Frebelius and his spouse Elizaveta Iakovlevna.

[There follows the addresses of the people mentioned.][94]

Even allowing for exaggeration on the part of Maria, Marius Petipa's explosive temper was a reality, as were his wife's numerous admirers, who no doubt stoked his jealousy. Equally, Maria's account of the intensification of Marius's violence conforms to the known pattern of physically abusive men. Given her many wit- nesses, she had a strong case and seems to have been taken seriously. On re- ceiving the written complaint, the examining magistrate Makalinsky opened a criminal case on 18 February. Some time further down the line, he warned Maria's lawyer Evgenii Zein that Petipa faced prison. The Litovsky fortress was the city's grim establishment for criminals.[95]

This never happened. In April both spouses notified the investigation that they had reached an out-of-court agreement.[96] Perhaps the severity of the punishment persuaded Maria to drop her complaint, conscious as she must have been that she had her children to consider; perhaps even the theatre directorate leaned on her, given the adverse publicity that would follow such a conviction. Either way, soon after, Maria moved to a separate address and it was arranged that eight-year-old Jean would live with her, while ten-year-old Marie would stay with her father. According to a new residence permit dated 19 January 1868, father and daughter were living at 86 Fontanka.[97] The marriage was not dissolved because of the difficulties surrounding divorce at that time, all the more complicated by the special imperial permission that had made the Franco-Russian marriage possible in the first place.[98]

Maria Petipa's health suffered; she appeared infrequently on stage and she gave her farewell on 11 February 1869. This was just three months before Marius made his own farewell to performing, appearing as Conrad on 8 May 1869. For her part, Maria chose *The Pharaoh's Daughter*; it was her seventieth performance as Aspichia and only four days short of her thirty-third birthday. Her technique had fallen far behind company standards and she performed a simplified version of the choreography. Although the theatre was full, just one newspaper, *Golos*, gave the evening a mention, a single line. A few weeks later she was accorded a state pension.[99]

Perhaps it was partly to steer clear of his wife that Marius had pronounced himself willing to move to Moscow, when the idea was mooted on 19 May 1867 in a letter from Borkh to his superior Vladimir Adlerberg. In his letter Borkh outlined the situation whereby the Moscow company lacked a permanent ballet master, able both to look after the existing repertoire and to mount new ballets and productions. (He had already been agitating to address this problem, as indicated by Saint-Léon's recommendation of Théodore the previous year.)[100] The hard-working Frédéric, now serving in Moscow as a teacher at the school and as a producer of ballets, could have been a candidate, but he was ruled out, partly because of his age (fifty-seven). Another candidate, the leading dancer Sergei Sokolov, had staged several ballets but the majority failed to impress. Although the company was in essence a satellite, Petipa must have been tempted by the prospect of being in charge. He would also have the benefit of the brand-new theatre, designed by Alberto Cavos with a six-tier auditorium and opened in 1856, after the fire which had destroyed all but the outer walls and portico of the old Bolshoi three years earlier. (In St Petersburg the ballet was still housed in the city's own Bolshoi (Kamennyi) Theatre.) Perhaps he was also seeing the Moscow appointment as a stepping stone to St Petersburg, once Saint-Léon was gone. But all those possibilities were to remain untested. The Ministry of the Court's response, made on 25 August to Borkh's successor Stepan Gedeonov, was that the move would be too expensive for the directorate's budget. Petipa was not only expecting to be reimbursed for the cost of his move and to receive the same salary as before, but others in St Petersburg, such as Alexei Bogdanov, would have to be paid extra to fill the gap.[101]

The same idea of moving Petipa, briefly revived in 1869 and indicated in another of Saint-Léon's letters, also came to nothing.[102] Eventually, in 1873, the Austrian ballet master Wenzel Reisinger was appointed, after the new minister, Count Alexander Adlerberg, on a visit to Moscow, made clear his dissatisfaction with the slipshod corps de ballet. Blame was laid on the absence of a permanent ballet master, and Reisinger, a second-rater, was chosen because there was nobody better.[103]

Around 1875, Maria Petipa went with her son Jean to live in Piatigorsk, a spa resort in the Caucasus, but she sometimes spent winter in St Petersburg with her daughter, by now a dancer in the company. She was still beautiful and charming and continued to have admirers, including, gossip said, a Georgian count and Nicholas I, prince of Montenegro.[104] In 1876 she gave birth to a son, named Jules (Iulii) Mariusovich Petipa, but Petipa—who had recognized his extramarital son Marius—never accepted Jules as his. In 1880 she made an unsuccessful attempt to return to the stage as an actress, appearing in St Petersburg and Novocherkassk near the Black Sea. It is in Novocherkassk that she is buried, after succumbing to smallpox in 1882.[105]

Marie Petipa

Jean (1859–1880s) attended cadet school, probably in Moscow, and became an officer. He died young, still a bachelor. Jules (1876–1951), a small boy at his mother's death, was largely brought up by his sister (or half-sister) Marie. He studied law and became a senior lawyer and civil servant; he was a victim of the Stalinist purges and was freed only at the end of the 1940s.[106] His granddaughter Tamara Petipa (1927–1992) was a distinguished marine biologist, the author of many published articles.

Petipa's daughter Marie (1857–1930) was the only one of his children with a prolonged career in dance.[107] Knowing the harsh conditions of the theatre school, her parents decided that she should be trained by her father at home. It was, perhaps, a rather isolated existence, particularly when her parents separated and she did not have frequent access to her mother. Later, she attended the *classe de perfectionnement* for company members with Christian Johansson. As Vazem recalled:

> There, she revealed what was, for a dancer, a very striking lack of understanding of the essence of the movements being set. When all of us panted from the strain during difficult, complicated tempi, Marie, not grasping what was involved, would be amazed at our struggles. According to her, there were no difficulties. But then she would perform movements that were not at all those set by the teacher.[108]

This might put into question Petipa's early teaching, except that his male students at the theatre school included Pavel Gerdt who graduated in 1866 and had
an outstanding outcome as a strict classical dancer.[109] Khudekov blames Marie's
lack of diligence and her unsuitable body shape.[110] Either way, Marie would often,
after Johansson's classes, ask him to let her spend time at the school, where she
received another kind of education, listening to the girls gossiping about ballet
fans—the obsequiousness of those who were impoverished and the generosity
of those who were rich.[111] A loftier result of Johansson's classes was that she soon
understood she was not suited to strict classical dance. Once in the company she
worked mostly as a character and *demi-caractère* dancer in roles which her father
created for her, always tailoring them to her strengths, as he had done with his
wife.[112]

However, for acceptance into the company she had to prove herself to the
directorate. To this end, Petipa gained permission from the minister of the
Court for her to appear on 12 January 1875 in a revival of the first act of one of
her mother's early ballets, *The Blue Dahlia*, as part of a mixed programme for
Pavel Gerdt's benefit performance. (The evening also marked the stage debut of
Platon Karsavin, father of Tamara Karsavina.)[113] Vera Petipa who, as the youngest
of Petipa's children, wasn't yet born, remembers in her memoir what her mother
Liubov (Petipa's second wife) said about the performance: 'When Marie made her
entry on stage, her beauty elicited a general explosion of admiration in the auditorium.' True, Marie contravened the laws of strict classical dance and Liubov, who
had returned home earlier from the theatre than Marius, waited for him, to hear
his usual implacably strict verdict. But, as Vera writes, 'she didn't even have time
to ask. She heard him say: "Mais elle est si belle." [But she is so beautiful.] He was
amazed by her success, he was overcome.'[114]

The reviewer of *Golos* was ecstatic, Marie triggering inevitable memories of
her mother. His single, somewhat optimistic, reservation was that 'if in relation to
technique the young debutante did not yet attain the loftiest limits of perfection,
accessible only to fully developed choreographic celebrities—then this is nothing
more than a matter of time.'[115] On 23 February she danced her mother's signature
number, 'La Charmeuse' from *The Beauty of Lebanon*, and was accepted into the
company with the standard 600 roubles salary for new entrants.[116]

With time she would not, contrary to *Golos*'s conviction, overcome her technical deficiencies. Shiriaev, another character and demi-character dancer, remembered that in Rimsky-Korsakov's opera *The Snow Maiden* (Snegurochka) 'to dance
with her was a rather difficult matter'. Not only did he find it impossible 'to locate
the waist of my partner, in order to lift her', but lacking technique she whipped
round on her legs as the fancy took her and, to make things worse, 'she would
constantly mix everything up, forgetting the arrangement of the dance.'[117] Even
Alexander Benois, who at thirteen fell head over heels in love with her, was obliged

to confess that 'in technique she was worse than the least of the corps de ballet. It was even an effort for her to rise on her toes, and she slipped down gratefully to the "half toes"; her movements were clumsy and she lacked suppleness. That was why her father, the choreographer, would allow her to dance only [sic] character roles in which she could project her sex appeal in a mad whirl.'[118] Predictably, the stern Vazem was unmoved by the mad whirl:

> As a character dancer, Maria [Marie] Mariusovna, to my eyes, did not have any outstanding merit, although she attracted attention in this capacity for several decades. Instead of dancing a given *pas*, she waved her arms in the air and stamped on the spot. [...] The fact that her father was ballet master played a decisive part in her career. He deliberately gave no opportunity to dancers who could be rivals to his daughter. Nevertheless, Petipa enjoyed a noisy success with the general public. Such were the powerful charms of this pretty woman.[119]

The photographs show that Marie's face had strong, regular features, like those of a classical statue, which must have transmitted well from the stage. However, her chunky torso and thin 'macaroni' legs deviated from the norms of an ideal ballet physique and, with the years, her tall body became matronly.[120] On the other hand, she had her mother's charm and, from both parents, she inherited an expressiveness in mime and irresistible élan in character dances. She learnt to distract attention away from her legs with her arms and eyes; she had an infectious, irresistible smile.[121] As she got older and, in Benois's phrase, 'her charms were usually spoken of as *des beaux restes* (beautiful remnants)', her costumes became more and more opulent, covered in the jewellery her admirers gave her. (The display of these trophies seems to have been a company tradition among the women.) For the mazurka in *Cinderella* (Zolushka), her bust glittered with priceless multicoloured gems.[122] For the Venetian dance in *Swan Lake* her diamonds were estimated to be worth several tens of thousands of roubles.[123] Fortified by this formidable armoury, Marie kept the hearts of a broad swathe of the public and occupied an enduring and prominent niche in the company.

Although Petipa was pleased, in another sense he was, writes Vera, disappointed. 'Her position as a character dancer did not give her the possibility of creating complete and profound roles in the classical ballet style.'[124] She appeared in a lot of travesti parts, for which her silhouette may have been well suited: for example, the predominantly mime role of a sea cadet in Petipa's *Daughter of the Snows*; and Cupid, disguised as a page, in Saint-Léon's *Fiametta*.[125] But she did also, against the odds, sometimes dance classical roles, edited by her father to conceal her inadequacies. She made her debut as Gulnare in *Le Corsaire* on 11 October 1881 and the following October replaced a sick Maria Gorshenkova for

Jean Petipa (1850–1855)

Marius (on the left), Lucien, Victorine, and their mother (1840s)

Lucien Petipa, a little older, still handsome (1860s); the inscription reads 'To my good and much-loved brother Marius'

Christian Johansson, admired classical dancer, revered teacher (1880–1890)

Maria Surovshchikova, Petipa's Galatea and first wife (1859)

Maria in her 'Little Muzhik' costume with Marie and Jean (c.1865)

Maria's rival Marfa Muraveva as the Tsar-Maiden in Saint-Léon's *Humpbacked Horse* (1864–1865)

Petipa as Lord Wilson in *The Pharaoh's Daughter* (1862–1867)

Petipa in the title role of Perrot's *Faust* (1854–1860s)

Felix Kshesinsky, the 'King of the Mazurka' (1890–1910)

The Pharaoh's Daughter Act I, with Matilda Kshesinskaya (1898)

Poster for the premiere of *La Bayadère*, a benefit performance for Ekaterina Vazem (23 January 1877)

Ekaterina Vazem as Nikiya in *La Bayadère* (1884)

Opening scene of the 1900 revival of *La Bayadère*, with Matilda Kshesinskaya
(photo taken 1901)

Petipa, aged fifty-four, first ballet master (1872)

A page from Petipa's working notes for *The Daughter of the Snows* (1879).

The list at the top says: '1) The Genie of the Cold and the Wind; 2) The horizon; 3) Snow—very little and small; 4) The decor changes, the gauze and the rain come down, ice floes are turning, an ice floe moves past; 5) the bear, the ship; 6) three or four bolts of lightning, thunder, the ship is smashed by the ice floes.' Diagonal note on the right: 'All this happens fairly quickly.'

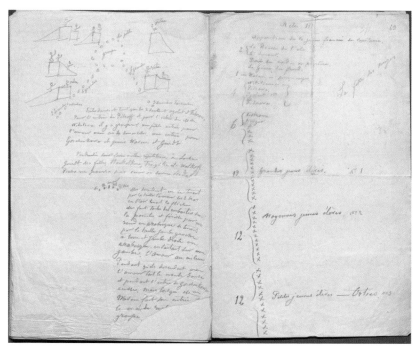

Two other pages for the same ballet.

The left-hand page: 'All the women dance while the two, Ogoleit and Fedorova, dance. For Petrov's entrance and for Mlle Nikitina's entrance, there is a group. A small entrance for Amor with her four companions. An entrance for Gorshenkova and then Vazem and Gerdt.

'Get a rehearsal on Friday night for Louba, Gerdt, my daughter, Stukolkin, Troitsky, and Volkov. Pisho won't be able to come, they are showing *Aida*.

'They come down, holding each other by the waist, Amor [has] her arms in the air holding an arrow. They all do *emboîtés* on point and finish with a circle in arabesque, holding each other by the waist, left leg on the ground and right leg in arabesque while jumping on one leg, Amor in the middle.

'While they come down with Amor everybody dances, and also during Gorshenkova's entrance, but when Mme Vazem makes her entrance …'

The right-hand page has a list for groups of dancers for Act III, including twelve tall pupils, twelve medium pupils, and twelve small pupils (all girls).

Petipa's new family with Liubov Savitskaya: on the left, Evgeniia; at the back, Nadezhda; on the right Vikor; centre, Liubov (1890–1892)

three performances as Nikiya's rival Gamzatti in *La Bayadère*. A reviewer declared that her beauty threatened to make a nonsense of Solor's preference for Nikiya.[126] She even danced the central role of Nisia in a 1900 revival of *King Candaules* (Tsar' Kandavl) when again the scheduled ballerina (Lina Campani) fell ill.[127]

Most famously, Marie was the original Lilac Fairy in *The Sleeping Beauty*. The best-known photo shows her in the fantastical floral costume and heeled shoes for the vision scene where the Lilac Fairy brings together Prince Désiré and Aurora's apparition. For a long time it was widely believed that the Lilac Fairy had been created exclusively as a mime role, matching Marie's abilities. The Prologue solo the Lilac Fairy dances in certain productions, such as the Royal Ballet's, is attributed to Fedor Lopukhov, in keeping with Lopukhov's claim that in 1914 he choreographed a solo which was inserted into the ballet.[128] The conviction there was a void before Lopukhov seemed to be substantiated not only by Marie's heeled shoes in the vision-scene photo, but by Bronislava Nijinska's childhood memory of the Prologue. 'As I carried the train of the Lilac Fairy, danced by Maria [Marie] Petipa, I could see that she was wearing shoes with a tiny heel, like a real lady.'[129] However, in contradiction to this, there *are Sleeping Beauty* photographs of Marie wearing a tutu and blocked ballet shoes. Moreover, the ballet master Sergei Vikharev's examination of the ballet's notation score in the Harvard Theatre Collection, in preparation for his 1999 Mariinsky reconstruction, confirmed that the Lilac Fairy did have a dance solo in the Prologue, as intimated in Petipa's own written plans. (Petipa describes it as a *variation voluptueuse*.)[130] In fact the notation score contains two alternative solos, both using point work. One has M[aria] Petipa written next to it and was almost certainly created by Petipa; the other resembles the solo in the Royal Ballet production, but like the first solo it seems to have been notated around 1903, which casts doubt on the Lopukhov attribution.[131] Either way, if Marie was indeed wearing heeled shoes for her first entry in the Prologue, then she must at some point have changed them.

As a character dance specialist, Marie was often partnered by the Hungarian Alfred Bekefi, who arrived in St Petersburg from the Moscow ballet in 1883. When Marie performed programmes of character dance abroad (the mazurka, the csardas, the *lezginka*), Bekefi accompanied her—to Warsaw, to Paris, to London, all in 1893.[132] Later she travelled with Sergei Legat, brother of Nikolai and son of the Swedish dancer Gustav Legat, who became her on- and off-stage partner. They danced at the Opéra-Comique in Paris (1902) and toured French cities (1904).[133] In the summer of 1899, with the Imperial Ballet's blessing, she gathered together twenty-two of the company's artists for performances in Budapest, Vienna, and Berlin. The repertoire emphasized character dance and jolly entertainment with *Coppélia*, *The Halt of the Cavalry* (Prival kavalerii), and a *divertissement* called *A Peasant Wedding* (Krest'ianskaia svad'ba).[134] One Budapest article wrote that in 1849 it was the Russian Cossacks who gained victory, but in 1899 it was the Russian ballet.[135] Following this warm reception, the company made a second visit in 1901. There had been foreign tours of concert groups on earlier occasions: variously composed of Matilda Kshesinskaya, Olga Preobrazhenskaya, Bekefi, Georgii Kiaksht, and others, they had appeared in Monte Carlo (1895, 1896, 1898) and Warsaw (1895).[136] But Marie's enterprise was much bigger. As such it represented the first-ever foreign tour undertaken by a Russian company, before the impresario Edvard Fazer brought a small troupe of Imperial Ballet dancers (including Pavlova and Shiriaev) to the Baltic countries and beyond (1908-1910), before Diaghilev launched the Ballets Russes (1909).

Back home, the appointment of Vladimir Teliakovsky as director of the Imperial Theatres gradually deprived her of roles. He extended his dislike of her father to herself, even though, on first seeing her in Petipa's *Raymonda* in 1901, he thought that 'she stood out from everybody with her costume, coiffure, her generally polished appearance' and that 'she danced with a great animation, with which she considerably enlivened the ballet.'[137] But by 1905, he would write of her 'big belly' and 'repellent' appearance, alongside which her 'lively face and flashing eyes were especially offensive'.[138]

Even if during her career she might have aroused resentment as the favoured daughter of the company's ballet master, she seems to have been without rancour. French-speaking, sociable, and humorous, with an inclusive habit of ending her sentences with a question—'What do you think?'; 'What would you say?'—she had a large circle of friends.[139] Fokine gratefully recalls a time when, as a tyro choreographer, he had to compose a csardas for her, as part of his 1906 ballet *The Grapevine* or *La Vigne* (Vinogradnaia loza, to Anton Rubinstein's ballet score), and felt overawed. 'She obviously sensed my embarrassment and, probably in order to encourage me, became enthusiastic from the very first step.'[140] She lived a dashing life, having moved into her own apartment on entering the company, perhaps because by then her father had set up house with Liubov Savitskaya. After several changes of address, she was by 1895 living in a seven-room apartment and owned her own coach and horses, complete with coachman. Subsequently, she acquired an independent house at 3 Sapernyi *pereulok* (Lane), a beautiful residential side street, just a fifteen-minute walk north of Nevsky Prospect. She loved to travel in Europe and to collect stray dogs, of which she always had about ten.[141]

Her beauty caused her father much anxiety.[142] She had many love affairs and often appeared in gossip columns. In 1892 she gave birth to a son from a liaison with D. F. Trepov, whose father was General Fedor Trepov, military governor of St Petersburg. Another lover, X. P. Von Derfelden, an adjutant to the tsar, recognized the son as his own; he was rumoured to have married Marie abroad. Yet another rumour says that Trepov gave 25,000 roubles for his child, to be held in safekeeping by Marie, but she spent it all and when the son reached maturity he demanded not only the money back, but the interest.[143] Later, when she was living in her seven-room apartment with Sergei Legat, tragedy struck. Enormously talented as a dancer and much loved as a teacher—Nijinsky was one of his pupils—Sergei also formed, with Nikolai, the partnership of the Legat Brothers, masterly caricaturists known for their witty portraits of members of the Imperial Theatres. But one evening, during the political unrest of 1905, Sergei committed suicide, returning home to slit his throat with a razor (about which more later).

In 1907, Marie married a French engineer, Paul Girard, in Paris; she was aged fifty, he, just thirty.[144] Returning to St Petersburg, she gave her farewell benefit on 11 November 1907; Nijinsky, Kshesinskaya, and Fokine were among the dancers. She suffered hardship in her final years, since she not only lost her considerable property to the October revolution, but inept Soviet bureaucracy withheld her pension. She moved to Paris in 1928 and died on 16 January 1930.[145]

6

Questions of Style and Structure

> *The artistic genre cultivated by Petipa was much more to the*
> *taste of the Petersburg public than that cultivated by Saint-Léon.*
> *During this time Petipa's principal concern was to show ballets*
> *à grand spectacle with an engaging, at times absorbing dra-*
> *matic narrative and brilliant mise en scène. For these he had an*
> *adroit gift for extracting very significant sums of money from the*
> *management.[1]*

The Big Ballets

Unlike Perrot and Saint-Léon, Petipa did not arrive in Russia with a suitcase full of compositions; yet from the 1870s onwards his ballets would dominate the Russian stage and give the Imperial Ballet a unique imprint that would spread far beyond Russia's borders. He is most closely associated with the 'grand' ballet or *ballet à grand spectacle* and its prototype was *The Pharaoh's Daughter.* As performed on the imperial stage, the Petipa *ballet à grand spectacle* was colossal, magnificent, and leisurely and would get bigger as the century progressed. Unfolding over three acts or more, it contained mime and action that alternated with the dancing. The choreography was Fabergé jewellery in motion, made out of patterned ensembles, elaborate pas de deux framed by a corps de ballet, and exquisite variations.

The *ballet à grand spectacle* was not an isolated manifestation, but part of a bigger nineteenth-century trend for the huge. Leading the way was European grand opera, displays of scale and magnificence where crowd scenes were an important feature. European winners in this genre quickly made their way to Russia. Auber's *La Muette de Portici* (1828) and Meyerbeer's *Robert le diable* (1831), for example, were staged in St Petersburg in 1834 and were popular for decades after. The spectacle of Vesuvius erupting in the final scene of *La Muette de Portici* (renamed *Fenella*) made a huge impression, trumped, even so, by *Robert le Diable* with its Gothic cloister scene and 'Ballet of the Nuns', in which Taglioni repeated her seminal role of Hélène for the first St Petersburg performances.[2]

Although the birthplace of many of these spectacles was the Paris Opera, ballet on the same stage remained more modestly scaled; but in Russia, as already noted, there was a liking for big full-evening productions, forcing Perrot and Saint-Léon to adapt. That said, of Petipa's fifty-eight or so original ballets, less than half had more than two acts. If any discussion of Petipa tends to be predicated on full-evening ballets it is because this is the model of most of his surviving ballets: *La Bayadère* (1877), *The Sleeping Beauty* (1890), *Raymonda* (1898), *Don Quixote* (1869), and the Ivanov-Petipa *Swan Lake* (1895). Among the shorter ballets, there is the other Ivanov-Petipa collaboration, *The Nutcracker* (Shchelkunchik, 1892). There is also the entertaining one-act *Halt of the Cavalry* (1896, to music by Johann Armsheimer), which depicts the disruptive effects on village life of a visiting regiment of hussars. The version in the recent repertoire of the Mikhailovsky (formerly Maly) Ballet comes from the eminent ballet master Petr Gusev's stagings in 1969 and 1975. The two-act *Millions d'Arlequin*, which became better known as *Harlequinade* (Arlekinada), enjoyed enormous success at its 1900 premiere. It was performed into the 1920s and shown round the world by Anna Pavlova, Alicia Alonso, and others. Balanchine, who appeared in it as a student, called it 'a model for comedy narrative' and remembered 'its wit and pace and its genius in telling a story with clarity and grace'. But in his own versions (1965 and 1973) he tried only 'to remain faithful to the spirit of Petipa's dances and drama without reproducing any of the actual steps'—adding 'who, in fact remembers them?'[3] Whether anything of Petipa survived in Fedor Lopukhov's *Harlequinade* (1933) for the Maly (Mikhailovsky) Ballet is open to question; and, although Gusev's 1975 version, again for the Maly, has always been held as *the* canonical staging, Gusev apparently had a heavy editorial hand, compressing the ballet into one act. The new production by Alexei Ratmansky, premiered by American Ballet Theatre on 4 June 2018, is this choreographer's latest attempt to return to 'the real' Petipa, a reconstruction (as far as this is possible) using the existing Stepanov notation score and Petipa's working notes (presumably those preserved in GTsTM).[4]

Another survivor in the Petipa oeuvre, the 'Grand pas from *Paquita*', preserved, reconstructed, and often performed today, seems to be more or less authentic, although it is not a ballet, but a *divertissement* amalgamating dances—a pas de trois, a children's mazurka, a grand pas—Petipa added to his 1881 production of Mazilier's *Paquita*. And finally there is the one-act anacreontic *The Awakening of Flora* (Probuzhdenie Flory, 1894), included because of Sergei Vikharev's reconstruction for the Mariinsky Ballet in 2007. Set to music, like *Harlequinade*, by Drigo, it was created at the Peterhof court theatre for the wedding of Alexander III's daughter and transferred the following year to the Mariinsky.[5]

Many of Petipa's short ballets were *pièces d'occasion* like *The Awakening of Flora*. As such, the odds were against their survival. Of the sixteen Petipa created, seven were destined to auto-destruct. Equally, there would surely have been a greater incentive to keep performing the big ballets, given their higher cost in terms of effort, time, and money. They would have had longer-lasting importance in Petipa's time.

But the most determinant factor common to half of the extant ballets was another genetic advantage: a musical heart, semi-inured to the ravages of time, thanks to two concert-hall composers, Alexander Glazunov and, especially, Tchaikovsky. This would explain, at least in part, the survival despite weak narratives of *The Nutcracker* (Tchaikovsky) and *Raymonda* (Glazunov), although the two one-act ballets created in 1900 with other Glazunov scores, *The Trial of Damis* (Ispytanie Damisa), also known as *Les Ruses d'amour*, and *The Seasons* (Vremena goda), have disappeared.[6]

Petipa's formulation of a definitive genre as early as *The Pharaoh's Daughter* suggests that he carefully studied the work of his predecessors in Russia during the fifteen years before the ballet's premiere. However, it is impossible to know with certainty how the ballets of Perrot and Saint-Léon looked. The few still with us—Saint-Léon's *Coppélia* (1870) and Perrot's *Giselle* and *Esmeralda*—appear for the most part in versions descended from Petipa's later stagings. Their authenticity has therefore been compromised, even if the consensus among ballet professionals is that Petipa's revisions consisted mainly of additions, enlarging the quantity of dance but preserving the style.[7]

Vazem's memoirs define Perrot more as a 'ballet dramatist' than a choreographer because he emphasized drama over dance.[8] Khudekov also wrote about Perrot: '[he] would first seek a theme, trying to make the ballet a complete, intelligent dramatic work in which all the artists were able to shine in both the dances and the mime.'[9] As such, Perrot, in the Romantic Ballet, was the exception; in the Romantic Ballet the typical narrative, behind rather involved detailing, was essentially simple, conceived as a pretext for dance and centred on a love triangle that was problematic—usually because of a social mismatch.[10] Saint-Léon was an expression of this genre, but he took it further. His dances often lacked narrative justification; instead they were accompanied by novel visual devices, such as the convex mirrors and electric light in *Fiametta*, used to produce an interplay of shadows.[11] This was what might be called the *divertissementization* of ballet in Russia. (*Coppélia*, his last and best ballet, created in Paris, avoids some of these weaknesses.) 'I never considered him a master at composing anything artistically complete,' writes Khudekov:

> Apparently aware of this weakness, Saint-Léon chose stories devoid of content, in which there was nowhere the ballerina could display her dramatic talent. In all the ballets composed by him, mime and story—the soul of a complete choreographic work—were always missing. His ballets are simple *divertissements*, with a quantity of dances that have little organic

connection with the action. In his work protagonists dance not out of narrative necessity, but are simply prompted as if by magic.[12]

Like Saint-Léon, Petipa allocated a large place to dance. However, as a great
mime artist himself, the narrative dimension of his ballets was stronger. True, set
against Perrot's *Faust* or *Esmeralda*, a ballet like *The Pharaoh's Daughter* had only a
simple dramatic thread, once all the gaudy surface trappings—the time-travel, the
dépaysement—were swept away. 'In their choreographic content Petipa's ballets
were in essence just as much *divertissements* as the ballets of Saint-Léon,' writes
Vazem, 'only here the *divertissement* was much more strongly stitched into the
narrative fabric.'[13]

In his most accomplished works Petipa seems to have absorbed the best of
both his predecessors. He had great respect for Perrot. In his diary entry of 6
June 1907 he wrote: 'As a ballet master Perrot was superior to Saint-Léon.'[14] Even
though he favoured a high proportion of dance, he valued, like Perrot, moving
mime scenes; he understood, like Perrot, the importance of a meaningful theatricality that exploited the magnificent Petersburg stage machinery, and he was able,
like Perrot, to respond to the Petersburg taste for lengthy spectacle more confidently than Saint-Léon. But although he attached more importance to solid narratives than Saint-Léon, some of these were still flawed or flimsy, and almost all were
moulded to an unvarying formula to provide arenas for dance. The vision scenes
which, located outside time, enabled extended sequences of pure classicism were
one element of this formula; so were the festivals, betrothals, marriages, and
birthdays which delivered a pretext for classical and national-dance *divertissements*.

It was also from Perrot that Petipa acquired the ability to manipulate large
numbers of dancers. For all his focus on narrative, Perrot was an expert at devising
substantial ensembles. Writing about Perrot's *Catarina* in 1849, shortly after the
choreographer's arrival in Russia, one critic was impressed at how, suddenly, 'the
gifted band of *coryphées* and *figurantes* came to life and began to stir, timidly at first,
but gradually becoming more animated and dashing up to the forestage, throwing
themselves into groups and elegant measures such as they had never been asked
to perform before, to the astonishment of the public'.[15]

This was beyond Saint-Léon, who in Khudekov's words 'did not know how to
deal with big numbers of people. […] All his *morceaux d'ensemble* are lifeless and
colourless.'[16] On the other hand, Saint-Léon was a ballerina's ideal maker of solos.
'He knew how to compose those correct, rhythmic movements which in ballet language are called classical dance-variations. Soloists used to say that it was always
comfortable for them to dance variations composed by this ballet master.'[17] (The
musical logic and delicate stitching of the Saint-Léon variation is evident in the reconstructions by Ann Hutchinson Guest and Pierre Lacotte of the pas de six from
La Vivandière.)[18] Iurii Slonimsky's 'Marius Petipa' essay is eccentric in many of its

assertions, but he is surely right to assert that Petipa learned from Saint-Léon's ballerina variations.[19]

So, the overarching feature of Petipa's grand ballets is heterogeneity; and within this heterogeneity are several elements. First, to repeat the obvious, there is a narrative—even the short ballets had a narrative—and this is often structured with a pivotal moment, when the heroine flips from one world into another, in a variant of Giselle's sudden madness, death, and entry into a spirit world.[20] In *The Pharaoh's Daughter* it is when Aspichia throws herself into the Nile and joins a watery realm; in *The Sleeping Beauty*, when Aurora pricks herself with the spindle and is plunged into her hundred-year sleep; in *La Bayadère*, when Nikiya is bitten by a snake planted by her rival Gamzatti, to appear in the next act in the Kingdom of Shades; and in *The Vestal* (Vestalka, 1888), when Amata is forced to abandon her home and fiancé Lucius, to become a Vestal virgin.

The narrative is mediated through codified mime, gestural action, and scenic effects, mostly separated from dance—a different procedure from the danced-through narratives of twentieth-century ballets where mime is excluded and the dance movement, combined with gestural action, carries the story. There are instances where Petipa does use actual dance steps to carry the story forward, but these are relatively rare. One example is Aurora's dance with the spindle, evading the anxious outreached hands of her parents and, when she has pricked herself, reeling, as Petipa writes in his plan, 'in a giddy madness as if bitten by a tarantula' (*un vertige de folie comme piquée par la tarentule*).[21] Another, in the same ballet, is Prince Désiré's encounter with a vision of Aurora, conjured up by the Lilac Fairy, during which he dances a pas de deux at a distance, pursuing Aurora who 'always evades him' (*lui échappe toujours*), until he finally asks to be taken to the briar-locked castle.[22] (Today's productions, however, show Désiré sometimes holding Aurora, as well as sometimes separated from her by the Lilac Fairy.) Petipa's 'Black Swan pas de deux' in *Swan Lake* could also be said to have narrative weight: Odile's calculated brilliance, aided by consultations with Rothbart on the margins, completely turns Siegfried's head. The dancing in the same ballet's two lakeside scenes moves the narrative forward even more, but then that was the work of Ivanov. (In combining dance and action so seamlessly, it could be said that Ivanov not only looked forward to twentieth-century ballet, but back to the second act of *Giselle*, where the dancing has the same organic narrative function.)

Dreams and Visions

Another component is the vision or dream scene, an extended grand pas suspended out of time and place during which the two main protagonists are brought together (again) and the narrative often (but not invariably) paused. The style is almost always strict classical dance, so that *La Bayadère*'s dream Kingdom of Shades comes as an interlude of flawless geometries, elaborations of form divorced from the ballet's Indian context. The underwater scene of *The Pharaoh's Daughter* where the river variations are based on national-dance motifs is, of course, an exception.

Vazem believed that these interludes were an imitation of 'François's Dream' in Saint-Léon's *Pâquerette* (1860), in which François, escaped from prison, falls into an exhausted sleep and dreams he is in a fantastical land, populated by nymphs and his beloved Pâquerette, who keeps eluding him.[23] The origins of both Petipa and Saint-Léon's visions or dreams, however, lie in the supernatural scenes of the early Romantic Ballet, the most famous being the deadly nocturnal sprites of *Giselle*'s second act and, before that, Filippo Taglioni's prototypical 'Ballet des Nonnes' for *Robert le Diable*. The diaphanous white tulle skirts of Taglioni's ghosts became an emblem of the Romantic Ballet, from which came the designation 'ballet blanc'; they contributed to the sense of spectral chastity, intangible disembodiment, and vaporous elusiveness. The underwater kingdom of *The Pharaoh's Daughter* has close links with Taglioni's *La Fille du Danube* (1837), where Fleur-des-Champs (Marie Taglioni) jumps from a balcony into the Danube to evade the clutches of Baron Willibald.[24] Rudolph, her lover, becomes so distraught he too throws himself into the Danube and, having fainted, is carried by undines to an underwater grotto where the Nymph of the Danube restores him to consciousness. To test his love for Fleur-des-Champs, she summons veiled nymphs who try to charm him, but he repulses them, until he sees a nymph whom he recognizes as Fleur-des-Champs. He pursues her and clasps her in his arms. The Nymph of the Danube, yielding to the lovers' entreaties, agrees to restore them to their terrestrial world and undines help them find the way.[25]

As in *La Fille du Danube*, Petipa's heroines—Aurora, Nikiya, Raymonda—inhabit the vision scenes as a part of the fantasy, into which the hero intrudes from the real world by various means. But sometimes it is the heroine who is the intruder, such as Aspichia and the Vestal Amata, following which their lovers appear as magical evocations. Meanwhile, in the Moscow *Don Quixote* (1869), the heroine Kitri did not take part in the dream at all; another character, Dulcinea, did instead. It was later, for the St Petersburg version (1871) that the two were merged, Kitri appearing in the guise of Dulcinea.

The vision in *La Bayadère* conforms to the more usual model. Like Achmet, the hero of Coralli's *La Péri* (1843), Solor has an opium-induced dream. In this, he finds himself in the Kingdom of Shades, where he finds his beloved Nikiya, the bayadère killed by Gamzatti. Alisa Sveshnikova, author of a monograph about Saint-Léon, considers that the Kingdom of Shades also has parallels with the final, celestial scene of Saint-Léon's *Météora, or the Valley of Stars* (1856), staged in St Petersburg in 1861 (Meteora, ili Dolina zvezd). She writes that Saint-Léon's dances, in which the newborn star Météora takes her place among other stars, have structural similarities with Petipa's. Météora is accompanied by the soul of a Scotsman,

John Barker, transformed to become her satellite; earlier, Météora had appeared during John Barker's wedding to Mary, in the manner of the dead Nikiya during Solor's wedding to Gamzatti, before claiming John Barker's soul for good.

It was widely known that the journalist and dance historian Sergei Khudekov was *La Bayadère*'s librettist. Vazem confirms this, as does Khudekov himself and the polished dramaturgy, even if Khudekov's name was not publicized. However, decades later Petipa would claim sole authorship in a letter to *Petersburgskaia gazeta*, following the newspaper's review of the ballet's revival.[26] Perhaps Petipa's insistence reflects the probability that it was he who pointed Khudekov towards previous stage works in the same genre. First there was Auber's opera-ballet, *Le Dieu et la bayadère* (1830): although it is possible that Khudekov had seen Auber's composition, Petipa would have been more familiar with it. He had danced in it in Bordeaux, as had, in St Petersburg, his first wife Maria, in a revival on 10 May 1854; Petipa even claims he staged the dances for Zina Richard as the bayadère in 1856 at the Paris Opera, when she appeared opposite the tenor Enrico Tamberlik.[27] Equally Marius was more likely than Khudekov to have known his brother Lucien's ballet *Sacountala*, based on the play of the same name by the Indian poet Kalidasa.[28] The clear narrative similarities show that both these works were important sources for *La Bayadère*, if not the only ones. (See chapter 7.)

Yet in retreading this Indian territory, Petipa and Khudekov produced something that was recognized from the start as a major achievement. No small credit went to the choreography of each act. The best-known scene, the Kingdom of Shades, has become justly famous for its extraordinarily radical, innovative choreography, so unprecedented it could qualify as experimental from a dance maker more often labelled as a conservative. The repeated arabesques *fondus*, performed by a single file of sixty-four women (their number in 1877) as they descend a sloping ramp down to the stage, was inspired by Gustave Doré's illustrations for Dante's *Paradiso*.[29] These ghostly bayadères, appearing like refractions of the ballet's dead heroine, Nikiya, establish the scene's otherworldly premise. Karsavina, who witnessed many performances at the turn of the century before herself dancing Nikiya, remembered that each row of bayadères was more tightly packed than in modern productions and that this, along with several front-cloth gauzes which were successively raised, accentuated the anonymity of the bayadères. The viewer, she said, would see not individual dancers, but ghostly figures, their long tulle tutus (just two inches above the knee) contributing to the spectral impalpability.[30]

The choreographic text prescribes that once all the bayadères have gathered on the stage, they form shimmering horizontal lines, white tulle fluttering as they move their arms in unison and balance in *développé* and arabesque before dropping into an eerily extravagant half-kneeling position. Standing again, *bourréeing*, they arch their torsos backwards and forwards with a preternatural abandon. Later Solor imagines himself reunited with Nikiya, for a pas de deux that coalesces out of the cold ghostly air and unfolds in the purest classical traditions.[31] But it is especially the lines of bayadères that are so remarkable—for example, the way they frame the pas de trois of the soloist Shades with dancing lines that slip back and forth from counterpoint to unison and animate the whole stage. With this, Petipa anticipated the juxtaposed dance units of twentieth-century *symphonism* visible in the plotless ballets of Balanchine and Leonid Massine, just as with the entrance of the bayadères he prefigured a modern minimalism.

Although recognizing the rhythmic melodiousness of Minkus's music, Skalkovsky wondered what mazurkas and *kazachoks* were doing in India.[32] But otherwise the ballet was enthusiastically received by the press. *Golos* praised the interesting subject, the 'elegant and original dances', and the extreme luxury of the staging. 'This subject has given Mr Marius Petipa full rein to deploy his fertile imagination, apply a masterly skill to the task, manage colossal corps de ballet ensembles.'[33] Reviewers were impressed by the character dances, several naming the 'Danse manu' (a solo for a dancer with a pitcher on her head, while two little girls pester her), which appears in the big *divertissement* honouring the Himalayan idol Badrinath. (In today's Western productions the festivities are attributed to the engagement of Solor and Nikiya's rival Gamzatti.) Among the other dances, the Lotus Dance (*Tanets lotusov*) in the final scene was singled out, as was Nikiya's Kingdom of Shades variation with a floating length of voile, performed to the accompaniment of Leopold Auer's violin. (Karsavina says that with Nikiya's final arabesque the fabric flew upwards out of sight, more vivid than today's resolution whereby Solor carries it off.)[34] But the entrance of the bayadères, which must have looked particularly sensational on the deep Bolshoi stage, did not get special mention, apart from a generalized homage paid to the corps de ballet for meeting their unprecedented challenges with such discipline and skill. Much later, in 1901, *Rossiia* wrote that 'the Kingdom of Shades is a choreographic scene full of taste and atmosphere, the best in the ballet', and *Birzhevye vedomosti* in 1907 referred to the plastique lyricism of the ballerina (Anna Pavlova) which 'created the impression of a magical vision, only just outlined in the misty glow of moon beams'.[35] The reference to moon beams suggests that, by then, the theatre had heeded *Peterburgskaia gazeta*'s advice after the 1877 premiere that the scene should be illuminated by the moon, not the sun.[36]

Most (but not all) of Petipa's ballets are a complete fit for this model of *ballet à grand spectacle*. The supernatural is absent from the three-act *Camargo* (1872), its narrative based on a real incident, when the eighteenth-century dancer Marie Camargo and her sister were 'abducted' by the comte de Melun. However, the entertainment which appears in scenes 5 and 6, during which dancers appear as incarnations of Summer and Winter, seems to have functioned as the vision scene, in the same way as 'Le Jardin animé' in *Le Corsaire*. The poster shows that for the Summer dances Adèle Grantzow (Marie Camargo) was a sylphide, Gerdt was the Spirit of the Air; for the Winter dances, she was the Queen of the Glaciers. Saint-Georges had actually written the libretto years before, in 1864, with Petipa's first wife in mind. The critic Konstantin Skalkovsky thought it slight, the dances unsuited to Grantzow's abilities, although Vazem who inherited the role chose an extract for her farewell benefit in 1884.[37] Skalkovsky reached the same verdict for Modest Tchaikovsky's libretto for *Calcabrino* (Kal'kabrino, 1891), set among simple folk in a *provençale* village, even though Modest was a dramatist and wrote the opera librettos of his brother's *Iolanthe* (Iolanta) and *Queen of Spades* (Pikovaia dama).[38] A 'fantastical ballet' in three acts, made for Carlotta Brianza, it belongs, like Perrot's *Faust*, to the gothic strand of romanticism and does not match the standard Petipa paradigm. Here, the supernatural is tightly woven into the action of the second and third acts, where evil spirits are intent on mischief. The pivotal character is a man, Calcabrino, a brutal smuggler who wants Brianza's Marietta for himself. He gets his just deserts when he is tricked into falling in love with a counterfeit Marietta, a demon who lures him into Hell.

Groups and Masses

Elaborate set-piece dances were a major feature of Petipa's ballets and, in most of his big ballets, these included a procession, a stratagem borrowed from grand operas such as Bellini's *Norma* (1831), Donizetti's *Les Martyrs* (1840), and Verdi's *Les Vêpres siciliennes* (1855). Petipa's processions usually appeared at the start of a celebratory scene and were, as mentioned in chapter 4, a means not only of introducing relevant characters, but also of feasting the eye with exotic costuming and cultural references. The procession in *King Candaules* (Tsar' Kandavl, 1868), another ballet with an atypical narrative structure, was especially magnificent, with more than 200 dancers, pupils, and extras, all representing the different social strata of the ancient Lydian kingdom (now part of Turkey). Celebrating victory in battle, it paraded young girls scattering flowers, triumphant warriors, prisoners, men and women slaves, and vestals. A golden chariot drawn by two white horses transported Candaules and the national hero Gyges, who had saved Candaules's queen, Nisia, from the enemy. She arrived on an elephant, an elaborate piece of stage machinery which had been constructed in a Paris workshop and was the subject of much anticipatory press coverage. As Anastasia Bagadaeva remarks in her essay on *King Candaules*, this begs the question of whether the elephant was the same as the one used later in *La Bayadère*.[39]

The dances for *King Candaules*, as for all Petipa's ballets, were listed on the poster. There was, for example: 'La Peltata', a Roman dance, performed by women with sickle-shaped shields; and the "Tortoise grand pas' (*Grand Pas de la tortue*), which refers to the Roman army's famous *testudo* tactic and, this being the world of ballet, featured Amazons. There was the 'Grand Pas de Vénus', which structurally seems to have been a familiar Petipa-esque grand pas (classique), consisting of an *entrée*, an adagio with partnering, variations, and a coda. It had no narrative function. However, in a (grand) pas d'action the same structure would normally contain elements that moved the story forward, perhaps also including the narrative dance described earlier. The set-piece that follows *The Sleeping Beauty*'s 'Garland Waltz' (*Valse villageoise*) and shows Aurora meeting her suitors, impressing them with her charm, and dancing the Rose Adagio, is designated as a pas d'action by Petipa in his own written plans.[40]

In Petipa's grands pas, ensembles often have a sweeping breadth and elaborate design, visible in the diagrams of his preparatory notes. To state the obvious, the geometric plan, at its most essential, placed the ballerina centre stage, surrounded by her immediate subordinates, the soloists, and at one remove the lines of the corps de ballet, a disposition mirroring the strict hierarchy that still rules ballet companies today. The ballerina's pas de deux with her partner was a climactic event, preceded by or interspersed with soloist and group dances. The corps de ballet's subservient lines framed the featured dances, mirroring their movement or creating a counterpoint. Or sometimes the corps de ballet was allowed its own moment of glory, in its own ensemble dance (*ballabile*), as in the Kingdom of Shades.

Petipa also made much use of props—garlands, fans, scarves—for cumulative visual effect. He used *practicables*, portable podiums or steps, carried around by male dancers to add an extra level of height to the ensemble patterns. Seven *practicables* are recorded in Petipa's working notes for the Roman Games scene of *The Vestal*.[41] Tamara Karsavina remembered how *practicables* were also used to spectacular effect in *The Pharaoh's Daughter* and *A Midsummer Night's Dream* (Son v letniuiu noch', 1876).[42] Similarly, Alexei Ratmansky's 2016 staging of *Swan Lake*, which reinstates the stools of the first-act waltz, shows how, when the men stand on them, they create the remarkable and convincing effect of a second tier.[43] Another device was using children to play with perspective: according to Alexandra Danilova, children would be placed at the back of the raked stage, their short height creating the illusion of greater depth.[44]

King Candaules was especially massive, with four acts and six scenes, mime alternating with a profusion of different dances and huge ensembles. The 'Grand Pas lydien', which followed the procession, included a *ballabile* for thirty-four dancers and thirty-two pupils; they were mulattos with tambourines and slaves with revolving marabou parasols. For Alexander Ushakov in *Golos* the most impressive part of the 'Grand Pas lydien' was 'the ensemble final coda in which all taking part [...] perform their own individual solo, and assembled together form a surprising ensemble, an astonishing combination of tempi. This completely new effect for ballet, à la Meyerbeer, is a *chef d'oeuvre*, which will give new impetus to choreographic art.'[45] Two decades later, the critic Nikolai Bezobrazov would be similarly impressed by the same beautiful and astonishing polyphonic finale.[46]

The eye-filling magnificence of such mass geometries, combined with props and stage machinery, was Petipa's answer to the tastes of the imperial court and social elite which made up much of the audience. In all this he was also matching the substantial proportions of the theatre at his disposal and, beyond its walls, the enormous architecture of the city itself. Most important to note, however, is that in elaborating his set-pieces he was pushing against the architecture of his ballets, squeezing the spaces for narrative. For the Moscow theatre critic Alexander Bazhenov the new focus on dance was to the detriment of the action. 'Ballet librettos no longer contain any drama,' he wrote in a review of the Moscow production of *The Pharoah's Daughter*, presumably with Saint-Léon as much in mind as Petipa. 'Instead, they are written, it seems, only so that the designers and machinists can find themes and pretexts for new designs, high-wire flying, transformations, while the ballet masters find a canvas on which they might deploy ready-made dances without any connection to the ballet's content.'[47] The *Contemporary Chronicle*'s writer also refers to the ballet's massive scale, citing 'a whole battalion of soldiers—all the corps de ballet and the whole theatre school—assembled on stage'.[48] But Bazhenov later concedes that the dances in *The Pharaoh's Daugher* 'shine with the variety and inventiveness of their patterns' and provides a graphic description of how ensembles looked in the new ballet genre:

> Modern ballet masters use everything they can just to fill the spectator's eyes, since the dancing by itself does not speak either to the mind or the soul. To that end, they place bright-coloured scarves in the dancers' hands, or tropical leaves tall enough to hide a person, or tambourines or torches; they put baskets of flowers on the dancers' heads and make them go up and down the steps of specially built stools; they invent difficult, striking poses, they assemble intricate patterns, they make the dancers converge and diverge in symmetrical lines. Out of all this emerges something which at first impression is really very pleasing and eye-catching; it all has the look of those variegated flakes in a kaleidoscope which continuously change position, creating completely new, highly symmetrical patterns.[49]

Saint-Léon, as one of the modern ballet masters, used similar props, but Petipa's ensembles were more inventive, more ambitious. Although Saint-Léon's versions tended to be distinguished by a certain monotony of construction, he himself, according to the dance historian Elizabeth Souritiz, later followed Petipa's lead: in his ballet *The Little Humpbacked Horse*, staged after *The Pharaoh's Daughter*, he devoted far more attention to his group dances.[50]

For Saint-Léon, though, *The Pharaoh's Daughter* was 'this interminable ballet (it began yesterday at 7.15 and we finished at 11.38)!!'[51] With the decades, Petipa would further increase the visual scale and the proportion of dance. The danger of this was a tendency to pile combination upon combination, overwhelming the narrative line and stretching the duration of a performance, as testified by his penultimate ballet *Raymonda*. In the 1920s, when Petipa had become outmoded, the dance writer Akim Volynsky would attack his big ballets as overgrown and overblown.[52]

In Petipa's heyday, though, the public had wanted these grand spectacles full of dance, so that emblems of the Romantic Ballet like *La Sylphide* and *Giselle* seemed meagre. It was in response to this that Petipa added substantial dance passages to existing ballets. Some of these additions have become justly famous: namely, the 'Jardin animé' in *Le Corsaire* and the 'Grand Pas from *Paquita*', performed as a separate ballet.

Petipa's adherence to a formula was not restricted to the matter of structure. Characters also tended to recur, only slightly altered for the occasion, so that, for example, John Bull, Lord Wilson's manservant in *The Pharaoh's Daughter*, returns as Sancho Panza in *Don Quixote*, while Aspichia and her unwelcome suitor the Nubian king are early versions of *Raymonda's* titular heroine and the moor Abderrakhman. Yet for all the recycling, Petipa's artistry was undeniable. Even Tamara Karsavina, a supporter of the post-Petipa, Fokine aesthetic, remembered how the Italian choreographer Achille Coppini, briefly invited to work in St Petersburg in 1902, made everybody understand just how exceptional Petipa was:

> Petipa certainly had a distinct leaning towards processions interrupting the action. His ballets [...] were all constructed after the same formula, with inevitable happy endings and a *divertissement* in the last act. Nevertheless, Petipa was a great master and had perfect command of masses. The intricate but always precise pattern of his grouping developed with facility and logic. He had an unerring tact in the use of *coups de théâtre*, a true sense of stage effect.[53]

Out of all this comes a paradox: as a superlative mime artist himself, Petipa was a defender of drama and expressive performance; yet in his ballets, in all the variations and ensembles he composed, he increasingly promoted the route of plotless dance that would lead to Balanchine. The fact is, a Petipa ballet was a composite of opposites, maintaining in delicate and sometimes precarious equilibrium the polar antitheses of narrative and abstraction.

National (Character) Dance

National or character dance featured prominently in nineteenth-century ballet, often as a *divertissement*, performed at special occasions. (It had a similar function in operas.) And, if Perrot and Saint-Léon were its enthusiastic proponents, Petipa was even more so; he clearly considered national dance as a fundamental ingredient and gave it generous space in the festivals and other gatherings of his narratives.

As Lisa C. Arkin and Marian Smith point out, national-dance *divertissements* in the Romantic Ballet actually replicated real-life balls where guests not only themselves performed national dances but were also entertained by professionals. For nineteenth-century audiences, therefore, national-dance *divertissements*, such as in the ballroom scene of *Swan Lake*, would be recognized as reproducing authentic social gatherings; they would have 'a certain immediacy and an air of reality' lost on today's audience.[54]

For Damien Mahmet, the same succession of national dances in *Swan Lake* also harks back to the so-called *ballet des nations*, the ritualized entries (*entrées*) and parade of exotic foreigners that was a common element of the *ballet de cour* of Louis XIII and XIV.[55] This model survived into the subsequent genre of opera-ballet, an early example of which was *L'Europe galante* (1697), with its *entrées* for France, Spain, Italy, and Turkey.[56]

A direct, conscious link to the *ballet des nations* was stitched into *The Sleeping Beauty*'s celebratory final Act III. Not only does this act begin with a series of courtly processional entries, for groups of foreigners, for fairy-tale characters and fairies, but Petipa also writes in his plan that the entry for foreigners was inspired by '*le carrousel Louis XIV*'—the parade and mock-tournament, staged by Louis XIV in 1662 near the Tuileries, to celebrate the dauphin's birth.[57] (The location is now called *la place du Carrousel*.) As well as a magnificently costumed procession of nearly 1,300 individuals, half of whom were on horseback, the carrousel featured five 'nations', each headed by a member of the highest nobility: the Romans (led by Louis himself), Persians, Turks, Indians, and Native Americans. Petipa eventually decided to feature the same nations, although it would seem that national dance was not part of the agenda. In his 'Instructions to Tchaikovsky', he specifies that they should perform a quadrille, 'a pompous and measured dance', set to a stately sarabande, so they would probably have been differentiated more by their costumes than their movements. He vacillated about the dance's positioning: towards the end of the act, just before the mazurka; or near the beginning, after the polonaise which accompanied the processional entries. Ultimately, it seems it was placed before the mazurka. One reviewer was disconcerted by the morphing of the sarabande into a mazurka (and thought the mazurka inappropriate for Versailles anyway); others, not knowing the history of Louis XIV's *Grand Carrousel* were puzzled by the quadrille's inclusion. At a later date it was removed.[58]

If national dance was absent from Petipa's quadrille, it was certainly part of another multinational grand pas in Petipa's *The Bandits* (*Bandity*, 1875), to music by Minkus. The story, in two acts with a prologue, tells of the abduction of Angela by gypsy bandits, her reunion with her family ten years later, and her marriage to a captain who unmasks the abductors. As such, it bears a similarity to Mazilier's *Paquita* and was based on Cervantes's novella *The Gypsy Girl* (La Gitanilla). But from the criticisms of Vazem, who created the main role, and Pleshcheev it would seem that it was too simple, overwhelmed by dances that had little narrative connection, especially those of the concluding *divertissement*, the ballet's highlight, the 'Allegory of the Five Continents of the World' (*Allegoriia piati chastei sveta*).[59] The ostensible reason for the Allegory was the wedding celebration of Angela and her captain, but its scale and ambition far outstripped the modest setting. Featuring some 200 participants, it started with a prolonged version of the Petipa procession, in which a parade of nations was accompanied by the changing colours of electric lighting.[60] Next came an elaborate flower-themed *pas* for soloists and the corps de ballet followed by national dances: a *tonga* for Australia, a tribal number for Africa, bayadères for Asia. Then, in a return to the floral theme, Vazem performed a lyrical classical solo, 'The Queen of Flowers' (*Tanets tsaritsy tsvetov*), to Leopold Auer's violin. This interlude was in turn interrupted by a particularly energetic dance for Inca warriors, led by Liubov Radina and Pavel Gerdt; Radina, in her ecstatic solo, appeared as though embraced by a flame, an impression created by coils of blue light along her arms. Finally came a complicated dance for Vazem, who, as 'Cosmopolitan Europe' (*Evropa-kosmopolitanka*, shades of Perrot's disputed 'Cosmopolitana'), performed five variations in quick succession: a Spanish cachucha, German waltz, French cancan, English jig, and Russian kamarinskaya.[61]

The 'Allegory of the Five Continents of the World', enhanced by elaborate corps de ballet patterns, rich costuming, and lighting effects, produced an explosion of colour and movement. Was this another variant of the *ballet des nations*? Possibly. But also, in its unprecedented scale, visual effects, and disconnection with the narrative it was, as Vazem writes, Petipa's first venture into the territory of *féeries*, spectacular stagings that were appearing all over Europe (and will be explored in more detail later). Western audiences loved *féeries*, and St Petersburg was no different. The Allegory elicited an ecstatic response, despite Vazem's disapproval of such 'rubbish' and of the cheap taste of a public who had failed to greet her classical solo to Auer's violin with the same noisy encores.[62] (By now it should be evident that a ballerina's *pas* to a featured violin accompaniment was another recurring device.)

Alexander Shiriaev, who achieved his greatest successes in character dances, considered Petipa's versions excessively balleticized: 'A devotee of ballet classicism,

Petipa approached character dance from the basis of the former, not from the basis of folk dancing.'[63] On the other hand, it could be argued that complete authenticity would have jarred with the overall ballet picture or with audience tastes of the day.[64] And where it is now common practice to denigrate the authenticity of Petipa's national dances, it is clear that he went to much trouble to research them and ensure the authenticity of the actual choreography, if not the style. His working notes contain long lists of national dances, with descriptions of their provenance, music, steps, and costumes.[65] For *Don Quixote*, he obviously drew upon his own firsthand knowledge of Spanish dance, although admittedly his versions of, for example, a *jota* and gypsy *zingara* would have been balleticized to a greater or lesser degree. The bullfighters' dance, on the other hand, performed by women *en travesti* was clearly more concerned with commercial appeal than authenticity.[66]

Character dances were always hugely popular with audiences and guaranteed wild applause not only for Shiriaev and Petipa's daughter, Marie, but also Felix Kshesinsky and Alfred Bekefi. For most of the century, the extreme demands of ballet training were considered sufficient preparation. But then Shiriaev came along and, while teaching at the school, took the initiative of devising a codified system of folk-dance training. Petipa, noting the progress made by Shiriaev's pupils, helped him persuade the directorate to open an official class in 1891.[67]

Dances of the Russian empire were not only popular in the programmes presented abroad by Marie Petipa, but they would later be exploited, with great success, by the Ballets Russes; later still, they would become an ideological feature of Soviet ballet, with the Shiriaev system used as a basis for training.[68]

Finales and Apotheoses

Typically, the finale of Petipa's big ballets was a big celebratory *divertissement*—or death. Then came the closing tableau, actually a painted backdrop mixed with real figures which conveyed a message of harmony restored. It was a satisfying way of sending audiences home. *The Sleeping Beauty*'s tableau, convincingly reproduced in Sergei Vikharev's 1999 reconstruction for the Mariinsky, is a beautiful assemblage of all the ballet's characters, creating a picture of mythic, emotionally overwhelming resonances.

If the ballet ended with death, the tableau would be an apotheosis, showing the dead united in eternity (*Swan Lake*, *La Bayadère*) or other evidence of supernatural will (*King Candaules*, *The Vestal*). There are variants. In *The Talisman*, Ella doesn't die, but she does forfeit immortality in order to stay with Nourredin, the Maharaja of Lahore, at which point the star, her protective talisman, flies away from her, back up to the heavens. This was followed by an apotheosis, mentioned but sadly not described in the published libretto.[69] The libretto for *Calcabrino*, which doesn't conform to type, doesn't mention an apotheosis at all—although, of course, that does not signify there wasn't one. The ballet's action ends with the demon Draginiazza revealing her true, horrifying identity, after she has tricked Calcabrino into thinking she is Marietta, the woman he wants. She shows Calcabrino a vision of the real Marietta's wedding to her sweetheart Olivier and then drags him with her into Hell.[70]

The apotheosis of *La Bayadère* has gone missing, as has the last act, although some recent productions have reintroduced them.[71] As in *Swan Lake* the lovers Nikiya and Solor are joined in heavenly reunion, in the skies above the Himalayas, after the gods have shown their wrath. The scenic complexities of the final act, requiring an earthquake and the temple's destruction, was one reason why this was not performed after the 1917 revolution. In fact, *La Bayadère* is the most altered of Petipa's surviving ballets.

King Candaules

For *King Candaules*, Pugni allegedly wrote his 312th ballet score: an amazing achievement whatever the merits or demerits of his music. *King Candaules* was his penultimate original score; his last was for Petipa's one-act anacreontic *The Two Stars* (Dve zvezdy). Meanwhile *King Candaules* had the further distinction of strong narrative content, being an adaptation by Saint-Georges of Herodotus's famous story about the titular eighth-century BC Lydian king who, so proud of his wife's beauty, wanted his servant Gyges to glimpse her naked. Khudekov claims that the libretto was originally devised by a St Petersburg journalist (Khudekov?), but that the new director of the Imperial Theatres Stepan Gedeonov insisted the famous Saint-Georges should tweak it for a vast fee.[72] Whatever the truth, the result on paper is a gripping drama, original in the way it breaks the mould with two *Macbeth*-type villains—King Candaules and his wife Nisia—as the central protagonists. Where most Petipa ballets are built around a simple love triangle, *King Candaules* uses a more oblique variant, woven with themes of guilt, hubris, and madness. Skalkovsky noted approvingly in *Novoe vremia* that '*King Candaules* [also] deserves attention as an artistic whole, without the slightest resemblance to previous choreographic creations devoid of dramatic intelligence.' He identified further dramatic themes. 'On stage it is not love that predominates [...] instead the most visible role in the intrigue is played out by other human passions: vengeance and a craving for glory.'[73]

The opening scene of a forest clearing and cave where the sibyl Pythia predicts Candaules's downfall has echoes of Shakespeare's three witches. It establishes Candaules's original sin—he is a usurper who killed the real king as a child—and signals the doom that will unfold with the ballet. Part of the story's deterministic march is Candaules's attempt to topple the gods by knocking the statue of Venus-Astarte from its pedestal and putting Nisia in its place. Nisia, whom power corrupts as much as her husband, plays into the hand of fate by fulfilling the next phases of the prophesied downfall. She is furious because Candaules, suddenly alerted to Venus's anger by a delegation of priests and fearing the terrible consequences, has followed the priests' advice and deprived Nisia of her crown. So she poisons him, encouraged by Pythia, and marries Candaules's favourite Gyges, named by the dying Candaules as his successor. However, she is wracked by guilt and loses her reason during the wedding celebrations. In a scene reminiscent of Macbeth with Banquo's ghost, Nisia is the only one to see the dead Candaules carried forward by dancing bacchantes. (A decade later, in *La Bayadère*, the dead Nikiya would only be visible to Solor during the wedding-scene.) Persuaded by Gyges, Nisia joins in their dancing, but her movements are strange, and she sees the ghost everywhere. Stricken with horror, she dementedly rushes from place to place among the gathered assembly, finally throwing herself at Gyges. The ghost, however, touches her with his icy hand, indicating that he waits for her in the grave where she has thrown him, and she dies in Gyges's embrace. Pythia appears and tells Gyges that the gods have saved him from a murderess, showing him the cup Nisia used to poison Candaules. The final tableau depicts Venus-Astarte, surrounded by other gods in the cloud-filled heavens and pointing at the corpse below of the hubristic queen who had dared to compete with the goddess of beauty.[74]

To reinforce this sombre drama was an unprecedented visual magnificence. 'The most ardent imagination cannot picture such luxury of design, splendour of costumes, or more brilliant sets,' wrote Skalkovsky. The stage effects were equally sensational. For the supernatural disorientation of the first scene, the designer Wagner devised owls that flew back to front in the semi-darkness.[75] The fourth scene showed Nisia revelling in her new deified status, as she and her slaves bathed in a luxurious pool (actually a mirror) surrounded by flowers and adjoining an impressive cascade of real water, illuminated by electric light.[76] (Perhaps this was not as kitsch as it sounds.) The 'Grand Pas de Vénus' followed, with Venus (Nisia), Adonis, Amour, and eight nymphs; it functioned, it seems, as an interlude and replacement for the standard vision scene. It also acted as a bridge to the next mime episode and coup de théâtre, in which Candaules, confronted by the priests and disbelieving their dire warnings, is brought to his senses by an explosion, signalling the anger of the gods. The explosion was planned by Petipa (for the 1891 revival) as an 'earthquake with firecrackers, as in Herculaneum'.[77] In the 1868 performances the effect was so violent it shook the theatre walls.[78]

For many reviewers the ballet was, overall, a triumph, both for its intelligent libretto and for its choreography, while Pugni's music served well and in certain passages had Wagnerian resonances.[79] Although he disapproved of Saint-Georges's deviations from Herodotus's original story, Skalkovsky gave full credit to Petipa's efforts: 'Our talented ballet master Mr. Petipa merits great praise, mounting this colossal ballet, which had a big and fully deserved success. All the dances are staged [...] with the evident wish to make sense of them, to give every one of them a certain character and subject.' Each dance was 'a small choreographic poem'.[80]

The French ballerina Henriette Dor played Nisia, Kshesinsky was Candaules, and Ivanov, Gyges. Vazem has an anecdote about Ivanov, whose role in the first act was only marginally better than that of an extra, as he strode back and forth in front of Nisia's tent before saving her from barbarians. 'Don't worr', Ivanov,' Petipa told him in his mangled Russian. 'In the last act yew will have large scene of mime.' Finally came the last act. '[But] it turned out that Gyges's big scene consisted of his entering and sitting on the throne, from where he watched the *divertissement*. We made fun of this episode for a long time.'[81]

Dor, viewed by balletomanes as a rival to Grantzow, played no small part in the ballet's popularity with the public. She was a formidable actress in the substantial mime scenes, while her virtuosity, displayed most memorably in the adagio of the 'Pas de Vénus', became the talking point of the season. The trick when 'standing on the toes of her left leg, she executed, simultaneously, five slow turns without support, while with the right leg she performed *battements*' seemed a physical impossibility and was dubbed the 'Pas Dor'.[82] She was rewarded at the premiere with gifts of flowers and a diamond tiara worth Petipa's salary, 7,000 roubles.[83]

When, after thirteen performances, she left, attendance slumped. Perhaps the heavyweight drama of the libretto, which impressed several reviewers, did not find favour with ordinary ballet-goers, accustomed to lighter entertainment. The ballet would also have benefitted from cuts. Fedor Lopukhov, who consulted the memories of older dancers, reports that the ballet's value was 'in the massed ensembles and war dances, staged with great art' but that the narrative was overextended and at times obscure. For Nikolai Soliannikov, the reliance on codified mime to push the story forward resulted in too much baffling arm-waving, particularly in the first scene where Pythia exposes Candaules's regicide and predicts his doom, so that crucial narrative premises remained a mystery.[84] Vazem, who led the 'Birth of the Butterfly' (*Naissance du papillon*) dances that followed the 'Grand Pas lydien', writes that, after Dor's departure, 'the ballet often reappeared in the repertoire, but usually not for long; the public obviously did not care for it and even Petipa himself called it "the sin of my youth".'[85] Echoing Soliannikov, she also states that where the mime in *The Pharaoh's Daughter* alternated skilfully with dance, in *King Candaules* it 'literally filled the whole ballet' and few could understand Pythia's voluminous predictions. 'Saint-Georges put together a multitude of melodramatic effects, but on the public the ballet only cast a pall of boredom.'[86]

Worse, she thought Petipa's choreography bland and uninteresting. She was underwhelmed by the 'Pas Dor' ('completely unaesthetic and even, frankly speaking, hideous') and by Dor herself ('devoid of any femininity').[87] Watching Dor in *The Pharaoh's Daughter*, Saint-Léon had a similar reaction: 'She does things that are so difficult that I wish they were impossible, for I have to look the other way, while as for charm, grace, and wit, there is nothing.'[88] Vazem, when the time came in 1875, was reluctant to take over the part of Nisia, its difficulties built on Dor's technique. She had even wanted to do away with the 'Pas Dor' and asked Petipa to compose a different dance for her. 'Yes, Madame,' Petipa answered, 'I know this number is not ver' beautiful. But if yew do not dans it, all artist will thinks yew cannot. I advise yew to dans it.'[89]

As a counterbalance, there is the possibility that the blame attached to the mime scenes was not wholly justified, reflecting instead the Soviet context in which Vazem, Soliannikov, and Lopukhov were writing.[90] It was, after all, the Soviets who systematically expunged mime from the nineteenth-century repertoire. Although not all the newspaper reviews have been accessible, of those that were, only *Peterburgskaia gazeta*, covering a much later performance, refers to an excess of mime, especially in the last three scenes. *Golos* actually praises the mime, spotlighting not only Dor, but Anna Kuznetsova as Pythia, especially in the first scene—or maybe the writer was focusing on performance, rather than text.[91] Either way, *King Candaules* managed to survive into the late 1870s, after which it was considered good enough to be revived several times between 1891 and 1908, the last revival staged by Nikolai Sergeyev.[92] (These are the later versions that Soliannikov would have seen.) It was also transferred to Moscow just a couple of months after its premiere, again with Dor, and found considerable success, not just with the public but also with the company who liked being in it. In its first year it was performed twenty-seven times and remained in the repertoire until 1889.[93]

Moscow acquired two other Petipa ballets in the same year (1868)—*The Parisian Market* (3 January) and *The Travelling Dancer* (27 November)—and, ten days before *King Candaules*, Petipa's production of *Le Corsaire*. (This last ballet had already become popular with Moscow audiences in the Mazilier-Perrot staging, mounted by Frédéric in 1858.) Perhaps the biggest surprise in all this was *The Parisian Market*, whose comedic genre pleased audiences to the point that it became a firm favourite, performed almost every year up to 1882, and revived in 1900 by Ivan Clustine (Khliustin).[94]

Don Quixote

Given that the possibility of permanently moving Petipa to Moscow had been mooted and ditched in 1867, the directorate's solution to Moscow's creative aridity was the flurry of Petipa ballets during 1868. In 1869 and 1870, when there was renewed talk of Petipa's relocation, he actually created two ballets there—*Don Quixote* and *Trilby* (Tril'bi)—which were then transferred to St Petersburg. *Don Quixote*, premiered in Moscow on 14 December 1869 and in St Petersburg on 9 November 1871, marked Petipa's first collaboration with the composer Ludwig

Minkus who, it seems, took over after Pugni became too ill to see the project through. Minkus was then on the staff of the Moscow Imperial Theatres; he had already collaborated with Blasis and Saint-Léon, starting in 1862 with Saint-Léon's *Météora*.[95]

The two versions of *Don Quixote* have been extensively analysed by the dance historians Elizabeth Souritz and Elena Demianovich, and the differences make clear that Petipa was well aware of the divergent ballet traditions of the two capitals.[96] In Moscow, the press did not approve of the new St Petersburg genre and its neglect of drama in favour of kaleidoscopic spectacle, elaborate group dances, and effects; in Moscow the company was notable for its expressiveness and mime, and for its character dancing. Playing, as always, to his performers' strengths, Petipa's concern was for colourful Spanish choreography and a strong (if flawed) narrative, which was his own adaptation of episodes from Cervantes's novel. It was a ballet full of *verismo* and verve, with a quantity of mime and a high proportion of vividly three-dimensional protagonists—nearly all simple Barcelona folk. As today, there were two parallel dramatic lines which occasionally converged: the story of Don Quixote's quest for heroic adventures, in which he is accompanied by Sancho Panza; and the love story of Kitri, an innkeeper's daughter, and Basilio, an impoverished barber, played by the company's star dancers Anna Sobeshchanskaya and Sergei Sokolov. With its rich narrative and tight connection of dance to drama, it was closer to the Perrot model, and although the climax of each act was a *divertissement*, this always arose out of the characters' actions. The scenes were expertly balanced, big massed episodes alternating with intimate lyrical ones and dance sequences with acting ones. Probably, not all the character dances were strictly authentic, but their effect was a colour-filled realism. There was little strict classical dance, most of it contained in the short vision scene of Dulcinea (Polina Karpakova) and her nymphs. Kitri's own dances were, in all probability, Spanish in style; her first-act pas de deux with Basilio was originally, as documented by *Sovremennaia letopis'*, a character dance called 'La Morena'. To give Sobeshchanskaya a chance to shine classically (the premiere was her benefit), Petipa inserted a small comic episode, 'Catching Larks', in the windmill scene, where travelling players stage a performance—which includes puppets—and force her to join in. Set to music by Pugni, this episode had originally been choreographed by Petipa in 1868 for Alexandra Vergina at the Krasnoselsky Theatre when she was still a pupil.[97]

But the folk dances, including the ensemble of bullfighters with women *en travesti*, were not enough to galvanize the public. *Novoe vremia* reported dwindling audiences, and although the ballet was performed up to 1873, where other ballets might last just three or four performances, its success was only relative.[98] It is hard to pinpoint the reasons. Perhaps, as Souritz suggests, the Muscovite public had become accustomed to the lavish Petersburg aesthetic as represented by *The Pharaoh's Daughter* and *King Candaules*. So Petipa had actually miscalculated

Moscow tastes: picturesque comedy about simple people mediated through mime and national dance ran counter to ballet fashion in the late 1860s. The press was also dissatisfied, pedantically objecting to the transformation of Cervantes's would-be knight (played by Vilgelm Vanner) into an out-and-out comic figure.[99] *Vseobshchaia gazeta*, however, praised the exuberance, passion, and variety of the dances.[100] *Novoe vremia* enjoyed the ingenious stage effects to represent the Don's delusions: the giant spider descending along its web, the large moon that cried and then laughed, the outsized cacti, dragons, and windmills.[101] The staging helped launch the career of the famous Bolshoi machinist, designer, and librettist Karl Valts, who also later wrote his memoirs.[102]

Even so, for the ballet's St Petersburg version, performed by Vergina as Kitri, Lev Ivanov as Basilio, and Timofei Stukolkin as Don Quixote, Valts's inventions would not be enough. The budget for the Moscow *Don Quixote* says it all: it cost just 8,913 roubles, half of the budget for the same theatre's *King Candaules* (16,389) and Saint-Léon's *Little Humpbacked Horse* (15,843).[103] For St Petersburg, consequently, Petipa enlarged the ballet from four to five acts and changed the order of the scenes. The Moscow production's comedy scene of Basilio's fake suicide—tricking Kitri's father into agreeing to a deathbed marriage—was replaced by Kitri's threat to kill herself rather than marry Gamache. The number of dances was significantly increased, notably in the much-enlarged dream where Kitri actually becomes Dulcinea, surrounded by a large corps de ballet and seventy-two children dressed as cupids.[104] The ballet's fifth act was a big *divertissement* at the court of the new characters of a duke and duchess. It featured a Nubian dance with goblets (maybe, for narrative justification, they were Nubian slaves), performed by a soloist and twenty-four corps de ballet dancers. Then came a big classical *pas* for Kitri, partnered not by Ivanov's Basilio, but (as was often the practice) by a young unnamed protagonist (Gerdt) who also had a variation; as today, there were two other female soloists in the mix.[105] Finally, the new epilogue showed the Don, sad and broken, returning home to die. *Novosti* consequently remarked: '*Don Quixote* is not a comic ballet, as many expected, but serious and dramatic.'[106] It was a long way from the good-humoured, high-spirited Moscow version which, in Souritz's opinion, Petipa sabotaged in trying to please St Petersburg.[107]

The St Petersburg Don Quixote remained the central character as before; only two acts were allocated to the story of Kitri and Basilio.[108] The Prologue's focus on the arm-waving, sword-brandishing ravings of the Don was one reason why the *Peterburgskii listok* was less than enthusiastic, concluding (in an echo of the criticism of *King Candaules*) that 'it was impossible to understand anything of this.'[109] And yet, other reviewers praised the same scene—'a *chef d'oeuvre*' (*Novosti*)—and Stukolkin's masterly portrayal of the Don, although in general they were lukewarm about the ballet.[110] But the box office did well, so well that the ballet was performed year after year and staged in Moscow in 1887 by Alexei Bogdanov, now the ballet master there, where it had equal success. The directorate was taken by surprise—otherwise they would have spent the 350 roubles needed to buy outright the special apparatus for the laughing and crying moon from its inventor, Moscow's lighting designer Franz Kun, rather than hiring it at 10 roubles a performance.[111] Later came Alexander Gorsky's productions of 1900 (Moscow) and 1902 (St Petersburg)—resented by the elderly Petipa—which restored some of the 1869 detail and the livelier scene of Basilio's mock-suicide. This is more or less the *Don Quixote* that has survived today, the earliest of Petipa's ballets to be still alive.

In 1874 the venerable ballet master Auguste Bournonville, former mentor of Petipa's colleague Johansson, visited St Petersburg. As the defender of the old Romantic Ballet in Copenhagen, he was horrified:

> I sought in vain to discover plot, dramatic interest, logical consistency, or anything which might remotely resemble sanity. And even if I were fortunate enough to come upon a trace of it in Petipa's *Don Quixote*, the impression was immediately effaced by an unending and monotonous host of feats of bravura, all of which were rewarded with salvos of applause and curtain calls. [...]
>
> The feminine costume, if one dares to call it that, was just as one sees it in the most caricatured pictures, and the excessively short skirts, which might possibly be suitable for valkyries riding through the air on winged steeds, do not seem to be appropriate for a Court festival, a wedding celebration, or a society ball. [...]
>
> I could not possibly suppress these and similar observations during my conversations with Johansson and the ballet master Petipa. They admitted that I was perfectly right, confessed that they privately loathed and despised this whole development, explained with a shrug of the shoulders that they were obliged to follow the current of the times, which they charged to the blasé taste of the public and the specific wishes of the high authorities.[112]

Bournonville's ballets were on a more modest, more intimate scale, reflecting in part the smaller stage and auditorium of the Royal Danish Theatre, whose new building, completed the same year, held 1,600 seats compared to the Bolshoi's 2,000 plus. Like Petipa, Bournonville had been a pupil of Auguste Vestris, but in the self-contained development of the Danish ballet he had chosen to build on the light filigree footwork, the bounce, and tasteful restraint of the old Romantic school.

Incidentally, in the following paragraph, Bournonville describes the Imperial Theatre School and gives a figure which presumably includes the smaller drama and opera sections: thirty-six girls and twenty-four boys, all boarders, plus an equal number of day pupils.[113]

Saint-Léon's Exit

In 1866, exhausted by work, Saint-Léon's health began to falter. He had always cast his ambitions wide and taken on multiple commitments, showing his work on four different stages—Moscow, St Petersburg, the Paris Opera, and the Théâtre-Italien. He had choreographed, composed music, written librettos, coached, and concerned himself with all the other details of producing a ballet. In this hyper-activity, he had spread himself too thin, forced to work quickly, to recycle and restage, and he had mostly failed to win over the Russian public. By the winter of 1868–1869 he was suffering from a disease of the kidneys and intestines, able to sleep only for short periods crouched in an armchair.[114] His contract had been extended to cover the 1870–1871 season, but he had resolved after that to leave Russia.[115] Given his acute ill-health, it is remarkable that he could have created a ballet so entertaining and endearing as *Coppélia*, premiered at the Paris Opera on 25 May 1870. He was in Paris when the Franco-Prussian war broke out and, as his return to St Petersburg neared, news was arriving of heavy French defeats and withdrawals. He collapsed with a heart attack in the fashionable Café du Divan, near the Opera, on the evening of 2 September 1870 and was dead before his friends could carry him back to the rue Laval, where he lived with Louise Fleury.[116]

With that, Petipa became first ballet master in practice and eventually in title since there was no attempt to find another replacement. Stepan Gedeonov, son of Alexander, was by then director of the Imperial Theatres, having come from the Hermitage museum, where he had achieved great distinction. He was responsible for the acquisition of one of Raphael's Madonnas and many important archaeo-logical artefacts; moreover, after becoming the museum's director, he had opened the collections to the public. His move to the Imperial Theatres in 1867 would prove a mistake: it meant a halt to the planned improvements at the Hermitage and saw him become paralysingly entangled with civil servants, in particular Baron Karl Kister.[117] (Kister would succeed Gedeonov at the Imperial Theatres in 1875.) A literary translator into French and a not-so-successful dramatist, Gedeonov's directorship of the Imperial Theatres was marked by a willingness to invite for-eign talent, as already hinted by his decision to enlist Saint-Georges's editorial help for *King Candaules*.

7

At Home and at Work

*The creation and staging of a big ballet presents enormous diffi-
culties; in outlining the scenario or programme, one must think
of all the individual roles; having completed the story and panto-
mimic part of the ballet, one must invent and create the appropriate dances, pas, and variations, and make them conform to
the music.*[1]

A Second Family

In 1872, five years after his separation from his first wife, Petipa set up house with
Liubov Savitskaya (1854–1919), the daughter of Leonid Leonidov, an actor at the
Maly Theatre in Moscow. (She took her mother's family name.) After graduating
from the Moscow theatre school she appeared on the Maly stage in small ballets
and vaudevilles, performing before the main show, while the audience were taking
their seats. On meeting Petipa she moved to St Petersburg where she served as a
dancer until her retirement in 1888. She was a pretty blonde but never achieved
any distinction. (Petipa might have striven to promote the female members of his
family onstage, but there were definite limits to his powers.) She was therefore
never Petipa's muse and there were never fanatical admirers.

When they met Petipa was fifty-five and she only nineteen, making her four
years younger than Petipa's oldest (illegitimate) son Marius (born 1850) and just
three years older than Marie. Despite her youth, it would seem that Petipa had
met his match. 'A very coarse and loose-tongued woman,' says Vazem, 'she often
argued with him at rehearsals and sometimes even showered him with the most
vulgar language.'[2] Pavel Gerdt's daughter, the dancer Elizaveta, remembered
Liubov's volcanic character, along with her habit of hitting people with her umbrella if she was in a hurry and wanted to get past. 'In the Petipa house, in order
to avoid coming to grief, everybody obeyed her implacable will. If they tried to op-
pose her, a violent scene would be ignited.'[3] Yet 'this vivid, temperamental household' never failed to impress Elizaveta. It was 'animated, charismatic, eccentric
even, but always busy, noisy, and interesting. Marius Petipa, as I remember, was,
in contrast to everybody, the quietest, calmest in the family.'[4] With age, it would

seem, Petipa learnt to control his temper; and maybe also the threat of prison had been a salutary lesson.

In Vera Petipa's description, Marius, a Frenchman born in Marseilles, and Liubov, who had Polish and Greek heritage, were complete opposites:

> Father was very mobile, punctual, completely immersed in his work and art, which he adored and which he missed during holidays. Mother was very lively, spontaneous, and mercurial. She paid no attention to time, was very absent-minded, and full of humour. Their conversations would make us, the children, laugh, for they were really opposites, which didn't prevent them from living together many years and loving each other. In the highly-strung and charged theatrical atmosphere in which we lived, mother brought a refreshing spontaneity and infectious humour.[5]

If the not-always-reliable Nikolai Legat is to be believed, the public Petipa could become 'the life and soul of every gathering' who 'kept things always on the go by his stories, jokes, and even juggling abilities, which he was fond of demonstrating at table'.[6] The composer and music critic Mikhail Ivanov also remembered Petipa's talent as a raconteur, able to communicate an inexhaustible wealth of interesting stories, something which did not transfer into the written words of his published memoirs.[7] Vazem, of course, thought this cheerfulness artificial, a product of the false, superficially courteous French national character. She also repeats gossip that he had a weakness for women (no news there), but adds that he 'started affairs with anybody available—from society ladies to theatre dressmakers and was extremely proud of his romantic successes'.[8] This begs the question of when he would have had the time.

Liubov and Marius had six children. The Petipa that emerges from the memoir of his youngest Vera (1885–1961) is biased by affection, but offers interesting glimpses. She says he taught his children modesty and did not like to publicize his titles and achievements loudly. He also insisted on sober dress and taught his sons life-saving—he had himself once saved someone from drowning. He had impeccable manners: even when old and ill, he stood up if a woman approached him. He liked to explore antique shops and markets, to buy art works and rare books; but essentially he lived for his work. Most of the time he dealt with people who understood French, although he did make attempts to learn Russian. He would learn phrases by heart, but then felt ridiculous after just a few words. His verbal mistakes became legendary. He regretted this lacuna greatly: Russia had become his homeland and, once, while ill in France, he had made his wife promise to take his body back home. He loved the St Petersburg company, for its high standards and hard-working approach. For his jubilee, he received many gifts but the one he valued most was a silver wreath from the corps de ballet on which were engraved all the dancers' names.[9]

When his first wife died in 1882, Petipa received permission to marry Liubov and have his children legitimized.[10] He didn't want his sons to enter the theatre school because the academic standards were poor; even so, all of them (apart from Jean his son with Maria Surovshchikova) became actors, which pleased him. Marius Mariusovich (1850–1919), whose mother was Marie-Thérèse Bourdenne, went to a commercial school, but became a successful actor, starting at the Alexandrinsky. Vera was already aged twelve when she first met him, but she often heard her parents speak of him. 'He had a lot in common with my father, especially a great delicacy in his relations with people and an enormous joie de vivre.'[11] Marius Mariusovich's three children also went on stage, one of them becoming an equally well-known actor, Nikolai Radin, whom Vera got to know in Odessa, when she had stopped dancing. Petipa's two sons from his second marriage became actors: Victor (1879–1939), whose career lasted thirty-five years and who was made an Honoured Artist of the Soviet Socialist Republic of Ukraine, and Marii (1884–1922) who did his military service in the cavalry before taking to the stage.[12] For a brief time (1910–1911) Victor and Marii worked alongside Marius Mariusovich and Nikolai Radin in the same troupe in Odessa. Marii, Vera writes, was a prankster who didn't always recognize boundaries. She describes an occasion when, playing the bit part of a sentry, he arrived wearing such ludicrously hideous makeup that he provoked long laughter in the audience, hindering the actor who, as the king, was trying to deliver a sombre monologue.[13] He had a son, Valerii, and died, aged only thirty-eight, after surgery for a hernia.[14]

Everything in the Petipa household was directed towards the arts. For his daughters, Petipa wanted dance careers; he wanted to see his artistic ideals flourish in them.[15] But if his hopes were disappointed by his eldest daughter Marie's limitations, they were dashed by the others. Like Marie, Nadezhda (Nadia, 1874–1945) and Evgenia (Eugénie, Génia, or Génie, 1877–1892) received a general education at home from tutors, and ballet training from their father in a studio installed in their apartment with a raked floor. The ballet lessons started very early in the morning, Petipa accompanying on the violin. Even with his own children, he was an unsparing teacher. The atmosphere was rarely calm, especially as the eldest, Nadezhda, would challenge her father's criticisms, while he, like his own father before him, expected unquestioning obedience. Nadezhda entered the company in 1892, but she, too, had a weak classical technique and concentrated on mime roles. She married and by 1904 already had five children. Later she became a teacher and moved to Kazan where she opened a school in 1912.[16]

By contrast, Evgenia had started well. However, Vera writes: 'A terrible calamity befell our family. Even now, I vividly remember the profound grief of my parents when their second daughter, Evgenia, the hope of my father, who believed her very talented, died of a sarcoma, her leg was amputated.'[17]

After Evgenia's death, the distraught Petipa dismantled the practice studio. He enrolled his other daughters, Liubov (Louba, 1880–1917) and Vera, at the theatre school. Liubov had outstanding promise. Even the exacting Vazem, who by then had retired and was teaching, was impressed: 'She undoubtedly had great ability and all the qualities to become an exceptional classical soloist and, probably, a ballerina with a soft, light style of dancing.'[18] She graduated into the company in 1899, together with Anna Pavlova, and the same year received enthusiastic notices in the major role of Myrtha in *Giselle*.[19] But just a year later she threw it all away to make an ill-considered marriage, followed by an unhappy life and early death aged thirty-seven.

All these setbacks taught Petipa 'that life has its own unavoidable rules' and he learnt to adopt a softer approach.[20] For all the squabbles, Petipa's diaries reveal a generous, involved, and adoring father; maybe it was the two youngest—Marii and Vera—who, still living in the parental home, were the focus of the most attention and indulgence. By the time Vera was ready for training, he was in poor health and no longer had the energy for prolonged teaching. She entered the school as a day pupil, aged eight, although she had started with her father the year before. Aged nine, in accordance with the rules, she became a boarder, going home only at weekends. She remembered how, when her father staged school performances, he would conduct rehearsals in a Russian so garbled only some of the older children could understand, while the others goggled in bewilderment. Fortunately, his assistant Alexander Shiriaev was usually on hand. The pupils were always anxious at these rehearsals because Petipa was such an unflinching fault-finder; but it was his own children who bore the greatest brunt, since the criticism continued at home, spoken in his execrable Russian—always Russian for such occasions, not French.[21]

Ballerinas were Petipa's muse, as they would be for Balanchine, a human clay that inspired him and gave shape to his ideas. Maria Surovshchikova-Petipa was his first ballerina-project and Vera was his last. He tried hard to develop her artistic sensibilities, drawing her attention to the colours and play of light in Gurzuf and encouraging her to comment on art works when they visited museums.[22] His efforts, it would seem, produced the desired result. Sergei Grigorev, Vera's contemporary in the company (and later *régisseur* of the Ballets Russes), wrote: 'She was nice, engaging, very well read, and to converse with her was extremely interesting.'[23] Petipa's surviving diaries show him, aged eighty-five, taking great pains to help Vera in her final years at the school, coaching her, consulting her teachers. He felt boundless paternal pride. 'She was the best,' he noted at her graduation performance on 2 May 1903, the day she received an examination mark of eleven out of twelve and was accepted into the company.[24] There, she quickly understood that she needed to improve, 'to occupy a position worthy of a daughter of my father'.[25] In the mornings she attended the company *classe de perfectionnement* which Evgenia Sokolova, now retired as ballerina and a friend of the Petipa family, had taken over from Johanssen; then came rehearsals; then, in the evening, if she wasn't performing, she went to an evening class.[26] In 1904 she was rewarded with *The Sleeping Beauty*'s White Cat, in which she was encored, and a featured role in *Harlequinade*, Petipa asserting, 'my dear daughter Vera was charming in every way.'[27] The same year, Petipa swallowed his pride and asked his arch-enemy the director of the Imperial Theatres Vladimir Teliakovsky to allow Vera to attend the ballerina Olga Preobrazhenskaya's classes when Sokolova was fired.[28] In the summer of 1905, as her sister Liubov had done six years earlier, she went with her parents to Milan to study with Caterina Beretta, teacher of the Italian stars.[29] But the gruelling toil had a price: the following spring she felt ill. On the advice of doctors, her parents hurriedly took her to the Crimea, where, disembarking in Yalta, she not only witnessed the horrible spectacle of cossacks brutally repressing a May Day demonstration, but at the hotel that same evening she coughed blood. It was tuberculosis; obviously a terrible blow. Although, with a year's rest, the disease was halted, dancing was out of the question.[30] In 1907 she resolved to switch to acting and, returning in mid-March to Crimea with her parents and brother Victor, she eventually started performing with Victor. (Petipa records performances in Sebastopol, Yalta, and Gurzuf.)[31] Later, she acted in other regions and in Moscow, attracted to the avant-garde in the exciting artistic ferment of the 1920s, but always reined in by her delicate health.[32]

Working Methods

Petipa worked like a slave—'*comme un nègre*', Saint-Léon said about Petipa's preparations for *King Candaules*.[33] (These were, of course, linguistically different times.) The monumental scale of Petipa's ballets demanded superhuman imagination and endless private preparation, besides the hours spent consulting the composer, the designers, teaching the steps to the company, and conducting rehearsals. For Petipa the choreographer, it wasn't just a matter of arranging attractive floor patterns, but of fitting steps to music, linking dance to narrative, arranging stage effects, and always inventing—pseudo-historical details for a group dance, pseudo-ethnographic accessories for incorporation in another dance, new twists on old formulas. In the background of all this was Petipa's indefatigable note taking. The Petipa's files in the GTsTM archive are full of lists of dancers and roles; reminders to himself of things to do; comments about costumes; references to images, paintings, and ethnographic illustrations that might jog his creativity. The notes for *The Vestal* include many detailed pencil drawings of the characters with their costumes and accessories—presumably as an aid to his thought processes.[34] And nothing ever escaped his attention: from the hair and baskets for a group of Virgins in *King Candaules* to the purchase of a broken-down horse for the part of *Don Quixote*'s Rosinante.[35]

In later years, according to Alexander Shiriaev—made *répétiteur* ('rehearser') in 1896—if Petipa didn't like the music, he would pass the job over to Ivanov or Shiriaev.[36] In collaborating with composers, surviving instructions signal that his procedure was largely unvarying, whether it was for Tchaikovsky and *The Sleeping Beauty* (1890) or Minkus and *Mlada* (1879).[37] He would write a breakdown of a ballet's dance numbers, with indications of their length, tempi, style, and context. As mentioned earlier, Wiley, in *Tchaikovsky's Ballets*, includes reproductions of what he calls the 'Ballet Master's Plans' (in the original French): that is, Petipa's outlines combining the scenario and musical specifications for *The Sleeping Beauty* and *The Nutcracker*, documents which appear to have been for his own use while mounting the ballets. Wiley also reproduces 'Petipa's Instructions to Tchaikovsky' (translated into English), for the same ballets, which were for the composer at an earlier phase.[38] Taking *The Sleeping Beauty*'s 'Instructions to Tchaikovsky', it is evident that they vary in their precision. So, for the ballet's Prologue, Tchaikovsky is allowed broad leeway:

No. 1. At the rise of the curtain a salon march for the entrance of the lords and ladies.

No. 2. For Catalabutte's little recitative, the march becomes somewhat more serious.

No. 3. Fanfares—broad grandiose music.

No. 4. 3/4, *grazioso*.

No. 5. 3/4, more broadly.

No. 6. 3/4, quite lively and *dansante* (pages and young girls enter dancing).[39]

But in Act I the instructions are more detailed. The famous Rose *adagio* and finger pricking are outlined in the following way:

No. 10. *Pas d'action*. Grand *adagio* of a very animated character (*mosso*). Rivalry of the princes. The music expresses their jealousy, then Aurora's coquetry. For the conclusion of the *adagio*, broad grandiose music.

No. 11. *Allegro* for the maids of honour. 48 b[ars], concluding with a polka *temps* for the pages.

No. 12. Aurora's variation. 3/4, *pizzicato* for violins, cellos, and harp. (Excuse me for expressing myself so oddly.) And then lute and violin.

No. 13. Coda. 2/4, *vivace*—96 b[ars].

No. 14. Suddenly Aurora notices the old woman. With a spindle she beats time in 2/4, then a transition to

No. 15. 3/4, a gay and very songful motif. When counting in 3/4 begins, Aurora seizes the spindle, which she waves like a sceptre—32 b[ars]. Suddenly (a pause) pain! Blood! 8 bars of 4/4, *largo*.

No. 16. Horror—2/4, *vivace*—she no longer dances—it is some kind of mindless turning, as if she had been bitten by a tarantula. At the end she falls dead. (For the circling, no more than 24 b[ars].)[40]

Petipa had to labour intensively. 'For all the merits of the music, Petipa was constrained by it and it was difficult for him to work on *Beauty*,' writes Shiriaev. 'This he actually admitted to me.'[41] Moreover, on a practical level, Petipa would have felt more freedom working with a staff composer. With Pugni or Minkus he could make numerous amendments and they would think nothing of late nights spent revising a whole act or composing it afresh. With Tchaikovsky and Glazunov, Petipa had to be more circumspect, partly because they had busy professional lives away from ballet.[42] Even so, Vera Petipa remembered how Tchaikovsky would come to their home to discuss and play passages on the piano, the children listening in another room, with their mother whispering explanations.[43] Vladimir Pogozhev, office manager during Ivan Vsevolozhsky's directorship, wrote that conferences and consultations with Vsevolozhsky, Petipa, and the ballet's director of music Riccardo Drigo became part of Tchaikovsky's life.[44] The first Aurora, Carlotta Brianza, recalled how Tchaikovsky would compromise and make changes:

> We rehearsed the ballet some three months on the little stage of the Theatre School in the presence of the old man Marius Petipa, Tchaikovsky, and Riccardo Drigo [...] Rehearsals took place to piano accompaniment, played by Drigo himself. Tchaikovsky met the wishes of the ballet master halfway, shortening, supplementing, and changing the music according to the dances.[45]

It seems likely that Tchaikovsky was consulted in the choice of Brianza; certainly he took an interest in casting, judging by an incident during a rehearsal. Tchaikovsky asked Petipa for the name of the young dancer he had seen as Amor in a performance of *The Vestal*, and Petipa answered 'Maria Anderson'. After searching for her with his eyes, Petipa beckoned her over with his usual appellation 'ma belle', and she approached, politely waiting at some distance while they continued their conversation in French.

> Petr Ilich discreetly threw a furtive glance in my direction, apparently appraising me as an artist. Judging by the slight smile on his face, he was satisfied with me. [...] Finishing the conversation, Petr Ilich took several steps towards me in his characteristic manner—with a slight inclination of

his body. Coming closer, he began to ask me various questions, mixing, as was his custom, Russian and French and playing with his pince-nez.

When Petr Ilich finished his questions, which I answered timidly and guardedly, M. Petipa, thinking that I did not understand French, began to explain to me in his broken Russo-French dialect what all the talk was about. According to the 'translation', the talk meant that in the ballet *The Sleeping Beauty* I would dance 'the little cat, as Tchaikovsky wished'.[46]

With Glazunov, Petipa worked as he had with Tchaikovsky, supplying his usual indications. But *Raymonda* (1898) was Glazunov's first ballet commission and he had to learn certain basic facts, like Tchaikovsky before him, such as the impossibility for dancers to cope with variations much longer than a minute, and the tendency for choreographers and ballerinas to demand changes. This aspect of Glazunov's inexperience prompted Petipa to write in frustration: 'Monsieur Glazunov does not want to change a single note, not in Mlle. Legnani's variation, nor even a small cut in the *galop*. It is awful to compose a ballet with a composer who has sold and published his score beforehand.'[47] But from Glazunov's side there were also frustrations. Responding to his publisher Mitrofan Beliaev's reproach that he was spending too much of his precious time watching beautiful ballerinas at rehearsals, he wrote that his presence was indispensable. His music was being played in a reduction for just two violins, which in no way could reproduce its complexities:

> Firstly, I mark out the tempo, secondly, Petipa is already old and forgets much of what he told me earlier; there are constantly clashes, which end quite well thanks to my presence. If I were not there, everything would be done any old how. Petipa would be angry, with justification, for they are pushing him to finish, and they would have subjected me to such cuts that I would have kicked up a real fuss.[48]

Petipa was seventy-eight years old. In the letter where he complains about Glazunov's obligations to his publisher, he also writes: 'I have two rehearsals every day and am very busy until two in the morning, writing down what is needed for the Hermitage productions.'[49] For Petipa, to cope with his huge workload, it had long been expedient to prepare beforehand at home. Shiriaev describes the process:

> As a rule, Petipa worked on the whole production of a new ballet at home, to which he usually summoned a pianist and violinist. Making them play excerpts of music numerous times, he planned a production on the table, using, especially for the mass dances and groups, small dolls made out of

papier mâché. They were moved by the ballet master into the most varied combinations which he noted down in great detail, marking the women with noughts, the men with crosses, and the different displacements with arrows, dashes, and lines, the meaning of which was known to him alone. In such a way, Petipa graphically created the whole of a future production.[50]

Many of the surviving diagrams in the GTsTM archive depict big ensembles; some are sketches and notes for smaller group dances and solos, such as those for *The Bandits*.[51] (There are also diagrams and notes for a few ballets, including *La Bayadère* and *The Daughter of the Snows*, in the Sergei Khudekov *fond* 1657 in RGALI.) Never late for rehearsals, Petipa would arrive armed with his drawings and, when Ivanov and Shiriaev were appointed as assistant ballet masters, he advised them to do the same. (Shiriaev did, Ivanov often didn't.) By this method, Petipa usually managed, by Shiriaev's reckoning, to compose a whole act in a few days and finish a big ballet in two and a half months.[52] Vazem, who belonged to an earlier generation, says that in a single season Petipa produced 'never less than two long ballets, not counting one-act ballets and separate dances'.[53]

However, Vazem also says that in the studio:

He was never certain of the rightness of his compositions, even though he worked them out at home, and he would quite often alter them while rehearsing. From this came the necessity of a great number of rehearsals, far more than Saint-Léon demanded. And at rehearsals Petipa would often fuss and fret, and this agitation would be transmitted to the artists.[54]

This is corroborated by Saint-Léon when he writes about Petipa's preparations for *King Candaules*: 'His ballet will not be ready until October. Mustapha Gedeonov [Stepan Gedeonov] is very surprised that he has already had sixty rehearsals for his three-act ballet. He will see many more of them.'[55]

The short-temperedness he displayed in his classes at the school sometimes also manifested itself at rehearsals. It provoked a member of staff to write to the directorate on 27 October 1865, complaining that Petipa had vented his frustration on one of the theatre's copyists, calling him a thief.[56] Vazem paints a damning picture of Petipa in his dealings with the company:

In his treatment of the company, Petipa was calculating to the point of impudence. If he was always courteous and gallant towards some artists, often paying them compliments with a quintessentially French unctuousness (one must take into account that among my colleagues were persons with 'friends' among the grand dukes and other powerful people on whom depended a ballet master's career), then with the 'small fry' he spoke with the peremptory tone of a dictator, not holding back his language. We often heard remarks such as: 'Listen *ma belle*', such was his favourite form of address for coryphées and corps de ballet dancers—'yew *dans* like my cook.'

Pathologically self-important, Petipa jealously defended his ballet master's authority and intensely disliked being contradicted. He would get very annoyed if artists criticized his productions. Second-rank dancers naturally kept submissively silent, but he often had clashes with leading soloists. He disliked me because I often contradicted him, although he always valued me as an artist. However, to give Petipa his due, if after several arguments he was fully convinced he was wrong, he was always ready to admit it. I danced in many of Petipa's ballets and he always showed complete satisfaction with my work and gratitude. Petipa greatly furthered my career, staging real dance gems for me, but I must say without boasting that I also considerably helped in the success of his productions by my participation. At any rate, the artistic results of our collaboration were very positive.[57]

That age eventually calmed Petipa down is confirmed by Nikolai Soliannikov, who graduated into the company in 1891, long after Vazem's retirement. He noted that, although Petipa could still get annoyed when things were going badly in rehearsal, the mercurial man of before 'rarely lost his self-control in his declining years'.[58] When things were going well, he composed quickly and precisely. 'Despite his old age, he demonstrated [what he wanted] himself, amazingly, powerfully, graphically, [while] at the same time he did not stifle the individuality of an artist, but allowed them to take the initiative and was extremely pleased when they managed to work out new sequences to be woven into the fabric of his choreography.'[59] Other dancers also remember Petipa as a man of few words, partly a symptom, maybe, of his limited grasp of Russian. Liubov Egorova, who graduated in 1898, writes that they all liked him very much, but the discipline was like iron. He expected dancers to grasp a given *enchaînement* (linked steps) quickly and didn't like repeating instructions more than two or three times. If a particular dancer was having problems mastering a series of steps, he would take her by the hand, lead her to the back row of dancers, and bring another out. (Such are actions that speak more pitilessly than words.) During performances, he would watch from a seat in the first wing. When somebody had performed well, he would nod in approbation and murmur '*Ma belle, ma belle*'; but if they had performed badly he would turn his back on them when they passed, or would look at the ceiling, but would never say anything.[60]

Soliannikov judged other aspects of Petipa's character more sympathetically than Vazem. 'Petipa carried himself with a dignity, bordering on self-importance, but this was the bearing of a person knowing his worth and respecting his art. If in his relations with artists there were glimpses of a certain haughtiness, then he did not fawn before his superiors either. True, Petipa was not a militant, he would go for compromise and would, with courtly diplomacy, avoid conflict. "C'est la vie," he would say with a light ironic smile. [...] All the same, despite his extreme caution and skilful manoeuvering in the world of court-theatre intrigues, Petipa in his working life remained a simple artist.'[61]

The Dance Language

Petipa's *enchaînements* articulate a spare and linear classicism that is recognized today as the defining style of the Russian Imperial Ballet. Unique to nineteenth-century Russia, these *enchaînements* were widely emulated in the twentieth century. That they represented a break with the vocabulary and syntax of the Romantic Ballet is clear from Vazem's comments, lamenting the loss of Saint-Léon's 'fine, "beaded" steps', which required 'genuine filigree work from a dancer', and their replacement by Petipa's 'coarser' style.[62] In the heterogenous context of a *grand* Petipa ballet this 'coarser' language appears like a chaste geometry threaded through a baroque fabric.

Vazem, who graduated into the company in 1867, is, however, talking generally, summarizing the mature Petipa; in the absence of evidence it is impossible to know if his early style was different. Although *The Pharaoh's Daughter* was notated, the system used was only devised by Vladimir Stepanov towards the end of the century. The notated *Pharaoh's Daughter* was therefore a much later version, following two revivals and many probable changes. So nobody can ever be sure whether Petipa's early vocabulary was closer to the fleet-footed, filigree dance of the Romantic Ballet, as exemplified by Perrot, Saint-Léon, and Bournonville whose ballets in Denmark have been uniquely preserved. And yet. All that said, if the individual evolution of today's choreographers is anything to go by, it seems more probable that Petipa found his movement language early on.

The working notes and sketches for *The Bandits* give a glimpse of technique in 1875. The partnering work described may not be as spectacular as the single-armed lifts and flying catches of Soviet ballet. However, in one lift the ballerina is raised high in what sounds like (to use an oxymoron) an upward fish dive: 'the legs encircle the man's body, the ballerina's body above the man's head, a tambourine in her hand.'[63]

In the school, technique was less demanding; it was viewed as the slow and sober inculcation of good habits and academic rigour. Shiriaev, who graduated from the school in 1885, describes the teaching, established by Petipa for the boys, as belonging to the strict canons of the French school. Reserve and smoothness were valued. Partnering and lifts were simple:

> They also taught us supports, but only the most primitive, reduced to holding the ballerina by the waist for two turns in adagio. At that time we

were not yet acquainted with ballerinas flying through the air, helped by their partner. A special class for lifts [...] was started up much later, not long before my graduation from the school.[64]

Any discussion of dance technique has to include Johansson, Petipa's Swedish near-contemporary whose career as a performer lasted forty-three years and who began teaching at the school in 1860. He had been trained in the French-derived school of Bournonville, with whom he perfected his technique in Copenhagen. As Petipa's workload increased and he relinquished much of his teaching, so Johansson increased his. He also taught the *classe de perfectionnement* for the leading women in the company. (The male dancers, being considered less important, didn't have a similar class; instead they had to ask permission to attend Pavel Gerdt's senior male class at the school. Later, though, with the arrival of the Legat brothers into the company, men were admitted into Johansson's class.)[65] Johansson had a great influence on dance standards: in the last decade of the nineteenth century every ballerina in the company had come under his guidance, either in the school or in his *classe de perfectionnement*.

Unlike other teachers such as Gerdt and Lev Ivanov, Johansson commanded universal veneration.[66] Tall and thin, his cool classicism on stage was translated into a laconic severity in the studio, transmitted, like Petipa, in a broken Russian mixed with French. His exceedingly complex classes, which in forty-three years of teaching never, legend says, repeated the same *enchaînement* twice, accustomed the dancers to difficulty. He always prepared the classroom floor himself with water sprinkled from the routine watering can and provided his own accompaniment on the violin.[67] Seated in front of the mirror, from time to time he would bring out his snuffbox, take a pinch of snuff, rise from his chair, pull a red handkerchief from his back pocket, and sneeze.[68] Like Petipa he disliked empty prowess, but he used the innovations of Italian technique if he counted them useful. Although he promoted an academic perfection, emphasizing the virtues of classical line, *épaulement* (the subtle angling of the torso in relation to the head), softness, smoothness, and clarity, he was known for his personalized approach, refusing to erase a particular idiosyncrasy if it preserved an attractive individuality. Reputedly it was he who did not try to interfere with Anna Pavlova's poor turnout, visible in later films.[69] Karsavina testifies to this approach when she reports Johansson's advice to her father Platon Karsavin: 'For God's sake don't polish her natural grace; even her faults are her own.'[70] By the time he was her teacher, he had sight in only one eye, but nothing escaped him and she, along with many newcomers to his class, was initially petrified by his impressive repertoire of insults.

Johansson taught until the year of his death in 1903. He produced the kind of dancers that Petipa wanted and their alliance was close. Given that Petipa was more comfortable creating solos for women than for men, he was happy to see male dancers go to Johansson for ideas and advice. According to Nikolai Legat, Petipa often visited his classes, taking out a notebook and jotting things down. 'At the end of the class, Johansson would wink and say: "The old man has pinched some more".'[71] They were two giants, Johansson and Petipa, one in the classroom, the other in the theatre, friends who grew old together and shaped the course of Russian ballet. Johansson is credited with bringing a Danish element of lightness and *épaulement* to the Russian style, both—the Danish and the Russian—based on the old French school. Later in the century would come the Italian influence, raising the stakes of virtuosity for men as well as women.

The style of nineteenth-century performance is, like the style of Petipa's early choreography, a matter largely of conjecture. Ballets have changed over the decades not only because of alterations to the choreography, but because of an evolution in performing manner. Written accounts don't offer much information. Rare early twentieth-century film footage—Anna Pavlova in *The Dying Swan* (1907), Tamara Karsavina in *Torch Dance* (1909)—suggests an emphasis on expressivity, fluidity, and upper body flexibility, although they are dancing choreography by Fokine, not Petipa.[72] (The last quality of flexibility contradicts the belief that ballerinas, because they were often encased in tightly corseted tutus, had intrinsically stiff backs; whale-boning, warmed by body temperature, was not rigid.) Petipa always stressed the importance of arms and their meaningfulness, which is how he moulded the eloquent plastique of his first wife Maria Surovshchikova. He often repeated to dancers that 'dancing with the legs is nothing, but knowing how to control the arms—this is the art of a harmonious, kinetic plastique.'[73] Especially apparent in posed and costumed photographs is a theatricality, an identification with the essence of a role, quite different from today's silhouette-focused dancers. The emphasis on expressiveness is confirmed by Vera Petipa:

> My father did not deny the great significance of technique to attain virtuosity, but he did not consider technique the one cornerstone. His artistic credo was that the ballet artist, besides necessarily possessing technique, had to have both an awareness of a given role in harmony with the music and the capacity to communicate it through facial expression and the plasticity and expressiveness of his movements.[74]

Petipa railed against empty virtuosity in newspaper interviews.[75] And in *divertissements*, where plotless dance was showcased, he would surely have insisted on an expressiveness in its widest sense—not 'emoting' or dramatizing, but modulating dance with the non-narrative qualities of texture and line, light and shade, musicality and an inner spirit.

The Variation

Although the famous dictum 'ballet is woman' belongs to Balanchine, Petipa was there before him. 'His speciality was women's solos,' Nikolai Legat writes. 'He had an amazing capacity for finding the most advantageous movements for each danseuse, so that the end result looked both simple and graceful.'[76]

For Vazem, however, Petipa lacked Saint-Léon's musicality. 'He did not feel the music or its rhythm; therefore, his dances were often extremely uncomfortable to perform, and the soloists had either to ask him to change the choreography or to rearrange it themselves illicitly.'[77] Fedor Lopukhov also criticized Petipa's musicality, but with arguments that were often eccentric and which he sometimes later contradicted or refuted.[78] The matter of Petipa's musicality is too big and specialized a question for this study. It will only note that dance musicality can sometimes be a subjective quality, dependent on personal and even national preferences, given the habit among Western writers not so long ago to criticize Russian dancers as unmusical.

The primacy of the ballerina on the nineteenth-century stage meant that her variations were generally viewed as the choreography's jewels. In composing a variation, Petipa's concern was not so much to make things easier for the ballerina as to make her truly glitter. Shiriaev writes:

> With the ballerinas Petipa always worked separately. Before mounting this or that solo, the ballet master painstakingly studied all the most characteristic traits and particularities of the ballerina with whom he would be working. He studied these not in order to adapt the dance to the individuality and aptitudes of the ballerina, but in order to fully uncover and expose them. And if the music of any variation did not correspond to the performer's qualities, he would change it with another inserted number, even if it was to the detriment of the musical entity of a production, but not to the detriment of a ballerina's success.[79]

The ever-pragmatic Petipa would, like Balanchine after him, also change steps if a ballerina had difficulties: 'It would happen that he showed the ballerina a new movement, [and] she struggled and struggled to no avail; [so] then he would rearrange the *pas*.'[80] He knew that choreography can only shine if the performer shines as well. But, besides taking into account his human material, he had to address the arduous task of composing something fresh, interesting, and appropriate over and over again. He had half a century of experience when he wrote: 'Those acquainted with ballet affairs know that in any *pas*, the most difficult part to create is the variations, because it is necessary to give them a completely new character every time.'[81]

Petipa built his variations on a repetition of motifs that produces a rhythmic patterning pleasing to the eye. He knew when and how to switch tempi to avoid monotony, how to build to a climax. His favoured device of repeating a step along a diagonal not only achieved a maximum clarity of display, but created suspense. The three famous Shades solos in *La Bayadère* are good examples of such tactics. The first solo, *allegro*, is initially composed of small runs and arabesques, followed by jumps and turns that seem to wind in on themselves, and ends with a diagonal of travelling arabesques. The second, to an expansive waltz, starts with a repeated diagonal of leisurely *cabriole* jumps before switching to a mosaic of turns and beats and profile arabesques. The third, which begins slowly and speeds up, elaborates a *développé-retiré* theme, the leg raised to the side, front, back, and reaches its finale with an exciting run on point.

As every ballet-goer knows, some dances portray character or mood, like the fairy-tale *pas de caractère* in the last act of *The Sleeping Beauty*, and like the fairies' variations in its prologue, each depicting a different quality. The variation for Canari is designated by Petipa in 'The Ballet Master's Plan' as 'qui chante' (who sings): the dancer's fluttering hands alternate between miming the music's piccolo and miming a bird's wings, while her feet travel with fast, tremulous running steps. Violente's variation is 'échevelé' (unbridled) and is remarkable for its bold energy and finger-pointing motif. 'Miettes qui tombent' (Falling Crumbs) has a *pizzicato* solo with small hops on point and scattering movements of the arms.[82] Also imbued with personality is Aurora's first-act opening solo or *entrée*—a distillation of girlish freshness and charm, Petipa taking advantage of Carlotta Brianza's youth and virtuosity.

The Ballerina, Not Forgetting Her Partner

The Romantic Ballet's exaltation of the ballerina in Western Europe was a process reinforced by advances in point technique and by the popularity of women *en travesti*, a strategy famously culminating in Eugénie Fiocre's creation of the role of Franz in *Coppélia*. When reviewers were not busy ignoring male dancers, they were demolishing them, since part of the problem was a paucity of outstanding male dancers. If someone was good enough, as was Lucien Petipa, he could, in the opinion of *Le Courrier des théâtres*, certainly draw deafening applause 'and dissipate the public's prejudices, prejudices unfortunately all too justified, but which talent could succeed in destroying'.[83] Perrot and Saint-Léon, in their youth, were other exceptions. Gautier complimented Saint-Léon for bringing masculinity back to the Paris stage. 'For a very long time we have not seen, properly speaking, a male dancer in France; the disfavour into which male dance has fallen has produced a dramatic reduction in the choreography allocated to men in ballets.' In the same breath, he reproached Lucien for not pushing himself forward enough: 'Petipa himself, an elegant actor, a mime full of flame and passion, always seemed to apologize for the fire of his dancing, by devoting himself completely to the impression made by his partner. Since Perrot's retirement, Saint-Léon is the only man who has dared present dancing for the sake of dancing and he achieved a surprise success.'[84]

In Russia the male presence had always been more robust and it continued that way, so that the Moscow correspondent of the French newspaper *Gil Blas*, reviewing Petipa's *Night and Day* for the 1883 coronation gala, could write: 'One point to make here is the importance of men's roles in ballets. Men are as much the stars as women; and by the way, it is only fair to say that they dance wonderfully.'[85] Even so, Petipa was not above sometimes casting women *en travesti*. And he adhered strictly to a classical pas de deux arrangement whereby the man stood behind the ballerina: a positioning, to use the words of the French academic Bénédicte Jarrasse, that relegates the man to the status of vassal, his masculine strength at the service of the ballerina. (The Romantic Ballet, by contrast, may have extended the standard gender-equal, side-by-side protocol for character dances to more classical sequences, as indicated by Bournonville's ballets and a number of nineteenth-century prints.) It is hard to gauge exactly what men did in a Petipa ballet, given the frugality of newspaper references. But the masculine-feminine divide was certainly accentuated by the man as *porteur*. He not only supported the ballerina in her steps, but lifted her in poses which were varied enough to display her many charms and increased in complexity decade by decade. Already in 1874, Bournonville, during his visit to St Petersburg, was dismayed by these lifts, judging them acrobatic in a letter to Sergei Khudekov.[86]

The accumulated evidence suggests that, since lead roles were assigned according to strict hierarchy, they belonged to the tiny number of senior, ageing, and sometimes aged dancers. Inevitably, therefore, they were tailored to their capacities, so that the central male role often consisted largely of mime with perhaps some light partnering: the kind of skills in which Petipa himself often specialized when playing characters such as Lord Wilson in *The Pharaoh's Daughter*. Unsurprisingly, the creator of a role tended to hang on to it as long as feasibly possible, which must have been frustrating for aspiring successors. The custom in present-day companies of any number of concurrent casts for a given ballet did not exist.

Lev Ivanov, who graduated from the school in 1852, took over most of Petipa's roles. Vazem paints the portrait of a good all-rounder, polished as a classical dancer, fond of character dances, effective in mime roles. 'His talent shone with an even light, without sudden flares.'[87] In earlier decades Petipa would have been replaced not by a Russian but another foreigner: so in that sense Ivanov was a sign of change in the male ranks. He thereby became the company's leading man, although he then gradually yielded that position to the more stellar Pavel Gerdt.[88]

In the St Petersburg company, bravura classical solos and taxing lifts were not, therefore, the property of the main character. Instead, pragmatically, they were assigned to younger, more junior dancers in secondary, sometimes unnamed roles, such as Pavel Gerdt. It was the twenty-four-year-old Gerdt who danced as Adonis in the classical 'Pas de Vénus', alongside the lead ballerina in *King Candaules*, while Ivanov created the mime role of Gyges.[89] It was also Gerdt who was Kitri's partner for the classical pas de deux in the finale of the St Petersburg *Don Quixote*, not Ivanov's Basilio. And when, aged forty-four and stout, Ivanov created the role of Solor in *La Bayadère*, it was Gerdt who danced with Maria Gorshenkova's Gamzatti in the *grand pas* of the festival scene, summoning 'loud applause with the lightness and legibility of his dances'.[90]

Handsome, always elegant and expressive, Gerdt became the company's leading man in a career that spanned fifty-two years, invariably kindling admiration. Starting with the mythological *Adventures of Peleus* (Prikliucheniia Peleia) in 1876, he created the leading parts in most of Petipa's ballets, including the three Tchaikovsky collaborations, the dance demands adapted to his changing capabilities. The fact that Gerdt was also a talented actor suggests that his roles might have merged the traditionally separate functions of mime and dance up to at least the early 1880s when he was still in his thirties, his body presumably in good trim. But Natalia Roslavleva claims it was only as Rudolph in Petipa's revival of Taglioni's *La Fille du Danube* (Deva Dunaia, 1880) that Gerdt played a role that truly exploited his dual gifts, in Rudolph's mad scene blending mime with dancing. She also says that he had to give up dancing before his acting was fully able to blossom, starting with the meatily evil role of Abderahman in *Raymonda* (1898).[91] As one of his students, Vera Petipa often used to watch him in class and remembers 'how exceptionally clear-cut and expressive his gestures were, the mime of his face, the turn of his head, the movement of his back, shoulders, qualities attainable only by a great artist'.[92]

Establishing exactly what Gerdt did or did not do in a given role is impossible. It is probably fair simply to say that with Gerdt the equation was reversed for male leads: his roles were more dance than mime. But by the time he was forty-five and cast as Prince Désiré in *The Sleeping Beauty* (1890), his dance solos were judiciously short, even if he still made an unforgettable impression. Vera Petipa writes that his pas de deux with Aurora 'stood out by its sculptural outlines and the skill of his partnering, while the grace of his small dance sequences ensured they were always accompanied by applause'.[93] In 1891, Nikolai Bezobrazov, reviewing the premiere of *Calcabrino*, lamented the fact that Gerdt in the title role had renounced dance, restricting himself to adroit partnering.[94] But even partnering was apparently a strain by the time of *Swan Lake* (1895). It was Alexander Oblakov as Siegfried's friend Benno who lifted Odette in the demanding lifts of the first lakeside scene, while Gerdt mimed. And it was the future ballet master Alexander Gorsky who danced the solos of the Black Swan pas de deux.[95]

As might be expected, mime roles were highly valued in the Petipa realm. The imposing veteran star Golts, who had started as an outstanding dancer in Didelot's time, was the pharaoh in *The Pharaoh's Daughter* and Gamache in the Petersburg *Don Quixote*. Skalkovsky, reviewing his appearance as the Guardian of the Cold in *The Daughter of the Snows*, called him the King Lear of our ballet stage.[96] Timofei Stukolkin specialized in comic or grotesque parts: Quasimodo in Petipa's staging of *Esmeralda*; Lord Wilson's manservant John Bull in *The Pharaoh's Daughter*; the titular knight of the Petersburg *Don Quixote*. Felix Kshesinsky, a national-dance specialist, was also a prominent mime artist: as well as Radivoi, the Muslim-Montenegrin rival of the heroic Ianko (Gerdt) in *Roxana*, his created roles included the Nubian king in *The Pharaoh's Daughter*, Candaules in *King Candaules*, and the Brahmin in *La Bayadère*.

There was, of course, no splitting of mime and dance functions for ballerinas. Petipa expended much effort not only in creating variations for them but also perfecting their mime. According to Shiriaev, the men were usually left to themselves:

> Petipa during the staging of ballets did not like to waste time on working out the mime scenes with the men, devoting all his attention to the ballerinas. Having given the general outline of a role, he would leave it up to male artists to elaborate it independently, according to their strengths and skills. Therefore I, like many others, made a point of writing my roles in a notebook.[97]

Like all choreographers, Petipa was an avid ballerina-watcher; he also attended classes at the school to keep pace with the progress of pupils. While he created small and large parts for promising young Russians, the directorate, with a beady eye on box-office returns, was often eager for imported celebrities. After the brief ascendency of Russian ballerinas, dramatized by the rivalry of Maria Petipa and Matilda Muraveva, had come a fresh wave of foreigners in the mid-1860s. As already noted, it was for the aerial Adèle Grantzow that Petipa created the 'Jardin animé' scene in his 1868 production of *Le Corsaire*. She also danced the lead in Petipa's 1870 revival of Perrot's *Catarina* and in the 1871 St Petersburg three-act version of Petipa's own *Trilby*, which, like *Don Quixote*, had earlier been premiered as a more modest two-act ballet in Moscow (1870).

Trilby would be Petipa's last complete creation for the Moscow stage, apart from his coronation ballets. During 1869 and 1870 he had virtually headed the Moscow company; but after *Trilby*, the connection ended. Even his existing ballets were mounted by others. As first ballet master, he was kept too busy in St Petersburg.

Ekaterina Vazem

Trilby was an anachronism, based by Petipa on the same Charles Nodier novella, *Trilby, or the Gremlin of Argyll* (Trilby, ou le lutin d'Argail), that had loosely inspired the much earlier *La Sylphide* (1832) and the *Trilby* (1846) of Jean Ragaine (choreographer of *Marco Bomba*) at the Théatre de la Porte-Saint-Martin. As such, it looked back to the familiar Romantic model of solid reality confronted with the misty, flickering creatures of a parallel fantastical world. But it was by all accounts an entertaining and popular ballet, although it survived much longer (into the 1880s) in St Petersburg than Moscow. In Moscow, Petipa kept to Nodier's original Scottish setting, creating the lead role of Mary for Polina Karpakova. In St Petersburg, Grantzow was Bettli, a beautiful Swiss villager, about to be married to Wilhelm. Trilby, a gremlin or elf, played *en travesti* by a student, Alexandra Simskaya, makes mischief by bewitching Bettli, to the extent that she forgets Wilhelm. He transforms her into a dove, an incarnation that ideally suited Grantzow, who danced as if she belonged in the air, not on the ground.[98] For her and the rest of the cast Petipa created a cascade of classical dances—for birds, for roses, a waltz for elves—to music by Iurii Gerber that was melodiously danceable. A pas de trois for cocaktoos (*Tanets kakadu*) wittily played with the contrasting sizes of Maria Broshel (tiny), Alexander Pisho (stocky), and Nikolai Troitsky (lanky); the comedy of the 'Canaries' Wedding' (*Svad'ba kanareek*), danced by students dressed as eggs, won particular praise from all but one reviewer, and even the hard-to-please Vazem remembered it fondly.[99] Bettli travels to various enchanted kingdoms and the designs and stage effects were appropriately magical. According to Khudekov, the most effective was a giant golden cage which occupied the whole stage, an idea borrowed from an unnamed *féerie* at the Châtelet in Paris. When it slid open, exquisite variegated groups of bird-dancers escaped.[100]

When a year later, in 1872, Petipa created *Camargo* on Grantzow, it would be the last ballet created on a foreigner for over a decade. A fresh generation of outstanding Russians was emerging and the first of these was Vazem. Her sometimes overt antipathy to Petipa notwithstanding, she became the ballerina on whom he created the greatest number of ballets—seven, in all. A virtuoso by Russian standards, she was a *terre-à-terre* dancer, more gifted in deftly intricate steps than jumps, although she took over Grantzow's roles in *Trilby* and *Camargo*. She was not so remarkable as an actress, but she improved to the extent that in 1876 the directorate cast her in the mime role of Auber's opera *La Muette de Portici* (or *Fenella*).

Vazem's first created role was in Petipa's *Two Stars* (1871), an anacreontic one-act 'scene', which was accompanied by Pugni's last score—he died a year before the premiere—and included Alexandra Vergina as the second star and Gerdt as Apollo. Her first major created role came with the four-act *Butterfly* (Babochka,

1874), Petipa's version of Marie Taglioni's 1861 ballet, for Emma Livry, in Paris. Saint-Georges's original libretto about a maharajah's daughter, Farfalla, turned into a butterfly by an ugly witch, seems to have been considerably simplified and Offenbach's score adapted. Not for the first time, Petipa introduced broad comedy into the fantasy: the third act, set in the maharajah's palace, featured courtiers with peacock feathers and much nose-tickling, all of which, reported Skalkovsky, put the audience at a loss. For the final act Petipa transferred the action to a kingdom of fairies, among whom were the fairies of gold and silver who would famously re-appear in *The Sleeping Beauty*. He added a variation for Vazem, to a popular waltz by Luigi Venzano, in which she performed two pirouettes *renversées* on point and finished with jumps, again on point. It was a hit and became known as the 'Pas Vazem'. The character dances—Persian, Malabar, Circassian—were, in Vazem's estimation, especially effective and the performers outstanding. But Skalkovsky thought the ballet was a damp squib.[101]

It was at the end of 1875 that Vazem made her debut in *King Candaules* and des-pite her misgivings, she emerged with honour. News of Vazem's brilliance had, though, travelled before that. In 1873 she received an invitation to appear in the United States over a period of three years, but the directorate considered the trans-atlantic crossing too dangerous. In the late 1870s the Paris Opera also offered her a contract, quashed this time by the French company's territorial young ballerinas.[102]

Meanwhile, Vazem not only disliked the 1875 *Bandits*, described in the previous chapter, but the three-act *Daughter of the Snows*, also created for her, even though Skalkovsky considered her performance outstanding, one of the best roles in her repertoire. Petipa produced Norwegian, gypsy, and sailor dances for the first act, set in a port, followed by classical dances for the other acts, their quantity under-lining the slender content of the fantastical, partly allegorical libretto. Since this shared some elements with the Russian Snow Maiden folk tale and Ostrovsky's 1873 play *Snegurochka*, Petipa's ballet can be considered one of the rare exceptions of his vigorously international repertoire. Mixed into this fairy tale dimension was the story of a polar expedition. The ship is stranded in the snow, punished by the Genie of the Cold (Golts) for its impudent intrusion into his domain, while the Norwegian captain (Gerdt) is fatally enraptured by the Daughter of the Snows (Vazem), who has only ice in her heart. The ballet was premiered on 7 January 1879 at a time when the Finnish explorer Adolf Erik Nordenskiöld was still iced up in his boat near the Bering Straits.[103] If, as Skalkovsky asserts, Petipa's libretto was indeed inspired by that expedition, the tragic end of the ballet's hero was clumsy in the extreme, but didn't put a jinx on Nordenskiöld, who returned to safety in the summer.[104] However, another source, as reported in *Vsemirnaia illiustratsiia*, might have been a much earlier polar expedition led by Sir John Franklin and declared lost in 1848.[105]

Either way, the ballet had a muted reception, despite Vazem's brilliance, which was thunderously applauded, and a first-act comic dance for Stukolkin as an elderly bosun saying goodbye to his vast gaggle of fifteen children.[106] The breakdown of the stage machinery for the opening performance, bungling the transformation of a wintery landscape into summer, didn't help matters.[107] (This event apparently triggered the mental breakdown of the machinist, Ivan Legat, a member of the famous dance family.) Like Skalkovsky, Petipa blamed the economies imposed by Baron Karl Kister, Stepan Gedeonov's replacement as director in 1875. 'To renovate, to repair, to touch up,' Petipa writes, 'became the only occupation of all the ateliers, during the staging of new works.'[108] This, in Skalkovsky's words, consigned the ballet to 'the ranks of the cheap', despite the appearance of polar bears in the second act. The sublime visual potential of icy landscapes was not fully exploited, and 'the ballet's finale came out as if crumpled.'[109] The production's meagreness was made all the more obvious by the magnificent staging at the same period of a spectacle with a similar subject, *Les Enfants du Capitain Grant*, by Jules Verne and Alphonse d'Ennery at Paris's Théâtre de la Porte-Saint-Martin.[110]

Vazem's favourite role was Nikiya in *La Bayadère*, created for her benefit performance in 1877, notwithstanding that she had quarrelled with Petipa. Petipa clearly did not have a monopoly on temperament; in fact, as Vazem herself reports, Baron Kister's successor Ivan Vsevolozhsky described her as having a difficult character (*terrible caractère*).[111] In the pressured, time-limited context of rehearsals, Vazem's complaints must have seemed unbearably obstructive to a ballet master who was probably at the end of his creative tether. First she objected to the costume and solo he had given her in the third scene which ends with Nikiya's death. 'I told him that such tempos did not agree with either the costume or the music. How can one perform cabrioles in baggy trousers? Petipa, as usual, began to argue.' Eventually they agreed that Nikiya would perform slow poses, in the nature of 'a choreographic monologue addressed by the bayadère to her beloved, Solor'. Then came her dance as Nikiya's ghost in the ballet's final grand pas d'action. She felt that Petipa was bearing a grudge against her because of the previous altercation and was now deliberately giving her an 'unsuitable' variation, made up of small movements, when the spectre's appearance demanded something more imposing. 'Without hesitating, I rejected his composition.' Although the last act was proving difficult for Petipa and he was anxious to finish it that same day, he nonetheless quickly put together another variation. This was 'even less successful' and Vazem again told him 'very calmly' that she would not dance it. 'He lost his temper completely and began to shout: "I don't *onderstan'* what is needed for *yew* to *dans*. *Yew* cannot this, *yew* cannot that! What kind of talent are *yew* if *yew* can nothing *dans*?"' At which point, Vazem 'without speaking a word' gathered her belongings and left, forcing the rehearsal to stop.

The following day, as though nothing had happened, she broached the subject of the same solo. 'It seemed as if his artistic imagination had completely dried up. In a hurry to finish the ballet, he exclaimed: "If *yew* cannot *dans* anything else then do same as Madame *Gorshenkov* does".' Vazem again took this as a deliberate provocation, because the solo started with jetés and, unlike her, Maria Gorshenkova was an aerial dancer. As a counterattack, she agreed, but her jetés, she told him, would travel not from the back of the raked stage, which gave a visual advantage, but, more difficult, from the wing nearest to the footlight. 'As *yew* wish, as *yew* wish,' replied Petipa. But, because Vazem only 'marked' her dances in the studio, he had to wait for the first orchestra rehearsal to see her perform. There, 'Petipa, as if wanting to disclaim any responsibility for his pas d'action, kept telling the other dancers: "I do not know what Madame Vazem will *dans*, she never *dans* at *rehearse*".' But Vazem was 'seething inside' determined 'to teach this jumped-up Frenchman a lesson'. She 'literally flew on to the stage, even jumping over the heads of a group of kneeling dancers' and covered the space in just three leaps. Everyone applauded and Petipa came up to her and said: 'Madame, forgive me, I am a fool.'[112]

Petipa's last ballet for Vazem was *Zoraiya, the Moorish Girl in Spain* (Zoraiia, mavritanka v Ispanii) in 1881, opulently designed with four acts and music by Minkus. Khudekov counted it as one of Petipa's best ballets, although his was perhaps a slightly biased judgement as he was the librettist.[113] Similarly, Vazem's avowed fondness for it may partly be linked to its genesis: she had proposed the idea after a vacation spent travelling round Spain. She had also suggested the scene in which the hero Soleiman (Gerdt) tries to kill himself under the wheels of the wedding carriage of Zoraiya and his rival, the African chief Tamarat (Ivanov, the mime counterpart). Even so, Khudekov-Vazem biases apart, the ballet was warmly received. It followed the usual Petipa structure: Soleiman's dream, for example, evoked a classical fantasy world that contrasted with the *verismo* of the real one. Petipa, writes Vazem, produced superb classical dances in addition to *villanos, morenas, and rondenios* which alternated with Bedouin, Abyssinian, and arabic dances.[114] Unfortunately, the premiere took place just four weeks before Alexander II's assassination on 1 March, an event that halted theatre activity for six months.[115] After that, it was performed only up to 1888, Gorshenkova taking over Vazem's role. Sadly, despite Pleshcheev's prediction that *Zoraiya* was destined to occupy one of the leading places in the repertoire, it did not survive.[116]

Also in 1881 Petipa revived Mazilier's *Paquita*, adding his elaborate grand pas, pas de trois, and children's mazurka.[117] Vazem counts the grand pas as one of Petipa's masterpieces, containing a pas de deux for the ballerina and her partner, supplemented by variations for seven soloists.[118] She chose this grand pas as part of her farewell benefit performance on 16 February 1884 and it continues today as a showcase for ballerinas.[119]

Vazem was undoubtedly the company's prima ballerina—'whom Europe envies us', as Skalkovsky wrote.[120] Others favoured by Petipa were Alexandra Vergina who graduated in 1868 and Evgenia Sokolova who graduated a year later. Vergina, the first Petersburg Kitri (*Don Quixote*), was a technically weak, graceful, expressive blonde. But then she abruptly retired on marrying in 1873. Sokolova meanwhile created almost as many lead roles (six) in Petipa's ballets as Vazem. Like Vazem she was a *terre-à-terre* dancer, but she lacked Vazem's strong technique, relying instead on grace and charm, as had Petipa's first wife Maria.[121] Among the ballets made for her was the four-act *Roxana, The Beauty of Montenegro* (*Roksana, krasa Chernogorii*), which had a libretto by Khudekov and which Vazem categorizes as one of Petipa's successes.[122] According to Slonimsky, however, that success was tied to the patriotic fervour that suffused daily life during the Russo-Turkish War (1877–1878) in the Balkans.[123] Although the ballet was not widely covered by contemporary writers, its premiere on 29 January 1878, just four weeks before the end of war, elicited enormous interest.[124] The narrative contains loud echoes of *Giselle*, but also has a setting showing the Slav Montenegrins under the yoke of the Muslim Ottomans. The Montenegrin heroine, Roxana, is the victim of a spell causing her to be a human by day and a *wili* by night. She has two suitors, Ianko, a Christian, and Radivoi, a Muslim, whose rivalry leads to a nocturnal battle. No sooner has Ianko defeated Radivoi and hurled him spectacularly off a bridge, he comes to the attention of the *wilis*, and is saved only by the rays of dawn. Roxana, back in human form, asks Ianko to help her; he kills the vampire responsible for the spell, and the ballet ends with Roxana and Ianko's wedding. Hariot, Lady Dufferin, wife of the British ambassador, attended a performance in 1879. She thought the last act very pretty, with its Montenegrin costumes and dances, including one for children which was encored.[125] This must have been the exhilarating finale, performed by the school's younger pupils (the jubilant youth of Montenegro) and remembered by Alexander Benois as a brilliant, uplifting sight, with floor patterns that advanced and retreated, 'forming a circle or spreading out like a fan'. Minkus's accompanying march became a huge favourite, adopted by Alexander II as military music and still played in parks twenty years later.[126]

Other dancers coming to the fore were Maria Gorshenkova, the creator of the role of Gamzatti in *La Bayadère*, who graduated in 1876; Varvara Nikitina (1877); and Anna Johansson, Christian's daughter (1878). All these Russians, however, with the possible exception of Vazem, could not compete with the virtuosity of dancers like Grantzow and Dor, or even Ferraris who had arrived in St Petersburg in the late 1850s already accompanied by the tag 'points of steel'. The Russians might have had as much artistry, but they were not trained in bravura technique. Judging by Vazem's remarks, point work in Russia was used sparingly: 'At the end of the 1880s, when ballet in Russia had still not been seduced by the endless running about on tiptoe of a whole series of visiting Italian ballerinas, dancing on point was not accorded such priority as it was later.'[127]

The evolution of the blocked shoe clearly had far-reaching implications for female technique. Surviving evidence shows that the shoes worn by Taglioni and Elssler in the 1830s and 1840s had little reinforcement apart from darning on the outside.[128] It is likely that these dancers balanced on point for just seconds; the Romantic style, promoting the ethereal, demanded that they skim the stage rather than balance in lengthily frozen poses. Some preserved shoes show signs of inserted strips of cardboard; Maria Petipa, as reported earlier, doubled the tips of her shoes; and, by 1866, Gautier could write that shoes were strengthened externally by stitching and internally by cardboard or leather at the tip.[129] But it was the Italians who developed the art to modern standards. They replaced the point technique of the Romantic Ballet, at the service of evanescence and yearning, with 'points of steel', which announced stability, strength, and confident virtuosity.[130] And in this Russia, like Paris, lagged behind.

The Exceptional Case History of Mlada

The four-act *Mlada*, staged on 2 December 1879, has a number of unusual features. Its pagan Russian setting makes it another exception in the Petipa repertoire, hot on the Slavic-tinged heels of *The Daughter of the Snows* and *Roxana*. However, rather than being confirmation of a reborn cultural nationalism, it was merely a piece of box-office opportunism. Although the Russo-Turkish war had ended early in 1878, patriotic emotion was still high. To capitalize on the communal Slav feeling manifested by the success of *Roxana*, the directorate's attention alighted on *Mlada*.

Actually, *Mlada* had been planned years earlier by Stepan Gedeonov, who wrote the scenario while he was director of the Imperial Theatres. In this way began the complicated genesis which makes the ballet both a prototype for *La Bayadère* and, by virtue of its later premiere, its successor. Originally, Gedeonov had envisaged an opera-ballet, the music's composition to be shared out between the individual members of the so-called Mighty Handful, champions of a Russian school of classical music. Minkus, however, was given responsibility for the ballet sections: either a recognition of the specialized nature of ballet music or, more likely, an indication of the low esteem accorded to it. Given that opera-ballet was, apart from a few imports, an unusual genre in Russia, Gedeonov's choice poses the question of why. Was he, as the dance writer Iulia Iakovleva surmises, searching for a simplified equivalent to the Wagnerian ideology of a transformative artistic fusion (*Gesamtkunstwerk*), assuming he was familiar with Wagner's theories?[131]

Eventually, despairing of such an ambitious collaboration, Gedeonov switched to the idea of a ballet. The music would be composed by Alexander Serov, a leading proponent of Wagner's music. That such a prominent figure as Serov should be enlisted for a ballet suggests he might have seen a Wagnerian dimension in Gedeonov's mythological libretto, completed after the St Petersburg premiere of *Lohengrin* in 1868. He even agreed in his contract to strictures, probably imposed by Petipa, that he should unquestioningly submit to musical changes, as well as insertions by other composers such as Minkus.

The libretto put before Petipa in 1870 was eclectic and not a little tangled.[132] Gedeonov took his narrative elements and characters from Filippo Taglioni's 1839 ballet *The Shade* (L'Ombre or, in Russian, Ten'), where a love triangle unfolds amid death, ghosts, and sorcery. As in Taglioni's ballet, the heroine Mlada is actually dead before the ballet starts, killed by a poisoned bouquet of flowers. The murderer is her rival Princess Voislava who, encouraged by her father, wants the hero Iaromir for herself. Iaromir, not knowing how Mlada has died, is drawn to Voislava, thanks to a spell cast on him by Voislava's ally, Morena, Goddess of the Underworld. Although another goddess, Lada, shows Iaromir a vision indicting Voislava for Mlada's death, he is still bewitched by Voislava and torn between her and Mlada's ghost which repeatedly appears, visible only to him. Following Mlada's ghost into the night, he comes to a valley where other ghosts or Shades flit about the trees and ground. Mlada charms Iaromir and reproaches him for his unfaithfulness, but eludes him as if fearful of his touch. Suddenly an ominous noise rumbles underfoot. Taking fright, the Shades disappear, and sinister goblins and other underworld demons crawl into sight, to begin a hellish dance. Chernobog, their ruler, also appears, as does Morena, who, alarmed by the turn of events, enlists Chernobog's help in recapturing Iaromir's soul. To this end Chernobog summons figures from Antiquity: the arch-seductress Cleopatra (played by Voislava) who confronts Helen of Troy (Mlada's alter ego), in an attempt to win over Iaromir. But Iaromir remains in a state of indecision. The final scene sees Iaromir arriving at the temple, to ask the oracle for guidance. Voislava, her father, and a crowd also arrive and he is trapped, swept up into the decision to start the marriage rites there and then, until Mlada's ghost again appears. Iaromir refuses to go ahead with the marriage, at which Morena, enraged, calls forth chaos. Thunder and lightning are followed by an earthquake and flood. The temple is destroyed, but Iaromir and Mlada are reunited in a celestial apotheosis where are also gathered the deities of the Slav pantheon.

In substituting Slav myth-making for Taglioni's Indian characters and setting, Gedeonov it would seem, was not far off Wagner's Scandinavian-Germanic gods and mortals. Moreover, Iakovleva sees similarities with Wagner's 1845 *Tannhäuser* in the theme of combat between earthly and spiritual forces—Voislava being the carnal counterpart of Mlada's ghost. (This duality is paralleled by the evil goddess Morena and her beneficent opposite, Lada, prefiguring Carabosse and the Lilac Fairy in *The Sleeping Beauty*.)[133] For all its chaotic mixture, Petipa apparently liked the libretto, seeing in it exceptional opportunities for mime and action scenes, exciting stage effects, and an enormous variety of dances. His notes attest to a quantity of national dances: Lithuanian, Czech, Bohemian, Serbian, Bulgarian, Russian. The inclusion of Cleopatra and Helen of Troy in the underworld scene is certainly an unexpected, not to say bizarre, complication, but maybe Petipa didn't care since it provided a further pretext for Egyptian, Greek, and bacchanal dances.[134]

However, in 1871 Serov died and the project was shelved. Six year later, Petipa and Khudekov recycled many of the narrative components and motifs into *La Bayadère*: the dead bayadère Nikiya, killed by her rival Gamzatti; Nikiya's ghost and the Kingdom of Shades; the aborted wedding ceremony and destruction of the temple; the celestial reunion of Solor and Nikiya. All this, and *La Bayadère*'s other probable sources—Auber's opera-ballet *Le Dieu et la bayadère*, Lucien Petipa's *Sacountala*—make the ballet's genesis as complicated as that of *Mlada*.[135]

Stepan Gedeonov died in 1878. A year later, the directorate decided to resuscitate *Mlada* and enrolled the musical services of Minkus. Reviewers of the premiere judged his melodious score highly congruous; they also especially liked the Slav dances and the circle dance (*khorovod*) performed by children.[136] (The circle becomes linked to Mlada's ghost, whereas Voislava is associated with rectilinear forms.) A 'Big Dance of the Shades' (*Bol'shoi tanets tenei*) begins with Iaromir's arrival in the remote valley. As in *La Bayadère*, it features a corps de ballet dressed in white, although here the formations are circular and the corps dancers made up of students of different ages, their uneven height allowing Petipa to exaggerate effects of perspective and distance.[137] Once again, Petipa turned to Gustav Doré's illustrations for Dante's *Paradiso*. He filled the entire stage with dancers, so tightly packed they seemed welded, moving as one, which is how Karsavina remembered *La Bayadère*'s shades in St Petersburg.[138] The sheer numbers—fifty-six corps dancers (they would be much reduced for the 1896 production), plus four soloists and two coryphées—must have produced a breathtaking effect, further dramatized by the floating veils attached to the dancers' wrists and heads, their arms moving the translucent material, now stretched, now loosened like coils of ectoplasm. (Mlada's ghost, like Nikiya's, also performed a dance with a tulle scarf.) Iakovleva's essay argues that what interested Petipa as a post-Romantic was not so much the symphonic patterning of lines, currently held to be the salient feature of the *Bayadère* Shades, but the eerily atmospheric play of sculptural mass. This was enhanced by blue electric lighting which permeated the stage, like twilight thickening the air. It created shadows and sudden illuminated patches that picked out limbs and white fabric, bringing to the dancing a ghostly sculpted relief which today has been evened out of *La Bayadère*.[139]

Surprisingly, reviews of *Mlada* did not upbraid Petipa for blatantly repeating himself so soon after *La Bayadère*, nor did they seem fazed by the inclusion of

Cleopatra and Helen of Troy. On the contrary, the frenzied bacchanal which concluded this scene was such a triumph it was reproduced in engravings.[140] But for all this, and its slavophile credentials, the ballet was not a critical success. Reviewers faulted the narrative structure for being cumbersome, tangled, and sluggish. Rather than a well-paced alternation between mime and dance, each section was overextended and dance dominated. 'The new ballet,' wrote the reviewer of *Sufler*, 'is an extensive *divertissement* consisting of character and classical dances and groups.'[141] The same writer noted that in composing the roles of Mlada's ghost and Voislava, played by Sokolova and Gorshenkova respectively, Petipa concentrated on dance, not on mime: a prioritization that was inverse to Sokolova's strength as an actress and her relatively weak technique. And, for all the magnificence of the costuming, the decor and stage effects were meagre, even downright shoddy.[142] 'The valley in itself would not be so bad,' said *Sufler*, 'if the sky were not torn and you were not to see, during the whole act, the twinkling light of the gas burners through the gaps.'[143] As often, the technical staff turned to the imperial soldiers for help—except this time the result was disconcerting. What should have been a spectacular closing scene of destruction and flood was sabotaged by slipshod machinery that revealed the temple's underpinning and allowed glimpses of soldiers' legs paddling furiously under stretched blue canvas. This, followed by the 'farcical' mix of tropical flora and Slav characters for the apotheosis, stirred the audience out of its torpor into bouts of laughter.[144]

Petipa continued tinkering with the ballet after its premiere and it survived the season, followed by a revival two years later. It then resurfaced in 1892 as an opera-ballet by Rimsky-Korsakov in which the dance segments were choreographed by the deputy ballet masters, Ivanov and Enrico Cecchetti. (Petipa was struggling through the difficulties of his daughter Evgenia's death and his own bouts of illness.) This version was no more successful.

Mlada was given a third and final chance in 1896, in the form of a ballet by Petipa, using Minkus's existing music. According to *Teatr i isskustvo*, all the dances were newly staged and the decor taken from Rimsky-Korsakov's version. The result was an improvement, if not a complete success.[145] The same review deemed the infernal creatures of the underworld scene too coarse for the imperial stage, reminiscent of fairground booths (*balagany*) and popular printed pictures (*lubki*). And, certainly, the horrifying god Chernobog has echoes of the folklore antagonist Kashchei (or Koshchei) who became the subject of Rimsky-Korsakov's opera *Kashchei the Deathless* (Kashchei bessmertnyi) in 1902. Kashchei also appears in the Ballet Russes' *Firebird* (1910), in which the choreographer Mikhail Fokine evokes the furious massed dances of *Mlada*'s demonic underworld.

Gedeonov's plans might or might not have had a connection with Wagner's *Gesamtkunstwerk* principles, but Alexander Benois thought *The Sleeping Beauty* certainly did.[146] However, Petipa's *ballets à grand spectacle*, including *The Sleeping*

Beauty, didn't achieve the same synthesis of art forms; as already suggested, a closer parallel would be the grand opera genre of Auber, Meyerbeer, and others. The mix of visual splendour, stimulating variety, and dramatic continuum was simply Petipa's solution to the eternal problem of sustaining audience interest over three or four hours. 'The richer the production, the bigger the takings,' observed the reviewer of *Sankt-Peterburgskii vedomosti* about *Mlada*, notwithstanding Kister's avarice vis-à-vis the decor.[147] This attests to the growing impact of the Franco-Italian *féerie* or *ballo grande*, which increased in importance in the 1880s and will be considered in the next chapter.

The Russian-ballerina phase that started in 1873 with the departure of Grantzow would be more pronounced than the one in the 1850s–1860s: for twelve years up to 1885 there were no major foreign dancers on the imperial stage. In parallel with this, the ballerina continued to dominate, until Enrico Cecchetti's arrival in 1887 opened up new possibilities for men.

The Assassination of Alexander II

The tsar's liberal reforms were too little for the different groups of Russian revolutionaries. One of these, The People's Will (*Narodnaia volia*), mounted an all-out terrorist offensive, believing that, because of the regime's centralized structure, crucial damage could be done by just a few assassinations. They designated the emperor as their chief target and made several attempts, but time and again he escaped by sheer luck. He even remained unharmed when the dining room of the Winter Palace was blown up. But on 1 March 1881 they finally hit him, with a bomb thrown in the street. Ironically, on that same day, he had indicated he would consider a proposal whereby elected members of the public could be consulted over administrative and political reforms.[148]

A period of mourning lasting six months followed, during which the theatres were closed. Alexander III's coronation in Moscow did not take place until 15 May 1883. The French newspaper *Gil Blas* carried a lengthy report of the celebratory gala evening on 18 May which seems to have been as colourfully exotic off the Moscow stage as on, the boxes occupied by splendid Asiatic princes and dignitaries. The national anthem had a grandiose impact, played by musicians, standing turned towards the tsar, and sung by 300 singers in national dress. Parts of Glinka's *A Life for the Tsar* occupied the first half of the evening, its finale provoking great emotion for fatherland and monarch. Then, after the interval, came Petipa's *Night and Day*, to music composed by Minkus. Appropriately devoted and allegorical, it depicted the Queen of Night (Sokolova), the Evening Star (Gorshenkova), and their acolytes being supplanted by the Queen of Day (Vazem). All of nature—the flora, the fauna—was thereby revived and from the mountain slopes came all the nations of the Russian Empire to perform their national dances: Crimean, Siberian, Finnish,

Cossack, Ukrainian, Polish. The appearance of shooting stars in the night sky was apparently particularly successful, as was the sunrise, one of the most beautiful transformations the writer had ever seen, and the travelling figure of Time, suspended high above the stage on an invisible wire.[149] The ballet's closing tableau displayed an eagle on whose wings was poised the personification of Russia, the empire's dominant state, spreading a protective veil over the arts, science, commerce, and other sociocultural cornerstones, while on the horizon church domes appeared.[150] As *Gil Blas* commented with understatement: 'Through all this mythology, the allusions are, we can see, easy to understand.'[151]

Bluff in manner and built like a colossus with immense physical strength to match, Alexander III was described by contemporaries as a 'mountain of stone'.[152] In his views he was equally stone-like, the antithesis of his father, who had introduced progressive reforms early in his rule, although he had later hardened his stance. Faced with the winds of revolution, Alexander III, like his grandfather Nicholas I, reacted with repression, bringing in counter-reforms to pull back the new freedoms. The moral pillar of his rule was his former tutor Konstantin Pobedonostsev, Chief Procurator of the Holy Synod and arch-conservative who hated the industrial revolution and urban growth and wanted 'to keep people from inventing things'.[153]

Yet, in contradiction to all this, Alexander III's initiatives for the performing arts would have a far-reaching, liberalizing effect.

8

The Vsevolozhsky Reforms

*On our ballet stage, the influence of the féerie could not be dis-
played too blatantly or shown in the form of inappropriate novelties. [However], with the unlimited resources of the theatre
directorate, lavish, féerie-style production values for ballet have
long been with us; and in mounting [such] ballet-féeries, the directorate has not found it necessary to undercut the choreographic
dimension. There is also a happy side to this, recently manifested
on our ballet stage and contributing to its revitalization. This
is the fact that the directorate is recognizing the importance of
music in ballet. Entrusting the composition of ballet scores to
our leading composers, the directorate has already succeeded in
giving us several beautiful ballet scores, headed by the pearl that
is Tchaikovsky's music for The Sleeping Beauty.[1]*

The End of the Monopoly

On 17 August 1881 Count Illarion Vorontsov-Dashkov became minister of the
Imperial Court, replacing Count Alexander Adlerberg. On 2 September the ballet
season reopened, with the patriotic choice of Saint-Léon's *The Little Humpbacked
Horse*. The following day Ivan Vsevolozhsky was named director of the Imperial
Theatres.[2]

In 1881 two public theatres in Moscow were under the umbrella of the state
monopoly—the Bolshoi and Maly—and five in St Petersburg—the Bolshoi,
Mariinsky, Alexandrinsky, Mikhailovsky, and, up to its closure in 1882, the sum-
mertime Kamennoostrovsky.[3] In 1879 the directorate had acquired another, brand-
new theatre, the 1,400-seat Petersburg Maly, rented from Count Apraksinii who
had built it by the Fontanka river, close to Theatre Street. It provided a second
stage for the Alexandrinsky troupe, but in 1882 passed back into private hands.[4]
Meanwhile, the days of St Petersburg's old Bolshoi Theatre, dedicated to Italian
opera and ballet, were also numbered: the glamorous Italian opera was dismantled
in 1885, a reflection of Alexander III's nationalist leanings, and the theatre itself
closed in 1887, demolished with gunpowder for the construction of a new home

for the St Petersburg Conservatoire which remains to this day. (The Conservatoire, headed by the pianist and composer Anton Rubinstein, opened in 1862.) The ballet moved to the Mariinsky, to share the stage with the Russian opera: an unpopular change-of-address, although the ballet had been making occasional appearances there since 1880. According to Khudekov, the general feeling among balletomanes was abasement by association: Russian opera at that time was held in less than low esteem. Moreover, the wider, but shallower stage meant problems with the old Bolshoi sets, detrimental to the decorative effects of existing productions. But the Bolshoi's machinists saw things from a different angle. Roller, now retired as chief machinist, told Khudekov that for all the visual advantages provided by the Bolshoi's deep stage, the theatre's basement where the machinery was located was permanently awash with water. 'One had to marvel at the patience and stamina of the Russian "evening soldiers" who for inconsequential pay spent almost six continuous hours up to their knees in water shifting equipment.'[5] Without doubt, twenty-five years after Gautier's rapturous endorsement in his *Voyage en Russie*, the Bolshoi was in dire need of renovation and the decision to pull it down was presented as a money-saving measure. Even so, Teliakovsky, for one, considered the demolition of the city's best theatre after the Alexandrinsky to be Vsevolozhsky's greatest mistake.[6] Either way, in 1890 the Mikhailovsky's German drama troupe followed the fate of the Italian opera, although there was still a season every year during the Lent closure by a German company at the Alexandrinsky Theatre. With this came an expansion of the activities of the Russian opera and drama companies.

Alexander III and his family were, like their forebears, famously fond of theatre and attended almost daily. Although generally viewed as a period of conservatism, Alexander III's reign inaugurated fundamental reform of the theatrical status quo in the two capitals. The most visible person driving this was Vsevolozhsky, prominent not only as director of the Imperial Theatres, but also as chairman of a commission established to examine the existing monopolistic provision and initiate reforms. In these two roles, he was fulfilling the directives formulated by his superior Vorontsov-Dashkov, who oversaw everything.[7] Ironically, it had been in Alexander II's liberalizing reign that the state had tightened its grip, banning new private theatres in the two capitals in 1856 before banning private theatres altogether in 1862, although certain private ventures were permitted at the directorate's discretion. Several women, for example, with an eye on their stage careers, were able to open their own theatres, but these were short-lived.[8] Also allowed were summer entertainments outside the theatre season—fairgrounds and fairground shows, pleasure gardens, cabarets, and concerts. In this way, during the 1870s and early 1880s Mikhail Lentovsky (about whom more later) organized summer amusements, including an operetta theatre, in Moscow's Hermitage garden.[9]

However, the commission now formulated two resolutions. The first, set out in a paper to Vorontsov-Dashkov in March 1882, reaffirmed the principle that the Imperial Theatres were 'a state pedagogical institution, meeting the educative tasks of the government' and also 'a court institution [...] a constant point of contact between the tsar's generosity and the aesthetic tastes of his subjects'. The Imperial Theatres, Vsevolozhsky concluded, should retain this dual position: they must be model theatres—cultural exemplars—and equally 'brilliant institutions, corresponding to the dignity of the Imperial Court'.[10] The second resolution was that the prohibitive tax which had previously strangled scattered attempts at private entrepreneurship without special permission should be abolished.[11]

The decree ending the monopoly was signed by Alexander III on 24 March 1882. In allowing a mix of public and private, the Russian government was following the examples of other European states. It was also responding to a growing urban population that was benefitting from capitalist expansion and was avid for entertainment. Deregulation had a rapid impact on ballet: for the first time in the many decades since serf companies, ballet expanded onto other stages.

The Ballet Company of the 1880s

In 1881 the St Petersburg dancers numbered sixty-two men and twice as many women. Petipa was the ballet master and Alexei Bogdanov, the *régisseur*, having succeeded Marcel in 1873. In the 1870s the company had been overshadowed in the public's mind by the Italian opera, its popularity so reduced *Teatral'nyi al'manakh na 1875* recorded ballet performances as being only once a week and rarely twice.[12] (This was in contrast to the imperial family's own devotion to ballet.) In the winter of 1876–1877, when *La Bayadère* was premiered, performances of opera outnumbered ballet by five or six to one.[13] Vsevolozhsky's predecessor Baron Kister undermined the ballet not only by restricting performances, but by the cheese-paring economies which affected design. Cheap fabric was now used for the costumes, impacting on both appearance and ease of movement; the permanent staff of skilled stage technicians was sacked, replaced by inexperienced workers hired from job to job.[14] Italian opera notwithstanding, Vazem and Sokolova had a strong following and benefit performances were always packed occasions.[15] But by the 1880s the public had grown weary of the same ballerinas, so that *Peterburgskaia gazeta* could write in 1882 that 'the time has gone when ballerinas produced good box office.'[16] And when Vazem retired in 1884 and Sokolova in 1886 an era seemed to have passed and the situation worsened. Anna Johansson, Maria Gorshenkova (Giselle in Petipa's 1884 production), and Varvara Nikitina (Swanilda in Petipa's production of *Coppélia*, also in 1884) were admirable, but simply not in the same league. The company's male contingent, although never ballet's raison d'être, was also in decline. In 1884 there were no evident replacements for the ageing or downright elderly Johansson (sixty-seven), Ivanov (fifty), Gerdt (forty), or the character dancers Kshesinsky (sixty-one) and Stukolkin (fifty-five).[17]

Skalkovsky, writing retrospectively in 1899, saw in this tired situation an irrefutable argument for the fresh oxygen of foreign talent:

> They said that the public grew cool because ballet is not in fashion. That is not correct; such an art as dance will always please, for it is in human nature. They assured us that Italian opera was not in fashion when it was poorly attended, but it was only necessary to invite Patti, Nilsson, Masini— and opera became fashionable. [...] With ballet it is the same story; it was always fashionable in Petersburg when Taglioni, Elssler, Grisi, Grantzow, Murav'eva, and so on were dancing; but when mediocrities were dancing, even in the 1840s and 1850s, the auditorium was completely empty. [...]
>
> The claim that there were no ballerinas in Europe, even if it was backed by the ballet master's official trips abroad, was also absurd. [...] There were several excellent Italian dancers, technically far superior to Russian ballerinas of recent times, and Milan was always preparing new ones.[18]

The Arrival of Vsevolozhsky

The arrival of Vsevolozhsky promised much that was antithetical to the widely disliked Kister regime. Although all ills were blamed on Kister—and nobody was more unpopular—the institutional sclerosis of the Imperial Theatres predated him by far. Either way, Kister and Vzevolozhsky were very different characters. Kister, a former cavalry officer, was a civil servant with little personal attachment to the theatre (apart from an attraction to a member of the French drama troupe). Vsevolozhsky, a scion of the old nobility, had studied oriental languages at the University of St Petersburg, had risen in the ranks of the Asian department of the civil service, and spent two years in Paris, attached to the Russian Embassy. Paris accentuated in him a love of French culture which had started in childhood; multilingual, he preferred to speak French and even thought in French.[19] Back home, he was also known to have participated in amateur French theatrics, specializing in comic parts. He wrote plays, some of which appeared during his directorship on the Alexandrinsky stage; he was a caricaturist and costume designer, but the pinnacle of his achievement would be as the initiator and librettist of some of Petipa's greatest work.[20] Aged forty-six when he was appointed, he was the epitome of the cultured grandee, urbane, mercilessly witty, erudite, seeing the world through a pince-nez with tortoiseshell frames. 'Here was a real *barin* [Russian nobleman] with the tastes of a European and the guile of a diplomat,' Teliakovsky writes, adding to this jaundiced portrayal the accusation of cowardly deceitfulness.[21] Others, including Petipa, reported only Vsevolozhsky's self-deprecation, benevolence, and attentiveness towards everyone.[22] V. Napravnik, the son of the Mariinsky's chief conductor and composer, Eduard Napravnik, remembers how in his father's archive he found and read some 160 letters and notes from Vsevolozhsky which showed 'how all the time he had to consider the wishes of the imperial family and during the eighteen years of his directorate had to manoeuvre between what he himself recognized as beneficial for the theatres, and the endless requests, even orders, raining down on him from all quarters.'[23]

Vsevolozhsky particularly favoured the ballet and French theatre companies: an inclination that mirrored his primary concern to please the court. He was, according to Teliakovsky, rather indifferent to Russian opera and the new music of The Mighty Handful. It was therefore 'curious that fate placed him at the head of opera affairs precisely when his beloved Italian opera, with leading Italian artists, ceased to exist'. However, the promotion at the Mariinsky of operas by Tchaikovsky 'whose music pleased all as melodic music', together with Napravnik's superlative service with the Mariinsky's orchestra, enabled Russian opera 'more and more to gain the public's sympathy'. He considered the plays by Ostrovsky at the Alexandrinsky to be vulgar and uninteresting. 'But, as director and a former diplomat he avoided saying so.' He preferred the theatre's other Russian dramatists and translations of French plays.[24]

Vsevolozhsky's tenure is divided into two periods: the first, 1881–1886, when he was director of the Imperial Theatres in both St Petersburg and Moscow; the second, 1886–1899, when he was director of the St Petersburg Imperial Theatres, and another director, subordinate, was in charge of the Moscow theatres.[25] The first years were tied up with introducing the large quantity of reforms formulated by the commission. For example, salaries for artists and workers were increased and rationalized. This was a popular move, needless to say: the Imperial Theatres' rigidly hierarchical and patriarchal system had the advantages of job security and a protective indulgence towards errant individuals, but the downside had been persistently low pay. (By contrast, the fees demanded by foreign celebrities routinely pushed the theatre budget into deficit.)[26] As part of the other reforms it was decided that the standards of design, props, and stage machinery were to be improved and new storage facilities built; central libraries of music, theatre, and production materials were to be established; a photographic studio was opened; and the opera budget was increased to augment the orchestra and chorus and raise standards.[27] There were also many changes in the theatre school, one of the last ones being the closure in 1888 of the drama and opera sections. The drama section was replaced by short courses for students no younger than sixteen (girls) and seventeen (boys).[28] Opera had been taught at the Petersburg Conservatoire right from its opening in 1862, making opera training at the theatre school redundant.[29]

But although the commission had invited the public to make suggestions and the reforms looked good on paper, in practice some of them proved unworkable or counterproductive. Strangely, considering Vsevolozhsky's ballet sympathies, ticket prices for ballet were raised in 1881, outstripping those for opera and excluding many regular ballet fans.[30] For several writers, the disappointing takings for the opening of the 1882 season on 2 September with the irreproachable *Zoraiya* were the result of these over-expensive seats, not lack of interest. Even the demagogic *Little Humpbacked Horse* was poorly attended.[31] The rise in ticket prices may have been a money-saving measure to compensate for the vastly increased expenditure instigated by the reforms, although from 1882 onwards a new funding arrangement meant that the Imperial Theatres were no longer subsidized by the Court Exchequer alone, but by the State Exchequer as well. Later came a second wave of reforms (1884–1890) to curb expenditure, including the closure of the Italian opera and the German drama troupe.[32]

Vsevolozhsky's first five years were challenging. Being in charge of the Moscow operations, as well as implementing top-to-bottom reforms, must have stretched his energies to the limit. Turning his attention to the Moscow ballet, which he considered provincial to the point of Siberian, he imposed savage cuts in budget and staff. There was even talk of liquidating the company altogether—until Petipa and Lev Ivanov pointed out that the opera would always need a supply of dancers.[33] Instead the Belgian ballet master Joseph Hansen was removed, leaving the company headless (not for the first time) for several months, and on 30 September 1883 more than 100 dancers—half the company—received notification from the office of the Moscow Imperial Theatres that they were fired. Admittedly, the company had grown too large and had too many elderly dancers, while a smaller company would enable those still employed to receive higher salaries. The arrival in 1883 of the widely reviled Alexei Bogdanov, the *régisseur* in St Petersburg, did at least improve corps de ballet standards by instituting an obligatory daily class. But generally the neglect of the company continued.[34] Bogdanov's transfer to Moscow must have been a welcome relief to Petipa, if, as Khudekov claims, he was a talentless dancer who, during the twenty-six years of the all-powerful Pavel Fedorov's regime, had busied himself off stage with intrigues against Petipa.[35] (The ensuing *régisseur* vacancy was filled by Lev Ivanov.)

The crowning achievement of Petipa's collaborations with Vsevolozhsky and Tchaikovsky was yet to come, once Vsevolozhsky had ceded responsibility for Moscow and had more time for his creative ideas. For most of the 1880s the ballet repertoire provoked little excitement and, where Perrot and Saint-Léon were aided by other ballet masters, Petipa did not acquire help in St Petersburg until the appointment of Lev Ivanov as second ballet master in 1885. According to Skalkovsky, who cites the 1883–1884 season as an example, Petipa was overworked:

Unfortunately, Petipa's works at this time were weaker than his earlier, similar compositions. They demanded too much of our esteemed ballet master, especially as it is not enough for the ballet master to create a ballet; he must teach it and stage it and then supervise all the performances— an enormous labour. Apart from the new ballet [*The Cyprus Statue, or Pygmalion*], dances for the opera *Nero* [by Anton Rubinstein], which take up an entire act, and separate *pas* for various operas, Mr Petipa had to compose in the one season even more dances, for the operas *Richard III* [Gaston Salvayre] and *Philémon et Baucis* [Gounod].[36]

Programming was dominated by revivals of existing ballets, Petipa enlarging them to match current tastes: as well as *Giselle* and *Coppélia* (both 1884), he mounted productions of Saint-Léon's *La Vivandière* (1881), *Pâquerette* (1882), and, with Lev Ivanov, *Fiametta* (1887); Mazilier's *Le Diable à quatre*, or *The Wilful Wife* (1885); Dauberval's *La Fille mal gardée* (1885); and Perrot's *Esmeralda* (1886).[37] He even, against his better judgement, revived Filippo Taglioni's *La Fille du Danube* (1880), following a request from Alexander II who had fond memories of Taglioni in the central part.[38]

He also suffered the flop of three new big ballets: the four-act *Cyprus Statue, or Pygmalion* (Kiprskaia statuia, 1883), a Parisian updating of Ovid's account, with music and libretto by Prince Ivan Trubetskoi and Sokolova's last created role; the three-act *Magic Pills* (Volshebnye piliuli, 1886), a mix of opera, ballet, and spoken drama using the devices of the *féerie*, to music by Minkus; and the four-act *King's Command* (Prikaz korolia, 1886) to music by Albert Vizentini. The February premieres of *The Magic Pills* and *The King's Command* within just five days of each other, along with insufficient rehearsal time, must again have placed huge pressure on Petipa. Ballet masters abroad, wrote Skalkovsky, had a much easier life.[39] *The Haarlem Tulip* (Garlemskii tiul'pan), a three-act ballet by Ivanov, had probable input from Petipa and music by Baron Boris Fitinhof-Schell; it premiered on 4 October 1887 and fared no better.

Ticket prices together with the dimmed lustre of company and repertoire contributed to the continuing slump in ballet attendances. However, another factor soon came into play, one which would, by its challenge, eventually help to reinvigorate the Imperial Ballet.

Commercial Enterprise

With the new private theatres came the importation of more commercial, middlebrow entertainments, in particular the *féerie*. Closer attention reveals that this French generic term, describing a fairy-tale subject and its associated magical effects, encompassed any combination of opera, drama, and dance. The Paris

Opera's repertoire in the 1820s and 1830s included two *ballet-féeries*; the Carafa-Gardel-Planard *Belle au bois dormant* (The Sleeping Beauty, 1825) was an *opéra-féerie*; the Hérold-Aumer-Scribe version (1829) was a *ballet-pantomime-féerie*; Perrot's later *Filleule des fées* (1849) was also a *ballet-féerie*. The *féerie* spread to the Châtelet and other theatres, where under slightly varying labels—*ballet féerique, grand spectacle féerique*, and suchlike—it designated any large-scale fantastical production using elaborate machinery and vivid lighting. In its more balletic forms it discarded the ambitious choreography of traditional ballet. Instead it used battalions of supernumeraries, moving about in colossal patterns, at the centre of which were a few superior ballet dancers, who executed brief sequences.[40] As such, the *féerie* prefigured the chorus lines of revues and musicals; it was also an ancestor of Busby Berkeley's film choreographies. In his visits abroad, Petipa would very likely have seen these super-productions. Although in later years he would decry the genre, his own already large-scaled work, following the lead of grand opera, was increasingly influenced by it. Where, in 1868, the polyphonic final coda of *King Candaules* had been described by a reviewer as 'à la Meyerbeer', at the 1891 revival *Russkie vedomosti* compared the ballet with the *féerie*.[41] Petipa went down this new road with Vsevolozhsky's encouragement and, if the *féerie* lacked interesting choreography, that was a failing which Petipa and Vsevolozhsky sought to remedy.

In Italy the parallel flamboyant genre of *ballo grande* dominated the stage at La Scala for more than fifty years. Its best-known example was Luigi Manzotti's *Excelsior*, created in 1881, the product, like Jules Verne's novels, of an age of optimism. *Excelsior* celebrates the victory of modern enlightenment over the forces of darkness in a succession of visually exciting allegorical tableaux which map scientific and technological progress, such as the invention of electricity and the building of the Suez Canal.[42] Surviving footage, filmed in 1913, shows large groups executing repetitive movements that required little expertise. The aim was to maximize the optical effect of mass, accentuated by props such as garlands and *practicables*, allowing the performers to appear in tiers. Any virtuosic movement is the monopoly of the ballerina Vittorina Galimberti who, as the figure of Civilization, performs eye-catching, but repetitive and not particularly attractive turns and balances on point.[43]

The commercial potential of *Excelsior* was such that, a stone's throw from the Paris Opera, a monster 4,000-seat theatre was speedily built.[44] The Eden-Théâtre opened in January 1883 with a programme that started with circus acts (a specially designed ring was lowered from the flies) and continued with *Excelsior*.[45] The scale of the production—several hundred performers had been gathered from all over Italy—completely dwarfed the traditional ballets presented at the Paris Opera. Vast ensembles moved with a hitherto unseen military precision; the simplistic choreography bore little relation to the poetic, elegant, and ethereal dancing of the French school. But so great was the Paris success of *Excelsior* that it ran nightly to full houses for more than nine months.[46] This was box-office profit out of the reach of conventional ballet and the Milanese ballerina Elena Cornalba, at the centre of the stage manoeuvres, became an overnight star.

Excelsior and similar shows were soon imported to the new theatres in the pleasure gardens of Russia's two capitals. (As Tim Scholl points out, although many of these shows were actually examples of the *ballo grande*, Russians lumped them all under the name of *féerie*.)[47] Even before the end of the monopoly, in the summer months when the Imperial Theatres were closed and the affluent de-camped away from urban heat, people had flocked to these gardens, to watch fireworks, acrobats, and performing animals. Now, in the recently constructed theatres, they could see variety shows, dramas, and operettas. They could also see the *opéra-féerie The Voyage to the Moon* (Le Voyage dans la lune), created in Paris in 1875 to music by Jacques Offenbach and inspired by Jules Verne's *From the Earth to the Moon* (De la Terre à la Lune). It had two ballet sequences, the second of which, 'The Grand Ballet of Snowflakes' (*Le Grand Ballet des flocons de neige*), launched the vogue for snow scenes which Petipa took up first with *The Daughter of the Snows* and *Camargo* (the winter *divertissement*), then with the 'Dance of the Snowflakes' (choreographed by Lev Ivanov) in *The Nutcracker*.

One of the best-known new impresarios was the larger-than-life Mikhail Lentovsky, an actor-turned-director who spent his finite money recklessly. In 1882, after acquiring the leasehold of Moscow's Hermitage Garden, he opened two theatres there.[48] Three years later in St Petersburg he took over the theatre in the Livadia Garden, on the bank of the Bolshaya Nevka in the Novaya Derevnia dis-trict, and renamed it Sans Souci or, in a more literal translation, Abandon Sorrow (*Kin' Grust'*). It was Lentovsky who the same year (1885) brought *The Voyage to the Moon* to St Petersburg, having already shown it, with great success, in Moscow. For the St Petersburg season, on Skalkovsky's recommendation, he invited the Milanese ballerina Virginia Zucchi—the 'divine Virginia'.[49] (He also presented, inter alia, Gilbert and Sullivan's *The Mikado* and Shakespeare's *A Midsummer Night's Dream*.)[50] *The Voyage to the Moon* cost Lentovsky nearly 40,000 roubles, largely because of the scenery and costumes bought from the London production. A company of 245 hastily assembled dancers from Milan and Vienna was directed by Joseph Hansen, not long departed from the Moscow ballet, who staged Zucchi's two ballet scenes.[51] The dancers wore ballet skirts in the short Italian style or just tights revealing the whole leg.

Excelsior came to Petersburg two years later, running simultaneously at the theatre in the Arcadia garden and the nearby Abandon Sorrow, both now under the control of the retired opera singer Iosif Setov, Lentovsky having run out of money.[52] The Abandon Sorrow production was staged by the Scala ballet master Giorgio Saracco (responsible for the Eden-Théâtre's) and featured a twenty-year-old Italian, Carlotta Brianza. The Arcadia production was by the Italian virtuoso

Enrico Cecchetti, dancing with an equally brilliant technician called Giovanna Limido. Cecchetti had assembled the company shortly before arriving in St Petersburg and was offering a cut-down version which, being unauthorized, provoked a lawsuit from Manzotti. At the Arcadia, Cecchetti also staged his own compositions and Manzotti's more conventionally balletic *Sieba*, created in Milan in 1878, whose plot was drawn from Norse mythology.

The Italian Invasion

Zucchi was the first major celebrity to arrive as part of the new wave of Italian dancers, forever changing the way Russians danced. However, although she had a good *terre-à-terre* technique and introduced several innovative feats, her real gift lay in a uniquely naturalistic expressiveness. Already her unruly black hair, which she used to dramatic effect, and vivid face gave her an arresting presence, but this was intensified by the blazing belief in her eyes and a mime that was articulated by her whole body. Her dramatic and unconventional charisma transfixed Russian audiences and created a furore unseen since Taglioni. She was a one-off, both in the theatre and beyond it; she was outside the strict academic mould, and heated arguments broke out between those against and those who had fallen madly in love with her. Pleshcheev wrote:

> If these admirers did not throw themselves in the Bolshaya Nevka, then it was only from fear of being pulled out by Mr Lentovsky himself, who, muffled up in a Spanish cloak, often swam for the sake of pleasure to Felicien's restaurant, reminding us of a sea-lion from the zoological garden.[53]

The circumstances of her Russian debut on 6 June 1885 were inauspicious: at thirty-six she was well into balletic middle-age; her brief dances didn't amount to much choreographically; the corps de ballet had yet to arrive from London; and the Abandon Sorrow (a former hay barn) was a far cry from the elegance of state theatres. It had a small, poorly carpentered stage and imperfect sightlines.[54] Yet Alexander Benois, a fifteen-year-old boy at the time, remembered Zucchi's mesmerizing performance at a pitifully attended performance; then he remembered how, on his return to St Petersburg six weeks later, he found the theatre packed night after night.[55]

Other productions followed with Zucchi and another Italian, Maria Giuri, at the same theatre. These included a much-abbreviated version of *Brahma*, an inferior but popular ballet created by the French choreographer Hippolyte Monplaisir at La Scala, Milan, in 1868. This was Zucchi's first opportunity to reveal to the St Petersburg public her supreme talent as a *tragedienne*; her performance reportedly reduced spectators to tears and on one occasion caused two ladies to faint.[56]

In this way, foreigners on the new stages revived the interest in ballet. Meanwhile the 'somnolent' state ballet was, as Skalkovsky saw it, 'stagnating after the departure of Grantzow and, with the retirement of the best soloists and absence of new talent, gradually managing to drive away the public and appeal only to a small circle of *papas*, little daughters and aunties'.[57] Skalkovsky was Zucchi's self-appointed guardian and he was lobbying hard for her—'the leading mime artist in Europe'—to be invited to the imperial stage.[58] (He was, according to Khudekov, largely responsible for her Petersburg success.)[59] He argued that she could show the company's artists just what the art of mime was; he even claimed that she could jolt out of his rut 'our ballet master' who 'had aged and, without the necessary stimulus, was in decline'. But he also knew there were opposing forces—among the more territorial dancers scenting competition and unaccustomed, these days, to guest artists, and among the management for whom 'pleasing the public has for long been the greatest crime'. The management, he said, was being duplicitous and facing 'the tricky task of having a ballet without ballerinas'.[60] However, the truth is, Vsevolozhsky had long been concerned by poor attendances. He had, in a report to Vorontsov-Dashkov, suggested the remedy of inviting foreign celebrities, but this came to nothing. On the other hand, he was unconvinced by Zucchi, fearing that her spontaneity and unconcern for academic rigour might not fit into the decorum of the Imperial Ballet. Petipa was of the same mind. She was, in his words, 'an unbridled Italian virtuosa who could not get an invitation from the Paris Opera'.[61]

All this was swept away by the imperial family who, having heard of Zucchi's successes, invited her to appear at the Krasnoe Selo summer theatre. She danced a few excerpts from *The Voyage to the Moon* and won over the illustrious audience. Not only were Petipa and Vsevolozhsky forced to reconsider, but so were those dancers who had even threatened strike action. The ballerina Varvara Nikitina had the courage to declare herself in favour of Zucchi, an attitude that was gradually adopted by some of the more intelligent dancers, seeing in Zucchi an opportunity to study her technique at close quarters. On 4 September Zucchi gave her final performance at the Abandon Sorrow and signed a contract with the Imperial Theatres for sixteen performances between December 1885 and March 1886.[62]

She was scheduled to perform *La Fille mal gardée*. However, because of an injury sustained by Sokolova she agreed to an earlier date, 10 November, in *The Pharaoh's Daughter*, requiring her to learn the role of Aspichia in less than a fortnight. Petipa, who as a classicist expected a certain reserve, despaired at her raw impulsiveness and dishevelled hair; Zucchi, for her part, try as she might, could not control herself.[63]

Her debut at the Bolshoi (the theatre's last season before closing) was sold out within a few hours; her performance was unlike anything the Mariinsky audience had ever seen and divided the critics. Some judged severely her unconventional style, her poor elevation, and schooling. But it was clear that she was a unique mime artist. Olga Racster reports an anecdote about how Zucchi's concern for realism provoked a brush with Petipa after the performance. In the scene near a river where Aspichia is chased by a lion, Zucchi had prepared for her entrance by tearing off her headdress and disarranging her costume. Petipa was horrified.

'How could you, a princess, think of appearing before the audience in such an untidy state?'
'Untidy, why not?'
'Where was your crown?'
'In the water, of course. Where else would it be?'
'But you are a princess. You ought not to be without it!'
La Zucchi's eyes twinkled.
'My crown I lost in the water, and I can tell you this, M. Petipa, had you been pursued by a lion, you would have lost not only your crown, but your trousers too!'[64]

Zucchi, nonetheless, would have found in Petipa a ballet master unequalled elsewhere, an artist unusually sensitive to the possibilities of each dancer. And, despite his concern for decorum, Petipa probably found in Zucchi a dancer who corresponded to at least part of his vision of dance. 'He hated soulless dancing, however perfect the technique. In Zucchi he had a wonderful dancer and an actress of exceptional power.'[65]

On 15 December Zucchi appeared in the premiere of Petipa's staging of *La Fille mal gardée*, the evening also celebrating Gerdt's twenty-five years of service. Here she had more opportunities than in *The Pharoah's Daughter* and the role of the peasant girl Lise was especially suited to her demi-caractère style. Her vivid portrayal left an imprint on future ballerinas in the role. Despite her un-steely points, even the conservative critic Bezobrazov was delighted, impressed by her double turns *en dehors* and other *tours de force*, as well as her grace and expressive face.[66] Benois remembered how in the second-act duet every step seemed to be a young girl's declaration of love, and how her sincerity was such that people wept, and an old family friend, the sculptor Aubert, had to retire to the *avant-loge*, to have a good cry—'his tears coming down in streams and choking him'.[67] Gerdt, in his address of thanks at the end, declared that ballet knew no national boundaries, at which Zucchi threw her arms impulsively round him and kissed him. Such an embrace had never been seen before on the imperial stage. Guest in his biography sees it as a personification of the coming together of two schools, from which would develop the Russian style of the twentieth century.[68]

Zucchi opened a floodgate to Italians on the imperial stage, dancers famous for a technical brilliance which she did not quite possess. In 1887, Emma Bessone, who had danced in Milan, London, and America, made her Russian debut in April; Elena Cornalba, in December. Later would come ballerinas such as Luigia Algisi, Antoinetta Dell'Era, Carlotta Brianza (on whom Petipa would create *The Sleeping Beauty*), and finally Pierina Legnani. Arguably the greatest and certainly the most durable of the Italians, Legnani became the company's *prima ballerina assoluta*, lasting eight seasons (1893–1901) and accumulating an enormous repertoire. Petipa clearly liked working with her; he created most of his new ballets on her; and conducted a friendly correspondence with her when she was abroad.[69]

Like Zucchi, two of these—Dell'Era and Brianza—had been appearing at the garden theatres which were tempting ballet fans to forgo their summer vacations. In this new environment, the Imperial Theatres were not above poaching talent originally spotted by private impresarios. (This practice would be famously applied to the opera: it was the railway magnate Savva Mamontov's Russian Private Opera which brought Fedor Chaliapin to the notice of the Imperial Theatres.) Cecchetti's garden theatre performances, in which he was causing a stir with his never-ending pirouettes and gymnastic tricks, also prompted an invitation for himself and his wife Giuseppina to the Petersburg imperial stage, although he had already danced with the Moscow company during the 1882–1883 season.[70]

These and many other Italian dancers would have a profound impact on Russian ballet—more profound than that of previous visitors, even Marie Taglioni in the 1830s–1840s. Actually, the Taglionis were émigré Italians—Marie herself was born in Stockholm. But her successors were products of remarkable training centres in Italy, one of the best known being the school at La Scala, Milan, directed from 1837 to 1850 by the great teacher and theoretician Carlo Blasis. His method created brilliant but elegant and expressive technicians, known for their exciting and varied turns, their speed, aplomb, and—in the case of ballerinas—their prioritization of point work. Some of the first generation of post-Romantic celebrities were his pupils: Fanny Cerrito, for example, Amalia Ferraris, and Carolina Rosati. But it was the Italian wave of the 1880s and 1890s—Brianza, Legnani, Emma Bessone, Maria Giuri, Giovanna Limido, and Adelina Rossi—which shook up the Russian status quo, arriving when they were not, for the most part, in the autumn of their careers, unlike earlier visitors.[71]

The Imperial Ballet had been in isolation for a dozen years, cut off from visiting foreigners able to show the newest developments in technique. Legnani's Russian debut in the new Ivanov-Cecchetti-Petipa *Cinderella* on 5 December 1893 jolted both company and audience. Not having appeared anywhere else in Russia, little was known about her. At the first rehearsal her unpromisingly dowdy, humble appearance meant that the shock was even greater when she started dancing. She executed *fouettés*, the turns in which the raised leg whips round, and repeated them at *Cinderella*'s premiere.[72] Where Bessone had performed fourteen *fouettés* in *The Haarlem Tulip*, Legnani, in *Cinderella*'s final act, trumped her with thirty-two. (She famously inserted the same number in *Swan Lake*.) She achieved this without travelling from her spot—even more difficult—and as an encore managed another twenty-eight.[73] Her Russian colleagues, starting with Matilda Kshesinskaya, lost no time in putting themselves through blood-and-sweat marathons to do the same.

Legnani was a pupil of another Milanese teacher, Caterina Beretta, who in 1877 had briefly been invited by the St Petersburg company as *maîtresse de ballet* and in 1879 opened her own studio in Milan. (Later, 1905–1908, she headed the school at La Scala.) Not only did Petipa's daughters Liubov and Vera go to study with her during the summer recess, so did Anna Pavlova, Olga Preobrazhenskaya, and Tamara Karsavina, all galvanized by their Italian rivals.[74] Where Blasis had always perceived technique as a means to artistry, Beretta concentrated on muscular strength and endurance. As such she provided an appropriate supplement to the graceful Russian school. Karsavina describes Beretta's teaching:

> The methods of Beretta were those of the Italian school, which does not care for individual grace of movements, but is implacable as to correctness of *attitudes* and *port de bras*. Exercises were set in the systematic pursuit of virtuosity; the class was forcible, not a second of rest allowed during the whole bar practice. The result of it for me was a considerable degree of endurance and amplitude of breath. [...]
>
> I stayed two months with Signora Beretta; at parting she embraced me fondly and congratulated me on my progress. I had undoubtedly improved considerably under her tuition; my jumps were higher, my 'points' were stronger, and my general standard of precision had improved beyond measure.[75]

Russian male dancing needed even more re-energising, and that was kindled by Cecchetti, the son of dancers, who had trained in Florence and became famous at La Scala. On 4 November 1887, when he made his debut on the St Petersburg imperial stage in *The Haarlem Tulip*, dancing a classical pas de deux with Varvara Nikitina, he was already aged thirty-seven. Even so, his stamina and virtuosity caused a sensation not elicited since Louis Duport nearly a hundred years earlier. As Shiriaev writes, male dancing can be divided into two periods: before Cecchetti and after Cecchetti.[76]

> At first glance nobody would have said that here was a ballet dance-soloist: he was not young, not too well built, stocky, even clumsy in appearance. However in dancing all these defects completely disappeared. Cecchetti vividly showed us the eye-catching art of the grotesque dancer, a performer of steps which we artists had not dreamed of [...] only the

strictly classical French school of male dance was accepted among us. Its chief representative and loftiest exemplar—the *premier danseur* P. A. Gerdt conquered spectators with softness, an elegance of movement, but he was devoid of virtuosity: in his dances there was not even a hint of *tours de force*. Gerdt was the measure by which our other dancer-soloists were judged.

Cecchetti brought to us a whole range of effective and difficult, almost acrobatic dance movements from Italy. His specialities were endless big pirouettes, often in thirty-two bars of music, double turns in the air with a landing on one leg, and big pirouettes during which he, without stopping, transferred the position of his leg from a side extension at 90° (*développé* [?]) to an *attitude*, and then finished in arabesque. However, sometimes he returned at the end of the pirouette to the initial pose. [...]

Big pirouettes [...] poured forth from him, as if from a horn of plenty. You could call him the King of Pirouettes. I remember one occasion when, in the ballet *The Vestal*, finishing his variation with pirouettes, he slipped and fell. The public broke into applause and demanded an encore. Angry with his clumsiness, Cecchetti, repeating the variation, executed its initial two or three jumps and immediately switched to pirouettes, varying them in different ways, now *à la seconde*, now in *attitude*, now in arabesque, and so on. Only this time all in all he executed up to one hundred pirouettes![77]

Supporters of tradition, like Khudekov, saw just tricks with little aesthetic value.[78] At the theatre school, the boys' section was under the influence of Petipa, with whom the other teachers invariably agreed. It was he, along with Johansson, who upheld the strict canons of the old French style which judged harmony, not athleticism to be all-important.[79] Shiriaev elaborates further:

Softness, smoothness, grace of movement, a cold, sculpturally finished style of performance were instilled in the students. The steps studied were very simple: *assemblés*, jumps, *développés*, turns, *ronds de jambe, entrechats, cabrioles, petits brisés*. Turns in the air were only exceptionally allowed—for specific dancers, displaying a special facility. So, my school fellow Platon Karsavin (father of the famous ballerina Tamara Karsavina), a very strong dancer, did these turns, and he also did pirouettes softly, calmly, smoothly.[80]

Even so, and notwithstanding that he was a ballerina's choreographer, Petipa immediately exploited Cecchetti's outstanding prowess. On 30 November 1887 he inserted a special pas de deux for Zucchi and Cecchetti in *The King's Command* called 'The Fisherman and the Pearl' (*Le Pecheur et la perle*) in which the Cecchetti casts his fisherman's net and he catches Zucchi, the pearl.[81] For the premiere on 25 January 1889 of *The Talisman* Petipa made the character-part of Hurricane

(*Uragan*) for Cecchetti, full of airborne turns and extraordinary jumps.[82] And on 24 November 1891 he gave Cecchetti full rein in the revival of *King Candaules* to show off his superlative partnering skills with Carlotta Brianza in the 'Pas de Vénus' and perform a variation of astonishing boldness.[83]

Cecchetti was also an intensely musical dancer: during all his incredible feats he never strayed from the music. He would leave an important mark on Russian ballet, still evident today in *The Sleeping Beauty*'s so-called Bluebird pas de deux. As the Bluebird he famously danced several sequences of flying beaten steps, including a solo diagonal of *brisés volés*. Even today, this stamina-sapping evocation of a fluttering, soaring bird defeats all but the most athletic of dancers. It is probable that here, as in the other roles mentioned, Cecchetti was responsible for at least part of the choreography. He was also a mime and the creator of *The Sleeping Beauty*'s Carabosse, for which role he devised a long passage of codified mime in the Prologue, so that, unusual for a man, he appeared in the ballet as two opposites—classical dancer and mime. The Soviet opposition to mime meant that this aspect of Carabosse's role was abbreviated in twentieth-century productions. However, it has been preserved in the Royal Ballet's version, where it appears with a wonderful graphic vividness, although it is impossible to know just how authentic it is. Krasovskaya calls Cecchetti's mime 'garish' and says it did not concord with the style of his Russian colleagues. Shiriaev agrees that it was rather coarse and close to caricature. Benois provides a more detailed assessment: 'Cecchetti's ardent southern temperament was perhaps a trifle out of tune with the severe *bon ton* of the imperial stage—as had also been Zucchi's. Now and again there would burst forth from Enrico something of Truffaldino and Pulcinella. But [...] in the role of the terrifying yet comical witch Carabosse, those traits were only an asset, as they helped to make him all the more alive and convincing.'[84]

Reacting like the company's ballerinas, the men tried to emulate Cecchetti's gymnastic displays either by imitation or by seeking out his guidance. One of these was Georgii Kiaksht, who spent day and night practising. He was the first to dance the Bluebird after Cecchetti, who taught him the role. Without epilepsy and alcoholism he might have had a notable career ahead of him.[85]

Shiriaev also caught the enthusiasm. When Petipa revived *Mlada*, he allowed Shiriaev as the Fool to beef up his dance with dangerous jumps. The solo, recorded on film, always had a big success.[86] But Shiriaev remembered: 'Petipa, sitting, as was his custom during a ballet, in the first stage-left wing, habitually turned his chair and back to the stage, so as not to see me break a leg. [...] The old ballet master turned out to be percipient. On tour in 1912 in London, I really did break my fibula in this dance and spent a month and a half in Charing Cross Hospital.'[87]

This new male generation became the next teachers and their pupils included Vaslav (*Vatslav*) Nijinsky, born in 1889. Nijinsky's first, much-loved teacher was Sergei Legat who, like his brother Nikolai and like Nijinsky's subsequent teacher

Mikhail Obukhov, was greatly influenced by Cecchetti.[88] But, of course, Nijinsky's rare talent was also genetic, inherited from his dancer-father Foma, particularly 'the ability to linger or hover in the air and then drop down at will, either softly and gently or as hard and fast as a stone'.[89] Nijinsky was a sublime freak and news of him spread like wildfire. The directorate of Imperial Theatres would have had him graduate a year early in 1906, had his mother not voiced her opposition.[90]

In addition to his talents as dancer and mime, Cecchetti was an exceptionally strong partner, 'a rare cavalier', as reported by *Peterburgskaia gazeta*, especially since supporting ballerinas 'is necessary in these days of modern technique, and not easy'.[91] But even before his arrival, pas de deux work, as briefly noted in the previous chapter, was evolving. In earlier times partnering was fairly simple, with straightforward supports and lifts where the ballerina stayed mostly in the same position. But now on stage it was being elaborated to include sequences where the ballerina was thrown or moved in the air, changing from one pose to another. This prompted the introduction at the school of specialized classes, taught by Gerdt, not long after Shiriaev's graduation in 1885.[92]

Wise old Petipa did not allow his head to be turned by the new 'leg-breaking feats', as Vazem called them.[93] Bravura moves for their own sake were what he denigrated as circus acrobatics. He probably gritted his teeth when Legnani was allowed to introduce her *fouettés* on the imperial stage. But presented with a *fait accompli* of such commercial appeal, he adapted these new steps in such a way as to extend the possibilities of classical dance without betraying his precepts of taste, grace, and expressiveness.[94] And certainly the *fouettés* in *Swan Lake* could be seen, by their mechanical brittleness, as an expression of Odile's evil supernaturalism.

As always, Petipa was guided by the qualities of the dancers before him; his aim was to show them to the best advantage. But perhaps he was affected by a lingering ambivalence towards Zucchi because he broke this rule in *The King's Command*. The ballet had a preposterous libretto taken from Delibes's comic opera *Le Roi l'a dit* (The King has Spoken) and its action was transferred from the France of Louis XV to medieval Spain, allowing Petipa to indulge his penchant for Spanish dances. Although Zucchi was celebrated for being Zucchi, and, the premiere being her benefit, she was showered with gifts of flowers and glittering jewellery, the consensus seems to have been that her talents as a dancer and especially a mime were given little scope in the role of Pepita, a kind of female Figaro.[95] Overlong and set to Vizentini's potpourri of melodies by Delibes, Auber, Massenet, and others, the word 'fiasco' was in the air.[96] Even so Petipa's choreography revealed a prompt response to the developed point work of the Italians and, for the first time, several Russian dancers were allowed to attempt similar feats.[97]

While Petipa was prepared to bow to the inevitable and absorb the new fashions, the other side, doubtless at his urging, began to meet him halfway. Carlotta Brianza made her debut on the St Petersburg imperial stage in *The Haarlem*

Tulip, where she also, as Khudekov reports, created a furore with sweeping *jetés en tournant*. However, she was the first to incorporate elements of the Russian style:

> When she was criticized for the extreme angularity and brittleness of her dancing, she tried to get rid of these characteristic defects of the Milanese school through intensive exercise. And in fact her work was rewarded by success. She introduced into her performance greater softness, roundedness, and pliancy, that is, those very features that are in general intrinsic to representatives of the Russian school. Her technically perfect dancing gained much, because she paid careful attention to the graceful Russian ballerinas, who never allowed themselves any inartistic deviations from the classical precepts of choreography.[98]

Legnani, on the other hand, already had that artistic sensibility, which is perhaps why Petipa liked working with her so much. 'Her movements were smooth, rounded, and completely feminine; they never disturbed the general harmony of her agreeable silhouette,' Khudekov writes. He jokes that, being always at one with the music, her extreme musicality could have earned her the name 'the choreographic chronometer'. She devised many new *tours de force*, performed without the slightest sense of effort, as if for fun, and without deviating from clarity and classical correctness. Khudekov attributes the success of *Cinderella*, a joint effort between Petipa (who worked out the general plan and production details), Lev Ivanov, and Cecchetti, exclusively to her. She was, he says, the last of the Italians and the virtuoso miracle of the nineteenth century.[99]

Petipa created many of his finest ballets with Italian ballerinas. While he may have felt doubts, the Italians gave fresh life to the St Petersburg ballet with his complicity. Their new, hard-edged bravura injected excitement, but it was tempered by the grace and expressiveness of the old French school. For this, Russian ballet was indebted to Petipa—for, on the one hand, his savvy recognition of what is popular, for, on the other, his understanding of what constitutes serious art. This is the style, exciting yet refined, that produced the outstanding generation of Anna Pavlova, Tamara Karsavina, and, a little later, Olga Spessivtseva—as well as, of course, Vaslav Nijinsky, since male dancing was also transformed. Mediated through Diaghilev's Ballets Russes, it had an enormous impact on Western audiences; in Russia it laid the foundations for Soviet ballet.

The Féerie *in Petipa's Ballets*

To the grand opera parallels of his big ballets, Petipa added elements of the even bigger-scale, visually magical *féerie*. From the mid-1880s, under Vsevolozhsky's stewardship, the process of *féerization* accelerated in Russia. In Moscow, in

February 1890, the new ballet master José Mendez's first ballet, *India*, epitomized European theatre fashion with dance numbers which were gaudily spectacular but devoid of narrative sense[100] But even before that, in December 1887, his predecessor Alexei Bogdanov had brought, from the unlikely crucible of the imperial Petersburg stage, a *féerie* to the Bolshoi. This was *The Magic Pills* and it had been staged by the Petersburg directorate on 9 February 1886, to mark the reopening of the Mariinsky Theatre after its refurbishment as the home of ballet and opera. *The Magic Pills* was not just ballet or opera with *féerie* components, but the full *féerie* package. The directorate pumped money with eyes closed to achieve the most sensational costumes, designs, and transformations and, although essentially aimed at children, the production became the talk of St Petersburg. Its scenario was based on *The Devil's Pills* (*Les Pilules du diable*), a *pièce féerique* by Ferdinand Laloue, Anicet Bourgeois, and Clément Laurent, premiered in 1839 in Paris and adapted in 1847 for the Alexandrinsky. This new version, split into three acts and thirteen scenes, incorporated dialogue, song, and dance to music by Minkus and followed the *féerie* strategy of excitingly varied locations, starting in a pharmacy and moving on to settings such as a Madrid square, the crater of a volcano, and the bedroom of a sorcerer. The narrative connections were unclear: the crater, for example, was a puzzle—'not one geologist present in the theatre could have explained the reasons for its sudden appearance.' But it was stunning, the theatre's huge stage 'a complete sea of fire'.[101]

Three separate scenes were dedicated to ballet, featuring the entire company. In the 'World of Amusements', male and female dancers embodied different games: croquet, draughts, knucklebones, chess, shuttlecock, and more. Although this ballet scene had already been staged the previous year by Hansen at the Abandon Sorrow as part of an *opérette-féerie* called *The Golden Apples* or *Les Pommes d'or* (Zolotye iabloki), Petipa's version worked wonderfully.[102] Several dozen female dancers, costumed (by Vsevolozhsky) as dominoes, lay on the stage in domino patterns, while thirty-two dancers representing cards were also spread out as in a game. Petipa choreographed a dance for a spinning top, performed by the young soloist Zinaida Frolova; the multicoloured ribbons, stitched to the bodice of her costume, produced a variegated blur as she whipped round, until, slowing down, she came to a stop by falling on to her side. Most admired, though, was the scene called 'The Kingdom of Laces' (*Tsarstvo kruzhev*), where, as described by 'Bukva' (Ippolit Vasilevskii) in *Russkie vedomosti*, the stage was hung with enormous swathes of delicate lace, now pale pink, now blue under flickering electric light. A hundred dancers surged into view, creating the effect of clouds of lace, each successive group led by a ballerina who, in a *ballet des nations*, performed a classical variation with national dance motifs linked to the origins of her lace— Belgian, English, and so on. 'Bukva' thought the visual magnificence unrivalled by anything he had ever seen in either Paris or London.[103]

For Petipa, subordinating ballet to a visual entertainment between dramatic scenes must have seemed a task akin to composing ballet scenes for opera. Actors of the Alexandrinsky Theatre performed the chief roles. But, for the *Teatralnyi mirok*, those sections were tedious, since the actors could make nothing of their colourless roles. The hero of the evening, the writer said, was the ballet master Petipa.[104] By now references in the press to Petipa were almost invariably accompanied by the epithets 'our gifted ballet master' or 'our venerable ballet master'. As early as 1872 he was considered 'one of the best and most talented choreographers and ballet masters in Europe' and ten years later he was 'the most talented and indisputably the best'.[105] Petipa's ballets might at times be criticized for their weak narratives or excessive length, but it was rare for his actual choreography to receive anything but praise. Over and over reviewers refer to the richness of his invention, the beauty of his group patterns, the variety of his individual dances, his unerring taste. The uniqueness of his talent shone even in less balletically rewarding contexts like *The Magic Pills*.

That said, *The Magic Pills* was a one-off, probably to Petipa's relief. The experiment taught the directorate that a straight importation of the *féerie*, where scenic effects overwhelm the choreography, might create a stir and be welcomed by the audiences of commercial theatres, but in the long term it would not satisfy the audience of the Imperial Theatres. The future of the St Petersburg ballet lay in something else.

That something else was classical ballet, incorporating *féerie* elements, but retaining the integrity of its core identity. *The Magic Pills* was followed a few days later by the four-act *King's Command*, with Zucchi; then came *The Haarlem Tulip*, the revivals of *Esmeralda* and *Fiametta*, and on 17 February 1888 *The Vestal* (Vestalka). It was with *The Vestal* that Petipa's ballets began to enlarge their already large scale—'*The Vestal*,' wrote one reviewer, 'has turned out bigger than the biggest of our ballets, *The Pharaoh's Daughter*.'[106] Size apart, though, it seems that *The Vestal*, with its muscular, historically rooted narrative, did not otherwise fit the *féerie* genre and was not advertised as a *ballet-féerie*. Others, based on fairy tales or fantasies, would be: *The Sleeping Beauty*, *The Nutcracker*, and *Bluebeard* (Siniaia boroda).[107] (*The Magic Pills* was given the reverse-designation of *féerie-ballet*.)

The *féerization* of ballet, together with its Italianization, was a commercially driven policy, thrust onwards by Vsevolozhsky. The final change instigated by his regime, however, was an artistic one with a nationalist subtext, and it was aimed at ballet music.

Music Reform

Ludwig Minkus (1826–1917), from Vienna, came to Russia in 1853 to take up a post as conductor of Prince Nikolai Iusupov's serf orchestra. By 1861 he was a solo violinist in the Moscow Bolshoi Theatre orchestra; by 1864, he was Inspector of the Moscow orchestras and had already composed ballet scores for Blasis and Saint-Léon. In 1866 he collaborated with the young Delibes on Saint-Léon's *La Source*, premiered in Paris.[108] The 1869 *Don Quixote* marked his first composition for Petipa and, despite alleged bouts of laziness, provoked perhaps by overwork and depression, he went on to provide Petipa with thirteen further scores, in addition to arrangements of existing music.[109] In 1872 he was appointed ballet composer, following Pugni's death.

Fourteen years later the post was abolished, as part of Vsevolozhsky's intention to improve and diversify musical standards by using non-specialist, preferably Russian, composers. 'Improve', however, is a problematic word in this context and at the time the new orientation provoked much debate. It is easy to belittle nineteenth-century ballet music as unambitious. Its composers were part of a tradition where music had to be written at great speed and be subservient to the ballet master's instructions. It had to be sonorously descriptive and, above all, danceable (*dansante*), its metre and melody clearly signalled to dancers who already had their own difficult and painful bodies to struggle with. Minkus was a master of all this. A reviewer of his farewell benefit on 9 November 1886 wrote the following summary: 'An enormous variety of melodies, brilliant orchestration, and, chiefly, consistency of musical style were guaranteed every time Minkus's name was placed on the poster.'[110]

There was now, however, an awareness of greater possibilities, based most probably on the foreign examples of Adolphe Adam, Léo Delibes, and Édouard Lalo. (Lalo composed the music for Lucien Petipa's 1882 ballet *Namouna*.) Closer to home, there was also the example of *Swan Lake*, premiered in Moscow on 20 February 1877, just one month after Petersburg's *La Bayadère* and its *musique dansante* by Minkus; *Swan Lake* had been the fulfilment of Tchaikovsky's long-held ambition, at odds with other leading composers, to write ballet music.[111] Rather than being subservient, ballet music, it was now proposed, could be an artistic creation in its own right, interesting enough—to paraphrase Balanchine's famous dictum—for any ballet-phobe to close their eyes and just listen. Choreography and music would join as two equals, the one enhancing the other.

The Haarlem Tulip, premiered on 4 October 1887, was, as noted by Riccardo Drigo, the first manifestation of Vsevolozhsky's reformist agenda.[112] As previously mentioned, the precise authorship of the choreography for this three-act ballet is unclear: Ivanov certainly wrote the libretto, but the staging is attributed to Ivanov and Petipa.[113] The composer, though, was without doubt Fitinhof-Schell. Pleshcheev calls the music 'very successful' and Skalkovsky considered it promising as a first attempt, lively and well-suited for dancing, with a particularly attractive violin solo for Leopold Auer. However, other reports are dismissive: 'boring'; 'little waltzes and galops'; 'a deft compilation of other men's things';

'it does not differ all that much from standard ballet music.'[114] These phrases, together with the qualified enthusiasm evinced by the musically conservative Skalkovsky, suggest that, if Vsevolozhsky's intention had been to initiate a new form of music, it was not realized with Fitinhof-Schell's conventional ballet score. Accordingly, Fitinhof-Schell did not trigger the polemic that Mikhail Ivanov, the composer of *The Vestal* did, four months later.

Petipa's previous collaborations with living ballet composers other than Minkus and Pugni were few. They were with theatre insiders: Iurii Gerber, music director of the Moscow ballet (for *Trilby*), and Vizentini, director of the Italian opera in the early 1880s (*The King's Command*). Or they were with aristocrats: Fitinhof-Schell, who was sufficiently esteemed to be chosen also for *Cinderella*; Petr, duke of Oldenburg (additional music for *Le Corsaire* and other productions); and the Paris-based prince Trubetskoi. None of these, insiders or aristocrats, seem to have pulled ballet music out of its stereotypical mould. Skalkovsky lays the blame for the flop of *The Cyprus Statue, or Pygmalion* on Trubetskoï's libretto and 'wretched' music, which by comparison made Minkus appear as a colossus, and lambastes the directorate for saddling Petipa with the choreography. For the premiere, the well-off gentry were not prepared to dig into their pockets for seats, preferring to stand, crammed like sardines (actually *seledki*, herrings), in the boxes that had been made free for the occasion. This produced a particularly curious impression, as the rest of the auditorium was virtually empty.[115]

The composer of *The Vestal* was Mikhail Ivanov who, rather than belonging to any ballet *côterie*, admitted that he had rarely attended ballet and had little idea of what was required.[116] He had briefly taken private composition lessons with Tchaikovsky and was a music critic with the St Petersburg newspaper *Novoe vremia*.[117] As such he was considered highly influential and probably exploited this to promote his creative ambitions. But most important, where previous commissions had slotted into the tradition of subservience—Vizentini's hurriedly assembled score for *The King's Command*, for example, followed the well-established practice of recycling existing compositions—Ivanov was widely seen as breaking new ground and extensively debated as such in the press.[118] Ivanov himself considered his score to be 'the first serious attempt in Russia to produce a symphonic genre in ballet'.[119]

He wrote this in his brief memoir of Petipa; in the same paragraph he dismisses the case for Tchaikovsky's *Swan Lake* as being an earlier representative of elevated ballet music, describing it as 'only of a series of waltzes'.[120] This may, for the most part, be factually correct and, from Ivanov's point of view, a fair criticism, since he is arguing for symphonic music, away from the straitjacket of the traditional dictates of dance. But it is also reductive, disregarding what the music critic Laroche described as the 'varied, graceful, and winning designs' of *Swan Lake*'s waltzes.[121] Tchaikovsky's score did suffer neglect: a fate caused not so much by the music's reception—mixed, but on balance favourable—or the indisputably poor choreography by Reisinger, but by what happened after. When in 1879 Hansen took over Reisinger's job, he produced a version (13 January 1880) which made a better impression. It was followed by a second version from Hansen on 23 October 1882. However, this second version lasted only up to 2 January 1883, when the sets started to fall apart. The theatre lacked the funds for repairs, so Tchaikovsky's score was parked off-piste—and several factors ensured that it languished there.[122] First, Hansen was fired and Vsevolozhsky's savage reforms produced a terrible upheaval. Then Bogdanov arrived from St Petersburg. Not only were his own ballets an abject failure—*Svetlana, the Slav Princess* (Svetlana, slavianskaia kniazhna, 1886) earned the verdict of 'farcical' from the playwright Alexander Ostrovsky— but when his superiors tried to redress the situation by instructing him to revive *Swan Lake* and other ballets from the Moscow repertoire, he replied he could not revive ballets he had never seen.[123] Bogdanov was finally shown the door in 1889. His successor, the more capable José Mendez, perhaps equally uneasy with the older Moscow repertoire, did not return to *Swan Lake* either.

An article just after *The Vestal*'s premiere in the monthly *Nuvellist* recalls the mixed reaction to the Moscow *Swan Lake* and is clearly aware of the highly specialized demands put upon ballet composers. Yet the writer comes down in favour of reform, denouncing the lazily hackneyed attitudes of both ballet masters and ballerinas to music, with their formulaic demands and their opposition to anything outside their expectations, forcing the composer to weaken and subordinate his artistic vision.[124]

The same writer might have mentioned a further symptom of the low regard for ballet music: the cavalier approach to existing scores, turning them into a patchwork of additions and cuts by other hands—*Le Corsaire*'s being a prime example. It will also be remembered that when the composer Alexander Serov signed a contract for *Mlada*, he was actually agreeing to possible changes and alien insertions. Even the illustrious Tchaikovsky had to submit to similar indignities with his Moscow *Swan Lake*, when the ballerina Anna Sobeshchanskaya decided she wanted a new pas de deux for Odile. Repeating a line of action that she had initiated a couple of years earlier for Reisinger's *Ariadne*, she had, without consulting the composer, travelled to St Petersburg where Petipa choreographed what she wanted to music by Minkus.[125] Unsurprisingly, Tchaikovsky saw red on discovering at the eleventh hour that this music was to be shoehorned into his score. But being a genius he hit upon a neat compromise: he composed replacement music that fitted Minkus's rhythmic patterns exactly. And apparently Sobeshchanskaya was so pleased with the result she asked Tchaikovsky to compose an extra variation.[126]

The anonymous writer of the *Nuvellist* seems remarkably well informed, in both his analysis of the issues and in his knowledge of how the collaboration between Mikhail Ivanov and Petipa worked in practice. ... But then it turns out that he was, most likely, Mikhail Ivanov himself.[127] True, he sidesteps any conflict of interest by focussing on an analysis of the issues—until near the end, when he can't resist blowing his own trumpet. 'With all its elegance, ease and melodiousness, the music [...] stands out by the creator's serious approach to his task.'[128]

One of his arguments holds that it should be possible to ally concert-hall standard music to ballet, since, when faced with creating dances in opera, the same musically philistine ballet masters and dancers show themselves perfectly up to the task:

> The truth of our remarks is attested by the fact that in operas we find on
> the contrary a quantity of superb ballet music. Why? Because ballet mas-
> ters do not dare in these cases to lay their hand on the music; since there
> are few ballet numbers in opera, they decide now and then to depart from
> tradition, to stir their imagination, if they have one.[129]

As well as his extensive encounters with superior music in opera, Petipa had used music by Mendelssohn for the one-act *Titania* and its reworking a decade later (1876) as *A Midsummer Night's Dream*.[130] He had used music by Delibes: most notably, for the 'Jardin animé' *divertissement* added to the 1868 *Corsaire* and for his 1884 version of *Coppélia*. Similarly, Delibes's music had been included in Minkus's score for *The Adventures of Peleus*, created for Sokolova in 1876 and revived in a one-act gala version as *Thetis and Peleus* (Fetida i Pelei) in 1896. (The mythological theme, although long absent from the imperial stage, did not prevent *The Adventures of Peleus* from being boring and short-lived.)[131] Yet, despite all this, Petipa belonged to the old school; his many collaborations with Pugni and Minkus were carried out according to his tightly prescriptive outlines. In fact, concerning *The Vestal*, he had lobbied hard for Minkus. In an undated letter to Khudekov, the ballet's librettist, he wrote:

> I did everything I could to ensure that Mr. Minkus should compose the
> music of our ballet. Alas! I failed in that regard. The person who will com-
> pose the music—you must know him—is a man called Mr. Ivanov who
> writes in *Novoe vremia*. I have met him, he's a charming person, very easy-
> going. As a composer, I think he is competent. The music he has com-
> posed is very melodious. Anyway, let's hope![132]

The Vestal

Although the Ivanov-Petipa *Haarlem Tulip* had a conventional ballet score, Wiley considers the ballet contained hints of the Vsevolozhsky agenda, with its high ratio of dance and Italian virtuosity.[133] The ballet's structure had obvious Petipa-esque influences: the first act was set in a suburb of Amsterdam; the second, a nocturnal Kingdom of the Tulips populated by personified flowers and butterflies, was a showcase for classical dances; the third finished with a festival (*kermesse*) featuring local and gypsy dances.[134] The story was weak, not always coherently elucidated, and lacking dramatic tension; nor was there any mime. But the dances were well-composed and, although the decor was disappointing, Evgenii Ponomarev's costumes were luxuriously beautiful. Most notably, the cast was led by Emma Bessone, one of the finest from Italy's production line of virtuosi. She was the centrepiece, her numerous, difficult variations dominated the ballet, her prodigious turns, fourteen *fouettés*, and balances on point eliciting near-disbelief. There also came censure from the anti-Italian guard, however: her undisputed technical marvels were to the complete detriment of grace and charm; she was 'a dance machine', her strong legs were 'inartistic' or 'sturdy' or 'muscular'.[135] (Photos, by modern standards, suggest the cruel word 'fat'.)[136]

But it was *The Vestal* that offered the first real example of the new Vsevolozhsky orientation. Besides testifying to the search for a new kind of ballet music, it represented a yet higher level of magnificence and scale. Billed as a ballet in three acts and four scenes, it demanded intervals of thirty minutes for the elaborate scene changes. It deployed a cast of between 500 and 600 performers, plus animals which, according to Petipa's preparatory notes, included a donkey (presumably real), monkey (possibly real), and camels and elephants (most likely not real).[137] It also relied on an Italian ballerina (Elena Cornalba) and had another novel dimension: an Ancient Roman setting, rare in ballet. Khudekov adapted the story of Gaspare Spontini's opera *La Vestale*, premiered in Paris in 1807, when fashion for the classical world was at its peak.[138]

As in *La Bayadère*, the long and detailed narrative pivots on romantic rivalry and external constraint: the lovers Lucius (*Lutsii*, played by Gerdt) and Amata (Cornalba) are torn apart by the cult of Vesta, with a little help from Amata's jealous sister Claudia (Maria Gorshenkova). In the published libretto, Lucius is a young centurion in whose honour the senator Julius (*Iulii*) Flak (Kshesinsky) gives a lavish banquet, an occasion for spectacular Andalusian and bacchanalian dances.[139] Flak's two daughters, Claudia and Amata, also take part in a mythological masque. Lucius asks Flak for permission to marry Amata and receives it. The banquet is not over, but Lucius has to leave for a military campaign. Soon after, a priest arrives to tell Flak that he must surrender a daughter to the cult of Vesta. The senator, distressed, tries to mislead the priest into thinking that Claudia is his only daughter; but Claudia, also in love with Lucius, exposes her father's deceit. The indignant priest demands that Amata be brought to the temple. Flak sinks into profound despair, while the revels continue. The act closes with a *kordak*, an energetic Ancient Greek dance with fast turns from the hip and jumps, performed by the corps de ballet. Knowing Petipa's habit of researching character dances, it is likely that he took the trouble to trace and preserve what was known of the dance. Either way, it seems to have pleased the public.[140]

The second act begins with Amata's consecration in the temple and her thirty-year vow of chastity. She is overwrought and exhausted, which is the cue for a Petipa dream and passages of classical dance.[141] Forest spirits appear, led by the allegorical figures of Cupid and Folly, then Venus herself in a seashell-shaped chariot, surrounded by nymphs personifying Hope, Sighs, Desires, Love, and more. Marie Petipa made a predictably sensational impact as Venus, luxuriant waves of ash-grey hair falling to her snowy-white shoulders—even if her appearance had been toned down for the premiere. (Petipa wrote in his rehearsal notes 'my daughter is too naked, her costume lacks drapery.')[142] The nymphs try to cheer Amata up and a corps de ballet of forty-two dancers perform a *ballabile*. Venus summons Lucius, but when Amata tries to embrace him, like Aspichia in *The Pharaoh's Daughter*, she clutches at air. This is interrupted by the arrival of the angry goddess Vesta, who causes all the other apparitions to take fright and flee. Vesta reminds Amata that her place is in the temple, not in the embrace of a lover.

A year has passed by the time of the third act. Lucius, returning from the campaign, learns of Amata's fate from Claudia who offers herself to him, but is rejected. When Flak confirms that Amata has become a Vestal virgin, Lucius tries to kill himself with his sword, but is saved by Amata who has just entered. Lucius tries to persuade her to run away with him, but she refuses to break her vow. In despair Lucius decides to find death among the gladiators in the upcoming games; the sisters follow to try to save him.

The final scene begins with a Petipa procession: children of the Roman nobility, athletes, slaves, lictors, and temple servants carrying statues of Roman gods. Then comes the emperor with his retinue and finally the gladiators who circle round the stadium and salute the emperor. After this come the entertainments: the Salii (priests of Mars) and their female counterparts perform war dances, leaping and waving swords; two gladiators enact a comical combat; and maenads from Thrace and Macedonia, carrying knives and snakes, churn the air with wild, aggressive postures.

As a contrast, the 'Danses des Muses au Parnasse', presided by Apollo (Alexander Oblakov) with his lyre and sun-ray crown, represent a haven of civilized, classical calm. Ivanov writes that Petipa attached particular importance to this scene in which Apollo invites the nine Muses to descend Parnassus, each wearing or carrying emblems of their individual skills.[143] For example, Thalia, the Muse of comedy and epigram, played by Claudia, had, as recorded by Petipa, 'a crown of ivy on her head, a mask and a pen in her hands, and is followed by a little monkey, symbol of imitation'. Terpsichore, the Muse of dance, comes last with 'a headdress of multicoloured plumes and a tambourine in her hand'.[144] She is played by Amata, who like her sister has joined the actors to watch over Lucius. Apollo asks each Muse to dance a variation reflecting her calling, with Phaethon (Cecchetti), not Apollo, partnering the two sisters. (Cecchetti looked 'dreadful' in his costume according to Petipa's rehearsal notes.)[145] The Muses then join hands in a circle dance representing the unity between science and art, and—no surprise— Terpsichore-Amata is crowned the *prima inter pares*. The Muses surround Apollo, forming a picturesque group before the enchanted forest of Parnassus disappears beneath the arena.[146]

After this scene, Amata runs from place to place, desperately lifting the gladiators' visors in a useless bid to find Lucius. A gladiatorial combat follows: one is armed with shield and sword, the other, with a trident and fishing net. The second is overpowered, his helmet and visor knocked off, and Lucius is revealed. Holding a foot against the fallen Lucius, his opponent turns towards the imperial box for the verdict. Lucius begs for death and tearing the sword from his opponent's hand, plunges it into himself. Amata rushes towards him and he recognizes her before dying. She kills herself with the same sword and the ballet ends with the usual apotheosis, described in the published libretto as 'the triumph of the goddess of chastity, Vesta'. (Whether this means that the lovers are not reunited is anybody's guess.)

For Skalkovsky the staging of such a monumental ballet with equal taste and knowledge was an outstanding achievement.[147] In fact all reviewers were agreed on the production's breathtaking scale and magnificence: the first act's enormous ensembles; the second act's sombre wood and temple of Vesta; the luxury and historical accuracy of the costuming. Khudekov's treatment was also generally well received, having been created, in *Syn otechestva*'s opinion, with a skilful theatricality. This, along with 'the inexhaustible fantasy of the ballet master Petipa', meant that 'the new ballet is an indisputably outstanding, masterly, and grand creation.'[148] The same paper the following day singled out the dances of the Muses as a *chef d'oeuvre*, as did Nikolai Bezobrazov in *Sankt-Peterburgskie vedomosti*; similarly *Birzhevye vedomosti* wrote that 'the appearance of the Muses [...] was such a magnificent and vivid scene it elicited stormy applause.'[149] But sadly Apollo and the Muses were later taken out, to shorten the ballet.[150] Most writers, though, did feel the ballet needed cuts. Bezobrazov judged that the classical dances of the vision scene, too numerous, and not so interesting, should be reduced by half.[151] And all the writers mentioned the theatre's underprepared, overstretched technical resources which not only diminished the effect of Mount Parnassus in the third act, but nearly caused a major calamity in the second. The machinists miscalculated the wire-flying trajectory of two ballerinas, Alexandra Vinogradova (Cupid) and Vera Zhukova (Folly), causing them to head straight for the temple altar and knock it over along with the flame and inflammable spirit, which then spread on to part of the stage and into the wings. Fortunately, prompt action by the theatre's firemen put the flames out in seconds before any widespread panic and the performance continued.[152]

As described by Ivanov, working relations with Petipa were cordial. Petipa proceeded with the usual written instructions, broken down into mime scenes and dance numbers with specifications of metre and intonation:

> He was patient, a true foreigner as regards courtesy, and never complained of the boredom which he probably suffered when explaining to novices the ABCs of his art. He listened through every page patiently, invariably submitting it to his censorship. He loved piquant music, lively and animated rhythms, but he never evaluated what had been written except for the arrangement of its parts—whether their length and dimensions, their general plan, corresponded with the dances he had already conceived.[153]

However, as communicated in his correspondence with Vsevolozhsky, Ivanov's poor knowledge of ballet led to misunderstandings and he did not, he claims, receive clear indication of the absolute need for variations.[154] The oddity of this situation begs the question of whether something else was afoot, such as the unwillingness of some dancers, especially Cornalba, to perform to Ivanov's music. The upshot was not only that he was subsequently asked to compose three variations, but an even greater number was ordered from Drigo—eleven according to *Syn otechestva* which also reported that Drigo was tasked with a pas de deux for Cornalba.

Notwithstanding this first-hand brush with the ballet world's casual and byzantine musical ways, Ivanov—if indeed it was he—wrote in the same *Nuvellist* article that the Ivanov-Petipa collaboration would be the harbinger of a new approach.[155] But other reviews of the music were lukewarm, criticizing those very characteristics—'operatic', 'symphonic'—which Ivanov was championing. The most damning verdict came from Bezobrazov who added a particularly cruel comparison:

> This is in no way possible as music for ballet. This is a kind of chaos of every possible sound, without rhythm, and one can only be surprised by how our dancers managed to dance to such music. [...] There are, however, a few charming musical numbers in *The Vestal*, but they are composed not by Mr Ivanov, but by the *kapellmeister* Mr Drigo. During these numbers the public relaxed.[156]

Other writers fished around gallantly for some positive elements (each one finding something different) but only 'Veto' in *Novosti i birzhevaia gazeta* was unequivocally enthusiastic. With the hindsight of a decade, Pleshcheev, his vision shaped perhaps by the Tchaikovsky collaborations, was another defender:

> Balletomanes opposing this music do not give any consideration to the fact that an independent composer cannot limit himself to polkas and waltzes, especially where there is a predominant dramatic dimension. The content of *The Vestal* demanded some divergence from the traditional ballet methods, whereby performers cry and suffer to the sounds of a waltz, and die to the accompaniment of a drum. Mr Ivanov has pursued an independent path, which has displeased balletomanes, and he has written music, which in the opinion of one musician, has the drawback that it is too good for ballet.[157]

But Shiriaev, giving the dancers' point of view at an even later date, was ambivalent:

> I confess that after such ballet composers as Pugni and Minkus, with their simple melody-making and rhythmic structures, it was not easy for us artists to get used to Ivanov's music. The complex score was difficult for dancing and forced both the ballet master and artists really to get down to work.[158]

Cornalba certainly didn't like the music—and Ivanov didn't like Cornalba: 'Cornalba,' he wrote, 'was, if not hard of hearing, unable to make out rhythms, even simple ones.'[159]

Invited directly from abroad, she made her Russian debut on 6 December 1887 in Saint-Léon's *Fiametta*. Her biggest success in this was an inserted pas de deux with Cecchetti where Cecchetti threw her up in the air and she seemed to float back to the ground like a piece of down.[160]

The Vestal was the first ballet made on her in Russia. She had a phenomenal technique and the Italian 'points of steel'. Unusually, she had an outstanding jump, at a time when most Italian ballerinas tended to be *terre-à-terre* dancers, because, as Skalkovsky quipped, Italian men could do the jumping. Her elevation was such that the stage of the Mariinsky seemed too small and in her second-act variation she began with twelve *entrechats-six* in succession, continuing with turns on point and *jetés en tournant*.[161] She moved gracefully, but her slightly high shoulders made her torso and arms look tense. Her biggest weakness, however, was an inexpressive face and weak mime.[162]

This marred her performance in a ballet where acting had such an important place. Unfortunately, the scenario had forced Petipa, normally so attuned to the individual qualities of a ballerina, to create a large quantity of dramatic scenes. 'This role is very mimetic and has places full of drama, in which Miss Cornalba was extremely weak,' wrote *Syn otechestva*. 'On the other hand, the ballerina danced beautifully, as always showing off her elevation, clean finish [...] and strong points.'[163]

The public failed to fill the Mariinsky's auditorium to the rafters for an unknown ballet which might turn out to be another of the 1880s disappointments.[164] They would have sold their coats for Zucchi; but the press reported on 26 November 1887 that she had rejected *The Vestal*.[165] It was also a fact that her contract had not been renewed for the following 1888–1889 season. (She was, however, in the audience for *The Vestal's* performance on 6 March and loudly fêted by her distressed fans.) The reasons were perhaps unconnected with her dancing: a member of the lofty Vasilchikov dynasty had become infatuated with her and at the final bows for the premiere of *The King's Command* he arranged for a necklace of enormous diamonds to be given to her in full view of the public. His alarmed family made representations to the tsar, who obliged them.[166] In Wiley's opinion, though, Vsevolozhsky had never warmed to Zucchi; she was certainly a box-office magnet, but given that she was pushing forty and her attractions necessarily in decline, his decision was vindicated. She continued to appear in Russia on commercial stages, but the enthusiasm for her abated.[167]

Although *The Vestal's* revival in 1891 with Varvara Nikitina attracted full houses, it disappeared after 1893, the final performance consisting of just its second act. The music remains as an orchestral score in the Mariinsky archives. On examining this, it becomes clear that Ivanov lacked nuance, that he tended to repeat the same devices—always a *tutti* orchestration for dramatic moments, always the same instruments for lyrical passages. A more skilled composer would have shown more finesse in manipulating his resources and would have given more time to thematic development.[168]

The Vestal was more important in its intentions that in itself. 'What really needs to be changed in *The Vestal*, from the beginning to the end, is the music composed by Mr Ivanov,' Bezobrazov wrote in one of his reviews. 'It destroys *The Vestal* and with it the ballet will not survive long.'[169] Bezobrazov was perhaps right in predicting that it was the music, intended to represent the future, that would consign *The Vestal* to the past. We will never see Petipa's Apollo and the Muses on Mount Parnassus.

Another disappeared ballet, *The Talisman*, was the second work in the same colossal genre, premiered a year later. Its libretto mixed an Indian setting with the supernatural and was credited to Petipa and the dramatist and writer Konstantin Tarnovsky: a compromise after Tarnovsky disputed Petipa's claim to single authorship.[170] (Tarnovsky had written a similar narrative some nine years earlier in an aborted collaboration with Petipa.) In a rare note of censure, Pleshcheev writes that the attribution was not worth fighting over, given the plot's weakness.[171] The choreography did not rise to the occasion either.[172]

However, Cornalba's aerial style was perfect for the heroine Ella, the celestial spirit who descends to Earth and falls in love. Equally adroit was Petipa's decision, noted earlier in this chapter, to exploit Cecchetti's virtuosity for the part of Hurricane, God of the Wind.

This time all the music was by Drigo. Although Pleshcheev judged it melodious in places, noisy in others, and not outstanding in originality, Benois became so carried away at a performance that his noisy approval earned him a disapproving finger-wagging from the governor of St Petersburg.[173] An Italian-born conductor and opera composer, Drigo had arrived in Petersburg in 1878 to work with the Italian Opera. His appointment as music director of the Imperial Ballet in 1886 followed the retirement of Alexei Papkov after long service. Because of the abolition of the post of ballet composer, his duties included making any necessary amendments and additions to ballet scores and he started by writing extra dances for Petipa's 1886 revival of *Esmeralda*. His first ballet score, for Lev Ivanov's one-act *Enchanted Forest* (Ocharovannyi les) in 1887, was well liked. Posterity considers him a superior ballet composer, although that is more from hearsay, since none of his ballets have survived on stage—with the exception of *The Awakening of Flora*, thanks to the Mariinsky's reconstruction, and *Harlequinade* (or *Les Millions d'Arlequin*), by way of Gusev and Balanchine. Harlequin's mandolin serenade became a popular stand-alone piece and Drigo, after returning to Italy, adapted it as an aria, 'Notturno d'amore', which was recorded in 1922 by the tenor Beniamino Gigli.[174]

The Talisman was revived in 1895 by Petipa with Legnani in the principal role and again in 1909, in a new production by Nikolai Legat which renamed the heroine as Niriti (danced by Preobrazhenskaya) and Hurricane as Vaiou (Nijinsky). The performances were doubtless superlative, but Legat's staging was particularly disappointing, which, like Ivanov's music for *The Vestal*, can't have helped the ballet survive.

Ivanov was not a gifted composer but his was the opening declaration in the search for concert-hall quality music. In the year after *The Vestal*, a one-act ballet, *The Whims of the Butterfly* (Kaprizy babochki), was premiered with music by Nikolai Krotkov, conductor at the Alexandrinsky and later the Mikhailovsky, who had already composed an opera, *The Scarlet Rose* (Alaia roza), based on the *Beauty and the Beast* story, for Mamontov's Private Opera in Moscow. The year 1890 saw the premiere of the Tchaikovsky-Petipa *Sleeping Beauty*, the greatest ballet of all, followed by other Petipa collaborations with Tchaikovsky, Petr Shenk, Krotkov, Fitinhof-Schell, Alexander Glazunov, Drigo, and Arsenii Koreshchenko. When Anton Rubinstein wrote his ballet score, *The Grapevine*, in 1881, he sent it speculatively to Vsevolozhsky, but despite constructive talks between the composer and Petipa, Vsevolozhsky rejected it.[175] The demand for composers deemed suitable outstripped the supply, leading to a reliance on Drigo, who consequently often fulfilled the duties of ballet composer in everything but name. All in all, finding a second Tchaikovsky was never going to be easy.

For or Against

Petipa's incorporation of new trends would meet with disapproval from the critic 'Svoĭ' in an article marking his fifty years' service in 1896: 'The Italian acrobatics which have noisily burst into our ballet,' he wrote, 'have been met by Mr Petipa affably and encouragingly instead of being completely and properly repulsed.'[176] In the same writer's review of *Bluebeard* (Siniaia boroda) two days later, premiered at Petipa's jubilee benefit, came another criticism:

> In the jubilee celebration of Marius Petipa, representing the apotheosis of his half century as ballet master, it would have been entirely natural to expect something outstanding, distilling the quintessence of his creative qualities, which are evident in even the weakest of his compositions. But, alas, the first sign of disappointment was given by the poster, announcing *Bluebeard*, a *ballet-féerie*. [...] This is so much the sadder that Mr Petipa, who made his debut here with the superb ballet *Paquita*, appears half a century later with a creation little befitting our exemplary stage. [...] *Ballet-féeries* make us think of a mosaic, shining with bright colour, but not communicating any clearly thought-out pictures.[177]

Yet a few days earlier, Petipa himself had been railing against both *féeries* and Italian bravura dancing in an interview for the *Peterburgskaia gazeta*. He considered that ballet had declined in Europe—but not yet in St Petersburg:

> 'How do you explain the decline abroad?'
> 'Chiefly by the fact that they have gradually turned away from real, serious art, dances have been transformed into clownish exercises. ... Ballet is a serious art, in which plastique and beauty must hold [?] the eye, not all possible kinds of jumps, meaningless spinning and legs lifted higher than the head. This is not art, but—I repeat—clownery.'
> 'In other words, the Italian school?'
> 'Yes. ... it corrupts the public, diverting it from serious ballets and turning it towards *féeries*, brought to the stage by people such as Manzotti, who created a *féerie*—yes, yes, not a ballet, but a *féerie*—*Excelsior*. In Paris [at the Opera] they have stopped staging big ballets and content themselves with small ones. ... There ballet is in decline—it is indisputably in decline. And there is nobody to champion it. [...] It now concerns itself with dances in a coarse, unbecoming style or with acrobatic exercises.'

'And this is not the case in Petersburg?'

'Not yet. ... I consider the Petersburg ballet the best in the world, precisely because in it is preserved that serious art which is lost abroad. ... The
Petersburg ballet is not in decline and will not be in decline as long as the
enthusiasm for the Italian school is kept at bay.'[178]

In fact, Petipa and Vsevolozhsky were not so divergent—although it is also true that
Petipa didn't have that much choice. Production details, narratives, and music
were Vsevolozhsky's domain; he had the final say. And what Vsevolozhsky seems
to have wanted was not the *féerie* as it was staged in Paris, but the *excitement* of
the *féerie*. To this would be added the sophisticated narrative, choreography, and
music which the Western model lacked, although the narrative, turning towards
fairy tales, would not equal the solidity of the historical-ethnographic Khudekov
collaborations. Put more reductively, Vsevolozhsky's vision was for an alliance of
the dance-led Petersburg grand ballet with the spectacular mise en scène of the
Franco-Italian *féerie*.[179] This was the goal as already understood by some contemporary writers, and its apex would be *The Sleeping Beauty*.[180]

Petipa, in the domain of choreography where he did have control, was a disciple
of the true, high tradition of classical ballet. Equally, however, he was a showman
who never forgot that ballet's raison d'être is to captivate its audience. At his best,
by using fashionable visual effects and massed dances judiciously in alliance with
his dedication to classical choreography, he preserved the integrity of his art, just
as under his influence, the 'coarse' dancing and 'acrobatic exercises' of the Italian
school were absorbed and transmuted into the Russian style.

It may well be, as indicated by Svoi above, that the mise en scène of *Bluebeard*,
six years after *The Sleeping Beauty*, was an example of an overblown *ballet-féerie*,
with its gimmicks and senseless succession of dance numbers. Tamara Karsavina
considered it to be so, and even included other late works. 'The productions following *The Sleeping Beauty* grew larger and larger. The subject was treated like a
peg on which to hang numerous *ballabiles*.' Although Petipa never lost his choreographic mastery, 'he had lost sight of the great lessons of the Romantic Ballet—the
inner motivation of the dance, and the right balance between the dramatic action
and dancing.' *Bluebeard* 'had several dancing displays with a loosely connected
plot. [...] Dancing knives, forks, spoons, and platters in one of them furnished
a pretext for dancing, not its motivation, reducing the classical dancing to ab-
surdity.'[181] Contemporary reviewers, apart from Svoi, however, made no mention
of the ballet's *féerie* elements, apart from the luxury of the costumes, designed in
Louis XIII style. *Peterburgskaia gazeta* and *Novoe vremia* praised Petipa's ability
always to find something new and avoid banality, his mastery in classical and character dances like the *gaillarde* and a *ballabile* for Norman country-folk (*paysannerie
normande*); they praised the effortless artistry of Legnani as the heroine Ysaure

(*Izora*) and singled out her 'pas de deux électrique' for its 'giddying' virtuosity; and they praised a scene for Ysaure's sister Anne (Olga Preobrazhenskaya), not only for its performance, but for its staging, Anna admiring herself before a mirror that was actually a transparent gauze behind which another dancer matched Anne's movements—a trick which Petipa's father had used years ago in Madrid for his ballet *Farfarella, or the Daughter of Hell*. They reserved their harsher judgements for Petr Shenk, who besides being one of the new composers was a friend of Vsevolozhsky. His music was variously described as derivative, indebted to Tchaikovsky, lacking a distinctive style, not without merit considering Shenk's youth, and more like the sounds of a musical snuffbox.[182]

Vsevolozhsky, in his search for the fireworks of virtuoso dancers, sent Petipa on ballerina-scouting trips abroad—including one in February 1898 to Vienna, Venice, Milan, Paris, and London, to find a replacement for Legnani, whose time in Russia was coming to an end.[183] In Milan, he was received by Manzotti with great reverence, despite his unflattering remarks about Manzotti's ballets to the press. But Petipa was apparently unabashed: during this meeting he expressed his hopes for a renaissance of serious ballet, pushing out the *féerie*.[184]

That, however, was all in the future. Now, on the eve of the century's final decade, Petipa was still faced with the most intractable component of Vsevolozhsky's equation: the music. For a conservative like him, it raised alarm bells. But, faced with the inevitable, he would buckle down to produce his greatest work with Tchaikovsky and Glazunov. (That said, maybe it was his petitioning which brought Minkus back on board for the 1891 *Calcabrino*, Minkus's last ballet score.)

The 1880s were therefore a period of preparation: the full effect of Vsevolozhsky's policies would be felt in the next decade. And that decade saw the late, remarkable renaissance of Petipa's creative powers, his golden age.

9

Big Music, Big Dance

*It requires much intelligence, a vast amount of taste, great under-
standing, and a rare love of work and patience to assemble such
a huge piece [The Sleeping Beauty], to work it down to the finest
details and then teach it to a hundred people.*[1]

Flora and Fauna

Vsevolozhsky's music reforms were destined to be his lasting legacy, forever changing the way ballet music is perceived. Without doubt Petipa owed the revitalization of his inventiveness to the terrain laid down by Vsevolozhsky, even if he was
dragged out of his comfort zone. The Italian practitioners of the 'acrobatics' he
so deplored and the ennobled ballet music which gave him so many headaches
jolted him out of an apparent rut. But it would take time for the right music to
come along.

As a librettist Vsevolozhsky could be superlative (*The Sleeping Beauty*, for example, *The Romance of the Rosebud and the Butterfly*) and less superlative (*The
Nutcracker*, in collaboration with Petipa). As a costume designer, he started with
revivals (such as *The Wilful Wife* and *The Pharaoh's Daughter*), then moved on
to original productions, the first being *The Devil's Pills*, followed by *The King's
Command* and *The Vestal*.[2] By the end of his directorship, he had, by the reckoning
of the Imperial Theatre's other costume designer, Evgeni Ponomarev, completed
no fewer than 1,087 costume drawings for ballet and opera.[3]

The costuming was part of the *féerization* process; the adjectives applied by
reviewers to his designs invariably denoted extreme luxury and originality. Such
were the costumes for the one-act *Whims of the Butterfly*, premiered at a private
performance at the Mariinsky on 5 June 1889, for the marriage of Grand Duke
Paul, the tsar's brother, to Alexandra of Greece.[4] (Its first public performance, on
the same stage, was on 25 October.) Personified flowers had long been a subject in
the Petipa repertoire, and so were insects. Petipa's libretto was poetic, not least because it was based on a poem by Iakov Polonsky, 'The Grasshopper Musician', and
featured a grasshopper (Sergei Litavkii) who defends his beloved butterfly (Varvara
Nikitina) from a predatory nightingale (Sergei Legat), even though she is in love

with a phoenix butterfly (Pavel Gerdt).[5] Saved, the butterfly marries the phoenix and all the insects celebrate, until night falls and the curtain descends on the badly wounded grasshopper, all alone, except for moths that have appeared. The melancholy ending was an arguably strange choice for a marriage celebration, but the lyrical, aerial possibilities were evident—except, for once, Petipa's choreographic muse mostly deserted him. The performances, however, were faultless. Nikitina fluttered about the stage—'what aplomb,' exclaimed a reviewer, 'what strength, lightness, and assurance!'[6] Gerdt was a seductive, handsome *danseur* and partner the likes of whom existed nowhere in Europe; he was full of grace, the epitome of irreproachable line, thrilling everyone by the way he would lift Nikitina in the air, throw and catch her. Krotkov's music worked splendidly, melodiously evoking the themes and characters.[7]

At its public premiere *The Whims of the Butterfly* also suffered from being presented with Lev Ivanov's *Enchanted Forest* and a revival of *A Midsummer Night's Dream*: too much fantastical flora and fauna on the same programme.[8] For *A Midsummer Night's Dream*, Vsevolozhsky not only designed new costumes, but persuaded Petipa to add green grasshoppers. These, Vsevolozhsky explained, would bring something fresh to the ballet and would be perfect roles for the school's pupils; moreover, grasshoppers being insect-musicians, they could each hold a violin.

Such ideas, expressed in a letter to Petipa with Vsevolozhsky's perfect tact, give a sense of Vsevolozhsky's detailed involvement in a production. He ends by reminding Petipa—'his steadfast commander'—how much the imperial family likes novelty. 'If we give *A Midsummer Night's Dream* then we are saved. I am aware that this is an enormous task—but I am turning towards a steadfast commander who has already conducted many campaigns and who is in charge of a magnificent army.'[9]

The Sleeping Beauty

The first indication of an approach by Vsevolozhsky to Tchaikovsky about composing a ballet score appears in the composer's diary on 8 November 1886, when his opera *The Enchantress* (Charodeika) was being rehearsed at the Mariinsky. He writes about a meeting proposed by Vsevolozhsky and attended also by Petipa; at this meeting he rejected the idea of a ballet based on Flaubert's *Salammbô*, in favour, seemingly, of a ballet called *Undine*.[10]

Tchaikovsky had already written an opera, *Undine*, and incorporated parts of it into his ballet score for the first, Moscow, version of *Swan Lake*. But the *Undine* ballet project was abandoned for unclear reasons, and on 13 May 1888 Vsevolozhsky wrote to Tchaikovsky with a new idea: Perrault's *Sleeping Beauty* adapted by himself, with a mise en scène in the style of Louis XIV and 'melodies composed in the spirit of Lully, Bach, Rameau, etc. etc.'[11] Although Tchaikovsky was Russia's most revered living composer, he had not been Vsevolozhsky's first choice for *The Sleeping Beauty*—Vizentini had. Perhaps understandably, Vsevolozhsky felt that a Frenchman would have the qualities and knowledge for the score as he envisaged it. But ultimately he abandoned the idea: 'I fear that if I order the music from Vizentini there will be an uproar in all St Petersburg, especially as he would not write a second ballet for free.'[12] (Vizentini was not paid for *The King's Command*, but quite why there would be an uproar is unclear.) It would also seem that at some point there was talk of transferring the action to Spain, most likely from Petipa's side. But for Vsevolozhsky keeping to the 'local colour' of Perrault and the costumes of Louis XIV was indispensable; moreover, transferring the action to Spain would 'firstly, be a repeat of *Zoraiya*, and, secondly, would destroy the charm and naivety of Perrault'.[13] Tchaikovsky took up the project enthusiastically. Wiley surmises that he viewed *The Sleeping Beauty* more seriously than the Moscow *Swan Lake* because of Petipa's involvement.[14] Tchaikovsky himself requested a written plan of Petipa's requirements and the two men seem to have got along very well.[15]

The *Sleeping Beauty* was premiered on 3 January 1890. Aurora was the young Carlotta Brianza, who, after dancing *Excelsior* at the Abandon Sorrow, had appeared in Moscow in Petipa's *Cyprus Statue*, followed by *Roxana*, both staged by Bogdanov. She then made her Mariinsky debut on 15 January 1889 in *The Haarlem Tulip*. Zucchi's departure had left a vacuum, and Benois was probably not the only one temporarily to neglect ballet-going, apart from a 'short infatuation with *The Talisman*'.[16] Among the younger Russian generation much hope had been pinned on Alexandra Vinogradova, who graduated in 1887 and was revealing a singular dramatic talent, a quality in short supply in the present company; she had even when still a student travelled to Paris to go through *Esmeralda*'s mime scenes with the elderly Perrot. However, she died in 1889, aged just twenty.[17] Meanwhile, attempts to find other foreign ballerina-glamour had so far yielded only average results. Bessone and Cornalba, although phenomenal technicians, did not win hearts, particularly among the Italo-sceptics. Another Italian, the very young and inexperienced Luigia Algisi, came and went, invited in 1888, on the recommendation of Alberto di Segni, who had been the Italian Opera's *régisseur* and became the ballet's in 1885 when Ivanov was appointed second ballet master. (Di Segni's death just before Algisi's arrival inspired wits to claim he had wanted to avoid her debut.)

In being signed up on 13 February 1889 at 20,000 roubles plus one benefit for 1889–1890, Brianza was the only foreigner to be engaged for that season, a cutback that reflected the money-saving decision to reduce ballet performances from twice a week to three times every fortnight.[18] (Performances of ballet, as recorded by the Yearbook of Imperial Theatres from 1890–1891 onwards, averaged some fifty performances a year, while the opera achieved about one hundred and thirty.) Even so, the directorate was vindicated in putting all their faith in Brianza, an attractive brunette with a small, but perfectly proportioned body, the only drawback being that she was rather swamped by the Mariinsky's enormous stage.[19] Her remarkable technique, evident in *Esmeralda* and especially in *The Haarlem Tulip*, raised expectations for *The Sleeping Beauty* and she did not disappoint. Given that she was not the match of Zucchi as a mime, Petipa avoided heavy-duty acting, instead building the role round her youth, pliancy, lightness, and virtuosity. Skalkovsky likens her style to that of a young panther, which might explain Petipa's inclusion of coltish *pas de chat* (to mix animal metaphors) for her first entrance, the perfect dance representation of a girlish princess. Most glitches came not from Brianza, but her dangerous partners. Gerdt, as Désiré, managed to tear a lock from her hair with his long sleeve; while Bekefi, as one of the four suitors, ripped her red costume with the sword he was wearing during a fast supported pirouette.[20]

Gerdt was well past his athletic days but, as noted in chapter 7, even his brief danced numbers always won applause. Benois, referring to the final act's evocation of the *ballet de cour*, confirms this:

> He gave the absolute illusion of a genuine prince—in fact, he seemed to be Louis XIV in person. Those who did not see this miracle for themselves can hardly imagine how perfectly suited this fine artist was to the role, how obvious were the traditions that he had inherited from Johannson and Petipa. [...] In the last act Gerdt performed a short variation. Although perfectly simple and lasting less than a minute, it aroused such enthusiasm in the public that even people who knew nothing of the history of the *Grand Siècle* seemed, during the dance, to achieve a clear vision of the distant past.[21]

Later, in 1904, when Nikolai Legat replaced Gerdt, he beefed up Désiré's solos, reflecting the revived taste for male virtuosity.

Skalkovsky gives a useful overview of the ballet's structure and provides a reminder that the original time-setting was the mid-sixteenth century for the first scenes and, after the hundred-year sleep, the early part of Louis XIV's reign (1643–1715).[22] This makes logical Petipa's references to Louis XIV's court for the last act, compared to subsequent productions which push the same act into the latter half of the eighteenth century. According to Benois, the change was first made by Konstantin Korovin's designs for the ballet's 1914 revival at the Mariinsky by Nikolai Sergeyev, helped by Alexander Gorsky.[23]

The public were enthusiastic even before the premiere, thanks to two open (and free) general rehearsals. The critics, though, were often ambivalent. Many, fixated by the ballet's designation as a *ballet-féerie*, had difficulty seeing beyond, ignoring the possibility that the word '*féerie*' might be as much a reflection of its fairy-tale origins as a description of its genre. Consequently, they underlined the magnificence of the staging, the eye-popping luxury of the costumes, the special effects. 'Bukva' in *Peterburgskie vedomosti* loved the dense forest that grew upwards and the different vistas that appeared during Désiré's journey to the castle.[24] Skalkovsky spotlights the graphic detail of 'a century's worth' of vegetation growing out of courtiers' mouths when everybody is asleep.[25] Beyond the Frenchness which bothered some critics (see chapter 5), the story was judged slight, lacking development and action. From that perspective, the ballet was bound to fail, in the opinion of 'N' (Dmitrii Koroviakov):

> Perrault's fairy tales represent good material for superficial spectacle by virtue of their poetic descriptions, but the internal content, in its ingenuousness, simplicity and child-like naïveté, cannot provide the imaginative material necessary for the composition of [...] a big ballet of the kind the public has become accustomed to. [...] If in fact ballet is only spectacle, a multicoloured kaleidoscope of costumes and decor, then no splendour of staging will compensate for its emptiness, lack of substance, and that boredom which towards the end inevitably takes hold of every 'grown-up', not to mention a spectator with sophisticated tastes.[26]

Although Laroche describes the narrative as 'a simple anecdote', in fact he stands out from other critics by spending a considerable part of his review defending it. For critics like 'N', fairy tales are only for children, but Laroche insists they have timeless significance: in them myth and fairy tale are intertwined, in them are resonances which go deep into our memories and humanity.[27] The closing tableau is an affirmation of natural order restored. If Carabosse is present, seated behind a painted cloud, it is because Evil exists, along with Goodness, represented by the Lilac Fairy. High above, overlooking the stage, stands Apollo in his chariot, the god of healing and the arts, surrounded by sun rays. The parallel reference to Louis XIV who famously danced The Sun/Apollo in court spectacles is also unmistakeable; indeed, Petipa in his 'Ballet Master's Plan' writes that 'Apollo is dressed as Louis XIV, lit by the sun.'[28] Linked to this is the whole act's evocation of the *ballet de cour*, as well as the salute to autocracy, mentioned in chapter 5. And there is yet another dimension to the ballet, in the figures of Aurora (Dawn) and Désiré (Desired), their union an image of continuation and, if the story is taken as an allegory for the seasons, of rebirth and fertility, after winter's long sleep.[29]

Despite the billing as a *ballet-féerie*, the creators of *The Sleeping Beauty* were united in their serious intent. As Wiley shows, Vsevolozhsky had more in mind than a mere display piece without lasting meaning. He wanted, he told Tchaikovsky, a work that is not 'a transient vision' but one, like *Giselle*, that will remain 'to enchant our grandchildren as it enchanted us'.[30] Tchaikovsky would have shared this aim; as a composer of profoundly meaningful music he would not have agreed to mere superficial entertainment.[31] Consequently, *The Sleeping Beauty* achieves an ideal balance of spectacle allied to an inspired story with allegorical and mythical undercurrents—although most reviewers did not allude to these at initial viewings. It owes much to Tchaikovsky's evocative music and its profundity makes it an exception in the Petipa canon.

Tchaikovsky might have been world famous but he had an artist's hypersensitivity. He recorded in his diary the now famous incident at the dress rehearsal when Alexander III crushed him with a curt 'very nice'. But, considering the ballet world's prejudices vis-à-vis music, he can't have been too surprised by the ambivalent reviews. Even so, there were more positive voices. Skalkovsky, albeit a defender of the specialist ballet composer, recognized the music's melodiousness and elegant orchestration, even if he called for more distinct rhythms to aid the performers.[32] Laroche, a staunch supporter of the music, writes that 'the local colour is French but the *style* is Russian': an interesting and valid point to anyone who in the final act's 'Vive Henri IV' theme, based on a popular French song, has heard a heart-tugging 'Slavic soul' in the orchestration.[33] The mysterious writer of *Nuvellist* singles out Ivanov's score of *The Vestal* as the first of a new genre of elevated ballet music (pointing again to the probability that Ivanov himself was writing) and names Tchaikovsky's as the second, summarizing it as 'one of the most successful creations of its gifted composer'.[34] He praises Tchiakovsky's rich instrumentation in particular, but criticizes the final act. This needs, he judges, more vigour and jubilation instead of succumbing to Tchaikovsky's tendency towards melancholia: an opinion which belittles the evocative undercurrents of Tchaikovsky's music and rather explains why Ivanov's is now forgotten. Meanwhile Nikolai Bezobrazov proclaims his unreserved delight with everything—the music, as a departure from 'the banal music of commonplace ballet composers', the orchestra under Drigo, the dancers—and predicts a glorious future for the ballet in every respect.[35]

All the reviews note the visual splendour and luxury of Vsevolozhsky's costumes. For Skalkovsky, the magnificence was even excessive, too heavy for a ballet, suggesting a new title—*The Sleeping Beauty, or the Triumph of the Art of Sewing*.[36] But Benois, writing much later, was a bluntly dissenting voice: 'The production of *La Belle au Bois dormant* [Sleeping Beauty] had all the usual qualities and shortcomings of the imperial stage—great luxury and at the same time lack of taste in the choice of costumes—especially with regard to colours.'[37]

That apart, Benois credits Vsevolozhsky as the indispensable glue that enabled a masterpiece to come into being. Vsevolozhsky's attentiveness to every detail was, he believed, the factor that enabled *The Sleeping Beauty* to be an example of a *Gesamtkunstwerk*, a total work of art, a synthesis of its constituent elements, with a unique coherence and polish. 'Vsevolozhsky had exceptional tact and never forced his ideas on anyone, striving to convince by persuasion, and, as Ivan Alexandrovich was a great charmer by nature, he found it very easy to convince.'[38]

The Sleeping Beauty, and even more so Tchaikovsky's opera *The Queen of Spades*, would be, for Benois, the two greatest achievements of Vsevolozhsky's directorship.[39] There was even talk of taking *The Sleeping Beauty* to the Eden-Théâtre in Paris, along with some twenty-five soloists from the Imperial ballet, which, if it had happened, would have been the company's first-ever tour.[40] As it was, it was Milan that gave the ballet its first showing outside St Petersburg, staged at La Scala by Giorgio Saracco in 1896. *Peterburgskaia gazeta* reported:

> Foreign audiences are becoming increasingly acquainted with the compositions of P. Tchaikovsky. This winter in Milan the ballet *Sleeping Beauty* is being staged at La Scala for the first time. La Scala's ballet master Mr. Saracco arrived in Petersburg yesterday and saw our ballet master Mr Petipa. Mr Saracco took this opportunity to receive directions from our ballet master. Dancing in *The Sleeping Beauty* will be Miss Brianza. No doubt this poetic ballet and Tchaikovsky's exquisite music will please the Italians.[41]

The Nutcracker

Tchaikovsky's next ballet commission was *The Nutcracker*. But before that came other ballets, including *The Water Lily* (Neniufar, 1890), a one-act 'choreographic fantasy', to music by Krotkov, led by a vivid and poetic Varvara Nikitina as the titular flower. There was also *Calcabrino* (1891), for which Minkus composed his last ballet score. Brianza created the double role of the flower-girl Marietta and the demon Draginiazza, not so different from the future Odette-Odile duality. Press consensus said that Brianza and the rest of the cast did much to overcome Modest Tchaikovsky's reputedly meagre scenario, briefly outlined in chapter 6. Shiriaev remembers how 'the ballet really suited Brianza's dance abilities', how everything was tailored on her and how, as 'a dark-complexioned brunette with black eyes, she really looked like some demon'.[42] Her superlative, assured technique— 'such an abundance of double turns [...] you marvel her head has not started whirling'—launched Bezobrazov, Skalkovsky, and others into rhapsodies. Petipa devised fiendishly difficult but always graceful *pas* in which she had three different partners—Gerdt, as the brutish smuggler Calcabrino, Nikolai Legat as Olivier, the man she loves, and Cecchetti as Robert, another smuggler.[43] The ballet showed Petipa's inventiveness at its best: a first-act ballabile was remarkable for its lace-work patterns; a *grand pas d'ensemble* offered an apparently original mix of classical and character dance. Also noted was Petipa's desire to push forward the company's newest talents: Varvara Rykhliakova, Olga Preobrazhenskaya, and Matilda Kshesinskaya.[44]

The ballet did not survive long, although with its final performances in 1895 it outlasted Brianza.[45] She also appeared in the 1891 revival of King Candaules, 'one of the grandest ballets of the 'good old times'.[46] The performances and production made a good impression on some levels, on others not (see also chapter 6). Contemporary audiences, accustomed to the high-wire excitement of the Italians, were no longer going to be blown away by the virtuosic tricks of the 'Pas Dor'; but, now modified, it was glitteringly performed by Brianza and Cecchetti. Several reviewers thought Brianza unsuited to her role's heavy emphasis on mime.[47] Pleshcheev says that Brianza, aware of the public's cooling towards her after King Candaules, decided, 'with great tact and dignity', to end her contract a year early. She appeared again in King Candaules for her farewell performance (16 February 1892), and her fellow-dancers, who loved her greatly, gave her a silver crown of laurels which moved her to tears.[48] The always colourful Skalkovsky, on the other hand, blames Nikitina's superlative performance in the same ballet's 'Les Amours de Diane' divertissement: the fiery Brianza objected to the bodice of Nikitina's costume being the same colour as hers and nothing could dissuade her from leaving.[49] Brianza went on to dance in Vienna, Italy, Paris, and London. After dancing Aurora in The Sleeping Beauty at La Scala, she returned to St Petersburg in 1896, appearing at the Maly Theatre in a one-act divertissement, In Venus's Grotto (V grote Veneri), staged by Saracco, where she seemed already faded and a great deal plumper.[50] On retiring she became a teacher in Paris. In 1921 she was in London, assisting Bronislava Nijinska in the Ballets Russes version of The Sleeping Beauty (renamed The Sleeping Princess) and appearing as Carabosse. However, the end of her life is a mystery: she is said to have committed suicide in Paris between 1930 and 1935.[51]

The two-act Nutcracker was conceived to be coupled, in the old manner of programming, with the premiere of Tchaikovsky's one-act opera Iolanthe. There is some uncertainty as to who was responsible for the libretto, based on E. T. A. Hoffmann's story The Nutcracker and the Mouse King. Roland John Wiley, in Tchaikovsky's Ballets, says it is normally attributed to Petipa and Vsevolozhsky (who also designed at least some of the luxurious costumes), but in his later Life and Ballets of Lev Ivanov, he veers towards Vsevolozhsky. Other sources, such as Benois, name Petipa alone.[52] Either way, evidence suggests that, after agreeing on the production, the collaborators came to realize the unsuitability of the libretto.[53] In fact, without its music the ballet would probably not have survived. The first act, the Silberhaus family's Christmas party, has more action than dancing and feels fragmentary, its separate incidents loosely strung together; the fantastical second act, which bears little relation to the first, is a divertissement and wholly static. The leading characters are children: Clara Silberhaus, her brother Fritz, and the

Nutcracker Prince, who do little dancing. There is a ballerina role, the Sugar Plum Fairy (*la Fée Dragée*), but she only appears in the second act, to perform a pas de deux with her cavalier Prince Coqueluche.[54] 'Above all,' Wiley writes, '*Nutcracker* loses the element of relation to human experience that *Sleeping Beauty* gained in the process of adaptation from story to ballet.'[55] The result remains a simple children's tale—which is what detractors wrongly said about *The Sleeping Beauty*—leaving adults at the end wondering whether there was anything else.

Tchaikovsky had vacillated over the project from the start. However, as Wiley argues, it perhaps acquired a deeper meaning for him after the death of his sister, Alexandra (Sasha). Perhaps he was inspired to identify Sasha with the Sugar Plum Fairy, and himself with Drosselmayer, the Silberhaus children's mysterious magician-godfather, played at the premiere by Stukolkin, who creates the harmonious second-act vision of the Kingdom of Sweets (*Confiturembourg*).[56] Another theory comes from Fedor Lopukhov, who reads into the ballet a progression from hardship to happiness, believing that Petipa's notes show traces of an original intention to invoke the French Revolution. (Lopukhov was writing during the Soviet era.) A ballet about childhood, he argues, may well have stirred up in Petipa memories of stories told by his parents about the French Revolution, as well as memories of his own first-hand experiences during the Belgian revolution.[57] A remnant of Petipa's allegedly early schema appears in the first act, when the adults dress up as *incroyables* and dance to Tchaikovsky's version of a well-known French song, 'Bon voyage Monsieur Dumollet'.[58] Petipa also originally listed a dance to 'La Carmagnole', the most popular song of the French Revolution, but removed it. With the resonances of the French Revolution (if indeed they were planned), the battle of the mice and tin soldiers would have taken on a whole new meaning. But such heavy-handed allusions were maybe judged unsuitable for the imperial stage, even if Petipa—as might be supposed—had envisaged an imperially correct resolution.[59] So instead the ballet was staged primarily with children, for children.[60] Later producers, frustrated by the structural flaws, have tried, like dance historians, to find unifying subtexts, notably the Soviet choreographer Vasilii Vainonen. His long-lived 1934 version downplayed Hoffmann's supernatural dimension to cast the narrative into an allegory about growing up.

On 26 August 1892, little more than three months before the premiere, *Peterburgskaia gazeta* reported: 'The ballet season is beginning with illnesses. The first ballet master M. Petipa has fallen rather seriously ill.' (It added that the second ballet master Ivanov had also fallen ill, so that all ballet rehearsals were being supervised by Cecchetti.) On 9 September 1892 the same newspaper announced that 'the health of the ballet master M. Petipa is still poor enough for the doctors not to allow him to leave his apartment.'[61] By 29 September Petipa's continuing illness, according to another newspaper, would necessitate Lev Ivanov's taking over the preparations.[62] Commentators have suggested Petipa's illness was tactical, to remove himself from a lost cause. But Petipa was certainly tired, tired enough already the previous year to ask Tchaikovsky to petition Vsevolozhsky on his behalf for a paid holiday. (It is not known if the request was successful.)[63]

He had, after all, followed *The Sleeping Beauty* with *The Water Lily*, the new three-act *Calcabrino*, and a revival of *King Candaules*. Then, just a few months later, he had staged a new production of Taglioni's *La Sylphide* (19 January 1892) and the one-act *Fairy Tale* (Volshebnaia skazka) for the school (10 February 1892).[64]

Not only that, but this was the time of family heartbreak, with his daughter Evgenia's death aged just fifteen, in 1892, after the amputation of her leg. According to his other daughter Vera, he was present at the operation and 'the suffering he experienced caused a nervous illness in him.'[65] This may be a reference to the skin ailment of painful itching lesions which, as recorded in his surviving diaries, tormented him in the last years of his life. After four months of medical observation, he was diagnosed on 10 March 1893 with the serious autoimmune disease pemphigus.[66] Since pemphigus was potentially fatal (today it is successfully treated by steroids), it is likely he had pemphigoid, a less severe variant unidentified in his time, which typically appears after middle age.[67] The medical report, sent to the directorate by his doctor Professor Poletebnov, underlined the absolute necessity for Petipa to take the waters in Levico, Southern Tyrol, famous for springs rich in iron and arsenic. The directorate's subsequent records show permission granted for a four-month break from 15 April, with full pay and an additional one-off allowance of 1,000 roubles for treatment.[68]

So with all this, it seems more than likely that Petipa was not playing truant. There remains, though, the further question of how much in *The Nutcracker* was Ivanov's work. According to Khudekov, Ivanov composed only one act; according to Vsevolozhsky's assistant Vladimir Pogozhev this was the second half of the ballet. Petipa attributed the mise en scène and choreography to Ivanov, but the libretto to himself, which, as evidenced by his written 'Instructions to Tchaikovsky' and his own 'Ballet Master's Plan' determined the detailed order of the action and musical numbers.[69] And although Petipa remained housebound during the preparations, he was, reported *Birzhevye vedomosti*, providing Ivanov with his 'counsel and instructions'.[70] What is certain is Ivanov's authorship of the 'Waltz of the Snowflakes', an outstanding symphonic sequence bridging the first and second acts. Pattern and dynamic build together in the manner of a blizzard, the thirty dancers in white tutus and bobbled headdresses spiralling and whirling, expanding and contracting, weaving and flurrying. True, as seen earlier, snow dances had long been fashionable, and Petipa had choreographed his own, in *Camargo* (1872) and *The Daughter of the Snows* (1879). But Skalkovsky in his review thought Ivanov's version better, and today it is viewed as a signpost to Ivanov's remarkable achievement in *Swan Lake*.[71] About the ballet as a whole, however, Skalkovsky in the same review concluded: 'For dancers there is very little in it, for art—absolutely nothing, and for the artistic fate of our ballet—this is one more little step downwards.'[72]

That, without the doom-laden prediction, seems to have been the overall critical consensus. Turning to separate elements, the first-act dances of the mechanical dolls—a *vivandière*, a soldier, Colombine, and Harlequin—were, mostly, noted approvingly, but the battle of the mice and tin soldiers was too long, too confused, and with too much aimless running about. The dances of the second act were variably successful, the Chinese dance representing tea was encored, and Shiraev's acrobatics, which included jumping through a hoop in the 'Danse des bouffons' were wonderfully deft. Meanwhile, the decor of the Kingdom of Sweets was an inventive profusion of all kinds of lollipops, sweets, and gingerbreads, to the extent that just to look at it was, for Skalkovsky, a cloying experience. Tchaikovsky himself thought the designs overdone: 'The eyes weary from this luxury.'[73]

The music was well received, but with some sniping about its failure to be *dansante*.[74] The music critic, Vladimir Baskin, saw the question from a different angle: *The Nutcracker* was the best of Tchaikovsky's ballet scores and wasted on such mindless nonsense.[75]

The Italian ballerina Antoinetta Dell'Era, engaged to replace Brianza on the imperial stage, had no rival in 'acrobatic' dance and was nicknamed the Goliath of Technique. She was blessed with remarkable elevation and an ability to execute triple tours on point without support, as well as to go straight on to her toes from a kneeling position.[76] But she was given little to do as the Sugar Plum Fairy, and so late in the ballet. Supported by Gerdt's Prince Coqueluche, she seemed, in the last part of the pas de deux's adagio, to glide along the stage, drawn on a piece of fabric pulled by Gerdt.[77] The dancer Vladimir Soliannikov was unimpressed: her heavy build, he wrote in his memoirs, was contrary to the role of the Sugar Plum Fairy. Petipa himself had ventured '*madame* no good', although his view was perhaps shaped by the disparaging remarks she had made about him in the Berlin press.[78]

Lev Ivanov

It was Petipa who persuaded Ivanov in 1882 to accept the post of *régisseur*, despite Ivanov's own qualms 'knowing my too kindly and weak character'. But it was also Petipa, by Ivanov's account, who was the first to complain to Frolov, supervisor of the ballet troupe, and to the director about Ivanov's performance of his duties. He was consequently succeeded in 1885 by Alberto di Segni who, when he died just three years later, was in turn briefly succeeded by his assistant Konstantin Efimov and then, in 1889, by Vladimir Langammer, dramatist, librettist, and the former *régisseur* of the now-defunct German troupe. Ivanov admitted he had found his duties 'most disquieting' and although his new appointment in 1885 as second ballet master 'was not especially calm, it was altogether better'.[79]

The testimonies of Ivanov's character are notable for their unanimity. 'A remarkably modest, undemanding, weak-willed, very good, mild, although occasionally also irascible person,' Vazem writes.[80] He was good-natured, states Pleshcheev, free of intrigue and loved by everyone.[81] He was also an eccentric with his sudden outbursts and his custom, throughout his life, of wearing the same khaki-green outfits; but he was also unfocussed and indolent and not by temperament suited to enforcing discipline. 'It is easy to imagine how Ivanov the person could endear while Ivanov the *régisseur* could falter,' writes Wiley.[82] As a teacher, he was, like Gerdt, somewhat mediocre. Kshesinskaya mentions how, while accompanying classes on the violin, he seemed to like his violin better than his pupils and was content to fall back on routine. 'In a lazy voice he would tell us: "Pliez!" or "Genoux en dehors!" but he never stopped us, made no corrections, did not interrupt the class to point out a pupil's wrong movement.'[83] Later, she discovered that he had another passion besides his violin: food. Although married, he rarely ate at home and was particularly fond of a restaurant called Dominique on Nevsky Prospect. When he was *régisseur*, artists wishing to speak to him would head for Dominique, knowing that probably they would find him there.[84]

He had an extraordinary memory, for both the ballet repertoire and music. Although untrained, he composed music and was able to play anything on the piano by ear. There was a striking example of this, when Anton Rubinstein was invited to play his ballet score *The Grapevine*, a fairly long and complex piece, in the company's rehearsal hall for Petipa and others. Having finished, Rubinstein was making his way out, when he was amazed to hear the sounds of his music being played again. It was Ivanov and Rubinstein, finding him, told him that he had never in his musical career encountered such a feat.[85] Even so, there were occasional strange lapses in Ivanov's musicality: he confessed to Shiriaev, for example, that he did not understand the Spanish dance in *The Nutcracker*, hardly a complicated piece of music.[86]

Ivanov's first composition as second ballet master was the brief one-act *The Enchanted Forest* (1887), to music by Drigo, for the school's graduation performance. After its premiere, it was deemed good enough to be transferred to the professional company, where it lasted, with changes, some twenty years. It already contained, in Wiley's estimation, certain defining characteristics: a flimsy libretto and, counterbalancing this, a flair for well-constructed dance, although Petipa's surviving work notes for an 1889 gala revival of *The Enchanted Forest* also endorse the claim that Petipa 'meddled' in the preparations of at least some of Ivanov's ballets.[87]

As described in the previous chapter, *The Haarlem Tulip*, which followed the same year, was on a different scale of ambition. Again, the scenario was weak, but the dances were strong. Arguing that Ivanov's choreographic inspiration grew directly out of the music, Natalia Roslavleva writes that he was particularly handicapped by the unremarkable scores that fell to his lot. It was only when Tchaikovsky came along that Ivanov's gifts fully surfaced. 'With his Russian soul and enormous talent,' she continues, 'Ivanov responded to the call of Tchaikovsky's genius, a genius equally Russian by its very nature.'[88]

Claims have been made for the wasted genius of Ivanov, on the basis of the 'Waltz of the Snowflakes' and *Swan Lake*. While Vsevolozhsky had made sweeping reforms in all areas of the Imperial Theatres, there remained the fact that two out of the three ballet masters in St Petersburg were foreigners—Cecchetti was made a ballet master around 1890.[89] This has contributed to the inference that Ivanov's career suffered from his balletically less glamorous nationality as well as from a self-effacing personality that stood no chance against the megalomaniac Petipa. Roslavleva refers to Ivanov as a 'fine and sensitive artist' who 'could and would have achieved much more under more favourable circumstances. The supposed bad luck arouse from his character: he was not a fighter and, besides, fighting could hardly have helped in his position.'[90] Vazem concurs:

> A true expert in ballet matters and in particular of classical dance, Ivanov not infrequently mounted separate dance numbers and even ballets for the theatre school's shows, and also for the big stage, especially when he was *régisseur* of the ballet troupe. However, Petipa did not give him much room in this direction, not wishing to create a rival for himself. Subsequently Ivanov fulfilled the duties of second ballet master, but in this post he did not manage in full measure to show his undoubted talent of choreographer.[91]

The notion that Petipa jealously suppressed Ivanov is refuted by Wiley, who has viewed Vsevolozhsky's letter (1 March 1885) to the minister of the Imperial Court proposing Ivanov's appointment as second ballet master. The idea was not that Ivanov should enjoy the limelight, but relieve the overworked Petipa.[92] It also seems that Petipa had a hand in the appointment: he was the one, after all, who was overworked; he had made representations about the need to replace Ivanov as *régisseur* and the new job might have seemed a neat solution for making everyone happy.[93] If Ivanov was given the ballets or opera dances Petipa didn't want to stage, or couldn't, it was simply because that was what Ivanov had been hired to do.

Maybe Petipa, at least in one part of himself, did proprietorially guard his position. After all, he was only human and had spent much time and effort to get where he was.[94] But in another part of himself, in his mature years, he seems to have known his worth, so that perhaps he did not fear competition, even dangerous competition, because he knew his mark would remain in history. Either way, there seems no reason not to accept at face value the rebuttal in his memoirs—'I certainly did not plot against the really capable, competent, gifted late Lev Ivanov.'[95] Later, Fedor Lopukhov came to his defence:

He treated Ivanov with great respect and Pavel Gerdt, Nikolai Legat, Alexander Shiriaev, and many others spoke to me personally about this. Enemies and persons envious as much of Petipa as of Ivanov spread the gossip about the hostility of Petipa towards Ivanov, and I stand here in defence of the great master from these mere apprentices. There have— alas!—always been far fewer masters than apprentices who are busy not so much with creativity as with self-promotion. […] If this great master were alive, I would advise him to change his surname Petit-pas to Grand-pas, it would only be right.[96]

What did probably go through Petipa's mind, though, was the worry that Ivanov was inexperienced: Ivanov was a fifty-one-year-old performer, with no choreographic apprenticeship apart from a handful of dances for opera. Small wonder, then, that Petipa might have felt it necessary to supervise preparations for *The Haarlem Tulip* and other Ivanov ballets, especially as by then Ivanov's haphazard approach to work would have become apparent.[97]

Ivanov had sudden flashes of genius that were not sustained for the longer time span and structural complications of a complete ballet. Indolent and eccentric, he lacked focus, rigour, ambition, and leadership: four qualities that Petipa possessed in abundance. Shiriaev, as a colleague, observed him at close quarters:

Lev Ivanov, on the advice of Petipa, prepared his dance productions at home, but, that said, with his very lazy nature, he often arrived unprepared at the theatre. Then he willingly allowed individual artists not only to refashion this or that element […] but also to mount complete dances. It seemed at times that he was even happy when someone came to his help. Modest and exceptionally kind by nature, Ivanov in general did not like to speak about himself, he never put his own goals first and gained nothing for himself personally.

But on the other hand it would happen that Ivanov would show flashes of such inventiveness, such originality of construction and movement, he would present something so vivid, that you were simply surprised, not knowing where it came from.[98]

The ballerina Tamara Karsavina was largely hostile to Petipa, an inclination she inherited from her father Platon. From Platon, who had been a staunch friend of Ivanov, she heard how Petipa allegedly used Ivanov and trampled over him for his own ends and glory. She also, as a member of Petersburg's modernist generation and follower of Fokine, opposed Petipa for representing the old order, for his antiquated methods of choreographing and formulaic subjugation of music. She admired Ivanov for his forward-looking originality, 'the excellence of the beautifully organic structure of his choreography' which 'you could not divide into sections as you could Petipa's brilliant adagios' but which had 'an inner cohesion [...] one *enchaînement* leading into another, a continuous flow of movement.' Yet, even she, years after, could see the fault lines in Ivanov's talent:

> Had Ivanov's talent been given an unchecked course, could he have become a representative of an epoch such as Petipa had been? Perhaps not. His inspiration welled up richly, but it was undisciplined and moody. Artists coming into a rehearsal might find him playing the piano, improvising. He hardly noticed them and continued playing. Sometimes, becoming aware of their presence, he would get up from the piano and dismiss them. More often, though, his creative mood fertile, he might go on composing, keeping the artists beyond all reasonable time. It is doubtful if he would have left behind him anything like the consistent, highly polished output of Petipa, but he might have left to us many unfading flowers of poetic inspiration, deeper far and of broader vision. In his use of integrated dance as distinct from mere uncoordinated steps, he was the precursor of Fokine.[99]

Ivanov's own assessment of his abilities is characteristically modest: 'Although I do not possess a talent such as Mr Petipa's,' he wrote in his short memoir, 'I nevertheless stage ballets no worse than other ballet masters.'[100] It was a view shared by Vsevolozhsky since, after *The Enchanted Forest* and *The Tulip of Haarlem*, Vsevolozhsky felt confident enough to entrust Ivanov with a dozen original ballets. Some were short 'trifles' for the school, or Peterhof, or the relaxed, away-from-scrutiny entertainments at Krasnoe Selo (where Ivanov was in charge of the programming), others, the high-profile projects of *The Nutcracker, Cinderella, Swan Lake*, and in 1897 *The Mikado's Daughter* (Doch' Mikado), although all these, with the exception of *The Mikado's Daughter*, were created collaboratively. In addition, Ivanov revived eighteen ballets—some in Moscow and Warsaw—and created dances for a further twenty-four operas, among them Borodin's *Prince Igor*, in which his choreography of the Polovtsian Dances would influence Fokine's more famous version. In his original creations he was linked with the search for fresh composers: Alexander Friedmann, a remarkable member of the corps de ballet who not only composed the scores for *Cupid's Prank* (Shalost' Amura, 1890) and *The Boatmen's Festival* (Prazdnik lodochnikov, 1891) but also conducted them; Andrei Kadlets, a violinist in the Mariinsky orchestra, for *Acis and Galatea* (Atsis i Galateia, 1896); and Baron Vasilii Wrangell (*Vrangel'*) for *The Mikado's Daughter* (Doch' Mikado, 1897). Untested, apart from Wrangell who had composed a couple of privately presented ballets, none of these individuals seems to have gone beyond the conventionally pleasant. They suggest either Vsevolozhsky was groping in the dark or cutting financial corners.

In July 1893 the announcement was made that the ballet orchestra would be abolished and its functions fulfilled by the opera's. The 1893–1894 season was difficult for further reasons: Gorshenkova and Nikitina left the stage, prompting complaints in the press about the treatment of native-born dancers; and the decision to invite Palmira Pollini as a replacement for Brianza in October turned out to be a mistake, since colourlessness seems to have been her principal attribute. Then came two calamities: on 6 November Tchaikovsky died suddenly, a victim of cholera; and on 3 December Maria Anderson, the promising twenty-three-year-old dancer, chosen by Tchaikovsky himself for the *Sleeping Beauty*'s White Cat, was seriously burnt in her dressing room while getting ready for a rehearsal of *Cinderella*. She had bent down to tie the ribbons of her shoes, when her tunic brushed against a spirit lamp used to heat curling tongs and went up in flames. Screaming, she ran into the foyer where Osip Palechek, stage teacher for the opera company, shouted to her to drop to the floor, following which he and Langammer smothered the flames with a coat and furs. Surrounded by weeping colleagues she was tended by a doctor; her life was saved, but not her career, and her farewell benefit took place the following season.[101]

Meanwhile, Petipa, also battling illness and tragedy, did not choreograph a complete ballet after *A Fairy Tale* for over two years, until *The Awakening of Flora* (23 July 1894). Almost all the ballets in the repertoire for the 1892–1893 and 1893–1894 seasons were collaborations in which Petipa was absent as choreographer (*The Nutcracker* and *Cinderella*) or revivals by Ivanov or Cecchetti, vindicating Cecchetti's appointment as a ballet master.[102] On 26 September 1893 Ivanov revived Petipa's one-act *The Offerings to Love, or Happiness Is Loving* (Zhertvy Amuru, ili Radosti liubvi, 1886). He also created his own *Magic Flute* (Volshebnaia fleita, 1893) and, in tandem with Cecchetti, the dances for Rimsky-Korsakov's 1892 opera-ballet version of *Mlada*. Finally, in the Yearbook of Imperial Theatres Petipa's name no longer appears as one of the school's teachers from 1893–1894 onwards. Perhaps the only positive event in his life during this period was his successful application in 1892 for Russian citizenship and the ceremonial oath-taking on 8 January 1894 in the offices of the directorate.[103]

True, he was involved in *Cinderella*: originally, he was to have been the choreographer, but was relegated to overseeing, while Cecchetti choreographed the first and third acts, Ivanov, the second.[104] Clearly an attempt to repeat *The Sleeping Beauty* genre with another fairy tale by Perrault, the adaptation was by a newcomer, Lidia Pashkova, variously described as an author, the St Petersburg correspondent for the *Figaro* newspaper, a dilettante with Court connections and possibly a relation of Vsevolozhsky.[105] (She would also be the librettist for *Bluebeard* and *Raymonda*.) Her libretto, amended by the directorate, was criticized as dull by the first-night reviewers and accompanied by the now familiar complaint that the staging emphasized spectacle to an excessive degree.[106] However, the magnificent designs for the ballroom of the second act were singled out for praise, as were Ivanov's Russian dance, mazurka, and grand pas d'action.[107]

All this, though, was overshadowed by Legnani's Russian debut. Not only did the thirty-two *fouettés* create a sensation, but so did other displays—such as a sequence of three single turns on point, followed by a double, repeated four times, and then encored, without the slightest hint of effort, all of which the enraptured Skalkovsky had never seen before.[108] Not only did Legnani's technique impress, so did her style—graceful, pliant, flowing, or, in Pleshcheev's choice of adjective, velvety.[109] And not only did her phenomenal technique and style impress, but so did her acting. Her impact was no less than that of Zucchi ten years before.[110] Since everybody wanted to see Legnani, ticket prices were raised for the second performance. The complete ballet remained in the repertoire for four years, after which it was transferred to Moscow.[111]

Swan Lake

The first sign of Petipa's improved health was the aptly named *Awakening of Flora* on 28 July 1894. This time the choreography was by Petipa and the libretto credited to Ivanov and Petipa, a reverse of the previous collaborations, where Ivanov had to fit the dances to Petipa's specifications. Watching a dress rehearsal, the *Peterburgskaia gazeta* welcomed 'the beauties of the picturesque groupings and general ensembles, the consistent classical character of the dances, the stamp of fine taste' as evidence that 'our first ballet master, M. I. Petipa, [is] found here in full strength.'[112] An anacreontic one-act ballet, to music by Drigo, it was staged at Peterhof to celebrate the wedding of Alexander III's daughter Grand Duchess Xenia and featured Matilda Kshesinskaya as Flora, Gerdt as Apollo, and Nikolai Legat as Mercury. On 8 January the following year it was brought to the Mariinsky, on the occasion of Maria Anderson's farewell benefit, sharing the programme with a revival of Petipa's *The Parisian Market* and various ballet extracts. *The Awakening of Flora*, as Wiley remarks, was not only the awakening of Petipa, but also the dawning of the last great flowering of his art. It was followed by the St Petersburg *Swan Lake*, the score and certain narrative components considerably revised since the last Moscow showing thirteen years before.[113]

Clearly the involvement of a composer of the calibre of Tchaikovsky meant that the Moscow *Swan Lake* did not go unnoticed. Early in 1886, long before *The Sleeping Beauty* was mooted, Vsevolozhsky was thinking of producing an extract from *Swan Lake* for a summer programme at Krasnoe Selo. However, although Tchaikovsky seems to have been happy to comply, insisting that they should use the music for the first lakeside scene—'the best in all respects'—there is no evidence that the project materialized. Instead, it was the ballet master August Berger in Prague who staged the first lakeside scene on 21 February 1888, for the second of two concerts at which Tchaikovsky conducted some of his own works.[114] That said, there are indications that back in St Petersburg further plans were being activated during Tchaikovsky's lifetime and that the composer approved certain modifications to his score (see below). Petipa in his memoirs claims that, believing the ballet's lack of success in Moscow could not be attributed to the music, he himself proposed a new version to Vsevolozhsky and the composer was delighted.[115] Moreover, Petipa's own working papers include diagrams and notes for the first and, especially, the second lakeside scenes, although as everybody knows these would in fact be choreographed in a different style by Ivanov.[116] (Petipa's notes also make clear that he envisaged introducing eight black swans, symbols of disaster, in the final scene.)

One certainty is that the composer's death galvanized the directorate. Within a month Vsevolozhsky had written to Voronstov-Dashkov asking permission for a memorial concert to raise funds for a monument to the composer. The programme he specifies includes one act of *Swan Lake*, a foretaste of a new complete production, which, he says, he wishes to propose for the next season. Since Petipa was still ill, the choreography for the memorial concert fell to Ivanov who, in accordance with Tchaikovsky's wish, chose the first lakeside scene. (Contrary to what has been suggested, the full production did not, therefore, result from Ivanov's success with this scene.)[117] The memorial concert took place on 17 February 1894 and was repeated on 22 February, during which Legnani danced the role of the Swan Princess Odette.[118] Although the concerts were poorly attended—the ticket prices had been pitched far too high—there was no doubt that Ivanov's choreography and Legnani's performance were triumphs.[119] The partnering adagio (accompanied by violin and cello) was 'a compete choreographic poem'.[120]

For the full version, the St Petersburg collaborators seem to have recognized that there were difficulties with both the Moscow libretto and the score. The libretto's origins are unclear: it was published anonymously, although Modest Tchaikovsky, in his brother's biography, and another memoirist Nikolai Kashkin name the Bolshoi Theatre's repertoire supervisor Vladimir Begichev. (Modest also includes the Moscow dancer Vasilii Geltser, but this attribution seems unlikely.) There are also signs that Tchaikovsky participated in the libretto, especially since he had already used a variant of the story before, for family theatricals at his sister's estate. The characters and themes contain echoes of Wagner, especially the Wagner of *Lohengrin*, which would most likely have come from Tchaikovsky.[121]

Modest Tchaikovsky revised the original libretto for St Petersburg with suggestions from Vsevolozhsky. The same scenes and premises remain, except that the original contained not one but two evil demons: Odette's evil sorceress stepmother, who had put Odette under a spell, and the rather superfluous Rothbart who first appears at the ball. Modeste sensibly merged the stepmother with Rothbart and ensured that Rothbart met his fatal retribution at the end. He also removed some of the narrative detail for greater performance clarity, such as Odette's crown, given to her as protection by her grandfather. And at Vsevolozhsky's request he dispensed with the climactic flood which engulfed Odette and Siegfried at the end—'these floods are trite and do not succeed well on our stage.'[122] (Instead the lovers throw themselves into the lake.)

Riccardo Drigo was designated to collaborate with the St Petersburg ballet masters to reorder, reshape, cut, and add to the musical numbers, as well as re-orchestrate them. It was, as Drigo wrote in his memoirs, 'a thankless yet utterly crucial task'; his duty, 'like a surgeon, to perform an operation'.[123] For all Drigo's humility, care, and skill, the obvious question is still whether Tchaikovsky would have approved all the changes. About 36 per cent of the original score was deleted.[124] There were also additions. Although the published St Petersburg score contains the claim that three inserted numbers (orchestrations of three of Tchaikovsky's piano pieces from Op. 72) were endorsed by the composer himself, it is still hard to believe that he would have authorized using the 'Valse bluette' (Op. 72, no. 11) in the final act with its dramatically jarring change of key.[125]

For the choreography it clearly made sense to keep Ivanov's successful lake-side choreography—'the second scene is composed,' Petipa wrote to himself in his working notes.[126] At some point it was also decided to assign the other lakeside scene to Ivanov, even though Petipa's working notes show that he had already prepared a great deal. Petipa has been accused of territorialism, determined not only to stamp out rivals but to keep the best for himself. Yet here it seems Petipa the artist recognized the importance of stylistic consistency for the lakeside choreography. Petipa therefore choreographed the first scene, where Siegfried celebrates his coming of age, and the ballroom scene, although for the national dance *divertissement* Petipa assigned the Venetian and Hungarian (csardas) numbers to Ivanov, keeping just the Spanish and mazurka numbers for himself.[127]

The division of labour was suited to the respective abilities of the two ballet masters. The scenes belonging to Petipa have a public formality entirely in keeping with the brilliant outward display and symmetry of his style. For the *valse champêtre* of the first scene he envisaged not only stools, allowing for variable levels, but also a maypole, the moving ribbons producing an effective picture.[128] Ivanov's choreography in the lakeside scenes has an entirely different, intimate, and melodic quality, Siegfried and Odette falling in love in the internalized narrative of the first scene's pas de deux. To repeat a much-repeated observation: Ivanov's structures are more fluid than Petipa's perfectly divided geometries; one section flows into the other, just as the movement seems to grow organically out of the soul of the music. For the final scene, he kept Petipa's idea of introducing black swans, which enter weaving their way through the white swans and add to the sense of doom.[129]

The partnership with Ivanov worked seamlessly, avoiding any sense of choreographic disjointedness, yet within the unity was a congruous contrast between the lyrical dream-like 'white' acts and the real world of the royal court. The designs were luxurious and appropriate, although the apotheosis, Odette and Siegfried seated on giant swans in the clouds, was considered rather absurd.[130] The score, though, failed to please the first-night critics and the ballet received mixed reviews. Even so, *Novoe vremia* exclaimed 'what a poetical ballet is *Swan Lake!*', *Novosti i birzhevaia gazeta* found the swans' waltz in Act I, Scene 2 'simple and beautiful', and the Hungarian dance and mazurka were unanimously praised.[131] One reason for the success of these last two was the popularity of their lead dancers: Marie Petipa and Bekefi (Hungarian dance), Marie, as always, looking sensational in her costume, adorned this time by 12,000 roubles' worth of diamonds; and the elderly Kshesinsky, 'the king of the mazurka' who danced with his daughter Matilda and created 'an absolute sensation'.[132] Unlike the 1877 Moscow premiere with its weak, if beautiful ballerina—Polina Karpakova—the St Petersburg version had a superlative Odette-Odile in Legnani: the lakeside pas de deux was 'a chef d'oeuvre in the performance of the ballerina', her brilliant technique accompanied by 'a lightness of movement and plasticity of pose'. Gerdt, as always, gathered praise as cavalier and mime, notwithstanding what Bezobrazov called in his review of the memorial concert programme 'the pas de deux à trois' with Alexander Oblakov (Benno) participating, or, as is usually inferred, helping out. In fact, so well accepted was this arrangement that when Nikolai Legat, replacing Gerdt, partnered the ballerina alone and danced the Black Swan pas de deux (previously danced by Gorsky), he only earned reproaches from the reviewers.[133]

The premiere on 15 January 1895 was the first ballet performance after the period of mourning for Alexander III, who had died in 1894 from kidney disease. Petipa followed the performance from his usual seat in the first wing and Drigo conducted, as he had done for the previous Tchaikovsky ballets.[134] *Swan Lake* was the last of the Ivanov-Petipa collaborations; from then on, Ivanov would have fewer opportunities, but more autonomy when they came along.[135] He would go on to compose *Acis and Galatea*, *The Mikado's Daughter*, and the produced but not performed *Egyptian Night* (Egipetskaia noch').

Set to a libretto by the *régisseur* Langammer, the mythological *Acis and Galatea* was premiered at a benefit on 21 January 1896 celebrating Marie Petipa's twenty-five years of service. On the same programme was another premiere: Petipa's jolly, if trivial *Halt of the Cavalry*, in which the pretty villagers Maria (Marie Petipa) and Teresa (Legnani) are rivals for the affections of Pierre (Gerdt). Using operetta-style music by Johann Armsheimer, a German-born brass player in the Imperial Theatres, Petipa's story sets forth the comical havoc caused among the three main characters and other villagers by the arrival of a regiment of gallant hussars. The ballet gives equal status to classical (as represented by Legnani) and character dance, and for maximum effect Marie wore a genuine Hungarian folk dress from

Budapest. After the performance she hosted a lavish dinner for company friends and various literary figures at Cubat's, the city's most fashionable restaurant.[136]

Ivanov's *The Mikado's Daughter*, premiered on 9 November 1897, had another libretto by Langammer, staged with great splendour and an unprecedented richness of ethnographic detail. Evgenii Ponomarev's new costumes totalled some 600. The press made much of rumoured factional disputes during the ballet's gestation and alleged that Petipa had declined to take it on. At least one report claimed this was because of the ballet's poor music and unsuitable narrative, although *japonaiserie* was not new on the Russian stage. (In fact, the previous year *Daita*, a Japanese-themed ballet, was imported from Paris for the Moscow Bolshoi, albeit with little success.) Either way, it fell to Ivanov's lot and the puzzle is that Vsevolozhsky persisted with what was accurately predicted to be a flop. Stuffed with dances, it was the *ballet-féerie* at its most overblown. Only the performers escaped unscathed: Kshesinskaya, given much to do as the titular heroine, won extravagant praise for her stamina, faultless technique, and charm.[137]

The last fourteen years of Ivanov's life were, Wiley records, plagued by debt, apparently brought on by illness in his family, educational expenses (his second surviving son was deaf-mute), and general difficulties, although the exact details remain unknown. The Ministry of the Imperial Court's responses to his numerous petitions were laudable, but on 26 April 1898 Ivanov's own health began a precipitous decline, necessitating further financial help for treatment. The first loan was guaranteed by Petipa, Drigo, and Cecchetti; the last loan, by Petipa and Drigo and was, it must be assumed, repaid by them after Ivanov's death on 11 December 1901.[138] At that time, Petipa was nearly eighty-three and also in poor health, but then, for all his faults, he had always been generous with money. He had done the same for Pugni, years ago.

The Coronation of Nicholas II

Marie Petipa's twenty-fifth anniversary began a celebratory year that continued with Petipa's own benefit in December marking fifty years of service. This is the benefit that showcased the premiere of the *ballet-féerie Bluebeard*, the last work to be based on a Perrault fairy tale. It was a moving occasion packed with Petipa's colleagues from all the theatres. He was showered with gifts and tributes, led by Lev Ivanov who made the first address. Legnani gave him a silver lyre with the inscription 'to the ballet master—poet, great artist, as a memento of my eternal gratitude'.[139] And from Emperor Nicholas II he received the title of Soloist of His Imperial Majesty, the first time a member of the ballet had ever received such a high honour.[140]

This was the period when an exciting new generation of Russian dancers was emerging. Olga Preobrazhenskaya graduated into the company in 1889, the same time as Alexander Gorsky. Matilda Kshesinskaya arrived a year later, becoming Kshesinskaya 2 since she already had a sister (Iulia) in the company, followed by Vera Trefilova in 1894. From Moscow in 1896 came Liubov Roslavleva, a representative of the 'new school' who, according to Marie Petipa, 'if she were to fall from the second floor, would confidently stand up on point without a totter.'[141] Also transferred from Moscow the same year was a young soloist, the future star Ekaterina Geltser; she would stay two years in Petersburg perfecting her art generally and learning from Preobrazhenskaya especially.[142] The same year (1898) as Geltser's return home, Liubov Egorova joined the company together with Iulia Sedova and Mikhail Fokine. They were followed by Anna Pavlova (1899) and Tamara Karsavina (1902).

The Petersburg ballerinas would owe much to the teaching of Beretta in Milan and Cecchetti, closer to home. Although indispensable during Petipa's illness, Cecchetti was an unremarkable choreographer and producer. But he was an outstanding teacher and as a representative of the Italian school was viewed with some hostility by the teaching establishment. When, in April 1893, he was appointed teacher of mime at the theatre school, he might well have resented not being asked to do more. Later, in recognition of the need to meet the demands of the new style and shape dancers able to replace the guest celebrities, the school changed this stance. In 1896 it gave him responsibility for the advanced classical class for girls.[143]

In the interim, however, in 1892, Cecchetti had opened his own private school in his large apartment, the first alternative to the theatre school and the first to teach the Milanese system.[144] If the theatre school was reluctant to accept Cecchetti, young company dancers immediately spotted the extramural possibilities. Preobrazhenskaya, once almost rejected by the theatre school because of an allegedly ungainly physique, benefitted enormously from her grinding work with Cecchetti (and Beretta in Milan) so that, for example, in *The Mikado's Daughter* she could follow a series of *entrechat-six* with turns on one leg, all the more difficult because of the slow tempo.[145] But she also transformed herself into a nuanced artist, with a delicate, musical quality. She seemed not to dance *to* the music so much as actually dance the music, absorbing every musical subtlety and creating something fresh.[146]

The Italian system did not replace, but enhanced the Franco-Russian school and Cecchetti can be credited with its transformation. He would be the last foreigner to exercise a pivotal influence on Russian ballet. As well as enabling ballerinas to indulge in the new trick steps, he instilled in them the importance of extreme precision and gave them the means to attain with greater ease the lyrical, elegant qualities of the old French school.[147] In this way, as described by Shiriaev, he solved Pavlova's difficulties with point work:

Quite a few of our best classical ballerinas studied with him. He toughened up their legs, giving them, through his exercises, that muscular strength which had marked him out. Anna Pavlova—the great ballerina for two decades of the twentieth century—is much indebted to him for the development of her talent. The high instep of Pavlova's feet prevented her from standing firmly on point. The French school of her teacher Gerdt paid little attention to this side of ballet training. At the beginning of her career, Pavlova coped so badly with her 'points' that once, turning in the finale of a variation, she could not remain on her feet and ended up sitting on the lighting box. The lessons with Cecchetti eliminated these shortcomings in her art and created real 'steel' points for her.[148]

Christian Johansson resented dancers going to Cecchetti.[149] He rebuked Kshesinskaya with the words, 'If you don't like my teaching, I can stop giving you classes altogether.'[150] But later, when she was assigned her first lead role, replacing Brianza in *Calcabrino* in November 1892, she hurried back to Cecchetti:

I worked diligently with Cecchetti, anxious to make myself ready for such an important role, and striving fully to attain the virtuosity which the Italian dancers were then demonstrating on the Russian stage. Italian technique called for abrupt, precise, clear-cut movements, while Russian and French techniques are more lyrical, softer, more expressive, even in steps most marked with brio and virtuosity.

Having acquired the power and precision of the Italian school, she returned 'to our own technique, realizing its grace and beauty'.[151] In the same way, Pavlova never lost her distinctive Franco-Russian style, even though she spent even longer studying with Cecchetti. When in 1902 Cecchetti was fired by the new director of the Imperial Theatres, Teliakovsky, he moved to the Imperial Theatre of Warsaw where he was ballet master, but it was with Pavlova's encouragement, in 1906, that he set up as a private teacher in St Petersburg again. In 1910 he joined the Ballets Russes as teacher and mime, creating roles such as the Showman in Fokine's *Petrushka*; and in 1918 he opened a school in London, from then on refining and codifying the Cecchetti method which would be adopted by the Royal Ballet School and widely disseminated long after his death in 1928.

Kshesinskaya also inherited Brianza's other role of Aurora on 17 January 1893. Like Vazem, she was a *terre-à-terre* dancer, lacking elevation. She was tiny, pretty, but not beautiful; her line was marred, detractors said, by legs that were too short and stocky. But she had, above all, fizz and extraordinary charm, both on and off stage. 'Almost every appearance by Miss Kshesinskaya was accompanied by the emptying of Petersburg's flower shops,' wrote one reviewer. 'They presented her not with baskets of flowers, but flower beds.'[152]

This was also the time of her liaison with the tsarevich, engineered largely through her own ploys. She was energetic, fiercely ambitious, and exceptionally determined. Already at her graduation performance she had managed to get herself noticed by Alexander III, although that may have been more to do with the emperor recognizing her as Felix Kshesinsky's daughter. She claims he commanded her to 'be the glory and the adornment of our ballet' and then arranged that she sit next to him and the tsarevich at the post-performance supper.[153] To facilitate her evenings with the tsarevich, she left her parental home in the autumn of 1892, to live at 18 Angliisky Prospect, a house that belonged to Rimsky-Korsakov.[154] (It was this house that the Bolsheviks commandeered as their headquarters in 1917.) The romance was the talk of St Petersburg, boosted by Kshesinskaya's own inability not to boast or put on airs. But, alas, the tsarevich's interest began to wane and his engagement to Princess Alix of Hesse was announced in April 1894. Kshesinskaya's despair was complete, unalleviated by a 'settlement' offered to her of 100,000 roubles and the house on Angliisky Prospect, bought for her by the tsarevich.[155] It was during this unhappy period that she created the title role of *The Awakening of Flora* at Peterhof, where she knew that the tsarevich was in the audience.

In her last letter to him she asked that she be able to continue to call him 'thou' (*ty*) and, when needed, go straight to him for help: requests which he granted in his reply.[156] He would be reminded of this many times, starting on the occasion of his coronation in Moscow as Nicholas II. Kshesinskaya discovered that Petipa's *pièce d'occasion* for the gala on 17 May 1896, *The Pearl* (Zhemchuzhina), would be led by Legnani as the White Pearl, while other ballerinas, drawn from both the Petersburg and Moscow companies, would personify pearls of other hues. Her name, however, was nowhere to be seen in the cast. The omission was perhaps driven by a concern for propriety and tact, since everyone (including the empress) knew of the romance; moreover, the ballet's rather obscure allegorical libretto was, rumour said, intended as a homage to the empress. Either way, Kshesinskaya lost no time in appealing to Nicholas via her old friend from Krasnoe Selo days, Grand Duke Vladimir Alexandrovich. Nicholas was in awe of his powerful uncle and the result was swift: Drigo speedily composed additional music and Petipa arranged a pas de deux for her as a Yellow Pearl.[157]

Meanwhile Kshesinskaya had pragmatically found herself another Romanov 'protector' in the shape of the immensely wealthy Grand Duke Sergei Mikhailovich, a cousin of the emperor. He gave her a luxurious seaside villa at Strelna near Peterhof, indulged her every whim, and would remain her devoted companion in the years ahead.[158] He continued even after she began a romance with another grand duke, Andrei Vladimirovich. (She eventually married Andrei in Cannes in 1921, but by then Sergei had been shot by the Bolsheviks.) When in 1902 the *ménage à trois* resulted in the birth of a son, Vladimir (known as Vova), the birth certificate gave Sergei as the father, although Vova claimed never to know who his real father was.[159]

With so many grand dukes in attendance, Kshesinskaya accumulated even more jewels than Marie Petipa and, like her, wore them on stage, a particularity that was widely reported during her London Ballets Russes appearances in 1911.[160] Her influential champions were public knowledge; unlike other dancers with 'protection', which was probably half the company's women, Kshesinskaya flaunted her conquests.[161] The further advantage of a hotline to the emperor himself, made her a formidable force, able to monopolize the best roles after Legnani's departure.

Raymonda

The reliance on fairy tales, which had marked nearly all the big ballets created in the last decade, was interrupted on 7 January 1898 by *Raymonda*, still performed today, although infrequently in its entirety outside Russia.[162] The penultimate of Petipa's *ballets à grand spectacle*, it represented, in Petipa's artistic evolution, an even greater emphasis on autonomous dance; its nearly stationary narrative pushed Petipa further along the line of dance for the sake of dance.

On 30 May 1896, thirteen days after *The Pearl*, Vsevolozhsky wrote to Petipa:

> If you are recovered from your Moscow tribulations, would you perhaps feel able to receive Mr Glazunov to give him your thoughts about the subject of the ballet he is to compose for the 1897–1898 season? I would like him to have more time to think about his music. At the last dinner at the Kremlin, the emperor's orchestra played a [illegible] by him which delighted me. It's Delibes fused with Tchaikovsky. He's definitely the man we have been looking for to compose ballets.[163]

As seen in chapter 7, the collaboration of Petipa with a ballet novice fifty years younger seems to have followed the usual modus operandi, notwithstanding Petipa's failing memory and Glazunov's reluctance to make changes. Despite this, both men spurred each other to excel. Glazunov produced a superlative score, strong on arresting melody, diversity, sonorous orchestration—and also colour, the music creating, for example, a vividly atmospheric sense of magical torpor in the scene where Raymonda (Legnani) and her friends fall under a spell. Also remarkable was the music's reception in the press: times had moved on. Critics, with only the rarest hesitation, now seemed completely unruffled by a score which, while offering strong rhythms and tunes, was a great deal more ambitious and complex than old-style ballet music. True, Bezobrazov still praised Glazunov in *musique dansante* terms and expressed relief 'after those scores they have been forcing on our exemplary ballet troupe'; but he also thought that 'Raymonda is indebted to a very significant degree to Mr. Glazunov's score.'[164] His specialist colleague Vladimir Baskin, analysing the music a few days later, was also enthusiastic, even if Glazunov had allowed the influence of Wagner and Delibes to show through.[165] Meanwhile, the music critic Vladimir Frolov wrote:

> Despite the subject's paucity and its almost total absence of content, Mr Glazunov has nevertheless known how to bring to it much imagination, taste, and beautiful, animated music, with rhythmic diversity, and interest, orchestrated sonorously and effectively.[166]

Equally appreciated was Petipa's inventiveness, at its most evident in the variations (no fewer than six, each very different, for Raymonda) and the climactic Act III, a glittering, swaggering showcase, some of which—the 'Pas classique hongrois'—is often performed today on its own, with maybe the Hungarian *palotás* which precedes it and additional variations, such as a solo for the hero Jean de Brienne since he didn't have one in the original.[167] Diaghilev included the 'Pas classique hongrois' in *Le Festin* (The Feast), an extended *divertissement*, presented by the Ballets Russes in its first 1909 season. The same *pas* contains Raymonda's most famous solo, unusual for the way it fuses classical and Hungarian dance. The ballerina's arms and repeated *retirés* have, like the music, resonances of Hungarian folk dance; she even claps her hands (or opts for a more 'refined' variant, fingers just brushing). But even more remarkable is her long winding *bourrée-ing* (rippling run) about the stage, repetitive, pared-down movement as drastically radical as the corps de ballet's repeated arabesques in *La Bayadère*. In an extraordinary leap of imagination, Petipa became a minimalist before minimalism; it is tempting to think it gave Fokine the idea for the similar *bourrée-ing* motif in the *Dying Swan* solo he choreographed for Anna Pavlova.

Although Sergei Legat as Jean de Brienne did not have a solo, he was part of a male pas de quatre, another striking component of the 'Pas classique hongrois'. Not being an expert in male dancing, Petipa, it is said, worked sedulously on the composition, making several visits to watch Gerdt's class.[168] Its inclusion mirrored the new abundance of athletic men, the result of Cecchetti's influence, and at the premiere it was encored.[169] 'For the first time Petipa has provided an ensemble variation for four men,' Pleshcheev wrote. 'On other European stages this would be unthinkable, because nowhere would be found four *premier danseurs*, and moreover dancers such as Legat 1 [Sergei] and 3 [Nikolai], Kiaksht, and Gorsky.'[170] Assuming the dance has survived unchanged, its unison jumps and *tours en l'air*, performed twice in canon, even today remain a considerable technical challenge for dancers and an exciting experience for spectators. As such it marks *Raymonda* as significant in the evolution of male dance, the start of

Russian ballet's famously strong male dancing, unequalled anywhere in the twentieth century.[171]

Raymonda's static libretto by Lidia Pashkova, however, is a real problem. Keen to be involved in ballet, she appears to have been persistent: 'You have me in despair,' she wrote to Petipa on 2 September 1898, after he had rejected another of her submissions. 'But if it [the submission] doesn't interest you, throw me a line for a Crimean ballet.'[172] Vsevolozhsky and Petipa clearly thought unsatisfactory her *Raymonda* libretto about medieval courtly love and crusading knights, and made revisions.[173]

Even so, the libretto is both narratively thin and geographically convoluted, visitors of different nationalities being a transparent pretext for wide-ranging national dances—Provençal, Spanish, Arab, Hungarian, Polish. The location, however, is the same for the first two acts: the Provençal castle of Raymonda, Countess of Doris. She, together with her aunt, awaits the return of her fiancé Jean de Brienne, a Crusader fighting under the banner of Andrei II of Hungary. The cast includes troubadours, in attendance to Raymonda, who provide a lyrical foil to the crusading knights, and the White Lady, a ghost (and feeble version of the Lilac Fairy) who protects the castle. Act I, Scene 1 is marked by the arrival of a letter for Raymonda announcing the triumphant return of Jean de Brienne and King Andrei. It is also Raymonda's name-day, which provides the reason for celebratory dances, including a 'Valse provençale' for twenty-two couples and a graceful *pizzicato* solo for Raymonda. The Saracen knight, Abderrakhman (Gerdt), unexpectedly enters, bearing gifts for Raymonda.[174] He is the brutal Islamic counterpart to the Christian Jean de Brienne: a male rivalry already used by Petipa in *Zoraiya* and *Roxana*. Although Raymonda declines the gifts, Abderrakhman, his head turned by her beauty, becomes determined to have her. The guests leave, night approaches, and Raymonda and her friends are left alone. Tired, they all lie down and fall into a strange sleep, except for Raymonda who sits up and looks at them in astonishment. At this point the scene segues into Scene Two, with the appearance of the White Lady, illuminated by moonlight. She beckons Raymonda to follow and leads her into a vision, in a mist-filled park.

De Brienne and allegorical figures appear in the vision, which is the occasion for classical dances, including a pas de deux for Raymonda and de Brienne and exquisite solos for two women. De Brienne disappears and Raymonda is horrified to find herself face to face with Abderrakhman. He is about to carry her off, when she falls unconscious and her real-life friends rush to her aid.

Act II takes place in the castle's courtyard. Knights, nobility, troubadours, and minstrels have gathered for a *cour d'amour* to welcome the Crusaders.[175] Uneasy at de Brienne's non-appearance, Raymonda becomes even more so when Abderrakhman appears with an enormous retinue. She wants to send them away, but her aunt persuades her to observe the laws of hospitality. There follow classical dances, from Raymonda's side, and character dances, from Abderrakhman's. Then, just as Abderrakhman's henchmen are abducting Raymonda, de Brienne enters with King Andrei. The king orders the rivals to settle their conflict in a duel. During the sword fight, the White Lady appears at the back of the stage, causing Abderrakhman suddenly to feel dazed and allowing de Brienne to deliver a mortal blow.

Thereafter the narrative gives up completely and Act III is a pure *divertissement*, a wedding celebration in the grounds of de Brienne's castle (presumably located close to Raymonda's). The presence of Andrei II gives the reason for the 'Pas classique hongrois' as well as Hungarian and Polish national dances (Poland, Petipa seems to have argued, being not so far from Hungary). A final *tableau vivant* depicts a tournament.

In the richness of its staging *Raymonda* surpassed even the ballets of the last seven years.[176] It was also Petipa's last big success. Nearly eighty, he applied himself with his usual meticulousness; no detail was too small for his note taking, right down to the mechanics of dancing with a garland—one end attached to a buttonhole, the other in the dancer's left hand, leaving the right arm free for partnering.[177]

Goodbye to Vsevolozhsky

On 1 February 1899 the mime artist Nikolai Aistov was appointed chief *régisseur* in replacement of Langammer, but that was a minor event in comparison with what was to come four months later. After seventeen years as director of the Imperial Theatres, Vsevolozhsky was moved sideways to the post of director of the Hermitage. He would joke that the Titian madonnas now in his care were far quieter than theatre people: they hung peaceably on the walls of the Hermitage and didn't complain if they were relocated.[178] In private, though, he admitted he had not wanted to exchange 'the movement of the theatre' for the 'stillness of the museum'. He enjoyed designing costumes; but at the Hermitage 'I am surrounded by goddesses and can't even clothe them.'[179] However, Vsevolozhsky was a casualty of the departure of Vorontsov-Dashkov as minister of the Imperial Court in 1897. His successor, Baron Vladimir Frederiks, disliked Vsevolozhsky. As someone who always kept finances in frugal order, Frederiks took a dim view of Vsevolozhsky's extravagance, exemplified at its most extreme by *The Mikado's Daughter*. He also distrusted Vsevolozhsky, considering him duplicitous and quick to shift the blame on the ministry when refusing a request. And he was riled by Vsevolozhsky's familiar manner, treating Fredericks as relatively young and inexperienced, rather than showing the reverence due to a superior.[180]

Vsevolozhsky's tenure was undeniably magnificent not only for ballet but for Russian opera, with the *Queen of Spades* its crowning glory. For ballet, his overseeing editorial eye was a real asset for Petipa, faced with the mountainous complexities of staging a new ballet. 'This work becomes pleasant,' Petipa writes, 'when one finds in the director such a well-informed and gifted adviser as was M. Vsevolozhsky.'[181] Vsevolozhsky's crucial presence would be lacking for Petipa's last performed ballet, *The Magic Mirror*; the then incumbent Vladimir Teliakovsky did little to avert its disaster and, even if he had wanted to, he lacked the understanding.

However, mixed into this stockpile of achievements were sclerotic elements. Vsevolozhsky, as Teliakovsky discerned, was a conservative, uncomfortable with the new, a typical representative of the elite.[182] In embracing the large-scale visual excitement of the *féerie* he was essentially mining the resources of a nineteenth-century commercial form, long popular in Western Europe. Although the *ballet-féerie* justified its presence on the imperial stage by winning back audiences, it is clear that by the end of the century it had reached exhaustion, each ballet becoming more and more bloated with dances, the narrative disappearing over the horizon.

The one segment of ballet tradition that Vsevolozhsky did radically overturn was its attitude to music. In so doing, he challenged the process of choreography and, above all, how that choreography actually sounded; in this domain at least, he pointed the way to the Diaghilevan project. True, the upgrading of ballet music was not so new in the bigger scheme of things since it was following the example of Delibes in France. Also true, Vsevolozhsky was anything but consistently triumphant in his choices of composer. But maybe he was just unlucky, Tchaikovsky being dead and Stravinsky still to come. Would he have embraced Stravinsky, even the early Stravinsky? Highly unlikely. His promotion of Glazunov seems true to type: a composer on the cusp of two centuries, who looked not forward stylistically, but back.

Vsevolozhsky's reform of ballet music was not accompanied by a reform of theatre design. The tradition of representational, *trompe l'oeil* sets remained, different designers responsible for separate scenes within one production. Three designers, for example, created the decor for *Raymonda*: Orest Allegri for Act I (Scene 1); Petr Lambin, Act I (Scene 2), Act III, and the Apotheosis; Konstantin Ivanov, Act II. That, plus two designers for the costumes—Vsevolozhsky and Evgeni Ponomarev—meant there was no strong, singular vision, apart from extravagant expenditure. The nineteenth-century designer was a staff craftsman, like the old ballet-composer, whose painstaking perspectives were intended to enhance the ballet master's intentions, not compete for attention. By contrast, the new set designers—Mikhail Vrubel, Victor Vasnetsov, Konstantin Korovin, Alexander Golovin, Valentin Serov—were also easel-painters. Employed by Savva Mamontov for the Private Opera Company he founded in Moscow in 1885, they were responsible for the elevation of theatre design. They tended to work singly or doubly, able to achieve a unique, cohesive signature. They brought a louder, more autonomous voice, an easel-painter's distinct, sophisticated concept, mediated through a rule-breaking vibrancy and, often, a Slav aesthetic that Diaghilev would make famous in the West.

Attached to the nineteenth century, Vsevolozhsky was disinclined to embrace this new thinking. This was evident in his work as a costume designer, which continued after his removal from the Imperial Theatres. Moreover, the extreme luxury which characterized his style could not conceal certain weaknesses. Benois's remarks about a poor understanding of colour and 'a rather helpless amateurishness' have already been noted.[183] Petr Gnedich, director of the Alexandrinsky Theatre, was less dismissive, but still felt that Vsevolozhsky failed to take into account the scenery's palette.[184] Harshest was Teliakovsky, champion of the new: Vsevolozhsky was sometimes a witty caricaturist, but as a costume designer he was 'a worse than mediocre artist and had the taste of a dilettante'.[185]

Another criticism to be levelled at Vsevolozhsky is that, although he gave preference to Russian composers, he did nothing to address the thematic foreign-ness of the ballet repertoire. On the contrary, as a francophile, one part of him actively pursued the *xenophilia* which had been endemic in the aristocratic class. But this was now outmoded, swept away by the tide of folk-art nationalism, Russia's equivalent of the Arts and Crafts movement, which Mamontov's Private Opera embraced. Mamontov promoted not only new-style neo-Russian design but also Russian music, especially that of Rimsky-Korsakov, who often drew on Russian themes; it was a combination that was able to outstrip Moscow's Imperial Opera Company in popularity.

But all that was not yet apparent to the conservative segments of the St Petersburg public or to the journal *Teatral*. In 1897 *Teatral* offered another perspective, pointing to the Imperial Ballet's privileged standing. Notwithstanding the popularity of opera with the public at large, which ensured it received more performances than ballet, notwithstanding the penny-pinching years of Baron Kister, the ballet company was prioritized in its status and finances, because the emperor wished it so:

Ballet long ago in the West gained almost equal rights with other branches of theatre arts, but here in Petersburg it actually occupies an exceptional position and enjoys the kind of attention and care from the directorate of Imperial Theatres, which unfortunately opera does not enjoy. It is very easy to find an explanation for this: almost all socially important gala performances, by tradition, consist of ballet numbers, and that is why our ballet stands out with the richness of its staging, brilliance, and artistry. This is why the directorate treats this branch of art so assiduously, does not spare the means for the staging and design of ballet productions, employs three ballet masters [Petipa, Lev Ivanov, Cecchetti] for the one Petersburg stage, has organized a special school for the training of new artists and yet still invites foreign ballerinas.[186]

Petipa occupied, as the composer Mikhail Ivanov wrote, 'an absolutely exceptional position, since he became the head of the Petersburg ballet when interest in the balletic arts was declining precipitously in the rest of Europe.'[187] Although that decline was also felt in Russia in the 1870s and 1880s, continued imperial enthusiasm for ballet meant that by the end of the century it had been well and truly reversed.

Enter Vladimir Teliakovsky

*He is terribly angry with me because I am throwing him out of
his dirty rut.*[1]

Prince Sergei Volkonsky

After the peaks of the 1890s came Petipa's decline and fall. The company was
growing ever stronger with Pavlova and Karsavina among its newest recruits, but
the wheels of company politics were turning. Petipa's days were numbered, even
if this was not immediately apparent and even if, in Soliannikov's recollection, he
still had an iron grip on company routine.

> He would carefully check out a performer before assigning him this or that
> role. If a role didn't immediately suit the performer, he would take it away
> [but] only after the performer had played it several times. [...]
>
> In appearance Petipa reminded one more of a dignitary than an artist.
> Especially on state occasions, when he wore all his decorations and medals.
> His gait was unique: tiny little steps and an immobile torso. [...]
>
> Always well-groomed, always used to taking charge, he held the ballet
> company firmly in his grip. The babbling crowd of dancers would instant-
> aneously fall silent when, without hurrying, the venerable ballet master
> walked past. He would answer the greetings of the young artists with a
> light nod; on rare occasions he would bestow a handshake. The strict dis-
> cipline, which Petipa demanded and which he obtained, played, of course,
> no small part in the general coherence of a production and in the develop-
> ment of a closely knit ballet company.[2]

Vsevolozhsky's successor on 22 July 1899 was Prince Sergei Volkonsky, his nephew
and a grandson of the famous Decembrist. Aged thirty-nine, he was highly intelligent, knowledgeable about theatre, and had, like his uncle, acted in amateur
productions. He was also full of plans. '[He] energetically set about reforming all
parts under his control,' writes Shiriaev. 'He especially turned his attention on
the ballet which, in his opinion, had very much fallen behind the other arts and

needed revitalizing.'³ Volkonsky was acquainted with a young law graduate, scion of minor provincial nobility, called Sergei Diaghilev and his circle of progressive or 'decadent' artists and writers. Among them were Alexander Benois, Léon Bakst (Lev Rosenberg), Konstantin Somov, and Dmitrii Filosofov, all linked to the magazine *World of Art* (Mir isskustva), which Diaghilev had recently founded.⁴ Faced with the conservatism of the Petipa-Vsevolozhsky era, Volkonsky wanted to let in the new ideas that were now circulating, notably in the visual arts and especially in Moscow. While Petersburg was, in Diaghilev's scathing words, 'a city of artistic gossiping, academic professors, and Friday watercolour classes', Moscow had become a major cultural centre, alongside Paris, Berlin, and Milan. It was the birthplace of the Russian avant-garde, patronized by a rich merchant class.⁵ The Moscow Arts Theatre, founded in 1898 by the theatre director and theorist Konstantin Stanislavsky and the playwright Vladimir Nemirovich-Danchenko, was committed to a new naturalism and plays about contemporary life. (The Moscow Arts Theatre's 1898 revival of *The Seagull* launched Chekhov's playwriting career.) The neo-nationalism of Mamontov's Private Opera Company not only reflected the late nineteenth-century craze for Russian folk art and legends, but served the interests of an artistic synthesis, fusing visual art, drama, and music and enrolling easel-painters to achieve this. The concept owed much to the Wagnerian idea of a total work (*Gesamtkunstwerk*), to be later emulated by Diaghilev for his own enterprise.⁶ But in the meantime Volkonsky, it would seem, was hoping to bring something of this to the Petersburg ballet.

Petipa made the welcoming speech at Volkonsky's first meeting with the ballet company and, judging by his memoirs, seems to have rather warmed to him, reforms notwithstanding.⁷ For his part, Volkonsky seems to have tactfully adopted much due deference towards his elderly subordinate and left him to get on with the series of shorter ballets planned during Vsevolozhsky's tenure. All these were small-scaled since they marked Petipa's debut at the Hermitage Theatre, newly reopened after an extensive three-year restoration, but still with a tiny stage and auditorium. As a court theatre, its performances were not open to the general public and it seems to have been directly controlled by the emperor and his minister.⁸

Petipa's ballets, four in all, were premiered in January–February 1900, and each, with the exception of *The Pupils of Dupré* or *Les Élèves de* Dupré (Ucheniki Dupré), was transferred after just a few days to the Mariinsky. Four ballets in four weeks is an amazing achievement, even if they consisted of just one or two acts and *The Pupils of Dupré* was a reduced version of the earlier *King's Command*. Glazunov composed two of the scores: for the one-act *Trial of Damis* and *The Seasons* (Vremena goda). As already seen, Drigo was the composer for the two-act *Harlequinade* (or *Millions d'Arlequin*). The costumes were all by Vsevolozhsky; and, although the librettos are attributed to Petipa alone, maybe Vsevolozhsky had at least some input. To add to the workload, the transfer of *The Trial of Damis* to the

Mariinsky was accompanied by the Petersburg premiere of the coronation ballet *The Pearl* (23 January). The intense pace of the preparations put paid to plans for a big ballet by Petipa, *Salammbô*, after Flaubert's novel, also to a score by Glazunov. The idea had long been in the air—Tchaikovsky had turned it down—and the setting of Ancient Carthage was ideal territory for Petipa. But Glazunov no longer had the time, nor did the company.[9]

The Trial of Damis (17 January) was a genre piece evoking eighteenth-century manners, with music and dances based on the dance styles of the time, and designs inspired by the paintings of Watteau and Nicolas Lancret. The plot came from *Les Ruses d'amour* (1748), a comic play by Philippe Poisson, a contemporary of Marivaux. The identity-swapping machinations were characteristic of eighteenth-century drama; in their ballet form they exactly repeated the premise of Petipa's *A Marriage during the Regency*, more than forty years earlier, except that the disguised character was now a woman, Isabelle (Legnani), not a man. Isabelle wants to test the sincerity of her new suitor Damis (as played by Gerdt) and for their first meeting she changes places with her maid Marinette. In the event, however, the ensuing incidents came across, in Benois's words, as 'too light to be moving', 'a bagatelle', and reviewers didn't like the absence of classical *pas* in favour of a small number of social dances—*passepied, courante, la musette, sarabande, farandole*—more suited to a salon and simple enough to be taught in a seminary.[10] The allegorical *Seasons* aroused more enthusiasm, with Glazunov at his vivid best and Petipa creating poetic dance images. Preobrazhenskaya was the Rose, Kshesinskaya was Kolosa, the 'Spirit of the Corn', and the young Anna Pavlova, who had graduated just the year before, was Hoar-Frost. Reading the libretto, it becomes clear how close Petipa was to plotless dance, just a short distance away from Fokine's *Chopiniana* (known in the West as *Les Sylphides*, 1907 and 1908).[11] Even more favourably received was the two-act *Harlequinade* or *Millions d'Arlequin* (10 February), with Kshesinskaya as Columbine, Georgii Kiaksht as Harlequin, and Preobrazhenskaya as Pierrette. The Hermitage Theatre's private audience, led by the emperor and empress, gave a tumultuous reception to Drigo's Italian music and the entertaining *commedia dell'arte* characters. The twelve dance numbers had great diversity, ranging from solos to ensembles, and were composed to highlight the dancers' different qualities.[12] Also popular with the general public, the ballet lasted, as already seen, up to the mid-1920s, and later in other versions.

If Petipa had stopped after this he would have ended on a climax of remarkable, admirable activity. But Volkonsky commissioned two more works from him: *The Heart of the Marquise* or *Le Coeur de la marquise* (Cerdtse markizy), a one-act 'pantomime' led by Preobrazhenskaya with members of the French drama company speaking verse; and a big ballet *The Magic Mirror*. However, Volkonsky was not long enough in his job to oversee the premieres. It was quickly apparent that he was completely inexperienced in administration. To Petipa and Shiriaev it seemed that he did not know how to approach his task calmly and methodically:

> The new director devoted himself enthusiastically to his new duties. But this very enthusiasm was dangerous: planning many reforms, he wanted to execute them at once, and to bring about a new order immediately, instead of by degrees. He gave neither himself nor others sufficient time to weigh and consider matters; thanks to this haste, there were of course many mistakes. But the prince himself realized this after a few weeks; he came to the conclusion that in order to reach the goal it would be necessary to go forward gradually, *pianissimo*.[13]

At the same time the savvy theatre personnel soon gauged Volkonsky's greenness and pitilessly started running rings round him, creating petty controversies and enlisting the press and influential outsiders. Being unusually young for such an appointment, he was surrounded by 'swarms of envious people' and men in the higher circles 'who had hoped to get the post and had been overlooked'. The directorate was 'a hot frying pan' where 'there were plots below, ill-will around me, and no support from above.'[14] All this reduced him to such a nervous state he couldn't sleep in his bedroom, feeling that he lacked fresh air, and he would sometimes take his bed into the hallway.[15]

If he hoped the situation could only improve, he was wrong. First came what might be called the Diaghilev crisis. Volkonsky had attached Diaghilev to the directorate as one of several functionaries 'for special missions'. At this appointment, Anatoly Molchanov, founder-editor of the *Yearbook of Imperial Theatres* (and husband of the leading Alexandrinsky actress Maria Savina), recognized his days were numbered and resigned, privately hoping that Diaghilev would make a mess of the job.[16] However, in taking over, Diaghilev's plan was 'to stagger the world' with the *Yearbook*. 'It would become plain to everybody that he was capable of "great deeds" [...] this would enable Volkonsky to make of him his chief and most active assistant. [...] He would, in time, replace Volkonsky himself and establish in the Imperial Theatres an era which would survive for posterity as The Diaghilev Era.'[17] The first number, published in 1901, was a metamorphosis, surpassing the most optimistic expectations with distinguished articles and lavish artwork by Léon Bakst, Valentin Serov, Ilia Repin, and Konstantin Somov.

Volkonsky also gave the outsiders Bakst and Alexander Benois their first small theatre design commissions for the Hermitage. Bakst was the designer of *The Heart of the Marquise*; Benois, of a twenty-minute opera, *Love's Revenge* (Mest' amura), by Alexander Taneev which rapidly came and went.[18] Finally, after much pressure from Diaghilev and his circle, Volkonsky agreed that they should mount a version of Delibes's ballet score *Sylvia* on the Mariinsky stage. Extracts from Louis

Mérante's 1876 production, a hit in Paris, had already appeared on Petersburg's commercial stages from 1886 onwards, performed by Dell'Era and Brianza, and in 1891 Giorgio Saracco had staged the complete ballet at Petersburg's Maly Theatre with Adelina Rossi and later Zucchi in the title role.[19] The excited friends were full of ideas and planned to invite the Legat brothers as ballet masters. However, Diaghilev's arrogant manner had made enemies. When Volkonsky announced the project, two of his assistants came immediately to tell him it would cause a revolt. And when Volkonsky consequently told Diaghilev he was forced partly to renege on his promise—not to take the project away from Diaghilev, but to announce officially that it would be under his own management—the result was pandemonium.

Diaghilev, full of the success of the *Yearbook*, was also in league with Kshesinskaya and her special friend Grand Duke Sergei Mikhailovich, who coveted Volkonsky's post. Diaghilev was consequently in no mood for compromise. He applied pressure by refusing to continue editing the next number of the *Yearbook*. In this deadlock Teliakovsky, who was then director of the Moscow Imperial Theatres, agreed to accompany Volkonsky to plead with Diaghilev—but to no avail. Ultimately, Diaghilev, refusing to continue as editor, but equally refusing to hand in his resignation, was dismissed by signed order of the emperor. Egged on by his powerful allies, he had been convinced of victory, so the shock was enormous. Worse, his dismissal was accompanied by the phrase 'according to article three': a rare sanction only applied in cases of disreputable behaviour, which meant he was permanently barred from any kind of state service.[20] His future with the Imperial Theatres was therefore finished—and in this way the seeds for the Ballets Russes were planted.[21]

Perhaps Diaghilev gained some comfort when Volkonsky himself resigned just a few months later. The cause was Kshesinskaya, whose hotline to the emperor encouraged her to expect privileges of the kind the actress Maria Savina enjoyed at the Alexandrinsky. She couched her petitions to the emperor in such a way as to make him think she was being wronged.[22] Teliakovsky, on assuming the directorship of the Imperial Theatres after Volkonsky, successfully set about removing Petipa, but against Kshesinskaya and Savina he was, he writes with only a little wry exaggeration, virtually powerless:

> A rather naive person once asked me: 'What is all this? In the Alexsandrinsky Theatre it is Savina, in the Mariinsky, Kshesinskaya, who gives orders. And who then are you?'
> I answered: 'The director.'[23]

Kshesinskaya habitually extended her vacation until the autumn season was well under way, forcing ballet masters to fit rehearsals round her diary.[24] Like Savina

she was consulted about the repertoire, except that with ballet it was easier because there were fewer performances:

> So, before the announcement of the repertoire the chief *régisseur* Aistov
> would appear in the director's office. He was a big, solid man, he spoke in
> a loud bass: 'Kshesinskaya has sent me to say that she will be dancing such
> and such a ballet on such and such a date. I feel that it is my duty to put
> your Excellency in the know.'
>   'Very well,' the director would reply. 'Let her dance. I had been thinking
> of giving the ballet to another dancer. ... Well, never mind, I will wait a
> little, we will postpone it for the next time.'[25]

She also demanded a monopoly over certain roles—more than half of the best—
and with this advantage, and Legnani's departure, she effectively became the
company's prima ballerina.[26] She clearly did not consider that an order, issued by
the directorate in 1899, establishing the principle of sharing leading roles on the
imperial stages, applied to her.[27] When, in the autumn of the same year, the Italian
guest Enrichetta Grimaldi, engaged to replace Legnani, was cast as Swanilda in
Coppélia, this was acceptable because she had already 'passed on the role to Olga
Preobrazhenskaya.' However, when Grimaldi was announced for *La Fille mal
gardée*, she quickly informed Volkonsky that 'the ballets in one dancer's repertoire
cannot, without her consent, be given to another'.[28] And when Volkonsky declined
to comply, because Grimaldi had been contracted by Vsevolozhsky to dance this
ballet and in any case there could be no monopoly of roles, she first asked Grand
Duke Sergei Mikhailovich to intercede with Volkonsky; and when the grand duke
failed, she went straight to the tsar, who had a telegram sent from Darmstadt,
Germany, where he was visiting, and the rehearsals with Grimaldi were stopped.

The final clash cost Volkonsky his job. Kshesinskaya, for her debut in *Camargo*,
wanted to discard the cumbersome farthingale from her traditional Russian costume, which was a copy of the one worn by Catherine the Great. The news that
she had been forbidden to do this entered the Petersburg rumour machine and
balletomanes waited with bated breath. When she emerged on stage without the
hooped petticoat, the following day it was announced that a fine would be imposed.
Once again, Kshesinskaya turned to the tsar and Volkonsky was forced to remit
the fine. But he also tendered his resignation, because his authority was being repeatedly and publicly undermined.[29] All these shenanigans, however, would dent
Kshesinskaya's popularity; the critic Valerian Svetlov attacked the monopolization
of roles and her rival Preobrazhenskaya became the audience's favourite.[30]

Later, when the Franco-Italian Carlotta Zambelli arrived for guest performances in October 1901, she asked to dance *Swan Lake*, not understanding this
was one of Kshesinskaya's ballets.[31] In the event, she made her debut in *Coppélia*

and then danced *Giselle*. By this time, Volkonsky had been replaced by Petipa's arch-enemy, Vladimir Teliakovsky; but, for once, Teliakovsky and Petipa shared the same enthusiastic opinion.[32] Black-haired and beautiful, Zambelli was also, Teliakovsky writes, 'a real ballerina of the highest schooling with an uncommon grace and a big talent for mime'.[33] The general public's reception, however, was lukewarm, their taste distorted by modern dance tricks, so that they did not understand the beautiful simplicity of her style.[34] Even Kshesinskaya praised her and, in a grand gesture of generosity, declared herself ready to yield *Paquita* and *The Sleeping Beauty*. Teliakovsky was keen to sign her up for a three-year contract, but maybe her own reluctance, or the Paris Opera's, meant she did not return.[35]

Volkonsky's tenure had lasted just two years. His halting attempts to introduce new artistic thinking in matters of design were cut short; his collision with corrupt internal practices left him bloodied and defeated. He also set in motion Petipa's last ballet, *The Magic Mirror*. Based on *Snow White*, it was in the same mould as the previous *ballets à grand spectacle*. Maybe the project was against Volkonsky's better judgement, but he doubtless knew that Petipa had a loyal following in the audience and the press.

Vladimir Teliakovsky

The forty-one-year-old Vladimir Teliakovsky, appointed director of the Imperial Theatres on 7 June 1901, was a completely different person from the well-meaning, tactful, beautifully mannered Volkonsky. Teliakovsky, an aristocrat like most high-ranking imperial bureaucrats, was a former colonel in the Horse Guards whose status contradicted his physically diminutive size. His commander had been Baron Fredericks, who was also his stepfather, as well as the current minister of the Imperial Court.[36] He had no connection with the arts except that he was an excellent pianist who had wavered between a musical and military career and that his wife, Gurlia, was an amateur artist with a special interest in designing costumes. He was, in Shiriaev's words, 'imperious, rude, and conceited'.[37] Benois, a little kinder, writes that Teliakovsky had retained all his military ways and 'under his mask of rough good-nature was concealed what the French call *une fine mouche* [a shrewd mind].'[38] Teliakovsky could be unscrupulous in his methods.[39] He ruffled feathers with radical reforms and his insensitive, sergeant-major manner of implementing them. The reforms included cutting out the so-called old wood, given that, in Teliakovsky-speak, the theatre arts were dominated by reactionaries, their stiffened minds fixated on the past.

However, before assuming the directorship, Teliakovsky had been in charge of the Moscow office of the Imperial Theatres since spring 1898, appointed by Fredericks. This apprenticeship gave him, by his own account, the training, lacked by Volkonsky, for the harsher difficulties of St Petersburg.[40] In Moscow he did much to revitalize the moribund ballet company, its neglect continued by Vsevolozhsky who used to advise visitors to see the plays at the Maly Theatre but avoid the ballet and opera.[41] Teliakovsky had moved to Moscow from St Petersburg and became enthused by the ferment of new artistic ideas there. He saw productions mounted by the Moscow Arts Theatre. He watched the operas of Mamontov's Private Opera Company and heard its star Fedor Chaliapin sing.[42] He discovered the work of young visual artists linked to Mamontov's company and the Russian craft centre at Abramtsevo, north of Moscow, one of several artistic colonies contributing to the slavophile tide of the late nineteenth century. It was maybe through his wife Gurlia—said to be the 'invisible *directrice*' by Benois and others—that Teliakovsky became acquainted with some of these painter-designers, notably Alexander Golovin and Konstantin Korovin.[43] During his first Moscow season he invited Golovin to design a production, making Teliakovsky the first to bring the Private Opera's style to the imperial stage.[44] The production was *The Ice Palace* (Ledianoi dom), by the young composer Arsenii Koreshchenko, premiered on 7 November 1900. Modest Tchiakovsky wrote the libretto and Chaliapin, enticed back to the Imperial Theatres by Teliakovsky, performed one of his first created roles at the Bolshoi.[45]

Golovin and especially Korovin would go on to collaborate with Alexander Gorsky, recently arrived at the Bolshoi from St Petersburg. As a friend of Vladimir Stepanov and adherent of the notation system he had invented, Gorsky used the Stepanov Notation to record *The Sleeping Beauty*. Rather than asking Petipa, whose knowledge of the ballet was certainly superior to Gorsky's notes, Teliakovsky commissioned Gorsky to stage *The Sleeping Beauty* in Moscow.[46] Teliakovsky, no ballet specialist, claims this was almost a faithful copy of the Petersburg original and the production, premiered on 17 January 1899, was a great success, considerably raising the company's spirits.[47] *Raymonda* followed on 23 January, again staged by Gorsky. Encouraged, Teliakovsky decided to attempt something more innovative, and his choice fell on *Don Quixote*. Gorsky was given complete freedom to revise Petipa's ballet, which also marked his first collaboration with Korovin, Golovin, and another painter-designer, Nikolai Klodt.[48] (His previous stagings had used other, more traditional, designers.) Young-ish (twenty-seven) and ambitious, Gorsky fell in with Teliakovsky's vision of a more expressionist and design-led ballet, away from the old Petipa aesthetic.[49] The premiere on 6 December 1900 received a muted response from the press, at a loss before this new genre. But the public, Teliakovsky writes, had no such problems, and tickets sold like hot cakes.[50] Gorsky reworked the crowd scenes to make everybody move in a more realistic, animated way.[51] In this he was expounding Stanislavsky's ideas that art should be true to life. Benois, no Gorsky enthusiast, describes this as 'novelties' consisting 'of making the crowds on stage bustle and move about fitfully and aimlessly'.[52] But, today, Moscow dance historians consider Gorsky to be a real innovator, the first to treat stage ensembles as choreographic drama, presenting them not as architectural compositions, but a living crowd of individuals, each with their life story and internal monologue.[53] (In 1911 Fokine adopted the same approach for *Petrushka*.) Teliakovsky, retrospectively shoring up his defence, wrote that the production was mould-breaking, marking a new era in the collaboration between dance and visual art. Meanwhile in Petersburg, he added, they were still performing the retrograde *Nutcracker*, with dancers in the 'Kingdom of Sweets' dressed as 'rich brioches'.[54]

At the start of the 1902–1903 season Gorsky was appointed first ballet master of the Moscow company, after just two seasons as *régisseur*, prompting Petipa to write:

> Formerly, every well-known ballet master began his career on second or even third-rate stages. But my pupil, Gorsky, in spite of the fact that he had never, anywhere, staged a work of his own, was immediately honoured with an invitation to the Bolshoi Theatre of Moscow, in the capacity of ballet master.[55]

Gorsky subsequently mounted his own versions of *The Pharaoh's Daughter, Swan Lake* (adding a jester who has since become a prominent feature), *La Bayadère*, and *Raymonda*. In these and other ballets he continued his reforms. Where Petipa built his patterns on classical symmetries, Gorsky disrupted them with an expressive dynamic. Where Petipa alternated traditional ballet *enchaînements* with national dances to provide cultural relevance, Gorsky, like Fokine after him, searched for naturalism, matching all the movement to character and context. This often meant discarding showy dance displays in favour of gesture and simple steps. Evocative stylization, though, was also a constituent: in *The Pharaoh's Daughter* he introduced—much to Petipa's distaste—profile movement, as well as making 'meaningless innovations and changes' such as changing the characters' names and giving the pharaoh not one but three daughters. 'Why didn't he give him a round dozen?' scoffs Petipa. 'How much talent do you suppose is necessary for such "innovations"? What a genius!'[56]

St Petersburg in Aspic

Moscow, now the city of new ideas, was a world away from the courtiers, high functionaries, and uniformed officers of St Petersburg. On moving back to St Petersburg, Teliakovsky was determined to show the traditionalists a thing or two.[57] True, the independent theatres presented a more mixed picture. Their numbers had multiplied in St Petersburg as a consequence of rapid industrialization in the century's final decade; some forty would open in the years up to 1917, although most were short-lived. (The Moscow Arts Theatre also played there in 1901 and 1902.)[58] But it was another, backward-looking story with the elegant imperial theatres: it was, after all, at the Alexandrinsky that the first performance of *The Seagull* famously flopped on 17 October 1896. The audience had been expecting a comedy in line with the repertoire's dominant style, a style epitomized by the dictum 'there is enough drama in real life.'[59]

So the state theatres were largely frozen in time. When it came to the ballet, several factors, in Teliakovsky's estimation, were involved. One was the audience: much bigger than in Moscow but different, populated by high society, the court, and important functionaries. As a result, the directorate not only lavished particular care and generosity on the ballet, but most importantly strove to gratify the not-always-artistic tastes of its influential patrons.[60] Another factor was the antiquated approach to theatre design, which Volkonsky in his brief time had only tentatively addressed. A third was the dominance in the ballet itself of the old guard, with its old ways, old tastes, and general aversion to change.

> When I used to say that in the theatre things were good and worthy, but boring, they would answer: 'How are things boring when before you arrived they were enjoyable? What is missing for you? Revive *The Maid of Orleans* by Schiller, *Coriolanus* by Shakespeare, *Ruslan and Liudmila*, by Glinka. What about *Fidelio* by Beethoven or the ballets *The Vestal*, *Zoraiya*, or *King Candaules*? Then things will be enjoyable. Aren't these all exemplary, proven works?'[61]

His run-ins with tenacious conservatism did not dissuade him, however. Beyond the ballet, he managed to increase the visibility of Wagner and Richard Strauss in the opera repertoire. He had Korovin appointed as artistic consultant to the directorate from 1 October 1901 and stage design was transformed across the board. He brought in a host of new producers to stage plays at the Alexandrinsky, culminating in an invitation to the avant-garde Vsevolod Meyerhold in 1908, which threw everyone into a flutter of apprehension—but in the event, Meyerhold toned down his more experimental precepts and stayed with the Imperial Theatres nearly a decade.[62]

Gorsky's Don Quixote

Actually, the Alexandrinsky's troupe was generally open to change—and not just the young members—while the principal concern of the all-powerful Savina was her roles.[63] But the ballet troupe was a different matter. Arriving from Moscow, Teliakovsky clearly felt—and was—faced with a panel of aged or ageing statesmen: Petipa (eighty-three), Ivanov (sixty-seven), Gerdt (fifty-six), Drigo (fifty-five), and Cecchetti (fifty-one). (He also clearly regarded the Imperial Theatres' chief conductor Eduard Napravnik, at sixty-two, as a has-been.) And with the ballet, broadly speaking, he managed only to inspire hostility. He declined to defer to the advanced age and venerable status of Russia's dance genius, while Russia's dance genius was shocked by Teliakovsky's unceremonious manners. He wanted to cut Petipa down to size; he would not 'make a great song and dance about Petipa' the way Vsevolozhsky did.[64] And so Petipa knew the door on his half-century career was closing.

Where Teliakovsky's memoirs have a carefully modulated frankness, the venom of his copious diaries makes disturbing reading. (By contrast, Petipa's own surviving diaries, although terse, reveal a more likeable personality.) The gaze Teliakovsky directs towards the people around him is not so much shrewd as cynical. So, when sick, debt-ridden Ivanov asks to be removed from the task of staging *Sylvia*, Teliakovsky notes that 'he nevertheless continues to work on the librettos of ballets in the hope, of course, that perhaps something will prove useful to the directorate, and then he will receive a separate payment.' He goes on to deplore the widespread practice among artists of absenteeism and 'fleecing the coffers'; he writes that 'Ivanov has the nerve to complain about the weak health of Shiriaev— his assistant.'[65] (Shiriaev assisted Ivanov as well as Petipa.) Shiriaev himself soon falls victim to Teliakovsky's harsh, military-style methods. When, on being offered the position of assistant *régisseur*, he asks for a raise of 1,000 roubles, Teliakovsky not only refuses, but adds that it will be necessary to reduce his existing salary, for trying to force the director's hand.[66]

Once Teliakovsky turns against someone, such as Petipa, he becomes obsessive. His diaries include a virulent vignette that creates a shocking contrast to Soliannikov's measured portrait, quoted at the start of this chapter:

> The nasty old geriatric bribe-taker, impudent Frenchman, who during fifty years spent in Russia at Russian expense, never learnt to speak Russian and feels instinctively all the contempt I have for him. With the inflated and completely unfounded reputation of an outstanding ballet master, he knows that in me he has met a director, who will not yield to the fraudulent spell he has cast around him and this he cannot excuse. [...] Frothing at the mouth, he defends his position and each day on stage his evil language in its toothless mouth tries to discredit me, like a snakebite. The ballet company fears him—his greed and his control—and keeps quiet. But of course they see how things are slipping away from him. It is enough to take a list of the ballets staged by Petipa to be convinced that almost all of them failed and have left no trace in the repertoire. Anything that works well belongs to Perrot and Saint-Georges [?] and Saint-Léon. The only successful Petipa ballets owe nothing to the choreography but to the success of Tchaikovsky's music.[67]

Not only that, but Petipa is 'a squeezed lemon' unable to move anything forwards, 'a malevolent, self-serving, dishonourable old man'. He 'talks nonsense' and 'lies as he breathes'.[68] It is absurd that Petipa should tell a designer how to draw and a composer how to compose, that he should have directly instructed Koreshchenko (composer of *The Magic Mirror*), 'here we need a violin, then the whole orchestra.' It beggars belief that 'a colossus like Tchaikovsky' was obliged to defer to Petipa's judgement of the merits or demerits of his music. All this might seem laughable, but the full horror is that Petipa is considered an expert. His reputation, however, is a fraud; he only reached his position because he was a foreigner with a wife who was a leading ballerina. For fifty-six years he has fooled the public which thinks that only he can stage ballets. He was a poor mime artist and a teacher of mime who hardly ever turned up for his classes, which is why the company lacks a good mime tradition.[69] And why is it that Johansson is not honoured on a par with Petipa, since his achievements are as good and longer-lasting?[70]

Where Teliakovsky handled Kshesinskaya with kid gloves, making time to talk to her, to reason with her, his methods for Petipa were brutal, compounded by what Petipa rightly describes as his lack of understanding of ballet.[71] (His attack against Petipa's method of collaborating with composers is clear evidence of this.) In practice, it seems that Petipa was too prominent as a Soloist of His Imperial Majesty to sack outright; instead Teliakovsky set about gradually pushing him out. 'Through my position as the ballet master's assistant,' Shiriaev writes, 'it fell on me more than anybody else in the ballet company, to be the unwilling witness of all the twists and turns of this systematic persecution of the eminent ballet master.'[72] There were the petty affronts, such as the crossing out of his name on the list of those who should receive thank-you gifts, after a gala performance for the French president, Émile Loubet—or that, at least, is what Petipa claims.[73] But far worse, substantiated insults came right at the start of Teliakovsky's tenure. First, Teliakovsky announced to Petipa his intention to promote Lev Ivanov, so that he would share the post of first ballet master with Petipa.[74] Ivanov's death three months later aborted the promotion; even so, it was an insensitive move vis-à-vis an elderly man who had achieved so much more than Ivanov.

The next attack followed soon after. Wanting to find something quickly with which to proclaim his modernist vision, Teliakovsky decided to show the Gorsky *Don Quixote* on the occasion of Johansson's benefit, on 20 January 1902.[75] True, in the nineteenth century, ballets were regarded as works-in-progress, the name of the original ballet master acknowledged (usually), but other hands also acknowledged for making additions and modifications.[76] Petipa explicitly writes this in his report (10 February 1892) about Vladimir Stepanov's notation system, which, besides being, in his opinion, too cumbersome to decode, was also redundant since 'a talented ballet master, reviving previous ballets, will create dances in accordance with his personal fantasy, his talent, and the tastes of the public of that time and will not start losing his time and effort copying what was done by others long before.'[77]

That said, the consensus among today's ballet producers seems to be that Petipa treated other people's work with care, responsible for additions but not wholesale distortions (see chapter 6), even if he was not above passing off a *pas* from an old friend like Perrot as his own. In any case, the issue of *Don Quixote* was on a far bigger scale. A new version of a multi-act ballet, when the original choreographer was alive, present in the same theatre, and opposed to the idea, was either a deliberate slap in Petipa's face or a demonstration of Teliakovsky's profound insensitivity.[78] (Worse, Petipa claimed in an interview that Teliakovsky had originally proposed the ballet be staged for his own benefit celebrating fifty-five years of service.)[79] The press sided with Petipa. 'Old Balletomane' (*Staryi baletoman*) in *Peterburgskaia gazeta* invited readers to imagine the same thing happening to the equally alive Rimsky-Korsakov and his opera *The Snow Maiden*—an impossibility.[80]

Having taken the decision, Teliakovsky insisted the elderly Petipa go to Moscow to see the ballet, with a view to staging Gorsky's version himself. Inevitably Petipa disliked his former pupil's revisions, even if modern research suggests Gorsky returned the ballet close to Petipa's jolly Moscow original. Petipa declined the task, arguing that there were so many changes it would be better for Gorsky to do it himself.[81]

He continued to bear a grudge so that when Gorsky arrived in St Petersburg, he not once offered to shake his hand during rehearsals, 'despite the fact that he had known him since childhood'.[82] Ballet legend also claims that Petipa said to the *régisseur* Aistov: 'Please ask that young man kindly to remember that I'm not dead yet.'[83] Meanwhile Teliakovsky confided to his diary that the press, 'led by Jews and a desire always to lambaste anything superior to the norm', was predictably disposed against Gorsky's *Don Quixote*.[84] It could not be otherwise, he wrote, when something new and illuminating appears on stage: 'this light disturbs the darkness which reigns over the whole theatre's atmosphere.'[85] And, anyway, the press has taken against Gorsky because Petipa has bribed them.[86]

The general public was more enthusiastic than the press and it is this version, along with the handsome Golovin-Korovin-Klodt designs, which largely survives in the Mariinsky repertoire.[87] A hundred years later, discussing what choreography belongs to whom in today's *Don Quixote*, Igor Belsky, the choreographer and the Vaganova Academy's artistic director, estimated that the classical dances must be by Petipa, and the rest a mix of Gorsky, Petipa, and others.[88]

Soon after his arrival, Teliakovsky had a meeting with Petipa, during which Petipa reported that the company had substantially declined in the past year and cited one reason as a lack of discipline.[89] He also talked of the deleterious practice of 'protection' (*protektsiia*), or the help of influential persons which determined whether a corps de ballet dancer was noticed for promotion.[90] There was nothing new there: already, the writer Volf had, during Stepan Gedeonov's tenure, identified a climate of corruption that made it difficult for promising young talents, financially unable to oil palms, to be noticed.[91]

Teliakovsky, who had a strict sense of propriety, made it his mission to uproot this. However, after this conversation, Teliakovsky's informers—his two stepsons—told him that gossip pointed not only to the *régisseur* Aistov but to Petipa himself as taking bribes.[92] Later, Baron Vladimir Kusov, manager of the technical department, told him that the assistant *régisseurs* were also guilty.[93] Convinced by now that he was standing on top of a seething mass of sleaze, Teliakovsky cast his suspicions wider to include the critic Nikolai Bezobrazov, who, he confided to his diary, was involved in an elaborate racket with Petipa, to further the fortunes of his mistress, the talentless dancer Anna Vasileva, and her friends.[94]

What to believe in all this? One perspective might be that it is difficult to take seriously such allegations against a man of Petipa's standing and artistic perfectionism, a man who had already condemned casting-by-'protection'. Although dancers did ask him for favours, there is no mention of money in his diaries: 'Mlle. Egorova came to bother me again about letting her dance *Naiad*,' he writes on 12 September 1903.[95] 'She is weak.' He was surely more interested in how his ballets were performed than in demanding routine backhanders. Even Vazem, although she repeats the same gossip, admits to not knowing how true it was.[96] And she clearly did not need to make payments for her advancement.

More damaging is Kshesinskaya's wish to take revenge on Petipa for not making a congratulatory speech at her father's fiftieth anniversary benefit on 19 January 1903. (Petipa writes that he couldn't because he had a sore throat; Teliakovsky, that, according to Kshesinsky, Petipa could not forgive Kshesinsky for being made a Soloist of His Imperial Majesty and had asked, during all the onstage gifts and tributes, whether this 'comedy' would soon be over.)[97] Kshesinskaya consequently made it known that throughout her career she had been obliged to pay Petipa bribes. Teliakovsky, repeating the gossip, specifies that she had to pay Petipa 100 roubles for each new ballet, to ensure that he would not create unflattering dances for her.[98]

Again, these allegations are hard to believe, given Kshesinskaya's string-pulling power, but they explain Petipa's indignant invectives against her in his surviving diaries.[99] A greater problem, however, is her later accusation that, the previous year (1902), on a visit to Petipa's apartment, she gave him 2,000 roubles in an envelope. Petipa's version to the directorate was that he had refused to accept the envelope and she had slipped it into the pocket of his jacket. He had wanted to return it; but his wife persuaded him that, rather than a bribe, it was a recompense, so he had kept it. Then he added, unfortunately scoring an own goal, that

Kshesinskaya had played a 'swinish' trick, telling others about the money, especially as it hadn't happened just the once.[100]

Kshesinskaya's gifts don't make Petipa a bribe-taker, for all his faults—at least, that has to be the hope. According to Nikolai Legat, Kshesinskaya extended her largesse to many others: in 1908, when he was appearing as her partner in Paris, she distributed banknotes of 500 and 1,000 roubles to all the dancers, conductors, and producers.[101] There is also the fact that other dancers gave gifts to ballet masters, as did Legnani at Petipa's fifty-year jubilee, to express thanks. (See chapter 9.) The truth is, human motivation is complex and the line between gifts and bribes inevitably porous. It is easy to see how gifts might have been construed as currying favour in the wild gossip-mongering ecology of a ballet company.[102] Even now, rumour and counter-rumour, corruption and scandal, are hazards that accompany companies everywhere.

Equally, the suspicions articulated in Teliakovsky's diaries often seem close to paranoia—or maybe not, given his unpopularity in certain circles. On several occasions, he claims the applause for Petipa is deliberately orchestrated to upset either him or Gorsky.[103] On 1 September 1904 he fires the former ballerina and *classe de perfectionnement* teacher Evgenia Sokolova, whom he had long disliked for being 'not a teacher, but a virus, who stirs the ballet up all the time' and who had the misfortune to be Petipa's friend.[104]

The Magic Mirror

The Petipa in Teliakovsky's diaries is an impossible old man, crotchety, capricious, amnesiac, spouting lies and nonsense, well on the way to senility, if not already there. And certainly some of this must have been true. His ill-health, in particular his painful skin ailment, can only have exacerbated his irritability. Yet his workload was still enormous, rehearsing ballets and preparing *The Magic Mirror*. It would become his nemesis, an allegory of his obsolescence, just five years after *Raymonda*. Created with music and designs that he disliked, this slow-motion four-act disaster came to epitomize two paradoxically opposing positions. To modernists, *The Magic Mirror* was an emblem of the decaying old school which was suffocating the St Petersburg ballet; to traditionalists, it was a victim of the so-called decadence of the new artistic concepts thrust upon it. In Petipa's own words, 'the ballet is a fiasco,' although he 'was much fêted'.[105]

The fiasco occurred on 9 February 1903, a glittering benefit performance, attended by the imperial family to celebrate Petipa's fifty-five years of service. The next day *Peterburgskaia gazeta* carried a long account, divided into subsections, including a list of 100 of the elite members of the audience and descriptions of some of the ladies' dresses.[106] On becoming director, Teliakovsky, who inherited *The Magic Mirror* from Volkonsky, had told Petipa with his customary bluntness that he felt little enthusiasm for it and suggested a revival of *The Sleeping Beauty* instead. At this, Petipa reacted head-on, complaining that it was usual practice to have a new ballet for his benefit performances, his earlier choice of *Salammbô* had disappeared with Vsevolozhsky's departure and now he was being told *The Magic Mirror* was to be aborted.[107] For once he prevailed.

The libretto by Petipa and Vsevolozhsky (announced as 'G **') replaced the seven knights of Pushkin's version of *Snow White*—called *The Story of the Dead Princess and the Seven Knights* (Skazka o mertvoi tsarevne i o semi bogatyriakh)—with the seven gnomes of the Brothers Grimm. The choice of Arsenii Koreshchenko as composer was on the recommendation of Glazunov, whom Petipa trusted. Several of Koreshchenko's operas had been staged over the past decade, but this was his first ballet.[108]

The hand of Teliakovsky, however, can be found in the choice of designers: Golovin for the sets and, helped by the so-called *directrice* Gurlia Teliakovskaya, the costumes, although her name is not listed.[109] The preparations are profusely mapped in Teliakovsky's diaries; more succinctly in Petipa's diary and memoirs. Rehearsals were slow and stressful, and by both accounts (but for different reasons) the atmosphere poisonous. On 14 October 1902, probably peeved by the invitation to Achille Coppini from La Scala to mount Saint-Léon's *La Source* (Ruchei), Petipa complained to Teliakovsky that, because Coppini's rehearsals were encroaching on his own, he wanted to be released from *The Magic Mirror*. Teliakovsky records his refusal and more of his hard-hearted thoughts about Petipa:

> I said that I cannot release him from the staging of *The Magic Mirror*. It is unacceptable to be ballet master, receive a salary of 9,000 roubles, and for two years refuse to make ballets. Last year, he turned down *Sylvia* (which Gerdt unsuccessfully mounted) and now it's *The Magic Mirror*. *The Magic Mirror* was postponed for a year, now the time has come to stage it and he is trying under this or that pretext to wriggle out. Of course the matter at issue is much simpler. Petipa has lost possession of his faculties and cannot stage anything new. [...] But he does not want to give in his notice, and this is the reason for these excuses.[110]

Rehearsals staggered on. Petipa revised and changed constantly: a modus operandi that Teliakovsky found alarming, given the looming premiere.[111] By 23 December 1902, however, he could report: 'Now, it seems, the project is getting organized, everything, except the last act is staged and there are several beautiful dances.'[112] But then on 3 January 1903 it was back to more chaotic changes:

> Petipa continues to be insufferable [...], he is dissatisfied with everything and berates the whole corps de ballet and management. The changes

continue all the time. New and yet newer dances appear. I simply don't
know when they will have time to sew the costumes.[113]

However, Petipa's diary entries at this time record his dogged attempts to
keep working, despite frustrations with the designs, music, and logistics. On 3
January, ten dancers are away sick; on other days, it's the turn of Kshesinskaya,
Preobrazhenskaya, Pavlova and Sergei Legat, and a couple of soloists. There are
other ballets to rehearse—*Le Corsaire*, *The Pharaoh's Daughter*, *The Trial of Damis*—
minutes lost waiting for unpunctual dancers, performances to attend. On 22
January he comes down with a heavy cold, but battles on, taking only 27 January
off. On 25 January half the ballet is rehearsed with the orchestra, half without;
either way, the music is 'terrible'. On 1 February he rehearses with some of the
'appalling' decor and without. During the break, he offers everyone lunch—as he
would for the orchestra on the day of the premiere, as well as buying five bottles of
champagne in the evening, noting 'expenditure quite heavy'. Not surprisingly he
is often tired.[114] On 29 January Vladimir Kusov, from the production department,
comes to see him on behalf of Teliakovsky who, because some of the costumes
are not going to be ready, wants to postpone the premiere by four days. Petipa refuses, persuaded, according to Teliakovsky, by Koreshchenko who points out that
the delay would diminish the number of performances before the season's end.[115]

The dress rehearsal, with borrowed costumes, took place on the morning
of 8 February. Kshesinskaya 2 (Matilda) danced the role of the princess, Legat 3
(Sergei), the prince, Gerdt, the king, and Petipa 1 (Marie), the wicked stepmother
queen.[116] Teliakovsky thought the ballet looked beautiful, and said in a speech after
the rehearsal that it was unlike anything ever done anywhere.[117] Petipa, however,
describes the designs as 'awful', adding, 'what bad luck for the ballet'.[118] It is clear
he did not understand the new 'decadent' school of design. 'A tree will always remain a tree, the sun, always the sun,' he had said about the Gorsky *Don Quixote* in
an interview. 'Is there really anything of Golovin's designs that resembles what we
see in nature?'[119] At some point after the rehearsal, the ballet's large mirror broke,
causing mercury to escape; this had an unnerving impact on the superstitious
stage staff who saw it as a bad omen.[120]

And it *was* a bad omen. Imperial presence notwithstanding, a section of the
audience noisily voiced its dislike of the 'decadent' designs from the second
scene onwards, provoking counter-protests from other spectators.[121] Golovin and
Koreshchenko were booed at the end and applause was frugal.[122] Teliakovsky acknowledged that the production did have some failings, but blamed Petipa and his
journalist-balletomane cronies for priming the protesters:

> The agitation, which all winter Petipa had been mobilizing, did its job
> and the ballet, despite the colossal efforts of the directorate, flopped. True,

the music is boring and very laboured. The ballet is not very successfully staged by Petipa, some of Golovin's designs are not quite finished, the costumes—some were taken from the Moscow *Swan Lake* and, of course, did not create an attractively unified picture. Nevertheless, much was successful and pretty. But the agitation of Petipa, Bezobrazov, Lappa, and others got the public, that is the balletomanes, ready to make a protest, and when the scene with the gnomes opened, insolent laughter rang out from the left side of the auditorium; even Grand Duke Vladimir Alexandrovich leaned out of his box to look at who was making the noise. When this act was finished, in the corridors, the public vehemently criticized the ballet.[123]

Benois's diagnosis of the core problem as being the absence of an overseeing eye is convincing:

> Both the composer, Koreshchenko, and the artist, Golovin, were disappointing. But the chief defect of the production was the absence of unified control—the control that had been so apparent during Vsevolozhsky's time, even in his less successful experiments. That is why my criticism, though dealing principally with Golovin's contribution, was in reality directed against Teliakovsky. [...] There is much in Golovin's sets that is beautiful. But where is the ensemble? Where is the central idea? Everything seems so badly patched together, so little thought out.[124]

While also blaming the 'decadent', non-realist decor, the hectic colours of the costumes, and the tedious music, reviewers showed mostly due reverence for Petipa's contribution. The opening 'Floral Waltz' (*Valse fleurie*) for gardeners celebrating the wicked queen's birthday caught the favourable attention of several reviewers who called it 'graceful', 'elegant', and 'poetic'.[125] Following this, the libretto explains that the king, so much older than his queen, tries to please her with gifts, brought by merchants of different lands, for her to choose. This is a cue for a *divertissement* of the different wares, in which the newly promoted first dancer Vera Trefilova featured prominently. There are animated precious stones, also Bohemian crystal, porcelain, and the tried-and-tested component of different styles of lacework—from Venice (Tamara Karsavina and Liubov Petipa or Petipa 3), England, Brussels, and, to finish, Russia, this last being a playful pas de trois for a merchant showing off his two lace-ballerinas. But it is a mirror that catches the queen's eye; it has, as its merchant explains, a magical peculiarity enabling it, when asked, to show the fairest woman in the land. The queen, looking into the mirror, but forgetting to ask the question, sees herself reflected, and, delighted, asks the king to buy her the mirror. She is so pleased, she leads a mazurka (a reminder that Marie Petipa was playing this role), before returning to the mirror and this time asking the fateful question. But, horror! Reflected as 'the fairest of them all' is Kshesinskaya's young princess, the queen's stepdaughter, in full view of all the courtiers. And by coincidence a fanfare now announces the arrival in person of the princess, who appears with a birthday bouquet for the queen. She is accompanied by her fiancé the prince (Legat) and two young couples—Anna Pavlova, Mikhail Fokine, Iulia Sedova, and Mikhail Obukhov. She dances a solo, chiefly remarkable, like her other solos, for its technical difficulties.[126] At the end of all this, the queen, very agitated, repeats her question to the mirror and it shows once again the young princess. The queen, overcome by jealousy and fury, faints, causing everybody to rush to her aid.

The second act starts with a mime scene in which the queen orders the princess's horrified nursemaid (Nadezhda Petipa or Petipa 2) to kill the princess. The nursemaid leads the young girl into a dense forest on the pretext of picking forget-me-nots. However, she can't bring herself to harm the much-loved princess who pleads with her to be spared, and instead leaves her in the forest, which is (of course) filled with twelve dryads. (This is not, though, the vision scene; this comes in the next act.) After the dances of the dryads, a curtain at the back lifts to show the queen in all her fury, having realized that the nursemaid, who is prostrate at her feet, has not followed her orders. She decides to do the job herself, disguised as a poor peasant woman.

The next scene shows a mountain landscape with huts and underground caves—gold mines worked by gnomes who appear from the caves and mountain slopes. The frightened princess runs into the midst of this and finds herself surrounded by the gnomes. Golovin's faux-primitivism apparently confused the audience, who mistook the mountains for trees or clouds.[127] *Novoe vremia* also objected to the knights of Pushkin's tale being replaced by shovel-carrying gnomes. But the gnomes gave Petipa a reason for introducing the school's students—one of them the twelve-year-old Nijinsky—their happy dance predictably raising much applause.[128]

Meanwhile the leader of the gnomes has taken the princess into one of the cabins. She re-emerges wearing a dress made of leaves covered with dewdrops and dances a solo, accompanied by the gnomes who hammer out the rhythms on an anvil. The gnomes then return to work, leaving the princess in her cabin with strict instructions not to let anyone in. The queen–peasant woman appears with stealthy steps and knocks on the door. The princess comes out and, feeling pity, gives her bread, at which the peasant woman insists on giving an apple (poisoned) in return. She watches as the princess takes a bite and drops lifeless to the ground. During her evil gloating, she does not notice she has dropped her handkerchief. She then hears the return of the gnomes and hurries away. The gnomes are naturally devastated to find the lifeless princess. Their leader spots the handkerchief and shows it as proof of the visit of an outsider. The act closes with a tableau vivant of the princess surrounded by the grieving gnomes.[129]

From Act III onwards the ballet is closer to the Pushkin version of the story. The prince is in a forest—and here, for once, Golovin's pale emerald designs, evoking the dewy freshness of spring, won general praise. The prince is searching for the princess and, sad and exhausted, he falls into a charmed sleep. In the ensuing vision appear the animated rays of the setting sun (led by Preobrazhenskaya), a 'shower of stars' (*pluie d'étoiles*, Karsavina and Liubov Petipa), and finally the lost princess, as a meteor, accompanied by Nikolai Legat as a zephyr. (Mikhail Fokine says that Nikolai, an excellent musician as well as a gifted visual artist, was always more interesting off stage than on.)[130] The prince and princess reach out to each other, but darkness falls and everything disappears. When the prince wakes, he realizes he is lost. He climbs a tree to try and see further; before him a panorama unfolds and in the far distance, under a sky filled with stars, he finally sees the castle.

The last act opens with a torchlit funeral procession, the gnomes carrying the princess in a crystal coffin covered with flowers. They place her in a cave, her final resting place. The princess is left alone, apart from one gnome who stays as a sentinel, and falls asleep. Everlasting flowers (*immortelles*) perform a dance.[131] Meanwhile, off stage, the leader of the gnomes, having heard about the disappearance of a princess and guessing that it is she in the coffin, sets off to the castle and brings back the king, queen, nursemaid, and other individuals. The prince also enters, running behind them. Seeing the princess, he is plunged in despair and he shatters the glass coffin with his sword. The apple rolls out in front of the prince and the princess comes back to life! Everyone is overjoyed—except the wicked queen. The gnome gives the king the handkerchief, evidence of whoever it was gave the apple. Recognizing the handkerchief, the king confronts the queen, who denies everything. Suddenly, the weeping nursemaid, unable to keep quiet any longer, explains what happened and her account is corroborated by the princess. The king with terrible anger threatens the queen with prison, but she, in a state of delirium and insanity, confesses—and drops dead. The ballet ends with a wedding celebration for the prince and princess, attended by foreign delegations—Polish, German, Swiss, Tyrolean who perform their dances, and then a massed *cracovienne*, set to music by Glinka. A grand pas de deux for Kshesinskaya and Sergei Legat follows, Kshesinskaya executing her difficult steps and triple turns with great lightness and style. Next comes a Saxon dance for six couples led by Preobrazhenskaya and Bekefi, which was encored; next, a classical pas de trois for Iulia Sedova, Anna Pavlova, and Fedor Kozlov, the costume worn by Kozlov arousing friendly mirth.[132] The closing climax is a Tyrolean dance with Kshesinskaya and Legat, rounded off by an elaborate coda full of brio bringing everybody together and enthusing the reviewers.[133]

The structure, therefore, followed Petipa's other grand ballets to the letter; it had all been seen many times before. Nevertheless it was decided not to kill the

Ivan Vsevolozhsky, director of the Imperial Theatres, seeing the world through his horn-rimmed pince-nez (1892)

Marie Petipa, in classical mode, as the Lilac Fairy in *The Sleeping Beauty*, with one of the fairy's attendants (Liubov Vishnevskaya) in the Prologue (1890–1891)

Marie was, however, principally a character dancer; here with Sergei Legat, in a burlesque dance of unknown origin, possibly called 'The Artist and Grizetka'

Matilda Kshesinskaya, pushy but charming, seen here as Niriti in Nikolai Legat's production of *The Talisman* (1910)

Matilda at home, maybe her villa at Strelna near Peterhof (1915)

Nadezhda, dancer, the least talented of Petipa's daughters, here in her father's *Les Millions d'Arlequin* (1900s)

Liubov, another of Petipa's daughters, had great talent as a classical dancer, but threw it all away; the hard-to-decipher dedication, to a Nadezhda Alexeevna (?), is from Liubov 'with warmth and devoted affection' (1900)

Victor, an actor, like Petipa's other sons (1910s)

Petipa's second wife, Liubov Savitskaya, with her children Victor and Vera in Gurzuf (1905–1910)

Pierina Legnani, warmth and a sense of fun, as Medora in *Le Corsaire*, with Alfred Bekefi as Said Pasha and Pavel Gerdt as Conrad (c. 1899)

Legnani, again in *Le Corsaire* with Olga Preobrazhenskaya (Gulnare), costumed for 'Le Jardin animé' (c. 1899)

Petipa, venerable ballet master; the dedication to 'Mademoiselle N. Bakerkina' (Nadezhda Bakerkina, Moscow ballerina) is dated 20 December 1896

Alexander Shiriaev, character dancer, memoir-writer, and assistant to Petipa, in the Spanish dance in *Swan Lake* with his wife Natalia Matveeva (1895)

Always graceful, always expressive, even in middle age: Pavel Gerdt as Solor in *La Bayadère* (undated)

Old-style theatre design: Konstantin Ivanov's set for Scene 2 in the 1900 revival of *La Bayadère*

The same production: Petr Lambin's set for Scene 3

Alexander Golovin's new approach to theatre design, which Petipa didn't understand: Act I, Scene 1 of *The Magic Mirror* (1903; picture taken from the Moscow staging of the same production in 1905)

The same production (*Magic Mirror*): Act III, Scene 6

Poster for the premiere of *The Magic Mirror* on 9 February 1903, a benefit performance for Marius Petipa, to be attended by the emperor and already sold out

Ivan Vsevolozhsky's costume designs for Petipa's last ballet, *The Romance of the Rosebud and the Butterfly*, more suited, according to Vladimir Teliakovsky, to the 'open-stage of the Zoological Gardens'; this drawing is for the Old Butterfly (*Vieux Papillon*), played by Pavel Gerdt.

Another butterfly costume, for corps de ballet dancers, including Vaslav Nijinsky, still at the theatre school

Costume for Olga Preobrazhenskaya as the Rosebud (*Bouton de Rose*)

The Daisy (*Pâquerette*), for Anna Pavlova: the note in Vsevolzhsky's handwriting says she is being pursued by the Old Butterfly

Costume for Mikhail Fokine as the handsome but inconstant butterfly (*le Beau Papillon*), also called the Sphinx Butterfly

Petipa in Gurzuf, shortly before his death: still impeccably turned out, with his clothes and his ballet-trained feet (c. 1910)

The funeral cortège to the Volkovo Lutheran Cemetery in St Petersburg (1910)

ballet after just one performance, but to make revisions to the music, designs, and choreography. On 6 September 1903 Petipa wrote: 'To the director's to hear on the piano the changes in the music that Mons[ieur] Koreshchenko has recomposed. It's even worse.'[134] The revising continued until the dress rehearsal on 27 December 1903. At the performance the following evening (a benefit for the corps de ballet) there was a full house and the dances were much applauded.[135] However, the critics were no more enthusiastic: *Novoe vremia* pointed to the ballet's excessive length, as well as to the previous defects; *Peterburgskaia gazeta* called the ballet 'a worthless and feeble creation'.[136] Unsurprisingly Petipa wasn't too pleased by this last judgement from his former collaborator's daily newspaper: 'That scoundrel Khudekov wrote again in his filthy paper against *Mirror*.'[137] The ballet was performed just twice more: on 14 April 1904, with Olga Preobrazhenskaya as the princess; and, in excerpted form, on 12 September 1904. It was, however, taken to Moscow, staged by Gorsky with the original libretto, designs, and, guessing from the description in the *Yearbook of Imperial Theatres*, many of Petipa's dances.[138] (This, though, doesn't mean they weren't modified.) After the premiere on 13 February 1905 the ballet was thought good enough to remain almost continuously in the repertoire until 1926.

On 17 February 1903 Petipa received notification that the emperor had approved the proposal to keep him as first ballet master without contract but with his salary intact (now 9,000 roubles) to the end of his days. In his diary he writes 'How splendid!,' also recording that he bought a large vase, which depicted a group of musicians and a singer—a way, perhaps, of celebrating.[139] On 19 February he had an audience with the emperor to express his gratitude, during which the emperor gave him his hand three times and 'said some charming and flattering things'. His impeccable manners holding sway, he also went to the director to thank him, although later in his memoirs he pointedly gives the credit to Baron Fredericks. (In this, he was doing Teliakovsky an injustice: it was Teliakovsky who drew up the conditions for Petipa's future as titular first ballet master; Fredericks only ratified them.)[140] On 3 March Petipa received the gift of a diamond ring from the emperor.[141]

Further Attacks

During the year 1903 alone Petipa rehearsed and revived an astonishing total of thirteen ballets, not counting *The Magic Mirror*.[142] He was eighty-five. Unsurprisingly, when the corps de ballet asked him to rehearse *The Talisman* for their benefit performance, he wrote in his diary, 'May God give me the strength.'[143] He was driven to distraction by his relentless, agonizing dermatological affliction, despite all medical efforts with ointments, drops, padding; he suffered his fair share of colds and bronchitis; his legs ached with rheumatism; his right eye was a worry; his 'nerves are bad, very, very bad'.[144] After the flop of *The Magic Mirror*, he had some kind of stroke, causing paralysis down one side, although only Vera mentions this, so maybe the effects were temporary.[145] Later, on 12 December 1903 came sad news: 'My old friend Johansson died this morning at seven.'[146]

The private man in Petipa's own diaries is certainly prone to bitterness and irritability, but he is also much more. By 1898 he has moved a few hundred yards from 53 Fontanka, right by the Theatre School, to 12 Zagorodnyi prospect. Like most people, he lives in rented property; even in Gurzuf, where he now spends the summer holidays, his accommodation is rented.[147] He does not live a flamboyant life, although he often buys a little something for himself (he smokes cigarettes) and for the apartment. He buys many gifts: toys for his grandchildren, a shelf and bonbons for his wife, a folding screen and a rug for his beloved Vera. He even finds a wardrobe for Vera at the market, the cost shared with his wife, but then sends it back, finding it poorly made.[148] He is warm-hearted and empathetic, commiserating, remembering anniversaries, regularly visiting the family graves, generous to a fault, a benefactor to charities, a prodigious tipper of attendants and servants. His means, though, are finite. He keeps a careful record of his expenses, no matter how small. (He also notes the box-office takings for each ballet performance.) In Gurzuf, the costs of accommodation and restaurant food with wine or beer add up, especially with visiting children and acquaintances. At one point during the 1904 vacation he has to delay the usual stipend to his sister Victorine for a few days because his month's salary has run out; at another point he writes that they will stay a further month, but only if the price of the accommodation is not raised.[149]

He is interested in current affairs and subscribes to the French newspaper *Le Gaulois*, he goes to the circus, he keeps framed photographs of the emperor and empress. On 19 March 1903 the chimney sweep cleans the sitting-room fireplace without telling anyone and covers the furniture with ash; on 15 May Vera's graduation is celebrated at an expensive restaurant.[150] Although Vera and her brother Marii are the only children still at home, it remains a close-knit family, with much letter writing and frequent visits by the others. Even Petipa's extra-marital first-born Marius Mariusovich makes an appearance. The household is also busy with other visitors: dancers, colleagues, Pavlova's patron Victor Dandré, Bezobrazov, even Khudekov, seemingly unaware that Petipa is annoyed by his articles.[151] Preobrazhenskaya, Pavlova, and Sedova are his favourites and often come.

As well as the inexorable reality of ageing, Petipa was also having to face the continuation of Teliakovsky's hostile manoeuvres. On 21 February 1903 Alexander Krupensky joined the directorate and Teliakovsky put him in charge of the ballet troupe to tighten what he considered the company's lax discipline. Krupensky's methods created an atmosphere of tense officiousness. No one, except Teliakovsky, has a good word to say about him: not Fokine ('a pampered, ambitious man'), not

Benois ('arrogant, overbearing, and insolent'), even less, of course, Petipa.[152] At first Krupensky tried to get along with Petipa, chattering and joking with him in French, but this didn't last long.[153] 'I could not reconcile myself,' Petipa writes, 'to the idea that a young man without the slightest comprehension of the art of choreography should be assigned to give orders and advice to a man who has devoted sixty years of his life to this business.' Appearing at rehearsals, 'he would sit down at a table, cross his legs, and acknowledge the greetings of the dancers with a slight nod of the head. I do not know where he was brought up, but in my old age it is hard to reconcile myself with such decadent manners, which, from childhood, I had believed were found only in taverns or in amusement establishments of the lowest order.'[154]

By 9 March, at the instigation of Vsevolozhsky who wrote the libretto, Petipa had started work on his final ballet, *The Romance of the Rosebud and the Butterfly* (Roman butona rozy i babochki), a 'ballet fantastique' with one act and two scenes and a score by Drigo. On 9 April 1903 he staged a new production of *King Candaules*, in which he inserted new dances, including a fresh version of the Pas de Venus for Sedova (Nisia) and Sergei Legat. And on 13 April *The Sleeping Beauty* celebrated its one hundredth performance—although, because 'that nasty swine' Kshesinskaya was dancing, he did not attend.[155]

Another of Teliakovsky's tactics, which had the effect of sidelining Petipa, was the creation of a ballet committee, initially consisting of Petipa, Gerdt, Drigo, and Aistov, to draw up the budget and discuss salary raises. According to Teliakovsky, this had previously been the responsibility of the *régisseur* and the theatre office's manager, so the involvement of others was certainly a democratic development.[156] However, when, after the summer vacation, the committee's remit was expanded to cover casting, Petipa vacillated, seeing this as a mortal blow to his authority, even if as chairman he had two votes. One accusation that can be fairly made against him is, as Vazem writes, nepotism, even though he had never been all-powerful, he had only ever been able to go so far, matters of casting and employment included.[157] In these later years he pushed his daughter Nadezhda into mime parts—the nurse in *The Magic Mirror*, Pythia in a revival of *Tsar Cadaules*—although by unanimous agreement she had no talent. In Vera, he seems to have discerned real classical potential and he may well have been right. So when, at the meeting of 13 October 1903 for the *Bluebeard* casting, his repeated attempts to replace Antonina Chumakova, offstage partner of Nikolai Legat, with his daughter Vera, were definitively stymied, he refused to attend any more.[158] The following day, he wrote a confirmation to Teliakovsky's assistant Georgii Vuich, adding that he would no longer rehearse the old ballets.[159]

In this way, Petipa unwillingly removed himself from the casting and from the control over some of his ballets—the beginning of their distortion over time. Now, he could only complain about the casting for the Grand Pas in *Paquita* ('It disgusts me! Poor sinking ballet!!') and about the performances of *The Sleeping Beauty* ('It's a disgrace for that committee').[160] Either because of administrative inefficiency or because the *régisseur* seized upon Petipa's letter to Vuich, he was being frozen out even with the newer ballets such as *The Sleeping Beauty* and *The Magic Mirror*. He was not notified of rehearsals, he did not receive the week's schedule, the carriage did not arrive.[161] By then Aistov had been sacked as *régisseur* and replaced on 28 September 1903 by Nikolai Sergeyev who around that time had also been given the responsibility, with two assistants, for notating the repertoire.[162] Aistov had squandered the initial goodwill of the dancers, but Sergeyev was, if possible, even more unpopular than Krupensky and widely believed to be a Teliakovsky informer.[163]

The Last Ballet

The Romance of the Rosebud and the Butterfly was a long time in preparation and scheduled for the Hermitage Theatre in January 1904, along with the revival of an early Petipa ballet, the 1865 *Travelling Dancer*.

Teliakovsky disliked Vsevolozhsky, that 'imbecile old man, who has been lying all his life, ingratiating himself and flattering his superiors', and 'whose brain, heart, understanding—everything—has been congealed for years'.[164] When Vsevolozhsky approached him about creating a new small ballet (*baletik*), a Vsevolozhsky-Petipa-Drigo project of has-beens (in Teliakovsky-speak), he had felt obliged to agree, although he feared that at curtain-rise the audience would see just 'three heaps of sand'.[165] Worse, as well as librettist, Vsevolozhsky had put himself forward as the costume designer. The full horror of the drawings could only make Teliakovsky gasp. 'My God, what is this primitive work, with pretensions to art, these drawings are more suited to [...] the open-air stage of the Zoological Gardens.' Vsevolozhsky had not only grown old, he had travelled backwards, but thinks that 'only his dilettante art will save the theatre'.[166]

The typewritten copy of Vsevolozhsky's libretto presents what it calls 'a poetic world' in which, as with the Glazunov *Seasons*, the emphasis is on dance, while flowers and butterflies provide the pretext.[167] This is not so far from, say, Balanchine's *Apollo*, a near-plotless ballet, with only a slender underlying narrative thread.

The curtain rises on a darkened stage, where all nature is asleep until dawn arrives and a daisy (*pâquerette*)—a special part for Pavlova—appears along with bell-shaped flowers (*campaniles*) who sway their heads and wake up the other flowers. They shake the dewdrops from their leaves and a morning breeze flurries through them. Small butterflies pursue the violets; but it is a handsome 'sphinx butterfly' (Mikhail Fokine) which attracts the flowers and they vie for his attention. At some point an old butterfly, played by Pavel Gerdt, chases after Pavlova's daisy.[168] A rosebud (Preobrazhenskaya) emerges from a crowd of roses and the sphinx butterfly chooses her; they leave together after a pas de deux and various group sequences. A bold nasturtium (*capucine*)—danced by Vera Trefilova— enters, carrying a leaf which serves as a parasol. She dances and flirts with her butterfly-admirers. The other flowers tell her about the rose and they decide to play a trick on her.

The second scene shows a different part of the garden, where the rose, now blossomed, and the butterfly are dancing. The nasturtium enters, determined to win over the butterfly—and succeeds, despite the rose's desperate attempts to keep him. There follows a triumphant dance for the other flowers, the rose has disappeared and the nasturtium and butterfly can be seen afar, arm in arm. A storm darkens the sky, bringing lightning and a downpour. The flowers revel in the freshness of the rain, but the butterflies seek shelter. Calm returns and the rose appears, faded and weeping, followed by marigolds (*soucis* in French, also meaning 'worries') and thistles. She asks the Queen of Gardens, an aristocratic lily (*lys*), to help bring back her inconstant lover. The queen causes the rose to be transformed back into a rosebud; other characters, including the nasturtium and butterfly, arrive in time to see the transformation and dance a *pas d'ensemble*. The sphinx's love is reignited and, pushing away the nasturtium, he begs the rose's forgiveness. After playing hard-to-get, she eventually falls into his arms. Finally comes the apotheosis of a setting sun, visible through a fine drizzle which delights the flowers and overpowers the butterflies.

There are no reviews of the Hermitage premiere, since it was cancelled. But Fokine leaves his own assessment:

> Petipa's choreography was as elegant and rich as in his other ballets. I can testify that Petipa's talent was not in its decline at all, as was claimed by his enemies; just the opposite—in spite of his greatly advanced age, he was, until the last days of his activities, full of artistic strength to which was now added his colossal experience.[169]

Perhaps the reason for the cancellation will never be fully elucidated. Already, Teliakovsky's misgivings about the ballet had escalated dramatically when he learnt about the casting. The issue was certainly not the presence of Pavlova or Trefilova— even less the student Nijinsky as a butterfly; it was that Kshesinskaya would not be the rose, but her rival Preobrazhenskaya. Teliakovsky interpreted this as a clear affront to Kshesinskaya. 'It cannot be that Vsevolozhsky, as former director, does not know and understand that to take part in a Hermitage performance is a great honour,' he writes in his diary. 'Since Kshesinskaya is the prima ballerina, she should take part.'[170] When Teliakovsky said this to Vsevolozhsky, he answered that as the ballet's author he had the right to choose the cast. Teliakovsky saw cunning in Vsevolozhsky's casting, exploiting Preobrazhenskaya's popularity—greater than Kshesinskaya's—and Petipa's antipathy to Kshesinskaya.[171] He also saw this as a base trick, a personal attack on himself, since it was landing him in an impossible position. He negotiated frantically: he pacified Kshesinskaya, explained the awkwardness to Baron Fredericks, asked him urgently to consult the emperor.[172] Ultimately, the emperor, after consulting the empress, decided to remove both ballets—*The Romance of the Rosebud* and *The Travelling Dancer*—from the mixed programmes. To his credit, Teliakovsky, on receiving this news, urged Fredericks to remind the emperor that one of the ballets was by no less a person than Vsevolozhsky.[173] But the following day the emperor personally confirmed the changes to Teliakovsky, saying 'it will be more convenient like this.' The decision made a huge impression on the company which had never been excluded from the Hermitage before. Speculation, according to Teliakovsky, went into overdrive, people wondering whether the imperial spouses were disturbed by the intrigues against himself or against Kshesinskaya.[174] If the emperor had another motive besides the desire not to step into the churning pit of rivalries, it remains a mystery.

Petipa was equally at a loss. 'All my work is wasted,' he wrote in his diary.[175] Those words, though, would ultimately turn out to be wrong. On 11 May 1919, for Drigo's farewell benefit, the ballet was revived by Alexander Chekrygin. Given that Chekrygin had been in the original cast as one of the blue butterflies and that, in 1903, he had become one of those assigned to notate the repertoire, his production is likely to have been reasonably authentic. It is also possible that Vsevolozhsky's costumes were used, since no name was indicated on the poster.[176]

Notwithstanding the extreme disappointment, Petipa kept as busy and involved as his body allowed. He enjoyed the scandal about Sergei Khudekov who spent the night with Vera Trefilova and on leaving her apartment was clubbed by a jealous Rimsky-Korsakov.[177] He took the trouble to buy a ticket for a violin concert given by a company dancer; he celebrated his eighty-sixth birthday *en famille*, receiving a cake from their housekeeper Hélène Mikhailovna; he rehearsed *Paquita*, then went to Vuich's office to deal with the raises for the ballet artists, ending up 'tired from walking up and down stairs'; he had to turn down an invitation from the family of the librettist Saint-Georges to mount *The Pharaoh's Daughter* in Paris ('my health is too poor').[178] Despite often being frozen out, he managed to work on ten ballets during 1904 and up to Preobrazhenskaya's benefit on 9 January 1905.[179] He could justifiably write with self-incredulity after a rehearsal lasting till 4:30 pm, 'I am amazing.'[180] He rehearsed Trefilova and Preobrazhenskaya for their debuts in *The Sleeping Beauty*.[181] He coached a new Italian guest Antoinetta Ferrero in *Coppélia*—'she could not do the adagio very well. She had difficulty learning. She has extraordinary ballon.'[182] Ever aware of a ballerina's individual needs, he was still modifying and choreographing, so for Ferrero's debut in *La Fille mal gardée* he composed two variations and three entrances in the coda 'in one hour'.[183] The chief beneficiary of Petipa's attention, though, was Vera. At the start of the family vacation in Gurzuf, he had a barre installed in their lodgings to give her daily lessons; three months later, when the barre was removed, she had had sixty-three. (She and her mother also went swimming sixty-three times; Petipa clearly had an addiction to counting.)[184]

Following the return on 23 August 1904 to St Petersburg, however, Petipa slowed down, staying increasingly at home and now writing his memoirs, fuelled by a desire to settle scores.[185] In his diary he obsessively monitors his aches and pains; he continues to complain about the distortion of his ballets. *The Sleeping Beauty* with the Italian ballerina Enrichetta Grimaldi has become 'awful' and 'a downright decadence of our art'.[186] He doesn't rate Grimaldi as a dancer; and anyway, the attraction of foreign ballerinas is clearly past, replaced by fabulously talented Russians, whom he cares for. Preobrazhenskaya comes to his apartment with a musician so he can choreograph a dance for her in *The Little Humpbacked Horse*.[187] As always he goes to immense trouble for Pavlova: in March he had coached her in *Paquita* and created a new variation to music by Drigo; and now, because she asked him, he showed her the mad scene again in *Giselle* and watched her rehearsing *Le Corsaire*.[188]

The Search for Other Choreographers

Petipa's age and Ivanov's death at the end of 1901 exposed the shortage of competent choreographers. Gorsky was in Moscow and despite rumours wasn't moving. Cecchetti, resented by Petipa because he was appointed ballet master over his head, had already been demoted in 1896, after filling the gap during a difficult period of ill-health and tragedy for Petipa. No longer ballet master, he also fell out with Teliakovsky and left in 1902.[189] Nor was Gerdt the answer: he had choreographed a couple of ephemeral ballets during the Volkonsky years and the subsequent one-act *Javotte* (1902), using Saint-Saëns's only ballet score, was a failure. The Legat brothers staged a version of Josef Hassreiter's widely popular *Die Puppenfee* or *Fairy Doll* (Feia kukol, 1903), created in Vienna in 1888; despite mediocre music by Josef Bayer, this also had much success in St Petersburg, helped by Bakst's costumes and the choreographic detail invented by the Legats.[190] But when Sergei Legat died, Teliakovsky had to recognize that Nikolaï's ballet productions were boring and monochrome; his *Puss in Boots* (Kot v sapogakh, 1906) disappeared without trace.[191] Attempts to find foreign ballet masters were no more successful. Achille Coppini, who had come from La Scala to mount Saint-Léon's *La Source* on 8 December 1902, left straight after, having made a decisively poor impression.[192] Three years later, Teliakovsky invited August Berger, the same Berger who, predating Petipa-Ivanov, had choreographed the first lakeside scene of *Swan Lake* in Prague. His three-week trial period in St Petersburg, however, led to nothing.[193] Teliakovsky might not have admitted it, but all these experiments highlighted the fact that Petipa was head and shoulders over everybody else.

Teliakovsky turned increasingly to Shiriaev, Petipa's able and loyal assistant. In 1903 Shiriaev was responsible for a revival of *The Haarlem Tulip* and *Giselle*, following which, on Petipa's recommendation, he was named second ballet master.[194] Required to rehearse Petipa's ballets, he was often instructed by Teliakovsky to make changes. This, naturally, upset Petipa and placed Shiriaev, who felt much indebted to Petipa, in an unpleasant position.[195] At the end of 1904, for a major new production of *Ruslan and Liudmila*, marking the centenary of Glinka's birth, Teliakovsky, who did not want any element of recycling to mar an occasion two years in the making, asked Shiriaev to replace Petipa's dances. These were, as Shiriaev writes, all excellent, but a Caucasian *lezginka* was especially thrilling— and authentic, choreographed after Petipa, with his usual thoroughness, had organized a lengthy demonstration by four Circassian dancers.[196]

Shiriaev, although a first-class rehearsal director, was not a gifted choreographer. Reluctantly, he composed new dances, but when it came to the *lezginka* he insisted to Teliakovsky that he could not better Petipa. 'However, the director could not stomach that Petipa's name should figure on the poster.' The resulting dance was, by Shiriaev's own admission, 'much less interesting than the old one', despite being performed by Pavlova.[197] 'There was something Spanish and something of the tarantella,' Petipa notes, 'but nothing of the *lezginka*.'[198] At the dress rehearsal Teliakovsky asked Petipa to modify it and, unsurprisingly, Petipa declined.[199]

Shiriaev was to suffer further: early in 1905 when Teliakovsky asked him to stage Petipa's *Talisman* he refused and decided to resign as ballet master, a position too onerous given the circumstances. But when he applied to Teliakovsky, rather than being allowed to continue as an ordinary dancer, as he had expected, he was fired. Teliakovsky, with his habitual cynicism, saw Shiriaev's request as a cunning attempt to swindle the directorate, because he had already received the proceeds of a dancer's farewell benefit on becoming a ballet master, and now he was announcing he wanted to resume as a dancer.[200]

Shiriaev officially left his post on 1 March 1905 but it was only on 24 November that his replacement Nikolai Legat was appointed.[201] As a consequence *Peterburgskaia gazeta* could accurately write on 4 September: 'The season is beginning in quite exceptional, simply unprecedented circumstances: without a ballet master!' Lamenting the absence of 'the venerable, irreplaceable Petipa' and the removal of Shiriaev, the article goes on to say that *La Bayadère* is currently being rehearsed by Sergeyev using notes. 'But can notes really replace a ballet master?'[202]

These issues were put directly to Teliakovsky a few days later as part of a long interview in the same paper:

[*Peterburgskaia gazeta*] How can you explain Mr Petipa's retirement from the ballet and how can the ballet actually be left without a ballet master?[203]

[Teliakovsky] Speaking frankly, we have been without a ballet master for a long time already. M. I. Petipa is too old to remain in his place, he is over eighty.

In the last years his memory has begun to fail him and things reached the point where he would ask for something one day, and the next day, having forgotten what he had said, would ask for something completely different.

Thanks to Mr Petipa we do not have, unfortunately, a replacement for him: Mr Petipa could not bear to hear about any candidate for his position and were he just to notice that some young artist was displaying the abilities of a future ballet master, he would push him aside. Accordingly, it was necessary to remove Mr Petipa's pupil Mr Gorsky, who was showing great promise, from Petersburg and transfer him to Moscow.[204]

Notwithstanding its questionable accuracy, this account doubtless contributed to the belief, which has persisted down the decades, that Petipa stamped on rivals. Meanwhile, it could only add fuel to the Teliakovsky-Petipa fire. Petipa lost no time in dispatching a smouldering letter, not to *Peterburgskaia gazeta* (presumably because it was Khudekov's paper) but *Novoe vremia*. 'In actual fact,' he wrote, 'I was removed as leader of the Petersburg ballet not because I have become old, have lost my understanding and artistic judgement, but because in all my long service I have been accustomed to work independently, obeying only the demands of art, and not the whims of civil servants, interfering in everything and dictating not only the distribution of roles, but also the way a ballet is staged.'[205] Teliakovsky considered Petipa's response to be 'the first instance of such impudence in all the directorate's existence'.[206] The matter sparked a debate in the press. One article, by Diaghilev, who detested Teliakovsky, described the programming of all the Imperial Theatres as weak; another, by Iurii Beliaev in *Novoe vremia*, mocked Teliakovsky for complaining about Petipa, 'who created Russian ballet and could not bear those without talent climbing all over the ballet masters'. However, in *Slovo* the dance writer Valerian Svetlov defended Teliakovsky's 'very positive merit' of 'opening the way to young artistic forces'.[207]

Petipa also took the opportunity to defend himself in the memoirs he was writing, not only denying that he had ever obstructed capable ballet masters such as Ivanov and Shiriaev, but insisting that he was never hostile to change:

I have never opposed reforms, but reasonable reforms. All my life I have believed that the young element must be given a chance, but they must be talented and capable people, and incompetents should not be pushed ahead just because they have influential friends.[208]

In his own memoirs Teliakovsky names another victim, Mikhail Fokine, but this is invalidated by the facts.[209] Petipa could not have suppressed Fokine's creative ambitions, which emerged only when Petipa was effectively out of the picture. It was in 1904 that Fokine wrote his first ballet libretto (*Daphnis and Chloë*); he sent it, with an attached list of ideas for aesthetic reforms, not to Petipa, but Teliakovsky—and received no answer. It was only in 1905 that, as a teacher, he choreographed his first ballet, a version for the school of Lev Ivanov's *Acis and Galatea*.[210] (As indicated in his diary, Petipa saw this in the school's concert on 10 April, but does not express any judgement.)[211] In the preceding years, Petipa seems to have approved of Fokine as a teacher, referring to him as *maître* Fokine, and as a dancer, casting him in the male lead of the *Romance of the Rosebud* and as Harlequin in *Harlequinade*.[212] And when in 1906 Fokine made his first work for professional dancers, *The Grapevine*, shown at an external fund-raising recital, he received a visiting card from Petipa with the inscription, 'Dear comrade, delighted by your composition, continue and you will become a great ballet master.' About this gesture Fokine could legitimately write: 'Never in my entire career as a ballet master did any compliment for my work please me more than this note from the great ballet master.'[213]

The 1905 Revolution

By now Teliakovsky had other exhausting problems. On 19 November 1904 the ballet company organized its first-ever petition against the directorate. The petition declared: 'This ballet troupe, saddened by the absence of Petipa from the theatre, [...] asks him to return to the theatre and occupy his proper place, for without him the art of ballet has started to decline.' The initiator, according to Teliakovsky, was Georgii Kiaksht. When Sergeyev stopped the collection of signatures at a rehearsal, they said they would continue after the rehearsal, at which point he called security. In all, seven dancers had already signed, among them Pavlova and Karsavina, but Teliakovsky claims that most of the artists were disturbed by 'Kiaksht's prank'.[214]

That, though, was only the beginning. The Russo-Japanese war, started on 8 February 1904 over rival ambitions in Manchuria and Korea, lurched into 'calamity', as Petipa records, when on 20 December the strategic naval base of Port Arthur fell to the Japanese.[215] The course of this war—Russia would eventually accept defeat in May 1905—helped stoke strikes and social unrest. On 9 January 1905 police fired on strikers marching peacefully to the Winter Palace with demands for the cessation of war and the abolition of the tyranny of capital over labour. This was the event which came to be known as Bloody Sunday. As loyal subjects the marchers were carrying icons and portraits of the emperor, but he wasn't even in St Petersburg and several hundred were killed or wounded. In his diary entry for that day Petipa writes that Preobrazhenskaya received 'gifts, flowers, etc. etc.' at her performance, but 'it's too much—here they're dancing and in the streets, they're killing.' He also mentions the Alexandrinsky performance that was suspended midway, after voices in the audience shouted, 'how can you act at such a time when blood is being spilt in the streets?'[216] In the following days there was rioting, the electricity was down, the theatres were closed, and the city in a state of siege. Petipa went with Marii to look at the broken shop windows on Nevsky Prospect.[217] The Bloody Sunday massacre could only give another boost to the stirrings of revolution. By 13 October the same year over 2 million workers were on strike. The unrest filtered into the ballet and on 15 October, after a meeting lasting seven hours, the 'progressives', led by an elected council including Fokine, Pavlova, and Karsavina, drew up demands. They wanted a say in budgetary decisions and in the appointment of *régisseurs*, an extra day off in addition to Saturday, and the reinstatement (again) of Petipa, Shiriaev, and Bekefi. (The last-named, considered superannuated by Teliakovsky, had also been forced out.)[218] The next day the progressives submitted a list of further demands and strike action disrupted the Mariinsky matinée of *The Queen of Spades*. While the dancers were getting ready, Karsavina, Fokine, and others ran through the dressing rooms shouting to them not to go on stage. Some also heaped abuse on the opera's performers and went so far as to douse them with water. As a result, the ball scene of Act II was omitted and the evening's performance cancelled. The turbulence was fraying the nerves of the Alexandriinsky troupe, a number of whom felt they were in no state to perform. But the decision was taken by Teliakovsky's superiors not to close the Imperial Theatres.[219]

When in the night of 18 October Sergei Legat slit his throat, some, like Karsavina, believed he had been driven to despair by the current situation. He had been 'nagged' to sign 'bitterly against his will' a declaration of loyalty to the directorate (the unnamed nagger being his offstage partner Marie Petipa) and 'the soul of loyalty, he felt himself a traitor'.[220]

However, his brother Nikolai (who also sided with the directorate) had a completely different version: 'He was highly imaginative and temperamental and conceived a mad and hopeless infatuation for a certain person attached with the ballet company.'[221] Teliakovsky, writing on 19 October, provides details about the events just before and after his death:

> Yesterday he was very agitated, he walked among the crowd on the street, he was shouting and in order to calm him down, they took him to the Mikhailovsky Theatre in the evening; returning home, [Marie] Petipa did not want to let him out and locked him in a room, where he cut his carotid artery with a razor and died from loss of blood. When the doctor arrived, he could only establish the fact of death.[222]

Although in his diary Petipa simply notes, 'Sergei went mad, biting Marie; then he killed himself,' in his memoirs he makes a genetic link with another Legat, Ivan, the machinist who lost his reason when, at the premiere of *The Daughter of the Snows*, the scenery toppled over and broke.[223] Perhaps he was not so wrong, given Teliakovsky's description which suggests not so much despair as some kind of psychosis. Naturally, the ballet company was deeply disturbed. Sergei's funeral took the form of a demonstration, Pavlova taking pains to make visible an inscription on a wreath's red ribbon—'the first victim at the dawn of artistic freedom'.[224]

Petipa had been observing all this second-hand. He was delighted by the demands for his reinstatement, but less enthused, it would seem, by other aspects. Preobrazhenskaya told Teliakovsky that much reformist agitation was coming from the Petipa *milieu*—not so much Petipa himself, but his wife, daughters, and Sokolova. When, apparently, Petipa repeatedly told them they should keep quiet, they quashed him, dismissing him as too old to reason properly. Perhaps this explains his diary entry on 29 October: 'I am ill of old age. My wife and Vera will never listen to a father's counsel. They are both stubborn mules.'[225] When Teliakovsky later writes that Preobrazhenskaya, so close to Petipa, has fallen out with his family because she could not sympathize with the dissidents, one can only hope that she fell out with the women rather than Petipa himself.[226]

The dissidents did not have the support of the opera and drama companies either, and were in fact a minority in the ballet itself. Their fellow dancers felt they had been tricked on 15 October into giving their signatures to economic and management reforms when in fact these had a political subtext; they even made several representations explaining this to the directorate. But disturbances continued to the end of the 1905–1906 season. On 21 November Pavlova berated a young dancer, Alexander Monakhov, for helping to draft a statement which opposed the progressives and was delivered to the directorate. Tempers flared and another progressive, Iosif Kshesinsky (Matilda's brother), slapped Monakhov's face. Kshesinsky, refusing to ask the minister of the Court for leniency, was fired, despite an official enquiry and interventions by other dancers, including Matilda who wrote from Cannes where she was on holiday. Monakhov received a formal reprimand and Pavlova a reproach.[227]

Also on 21 November the dissidents elected an executive committee to pursue their utopian aim of artistic autonomy. Marie Petipa and Preobrazhenskaya declined to take part, as did Petipa ('stupid committee'). The committee would not only decide salaries but also artistic matters such as promotions and invitations to foreign dancers and ballet masters. 'In short,' Teliakovsky remarks drily, 'the directorate would have nothing left to do, apart from cleaning the theatres and transferring money to the [...] committee.'[228]

It all came to nothing. However, except for Iosif Kshesinsky and another dancer, Petr Mikhailov, dismissed as the driving force behind the insurgency, little action seems to have been taken against the other activists.[229] Teliakovsky wanted to take a tougher line against 'hooligans' such as Fokine, but his superiors were more emollient.[230] The careers of neither Fokine, nor Karsavina, nor Pavlova seem to have suffered in the long term. Perhaps they were simply too talented. Fokine, despite Teliakovsky's antipathy to him as a political ringleader, would soon emerge as the choreographer the company needed, his trail-blazing premises aligning him with Teliakovsky's new-wave sympathies—except that with the launch of the Ballets Russes in 1909 his loyalties, like those of Karsavina, became divided. Meanwhile Pavlova, who was now earning 'head-spinning' quantities of money, made her debut in *The Pharaoh's Daughter* for Bekefi's farewell benefit on 29 January 1906: a performance which marked the end of Kshesinskaya's monopolies and consequently provoked huge public interest.[231] Despite changing her status to guest ballerina in 1904, Kshesinskaya had campaigned to retain her exclusive rights, but Teliakovsky's ears were now deaf to her pleas.[232] A fortnight earlier (15 January) he gave another Kshesinskaya ballet, *La Fille mal gardée*, to Preobrazhenskaya. Company legend says that Kshesinskaya still managed to sabotage Preobrazhenskaya's debut: someone allowed the ballet's live chickens to escape from their coop and create a commotion during one of Preobrazhenskaya's dances.[233]

The Final Years

The preparations for Preobrazhenskaya's benefit on 9 January 1905 were Petipa's last activities as ballet master with the company. (The programme consisted of the snowflakes scene from *The Nutcracker*, a *divertissement* called *Masquerade*, *The Travelling Dancer*, and *The Whims of the Butterfly*.) A few days earlier, on 4 January, even though the management had again failed to send a carriage for him, he had gone to the theatre for a rehearsal with orchestra of *The Travelling Dancer*, which the present crop of dancers scarcely knew. This was followed by a rehearsal without orchestra of *The Whims of the Butterfly*. Back home the same evening he composed a variation for Preobrazhenskaya for *The Travelling Dancer* and in his diary recorded, 'It's my last variation. It's finished!!!' Did he know that it would indeed be his last variation? Is that what he meant?[234]

Mid-February, watching a rehearsal of *The Blue Dahlia*, he is appalled. The ballet is 'dreadfully mounted' with new dances by 'that swine Gerdt' and he asks for his name to be removed.[235] (In his memoirs, though, he complains that his name is sometimes omitted from other ballets.)[236] Meanwhile, the reduction of purposeful activity weighs heavily on him: 'Tedium,' he writes, 'is one of the worst things in life.'[237] After the summer trip to Milan, accompanying Vera on her pilgrimage to Beretta's classes, there are still occasional outings—to important ballet performances, to the Farce Theatre where Victor is performing—but he feels increasingly isolated, poorly, and sorry for himself.[238] Yet occasionally there is good news: Marii passed the exams to enter the cavalry for his military service, joining a regiment based at Peterhof.[239] And much later, the public reminds him that he is not forgotten: at Glazunov's benefit performance on 28 January 1907, where the company performed *The Trial of Damis*, the third act of *Raymonda*, and *The Seasons* in a new, very bad staging by Legat, the audience stood up to give him, seated in the sixth row of the stalls, a momentous ovation.[240]

On 7 March 1907 *Peterburgskaia gazeta* announced the imminent sixtieth anniversary of Petipa's arrival in Russia. It asked, with indignant incredulity, 'is it really possible that the Directorate will not give a benefit [...] for so many years of service?' and concluded, 'as before the Directorate does not stand on ceremony with Mr Petipa'.[241] In mid-March Petipa left for Crimea, but before leaving gave an interview to *Peterburgskaia gazeta*, published on 2 May, which noted that he would not spend his May jubilee in Petersburg. In his absence, on the due date, the ballet company gathered informally 'to honour their old teacher'.[242]

He gave his last interview in Gurzuf, a month before his death. He declared himself saddened by the fate of his company and unimpressed by Diaghilev's Paris success: 'It's not the victory of Russian ballet, but the triumph of twentieth-century clamour. When I hear about the victory of Russian ballet abroad, my heart weeps. [...] Everything I cared for and nurtured over many years, is going through its death throes.'[243] The Fokine ballets which made up most of the two Ballets Russes programmes had all been premiered in St Petersburg during 1907–1908 by the Imperial Ballet. Maybe he didn't see them; it is tempting to think that he might have felt less desolate if he had seen *Chopiniana* in Paris, not so far removed from his own one-act ballets.

After his death in Gurzuf on 1 July 1910, his body was transported, as he had requested, to St Petersburg. He was buried in the family plot at the Volkovo Lutheran Cemetery alongside his father, daughter, and brother. The journal *Teatr i iskusstvo* noted the shocking absence of any representative or wreath or telegram from the directorate. Many dancers could not come, many were in Paris with Diaghilev's company. Even so, among the mourners were Vazem, Kshesinskaya, Gerdt, Aistov, Glazunov, and Pleshcheev.[244] Much later, in 1948, his remains were transferred to the Alexander Nevsky Monastery (*Aleksandro-Nevskaia Lavra*), to lie in the company of Tchaikovsky, Rimsky-Korsakov, and Dostoevsky.[245]

Especially moving is Vera Petipa's dedication in her memoir to her family and 'to my dear father, who surrounded my childhood and youth with loving care'. She remembered as a child

his trembling hand, guiding me towards the entrance on stage, when I, disoriented and frightened, hesitated before the dark chasm of the auditorium and shrank back. In my youth, when I was appearing before the public for the first time as a professional artist, in the ballet *Harlequinade*, I can never forget my father's agitation and his whispered blessing in the wings. When I fell ill in Yalta and lay in a serious state with tuberculosis, my father, although an old man, somehow immediately stood alongside my mother as she bustled around me, and not knowing how to help me, whispered gentle words, stroked my head, and looked into my eyes, and offered to read to me—there was much, much reading.

Finally, the last sad memory—his death in Gurzuf, when we were all crowded round his bed and he says my name faintly and his fingers, growing cold, grip my hand.[246]

Apotheosis

In recent times there has been a re-evaluation of artistic values in all areas of art, views on art have changed in many ways, new trends have appeared and the ballets of Petipa have, of course, receded into the background. But the merit of Petipa has not diminished at all, it will remain eternal in the annals of Russian choreography, which today has earned worldwide fame and universal recognition.[1]

AFTER PETIPA'S DEATH the position of first ballet master went, in the immediate, to Nikolai Legat, an excellent teacher, but widely recognized as a poor producer and choreographer. By then, Karsavina, Nijinsky, Pavlova, Sergei Grigorev, and Fokine had joined the Ballets Russes, although initially they divided their time between the two companies. Pavlova, who appeared with the Ballets Russes up to 1911, also formed her own company abroad; with it, she travelled the globe, initiating audiences in far-flung places, until her death in The Hague in 1931.

For this generation (with the exception of the more conservative Pavlova), the future of ballet lay with one-act works where the style of movement was determined by the subject and the narrative was articulated through an expressionist body language. In *Le Spectre de la rose* (1911) Nijinsky floated about the stage and curved his arms like tendrils because he was the spirit of a rose in a young girl's dream. He was the supreme incarnation of the rehabilitated male dancer, the school of Gerdt and Johanssen, with its modulated elegance, expressiveness, and restraint, merging with the pyrotechnics of Cecchetti. Always centre stage, he ended his stamina-draining dance with a leap that became a legend, still spoken of today. In *Petrushka* (1911), though, it was irrelevant that he could perform such a leap, because as Petrushka he was a badly made puppet and could only move with turned-in, jerky shapes. The Russian subject, mediated through a synthesis of Benois's designs, Igor Stravinsky's score, and Fokine's choreography, each component accorded equal importance, made *Petrushka* one of the defining works of the Ballets Russes.

Petipa represented the past, and to some extent he knew it. For him, choreography was, as he said in an interview, 'like architecture, based on the beauty and harmony of lines', something he could not find in the ballets of young rivals like Gorsky.[2] He admitted that he could not understand the new 'decadent' school of stage design.[3] Nor, he said, could he 'be reconciled to the contemporary *grotesque-ries* and *tours de force*' of the Italian school, because he found them 'inelegant', although history says he managed to reach a compromise.[4] He also rose to the challenge of a more ambitious form of ballet music, even if by inclination he might have preferred to keep to the old ways. Khudekov divides Petipa's work into two periods. In the first, which ended with *The Vestal*, Petipa's ballets had a strong storyline, a real dramatic development, authored by Saint-Georges and Khudekov. In the second, Petipa fell under Vsevolozhsky's influence and produced a series of *féeries* with 'microscopic' narratives taken from fairy tales, in which the dances often bore little relation to the subject.[5] Judging by the reviews, though, the Petipa of the first period also had a tendency to overstuff his ballets with dances, nor did he always avoid feeble narratives, especially when he wrote them himself. There was always a tension between his loyalty to drama, underpinned by his own career as a great mime artist, and his unstoppable urge to create dances. But, certainly, in the century's final decade, the proportion of dance to drama increased in dance's favour, opening the door to the plotless ballets of the twentieth century. It is the composition of his dances, everlastingly fresh and interesting, which is his most lasting legacy, able to transcend the boundaries of fashion and time.

Petipa was more an evolutionist than an innovator. Contrary to what he thought, it was not, Diaghilev bluntly argued in a letter to *Peterburgskaia gazeta*, the designs or 'the unsuccessful, heavy music' that brought about the downfall of *The Magic Mirror*, but the ballet itself, its form, its procedures, 'unnecessary, boring, long, complicated, and pretentious'.[6] In not recognizing this, Petipa had indeed completely lost touch. Even before joining the Ballets Russes, Bronislava Nijinska, who graduated into the Imperial Ballet in 1908, felt the 'absurdities' of the Petipa style: the mime, the virtuoso steps which did not match the action (although the blame, here, might not just rest with Petipa), the geographic and ethnographic incongruities, and the way, in *Paquita*'s final act, a superlative classical grand pas, performed by dancers in short tutus, was presented alongside an archetypal ma-zurka for the school's pupils. After she became a Ballets Russes dancer, the alien-ation from Petipa's work grew more acute. 'The ballet of the imperial theatres was becoming foreign to me [...] it was as if I was living on another planet.' With Petipa gone, the gulf had widened even more because the company no longer had his creative leadership. Sergeyev, who rehearsed Petipa's ballets, devoted all his at-tention to what he saw as the inviolable lines of a dance, so that the corps de ballet moved without 'reflecting any of the nuances of the music, only adhering to the snapping of Sergeyev's fingers, marking out beats'. There were also times when a dancer would perform a phrase that did not tally with the music and Sergeyev would not notice.[7]

In 1921, after Sergeyev had left Russia in the tumult of revolution, taking with him all the repertoire's notations, Diaghilev engaged him for the Ballets Russes production of *The Sleeping Beauty* (*The Sleeping Princess*) in London. It was maybe in this production that the erosion of Petipa's passages of mime first began. When Diaghilev brought in Nijinska to counterbalance the dryness of Sergeyev's notations and snapping fingers, Diaghilev and Nijinska both agreed that, although most of the dances should be preserved, the mime, which to them seemed absurd, should be presented differently, more naturally. However, the more Nijinska worked on this and other Petipa ballets, the more she 'became imbued with a profound respect for Petipa, for the genius of his choreography', those dances embedded in the sometimes dated paraphernalia of nineteenth-century theatre.[8] While Petipa provided the new generation with a tradition to kick against, so the new generation revered, or came to revere, the Petipa tradition.

The Ballets Russes grew from the soil that Petipa had tended. Excepting Leonid Massine, who had trained in Moscow, all the company's choreographers came from St Petersburg, as did many of its dancers. And from the start, Diaghilev included Petipa's works in his programming. Excerpts from *Raymonda* were incorporated into *Le Festin*, a *divertissement* for the 1909 Paris launch; *Swan Lake* received its Ballets Russes premiere in London in 1911. The West owes *Giselle* to Petipa and Diaghilev, since it was the huge success of Petipa's production in Paris 1910 which returned a French classic to a nation that had forgotten it. Finally, Benois went so far as to claim: 'The Ballets Russes themselves would never have seen the light of day had not the *Belle au Bois dormant* [The Sleeping Beauty] awakened in a group of Russian youths a fiery enthusiasm that developed into a kind of frenzy.'[9] It was because he was determined to do full justice to *The Sleeping Beauty* that Diaghilev famously brought his company to the brink of bankruptcy.

As everyone knows, the Ballets Russes had a colossal impact in Paris and London where ballet had been demoted from art to entertainment and serious-minded people took no interest. Suddenly all that changed, sparked by the company's modernist credentials, the high calibre of its participants, and its 'exoticism'. If the vividly coloured otherness of *The Firebird* and *Petrushka* was in fact a *faux-Russianness*, modelled on the slavophile folk art of privileged artistic colonies such as the one at Abramtsevo, it didn't matter. Suddenly, after nearly two centuries of aping Western Europe, ballet from Russia had a blazing, singular identity. It was the 'Russian Ballet', adopted by the twentieth century as a separate category. And at its root, as the critic Valerian Svetlov wrote, was Petipa, even if the old Petipa himself had denounced it.

Of course, this triumph, this victorious march of Russian choreography around the cities of the New and Old World is the immediate result of the feverish and talented activity of Diaghilev, Fokine, and the brilliant galaxy of their like-minded performers and artists. But this to be exact is a *result*, the result of that mighty creative work, which in the course of many decades was shouldered by the genius of the old ballet—Petipa.[10]

The Ballets Russes produced its own important offshoots, after Diaghilev's death and the company's dissolution in 1929—the Ballets Russes de Monte Carlo, the Ballets Russes du Colonel de Basil, the Ballets 1933, and more. George Balanchine, Diaghilev's last choreographer, whose plotless classical style was most closely indebted to Petipa, founded in 1935 what would become the New York City Ballet. British ballet owes its existence to Diaghilev: Marie Rambert, a Jaques-Dalcroze eurythmics expert, engaged by Diaghilev to help Nijinsky with *The Rite of Spring*, created Britain's first ballet company in 1926, the Ballet Rambert (now called just Rambert); and an Anglo-Irish dancer, Ninette de Valois, who had joined the Ballets Russes in 1923, founded the Vic-Wells Ballet (later Royal Ballet) in 1931. All this was touched upon at the beginning of this book, but it bears repeating here.

With de Valois the ties with Petipa were considerably strengthened. For the first time, somebody wanted to use the nineteenth-century Petersburg repertoire to build the pillars of a company. In this de Valois was aided by Sergeyev and his notation scores. Sergeyev also had the advantage of knowing at least some of the steps and structures of the ballets.[11] Joining de Valois as ballet master he was instrumental in enabling the company to mount *Swan Lake, Giselle, Coppélia, The Sleeping Beauty*, and *The Nutcracker*. Of all the extant companies in the West, therefore, the Royal Ballet is the one which has been the closest, in its repertoire, to the Petersburg ballet and its example has had considerable influence round the world.[12]

While audiences were ecstatically discovering Diaghilev's Ballets Russes, Russia was in turmoil and its ballet haemorrhaging dancers who eventually stopped returning and settled permanently in the West. Worse, in the swirl of contradictory forces immediately after 1917, ideas of a proletarian culture were threatening ballet's very existence. Eventually, with the appointment of Anatolii Lunarchasky as the People's Commissar of Education came the possibility of rescue. In fact it was a stroke of luck that in a previous incarnation Lunarchasky had followed the early performances of the Ballets Russes and written articles about them. As commissar, he not only argued for the protection of historic buildings, but he also enlisted ballet as a revolutionary cause, to bring art to the masses. Speaking in 1921 about Russian ballet's important tradition, he announced that 'to lose this thread, to allow it to break before being used as the foundation of a new artistic culture belonging to the people, this would be a great calamity.'[13]

Under the ballet master Fedor Lopukhov, the Mariinsky ballet, now renamed, with the opera, the State Academic Theatre of Opera and Ballet or GATOB (Gosudarstvennyi akademicheskii teatr opery i baleta), modernist experimentation was balanced with a will to preserve at least some of the Petipa classics.[14] Even a ballet as unlikely as *The Sleeping Beauty* survived, fairy-tale royalty notwithstanding, although the score was certainly an important factor. In Moscow, the influential dancer, ballet master and teacher Vasilii Tikhomirov also fought successfully to keep certain classics. And in Leningrad, Agrippina Vaganova, never an outstanding ballerina—the adjectives 'awful' and 'dreadful' accompany Petipa's diary entries—emerged as an exceptional teacher and theoretician.[15] To Petipa's language of movement, she gave a whole-bodied spaciousness, an audacious plasticity and flow that corresponded to the heroic dimension of the Soviet ideal. The Moscow ballet evolved in a similar way, only even more so, with an epic athleticism and drama; while Leningrad conserved a more aristocratic restraint, in keeping with its past.

This then was Soviet ballet, sealed off from foreign influences by the Iron Curtain: a complete reversal of the internationalism of the Petipa era. When in 1956 the Moscow Bolshoi Ballet appeared in London, it was the first time a major Russian company had danced outside the Soviet Bloc. They brought *Swan Lake*, *Giselle*, and two *drambalets*—the Soviet version of classical ballet, narrative, full-evening, and ultra-conservative. Galina Ulanova in one of these, the Prokofiev–Leonid Lavrovsky *Romeo and Juliet*, was a revelation equal to the Ballets Russes in 1909. Western audiences had not seen such technical mastery since the days of Nijinsky and Pavlova, such artistry, such wholehearted commitment. It was the 'Russian Ballet' all over again.

Petipa was the father of all this. With his death went the last foreigner to shape Russian ballet, completing the task started by Jean-Baptiste Landé 172 years before.

Appendices

THE CHAIN OF COMMAND DURING PETIPA'S TIME

THE EMPEROR

Nicholas I 1825–1855
Alexander II 1855–1881
Alexander III 1881–1894
Nicholas II 1894–1917

THE MINISTER OF THE IMPERIAL COURT

Prince Petr Volkonsky 1826–1852
Count Vladimir Adlerberg 1852–1870
Count Alexander Adlerberg 1870–1881
Count Illarion Vorontsov-Dashkov 1881–1897
Baron Vladimir Fredericks 1897–1917

THE DIRECTOR OF THE IMPERIAL THEATRES

Alexander Gedeonov 1833–1858
Andrei Saburov 1858–1862
Count Alexander Borkh 1862–1867
Stepan Gedeonov 1867–1875
Baron Karl Kister 1875–1881
Ivan Vsevolozhsky 1881–1899
Prince Sergei Volkonsky 1899–1901
Vladimir Teliakovsky 1901–1917

THE PETIPA FAMILY

*Parents**

Jean Antoine Petipa (1787–1855), ballet master

Victorine Morel or Maurel (c.1794–1860), actress

Siblings

Joseph **Lucien** (1815–1898), dancer and ballet master

Élisabeth Marianne (1816–?)

Victor **Marius** Alphonse Petipa (1818–1910), dancer and ballet master

Jean Claude Tonnerre (1820–1873), dancer and actor

Aimée (Amata) **Victorine** Anna (1824–1905), opera singer

Adélaïde Antoinette (1826–?)

Wives

Maria Sergeevna Surovshchikova (1836–1882), dancer

Liubov Leonidovna Savitskaya (1854–1919), dancer

Children

From liaison with Marie-Thérèse Bourdenne (d. 1855)

Marius Mariusovich Petipa (1850–1919), actor

From marriage with Maria Surovshchikova

Maria (Marie) Mariusovna (1857–1930), dancer (she had a son)

Jean Mariusovich (1859–1880s)

From relationship (and presumed marriage) with Liubov Savitskaya

Nadezhda Mariusovna (1874–1945), dancer and teacher, married Konstantin Matveevich Chizhov, son of a famous sculptor, Matvei Chizhov. (They had five children.)

Evgenia Mariusovna (1877–1892)

Victor Mariusovich (1879–1939), actor

Liubov Mariusovna (1880–1917), dancer (retired early to get married)

---

*The format for this Petipa genealogy has been modelled with gratitude on Lynn Garafola's in her edition of Petipa's diaries.

Marii Mariusovich (1884–1922), actor

Vera Mariusovna (1885–1961), dancer and actress

Some of the Grandchildren

Nikolai Mariusovich Radin (1872–1935), actor, son of Petipa's eldest child Marius Mariusovich

Nadezhda Konstantinovna Petipa-Chizhova (1896–1977), actress, daughter of Nadezhda Mariusovna and Konstantin Chizhov

Xenia Konstantinovna Petipa-Chizhova (1905–1975), dancer, daughter of Nadezhda Mariusovna and Konstantin Chizhov

Other Relatives

Joseph Jacob Victor Mendès de Léon (1846–1896), son of Victorine from her marriage with Josua Mendès de Léon; he was therefore Petipa's nephew. Joseph Jacob had many children, including the following:

Lucienne (1873–1942) and Jeanne Mendès de Léon (1873–1956?), twin daughters and Petipa's great nieces. Lucienne was an opera singer.

Berthe Mendès de Léon (1878–1961), another great niece of Petipa. She was a soprano at the Paris Opera and Opéra-Comique.

WORKS BY MARIUS PETIPA IN RUSSIA*

Paquita, ballet in two acts and three scenes. Music: Edward Deldevez. Libretto: Paul Fouché and Joseph Mazilier. Choreography: Mazilier, staged by Petipa and Frédéric. Design: Jourdeuil (Scenes 1 and 2); Heinrich Wagner (Scene 3). Principal dancers: Elena Andreianova (Paquita); Marius Petipa (Lucien d'Hervilly); Frédéric (Inigo).

Production premiere: 26 September 1847, Bolshoi Theatre, St Petersburg.

23 November 1848: the production was staged by Petipa in Moscow, dancing with Andreianova.

27 December 1881: revival at the Bolshoi Theatre, St Petersburg, by Petipa with additional music by Minkus and a new pas de trois, grand pas, and children's mazurka. Principal dancers: Ekaterina Vazem (Paquita); Pavel Gerdt (Lucien d'Hervilly).

The original was staged on 1 April 1846 at the Paris Opera with choreography by Mazilier.

Satanilla, or Love and Hell, pantomime ballet in three acts and seven scenes. Music: Napoléon Henri Reber and François Benoist. Libretto: Henri Vernoy de Saint-Georges and Joseph Mazilier. Choreography: Jean Petipa and Marius Petipa, after Mazilier. Design: Heinrich Wagner and Andrei Roller. Principal dancers: Elena Andreianova (Satanilla); Marius Petipa (Fabio); Jean Petipa (Hortensius).

Production premiere: 10 February 1848, Bolshoi Theatre, St Petersburg.

19 January 1849: the production was staged in Moscow by the Petipas with Andreianova in the title role.

18 October 1866: revival at Bolshoi Theatre, St Petersburg. Dancers: Praskovia Lebedeva (Satanilla); Lev Ivanov (Fabio).

The original was staged on 21 September 1840 with choreography by Mazilier at the Paris Opera as *Le Diable Amoureux*.

[*Lida, the Swiss Milkmaid*, demi-caractère ballet in two acts and three scenes, based on Filippo Taglioni's ballet, whose first version, *The Swiss Milkmaid*, was created in 1821. Music: Adalbert Gyrowetz. Choreography: probably Jean Petipa or Jules Perrot, although Petipa in his memoirs claimed it as his own. Design: Heinrich Wagner. Principal dancer: Fanny Elssler.

Production premiere: 4 December 1849, Bolshoi Theatre, St Petersburg.]

---

*This list is based, not on Petipa's own unreliable list in his memoirs, but on Lynn Garafola's masterly compilation and explanatory notes in her edition of *The Diaries of Marius Petipa*. The small number of additions and modifications come principally from *Peterburgskii balet. Tri veka. Khronika*, eds. Irina Boglacheva, V. Mirovana, and N. Zozulina, 6 vols. The additions for the Moscow stagings were sourced in Elizabeth Souritz, *Balet moskovskogo Bol'shogo teatra vo vtoroi polovine XIX veka*, and in *Baletmeister A. A. Gorskii*, eds. Elizabeth Souritz and E. Belova.

The Star of Granada, divertissement. Music: Cesare Pugni. Choreography: Marius Petipa (uncredited).

Premiere: 22 January 1855, Mikhailovsky Theatre, St Petersburg. Dancer: Maria Surovshchikova.

[*The Rose, the Violet, and the Butterfly,* dance scene in one act. Music: Petr, duke of Oldenburg. Libretto: Jules Perrot. Petipa claimed the choreography as his own but it seems more likely to be Perrot's. At the Bolshoi Theatre, the performers were: Liubov Radina (Rose); Nadezhda Amosova (Violet); Marfa Muraveva (Butterfly).

Premiere: 8 October 1857, Tsarskoe Selo (court performance) or Bolshoi Theatre.]

A Marriage During the Regency, ballet in two acts. Music: Cesare Pugni. Libretto: Petipa. Design: Andrei Roller. Principal dancers: Anna Prikhunova (Nathalie); Maria Surovshchikova-Petipa (Matilda); Marfa Muraveva (Carolina); Timofei Stukolkin (Sylph, dancing master); Christian Johansson (Count); Marius Petipa (Prince Oscar); Lev Ivanov (Marquis).

Premiere: 18 December 1858, Bolshoi Theatre, St Petersburg.

23 October 1859: premiere at Bolshoi Theatre, Moscow, staged by Théodore.

The Sleepwalker Bride, ballet in three acts, four scenes. Music: Ferdinand Hérold. Libretto: Eugène Scribe. Choreography: Jean Aumer, staged by Marius Petipa (choreography) and Ekaterina Friedberg. (The poster mistakenly attributed the choreography to Aleksei Bogdanov.) Design: Heinrich Wagner. Principal dancers: Marius Petipa (Edmond); Ekaterina Friedberg (Teresa).

Premiere: 29 January 1859 at the Bolshoi Theatre, St Petersburg.

The original by Jean Aumer was premiered at the Paris Opera on 19 September 1827 as *La Somnambule.*

Venetian Carnaval, grand pas de deux. Music: Cesare Pugni, on a theme by Paganini. Choreography: Petipa (uncredited). Principal dancers: Amalia Ferraris; Marius Petipa.

Premiere: 12 February 1859, Bolshoi Theatre, St Petersburg.

The Parisian Market, comic ballet in one act. Music: Cesare Pugni. Libretto: Petipa. Choreography: Petipa. Principal dancers: Maria Surovshchikova-Petipa (Lizetta); Timofei Stukolkin (Marquis de Maigrelet); Marius Petipa (Simon).

Premiere: 23 April 1859, Bolshoi Theatre, St Petersburg.

29 May 1861: the ballet was staged at the Paris Opera as *Le Marché des Innocents* with some changes. Principal dancers: Maria Surovshchikova-Petipa (now called Gloriette); Louis Mérante (Simon).

3 January 1868: staged at the Bolshoi Theatre, Moscow.

8 January 1895: revival for Maria Anderson's farewell benefit. Principal dancers: Anderson (Lizetta); Enrico Cecchetti (Marquis de Maigrelet).

The Blue Dahlia, fantastic ballet in two acts. Music: Cesare Pugni. Libretto: Petipa. Choreography: Petipa.

Premiere: 12 April 1860, Bolshoi Theatre, St Petersburg. Principal dancers: Maria Surovshchikova-Petipa (Blue Dahlia); Marius Petipa (Gautier); Timofei Stukolkin (Beausoleil).

Euterpe and Terpsichore, divertissement. Music: Cesare Pugni. Choreography: Petipa. Performers: Maria Surovshchikova-Petipa (Terpsichore); opera singer Zhosefina Mikhailovskaya (Euterpe).

Premiere: 15 November 1861, Tsarskoe Selo (court performance).

The Pharaoh's Daughter, ballet in three acts and nine scenes, with prologue and epilogue. Music: Cesare Pugni. Libretto: Henri Vernoy de Saint-Georges and Marius Petipa. Choreography: Petipa. Sets: Heinrich Wagner (Prologue, Scene 1; Act I, Scene 1; Act II, Scene 2; Act III, Scene 1); Andrei Roller (Prologue, Scene 2; Act I, Scene 2; Act II, Scene 1; Act III, Scenes 2 and 3). Costumes: Philippe Calver and Alexei Stoliarov. Principal dancers: Carolina Rosati (Aspichia); Marius Petipa (Lord Wilson/Taor); Timofei Stukolkin (John Bull/Passifont); Nikolai Golts (pharaoh).

Premiere: 18 January 1862, Bolshoi Theatre, St Petersburg.

17 November 1864: staged at the Bolshoi Theatre, Moscow.

10 November 1885: revival at the Bolshoi Theatre, St Petersburg. Principal dancers: Virginia Zucchi (Aspichia); Pavel Gerdt (Lord Wilson/Taor)

21 October 1898: revival at the Mariinsky Theatre. Principal dancers: Matilda Kshesinskaya (Aspichia); Pavel Gerdt (Lord Wilson/Taor).

27 November 1905: new version by Alexander Gorsky for the Bolshoi Theatre, Moscow, based on the libretto by Henri Vernoy de Saint-Georges and Marius Petipa.

Le Corsaire, ballet in four acts and five scenes. Music: Adolphe Adam and Cesare Pugni. Libretto: Henri Vernoy de Saint-Georges and Joseph Mazilier. Choreography: Mazilier, staged by Petipa. Decor: Andrei Roller and Heinrich Wagner. Principal dancers: Maria Surovshchikova-Petipa (Medora); Marius Petipa (Conrad); Anna Kosheva (Gulnare). Production premiere: 24 January 1863, Bolshoi Theatre, St Petersburg.

25 January 1868: revival at the Bolshoi Theatre, St Petersburg, with the addition of 'Le Jardin animé' to music by Léo Delibes. Principal dancers: Adèle Grantzow (Medora); Marius Petipa (Conrad).

12 December 1868: this new production was staged at the Bolshoi Theatre, Moscow. (The first Moscow production was by Frédéric in 1858).

30 November 1880: revival at the Bolshoi Theatre, St Petersburg with new designs. Principal dancers: Evgenia Sokolova (Medora); Lev Ivanov (Conrad); and Marie Petipa (Gulnare).

13 January 1899: revival at the Mariinsky Theatre, St Petersburg, with additional music by Riccardo Drigo for a new adagio and waltz Principal dancers: Pierina Legnani (Medora); Gerdt (Conrad); and Preobrazhenskaia (Gulnare).

Le Corsaire was created on 23 January 1856 at the Paris Opera with choreography by Mazilier. The first Russian production was by Perrot on 12 January 1858 at the Bolshoi Theatre, St Petersburg and included a new 'Pas d'esclaves' by Petipa to music by the duke of Oldenburg.

The Beauty of Lebanon, or The Mountain Spirit, fantastic ballet in three acts and seven scenes, with prologue and apotheosis. Music: Cesare Pugni. Libretto: Mavrikii Rappaport and Petipa. Choreography: Petipa. Decor: Andrei Roller; Heinrich Wagner; Albert Bredov. Costume designs: Adolf Charlemagne. Principal dancers: Maria Surovshchikova-Petipa (Mirana); Marius Petipa (Livan); Christian Johansson (Esmar).

Premiere: 12 December 1863, Bolshoi Theatre, St Petersburg.

The Travelling Dancer, episode in one act. Music: Cesare Pugni. Libretto: Petipa. Choreography: Petipa. Principal dancers: Maria Surovshchikova-Petipa (Alma); Liubov Radina (Carmen); Timofei Stukolkin (Verra).

Premiere: 4 November 1865, Bolshoi Theatre, St Petersburg.

27 November 1868: staged at the Bolshoi Theatre, Moscow.

Based on Paul Taglioni's *The Prima Ballerina, or the Ambush* (La Prima Ballerine, ou l'embuscade), created in London on 14 June 1849.

Florida, ballet in three acts and five scenes. Music: Cesare Pugni. Libretto: Petipa. Choreography: Petipa. Decor: Andrei Roller; Heinrich Wagner; S. Gvalio. Costume designs: Adolf Charlemagne. Principal dancers: Maria Surovshchikova-Petipa (Florida); Christian Johansson (Florida's father); Lev Ivanov (Ernest).

Premiere: 20 January 1866, Bolshoi Theatre, St Petersburg.

Titania, ballet in one act. Music: Mendelssohn/Pugni. Choreography: Petipa. Principal dancers: Maria Surovshchikova-Petipa (Titania); Marius Petipa (Oberon).

Premiere: 18 November 1866, Palace of the Grand Duchess Elena Pavlovna, St Petersburg.

Faust, fantastic ballet in three acts and seven scenes. Music: Giacomo Panizza and Cesare Pugni. Libretto: Jules Perrot. Choreography: Petipa, after Perrot. Decor: Pavel Isakov (Act I, Scene 1; Act III, Scene 2; Act II, Scene 2); Fedor Serkov (Act I, Scene 2; Act II, Scene I); Andrei Roller (Act I, Scenes 3 and 4; Act II, Scene 3); Heinrich Wagner (Act I, Scene 5; Act III, Scenes 3 and 4; Apotheosis); Ivan Shangin (Act II, Scene 1). Costumes: Philippe Calver and Alexei Stoliarov. Principal dancers: Lev Ivanov (Faust); Alexei Bogdanov (Mephistopheles); Guglielmina Salvioni (Marguerite); Christian Johansson (Valentin).

Production premiere: 2 November 1867, Bolshoi Theatre, St Petersburg.

Perrot created *Faust* in Milan on 12 February 1848. He restaged it at the Bolshoi Theatre, St Petersburg on 2 February 1854. Principal dancers: Marius Petipa (Faust); Perrot (Mephistopheles); Gabriele Yella (Marguerite); Johansson (Valentin).

The Benevolent Cupid, ballet in one act. Music: Cesare Pugni. Libretto: Petipa. Choreography: Petipa. Principal dancer: Evgenia Sokolova (pupil).

Premiere: 6 March 1868, Imperial Theatre School, St Petersburg.

The Slave Girl, divertissement in one act. Music: Cesare Pugni. Choreography: Petipa.

Premiere: 27 April 1868, Tsarskoe Selo (court performance).

King Candaules, ballet in four acts and six scenes. Music: Cesare Pugni. Libretto: Saint-Georges and Petipa. Choreography: Petipa. Decor: Heinrich Wagner (Scenes 1 and 2); Vladimir Egorov and Vasilii Prokhorov (Scene 3); Albert Bredov (Scene 5); Andrei Roller (Scene 6). Costumes: Evgenii Ponomarev. Principal dancers: Henriette Dor (Nisia); Felix Kshesinsky (Candaules); Lev Ivanov (Gyges); Anna Kuznetsova (Pythia).

Premiere: 17 October 1868, Bolshoi Theatre, St Petersburg.

22 December 1868: the ballet was staged at the Bolshoi Theatre, Moscow.

24 November 1891: revival at the Mariinsky Theatre, St Petersburg. Principal dancers: Carlotta Brianza (Nisia); Pavel Gerdt (Candaules); Alexander Oblakov (Gyges); Giuseppina Cecchetti (Pythia).

9 April 1903: revival at the Mariinsky Theatre, St Petersburg, with several new dances. Principal dancers: Iulia Sedova (Nisia); Nadezhda Petipa (Pythia).

Don Quixote, ballet in four acts and eight scenes. Music: Ludwig Minkus. Libretto: Petipa, after Cervantes. Choreography: Petipa. Decor: Pavel Isakov (Act I, Scenes 1 and 2); Ivan Shangin (Act II, Scene 3; Act III, Scene 5; Act IV, Scene 8); Fedor Shenian (Act II, Scene 4; Act III, Scenes 6 and 7). Principal dancers: Anna Sobeshchanskaya (Kitri); Sergei Sokolov (Basilio); Wilhelm Vanner (Don Quixote).

Premiere: 14 December 1869, Bolshoi Theatre, Moscow.

9 November 1871: revised version at the Bolshoi Theatre, St Petersburg, in five acts and eleven scenes. Principal dancers: Alexandra Vergina (Kitri/Dulcinea); Lev Ivanov (Basil); Timofei Stukolkin (Don Quixote).

13 February 1887: the St Petersburg redaction was mounted at the Bolshoi Theatre, Moscow, by Alexei Bogdanov.

6 December 1900: Alexander Gorsky produced his version at the Bolshoi Theatre, Moscow, and brought it to the Mariinsky, St Petersburg, on 20 January 1902.

Trilby, fantastic ballet in two acts and three scenes. Music: Iurii Gerber. Libretto: Petipa, after the novel by Charles Nodier. Choreography: Petipa. Decor: Karl Valts; Pavel Isakov. Principal dancer: Polina Karpakova.

Premiere: 25 January 1870, Bolshoi Theatre, Moscow.

17 January 1871: revised version at the Bolshoi Theatre, St Petersburg. Decor: Andrei Roller and Heinrich Wagner. Costumes: Philippe Calver and Alexei Stoliarov. Principal dancers: Adèle Grantzow (Bettli); Alexandra Simskaya, pupil (Trilby); Lev Ivanov (Wilhelm).

Catarina, ou la Fille du bandit, ballet in three acts and four scenes. Music: Cesare Pugni. Libretto: Jules Perrot. Choreography: Petipa, after Perrot. Decor: Heinrich Wagner (Scenes 1 and 3); Andrei Roller (Scenes 2 and 4). Principal dancer: Adèle Grantzow (Catarina).

Production premiere: 1 November 1870 at the Bolshoi Theatre, St Petersburg.

Perrot created *Caterina* on 3 March 1846 in London. He restaged it on 4 February 1849 at the Bolshoi Theatre, St Petersburg. Enrico Cecchetti was responsible for another revival on 25 September 1888 at the Mariinsky Theatre.

The Two Stars, anacreontic scene in one act. Music: Cesare Pugni. Libretto: Petipa. Choreography: Petipa. Decor: Andrei Roller. Principal dancers: Ekaterina Vazem and Alexandra Vergina (The Stars); Pavel Gerdt (Apollo).

Premiere: 31 January 1871, Bolshoi Theatre, St Petersburg.

25 February 1878: staged at the Bolshoi Theatre, Moscow, with the title *Two Little Stars* (Dve Zvezdochki).

Camargo, ballet in three acts and nine scenes. Music: Ludwig Minkus. Libretto: Henri Vernoy de Saint-Georges and Petipa. Decor: Andrei Roller (Scenes 1, 3, 7, and 9); Heinrich Wagner (Scenes 2, 4, 5, and 6); Mikhail Bocharov (Scene 8). Costumes: Evgenii Ponomarev. Principal dancers: Adèle Grantzow (Marie Camargo); Anna Kuznetsova (Madeleine, her sister); Alexandra Simskaya (Vestris); Lev Ivanov (Comte de Melun).

Premiere: 17 December 1872, Bolshoi Theatre, St Petersburg.

The ballet was restaged in 1901 at the Mariinsky Theatre by Lev Ivanov, after Petipa, but with additional dances. Pierina Legnani performed the title role.

The Butterfly, fantastic ballet in four acts. Music: Ludwig Minkus. Libretto: Saint-Georges and Petipa. Choreography: Petipa. Decor: Lev Lagorio (Act I); Mikhail Bocharov (Act II); Matvei Shishkov (Act III); Heinrich Wagner (Act IV). Costumes: Ivan Panov. Principal dancers: Ekaterina Vazem (Farfalla); Pavel Gerdt (Maharajah); Lev Ivanov; Matilda Madaeva; Liubov Radina.

Premiere: 6 January 1874, Bolshoi Theatre, St Petersburg.

This was a version of *Le Papillon*, choreographed by Marie Taglioni to music by Jacques Offenbach and staged on 26 November 1861 at the Paris Opera.

The Naiad and the Fisherman, fantastic ballet in three acts and five scenes. Music: Cesare Pugni. Libretto: Jules Perrot. Choreography: Petipa, after Perrot. Decor: Andrei Roller (Scenes 1, 3, 5 and 5); Heinrich Wagner (Scenes 2 and 6).

Principal dancers: Evgenia Sokolova (Ondine); Pavel Gerdt (Matteo); Alexandra Kemmerer (Giannina).

Production premiere: 27 October 1874, Bolshoi Theatre, St Petersburg.

20 September 1892: revival at the Mariinsky Theatre, St Petersburg. Principal dancers: Varvara Nikitina (Ondine); Pavel Gerdt (Matteo); Marie Petipa (Giannina).

7 December 1903: revival at the Mariinsky Theatre, St Petersburg, staged by Alexander Shiriaev. Principal dancers: Anna Pavlova (Ondine); Sergei Legat (Matteo); Vera Trefilova (Giannina).

Perrot created *Ondine, ou la Naïade* on 22 June 1843 in London and restaged it at the Bolshoi Theatre, St Petersburg, on 30 January 1851 as *The Naiad and the Fisherman* with Carlotta Grisi and Perrot in the lead roles. Petipa worked on the ballet for a long time; as early as 31 January 1871, he showed one act of what would be his 1874 production. Garafola also writes that: 'already in 1867, when he rehearsed the ballet for Ekaterina Vazem, he added two new variations and elaborated the Pas de l'Ombre to include double turns and additional point work' (*The Diaries of Marius Petipa*, ed. Garafola, 84).

The Bandits, ballet in two acts and five scenes, with prologue. Music: Ludwig Minkus. Libretto: Petipa, after the novella *La Gitanilla* by Cervantes. Choreography: Petipa. Decor: Heinrich Wagner (Act I and Apotheosis); Andrei Roller (Act II). Costume design: Ivan Panov. Principal dancer: Ekaterina Vazem.

Premiere: 26 January 1875, Bolshoi Theatre, St Petersburg.

The Adventures of Peleus, mythological ballet in three acts and five scenes. Music: Minkus with possible additional music by Léo Delibes. Libretto: Petipa. Choreography: Petipa. Decor: Heinrich Wagner (Scenes 1 and 3); Matvei Shishkov (Scene 2 and, with Ivan Andreev, Scene 4); Andrei Roller (Scene 5). Principal dancer: Evgenia Sokolova (Thetis).

Premiere: 18 January 1876, Bolshoi Theatre, St Petersburg.

A Midsummer Night's Dream, fantastic ballet in one act. Music: Felix Mendelssohn, with additional music by Ludwig Minkus. Libretto: Petipa, after Shakespeare. Choreography: Petipa. Principal dancers: Evgenia Sokolova (Titania); Pavel Gerdt (Oberon).

Premiere: 14 July 1876, Peterhof (court performance).

25 September 1876: Mariinsky Theatre, St Petersburg.

La Bayadère, ballet in four acts and seven scenes, with apotheosis. Music: Minkus. Libretto: Petipa and Sergei Khudekov. Choreography: Petipa. Decor: Michael Bocharov (Scene 1); Matvei Shishkov (Scenes 2 and 3); Ivan Andreev (Scenes 4 and 6); Heinrich Wagner (Scene 5); Andrei Roller (Scene 7 and Apotheosis). Costume design: Ivan Panov. Principal dancers: Ekaterina Vazem (Nikiya); Lev Ivanov (Solor);

Maria Gorshenkova (Gamzatti); Christian Johansson (Rajah Dugmanta); Nikolai Golts (Great Brahmin).

Premiere: 23 January 1877, Bolshoi Theatre, St Petersburg.

3 December 1900: revival at the Mariinsky Theatre, St Petersburg. Decor: Adolf Kvapp (Scene 1); Konstantin Ivanov (Scenes 2 and 6; Apotheosis); Petr Lambin (Scenes 3 and 5); Orest Allegri (Scene 4). Principal dancers: Matilda Kshesinskaya (Nikiya); Nikolai Aistov (Rajah Dugmanta); Olga Preobrazhenskaya (Gamzatti); Pavel Gerdt (Solor); Felix Kshesinsky (Great Brahmin).

24 January 1904: production after Petipa by Alexander Gorsky at the Bolshoi Theatre, Moscow.

Roxana, The Beauty of Montenegro, fantastic ballet in four acts. Music: Minkus. Libretto: Sergei Khudekov and Petipa. Choreography: Petipa. Decor: Mikhail Bocharov (Acts I and IV); Matvei Shishkov (Act II); Heinrich Wagner (Act III). Costume design: Pavel Grigorev. Principal dancers: Evgenia Sokolova (Roxana); Marie Petipa (Zoia, Roxana's friend); Nikolai Golts (Peiko); Pavel Gerdt (Ianko); Felix Kshesinsky (Radivoi); Lev Ivanov (Marko); Christian Johansson (Bozhko); Maria Smirnova (vampire-ghost of Roxana's mother).

Premiere: 29 January 1878, Bolshoi Theatre, St Petersburg.

27 November 1883: Petipa's ballet was staged at the Bolshoi Theatre, Moscow, by Alexei Bogdanov.

The Daughter of the Snows, fantastic ballet in three acts and five scenes. Music: Ludwig Minkus. Libretto: Petipa. Choreography: Petipa. Decor: Matvei Shishkov (Act I); Heinrich Wagner (Act II); Mikhail Bocharov (Act III). Costumes: Adolf Charlemagne. Principal dancers: Ekaterina Vazem (Daughter of the Snows); Nikolai Golts (Genie of the Cold); Maria Gorshenkova (Goddess of Summer); pupil Evgenia Voronova (Amor); Pavel Gerdt (ship's captain); Alexander Pisho (rich Norwegian); Petipa's future wife Liubov Savitskaya (his daughter and the captain's fiancée); Timofei Stukolkin (old sailor); Marie Petipa (his son).

Premiere: 7 January 1879, Bolshoi Theatre, St Petersburg.

Frisak, the Barber, or, The Double Wedding, comic ballet in one act. Music: Jean-François Snel, orchestrated by Ludwig Minkus. Libretto: Petipa, based on the ballet produced by Jean Petipa in Brussels on 10 February 1822. Choreography: Petipa. Principal dancers: Alexander Pisho (Duchamp, innkeeper); Elena Shamburskaya (his wife); Varvara Nikitina (Victorine, their daughter); Nikolai Troitsky (barber, in love with Victorine); Platon Karsavin (Laviron, in love with Victorine).

Premiere: 11 March 1879, Bolshoi Theatre, St Petersburg.

Mlada, fantastic ballet in four acts and nine scenes. Music: Ludwig Minkus. Libretto: Stepan Gedeonov. Choreography: Petipa. Decor: Matvei Shishkov; Mikhail

Bocharov; Heinrich Wagner; Vladimir Egorov; Alexei Lupanov. Costumes: Vasilii Prokhorov and Ivan Panov. Principal dancers: Evgenia Sokolova (Mlada's ghost); Felix Kshesinsky (Prince Mstivoi); Maria Gorshenkova (his daughter Princess Voislava); Pavel Gerdt (Iaromir); Liubov Savitskaya (Sviatokhna, friend of Voislava); Platon Karsavin (Mstivoï's jester); Anna Simskaya (Morena); Alexander Orlov (Chernobog); Maria Valter (Lada).

Premiere: 2 December 1879, Bolshoi Theatre, St Petersburg.

22 September 1896: revived with revisions at the Mariinsky Theatre, St Petersburg, ballet in four acts and six scenes. Principal dancers: Matilda Kshesinskaya (Mlada's ghost); Felix Kshesinsky (Prince Mstivoi); Marie Petipa (Princess Voislava); Pavel Gerdt (Iaromi); Nadezhda Petipa (Sviatokhna); Alexander Shiriaev (jester).

In 1892 Nikolai Rimsky-Korsakov staged an opera version, with choreography by Lev Ivanov and Enrico Cecchetti, at the Mariinsky; the decor (by Ivan Andreev and Mikhail Bocharov) was used for the ballet's 1896 revival.

La Fille du Danube, ballet in two acts and four scenes. Music: Adolphe Adam. Libretto: Filippo Taglioni. Choreography: Petipa, after Taglioni. Decor: Heinrich Wagner. Principal dancers: Ekaterina Vazem (the Maid of the Danube); Pavel Gerdt (Rudolph).

Production premiere: 24 February 1880, Bolshoi Theatre, St Petersburg.

This ballet, with Marie Taglioni (Fleur-des-Champs, the heroine's original name), was created by Filippo Taglioni at the Paris Opera on 21 September 1836; and, as *Deva Dunaia*, shown by them, with Nikolai Golts (Rudolph), at the Bolshoi Theatre, St Petersburg on 20 December 1837.

Zoraiya, or The Moorish Girl in Spain, ballet in four acts and seven scenes. Music: Ludwig Minkus. Libretto: Sergei Khudekov and Petipa. Choreography: Petipa. Decor: Mikhail Bocharov (Scenes 1 and 5); Heinrich Wagner (Scenes 2 and 3); Matvei Shishkov (Scenes 4 and 5). Costume design: Adolf Charlemagne. Principal dancers: Ekaterina Vazem (Zoraiya); Felix Kshesinsky (Abderraman); Liubov Savitskaya (Tisbah, confidante of Zoraiya); Lev Ivanov (Tamarat), Pavel Gerdt (Soleiman).

Premiere: 1 February 1881, Bolshoi Theatre, St Petersburg.

13 May 1883: staged at the Bolshoi Theatre, Moscow, but for just two performances as part of the coronation celebrations.

La Vivandière (Markitantka), ballet in one act. Music: Pugni. Libretto: Arthur Saint-Léon. Choreography: Petipa, after Saint-Léon and Jules Perrot. Principal dancers: Ekaterina Vazem (Kathi); Pavel Gerdt (Hans); Lev Ivanov (first postman); Felix Kshesinsky (Hungarian count); Liubov Savitskaya (his wife).

Production premiere: 8 October 1881, Mariinsky Theatre, St Petersburg.

Saint-Léon created this ballet in collaboration with Fanny Cerrito in Rome in 1843, to music by Enrico Rolland; later productions had music by Pugni. The first Russian production was staged by Jules Perrot on 13 December 1855, Bolshoi Theatre, St Petersburg and brought to the Bolshoi Theatre, Moscow, on 30 August 1856.

Pâquerette, ballet in four acts and seven scenes. Music: François Benoist; Cesare Pugni; Ludwig Minkus. Libretto: Théophile Gautier. Choreography: Petipa, after Arthur Saint-Léon. Decor: Heinrich Wagner (Scenes 1, 3, and 4); Alexei Lupanov and Vladimir Egorov (Scenes 2 and 5); Mikhail Bocharov (Scenes 6 and 7). Principal dancers: Evgenia Sokolova (Pâquerette); Fedor Geltser (Martin); Pavel Gerdt (Franz).

Production premiere: 10 January 1882, Bolshoi Theatre, St Petersburg.

17 February 1884: this production was mounted at the Bolshoi Theatre, Moscow, by Alexei Bogdanov.

Saint-Léon created this ballet on 15 January 1851 at the Paris Opera and staged it with additional music by Pugni at the Bolshoi Theatre, St Petersburg, on 28 January 1860.

Night and Day, fantastic ballet in one act. Music: Ludwig Minkus. Libretto: Petipa. Choreography: Petipa. Decor: Mikhail Bocharov and Karl Valts. Costumes: Adolf Charlemagne; Pavel Grigorev; Nikolai Klodt. Principal dancers: Evgenia Sokolova (Queen of the Night); Ekaterina Vazem (Queen of the Day); Maria Gorshenkova (Night Star); Varvara Nikitina (a dove).

Premiere: 18 May 1883, Bolshoi Theatre, Moscow (for the coronation gala).

The Cyprus Statue, or Pygmalion, ballet in four acts and six scenes, with apotheosis. Music: Prince Trubetskoi. Libretto: Prince Trubetskoi. Choreography: Petipa. Decor: Matvei Shishkov with Mikhail Bocharov (Act I, Scene 1; Act II, Scene 2); Mikhail Bocharov (Act III, Scenes 3 and 4); Heinrich Wagner (Act IV, Scene 6; Apotheosis). Costumes: Pavel Grigorev. Principal dancers: Evgenia Sokolova (Galatea); Felix Kshesinsky (Pygmalion); Pavel Gerdt (Osiris); Liubov Radina (Ramses).

Premiere: 11 December 1883, Bolshoi Theatre, St Petersburg.

6 October 1888: the ballet was brought to the Bolshoi Theatre, Moscow by Alexei Bogdanov and marked Carlotta Brianza's debut at that theatre.

Giselle, fantastic ballet in two acts. Music: Adolphe Adam. Libretto: Saint-Georges; Théophile Gautier; Jean Coralli. Choreography: Petipa, after Coralli and Jules Perrot. Principal dancers: Maria Gorshenkova (Giselle); Pavel Gerdt (Albrecht); Sofia Petrova (Myrtha).

Production premiere: 5 February 1884, Bolshoi Theatre, St Petersburg.

14 December 1886: Alexei Bogdanov staged this version at the Bolshoi Theatre, Moscow.

23 September 1901: Alexander Gorsky based his production on Petipa's for the Bolshoi Theatre, Moscow.

Giselle was created by Coralli and Perrot on 28 June 1841 at the Paris Opera. The first Russian production was staged by Titus at the Bolshoi Theatre, St Petersburg, on 18

December 1842. According to Guest, Perrot then produced his own version in Russia for Carlotta Grisi on 8 October 1850 (*Jules Perrot*, 252–53). For the 1884 production, Petipa choreographed the 'Grand Pas des *wilis*'.

Coppélia, ballet in three acts. Music: Léo Delibes. Libretto: Charles Nuitter and Arthur Saint-Léon. Choreography: Petipa, after Saint-Léon. Principal dancers: Varvara Nikitina (Swanilda); Pavel Gerdt (Franz); Timofei Stukolkin (Dr Coppélius).

Production premiere: 25 November 1884, Bolshoi Theatre, St Petersburg.

25 February 1905: Alexander Gorsky based his *Coppélia* on Petipa's production and other sources.

Saint-Léon created his ballet on 25 May 1870 at the Paris Opera. The first Russian production was by Joseph Hansen after Saint-Léon, staged on 24 January 1882 at the Bolshoi Theatre, Moscow. In 1894, the ballet was revived at the Mariinsky by Enrico Cecchetti, with choreography after Petipa and with Pierina Legnani.

The Wilful Wife, ballet in four acts and five scenes. Music: Adolphe Adam, with additional music by Ludwig Minkus. Libretto: Adolphe de Leuven and Joseph Mazilier. Choreography: Petipa, after Mazilier and Jules Perrot. New decor: Mikhail Bocharov; E. Aubet; Matvei Shishkov. Costume design: Ivan Vsevolozhsky and Pavel Grigorev. Principal dancers: Evgenia Sokolova (Countess Berta); Maria Gorshenkova (a basket-maker); Pavel Gerdt (the count).

Production premiere: 23 January 1885, Bolshoi Theatre, St Petersburg.

Mazilier created this ballet on 11 August 1845 at the Paris Opera as *Le Diable à Quatre*. The first Russian production was by Ekaterina Sankovskaya for the Bolshoi Theatre, Moscow, in 1846. Perrot staged a version with additional music by Cesare Pugni on 14 November 1850 and Mazilier yet another on 18 October 1851, both at the Bolshoi Theatre, St Petersburg.

La Fille mal gardée (Tshchetnaia predostorozhnost'), comic ballet in three acts and four scenes. Music: Peter Ludwig Hertel. Libretto: Jean Dauberval. Choreography: Petipa and Lev Ivanov(?). Principal dancers: Virginia Zucchi (Lise); Pavel Gerdt (Colin); Gustav Legat (Marcelina).

Production premiere: 15 December 1885, Bolshoi Theatre, St Petersburg.

Dauberval created this ballet at the Grand-Théâtre, Bordeaux, on 1 July 1789. There were many Russian productions from 1800 onwards. According to *The Diaries of Marius Petipa*, ed. Garafola (87) and other sources, the 1885 production marked Ivanov's first important undertaking as a choreographer; according to Wiley, *The Life and Ballets of Lev Ivanov* (223), Ivanov only staged the later revivals in 1894 and 1901.

The Magic Pills, ballet-féerie in three acts and thirteen scenes. Music: Ludwig Minkus. Libretto: Ferdinand Laloue; Anicet Bourgeois; Clément Laurent. Choreographic scenes: Petipa. Decor: Konstantin Ivanov (Scenes 1 and 2); Mikhail Bocharov (Scenes 3, 4, 5, and 10); Matvei Shishkov (Scenes 6, 7, and 11); Heinrich Wagner (Scene

8); Heinrich Levogt (Scenes 9, 12, and 13). Costumes: Evdokia Ivanova; Christian Pipar; and Ekaterina Ofitserova (women); Ivan Vsevolozhsky (men). Principal dancers: Varvara Nikitina and many others.

Premiere: 9 February 1886, Mariinsky Theatre, St Petersburg.

13 December 1887: Alexei Bogdanov mounted this production, with Petipa's choreography at the Bolshoi Theatre, Moscow.

The King's Command, ballet in four acts and six scenes. Music: Albert Vizentini. Libretto: Petipa and Vizentini after Edmond Gondinet. Choreography: Petipa. Decor: Francesco Zuccarelli (Act I, Scene 1); E. Aubet (Act I, Scene 2); V. Ovsiannikov (Act II, Scene 1); Heinrich Levogt (Act III); Ivan Andreev (Act IV). Costumes: Evdokia Ivanova and Ekaterina Ofitserova (women); Ivan Vsevolozhsky and Evgenii Ponomarev (men). Principal dancers: Viriginia Zucchi (Pepita); Lev Ivanov (Milon, dance teacher); Pavel Gerdt (Markino, in love with Pepita).

Premiere: 14 February 1886, Bolshoi Theatre, St Petersburg.

30 November 1887: modified production with two additional dances, the Gallarda in the last act and a pas de deux 'The Fisherman and the Pearl' for Virginia Zucchi and Enrico Cecchetti.

The Offerings to Love, or Happiness Is Loving (Les Offrandes à l'amour, ou le Bonheur est d'aimer), ballet in one act. Music: Ludwig Minkus. Libretto: Petipa. Choreography: Petipa. Principal dancers: Maria Gorshenkova (Lisa); Marie Petipa (Venus); Evgenia Sokolova (Chloë); Pavel Gerdt (Amor).

Premiere: 22 July 1886, Peterhof (gala performance).

25 November 1886: staged at the Mariinsky Theatre, St Petersburg.

Esmeralda, ballet in four acts and five scenes. Music: Cesare Pugni, with additional music by Riccardo Drigo. Libretto: Jules Perrot, after Victor Hugo. Choreography: Petipa, after Perrot. New decor: Ivan Andreev (Act I); Heinrich Levogt (Act III; Act IV, Scenes 1 and 2). Principal dancers: Virginia Zucchi (Esmeralda); Pavel Gerdt (Pierre Gringoire); Felix Kshesinsky (Claude Frollo); Iosef Kshesinsky (Phoebus or Feb); Alfred Bekefi (Quasimodo).

Production premiere: 17 December 1886, Mariinsky Theatre, St Petersburg.

21 November 1899: revival with new decor. Designers: Ivan Andreev and Orest Allegri (Act I); Vasilii Shiriaev (Act II); Gavriel Kamensky and Grigori Iakovlev (Act III); Sergei Vorobev (Act IV, Scene 1); Orest Allegri (Act IV, Scene 2). Principal dancers: Matilda Kshesinskaya (Esmeralda); Pavel Gerdt (Pierre Gringoire); Nikolai Aistov (Claude Frollo); Iosef Kshesinsky (Phoebus); Alfred Bekefi (Quasimodo).

Perrot created this ballet on 9 March 1844 in London and staged it, with Elssler and Petipa's help, at the Bolshoi Theatre, St Petersburg, on 21 December 1848. Referencing Ivor Guest (*Jules Perrot*, 349), Garafola writes that Petipa had been making additions to the ballet since 1866 (*Diaries of Marius Petipa*, 87). In that year he added the pas de deux for Claudina Cucchi that became long remembered as the 'pas Cucchi'; in the early 1870s he also arranged a pas de dix for Evgenia Sokolova; and in 1872, for Adèle Grantzow's debut as Esmeralda, he inserted a new pas de cinq.

The Haarlem Tulip, fantastic ballet in three acts and four scenes. Music: Boris Fitinhof-Schell. Libretto: Lev Ivanov. Choreography: Lev Ivanov and Petipa. Decor: Heinrich Levogt. Costumes: Evgenii Ponomarev. Principal dancers: Emma Bessone (Emma); Pavel Gerdt (Peters); Alfred Bekefi (Andres).

Premiere: 4 October 1887, Mariinsky Theatre, St Petersburg.

22 March and 1 April 1902: second act staged by Klavdia Kulichevskaya for two school performances at the Mikhailovsky Theatre.

16 April 1903: staging by Alexander Shiriaev, with the interpolation of the pas de six from Pavel Gerdt's *Javotte*, reworked as a pas de trois. Principal performers: Vera Trefilova (Emma); Pavel Gerdt (Peters); Tamara Karsavina, Elena Poliakova, Mikhail Obukhov (pas de trois).

The precise authorship of the choreography for this three-act ballet is unclear: Petipa included it in his list of ballets as a collaboration and reviewers referred to his involvement. It seems likely that Ivanov wrote the libretto, but Petipa kept an overseeing eye on Ivanov's work as choreographer.

Fiametta, fantastic ballet in four acts. Music: Ludwig Minkus. Libretto: Arthur Saint-Léon. Choreography: Petipa and Lev Ivanov, after Saint-Léon. Principal dancers: Elena Cornalba (Fiametta); Marie Petipa (Amor); Anna Johansson (Terpsichore); Pavel Gerdt (Sterngold).

Production premiere: 6 December 1887, Mariinsky Theatre.

30 January 1905: this production was mounted by Alexander Gorsky and Nikolai Legat at the Bolshoi Theatre, Moscow.

Saint-Léon created this ballet on 12 November 1863 at the Bolshoi Theatre, Moscow, as *The Flame of Love, or The Salamander*. He then mounted it on 13 February 1864 at the Bolshoi Theatre, St Petersburg, with the title *Fiametta, or the Triumph of Love*.

The Vestal, ballet in three acts and four scenes. Music: Mikhail Ivanov. Libretto: Sergei Khudekov. Choreography: Petipa. Decor: Francesco Zuccarelli (Act I); Mikhail Bocharov (Act II); Heinrich Levogt (Act III, Scenes 1 and 2). Costume designs: Ivan Vsevolozhsky and Evgenii Ponomarev. Principal dancers: Elena Cornalba (Amata); Pavel Gerdt (Lucius); Maria Gorshenkova (Claudia); Felix Kshesinsky (Julius Flak); Marie Petipa (Venus).

Premiere: 17 February 1888, Mariinsky Theatre, St Petersburg.

The Talisman, fantastic ballet in four acts and seven scenes, with prologue and epilogue. Music: Riccardo Drigo. Libretto: Konstantin Tarnovsky and Petipa. Decor: Heinrich Levogt (Prologue and Epilogue); Ivan Andreev (Acts I and IV);

Mikhail Bocharov (Act II, Scenes 1 and 2); Matvei Shishkov (Act III). Principal dancers: Elena Cornalba (Ella); Pavel Gerdt (Nurredin); Enrico Cecchetti (Uragan).

Premiere: 25 January 1889, Mariinsky Theatre, St Petersburg.

22 October 1895: revival at the Mariinsky Theatre for Pierina Legnani.

29 November 1909: revival staged by Nikolai Legat with changes (including character's names) and with a new orchestration by Drigo of his score. Principal dancers: Olga Preobrazhenskaya (Niriti); Pavel Gerdt (Akdar); Vaslav Nijinsky (Vaiiu, God of Wind).

The Whims of the Butterfly, ballet in one act. Music: Nikolai Krotkov. Libretto: Petipa, after the poem 'The Grasshopper Musician' by Iakov Polonsky. Choreography: Petipa. Decor: Mikhail Bocharov. Costumes: Pavel Kamensky. Principal dancers: Varvara Nikitina (Butterfly); Maria Anderson (Fly); Pavel Gerdt (Phoenix Butterfly); Enrico Cecchetti (Grasshopper); Alexander Shiriaev (Spider); Nikolai Legat (Nightingale).

Premiere: 5 June 1889, Mariinsky Theatre, St Petersburg (gala performance); 25 October 1889, Mariinsky Theatre (public performance).

The Sleeping Beauty, ballet-féerie in three acts, with prologue. Music: Tchaikovsky. Libretto: Ivan Vsevolozhsky, after Charles Perrault. Choreography: Petipa. Decor: Heinrich Levogt (Prologue); Mikhail Bocharov (Act II, Scene 1; with Ivan Andreev, Act I); Konstantin Ivanov (Act II, Scene 2); Matvei Shishkov (Act III and Apotheosis). Costume design: Ivan Vsevolozhsky. Principal dancers: Carlotta Brianza (Aurora); Pavel Gerdt (Prince Desiré); Marie Petipa (Lilac Fairy); Enrico Cecchetti (Carabosse and the Bluebird); Varvara Nikitina (Princess Florine).

Premiere: 3 January 1890, Mariinsky Theatre, St Petersburg.

17 January 1899: Alexander Gorsky staged the ballet, using the Stepanov notations, for the Bolshoi Theatre, Moscow, with new designs.

16 February 1914: revival at the Mariinsky Theatre by Nikolai Sergeyev, helped by Alexander Gorsky, with new designs by Konstantin Korovin. Principal dancers: Tamara Karsavina (Aurora); Ivan Kusov (Prince Desiré); Liubov Egorova (Lilac Fairy and Princess Florine); Alexander Chekrygin (Carabosse); Victor Semenov (Bluebird).

Fedor Lopukhov claims that a new solo he created for the Lilac Fairy was inserted into this production, but a question mark remains.

The Water Lily, choreographic fantasy in one act. Music: Nikolai Krotkov. Libretto: Petipa. Choreography: Petipa. Decor: Mikhail Bocharov. Costume design: Evgenii Ponomarev. Principal dancers: Varvara Nikitina (Waterlily); Timofei Stukolkin (Iodokus, teacher); Pavel Gerdt (Franz, one of several students).

Premiere: 11 November 1890, Mariinsky Theatre, St Petersburg.

Calcabrino, fantastic ballet in three acts. Music: Ludwig Minkus. Libretto: Modest Tchaikovsky and Petipa. Choreography: Petipa. Decor: Vasilii Vasilev (Act I); Mikhail

Bocharov (Act II); Ivan Andreev (Act III). Costumes: Evgenii Ponomarev. Principal dancers: Carlotta Brianza (Marietta/Draginiazza); Pavel Gerdt (Calcabrino); Nikolai Legat (Olivier).

Premiere: 13 February 1891, Mariinsky Theatre, St Petersburg.

La Sylphide, ballet in two acts. Music: Jean Schneitzhoeffer, with additional music by Riccardo Drigo. Libretto: Adolphe Nourrit. Choreography: Petipa, after Filippo Taglioni. New decor: Heinrich Levogt (Act I); Mikhail Bocharov (Act II). Costumes: Evgenii Ponomarev. Principal dancers: Varvara Nikitina (Sylphide); Pavel Gerdt (James); Maria Anderson (Effie), Timofei Stukolkin (Madge).

Production premiere: 19 January 1892, Mariinsky Theatre, St Petersburg.

Taglioni created this ballet on 12 March 1832 at the Paris Opera; Titus staged the first Russian production on 28 May 1835 at the Bolshoi Theatre, St Petersburg.

A Fairy Tale, fantastic ballet in one act for the Theatre School. Music: ?. Choreography: Petipa.

Premiere: 10 February 1892, Imperial Theatre School, St Petersburg.

The Nutcracker, ballet-féerie in two acts and three scenes. Music: Tchaikovsky. Libretto: Petipa, after E. T. A. Hoffmann. Choreography: Lev Ivanov. Decor: Konstantin Ivanov (Scenes 1 and 3); Mikhail Bocharov (Scene 2). Costume design: Ivan Vsevolozhsky and Evgenii Ponomarev. Principal dancers: Antonietta Dell'Era (Sugar Plum Fairy); Pavel Gerdt (Prince Coqueluche); Timofei Stukolkin (Drosselmeyer); Sergei Legat (Nutcracker); Olga Preobrazhenskaya (Columbine); Georgii Kiaksht (Harlequin).

Premiere: 6 December 1892, Mariinsky Theatre, St Petersburg.

Cinderella, fantastic ballet in three acts. Music: Boris Fitinhof-Schell. Libretto: Lidia Pashkova, after Charles Perrault. Choreography: Petipa (general plan and certain details); Enrico Cecchetti (Acts I and III); Lev Ivanov (Act II). Sets: Heinrich Levogt (Act I); Matvei Shishkov (Act II); Mikhail Bocharov (Act III). Costume design: Ivan Vsevolozhsky and Evgenii Ponomarev. Principal dancers: Pierina Legnani (Cinderella); Pavel Gerdt (Prince Charming); Matilda Kshesinskaya and Klavdia Kulichevskaya (Stepsisters); Anna Johansson (Good Fairy).

Premiere: 5 December 1893, Mariinsky Theatre, St Petersburg.

1 September 1898: Lev Ivanov brought the ballet to the Bolshoi Theatre, Moscow.

The Awakening of Flora, anacreontic ballet in one act. Music: Riccardo Drigo. Libretto: Petipa; Lev Ivanov. Choreography: Petipa. Decor: Mikhail Bocharov. Costume design: Evgenii Ponomarev. Principal dancers: Matilda Kshesinskaya (Flora); Anna Johansson (Aurora); Klavdia Kulichevskaya (Diana).

Premiere: 28 July 1894, Peterhof (gala performance).

3 May 1896: first performance of the ballet (as part of the coronation celebrations) by members of the St Petersburg company at the Bolshoi Theatre, Moscow.

Swan Lake, fantastic ballet in three acts and four scenes. Music: Tchaikovsky. Libretto: Vladimir Begichev, edited by Modest Tchaikovsky. Choreography: Petipa (Act I, Scene 1; Act II); Lev Ivanov (Act I, Scene 2; Act III). Decor: Ivan Andreev (Act I, Scene 1); Mikhail Bocharov (Act I, Scene 2; Act III; Apotheosis); Heinrich Levogt (Act II). Costume design: Evgenii Ponomarev. Principal dancers: Pierina Legnani (Odette/Odile); Pavel Gerdt (Siegfried); Alexei Bulgakov (Rothbart).

Premiere: 15 January 1895, Mariinsky Theatre, St Petersburg.

5 May 1896: first performance of this ballet by the St Petersburg company at the Bolshoi Theatre, Moscow, for the coronation celebrations.

24 January 1901: Alexander Gorsky brought the production to the Bolshoi Theatre, Moscow, with some changes and designs by Alexander Golovin, Konstantin Korovin and Nikolai Klodt.

Wenzel Reisinger choreographed the first version on 20 February 1877 in Moscow. Act I, Scene 1, choreographed by Ivanov for a Tchaikovsky memorial programme was first shown on 17 February 1894.

The Little Humpbacked Horse, or the Tsar-Maiden, magic ballet in four acts and eight scenes, with apotheosis. Music: Cesare Pugni. Libretto: Arthur Saint-Léon, after Petr Ershov. Choreography: Petipa, after Arthur Saint-Léon. Decor: Vasilii Perminov (Act I, Scenes 1 and 2); Konstantin Ivanov (Act II, Scene 1); Heinrich Levogt (Act III, Scenes 1, 2, and 3); Petr Lambin (Act IV, Scene 1; Apotheosis). Costume design: Evgenii Ponomarev. Principal dancers: Pierina Legnani (Tsar Maiden); Alexander Shiriaev (Ivanushka); Felix Kshesinsky (Khan).

Production premiere: 6 December 1895, Mariinsky Theatre, St Petersburg.

Arthur Saint-Léon created this ballet on 3 December 1864 at the Bolshoi Theatre, St Petersburg.

Halt of the Cavalry, character ballet in one act. Music: Johann Armsheimer. Libretto: Petipa. Choreography: Petipa. Decor: Heinrich Levogt. Costume design: Evgenii Ponomarev. Principal dancers: Pierina Legnani (Teresa); Pavel Gerdt (Pierre); Marie Petipa (Maria); Alfred Bekefi (Hussar Captain); Sergei Legat (Lancer Cornet).

Premiere: 21 January 1896, Mariinsky Theatre, St Petersburg.

26 April 1896: first performance of the ballet at the Bolshoi Theatre, Moscow, by members of the St Petersburg company for the coronation celebrations.

15 November 1898: Petipa's ballet was mounted for the Moscow company (Bolshoi Theatre) by Ivan Clustine.

The Pearl, ballet in one act. Music: Riccardo Drigo. Libretto: Petipa. Choreography: Petipa. Decor: Petr Lambin, after Mikhail Bocharov. Principal dancers: Pierina Legnani (White Pearl); Pavel Gerdt (Genie of Winter); Matilda Kshesinskaya (Yellow Pearl).

Premiere: 17 May 1896, Bolshoi Theatre, Moscow (gala coronation performance); 23 January 1900 first public performance at the Mariinsky Theatre.

Bluebeard, ballet-féerie in three acts and seven scenes, with apotheosis. Music: Petr Shenk. Libretto: Lidia Pashkova, after Charles Perrault. Choreography: Petipa. Decor: Petr Lambin (Act I); Konstantin Ivanov (Act II, Scene 1; Act III, Scene 1); Heinrich Levogt (Act II, Scenes 2, 3, and 4); Konstantin Ivanov and Vasilii Perminov (Act III, Scene 2). Costume design: Ivan Vsevolozhsky. Principal dancers: Pavel Gerdt (Bluebeard); Pierina Legnani (Ysaure); Olga Preobrazhenskaya (Anne, her sister); Iosef Kshesinsky and Andrei Oblakov (Ebremard and Raymond, their brothers); Sergei Legat (Arthur, Bluebeard's pageboy).

Premiere: 8 December 1896, Mariinsky Theatre, St Petersburg, marking Petipa's half-century of service.

12 December 1910: revival with new choreography by Nikolai Legat at Mariinsky Theatre, St Petersburg, with Matilda Kshesinskaya and Pavel Gerdt in the lead roles.

Thetis and Peleus, mythological ballet in one act. Music: Ludwig Minkus, with additional music by Léo Delibes. Libretto: Petipa. Choreography: Petipa. Decor: Petr Lambin; Pavel Kaminsky. Costume design: Evgenii Ponomarev. Principal dancers: Pavel Gerdt (Peleus); Matilda Kshesinskaya (Thetis); Olga Leonova (Venus); Olga Preobrazhenskaya (Amor); Liubov Roslavleva (Flora); Sergei Legat (Adonis); Alexei Bulgakov (Jupiter).

Premiere: 28 July 1897, Peterhof (gala performance for the German emperor William II).

This was a shortened version of Petipa's *The Adventures of Peleus*, premiered on 18 January 1876.

Raymonda, ballet in three acts and four scenes. Music: Alexander Glazunov. Libretto: Lidia Pashkova. Choreography: Petipa. Decor: Orest Allegri (Act I, Scene 1); Petr lambin (Act I, Scene 2; Act III; Apotheosis); Konstantin Ivanov (Act II). Costume design: Ivan Vsevolozhsky and Evgenii Ponomarev. Principal dancers: Pierina Legnani (Raymonda); Pavel Gerdt (Abderrakhman); Sergei Legat (Jean de Brienne); Olga Preobrazhenskaya (Henriette); Klavdia Kulichevskaya (Clémence); Georgii Kiaksht (Bernard); Nikolai Legat (Béranger).

Premiere: 7 January 1898, Mariinsky Theatre, St Petersburg.

23 January 1900: Petipa's ballet was staged at the Bolshoi Theatre, Moscow, by Alexander Gorsky and Ivan Clustine.

The Trial of Damis (also known as *Les Ruses d'amour*), ballet in one act. Music: Alexander Glazunov. Libretto: Petipa. Choreography: Petipa. Decor: Petr Lambin. Costumes: Evgenii Ponomarev. Principal dancers: Pierina Legnani (Isabelle); Pavel Gerdt (Damis); Klavdia Kulichevskaya (Marinette); Giuseppina Cecchetti (Countess Lucinda).

Premiere: 17 January 1900, Hermitage Theatre, St Petersburg; 23 January 1900, Mariinsky Theatre, St Petersburg.

The Seasons, allegorical ballet in one act and four scenes. Music: Alexander Glazunov. Libretto: Petipa. Decor: Petr Lambin. Costumes: Evgenii Ponomarev. Principal dancers: Matilda Kshesinskaya (Spirit of the Corn); Anna Pavlova (Hoar-Frost); Iulia Sedova (Ice); Liubov Petipa (Snow); Vera Trefilova (Hail); Olga Preobrazhenskaya (Rose); Alexei Bulgakov (Winter); Pavel Gerdt (Bacchus); Marie Petipa (Bacchante); Mikhail Obukhov (Faun); Nikolai Legat (Zephyr).

Premiere: 7 February 1900, Hermitage Theatre, St Petersburg; 13 February 1900, Mariinsky Theatre, St Petersburg.

28 January 1907: new production by Nikolai Legat, after Petipa, at the Mariinsky Theatre, St Petersburg.

Les Millions d'Arlequin (also known as *Harlequinade*), harlequinade in two acts. Music: Riccardo Drigo. Libretto: Petipa. Choreography: Petipa. Decor: Orest Allegri. Costumes: Evgenii Ponomarev. Principal dancers: Matilda Kshesinskaya (Colombine); Georgii Kiaksht (Harlequin); Olga Preobrazhenskaya (Pierrette); Sergei Lukianov (Pierrot); Enrico Cecchetti (Cassandre).

Premiere: 10 February 1900, Hermitage Theatre, St Petersburg; 13 February 1900, Mariinsky Theatre, St Petersburg.

21 January 1907: *Harlequinade* by Alexander Gorsky, after Petipa, for the Bolshoi Theatre, Moscow.

The Pupils of Dupré (also known as *Les Élèves de Dupré*), ballet in two acts. Music: Alberto Vizentini, Léo Delibes, and others. Libretto: Petipa. Choreography: Petipa. Decor: Orest Allegri (Act I); Heinrich Levogt and Orest Allegri (Act II). Costumes: Evgenii Ponomarev. Dancers included: Lev Ivanov (Comte de Montignac); Olga Preobrazhenskaya (Violette); Pierina Legnani (Camargo); Alexander Shiriaev (Dupré); Sergei Legat (Vestris); Pavel Gerdt (Louis XV); Marie Petipa (Madame de Pompadour).

Premiere: 14 February 1900, Hermitage Theatre, St Petersburg.

This was a shortened version of Petipa's *The King's Command*, premiered on 14 February 1886.

The Heart of the Marquise (also known as *Le Coeur de la marquise*), pantomime in one act, with a prologue and epilogue in verse. Music: M. G. Giraud. Choreography: Petipa. Sets and costumes: Léon Bakst. Principal dancers: Olga Preobrazhenskaya (Lisette); Nadezhda Petipa (A Young Woman); Enrico Cecchetti (Doctor Pierrot); Pavel Gerdt (Vicomte); Sergei Lukianov (Street Singer); Nikolai Legat, Sergei Legat, Georgii Kiaksht (Officers). Members of the French drama troupe also took part.

Premiere: 22 February 1902, Hermitage Theatre, St Petersburg.

The Magic Mirror, fantastic ballet in four acts and seven scenes. Music: Arsenii Koreshchenko. Libretto: Petipa and Ivan Vsevolozhsky, after Alexander Pushkin and the Brothers Grimm. Choreography: Petipa. Decor: Alexander Golovin. Principal dancers: Matilda Kshesinskaya (Princess); Sergei Legat (Prince); Pavel Gerdt (King); Marie Petipa (Queen); Nadezhda Petipa (Nurse); Anna Pavlova and Liubov Egorova (Princess's retinue); Mikhail Obukhov and Mikhail Fokine (Prince's retinue).

Premiere: 9 February 1903, Mariinsky Theatre, St Petersburg, marking the 55 years of Petipa's service.

13 February 1905: staged at the Bolshoi Theatre, Moscow, by Alexander Gorsky with the same designs by Alexander Golovin.

The Romance of the Rosebud and the Butterfly, ballet in one act and three scenes. Music: Riccardo Drigo. Libretto and costume design: Ivan Vsevolozhsky. Choreography: Petipa. Principal dancers: Olga Preobrazhenskaya (Rosebud); Mikhail Fokine (Sphinx Butterfly); Anna Pavlova (Daisy); Vera Trefilova (Nasturtium).

Premiere: scheduled for 23 January 1904 at the Hermitage Theatre, St Petersburg, but cancelled.

DANCES FOR OPERA

The dates given are for the first performance of an opera with Petipa's choreography.

Alessandro Stradella, music by Friedrich von Flotow.
First performance: 7 January 1849, Bolshoi Theatre, Moscow.
Polka (Act II).

Rusalka, music by Alexander Dargomyzhsky.
First performance: 4 May 1856, Theatre-Circus, St Petersburg.
Slavonic Dance (Act II), Gypsy Dance (Act II), Dance of the Mermaids (Act IV), all choreographed with Nikolai Golts.

Martha, music by Friedrich von Flotow, with additional music for the *divertissement* by Cesare Pugni.
First performance: 10 January 1859, Bolshoi Theatre, St Petersburg.
National Dance, Character Dance, English Dance (Act I).

Orfeo ed Euridice, music by Christoph Willibald von Gluck.
First Performance: 15 April 1868, Bolshoi Theatre, St Petersburg.
Dances and mime groups.

Hamlet, music by Ambroise Thomas.

First performance: 14 October 1872, Bolshoi Theatre, St Petersburg.

Traveling Players (Act III), Spring Festival (Act V).

Tannhäuser, music by Richard Wagner.

First performance: 13 December 1874, Mariinsky Theatre, St Petersburg.

Groupings of Bacchantes, Nymphs, Graces, etc. (Act I).

New production: 17 September 1899, Mariinsky Theatre, St Petersburg.

The Demon, music by Anton Rubinstein.

First performance: 13 January 1875, Mariinsky Theatre, St Petersburg

Oriental Dance (Act III), Lezginka (Act III).

New production: 1 October 1884, Bolshoi Theatre, St Petersburg.

Aïda, music by Giuseppe Verdi.

First performance: 19 November 1875, Bolshoi Theatre, St Petersburg.

Dances of the Priestesses (Act I), Dances of the Negroes (Act II), Dances of the Almées (Act II).

Il Guarany, music by Carlos Gomes.

First performance: 31 January 1879, Bolshoi Theatre, St Petersburg.

Dance of the Savages, Arrow Dance, March.

The Queen of Sheba (Die Königin von Saba), music by Karl Goldmark.

First performance: 11 February 1880, Bolshoi Theatre, St Petersburg.

Amazons, Slaves, Negroes (Act I), Dance of the Almées, Dance of the Bayadères, Devil's Dance, Bacchanalia (Act IV).

Mefistofele, music by Arrigo Boito.

First performance: 12 January 1881, Bolshoi Theatre, St Petersburg.

Obertas (Act I), Sabbath Round Dance (Act II), Chorea (Act IV).

Le Roi de Lahore, music by Jules Massenet.

First performance: 30 December 1881, Bolshoi Theatre, St Petersburg.

Dances of the Almées (Act II), Fantastic Ballet—Adagio, Theme and Variation, Waltz, and Coda (Act III).

Robert le Diable, music by Giacomo Meyerbeer.

First performance: 27 September 1882, Mariinsky Theatre, St Petersburg.

Pas de cinq (Act II), Dances (Act III).

3 December 1882, Bolshoi Theatre, St Petersburg.

Dances (Act III).

Carmen, music by Georges Bizet.

First performance: 29 October 1882, Mariinsky Theatre, St Petersburg.

Morena (Act II), Running of the Bulls, Stocking Weavers, Picadors, Fandango, Olé (Act IV).

Faust, music by Charles Gounod.

First performance; 19 November 1882, Bolshoi Theatre, St Petersburg.

Waltz (Act II), Walpurgisnacht (Act IV).

Les Huguenots, music by Giacomo Meyerbeer.

First performance: 27 December 1882, Mariinsky Theatre, St Petersburg.

Nymphs (Act III), Gypsy Dance (Act III).

New production: 25 March 1899, Mariinsky Theatre, St Petersburg.

La Gioconda, music by Amilcare Ponchielli.

First performance: 18 January 1883, Mariinsky Theatre, St Petersburg.

New production: 21 January 1888, Mariinsky Theatre, St Petersburg.

Furlana (Act I), dance of the hours—Morning, Afternoon, Evening, Night (Act III).

A Prisoner in the Caucasus, music by César Cui.

First performance: 4 February 1883, Bolshoi Theatre, St Petersburg.

Oriental Dance (Act III), Lezginka (Act III).

L'Étoile du Nord, music by Giacomo Meyerbeer.

First performance: 17 February 1883, Mariinsky Theatre, St Petersburg.

Richard III, music by Gervais Bernard Gaston Salvayre.

First performance: 9 December 1883, Mariinsky Theatre, St Petersburg.

Philémon et Baucis, music by Charles Gounod.
First performance: 19 December 1883, Mariinsky Theatre, St Petersburg.
Dance of the Bacchantes (Act II).

Lallah-Roukh, music by Félicien César David.
First performance: 24 January 1884, Bolshoi Theatre, St Petersburg.
Dance of the Kashmiris (Act I).

Nero, music by Anton Rubinstein.
First performance: 29 January 1884, Mariinsky Theatre, St Petersburg.

Rogneda, music by Alexander Serov.
First performance: 6 September 1884, Bolshoi Theatre, St Petersburg.
Round Dance and Dance of the Wandering Players (Act II).

Aldona, music by Amilcare Ponchielli.
First performance: 8 November 1884, Mariinsky Theatre, St Petersburg.
Folk Dance (Act I), Andalusian Dance, Dances of the Greek Slaves, Soldiers' Dance (Act II).

Lakmé, music by Léo Delibes.
First performance: 6 December 1884, Mariinsky Theatre, St Petersburg.
Dances of the Bayadères, Tirana, Charming of the Snake (Act II).

Manon, music by Jules Massenet.
First performance: 19 December 1885, Bolshoi Theatre, St Petersburg.
Dances (Act III).

Tamara, music by Boris Fitinhof-Schell.
First performance: 22 April 1886, Mariinsky Theatre, St Petersburg.
Bayadères, Lezginka (Act II), Tamara's Visions (Act IV).

Ruslan and Liudmila, music by Mikhail Glinka.
First performance: 31 August 1886, Mariinsky Theatre, St Petersburg.
Veil Dances and Groups (Act II), Dances of the Black Sea Slaves, Oriental Dances, Lezginka (Act IV).

New production: 10 December 1904, Mariinsky Theatre, with new choreography by Alexander Shiriaev.

Fenella (La Muette de Portici), music by Daniel François Esprit Auber.
First performance: 20 January 1887, Mariinsky Theatre, St Petersburg.
Guaracha, Bolero, Tarantella (Act I).

The Queen of Spades, music by Petr Tchaikovsky.
First performance: 7 December 1890, Mariinsky Theatre, St Petersburg.
Interlude 'The Sincerity of the Shepherdess'—Shepherdesses, Shepherds, Zlatogor's Retinue (Act II, Scene 1).

Johann von Leyden, music by Giacomo Meyerbeer.
First performance: 15 October 1891, Mariinsky Theatre, St Petersburg.
Waltz (Act II), Redova, Skating Quadrille, Pas des Frileuses (Act II), Groups and Dances (Act V).

Dubrovsky, music by Eduard Napravnik.
First performance: 3 January 1895, Mariinsky Theatre, St Petersburg.
Quadrille (later called *Contredanse*) and Polonaise (Act IV).

Hansel and Gretel, music by Englebert Humperdinck.
First performance: 24 October 1897, Mariinsky Theatre, St Petersburg.
Groups of angels.

Fran Diavolo, music by Daniel François Esprit Auber.
First performance: 21 November 1897, Mariinsky Theatre, St Petersburg.
Tarantella (Act III).

Don Giovanni, music by Wolfgang Amadeus Mozart.
First performance: 22 January 1898, Mariinsky Theatre, St Petersburg.
Entrance of the Masks, Dance of the Roses and Butterflies, Minuet (Act II).

Feramors, music by Anton Rubinstein.
First performance: 15 September 1898, Mariinsky Theatre, St Petersburg.
Dances of the Bayadères, Dances of the Fiancées, General Dance (Act I), groups of Bayadères (Act III).

Illustration Credits

All the illustrations are reproduced by kind permission of the St Petersburg State Museum of Theatrical and Musical Art (GMTMI), except for those listed below.

Illustrations reproduced by kind permission of the Russian State Archive of Literature and Art (RGALI):

> Gallery A, pictures 16 and 17, working notes for *The Daughter of the Snows* (Sergei Khudekov collection, *fond* 1657, *op.* 3, *ed. khr.* 125, *l.* 37 and 68ob–69)
>
> Endpiece, cartoon of Marius Petipa by the Legat Brothers (*fond* 3045, *op.* 1, *ed. khr.* 522, *l.*1)

Illustrations reproduced by kind permission of the St Petersburg State Theatre Library:

> Gallery B, pictures 15 and 16, *La Bayadère* set designs, taken from the *Yearbook of Imperial Theatres, 1900–1901* (Part 1, 159–160)
>
> Gallery B, pictures 17 and 18, *The Magic Mirror* set designs, taken from the *Yearbook of Imperial Theatres, 1904–1905* (Part 1, 197 and 208)

The frontispiece cartoon of Marius Petipa by the Legat brothers has been reproduced by kind permission of the National Library of Russia and taken from N. Legat and S. Legat, *Russkii balet v karikaturakh* [Russian Ballet in Caricatures] (St Petersburg: Progress, 1902–1905).

Archives and Libraries

MOSCOW

GTsTM: Gosudarstvennyi tsentral'nyi teatral'nyi muzei imeni A. A. Bakhrushin [State Central Theatre Museum named after A. A. Bakhrushin], *fond* 205.*

RGALI: Rossiiskii gosudarstvennyi arkhiv literatury i iskusstva [Russian State Archive of Literature and Art], *fond* 1945 (Petipa collection) and *fond* 1657 (Sergei Khudekov collection)

ST PETERSBURG

GMTMI: Sankt-Peterburgskii gosudarstvennyi muzei teatral'nogo i muzykal'nogo iskusstva [St Petersburg State Museum of Theatrical and Musical Art]

Muzykal'naia biblioteka Mariinskogo teatra [Music Library of the Mariinskii Theatre]

RGIA: Rossiiskii gosudarstvennyi istoricheskii arkhiv [Russian State History Archive]: *fond* 497 (Directorate of Imperial Theatres collection), *on.* 5, *ed. khr.* 2467 (Marius Petipa); *op.* 2, *ed. khr.* 14655 (Maria Surovshchikova-Petipa).

Rossiiskaia natsional'naia biblioteka [National Library of Russia]

Sankt-Peterburgskaia gosudarstvennaia teatral'naia biblioteka [St Petersburg State Theatre Library]

TsGIA: Tsentral'nyi gosudarstvennyi istoricheskii arkhiv [Central State History Archive]: *fond* 487, *op.* 1, *d.* 348.

* This book keeps to the Russian classification system of *fond, op[is'], ed[initsa], kh[raneniia]* or *d[elo]*, and *l[ist]*. (GTsTM uses a simplified version of this.)

FRANCE

Archives Bordeaux Métropole
Archives de Nantes
Archives départementales de la Gironde
Bibliothèque municipale de Bordeaux
Bibliothèque-musée de l'Opéra de Paris (Bibliothèque nationale de France)

UNITED STATES

Harvard Theatre Collection
Library of Congress
New York Public Library for the Performing Arts
New-York Historical Society

Notes

OVERTURE

1. Marius Petipa, *Russian Ballet Master: The Memoirs of Marius Petipa*, xv.

2. Ibid., 22–23.

3. This information comes from Sergei Konaev's commentary in *Marius Petipa. 'Memuary' i dokumenty*, 13, 22–23, 133, and 135. Konaev also points to Petipa's diary entry of 1 June 1907 (not included in published editions of the diaries) which shows Petipa's confusion: 'The 24 May', Petipa notes, 'I arrived in St Petersburg sixty years ago.' ('Le 24 mai il y a soixante ans que je suis arrivé à Pétersbourg.')

4. Léontine Fay (1810–1876), later Volnys, started as a successful child actor and made a smooth transition into adult roles, performing at the Comédie-Française. She acquired the name Volnys when she married her fellow actor Claude François Charles Joly (known as Volnys) in 1832. She worked for many years in Russia and is mentioned as being a member of the French troupe at the Mikhailovsky Theatre by Théophile Gautier in *Voyage en Russie* (154). She returned to France only in 1873, rejoining her husband in Nice, where she died. See Petipa, *Russian Ballet Master*, 26, n. 4.

5. Ibid., 23; Marquis de Custine, *Lettres de Russie*, 71–72, 80–82. Actually, as Konaev shows, although such a dispensation from customs duty had recently been introduced for foreign artists, there was some confusion over exactly what this meant. In a letter to the directorate of Imperial Theatres, the minister of finance insisted that the dispensation only applied to items destined for professional use (for example, stage costumes), so Petipa's luggage would necessarily have been inspected. In addition to his own luggage, Petipa was seemingly asked by the directorate to bring two boxes from Paris, filled with bolts of cloth, shawls, gloves, and other articles. See Konaev, *Marius Petipa. 'Memuary' i dokumenty*, 135–38.

6. Petipa, *Russian Ballet Master*, 23. Petipa's original French manuscript, reproduced by Konaev in *Marius Petipa. 'Memuary' i dokumenty*, is less detailed here, more euphemistic: 'mon couvre-chef [...] s'était envolé' (my hat had flown away), 56.

7. See also the British travel writer Edward Dicey in *A Month in Russia during the Marriage of the Czarevitch* about droshkies: 'There is nothing to hold on by—nothing whatever to hinder you from falling off,' 14.

8. Petipa, *Russian Ballet Master*, 23–24.

9. Ibid., 24.

10. These days the meaning of 'ballet master' varies from company to company. Balanchine was 'ballet master' at New York City Ballet, a job title that retains much of the nineteenth-century meaning of a person working as a choreographer as well as a coach and producer mounting versions of existing ballets. But at the Royal Ballet, 'ballet master' denotes a person who rehearses the corps de ballet and junior soloists.

    Antoine Titus Dauchy (1780–1860) was a dancer at the Paris Opera, making his debut there in 1804. He spent a long time in Berlin as ballet master, before arriving in St Petersburg in 1832 as second ballet master, assisting his French compatriot Alexis Blache. When Blache left in 1836 he became first ballet master and remained until around the end of 1848, to be replaced by Jules Perrot.

    Émile Gredelue had been a leading dancer in Bordeaux under Jean Petipa (Marius's father) from 1835 to 1836. In 1837 he partnered Marie Taglioni in *La Sylphide*, a performance which marked their respective Russian debuts.

11. Part of the contract is reproduced in *Marius Petipa. Materialy, vospominaniia, stat'i*, ed. A. Nekhendzi, 113–14. *Premier danseur*: in British companies the equivalent category would be 'male principal'.

12. 'Ялта, 3 июля (по телеграфу). В Гурзуфе скончался солист Его Величества Мариус Иванович Петипа. Тело для погребения будет отправлено в Петербург. Сошел в могилу Мариус Иванович Петипа, который мог смело сказать: "Русский балет—это я …" Петипа отдал ему все силы, все творчество, свой художественный талант. Шестьдесят лет он непрерывно сочинял и ставил балет за балетом, и воспитывал русскую танцовщицу, которая совершенствовалась и расцветала под руководством верного хореографа.' 'M. I. Petipa', *Peterburgskaia gazeta*, 4 July 1910, 3.

13. The authorship of a small number of ballets is uncertain.

14. Dame Adeline Genée (1878–1970) was born Anina Jensen in Hinnerup, Aarhus, Denmark, and died in Esher, England. She received her early training in Denmark before enjoying wide-ranging international success, most notably in London where she became the founder of the Royal Academy of Dancing.

    Maud Allan (1873–1956), a Canadian dancer, performed barefoot 'Greek dance', whose most famous proponent was Isadora Duncan (1877–1927). Allan finally settled in England where she established her own school.

15. 'If Pavlova Had Never Danced', *The Times*, 18 July 1910, 3.

16. Tati'iana Smirnova (1821–1871) had been a pupil in St Petersburg of the famous ballet master Charles Didelot; Elena Andreianova (1819–1857) was the

first Russian Giselle; Ekaterina Sankovskaia (1816–1878) was a big star of the Moscow stage; Nadezhda Bogdanova (1836–1897), trained by her father, and Marfa Murav'eva (1838–1879) belonged to the next generation. The ballerinas are listed by Aleksandr Pleshcheev, *Nash Balet*, 38; see also *Gautier on Dance*, 144–45, 163, 228–29, 233, and 238.

17. About Zina Richard see Vera Krasovskaia, *Russkii baletnyi teatr vtoroi poloviny XIX veka*, 127–29. Her mother, Dar'ia Richard (née Lopukhina), was a Moscow dancer who in 1848 became a teacher at the St Petersburg theatre school; her French father, Joseph, was from a ballet family and moved to Russia in 1823. Zina was born in 1832, and graduated from the St Petersburg school in 1850. Félicité Hullin Sor, a dancer and ballet mistress (1823–1839) with the Moscow company, was her aunt or cousin.

18. Didelot's famous two-act *Zéphire et Flore*, created at the Paris Opera in 1815, appears to have been a considerable elaboration, not a copy or adaptation, of his 1804 one-act ballet of the same name at the Hermitage Theatre, St Petersburg. The 1804 ballet was, in turn, probably similar to the same choreographer's *La Métamorphose* (Lyons, 1795) and inversely titled *Flore et Zéphire* (London, 1796). See Mary Grace Swift, *A Loftier Flight*, 52–53, 60, 63, 130–34, 194–95, and 197.

19. Diagilev's death in 1929, which brought to an end the Ballets Russes, prompted a succession of other Ballets Russes companies, among them the Ballets Russes de Monte Carlo (founded in 1932), the Ballets Russes du Colonel de Basil (1936), and the Original Ballet Russe (1939).

20. Ballet Rambert dates its first performances from 1926; in 1987 it changed its name to Rambert Dance Company and in 2014 to just Rambert.

21. The Royal Ballet grew out of the Academy of Choreographic Art, established by de Valois in 1926. The school gave its first full evening of ballet at the Old Vic in 1931 and became known the same year as the Vic-Wells Ballet, because it divided its time between the Old Vic and Sadler's Wells theatres. Based solely at Sadler's Wells by 1935, it became the Sadler's Wells Ballet in 1941. Five years later it moved to the Royal Opera House and in 1956 became the Royal Ballet.

22. Nikolai Sergeev (1876–1951) graduated from the St Petersburg Imperial Theatre School into the company in 1884, became responsible for notating the ballet repertoire (see below), and was appointed *régisseur* in 1903, a post broadly equivalent to that of company manager.

23. Another leading nineteenth-century choreographer, Auguste Bournonville, is an exception: many of his ballets have been preserved, with or without modifications, in the repertoire of the Royal Danish Ballet.

24. 'Дидло венчался славой', *Evgenii Onegin*, Chapter 1, stanza 21, line 12.

25. Vladimir Stepanov (1866–1896) published his system in Paris in 1892 with the title *Alphabet des mouvements du corps humain* and the following year it was introduced into the theatre school's curriculum. The future Moscow ballet master Aleksandr Gorskii refined the system, publishing several pamphlets in 1899,

and taught it at the St Petersburg school. By 1903 Nikolai Sergeev had two assistants, Aleksandr Chekrygin and Sergei Rakhmanov, for the task of notating
the ballet company's repertoire (*Materialy po istorii russkogo baleta*, ed. Mikhail
Borisoglebskii, vol. 2, 76–79 (76)). In the West Sergeev, besides helping with the
Ballet Russes *Sleeping Princess* (1921), mounted several works from the Petersburg
repertoire, including the Kingdom of Shades act from *La Bayadère*, for his own
ensemble in Riga; he followed this with Petipa's production of *Giselle* for the Paris
Opera Ballet (1924) and the London-based Camargo Society (1932). He mounted
the first lakeside scene from *Swan Lake* (1932) and the first British production
of the full ballet (1934) for Ninette de Valois's Vic-Wells company. For the same
company, he staged Petipa's production of Saint-Léon's *Coppélia* (Acts I and II in
1933, the complete version in 1940), *Giselle, The Nutcracker* (first showing outside
Russia) and *Swan Lake* (all 1934), and *The Sleeping Beauty* or *Princess* (1939). In
1941 he moved to the International Ballet, a British touring company led by the
ballerina Mona Inglesby, where he mounted the same Petipa ballets.

26. Sergei Vikharev (1962–2017) used the Stepanov notations and other archival materials for productions of *The Sleeping Beauty* (1999), *La Bayadère* (2002), and *The
Awakening of Flora* (2007), all for the Mariinsky Ballet, plus *Raymonda* (2011) for
the ballet company of La Scala, and Petipa's version of *Coppélia (2009)* for the
Moscow Bolshoi. Aleksei Ratmanskii's reconstructions, using the same sources,
include *The Sleeping Beauty* (2015) for American Ballet Theatre, *Swan Lake*
(2016) for the Zurich Ballet and the ballet of La Scala, and *La Bayadère* (2018) for
the Berlin State Ballet.

27. Rafail Zotov (1795–1871), dramatist and writer, was a critic for *Severnaia pchela*,
a daily politcal and literary newspaper (1825–1864). Fedor Koni (1809–1879),
man of letters and theatre historian, was editor of the monthly journal *Panteon*,
later called *Panteon i repertuar russkoi stseny*. Mavrikii Rappaport (1824–1884), a
civil servant by day, edited the weekly *Muzykal'nyi i teatral'nyj vestnik* (1856–1860)
and wrote for *Syn otechestva* and other publications.

28. Murray Frame, *The St. Petersburg Imperial Theaters: Stage and State in
Revolutionary Russia, 1900–1920*, 65.

29. Konstantin Skal'kovskii (1843–1906) wrote witty reviews which appeared in
Novoe vremia, Birzhevye vedomosti, Peterburgskaia gazeta, and specialist publications. Nikolai Bezobrazov (1848–1912), a civil servant by day, wrote for
Sankt-Peterburgskie vedomosti and *Peterburgskaia gazeta*. Aleksandr Pleschcheev
(1858–1944) began as an actor before switching to journalism and books; his articles appeared in *Birzhevye vedomosti, Novoe vremia, Rossiia*, and *Peterburgskaia
gazeta*.

30. Vera Petipa, *Moia sem'ia: Petipa v zhizni i iskusstve*. The typescript is in the Marius
Petipa collection, *fond* 1945, *op.* 1, *ed. khr.* 66 in RGALI in Moscow. An abridged version
is reproduced in *Marius Petipa. Materialy, vospominaniia, stat'i*, ed. Anna Nekhendzi
(see below) and (translated) in *Marius Petipa: Mémoires*, ed. Galia Ackerman and
Pierre Lorrain, and Laura Hormigón, *Marius Petipa en España 1844–1847*.

31. These working papers can be found in Moscow in the Sergei Khudekov collection, *fond* 1657 in RGALI and in the Marius Petipa collection, *fond* 205 in GTsTM.

32. The diaries are preserved in *fond* 1945, *op.* 1, *ed. khr.* 1 in RGALI.

Lynn Garafola's edition of *The Diaries of Marius Petipa* is a slightly abridged translation which includes a long and perceptive introduction by Garafola and a detailed list of Petipa's works. While finishing this book Pascale Melani's handsome, very complete French edition appeared, *Journal du maître de ballet des Théâtres Impériaux*, also with a long introduction by its editor, but too late, alas, for more than a brief look. All references to the diaries use the Garafola edition except where stated.

33. *The Diaries of Marius Petipa*, xiv (introduction).

34. The title of the original publication *Memuary Mariusa Petipa, solista ego Imperatorskogo Velichestva i baletmeistera Imperatorskikh teatrov* (St Petersburg: 'Trud', 1906) translates as *The Memoirs of Marius Petipa, Soloist of His Imperial Majesty and Ballet Master of the Imperial Theatres*. In addition to the version published in the 1971 collection *Marius Petipa. Materialy, vospominaniia, stat'i*, ed. Anna Nekhendzi, there have been two unedited reprints: in 1996 (St Petersburg: Predpriiatie S.-Peterb. soiuza khudozhnikov) and 2003, in a volume including articles from *Sankt-Peterburgskie vedomosti* and other writings about Petipa (St Petersburg: Soiuz khudozhnikov). Then, in 2018 came a forensically annotated, very complete edition, *Marius Petipa. 'Memuary' i dokumenty*, ed. Sergei Konaev, which is referred to later in this section (Overture). The incomplete manuscripts in French are preserved both in GTsTM (*fond* 205) and, together with the diaries, in RGALI (*fond* 1945, *op.* 1, *ed. khr.* 1). Petipa first mentions working on his memoirs in his diary entry for 31 January 1904.

35. Petipa, *Russian Ballet Master: The Memoirs of Marius Petipa*, ed. Lillian Moore, 91. About this English translation of Petipa's memoirs, which my book quotes from extensively, see later in Overture.

36. 'Человек, прослуживший 60 лет в России, мог бы многое порассказать о положении театрального дела. Но, к сожалению, "мемуары" г. Петипа только на одну треть мемуары, да две трети же представляют отповедь нынешнему директору Императорских театров В. А. Теляковскому, жестоко "обидевшему" почтенного балетмейстера.' Nikolai Negorev, 'Baletnye memuary', *Teatr i iskusstvo*, 2 April 1906, 220–22.

37. Ekaterina Vazem, *Zapiski baleriny Sankt-Peterburgskogo Bol'shogo teatra*; Aleksandr Shiriaev, *Peterburgskii balet. Iz vospominanii artista Mariinskogo teatra*; Vladimir Teliakovskii, *Vospominaniia* and *Dnevniki Direktora Imperatoriskikh teatrov*.

38. Matil'da Kshesinskaia [Mathilde Kschessinska], *Dancing in Petersburg: The Memoirs of Mathilde Kschessinska*.

39. The Marius Petipa file in RGIA, *fond* 497, *on.* 5, *ed. khr.* 2467.

40. Aleksandr Pleshcheev, 'M. I. Petipa (1847–1907). K 60-letiiu ego khoreograficheskoi deiatel'nosti v Peterburge', *Istoricheskii vestnik*, May, 1907, 561–68.

The centenary tributes are: Denis Leshkov, *Marius Petipa (1822–1910): K stoletiiu ego rozhdeniia*; M. Iakovlev, *Baletmeister Marius Petipa*; and I. Ivanov and K. Ivanov, *Marius Ivanovich Petipa 1822–1922: K stoletiuu dnia rozhdeniia*. The last three tributes marked what was still believed to be the centenary of Petipa's birth, since he had claimed to be born in 1822 rather than 1818, although Iakolev's was not published until 1924.

41. Sergei Khudekov, *Istoriia tantsev*, 4 vols. Other histories with important Petipa coverage are: Iurii Slonimskii, *Mastera baleta* (Leningrad: Iskusstvo, 1937), the chapter on Marius Petipa later translated and published in Dance Index (1947); and Vera Krasovskaia, *Russkii baletnyi teatr vtoroi poloviny XIX veka*. Krasovskaia's book is the second of a two-volume history, the first being *Russkii baletnyi teatr ot vosniknoveniia do serediny XIX veka*.

42. This volume contains helpful notes by Moore but is the product of a chain of translations, coming from the published Russian text which was itself a translation of the French manuscript. Moore also wrote an essay, 'The Petipa Family in Europe and America', which was the product of research conducted with the unfulfilled aim of producing a biography of Petipa and was published in *Dance Index*, 1/5 (May 1942).

43. *Marius Petipa, Meister des Klassischen Balletts: Selbstzeugnisse, Dokumente, Erinnerungen*, ed. Eberhard Rebling (Berlin: Henschelverlag, 1975); *Marius Petipa: Mémoires*, trans. and ed. Galia Ackerman and Pierre Lorrain (see also above n. 30).

44. Examples are: extracts from Vazem's book, published as 'Memoirs of a Ballerina of the St Petersburg Bolshoi Theatre', trans. Nina Dimitrievich, in *Dance Research*; extracts from Vladimir Teliakovskii's memoirs, published as 'Memoirs', trans. Nina Dimitrievich, in *Dance Research*; and the Petipa chapter in Iurii Slonimskii's *Mastera baleta*, published as 'Marius Petipa', trans. Anatole Chujoy, in *Dance Index*. See the bibliography for full references.

45. Like Lillian Moore, the US-based writer Gennady Smakov died (in 1988) before completing a projected biography.

CHAPTER 1

1. 'Se faire applaudir pour un pas, à Saint-Pétersbourg, n'est pas chose facile. Les Russes sont très connaisseurs en ballet, et le feu de leur lorgnettes est redoutable.' Théophile Gautier, *Voyage en Russie*, 152.

2. There had been previous Italian opera companies; the last, which made its debut on 17 January 1829, lacked the first-class singers to ensure box-office success and folded two years later. See Vol'f, *Khronika peterburgskikh teatrov s kontsa 1826 do nachala 1881*, Part 1, 20 and 26.

    When the Russian opera company returned from Moscow after a few years it had to make do with the Theatre-Circus opposite the Bolshoi. Much the same happened to the Russian opera company in Moscow during the 1860s: the Moscow branch of the Imperial Italian Opera moved into the Bolshoi Theatre where it performed up to five nights a week, leaving the Russian company with just one night. See Marina Frolova Walker, 'Grand Opera in Russia: Fragments of an unwritten history', in *The Cambridge Companion to Grand Opera*, 348.

3. Gautier, *Voyage en Russie*, 148–50.
4. 'Du velours, de l'or, de la lumière à profusion, que faut-il de plus?' Ibid., 151.
5. 'Зрительный зал Большого театра имел очень нарядный вид и являл собой ч резвычайно оживленную картину. Хотя самым модным театральным местом встреч "бомонда" тогда считалась итальянская опера и балетные зрители в их массе с внешней стороны выглядели как будто скромнее итальянск их, все же театральный зал балета, особенно в бенефисы, мало чем уступал "итальянскому". Первый ряд партера занимали главным образом гвардейск ие офицеры—кавалергарды и конногвардейцы—клавшие свои медные каски или белые фуражки перед собой на барьер, отделявший кресла от оркестра. Среди них выделялись темными пятнами штатские. [...]

'Часто бывали в балете и иностранные дипломаты. Среди них особенно ревностно посещали балет посланник испанский, маркиз Кампосаградо, и итальянский—граф Греппи. Первый отличался необыкновенной тучностью. Он не помещался в театральном кресле, и для него всегда ставили в первый ряд диванчик шириной в два кресла. Напротив, Греппи был очень худощав, и при встречах друг с другом они контрастами своих фигур производили весьма комичное впечатление.

'Рядом с аристократией значительное место в составе балетной публики занимала крупная буржуазия—железнодорожные концессионеры, заводовладельцы, директора банков и акционерных компаний, откупщики. Мужской контингент ее представлял собой обыкновенно малопримечательного с внешней стороны, зато дамы очень выделялись роскошью своих нарядов и ценных украшений. Недаром в старину назывался "бриллиантовым рядом" бельэтаж Большого театра, где они любили восседать, особенно на бенефисах и других выдающихся спектаклях.' Ekaterina Vazem, *Zapiksi baleriny Sankt-Peterburgskogo Bol'shogo teatra*, 193–94. See also Murray Frame, *The St Petersburg Imperial Theatres: Stage and State in Revolutionary London, 1900–1920*, which offers a description of audiences in late Tsarist Russia, 70–84.
6. 'Les vols, les engloutissements, les transformations à vue, les jeux de lumière électrique et tous les prestiges que nécessite une mise en scène compliquée s'y exécutent avec la promptitude la plus certaine.' Gautier, *Voyage en Russie*, 153.
7. Vazem, *Zapiksi baleriny Sankt-Peterburgskogo Bol'shogo teatra*, 49.
8. Joseph Mazilier's *Le Corsaire* received its world premiere at the Paris Opera on 23 January 1856.
9. *Sankt-Peterburgskie vedomosti*, 12 January 1858, quoted in translation by Ivor Guest in *Jules Perrot: Master of the Romantic Ballet*, 307.

10. Irina Boglacheva, *Artisty Sankt-Peterburgskogo baleta. XIX Vek*, 21.

11. 'Comme la danse doit seule former tout le spectacle, les ballets ont plus de développement que chez nous: ils vont jusqu'à quatre ou cinq actes, avec beaucoup de tableaux et de changements, ou bien l'on en joue deux dans la même soirée.' Gautier, *Voyage en Russie*, 152.

12. 'A force de roubles et de bon accueil, l'on a vaincu la crainte chimérique des extinctions de voix et des rhumatismes. Nul gosier, nul genou n'a souffert dans ce pays de neige ou l'on voit le froid sans le sentir.' Ibid., 152.

13. 'Leur Conservatoire de danse fournit des sujets remarquables et un corps de ballet qui n'a pas son pareil pour l'ensemble, la précision et la rapidité des évolutions. C'est plaisir de voir ces lignes si droites, ces groupes si nets qui ne se décomposent qu'au moment voulu pour se reformer sous un autre aspect; tous ces petits pieds qui retombent en mesure, tous ces bataillons chorégraphiques qui ne se déconcertent et ne s'embrouillent jamais dans leur manoeuvres!' Ibid., 152.

14. 'Il est inouï que pareilles pauvretés soient présentées à un public d'élite sur la première scène du monde.' *Le Journal des théâtres*, 4 July 1844; quoted by Sylvie Jacq-Mioche, 'Ombres et flamboiements du ballet romantique à Paris' [The Shadows and Flares of the Romantic Ballet in Paris], in 'De la France à la Russie, Marius Petipa', ed. Pascale Melani, 23–39 (35).

15. 'Ce n'est pas lorsqu'on touche des appointements de soixante francs par mois que l'on peut consacrer beaucoup de temps à la danse.' Gautier, *La Presse*, 20 January 1845; quoted by Jacq-Mioche, 'Ombres et flamboiements du ballet romantique à Paris', 35. The figure of 400 roubles was given to Jacq-Mioche by Ol'ga Fedorchenko.

If Gautier's appreciation of Russian dancers makes no reference to their expressiveness, Soviet writers were quick to claim that even early on they had a distinctive quality. Taking Pushkin's line in *Eugene Onegin*, 'will I see the soul-inspired flight of the Russian Terpsichore', as their signpost, they believed that Russians infused Western shapes with a Slavic depth. See, for example, Natalia Roslavleva, *Era of the Russian Ballet 1770–1965*, 50. (Pushkin's original Russian is: 'Узрю ли русской Терпсихоры/Душной исполненный полет?', *Evgenii Onegin*, chapter 1, stanza 19, lines 6–7.) On the other hand, Pushkin might have written the same about Western dancers.

16. The sources for the St Petersburg figures are: A. Vol'f, *Khronika peterburgskikh teatrov s kontsa 1826 do nachala 1881*, Part 3, 150–51; and Murray Frame, *School for Citizens: Theatre and Civil Society in Imperial Russia*, 79–80, which quotes Vladimir Pogozhev, *Proekt zakonopolozhenii ob imperatorskikh teatrakh* [Draft Statute for the Imperial Theatres], 3 vols. (St Petersburg, 1900), vol. 3, 487. The Frame and Pogozhev figures are part of the findings of a committee formed in 1858 to explore ways of reducing deficits in the Imperial Theatres' budget. The committee compared the Imperial Theatres with theatres in Western Europe

and found, among other things, that the St Petersburg Ballet had 261 more members than the Paris Opera. This number seems excessive, but it includes the pupils of the Theatre School. Perhaps, also, the Paris Opera Ballet was much smaller than today. My thanks to Dr Frame for his help in trying to understand all this.

I do not have nineteenth-century statistics for the ballet of the Paris Opera, the most important company of that time, but Marian Smith publishes figures for the repertoire from 1825–1850, in which forty ballets (plus a ballet-opera) were created. See Marian Smith, *Ballet and Opera in the Age of Giselle*, 210–12. Today's Paris and London figures are for the 2017–2018 season.

17. Gautier, *Voyage en Russie*, 153; about Perrot's appointment to the St Petersburg ballet, see Guest, *Jules Perrot*, 251–52.

18. The culmination of this trend came in Paris with Saint-Léon's *Coppélia* (1870), in which the central role of Franz was created by the ballerina Eugénie Fiocre.

19. Nicholas V. Riasanovsky and Mark D. Steinberg, *A History of Russia*, 221.

20. Frame, *The St Petersburg Imperial Theatres, 1900–1920*, 9–10.

21. The technical date of the founding of state theatre is 30 August 1756 when the empress Elizabeth signed a decree founding a Russian theatre in the Golovkin Mansion on Vasilevsky Island (*Vasilevskii ostrov*). (From then on Imperial Theatre seasons always started on 30 August, usually ending by March or April.) However, despite first intentions, the theatre stayed closed to the general public for some twenty years and was then superseded by the Kamennyi Theatre. For a fuller account of early Russian theatre, see Frame's chapter 'Emblem of Enlightenment', in *School for Citizens*, 10–44.

22. Roslavleva, *Era of the Russian Ballet, 1770–1965*, 40.

23. Vol'f, 12–13, 23–24; T. A. Stukolkin, 'Vospominaniia artista Imperatorskikh teatrov', in *Artist*, 45 (January 1895), 126–27; see also translated version in Wiley, *A Century of Russian Ballet*, 108–34 (108–9).

24. In 1862 the Ministry of the Court issued an edict for the distribution of companies in the four main theatres. For a summary of this, see *Peterburgskii balet. Tri veka. 1851–1900*, ed. Boglacheva, 95.

25. It was also just a block away from the Hotel Klee where Petipa stayed on arrival.

26. The Kamenny Island theatre was closed in 1882 and became a depot for theatre sets, but has since been restored and today is the second stage of the Bolshoi Dramatic Theatre (*Bol'shoi dramaticheskii teatr im. G. A. Tovstonogova*). See *Peterburgskii balet. Tri veka. 1851–1900*, ed. Boglacheva, 377.

27. Roland John Wiley, *The Life and Ballets of Lev Ivanov*, 55–56.

28. Kshesinskaia [Kschessinska], *Dancing in Petersburg*, 32–33, 40–42.

29. Natalia Rozhdestvenskaia, 'The Hermitage Theatre', *Petersburg City/Guide to St. Petersburg, Russia*, http://petersburgcity.com/theaters/hermitage.

30. Frame, *School for Citizens*, 43 and 49. However, as will later be seen, there were exemptions, contingent upon special permission.

31. Ibid., 42.
32. Ibid., 49.
33. Solomon Volkov, *St Petersburg*, 254–56.
34. Franz Anton Christoph Hilverding (1710–1768) was appointed court dancer in Vienna in 1735 and then ballet master in 1749. He was considered by some of his contemporaries, notably his disciple Gaspero Angiolini, as the true pioneer of the *ballet d'action*, rather than Jean-Georges Noverre, who claimed to be the inventor.
35. After training in Italy, Gaspero Angiolini (1731–1803) went to Vienna where he came under the influence of Hilverding and succeeded him as ballet master, after Hilverding's departure to St Petersburg. When in turn Angiolini arrived back from St Petersburg in 1772, he was driven to contest publicly Noverre's claim to be the inventor of the *ballet d'action*. This began a long controversy and enmity. A vociferous supporter of democratic and republican ideals who saw theatre as an arena for ideas and inspiration, he was imprisoned for his opinions and exiled from Milan in 1799. He returned to Milan in 1801 where he died two years later.
36. Charles Le Picq (1744–1806) had an international career as ballet master and dancer which included two stints (1783 and 1785) in charge of the troupe at the King's Theatre, London. A pupil and disciple of Noverre, he was responsible for the St Petersburg edition of Noverre's seminal publication, *Lettres sur la danse*.
37. Jean-Georges Noverre (1727–1810) graduated from the Paris ballet school. He created ballets in many cities, including London where the actor David Garrick considered him 'the Shakespeare of the Dance', and spent large portions of his long career in Stuttgart and Vienna. His *Lettres sur la danse* were first published in 1760 and he is recognized as a major reformer and theoretician, overshadowing his forerunners Hilverding and Angiolini, and inspiring later choreographers.
38. 'Весь Петербург жаждал ее видеть.' P. Bolotov, *Zhizn' i prikliucheniia Andreia Bolotova* [The Life and Adventures of Andrei Bolotov] (Russkaia starina: 1873), vol. 4, 699–700; quoted in Vera Krasovskaia, *Russkii baletnyi teatr ot vozniknoveniia do serediny XIX veka*, 67.
39. 'Прикидываясь охотниками до театральных представлений на драматические пьесы и игру актеров, ведут себя во время спектакля шумно и неприлично, и что молчание и тихость восстанавливаются среди них только на балете.' V. Mikhnevich, *Istoricheskie etiudy russkoi zhizni* [Historical sketches of Russian Life] (St Petersburg, 1882), 323; quoted by Tat'iana Kuzovleva, 'Inostrantsy i formirovanie russkogo baletnogo teatra', in *Teatral'nyi Peterburg: Interkul'turnaia model'*, 37.
40. The Italian school was known for virtuosity and technical innovation from early on. The performers, who had humorous, proletarian stage names, excelled in the so-called comic genre, which featured acrobatic jumps and turns. The French school as represented by Landé was more accessible to amateurs, being

related to ballroom dancing, especially the minuet, so that the style was stately and geometric with frugal jumps and turns. Rinaldi, an Italian, and his wife Julia taught alongside Landé at the theatre school, and when Landé died in 1748, Rinaldi succeeded him. In this way, the French and Italian schools were fused, as they were elsewhere in Europe.

41. Frame, *School for Citizens*, 12–20.
42. Krasovskaia, *Russkii baletnyi teatr ot vozniknoveniia do serediny XIX veka*, 70–71.
43. Hans Rogger, *National Consciousness in Eighteenth-Century Russia*, 140.
44. Krasovskaia, *Russkii baletnyi teatr ot vozniknoveniia do serediny XIX veka*, 118–20.
45. Frame, *School for Citizens*, 35–36. By 1816 the French theatre had been restored to St Petersburg, and to Moscow in the late 1820s.

The narrative for Cavos's opera would be reused by Mikhail Glinka in 1830 for the opera which became known as *A Life for the Tsar* (Zhizn' za Tsaria).

46. Krasovskaia, *Russkii baletnyi teatr ot vozniknoveniia do serediny XIX veka*, 168–70.
47. Ibid., 121–22.
48. 'Тогда мало давалось балетов во французком роде, а больше русские национальные дивертисманы.' Adam Glushkovskii, *Vospominaniia baletmeistera*, 176.
49. 'Многие нарочно ездили к цыганкам и платили им большие деньги, чтобы только перенять их манеры в народной пляске.' Ibid.
50. As noted earlier, Didelot's career in Russia had a five-year interruption halfway: 1801–1811, resuming 1816–1831.
51. Frame, *School for Citizens*, 33–35 and 58.
52. Riasanovsky and Steinberg, *A History of Russia*, 298.
53. 'Le pouvoir absolu devient par trop redoutable quand il a peur'. Custine, *Lettres de Russie*, 124.
54. Frame, *School for Citizens*, 67–68.
55. Ibid., 76–77.
56. Ibid., 62.
57. Nikolai Gogol, 'Petersburg Notes for 1836', in *Russian Dramatic Theory from Pushkin to the Symbolists*, ed. and trans. Laurence Senelick (Austin, TX, 1981), 24; quoted by Frame, *School for Citizens*, 65.
58. Ibid., 51–52.
59. Riasanovsky and Steinberg, *A History of Russia*, 302–303.
60. Ia. Nazakulisnyi, 'Teatral'naia khronika', *Molva*, 21 (1834), 325; quoted and trans. Mary Grace Swift, *A Loftier Flight: The Life and Accomplishments of Charles-Louis Didelot, Balletmaster*, 185.
61. Taglioni's 1832 Paris version was danced by his daughter Marie. Despite her phenomenal talent, the ballet, shown in London the following year, stirred *The Times* to dismiss it in a single line as being 'very insipid' (Cyril W. Beaumont, *Complete Book of Ballets*, 110). According to Ivor Guest, Titus first staged his own *Swiss Milkmaid* at Paris's Théâtre de la Porte-Saint-Martin on 25 September

1823. It was set to the same score by Adalbert Gyrowetz, but didn't acknowledge Taglioni's original authorship (Guest, *The Romantic Ballet in Paris*, 225–26).

62. 'В первом акте танцуют, толпятся, бегают, и похищают молочницу, а во втором женятся на ней, бегают, толпятся, и танцуют. [...] Зрители расстались с ней [швейцарской молочницей] так точно, как расстаются с человеком, который надоел продолжительной болтовней.' 'Peterburgskii teatr', *Severnaia pchela*, 23 April 1832, 1–2.

63. Sandra Noll Hammond, 'Dancing *La Sylphide* in 1832: Something Old or Something New?', in *La Sylphide: Paris 1832 and Beyond*, ed. Marian Smith, 31–56 (50).

64. Théophile Gautier, 'La Sylphide', *La Presse*, 24 September 1838, in *Gautier on Dance*, ed. and trans. Ivor Guest, 51–55 (53).

65. In fact, his first contract, like Marius Petipa's, officially designated him as *premier danseur*.

66. Serfs comprised 49 per cent of the population of 36 million in 1796; they were 44.5 per cent in 1858 (Riasanovsky and Steinberg, *A History of Russia*, 321).

67. Frame, *School for Citizens*, 36.

68. Ibid., 37.

69. Ibid., 39.

70. Victor Borovsky, 'The Organisation of the Russian Theatre 1645–1763', in *A History of Russian Theatre*, 43.

71. Iurii Shamurin, 'Podmoskovnye kul'turnye sokrovishcha Rossii' [Russian Cultural Treasures in Moscow] (extract), in *Moscow: A Traveller's Companion*, ed. by Laurence Kelly, 218. See later in this chapter about the entrepreneur Michael Maddox.

72. Frame, *School for Citizens*, 39, and Krasovskaia, *Russkii baletnyi teatr ot vosniknoveniia do serediny XIX veka*, 89–90.

73. Ibid., 87.

74. Frame, *School for Citizens*, 40, quoting Martha Wilmot, an Irish traveller. See Martha and Catherine Wilmot, *The Russian Journals of Martha and Catherine Wilmot, 1803–1808*, ed. by the Marchioness of Londonderry and H. M. Hynde (London, 1934), 56–57. Also Krasovskaia, *Russkii baletnyi teatr ot vosniknoveniia do serediny XIX veka*, 90.

75. Ibid., 96–97.

76. Sheremet'ev artists were given the stage names of gems and the third element of Praskovia Kovaleva-Zhemchugova's name means 'pearl'; see Douglas Smith, *The Pearl*.

77. Frame, *School for Citizens*, 40–41.

78. Krasovskaia, *Russkii baletnyi teatr ot vosniknoveniia do serediny XIX veka*, 99–100.

79. Petipa, *Russian Ballet Master*, 27. The Hermitage was only opened to the general public in 1852 but perhaps as an employee of the Imperial Theatres he was given a special pass.

80. Rosamund Bartlett, *Chekhov: Scenes from a Life*, 86–87.

81. This study will refer to the ballet's Russian production as *Satanilla*.

82. Frame, *School for Citizens*, 34–35. Frame's figures are taken from V. Vsevolodskii-Gerngross, *Teatr v Rossii v epokhu otechestvennoi voiny* [Theatre in Russia at the Time of the Patriotic War] (St Petersburg, 1912), 40–41.

83. 'Во фраках, офицеры со шпорами и с особыми усами, дамы с обнаженной, белой как снег грудью—бриллианты, духи, кружева … Здесь и без балета есть на что поглядеть. Царская ложа не пустая, как часто бывает в Москве. Все на своих местах. […] тут все знакомы, все друг другу кланяются, все свои. А капельдинеры как вежливы и как хорошо одеты—в Москве часто ливреи мешками сидят, а здесь как будто на каждого сделаны по мерке.' Vladimir Teliakovskii, *Vospominaniia*, 152.

84. Elizaveta Surits, 'Moscow v Petersburg: The Ballet Master Alexis Bogdanov and Others', unpublished paper presented at the International Symposium of Russian Ballet, Harriman Institute, New York, 2007.

85. M. A. S. Burgess, 'The Early Theatre', in *An Introduction to Russian Language and Literature*, ed. Robert Auty and Dimitry Obolensky, 237–39; and Simon Morrison, *Bolshoi Confidential: Secrets of the Russian Ballet from the Rule of the Tsars to Today*, 3–7. Morrison has uncovered much detail about Maddox. He also writes that Maddox's stage career seems to have included magic shows and that he later applied his mechanical skills to clock making and automata, including music-box dancers. For his benefactress Catherine the Great he designed an elaborate clock with figurines allegorizing her achievements (5–6).

86. Ibid., 9–10.

87. Ibid., 18–19.

88. Ibid., 30.

89. Ibid., 31–41.

90. Frame, *School for Citizens*, 25.

91. Nicholas Riasanovsky, *Nicholas I and Official Nationality in Russia, 1825–1855*, 28–29.

92. Richard S. Wortman, *Scenarios of Power: Myth and Ceremony in Russian Monarchy*, vol. 2, 6.

93. Nicholas I apparently didn't hold a grudge: when the landowner suddenly drowned and Volkova, a victim of his family, found herself destitute, since she had also left the company, he granted her request that she be allowed back. She left the company a second time, for the love of an engineer who embezzled a large sum of money and shot himself. Nicholas again allowed her back into the Imperial Theatres, but as a teacher this time in the school (*Materialy po istorii russkogo baleta*, ed. Borisoglebskii, vol. 1, 150).

94. 'Государь очень интересовался постановкой балета *Восстание в серале*, где женщины должны были представлять различные военные эволюции. Для обучения всем приемам были присланы хорошие гвардейские

унтер-офицеры. Сначала это занимало танцовщиц, а потом надоело, и они стали лениться. Узнав об этом, государь приехал на репетицию и строго объявил театральным амазонкам: "Если они не будут заниматься как следует, то он прикажет поставить их на два часа на мороз с ружьями, в танцевальных башмачках." Надобно было видеть, с каким жаром перепуганные рекруты в юбках принялись за дело.' Fedor Burdin, 'Vospominaniia artista ob imperatore Nikolae Pavloviche' [Memories of an Artist about the Emperor Nicholas Pavlovich], *Istoricheskii vestnik*, 23 (1886), 151; quoted by Krasovskaia, *Russkii baletnyi teatr ot vosniknoveniia do serediny XIX veka*, 259.

95. *Catarina, ou la Fille du bandit* was first created by Perrot at Her Majesty's Theatre, London on 3 March 1846.

96. Petipa, *Russian Ballet Master*, 32–33.

97. Solomon Volkov, *St Petersburg*, 251.

98. '[Тальони командует целой армией солдат, вооруженных] […] белым оружием полных плеч и кругленьких ручек.' 'P. M.', 'Bol'shoi teatr', *Severnaia pchela*, 9 October 1837, 909–11 (911).

99. Nicholas Riasanovsky, *Nicholas I and Official Nationality in Russia, 1825–1855*, 10.

100. Ibid., 8–9.

101. Richard S. Wortman draws a similar analogy between ballet and the parade ground in Alexander I's time (*Scenarios of Power: Myth and Ceremony in Russian Monarchy*, vol. 1, 210).

102. Ekaterina Sankovskaia trained at the Theatre School in Moscow and graduated into the company in 1836. As mentioned in this book's introduction, she became the city's pre-eminent ballerina, an exemplar of the Romantic style, admired for her stirring and engaging interpretations. She danced in the first Moscow staging of *La Sylphide* and was much appreciated in roles such as Giselle and Esmeralda.

103. The Soviet impulse to give political ascendency to Moscow prompted the transfer of several dancers from Leningrad to boost standards: Marina Semenova and Galina Ulanova, two of the century's greatest ballerinas, moved to Moscow in 1930 and 1944 respectively, as did the choreographer Iurii Grigorovich in 1964.

104. Riasanovsky, *Nicholas I and Official Nationality in Russia, 1825–1855*, 1–3.

105. Custine, *Lettres de Russie*, 116–17.

106. Frame, *The St Petersburg Imperial Theatres*, 19.

107. 'Достаточно было, чтобы царь о ком-нибудь из последних обмолвился добрым словом, и дальнейшая карьера могла считаться обеспеченной. Не уд ивительно, что ловкий, угодливый француз Петипа всегда заглядывал в глаза членам императорского дома, зорко следя за впечатлением, производимым его балетами.' Vazem, *Zapiksi baleriny Sankt-Peterburgskogo Bol'shogo teatra*, 190.

108. 'Для нас сделал так много добра, любил нас и относился к нам, как к своим детям.' Timofei Stukolkin, 'Vospominaniia artista Imperatorskikh teatrov', in

Artist, 46 (February 1895), 119. See also translated version in Wiley, *A Century of Russian Ballet*, 123.

109. *The Diaries of Marius Petipa*: entries for 23 April 1903, 14; 21 October 1904, 56; 20 October 1904, 56; and 2 February 1904, 44.
110. Frame, *The St Petersburg Imperial Theatres*, 33.
111. Petipa, *Russian Ballet Master*, xv.
112. Benefit performances were a standard component of an artist's contract, entitling him or her to at least part of the box-office takings for one or more performances in a year. Tamara Karsavina in *Theatre Street* tells how her father pawned the emerald ring he received at his farewell benefit (38).

CHAPTER 2

1. 'Después de haber recogido abundante cosecha de aplausos en Sevilla, han marchado a Cádiz la aérea Guy-Stephan y el señor Petipa, donde llegaron el 3 del actual, y el día 5 debían hacer su primera salida en el teatro principal de esta ciudad, donde indudablemente les espera el mismo triunfo que han obtenido en Sevilla.' 'Boletin de provincias', *El Espectador*, 12 May 1846; quoted by Laura Hormigón, *Marius Petipa en España 1844–1847*, 286–87.
2. Mikhail Ivanov, 'Marius Ivanovich Petipa', *Novoe vremia*, 12 July 1910, 2; reprinted and translated in Roland John Wiley, *A Century of Russian Ballet*, 350–56. RGIA, *fond 497, op. 5, ed. khr.* 2467 (all the passport permissions). Ekaterina Vazem, *Zapiski balleriny*, 66. Vera Petipa, *Moia sem'ia*, l. 1–33.
3. The passport is in the Archives départementales de la Gironde. Passeport de Marius Petipa, 4 M 724/213. It can be viewed online at http://gael.gironde.fr. It is also reproduced in Hormigón, *Marius Petipa en España 1844–1847*, 17.

    Details of average male height in France come from Natalie Morel Borotra, 'Marius Petipa *second danseur* au Grand-Théâtre de Bordeaux', in 'De la France à la Russie, Marius Petipa', ed. Pascale Melani, 93–112 (p. 93).
4. Kshesinskaia [Kschessinska], *Dancing in Petersburg*, 45.
5. Petipa, *Russian Ballet Master*, 91.
6. 'You should go for a stroll.'
7. Actually, the sum recorded in the directorate files is 250 roubles: RGIA, *fond 497, op 5, ed. khr.* 2467, l. 25.
8. Petipa, *Russian Ballet Master*, 24–25.
9. The beginning of the contract, dated May 1847, reads: 'Я, нижеподписавшийся Марий Петипа, заключил сей контракт с дирекцией императорских театров на нижеследующих условиях:

    '1) Контракт сей приемлет силу и действие с 24 мая 1847 года и продлится впредь до 24 мая 1848 года с условием возобновить оный контракт еще на 2 года буде пожелает того дирекция.

'2) В продолжение сего времени обязуюсь исполнять должность в качестве первого танцора и мимика.' RGIA, *fond* 497, *op.* 1, *ed. khr.* 11289, *l.* 61–62. Reprinted in *Marius Petipa. Materialy, vospominaniia, stat'i*, ed. A. Nekhendzi, 113–14.

The contract gives the salary only in francs, not roubles.

10. The information about Petipa's fluctuating age comes from Sergei Konaev who consulted various archives in St Petersburg. See his commentary to *Marius Petipa. 'Memuary' i dokumenty*, 13–14. The centenary tributes to Petipa (already mentioned in Overture) are: Denis Leshkov, *Marius Petipa (1822–1910): K stoletiiu ego rozhdeniia*; I. Ivanov and K. Ivanov, *M. I. Petipa*; and (published in 1924), M. Iakovlev, *Baletmeister Marius Petipa*.

11. See Hormigón, *Marius Petipa en España*, 150.

12. Petipa, *Russian Ballet Master*, 8.

About Jean Petipa and the various members of his family see Natalia Roslavleva, 'Sem'ia Petipa v Evrope', in *Marius Petipa. Materialy, vospominaniia, stat'i*, ed. A. Nekhendzi et al., 335–47; M. A. Il'icheva, 'Jean Petipa', in *Baletmeister Marius Petipa*, ed. Ol'ga Fedorchenko, 274–87; Hormigón, whose exhaustive sifting through French and Spanish archives and newspapers for *Marius Petipa en España* also illuminates hitherto unknown details of Marius Petipa's early career; and Lillian Moore, 'The Petipa Family in Europe and America', *Dance Index*. The *Dance Index* essay is also reproduced in a collection of Moore's writings, *Echoes of American Ballet: A Collection of Seventeen Articles*, ed. Ivor Guest, 82–102, but this study uses the *Dance Index* pagination.

13. Hormigón, *Marius Petipa en España 1844–1847*, 148–49.

14. As previously noted, Taglioni only brought *The Swiss Milkmaid* to Paris in 1832, reworked and renamed *Nathalie, or the Swiss Milkmaid*. Jean, for his much earlier Brussels revival, relied on Titus's pirated version, shown in Paris in 1823. See Jean-Philippe Van Aelbrouck, *Dictionnaire des danseurs à Bruxelles de 1600 et 1830*, 253.

15. This is suggested by an unsigned account in the Lucien Petipa papers at the Bibliothèque Musée de l'Opéra de Paris, Dossiers d'Artistes.

16. Ivor Guest, *The Romantic Ballet in Paris*, 297 and 299.

17. 'Petipa est toujours ce mime intelligent et passionné, ce danseur hardi et souple qui a contribué pour une large part au succès de la plupart des ballets modernes.' 'Feuilleton de la presse', *La Presse*, 1 December 1845, 1.

18. 'Petipa est partout élégant, gracieux, et distingué.' 'Théâtres de Paris', *Le Journal des théâtres*, 17 February 1847, 1.

19. '[Donc, M. Petipa, s'étant mis à la première place dès son apparition à l'Opéra, fut longtemps et] sans partage le héros et le prince aimé de tous les ballets de [L'Académie Impériale de la danse].' Théodore Massiac, 'Petipa', *Gil Blas*, 28 July 1896, 3.

20. 'Petipa, par l'expression et la chaleur de sa pantomime, par la vigueur de sa danse, s'est montré digne d'un tel voisinage; bien que la mode ne soit guère favorable aux danseurs, ils s'est fait applaudir à plusieurs reprises.' 'Représentation au bénéfice de Mlle Taglioni', *La Presse*, 1 July 1844, 1.

21. Gautier, *La Presse*, 25 July 1843, in *Gautier on Dance*, ed. and trans. Ivor Guest 112–21 (119).

22. *Le Petit Journal*, 31 July 1863, 2.

23. Gautier, *Le Moniteur universel*, 19 July 1858 (reprinted in *Théâtre*, 2nd ed., 376–81), in *Gautier on Dance*, ed. and trans. Ivor Guest, 281–87 (286).

24. 'Inoffensif, tutoyant tout le monde, [il n'a ni les célèbres colères de l'excellent père Coralli, ni la mimique de Mazilier, ni l'imagination de Perrot, ni la fantaisie de Saint-Léon].' Albert Vizentini, *Derrière la toile (foyers, coulisses, et comédiens): Physiologies des théâtres parisiens* [Behind the Scenes (Foyers, Backstage, and Actors): About Parisian Theatres] (Achille Faure: Paris, 1868), 28.

25. 'Petit Journal de la semaine' [Little Chronicle of the Week], *L'Europe artiste*, 20 December 1868, 3.

26. Ivor Guest, *The Ballet of the Second Empire*, 227. Jean-Philippe Van Aelbrouck identifies Lucien's wife as Angélique Brard (*Dictionnaire des Danseurs à Bruxelles de 1600 à 1830*, 197). However, she is either Hélène or Eloïse in the documents at the Bibliothèque-Musée Opéra de Paris (Dossiers d'Artistes, 'Lucien Petipa').

27. Jacques Isnardon, *Le Théâtre de la Monnaie depuis sa fondation jusqu'à nos jours*, 588.

28. 'Courrier des théâtres' [Theatre Bulletin], *Gil Blas*, 17 August 1881, 4; 'Saison theatrale', *Gil Blas*, 9 August 1888, 3.

29. Vera Petipa, *Moia sem'ia, l.* 2.

30. 'Courrier des spectacles' [Theatre Bulletin], *Le Gaulois*, 8 July 1898, 5.

31. Lillian Moore, 'The Petipa Family in Europe and America', *Dance Index*, 76; Petipa, *Russian Ballet Master*, 10 and 12, n. 3. Natalia Roslavleva first reported Slonimskii's findings in *Le Coureur des spectacles* (26 and 27 October 1842) about the benefit for Lucinde Paradol. See Roslavleva, 'Sem'ia Petipa v Evrope', in *Marius Petipa. Materialy, vospominaniia, stat'i*, ed. Nekhendzi, 335–47 (345). Sergei Konaev provides further details in his edition of Petipa's memoirs, *Marius Petipa. 'Memuary' i dokumenty*, 40.

32. Van Aelbrouck, *Dictionnaire des danseurs à Bruxelles*, 164. Lillian Moore's research files at the New York Public Library of the Performing Arts show that a French dancer, Anna (?) Lecomte, accompanied by her husband the singer Jean Lecomte, was employed by the Imperial Theatres 1836-1837 (*ZBD-157, box 3, folder 123).

33. Moore's 'The Petipa Family in Europe and America', *Dance Index*, 72–84, has also been an important source for the New York season, as has her extended editorial note in Petipa, *Russian Ballet Master*, 11–12, n. 1.

My thanks again to Laura Quinton for unearthing much additional detail about the season.

34. I am indebted to Lynn Garafola for discovering the certificate of arrival for Jean Petipa (Boulogne-London) at www.ancestry.com. For the voyage to New York, arriving on 21 September 1839, Lecomte's name appears in the British Queen's passenger list, but not Jean Petipa's. (See the National Archive microfilm online at https://archive.org/details/passengerlistsof0040unix.) Perhaps his name is one of those made illegible by damage to the paper; or maybe the surviving list is incomplete. Either way, he certainly came to New York, as attested by the advertising and at least one review.

35. George Odell, *Annals of the New York Stage*, vol. 4 (1834–1843), 336.

36. For example, the *Boston Recorder*, 27 September 1839, 155; the *New York Mirror*, 28 September 1839, 111; and *The Albion*, 28 September 1839, 311.

37. For example, see *Spirit of the Times*, 28 September 1839, 360; *The Albion*, 28 September 1839, 311; and *The Corsair*, 5 October 1839, 475.

38. Odell, *Annals of the New York Stage*, vol. 4 (1834–1843), 338. Jean Coralli, from a Bolognese family, studied at the school of the Paris Opera and graduated into the company in 1801. He created works in the major cities of Europe and in 1825 was appointed ballet master at the Théâtre de la Porte-Saint-Martin, Paris's leading lyric theatre after the Paris Opera. In 1831 he took on the same function at the Paris Opera where in 1841 he and Jules Perrot choreographed *Giselle*. *La Tarentule* was created on 24 June 1839.

39. 'Things Theatrical', *Spirit of the Times*, 2 November 1839, 420.

40. Jean-Philippe Van Aelbrouck, *Dictionnaire des danseurs*, 198 and 253; Jean-Philippe Van Aelbrouck, 'Marius Petipa, une enfance bruxelloise' [Marius Petipa, a Brussels childhood], in 'De la France à la Russie, Marius Petipa', ed. Pascale Melani, 41–81 (47, 65, 76, and 81). Jean Petipa seems to have created his own version, based on the play by Edmond Rochefort, which was in turn inspired by Charles de Pougens's novel.

41. The playbill for 9 November 1839 in the Harvard Theatre Collection is not reproduced in the original *Dance Index* publication of Lillian Moore, 'The Petipa Family in Europe and America', but in its republication in Moore, *Echoes of American Ballet: A Collection of Seventeen Articles*, 82.

42. *New York Evangelist*, 23 November 1839, 181; *Spirit of the Times*, 23 November 1839, 12.

43. Odell, *Annals of the New York Stage*, vol. 4 (1834–1843), 366; Moore, 'The Petipa Family in Europe and America', 77–78.

44. Van Aelbrouck, *Dictionnaire des danseurs à Bruxelles*, 207.

45. Ivor Guest, *Jules Perrot: Master of the Romantic Ballet*, 356.

46. *Morning Herald*, 23 November 1839, 3. Previous issues of this newspaper provide a daily record of the company's activities.

47. Petipa, *Russian Ballet Master*, 9–10.

48. Moore, 'The Petipa Family in Europe and America', 78.

49. Sergei Konaev's annotation in *Marius Petipa. 'Memuary' i dokumenty*, 38–39.

50. Nantes Archives, Documents des dossiers d'exploitation théâtrale, 2R611 and 2R612.

51. Hormigón, *Marius Petipa en España 1844–1847*, 363–64. Étienne-Hughes Laurençon's career in Brussels was cut short by his arrest and imprisonment on six counts of theft: more details will be provided in chapter 4. See also Lillian Moore, 'The Petipa Family in Europe and America', 75, and Jean-Philippe Van Aelbrouck, *Dictionnaire des danseurs à Bruxelles*, 160–62.

52. Petipa, *Russian Ballet Master*, 8.

53. 'Grand-Théâtre—Aujourd'hui jeudi, 16 juillet 1840 à 6 heures. 1. *Don Juan d'Autriche*, comédie en 5 actes, par M. Casimir Delavigne; 2. *L'Étourdi, ou l'Intrigue amoureuse*, ballet en 2 tableaux, par M. Marius Petipa'. *Le Breton*, 16 July 1840, 4; reproduced in *Marius Petipa. 'Memuary' i dokumenty*, annotated by Sergei Konaev, 12 and 34. The list of dances created by Petipa also come from Konaev's findings in the same publication, 34.

54. Further references to Petipa as a dancer include: 'Opéra en cinq actes *Les Huguenots* […] danses de M. Pizzarello […] au troisième acte: Pas de six exécuté par MM. Pizzarello, Marius Petipa, Duchâteau jeune, Mlles Armande, Thérèse Ferdinand, et Giraudier; au cinquième acte: Menuet, exécuté par MM. Pizzarello, Marius Petipa, Duchâteau jeune, Mlles Armande, Thérèse Ferdinand, et Giraudier'. *Le Breton*, 14 January 1840, 3. Also, '*La Tyrolienne*, composée par M. Constant Telle et exécutée par MM. Marius Petipa, Constant Telle, Mlles Armande, et Thérèse Ferdinand'. *Le Breton*, 10 October 1840, 3. Konaev has also found other references which he lists in *Marius Petipa. 'Memuary' i dokumenty*, 36–39.

55. Ibid., 34–35.

56. Petipa, *Russian Ballet Master*, 8–9.

57. Konaev annotation in *Marius Petipa. 'Memuary' i dokumenty*, 36–37.

58. Petipa, *Russian Ballet Master*, 11.

59. Natalie Morel Borotra, 'Marius Petipa, *second danseur* au Grand-Théâtre de Bordeaux', in 'De la France à la Russie, Marius Petipa', ed. Pascale Melani, 105.

60. Difficult to translate: an approximation might be *A Countryside* (lit. *Straw*) *Ballet, or There Is Only a Step from Misery to Happiness*.

61. Jean Latreyte, *Le Grand Théâtre de Bordeaux: Des scènes dans la pierre*, 97–100; Jacques d'Welles, *Le Grand Théâtre de Bordeaux: Naissance et vie d'un chef-d'oeuvre*, 63–64.

62. http://www.archives.nantes.fr/PAGES/DOSSIERS_DOCS/expo_virtuelle_theatre/troupe.html.

63. Petipa, *Russian Ballet Master*, 10–11.

64. 'Grand-Théâtre', *Mémorial bordelais*, 18 May 1843. 'Petipa [qui a été alternativement applaudi et sifflé] n'obtiendra pas les succès sur lesquels on a dit

qu'il comptait.' 'Rapport du 14 mai 1843', *Théâtres. Direction Devéria. 1842–1848*, Bordeaux Municipal Archives, 1710R14. Quotes from Natalie Morel Borotra, 'Marius Petipa, *second danseur* au Grand-Théâtre de Bordeaux', in 'De la France à la Russie, Marius Petipa', ed. Pascale Melani, 96–97.

65. 'De la jeunesse, un joli physique, de la légèreté et une bonne école, mais un peu de raideur et d'inexpérience, tel est l'ensemble des qualités et des défauts qu'il nous a montré […] le travail lui fera acquérir ce qui lui manque.' 'Semaine dramatique [The Theatre Week]. Grand-Théâtre', *La Sylphide*, 18 May 1843 quoted in ibid., 97.

66. 'M. Petipas [*sic*] est un tout jeune danseur qui montre déjà d'excellentes dispositions; sa danse est un peu molle, il est vrai, mais sa tenue est bonne; il mime et pose bien.' 'Feuilleton. Chronique théâtrale', *L'Indicateur*, 21 May 1843, quoted in ibid., 97.

67. Sergei Konaev in *Marius Petipa. 'Memuary' i dokumenty*, 41; Natalie Morel Borotra, 'Marius Petipa *second danseur* au Grand-Théâtre de Bordeaux', in 'De la France à la Russie, Marius Petipa', ed. Pascale Melani, 96. The quote about Petipa notating *Giselle* comes from Pierre Lacotte, '*Giselle*: le style romantique', in *L'Avant-scène Ballet/ Danse*, 1. 1980, 25.

68. François-Ferdinand Décombe, called 'Albert' (1787–1865), a leading dancer at the Paris Opera, appeared on many European stages and choreographed a number of ballets, including *The Beautiful Maid of Ghent* (La Jolie Fille de Gand).

69. X. Gt., 'Théâtres', *L'Homme Gris*, 27 May 1843; 'Depuis que M. Marius Petipas [*sic*] a fait annoncer qu'il prendrait un emploi plus modeste que celui auquel il semblait d'abord prétendre, son horizon, assez noir, s'est légèrement éclairci.' Duboul, 'Feuilleton du Mémorial bordelais', *Mémorial bordelais*, 4 June 1843, quoted in Natalie Morel Borotra, 'Marius Petipa *second danseur* au Grand-Théâtre de Bordeaux', in 'De la France à la Russie, Marius Petipa', ed. Pascale Melani, 98.

70. 'Plus de Petipa—à aucun prix'. No. 2277, *Théâtres, Direction Devéria. 1842–1848*, Bordeaux Municipal Archives, 1710R14, quoted in ibid., 99–100.

71. Report of 8 June 1843, *Théâtres, Direction Devéria. 1842–1848*, Bordeaux Municipal Archives, 1710R14, quoted in ibid., 99.

72. '[J'éprouve le besoin de dessiner ma position de manière] à rassurer ceux qui pourraient me tenir rigueur en me croyant la prétention de danser le premier emploi, tandis que je me borne à remplir celui de deuxième danseur.' 'Chronique théâtrale', *Mémorial bordelais*, 11 June 1843, reproduced in ibid., 100.

73. Ibid., 94, 101–3, and 106.

74. 'Il y a eu, dans son execution, des progrès que le public a su apprécier.' 'X. Gt.', 'Théâtres', *L'Homme gris*, 16 March 1844 (supplement), quoted in ibid., 104.

75. Ibid., 108; 'M. Marius Petipa se pose tous les jours avec plus d'avantage [*sic*] dans la faveur du public.' 'Semaine dramatique. Grand-Théâtre', *La Sylphide*, 14 March 1844, quoted in ibid., 108–9.

76. The list of roles and ballets comes Laura Hormigón, *Marius Petipa en España 1844–1847*, 307, n. 15, and Natalie Morel Borotra, 'Marius Petipa *second danseur* au Grand-Théâtre de Bordeaux', in 'De la France à la Russie, Marius Petipa', ed. Pascale Melani, 108.

77. Ibid., 109.

78. 'M. Petipa est bien vu et le mérite.' 'Semaine dramatique. Grand-Théâtre', *La Sylphide*, 15–16 June 1844, quoted in ibid., 111.

79. The ballets listed in the memoirs are: *The Beautiful Girl from Bordeaux* (La Jolie Bordelaise); *The Grape Harvest* (Les Vendanges); *The Love Intrigue* (L'Intrigue amoureuse); and *The Language of Flowers* (Le Langage des fleurs). See Marius Petipa, *Russian Ballet* Master, 11. *The Beautiful Girl from Bordeaux* appears to be the same ballet as *Grisette de Bordeaux*, which is recorded but not attributed to Petipa (Hormigón, *Marius Petipa en España*, 308, n. 16).

80. Natalie Morel Borotra, 'Marius Petipa, *second danseur* au Grand-Théâtre de Bordeaux', in 'De la France à la Russie, Marius Petipa', ed. Pascale Melani, gives the date of Devéria's bankruptcy as 13 May (111); Arnaud Detcheverry, *Histoires des théâtres de Bordeaux depuis leur origine dans cette ville jusqu'à nos jours*, says 13 June (238).

81. See note 3 of this chapter for the archival reference for the passport. The Teatro del Circo was the place for the best opera and French ballet in Madrid up to 1850, when the Teatro Real (Royal Theatre) was opened. Thereafter the Teatro del Circo was mostly dedicated to the *zarzuela*.
    Much of the information about Petipa in Spain comes from Laura Hormigón, *Marius Petipa en España*.

82. *Le Figaro: Journal littéraire et d'arts*, 14 May 1840, 2. Guy-Stéphan returned several times to Bordeaux's Grand-Théâtre; for example, she performed the mime role of Fenella in *La Muette de Portici* in mid-September 1842 (*La Tribune dramatique*, 25 September 1842, 108).

83. '[El nuevo bailarín que ya anunciamos, el Sr. Mario Petipa, que] fue recibido con general aplauso. […] Su escuela de baile, así como la mímica, son muy buenas.' 'Coreo de Madrid. Circo', *El Heraldo*. Parte Literaria, 30 June 1844; reproduced in Hormigón, *Marius Petipa en España*, 234.

84. The Spanish modifies the title of *The Beautiful Maid of Ghent* to *Beautiful Beatrix or the Dream*.

85. 'Su escuela es moderna, reúne buen gusto y bastante ejecución'. 'Seccion literaria', *El Clamor Publico*, 10 September 1844, reproduced in Hormigón, *Marius Petipa en España*, 237; 'El primero en particular, nos hizo sentir to corto de la parte que desempeñaba.' 'Boletin de Madrid', *El Globo*, 20 November 1844, reproduced in ibid., 240; '[El primero sobre todo] espresó con sumo acierto y comprendió con intelligencia el papel del conde Federico.' 'Gacetilla de la capital', *El Heraldo*, 30 January 1845, reproduced in ibid., 242.

86. 'Quedando tan solo para el año próximo la inimitable Guy-Stephan y el señor Petipá.' 'Boletin de Madrid', *El Globo*, 8 March 1845; reproduced in ibid., 244.

87. Ibid., 18, 108–9. Frédéric Montessu (1823–1889) later found employment in Moscow as a dancer and teacher, as will be seen.

88. 'El señor Petipa, en el baile heroico, no es más regular, pero en los bailes caracteristicos ó de sala es sobresaliente [...] su acción en la fábula, es natural y verdadera.' 'Semanario Pintoresco Español', *Crónica de Madrid*, 18 May 1845, reproduced in ibid., 245–46 (246).

89. 'Obtendrán sin duda no menores aplausos que otras veces la graciosa y aérea Guy-Stephan y el infatigable e inteligente Petipa.' 'Varidedades. Crónica de Madrid', *El Heraldo*, 12 August 1846, quote in ibid., 263.

90. Ibid., 108–9.

91. Ibid., 275–94; Petipa, *Russian Ballet Master*, 14–15.

92. Perrot created the one-act *Aurore* in London in 1843, to music by Pugni, with Adèle Dumilâtre as Dawn. Dumilâtre was about to perform the central pas de deux with Perrot, when suddenly, as Perrot was performing an introductory sequence, a sound like the crack of a whip was heard. Perrot stopped in his tracks, clutched his leg in agony and hopped towards the wings, unable to continue (Guest, *Jules Perrot, 92-93, 353*).

93. Hormigón, *Marius Petipa en España*, 199–206 and 416. The ballets listed by Petipa are: *The Pearl of Seville; The Adventure of the Daughter of Madrid; The Flower of Granada; The Departure for the Bullfight*. See Petipa, *Russian Ballet Master*, 16.

94. Hormigón, *Marius Petipa en España*, 149–50 and 244.

95. Ibid., 150.

96. 'El Sr. Petipa comprendió perfectamente el carácter del paso que desempeñaba, por lo que es inútil decir que estuvo inimitable.' 'Revista Teatral', *El Cinife*, 18 September 1845, reproduced in Hormigón, *Marius Petipa en España*, 251.

97. Petipa, *Russian Ballet Master*, 16–17.

98. 'El público, al llegar al *beso* aplaudió a la besada, al besador, y también a la autoridad que permitió el inocente y disputado beso.' 'Folletin. Crónica de Madrid. Circo.', *El Globo*, 26 September 1845; reproduced in Hormigón, *Marius Petipa en España*, 251–52 (252).

99. For example, 'Crónica des Teatros', *El Clamor Publico*, 7 March 1846, reproduced in ibid., 259–60 (259).

100. 'Variedas. Crónica de San Sebastian', *El Heraldo*, 26 August 1846, reproduced in ibid., 263; 'Gacetilla de la Capital', *El Heraldo*, 11 September 1846, reproduced in ibid., 264; 'Revista de Madrid', *La Epoca*, 6 September 1864, reproduced in ibid., 272.

101. Petipa, *Russian Ballet Master*, 17–18.

102. Ibid., 19.

103. Ibid., 20.

104. Konaev, who has tried to find precise details about the count's identity, has located a comte Jean Alexis de Cadoine de Gabriac who was a French diplomat in Frankfurt, not Copenhagen, in 1844 (*Marius Petipa. 'Memuary' i dokumenty*, 129. He gives two different dates for *Der Bayerische Eilbote*: 4 October 1844 (11) and 6 October 1844 (127).

105. Hormigón, *Marius Petipa en España*, 21–27; the findings in this book have since been updated by Hormigón, 'La apasionante fuga de España de Marius Petipa. Una cuestion de Estado' [Marius Petipa's Passionate Flight from Spain. A Matter of State], in *Revista ADE-Teatro*, 169, Madrid, January–March 2018, 8–19. My knowledge of Hormigón's latest research, however, is through Sergei Konaev's commentary for *Marius Petipa. 'Memuary' i dokumenty*, to which he has added his own findings (11–13 and 125–29). Carmen's full name was originally recorded in Hormigón's *Marius Petipa en España* as Maria del Carmen.

106. 'Je croyais que M. Petitpas [*sic*] en voulait à la marquise de Villagarcia elle-même et non à sa fille. Mais il paraît que c'est un homme sans préjugés qui mange le fruit mûr d'abord et le vert après.' Prosper Mérimée, *Lettres de Prosper Mérimée à la comtesse de Montijo*, vol. 1, 202–3. Also quoted by Hormigón, *Marius Petipa en España*, 22.

107. 'La desaparición de una joven de las mas elegantes de la corte […] haber coincidido con la desaparición repentina de alguna de las notabilidades que actualmente llamaban la atención en uno de los principales teatros de Madrid.' 'Gacetilla de la capital', *El Heraldo*, 12 January 1847, and 'Gacetilla de Madrid', *El Tiempo*, 13 January 1847; reproduced in Hormigón, *Marius Petipa en España*, 265–66.

108. 'Si la familia de esta alucinada cuanto interesante joven, pretende seguir la pista del raptor, no debe descuidarse […] la cualidad que mas le distingue es una ligereza de pies casi fabulosa.' *La Opinion*, 13 January 1847, reproduced in Hormigón, *Marius Petipa en España*, 266.

109. 'Revista de Madrid', *El Español*, 13 January 1847, and *La Opinion*, 17 January 1847, reproduced in Hormigón, *Marius Petipa en España*, 266–67 (267) and 268–69 (268).

110. 'El más notable acontecimiento doméstico que ocupa en el día á la malas lenguas es la fuga del bailarín Petipá con la hija de la marquesa de V. Dicen que esta romancesca señorita desapareció de su casa á la hora de comer, dejando una carta para su mamá, en la que exponía los motivos que la habían obligado á tomar una determinación tan excéntrica, siendo el de más peso el amor vehementísimo que profesaba al aéro y vaporoso amante con quien se ha fugado.' Juan Valera, *Correspondencia, 1847–1857*, vol. 1, 13–14; also quoted by Hormingnón, *Marius Petipa en España*, 24–25.

111. 'Los amantes fugitivos han sido descubiertos y sorprendidos.' *La Opinion*, 17 January 1847, reproduced in Hormigón, *Marius Petipa en España*, 268–69 (269).

112. 'Este acto de seducción amorosa es un *petit-pas* (pequeño paso) hacia un *matrimonio de conciencia.*' 'Crónica de la capital', *El Clamor Publico*, 13 January 1847, reproduced in Hormigón, *Marius Petipa en España*, 267–68.

113. 'Les acteurs français ont, à l'étranger, des succès de plus d'un genre; car voici qu'on nous annonce de Madrid le mariage de M. Marius Petipa, premier sujet du théâtre d'El Circo, et frère de Lucien Petipa, notre danseur français, avec Mlle Carmen de Medina, marquise de Villa-Garcia.' 'Feuilleton de la presse', *La Presse*, 9 February 1847, 2.

114. 'Mademoiselle Carmen Mendoza y Castro, fille du marquis de Villagarcia, a quitté Madrid le 10 de ce mois sans consentement de ses parents [sic] pour suivre en France le Sr. Petipas [sic], danseur. J'ai recours à l'obligeance de V[otre] E[xcellence] pour le prier de vouloir bien donner les ordres nécessaires pour que la demoiselle Mendoza y Castro soit recherchée avec soin et déposée dans un lieu convenable jusqu'à ce que les parents puissent envoyer la reprendre.

'D'après les renseignements qui me sont parvenus le Sr. Petipas voyage sous un nom supposé et a dû quitter Bayonne le 14 de ce mois pour se rendre à Paris, où il aurait été vu le 23 au débarcadère du chemin de fer de Rouen.' The original letter has not been found, only a copy in the Archivo Historico Nacional (Spain), 7 135, which is reproduced by Sergei Konaev, 'Le Señor Petipa voyage sous un nom supposé' [Señor Petipa is travelling under a false name], in 'De La France à la Russie, Marius Petipa', ed. Pascale Melani, 113–22 (118).

115. Konaev in his introduction to *Marius Petipa. 'Memuary' i dokumenty* (12–13), using information from Hormigón, '*La apasionante fuga de España de Marius Petipa. Una cuestion de Estado'.*

In 1855 Carmen married Raoul Grandemont, equerry to Napoleon III, in Paris (Hormigón, *Marius Petipa en España*, 26).

116. Petipa, *Russian Ballet Master*, 22. See Susan Au, 'Elssler Sisters', in the *International Encyclopedia of Dance*, ed. Selma Jeanne Cohen, vol. 2, 504.

117. 'Svoǐ, *Birzhevye vedomosti*, 8 December 1896, no. 339, 3; Pleshcheev, *Nash balet*, 183. Iuri Slonimskii echoes the theory put forward by 'Svoǐ' in 'Marius Petipa', *Dance Index*, 100. But Nikolai Legat's account that Marius arrived in Russia before his brother Ivan (?) and 'stole' his job cannot be taken seriously. See Legat, *The Story of the Russian School*, 33–34.

118. Il'icheva, *Neizvestnyi Petipa*, 81.

CHAPTER 3

1. 'Петипа сын [...] дебютировал в *Пахите* и танцевал с Андреяновой "Pas de folie", в котором выказал много искусства.' A. Vol'f, *Khronika peterburgskikh teatrov s kontsa 1826 do nachala 1881*, Part 1, 128.

2. About the ballet, see, for instance, Cyril W. Beaumont, *The Complete Book of Ballets*, 222–31, and Théophile Gautier, 'Opéra: Paquita', *La Presse*, 6 April 1846, in *Gautier on Dance*, 166–70.

3. Petipa claims that 'at the director's request, I started staging the ballet *Paquita*'. *Russian Ballet Master*, 27.

Coralli's ballet *La Péri*, to a scenario by Gautier, had almost as big a success as *Giselle* when it was premiered in Paris in 1843. Lucien Petipa danced the role of Ahmet who falls in love with a *péri* (oriental fairy) and Carlotta Grisi was the *péri*. The ballet's first-act pas de deux, full of spectacular aerial supports and a perilous leap by Grisi from the back of the stage into Lucien's arms, made an unforgettable impression both in Paris and in London where it was shown a few months later.

4. Marina Il'icheva, *Neizvestnyi Petipa*, 78–80.

5. *Russian Ballet Master: The Memoirs of Marius Petipa*, 27. 'Он танцевал в "pas de folie" и *el jaleo*, следственно, в двух характерных танцах. Легкость и сила в нем удивительные, но мы подождем будущих его дебютов в танцах благородного и серьезного рода и тогда отдадим о нем подробный отчет; [теперь же мы видели, что это] прекраснейшее приобретение для нашей труппы.' R[afael] Z[otov], 'Fel'eton. Teatral'naia khronika', *Severnaia pchela*, 6 October 1847, no. 225, 897–98 (898).

6. M. A. Il'icheva, 'Jean Petipa', in *Baletmeister Marius Petipa*, ed. Fedorchenko, 274–87 (285).

7. *Marius Petipa. 'Memuary' i dokumenty*, ed. Sergei Konaev, 145. The three-year contract, as opposed to Marius's one-year contract, is perhaps an indication of Jean's distinguished reputation.

8. Petipa's memoirs incorrectly assert that the ballet was staged for his own benefit performance (*Russian Ballet Master*, 28).

9. M. A. Il'icheva, 'Jean Petipa', in *Baletmeister Marius Petipa*, ed. Fedorchenko, 274–87 (286).

10. '[Бенефис...] Был истинным торжеством [...] Г-жа Андреянова была более чем превосходна [...] Можно почти побиться об заклад, что в "Большой опере" в Париже она [*Сатанилла*] никогда не была играна с таким великолепием и фантастическим очарованием. [...]

'Г-н Петипа-сын с одушевлением исполняет роль графа Фабио. В этом артисте есть одно неоценимое достоинство: он старается передавать балетные характеры просто и естественно [...] Лицо Петипа выразительно, и он мимикой дополняет то, что отвергает в пластике.

'Роль Ортензиуса, наставника графа, выполняет г-н Петипа-отец. В нем виден ловкий и опытный артист, комик благородный, не позволяющий себе ничего лишнего на потеху невежества, но умеющий быть забавным без фарса, одной тонкой иронией и простодушием.' F[edor] Koni, *Panteon*, 3, 1848; reprinted in *Russkaia baletnaia kritika kontsa XVIII–pervoi poloviny XIX veka*, ed. Oleg Petrov, 233–39 (233 and 236).

11. 'Эта прелестная танцовщица вполне утешает за отсутствие Тальони.' R[afail] Z[otov], 'Zhizel', ili Vilisy', *Severnaia pchela*, 29 December 1842, 1161–62 (1162); also reprinted, *Russkaia Baletnaia kritika kontsa XVIII–pervoi poloviny XIX veka*, ed. Petrov, 211–15 (214).

12. 'Есть прелестные танцовщицы, искусные танцоры, удивительный кордебалет, есть ежедневно распускающийся рассадник самых редких дарований: нет только в публике охоты смотреть на них. Единственным средством к возбуждению этой охоты было бы, может быть, сочинение новых, занимательных балетов; но для этого нужен новый Дидло, новый Прометей, новый гениальный хореограф, а теперь такого, кажется, нет во всей Европе.' R[afail] Z[otov], 'Fel'eton. Teatral'naia xronika'. *Severnaia pchela*, 27 January 1847, 81–82 (81); also reprinted in *Russkaia Baletnaia kritika kontsa XVIII–pervoi poloviny XIX veka*, ed. Petrov, 231–33 (233).

13. 'Вообще 1847 год можно отметить в театральной хронике годом возрождения балета, что доказал новый успех двух балетов: *Пахиты* и *Сатаниллы* и общим стремлением публики к этому роду представления.' *Literaturnaia gazeta*, 9 October 1847, 650–51, and 8 April 1848, 217; reprinted in ibid., 240.

14. August Bournonville, *My Theatre Life*, 47; also quoted by Ivor Guest, *Jules Perrot*, 12.

15. Charles Maurice, *Courrier des Théâtres*, 16 March 1831, quoted by Guest, *Jules Perrot*, 22.

16. Ibid., 22. Perrot's salary, however, pales when compared with Taglioni's contract around the same time for 30,000 francs a year, a guaranteed benefit and *feux*.

17. *Le Ménestrel*, 2 February 1834, quoted by Guest, *Jules Perrot*, 28.

18. Ibid., 183–84.

19. Sergei Konaev annotation, *Marius Petipa. 'Memuary' i dokumenty*, 148.

20. Guest, *Jules Perrot*, 224–29. See also Vol'f, *Khronika peterburgskikh teatrov s kontsa 1826 do nachala 1881*, Part 1, 134; Pleshcheev, *Nash balet*, 184–87; and Petr Karatygin, *Zapiski*, 311–12.

21. 'Лицо Фанни Эльслер без слов передавало зрителю сокровенные тайны души и сердца, заставляло вместе с артисткой радоваться и страдать. [...] У нее не было воздушности, которую вообще трудно сохранить до 38 лет, но это искупалось силой, виртуозностью, пластичностью, идеальной грацией, чарующею красотой, полнотою ума, глубоко действовавшею на зрителя мимикой!' Pleshcheev, *Nash balet*, 189–90 (189).

22. Guest, *Jules Perrot*, 224–30.

23. Irina Boglacheva, *Artisty Sankt-Peterburgskogo imperatorskogo baleta. XIX Vek* (Saint Petersburg: Chistyi list, 2015), 31.

24. Sergei Konaev annotation, *Marius Petipa. 'Memuary i dokumenty*, 150.

25. In his final years he was painted by Degas, a stocky figure, seated (*Le Danseur Perrot, assis*) or teaching class at the Paris Opera (*La Classe de danse de M. Perrot* and *La Classe de danse, adage*).

26. Anna Natarova, 'Iz vospominanii artistki A. P. Natarovoĭ', in *Istoricheskii vestnik*, November 1903, 420–42 (431–32). Extracts of this memoir are translated in Wiley, *A Century of Russian Ballet*, 135–69.

27. Petipa wrongly claims that he played Phoebus at the first performance (*Russian Ballet Master*, 31). He was actually in Moscow at the time.

28. Guest, *Jules Perrot*, 230–32.

29. Vol'f, *Khronika peterburgskikh teatrov s kontsa 1826 do nachala 1881*, Part 1, 134; Timofei Stukolkin, 'Recollections of T. A. Stukolkin, Artist of the Imperial Theatres', in *Artist*, February 1895, 119; also translated and reprinted in Wiley, *A Century of Russian Ballet*, 108–34 (124).

30. Karatygin, *Zapiski*, 309–10.

31. 'Меня удивляла смелость Андреяновой, но в то же время мне было приятно видеть, как гроза всех артистов смиренно повиновался ее приказанию'. Avdot'ia Panaeva, *Vospominaniia*, 56.

32. Pleshcheev, *Nash balet*, 167–68.

33. Ibid., 322.

34. An account was published by S. Taneev in *Iz proshlogo Imperatorskikh teatrov 1825–1856* [From the Past of the Imperial Theatres …] (Moscow, 1886) and is reproduced in *Peterburgskii balet. Tri veka. 1801–1850*, ed. Boglacheva, 297. (Contrary to other sources Boglacheva gives the year of the incident as 1847.) In his memoirs, Petipa uses more hyperbolic language and says Andreianova was carried offstage, unconscious, by Montessu (*Russian Ballet Master*, 28). See also Pleshcheev, *Nash balet*, 174–76; and Simon Morrison, *Bolshoi Confidential*, 105–9.

35. This letter, dated Moscow, 6 December 1848, was published in the journal *Archives internationales de la danse*, no. 3, 15 July 1934, 106. Accessed online 2 February 2017 at www.mediatheque.cnd.fr.

36. See editorial note accompanying the letter in ibid.; also Pleshcheev, 176, and Petipa, *Russian Ballet Master*, 30, n. 3–4. Yrca Matthias, born in Lyons in 1829, was a pupil of Joseph Mazilier and made her Moscow debut in 1847.

37. Petipa, *Russian Ballet Master*, 30, n. 3.

38. Panaeva, *Vospominaniia*, 57.

39. Ibid., 28–29.

40. Panaeva in *Vospominaniia* (57) and Karatygin in *Zapiski* (323) identify Mlle Mila as Mila Deschamps; Irina Boglacheva calls her Marie Deschamps in *Artisty Sankt-Peterburgskogo imperatorskogo baleta*, 97. However, Lillian Moore's editorial note in Petipa, *Russian Ballet Master* (48, n. 1) says that Mlle Mila (here spelt Milla) was Laure Dordet, a soubrette and operetta star.

41. *Peterburgskii balet. Tri veka. 1851–1900*, ed. Boglacheva, 30–31 and 41; Valerii Kulakov, 'Andreianova, Elena', in *International Encylopedia of Dance*, ed. Selma Jeanne Cohen, vol. 1, 86–87; Pleshcheev, *Nash balet*, 176–77.

42. 'Все шло crescendo, [открылся абонемент, а оставшиеся от него места брались в кассе] приступом.' Vol'f, *Khronika peterburgskikh teatrov s kontsa 1826 do nachala 1881*, vol. I, 134.

43. Wiley, *A Century of Russian Ballet*, 175.

44. 'Тут видели мы не одну восхитительную танцовщицу, но и высокую актрису. Самые танцы ее [...] представили новый тип этого искусства. Мы до сих пор требовали только грациозных поз, пластических движений, лекости, быстроты, силы: тут увидели игру в танцах. Каждое движение говорило уму и сердцу; каждая минута выражала какое-нибудь чувство; каждый взгляд соответствовал ходу сюжета. Это было новое, прелестное открытие в области хореографии.' R[afail] Z[otov], 'Pchelka. Teatral'naia Khronika', *Severnaia pchela*, 1 March 1849, 181. See also the same passage translated in Wiley, *A Century of Russian Ballet*, 176.

45. The St Petersburg staging was not for Elssler's benefit as Petipa incorrectly states (*Russian Ballet Master*, 32).

46. 'Иогансон удивлял всех своими пируэтами. После своих дебютов во времена Тальони, он быстро совершенствовался и стал первым любимцем публики.' A. Vol'f, *Khronika Peterburgskikh teatrov s kontsa 1826 do nachala 1881*, Part 1, 116. See also Boglacheva, *Artisty Sankt-Peterburgskogo imperatorskogo baleta XIX vek*, 23–24; and Pleshcheev, *Nash balet*, 177–78.

47. Pleshcheev, *Nash balet*, 208.

48. *Sankt-peterburgskye vedomosti*, 17 February 1849, quoted and translated in Guest, *Jules Perrot*, 233.

49. Sergei Konaev annotation, *Marius Petipa. 'Memuary' i dokumenty*, 150.

50. Petipa claims this ballet as his own (*Russian Ballet Master*, 32). Vol'f attributes its production to Perrot (*Khronika peterburgskikh teatrov s kontsa 1826 do nachala 1881*, Part 1, 141); Pleshcheev, to Jean Petipa, with a *scène dansante* by Perrot (*Nash balet*, 193); Boglacheva, to Titus, with additions by Perrot (*Peterburgskii balet. Tri veka. 1801–1850*, ed. Boglacheva, 311); and Guest, to Jean Petipa, with two *pas* by Perrot (*Jules Perrot*, 245). About Elssler's previous performances in *Nathalie, or the Swiss Milkmaid*, see ibid., Hormigón, *Marius Petipa en España 1844–1847*, 148–49, and Guest, *Fanny Elssler*, 72 and 76.

51. 'Лида—весьма слабая и очень неудачно подогретая старина. [...] [Г–жа Эльслер играла Лиду, Перро—Фрица, он приделал даже к балету танцевальную сцену (*scène dansante*) своего изобретения, но все это не спасло балет, скудный по содержанию, [жалкий по содержанию,] жалкий по вымыслу. [Лида выдержала только два представления.]' F[edor] Koni, 'Balet v Peterburge', *Panteon i repertuar russkoi stseny*, 1850, vol. 2, no. 3, 42–43.

52. Guest, *Jules Perrot*, 245.

53. Ibid., 246–48.

54. Ibid., 251–52.

55. Simon Morrison, *Bolshoi Confidential*, 152.

56. Petipa, *Russian Ballet Master*, 91; Timofei Stukolkin, 'Recollections of T. A. Stukolkin, Artist of the Imperial Theatres', in *Artist*, February 1895, 117; also translated and reprinted in Wiley, *A Century of Russian Ballet*, 120. Pugni's

grandson would be the Russo-French avant garde painter Ivan Puni (Jean Pougny).

57. The expression *le diable à quatre* denotes a turbulent person who creates a lot of noise and upset. According to Cyril Beaumont's *Complete Book of Ballets*, 2nd ed. (London: Putnam, 1949, 215), the ballet was based on two English stage presentations, Thomas Jevon's *The Devil of a Wife* (1686) and C. Coffey's *The Devil to Pay* (1731).

58. Guest, *Jules Perrot*, 255. The date for *The Naiad and the Fisherman* comes from *Peterburgskii balet. Tri veka. 1851–1900*, ed. Boglacheva, 15, and differs from Guest (356).

59. Guest, *Jules Perrot*, 261.

60. 'Несмотря на громкую парижскую репутацию'. Pleshcheev, *Nash balet*, 217. *Vert-Vert* (Green-Green) was based on an eighteenth-century pseudo-heroic poem which told the humorous story of a devout parrot called Vert-Vert.

61. Guest, *Jules Perrot*, 261–63; *Peterburgskii balet. Tri veka. 1851–1900*, ed. Boglacheva, 24.

62. Olga Fedorchenko, 'Marius Petipa v baletakh Zhiulia Perro' [Marius Petipa in the Ballets of Jules Perrot], in *Baletmeister Marius Petipa*, ed. Fedorchenko, 267–74 (267). A later, expanded version of this study appears as 'Marius Petipa dans les ballets de Jules Perrot', in 'De la France à la Russie, Marius Petipa', ed. Melani, 135–46.

63. Fedorchenko, 'Marius Petipa dans les ballets de Jules Perrot', 139.

64. '[А второй [[балет—*Сатанилла* был поставлен]] балетмейстером Петипа, прибывшим вместе со своим сыном,] молодым, довольно ловким танцовщиком.' F[edor] Koni, 'Balet v Peterburge', *Panteon i repertuar russkogo teatra*, vol. 2, book 3, 1850; reproduced in *Russkaia baletnaia kritika kontsa XVIII–pervoi poloviny XIX veka*, ed. Petrov, 254–64 (259).

65. 'Novosti peterburgskikh teatrov' [News of the Petersburg Theatres], *Sovremennik*, 1851, vol. 25, 275; quoted in Fedorchenko, 'Marius Petipa v baletakh Zhiulia Perro', in *Baletmeister Marius Petipa*, ed. Fedorchenko, 269.

66. I. Ivanov and K. Ivanov, *Marius Ivanovich Petipa. 1822–1922. K stoletiiu dnia rozhdeniia*, 6.

67. 'Классические танцы у него выходили неважно, во всяком случае, очень некрасиво. С классикой не увязывались его ноги, лишенные подъема и с большими плоскими ступнями.' Ekaterina Vazem, *Zapiski baleriny sankt-peterburgskogo bol'shogo teatra*, 114.

68. 'Он был превосходен в характерных танцах, декоративен, увлекателен, полон темперамента и выразительности. Особенно удавались ему испанские пляски, которые он досконально изучил, когда в своих юных годах подвизался на сценах Испании.' Ibid.

69. Il'icheva, *Neizvestnye Petipa*, 196.

70. 'Венцом искусства Петипа как балетного артиста была мимика. Здесь он был положительно выше всяких похвал. Темные жгучие глаза, лицо, выражавшее целые гаммы переживаний и настроений, широкий, понятный, убедительный жест и глубочайшее проникновение ролью и характером изображаемого лица, граничащее с настоящим перевоплощением мима в его роль, ставили Петипа как "немого артиста" на высоту, которой достигали очень немногие его собратья по искусству. Его игра могла, в самом серьезном смысле слова, волновать и потрясать зрителей.' Vazem, *Zapiski baleriny*, 114.

71. Fedorchenko, 'Marius Petipa dans les ballets de Jules Perrot', in *De la France à la Russie, Marius Petipa*, ed. Melani, 139–40. Konaev gives the date of Petipa's debut as Phoebus, slightly earlier, as 27 September 1849 (*Marius Petipa. 'Memuary' i dokumentyi*, 153).

72. '[В первом представлении *Эсмеральды*, Петипа исполнял роль Феба и заслужил комплимент Эльслер, заявившей,] что это лучший Феб из всех, с которыми ей приходилось танцевать', D[enis] Leshkov, *Marius Petipa*, 10. Contrary to what Leshkov writes, Petipa did not appear in the premiere of *Esmeralda*. If Fedorochenko's sources are correct and Petipa made his debut in the role in January 1850, then Elssler would still have been in St Petersburg, before being replaced by Grisi in the autumn.

73. Fedorchenko, 'Marius Petipa dans les des ballets de Jules Perrot', in *De la France à la Russie, Marius Petipa*, ed. Melani, 141–42.

74. Ibid., 142–43.

75. The photograph is in *Marius Petipa. Materialy, vospominaniia, stat'i*, ed. Nekhendzi (without page no.).

76. Fedorchenko, 'Marius Petipa dans les ballets de Jules Perrot', in *De la France à la Russie, Marius Petipa*, ed. Melani, 143; Guest, *Jules Perrot*, 278–80.

77. 'Г-жа Суровщикова подает самые блистательные надежды как танцовщица и как мимистка [...] Природа дала ей все, что нужно, чтоб сделаться отличной танцовщицей, и мы не сомневаемся, что она исполнит свое призвание.' 'Peterburgskaia letopis' [Petersburg Chronicle], *Sankt-Peterburgskie vedomosti*, 19 February 1854, reproduced in *Peterburgskii balet. Tri veka. 1851–1900*, ed. Boglacheva, 34.

78. '*Фауст* делал постоянно полные сборы, возбуждая единодушные похвалы. [...] Он вышел победителем из трудной борьбы с этим громадным сюжетом. Кроме небольших [...] недостатков и одной немного длинной картины, весь балет составлен прекрасно, и успех его был совершенно заслуженный.' 'V. Z.', 'Balet v Peterburge. Sezon 1853–1854 goda', *Panteon*, vol. 14, book 3, 1854; re-produced *Russkaia baletnaia kritika kontsa XVIII–pervoi poloviny XIX veka*, ed. Petrov, 281–93 (287 and 291–92).

79. '[Такой характер толкования о Фаусте был в либретто того времени, но] М. И. постарался дать тип более близкий по духу к поэме Гете. И его исполнение Фауста значительно отличалось от игры других артистов. В первом акте перед

зрителем был робкий, несмелый человек, не понимающий еще всей силы того чувства, которое впервые в нем зародилось; в последующей картине (сад) это робкое чувство разрасталось в ту страстную любовь, в которой был виден один лишь земной порыв, заслоняющий платоническую идеологию любви. После этой сильной сцены игра М. И. Петипа не понижалась, а возрастала, и его страданья, раскаянья (сцена в тюрьме) вызывали чувство глубокой симпатии и сожаленья.' I. Ivanov and K. Ivanov, *M. I. Petipa*, 8.

80. 'Я помню его в ролях Фауста в балете *Перро* того же названия и лорда Вильсона–Таора в *Дочери фараона* и сама выступала с ним в *Корсаре* весной 1868г., т.е. в первый сезон моей службы. В этот вечер Петипа вообще появился на сцене в последний раз. Созданный им образ предводителя корсаров Конрада был совершенно незабываем. В каждом его движении сказывалась привычка вл аствовать и повелевать. Вместе с тем было видно огромное мастерство в п ользовании жестами, которые у него были чрезвычайно уверенными. К бессмысленному размахиванию руками, которое мне сплошь и рядом прихо дилось наблюдать у других исполнителей роли Конрада, Петипа не прибегал никогда. Его игре можно было учиться, но не рабски подражать, так как артист слишком много вкладывал в роль своего художественного "я". В галантной сцене в гроте Петипа очень увлекался. При объяснении в любви Медоре он весь содрогался и, судорожно сжимая в объятьях, шептал: "Je t'aime! … Je t'aime! …" Тогда я была совсем молодой девчонкой, и такой мимический натурализм меня немало поражал. На репетициях Петипа, показывая в качестве постановщика сцены артистам, обыкновенно играл за всех, и здесь его мимика была всегда очень выразительной.' Vazem, *Zapiski baleriny*, 114–16.

81. Nikolai (Nicolas) Legat, *The Story of the Russian School*, 37.

82. Olga Fedorchenko says 8 May 1869 in 'Marius Petipa dans les ballets de Jules Perrot', in 'De la France à la Russie, Marius Petipa', ed. Melani, 145; Irina Boglacheva, 4 May 1869 in *Peterburgskii balet. Tri veka. 1851–1900*, ed. Boglacheva, 143.

83. In Soviet productions this would become a dance for Medora's friend Gulnare and the slave trader Lanquedem.

84. S. Boglachev and Irina Boglacheva, 'Mariia Sergeevna Surovshchikova-Petipa', in *Baletmeister Marius Petipa*, ed. Fedorchenko, 287–325 (307). The same essay, which has provided much material for my book, reappears in Irina Boglacheva, *Artisty Sankt-Peterburgskogo baleta. XIX Vek*; however, the pagination used here is that of *Baletmeister Marius Petipa*.

About 'Le Petit Corsaire' see Tamara Karsavina's account in *Theatre Street*, 215–16, and Natali'ia Matveeva's performance, recorded by Aleksandr Shiriaev on film in the 1900s, available on *Zapozdavshaia prem'era: A Belated Premiere* (DVD: Kinokompaniia Miris, 2003).

85. Garafola, *The Diaries of Marius Petipa*, 81–82 (editorial information).

86. My thanks to Doug Fullington for pointing to Maria Bananina's work in tracing the origins of the 'Corsaire pas de deux'. See Babanina, Maria, 'Prima la musica, dopo la coreografia?—Prima la coreografica, dopo la musica?' [The Music First, before the Choreography?–The Choreography First, before the Music?], programme book, *Le Corsaire*, Bayerisches Staatsballet, January 2007, 31–37. See also Natalie Lecomte, 'Dans le sillage du Corsaire: de Paris (1856) à Saint-Pétersbourg' [On the Trail of *Le Corsaire*: from Paris (1856) to St Petersburg], in 'De la France à la Russie, Marius Petipa', ed. Melani, 149–61.

87. 'Obzor deistvii. S. Peterburgskikh teatrov' [A Round-Up of St Petersburg Theatres], *Severnaia pchela*, 3 May 1854, 429.

88. Théophile Gautier, 'Giselle, ou les *wilis*', *La Presse*, 5 July 1841; reprinted in *Gautier on Dance*, ed. and trans. Ivor Guest, 94–102 (101).

89. Sylvie Jacq-Mioche, 'Ombres et flamboiements du ballet romantique à Paris', in *De la France à la Russie, Marius Petipa*, ed. Melani, 32 and 36.

90. Guest, *Jules Perrot*, 273–74.

91. Ibid., 285.

92. Ibid., 282.

93. Ibid., 285–86. Perrot created the *Pas de Quatre* in London 1845 for four of the Romantic Ballet's most iconic ballerinas: Marie Taglioni, Cerrito, Grisi, Grahn.

94. '[Техническая часть, то есть собственно танцы, уже доведена ею до] замечательной степени развития.' *Sankt-Peterburgskie vedomosti*, 29 November 1855; reprinted in *Russkaia baletnaia kritika kontsa XVIII–pervoi poloviny XIX veka*, ed. Petrov, 298–302 (302).

95. Guest, *Jules Perrot*, 295.

96. Konstantin Skal'kovskii, *Balet: Ego istoriia i mesto v riadu iziashchnykh iskusstv*, 229–31.

97. Vazem, *Zapiski baleriny*, 138–40; *Materialy po istorii russkogo baleta*, ed. Borisoglebskii, vol. 1, 220–27.

98. Khudekov, *Istoriia tantsev*, vol. 4, 148 and 154.

99. Lev Ivanov, 'Moi vospominaniia' (dated 2 February 1899), published in *Sovetskii balet*, no. 32 (January–February 1987), 39–43 (42). The manuscript is in the St Petersburg State Museum of Theatrical and Musical Art (GMTMI). Parts were also published in *Peterburgskaia gazeta*, 13 December 1901, and a full translated version is in Wiley, *The Life and Ballets of Lev Ivanov*, 5–20.

100. *Materialy po istorii russkogo baleta*, ed. Borisoglebskii, vol. 1, 378.

101. Boglacheva, *Artisty sankt-peterburgskogo imperatorskogo baleta XIX vek*, 13. Marcel' served as *régisseur* from 1842 to his death in 1873.

102. Karatygin, *Zapiski*, 299–303.

103. Ibid., 304.

104. Frame, *School for Citizens*, 79–82.

105. Petipa, *Russian Ballet Master*, 46.

106. Ibid., 44–46.

107. 'А ты не хочешь туда ехать?' 'Нет, Ваше Превосходительство.' 'Ну, так ты поедешь туда, здесь ты совсем не нужен.' Karatygin, *Zapiski*, 305–6.

108. 'Дура […] ведь у него ничего нет, кроме долгов и золотого мундира; он тебя через месяц прогонит. Плюнь ты на него!' Ibid., 307.

109. 'Без церемонии и улыбается [в кресла на правую сторону,—и добро бы, смотрела] на порядочного человека [а то на] N.N., у которого гроша за душой нет.' Ibid.

110. 'J'ai été fort surpris en lisant que vous écririez au Général mon directeur pour réclamer la somme que je vous suis redevable. Je crois [que] si vous le feriez le Général déchirerait votre lettre et que lui-même n'a aucun droit de retenir mes appointements et même que je le connais trop aimable pour jamais le faire.' Letter dated 26 May 1848, RGIA, *fond 497, op. 5, ed. khr. 2467, l. 47.*

111. Il'icheva, *Neizvestnyi Petipa*, 104.

112. RGIA, *fond 497, op. 5, ed. khr. 2467, l. 44, 46–54, 56, 60–62,* and 86; see also GTsTM *fond 205, ed. khr. 13.*

113. Prince Petr Volkonskii married Princess Sofia Volkonskaia, sister of the Decembrist. The two therefore had the same family name and were maybe related.

114. Frame writes: 'As court institutions, the St Petersburg Imperial Theatres were regarded as the property of the tsar, a fact that is readily apparent from their original Russian title, "imperatorskie teatry". The Russian word "imperatorskii" pertains to the person of the emperor, not to the empire as a territorial unit ("imperskii") and therefore a more accurate rendering of "imperatorskie teatry"—and one that would express more accurately the formal status of the Imperial Theatres—would be "The Emperor's Theatres".' *The St Petersburg Imperial Theatres: Stage and State in Revolutionary Russia, 1900–1920,* 19.

115. Petipa, *Russian Ballet Master*, 49.

116. Alisa Sveshnikova, *Peterburgskie sezoni Artura Saint-Leona*, 70.

117. Guest, *Jules Perrot*, 319–20; *Peterburgskii Balet. Tri veka. 1851–1900,* ed. Boglacheva, 81.

118. Sveshnikova, *Peterburgskie sezoni Artura Saint-Leona*, 69 and 103.

CHAPTER 4

1. 'Depuis trois ans j'ai rendu de grands services à l'administration des théâtres Impériaux comme compositeur de ballets et divertissements, sans jamais avoir reçu un cadeau, ni indemnité pour toutes les peines et fatigues que je me suis données. […] J'aurai l'honneur de faire encore remarquer à Votre Excellence que je ne suis engagé que comme premier danseur, mime et maître de danse à l'école des théâtres impériaux. Je viens donc prier votre Excellence de me faire avoir une récompense pour toutes les peines que je me suis données en remplissant le service de maître de ballet.' Letter from Petipa to the director of

the Imperial Theatres Andrei Saburov dated 28 February 1862; RGIA, *fond 497, op. 5, ed. khr. 2467, l.* 137. The letter, translated into Russian, is also reproduced in *Marius Petipa. Materialy, vospominaniia, stat'i*, ed. Nekhendzi, 114–15.

2. Guest, *Jules Perrot*, 285.

3. 'Ci-git/Un père bien aimé/Jean Antoine Petipa/Décédé le 16 juillet 1855 à l'age de 68 ans.'

4. 'Среднего роста, подвижный, живой, с мягкими и изящными манерами, добрый до самозабвения, он был обожаем учениками.' A. Sokolov, 'Teatral'nye vospominaniia', *Novoe slovo*, 3 (1894), 345.

5. 'С поступлением Петипа введена была новая школа танцев, и обращено было внимание на мимику. Отец Петипа был очень хороший актер-мимист.' Anna Natarova, 'Iz vospaminanii artistiki A. P. Natarova', in *Istoricheskii vestnik*, October 1903, 25–44 (43).

6. *Materialy po istorii russkogo baleta*, ed. Borisoglebskii, vol. 1, 159 and 366; Vazem, *Zapiski baleriny*, 30. The Russian transliteration of Huguet's name is Giuge (Гюге).

7. Il'icheva, *Neizvestnyi Petipa*, 224.

8. '[Она, танцуя народные испанские танцы так,] как, они именно исполняют ся народом на улицах Гренады, Севильи и Мадрида, не заботится придать им той французской грациозности, которые наша публика привыкла видеть в балетах.' F[edor] Koni, 'Benefis' g-zhi Mila', *Panteon*, 19 (1855); reprinted in *Peterburgskii balet. Tri veka. 1851–1900*, ed, Boglacheva, 42.

9. A. Sokolov, 'Teatral'nye vospominaniia', in *Novoe slovo*, 3 (1894), 345–46; C. Boglachev and I. Boglacheva, 'Mariia Sergeevna Surovshchikova-Petipa', in *Baletmeister Marius Petipa*, ed. Fedorchenko, 290.

10. Il'icheva, *Neizvestnyi Petipa*, 186–87; S. Durylin, in *N. M. Radin*, a biography of the actor Nikolai Radin, gives the name as Thérèse Bourdin, 23–24. Radin was Petipa's grandson, since his father was Marius Mariusovich Petipa. Online sources such as www.geni.com say that Marie-Thérèse Bourdenne was an actress, not a milliner—but perhaps she was both.

11. RGIA, *fond 497, op. 5, ed. khr. 2467, l.* 75–83.

12. Boglachev and Boglacheva, 'Mariia Sergeevna Surovshchikova-Petipa', in *Baletmeister Marius Petipa*, ed. Fedorchenko, 291.

13. RGIA, *fond 497, op. 5, ed. khr. 2467, l.* 84–85.

14. Boglachev and Boglacheva, 'Mariia Sergeevna Surovshchikova-Petipa', in *Baletmeister Marius Petipa*, ed. Fedorchenko, 291.

15. Mademoiselle Petitpas is mentioned in the catalogue for a Bibliothèque Nationale exhibition featuring the composer Jean-Philippe Rameau (Paris, 1964), 26–27. Apparently, she sang in *L'Endriague*, an *opéra-comique*, staged in 1723, following which she was accepted into the Paris Opera company. Jean Petitpas is listed in *Wagner et la France*, the catalogue for an exhibition mounted by the Bibliothèque Nationale/Théâtre National de l'Opéra de Paris,

ed. by Martine Kahane and Nicole Wild (Paris: Herscher, 1983), 169. French archives presumably have additional records.

16. Marina Il'icheva, 'Jean Petipa', in *Baletmeister Marius Petipa*, ed. Fedorchenko, 274–87 (274).

17. The entry for Jean Antoine Petipa in Jean-Philippe Van Aelbrouck, *Dictionnaire des danseurs à Bruxelles de 1600 à 1830*, 193–96, has provided a quantity of material for these pages.

18. Ibid., 194. The Restoration brought the Bourbons back, in a constitutional monarchical regime, after the fall of Napoleon in 1814.

19. 'Sérieux et demi-caractère'; 'les fortes jeunes premières, amoureuses'. *Journal général des Théâtres*, 19 (16 June 1816), 292 and 294.

20. Ibid.

21. Il'icheva, 'Jean Petipa', in *Baletmeister Marius Petipa*, ed. Fedorchenko, 277; Roslavleva, 'Cem'ia Petipa v Evrope' in *Marius Petipa. Materialy, vospominaniia, stat'i*, ed. Nekhendzi, 338; and Van Aelbrouck, *Dictionnaire des danseurs à Bruxelles*, 195.

22. The birth certificate (no. 375) is in the Marseilles Archives municipales, R375-IE375. It can be viewed online: http://marius.marseille.fr/marius/jsp/site/Portal.jsp?action=fulltext&page=imagespatrimoine&recStr=Petipa.

23. Van Aelbrouck, *Dictionnaire des danseurs à Bruxelles*, 106 and 144. The description of Victorine's employment comes from the *Almanach royal de la Cour, des Provinces méridoniales et de la Ville du Bruxelles. Pour l'An 1820*, 448. Given the time lag required for publication, the arrival of the Petipas is recorded in the 1820, not the 1819 volume.

24. Van Aelbrouck, *Dictionnaire des danseurs à Bruxelles*, 195.

25. *Almanach royal* (1820), 449. Where there are discrepancies between the lists of dancers in the Almanach royal, in Frédéric Faber, *Histoire du théâtre français en Belgique*, and Jacques Isnardon, *Le Théâtre de la Monnaie depuis sa fondation jusqu'à nos jours*, I have chosen to follow the *Almanach royal*.

26. *L'Oracle*, no. 137, 17 May 1819; quoted in Frédéric Faber, *Histoire du théâtre français en Belgique*, vol. 3, 52–53.

27. *L'Oracle*, no. 147, 27 May 1819; quoted in ibid., 54.

28. Van Aelbrouck, *Dictionnaire des danseurs à Bruxelles*, 195. *La Revue des spectacles* published a pernickety and prudish notice, attacking the ballet as an orgy with the cast in costumes bearing no relation to the Belgian subject, and the presence of two Quakers, who didn't belong in a *kermesse*, especially when they were drunk. ('Ce qu'il y a de plus ridicule dans cette orgie, c'est qu'elle n'a même pas le mérite de la vérité: le nom de *Kermesse* et une partie des détails indiquent suffisamment que c'est d'une fête de notre pays qu'il s'agit, et cependant les paysannes ont des costumes suisses, les paysans portent des costumes de toutes les nations; on fait figurer, d'une manière dégoûtante, deux *quakers*, que l'on outrage de toutes les façons, et, je le demande, a-t-on jamais

vu des *quakers* dans nos kermesses, et surtout s'y enivrer?' June 1822, 69–70; quoted in Frédéric Faber, *Histoire du théâtre français en Belgique*, vol. 3, 88.

29. Van Aelbrouck, *Dictionnaire des danseurs à Bruxelles*, 248.
30. Il'icheva, 'Jean Petipa', in *Baletmeister Marius Petipa*, ed. Fedorchenko, 279.
31. 'M. Petipa, danseur vif et gracieux, qu'on a vu au Théâtre de la Porte-Saint-Martin: il dirige le ballet avec beaucoup de goût et d'intelligence.' *Almanach des spectacles pour l'an 1822*, 257.
32. '*Cendrillon*, ballet, a fait le plus grand plaisir, et quoiqu'on le donne souvent, il est toujours reçu avec le même accueil. M. Petipa, dont le zèle et le talent sont infatigables, a monté cette pièce avec tout le goût et la fraîcheur qu'on pouvait désirer.' *Almanach théâtral, ou Résumé des représentations données sur le Théâtre royal de Bruxelles*, 16 May 1824, 26.
33. Van Aelbrouck, *Dictionnaire des danseurs à Bruxelles*, 196, quoting the *Revue des spectacles*, 1822.
34. 'Notre ballet est, sans contredit, le meilleur qu'il y ait dans aucune ville de France; [bien entendu qu'il faut excepter celui du Grand-Opéra de Paris,] le plus beau qu'il y ait dans l'Europe dansante.' *L'Aristarque des spéctacles*, 15 August 1824; quoted by Van Aelbrouck, *Dictionnaire des danseurs à Bruxelles*, 29.
35. '[Votre ballet] […] est bien monté, bien organisé, bien conduit, et il travaille sans relâche; tout le monde fait des progrès; et depuis le dernier figurant qui ne gagne que trente francs par mois, jusqu'aux premiers sujets qui gagnent cinquante francs par jour, chacun cherche à se faire remarquer par son talent et par son zèle.' *L'Aristarque des spectacles*, 19 September 1824; quoted by Van Aelbrouck, *Dictionnaire des danseurs à Bruxelles*, 29–30.
36. See, for example, Frédéric Faber, *Histoire du théâtre français en Belgique*, vol. 3, 102, 110, 114, and 117.
37. Petipa, *Russian Ballet Master*, 5.
38. Van Aelbrouck, *Dictionnaire des danseurs à Bruxelles*, 195. The existence of the sixth child, Adelaide, was discovered by Van Aelbrouck.
39. Victorine is listed in the 1822 *Almanach royal*, but not in the 1824 one. (It has not been possible to access the 1823 volume online.) However, Frédéric Faber gives the 1823 list in *Histoire du théâtre français en Belgique*, vol. 3, 97–99.
40. Van Aelbrouck, *Dictionnaire des danseurs à Bruxelles*, 144–45.
41. This was published in *L'Aristarque des spectacles* on 30 April 1826, with the invitation for any interested parents to contact Jean Petipa, the director of the Conservatoire de danse and ballet master of the Théâtre de la Monnaie, for further information. It is reprinted by Van Aelbrouck, *Dictionnaire des danseurs à Bruxelles*, 40–41.
42. Van Aelbrouck, *Dictionnaire des danseurs à Bruxelles*, 41.
43. Petipa, *Russian Ballet Master*, 2.

44. Van Aelbrouck, 'Marius Petipa, une enfance bruxelloise', in 'De La France à la Russie, Marius Petipa', ed. Melani, 45. He is quoting the *Annuaire* [Directory] *du Conservatoire royal de musique à Bruxelles* (Bruxelles: C. Muquardt, 1877), vii–viii.

45. Franz Anton Schubert the Younger (1808–1878), violinist and composer, born in Dresden. He studied in Paris and worked under the name François Schubert.

46. 'Petitpas Marius, né à Marseille, quinze ans et demi, entré en Xbre [décembre] 1832. Pas de disposition, conservé par des raisons particulières.' Quoted by Van Aelbrouck in 'Marius Petipa, une enfance bruxelloise', in 'De La France à la Russie, Marius Petipa', ed. Melani, 3.

47. Petipa, *Russian Ballet Master*, 2.

48. Van Aelbrouck, 'Marius Petipa, une enfance bruxelloise', in 'De La France à la Russie, Marius Petipa', ed. Melani, 17–26.

49. Moore, *The Petipa Family in America and Europe*, 73. Moore explains in detail that David liked ballet: as Fragonard's assistant he had helped paint the frescoes for the house of the dancer Marie Madeline Guimard, who then, it was said, paid for his studies before he won the Prix de Rome. Exiled from France after Waterloo, he lived close to the Monnaie and often attended performances; he had a designated seat which was left empty even if he did not come. He must therefore have often seen Jean Petipa dance. Apparently, he was so impressed by Jean's *Birth of Venus* (La Naissance de Vénus), staged in Brussels in 1821, it inspired him to paint *Mars Disarmed by Venus*. He finished it in 1824 and it hangs in the Musées royaux des Beaux-Arts in Brussels. Mars was modelled by a subscriber to the Monnaie, the central figure of the Three Graces was the dancer Mlle Philippont, who was the mistress of the prince of Orange, and although Mlle Lesueur was Venus, her feet, which presumably showed the stresses of her profession, were replaced by those of a little servant girl. See also Van Aelbrouck, *Dictionnaire des danseurs à Bruxelles*, 170.

50. Petipa, *Russian Ballet Master*, 2.

51. There is a painting of the young Marius in *Jocko, or the Ape of Brazil*, which shows him with a monkey on his arm and wearing the costume of a Savoyard. (Savoyards became synonymous with street performers.) Russian writers, basing themselves on Petipa's memoirs, have assumed the painting was related to *La Dansomanie*.

52. '[Dans le ballet des *Meuniers*, la jeune Martin et] Marius Petipa, le danseur comique, [se sont distingués, l'un par la gentillesse de ses manières enfantines, la vivacité de sa petite physionomie pétrie de grâces, l'autre,] par son aplomb imperturbable et extraordinaire pour son âge.' *L'Aristarque*, 14 June 1827; quoted by Van Aelbrouck, 'Marius Petipa, une enfance bruxelloise', in 'De La France à la Russie, Marius Petipa', ed. Melani, 3.

53. *Almanach royal*, 1825, 452.

54. Ibid., 1824, 467.

55. 'Messieurs, je n'ai plus que deux mois à jouer, laissez-moi finir la pièce.' Quoted in Frédéric Faber, *Histoire du théâtre français en Belgique*, vol. 3, 117. In fact, she carried on dancing a little beyond the two months specified, but by late summer repeated bouts of illness defeated her career.

56. Van Aelbrouck, *Dictionnaire des danseurs à Bruxelles*, 169–71.

57. Ibid., 161–62.

58. From 1794 to 1814, Brussels was under French control and from 1814 to 1830, Dutch control.

59. This opera was shown in St Petersburg under the title *Fenella*; it was an enormous success, remaining long in the repertoire with many distinguished ballerinas in the titular dance role. Anna Pavlova was one of them and she later appeared in a 1915 Hollywood film version with the original title.

60. Petipa, *Russian Ballet Master*, 2–3.

61. Tim Wencker, *The Belgian Coincidence* (Dissertation Utrecht University, 2013), 14–16. www.dspace.library.uu.nl.

62. Petipa, *Russian Ballet Master*, 3.

63. Ibid., 4.

64. Ibid., 4–5.

65. Ibid., 7.

66. Isnardon, *Le Théâtre de la Monnaie depuis sa fondation jusqu'à nos jours*, 240; Il'icheva, 'Jean Petipa', in *Baletmeister Marius Petipa*, ed. Fedorchenko, 283.

67. Isnardon, *Le Théâtre de la Monnaie depuis sa fondation jusqu'à nos jours*, 258.

68. Van Aelbrouck, *Dictionnaire des danseurs à Bruxelles*, 196.

69. Isnardon, *Le Théâtre de la Monnaie depuis sa fondation jusqu'à nos jours*, 311, 319, and 327.

70. Ibid., 326 and 329–30.

71. 'Au profit des victimes les plus nécessiteuses de l'incendie du Théâtre Royal de la Monnaie [...] ce beau théâtre qui n'est plus aujourd'hui qu'un monceau de cendres.' Ibid., 409.

72. Ibid., 374.

73. *Le Journal des théâtres*, 19 November 1845, 4.

74. 'C'est toujours la jolie *prima donna*, l'enfant gâté du public, qu'elle séduit par la souplesse et suavité de son chant.' *Le Journal des théâtres*, 18 September 1847, 3.

75. See, for example, *Le Journal des théâtres*, 7 July 1847, 3, and *L'Argus*, 7 July 1850, 1.

76. Van Aelbrouck, 'Marius Petipa, une enfance bruxelloise', in 'De La France à la Russie, Marius Petipa', ed. Melani, 61–62. Like her father and brother Marius, Victorine made herself younger: the certificate says she was thirty-two, when in fact she was thirty-seven.

77. *The Diaries of Marius Petipa*: for example, 24 December 1903, 29; 21 January 1904, 44; and 13 February 1905, 65. Lucienne, Jeanne, and Berthe Mendès were, more precisely, Petipa's great-nieces. See online genealogy sites such as www.geneanet.org and www.geni.com.

78. *Le Petit Parisien*, 6 December 1901, 2.

79. Vera Petipa, *Moia sem'ia*, RGALI, *fond* 1945, *op.* 1, *ed. khr.* 66, *l.* 2–3. 'Тетя же Викторина была чудная старушка, напоминавшая отца, худенькая, прямая и очень подвижная. Я изумлялась, с какой быстротой и легкостью она взбиралась, постукивая каблуками, по лестнице наверх 2-х этажного омнибуса, на который мама моя, гораздо ее моложе, только со страхом погл ядывала.' Ibid., *l.* 2.

80. Petipa, *The Diaries of Marius Petipa*, 64. The entry for 23 February 1905 (66) says that Marius sent 25 roubles for Victorine's grave.

81. Van Aelbrouck, 'Marius Petipa, une enfance bruxelloise', in 'De La France à la Russie, Marius Petipa', 5.

82. Ibid., 9.

83. Guest, *The Romantic Ballet in Paris*, 384–85; *Le Coureur des spectacles*, 12 September 1844.

84. *Vseobshchaia adresnaia kniga S.-Peterburga* [General Directory of St Petersburg] (St Petersburg: Goppe and Kornfel'd, 1867–1868), 367. The same directory gives Marius's address, with his wife Mariia, as 101 Fontanka. Confusingly, it also records a 'Jules Petipa, glove-maker'—clearly a mix-up, given the address is the same as Jean's glove shop. See also Natalia Roslavleva, 'Sem'ia Petipa v Evrope', in *Marius Petipa. Materialy, vospominaniia, stat'i*, ed. Nekhendzi, 344.

85. *The Diaries of Marius Petipa*, 29.

86. RGIA, *fond* 497, *op.* 5, *ed. khr.* 2467, *l.* 87–88.

87. 'Петипа был настоящей нашей грозой. Отличный балетмейстер и большой знаток своего дела, он не стеснялся быть вспыльчивым, дерзким, а иногда и до невозможности грубым. Малейшая ошибка или непонимание ученика выводили его из себя. Мы все боялись его, как огня, хотя за спиной у него и посмеивались, потому что он плохо говорил по-русски и выходило это у него очень смешно.' Quoted in *Materialy po istorii russkogo baleta*, ed. Borisoglebskii, vol. 1, 236. Another possibility is that Alexandra Kemmerer is repeating what the boys told her.

88. 'Дед говорил: "Когда вырастешь и будешь сам учителем, тогда говори, а пока учишься, слушай, и молчи." Vera Petipa, *Moia sem'ia*, RGALI, *fond* 1945, *op.* 1, *ed. khr.* 66, *l.* 3.

89. 'Он хорошо понимал из своего жизненного опыта, что в искусстве, как и в каждом деле нужно работать, работать и работать.' I. Ivanov and K. Ivanov, *Marius Ivanovich Petipa 1822–1922*, 8.

90. Elvira Roné, *Olga Preobrazhenskaya*, 23–24 and 33; Tamara Karsavina, *Theatre Street*, 150.

91. RGIA, *fond* 497, *op.* 5, *ed. khr.* 2467, *l.* 295 and 296; *Materialy po istorii russkogo baleta*, ed. Borisoglebskii, vol. 1, 283.

92. 'Метод преподавания в этом классе мне не нравился. Петипа заставлял учеников точно копировать все изменения его лица, все его жесты. И

только несколько лет спустя после окончания школы я по достоинству оценил школу мимики Петипа. В роли Квазимодо из *Эсмеральды* или паши из *Корсара*,—везде Петипа своими уроками подготовил почву для создания этих ролей.' Shiriaev, *Peterburgskii balet*, 28.

93. Vol'f, *Khronika peterburgskikh teatrov s kontsa 1826 do nachala 1881*, Part 1, 177. Contemporaneous Russian writers called her Miss/Mrs (*gospozha*) Petipa, or M. S. Petipa; to avoid confusion this text will refer to her as Mariia or Mariia Petipa.

94. S. Boglachev and I. Boglacheva, 'Mariia Sergeevna Surovshchikova-Petipa', in *Baletmeister Marius Petipa*, ed. Fedorchenko, 292–93.

95. Khudekov, *Istoriia tantsev*, vol. 4, 76–77.

96. Vazem, *Zapiski baleriny*, 87.

97. Sergei Khudekov, 'The First Performance of the Ballet *The Pharaoh's Daughter*', *Peterburgskaia gazeta*, 15 October 1898; reproduced and translated in Wiley, *A Century of Russian Ballet*, 235–37 (236–37).

98. S. Boglachev and I. Boglacheva, 'Mariia Sergeevna Surovshchikova-Petipa', in *Baletmeister Marius Petipa*, ed. Fedorchenko, 290.

99. Guest, *Jules Perrot*, 288–89.

100. The Petipas were given permission from 12 May to travel abroad for six weeks (RGIA, *fond* 497, *op.* 5, *ed. khr.* 2467, *l.* 97).

101. Guest, *Jules Perrot*, 297–98.

102. S. Boglachev and I. Boglacheva, 'Mariia Sergeevna Surovshchikova-Petipa', in *Baletmeister Marius Petipa*, ed. Fedorchenko, 293.

103. Petipa, *Russian Ballet Master*, 95.

104. *Peterburgskii balet. Tri veka. 1851–1900*, ed. Boglacheva, 57. In dating the premiere Denis Leshkov contradicts himself, writing summer 1857 (*Marius Petipa*, 12), then 8 October (59); the dancers listed are Petipa, Murav'eva, and the student Matil'da Madaeva. Konstantin Skal'kovskii, *Balet: Ego istoriia i mesto v riadu iziashchnykh iskusstv*, 229.

105. Petipa's daughter becomes Mariia in Russian dance writing; her family, however, like her father, seem to have used the French version of her name. To avoid confusion between the different Mariias, this study calls her Marie.

106. This was followed by Aleksandr Dargomyzhskii's *Rusalka* on 4 May 1856, where Petipa created, in collaboration with Nikolai Gol'ts, a Slavonic Dance (Act II), Gypsy Dance (Act II), and Dance of the Mermaids (Act IV).

107. Petipa, *Russian Ballet Master*, 49.

108. 'Quant à Madame Petipa [...] elle est fine, jolie, légère, et digne d'appartenir à cette famille de chorégraphes distingués.' Gautier, *Voyage en Russie*, 340.

109. Il'icheva, *Neizvestnyi Petipa*, 302–5.

110. The close narrative parallels with Petipa's much later one-act *Trial of Damis* (1900), which was based on an eighteenth-century play by Philippe Poisson,

pose the question of whether Petipa's libretto for *A Marriage during the Regency* shared the same source. See chapter 10.

111. 'Он сумел сочинить для каждой из четырех танцовщиц па, соответствующее характеру ее дарования и выставившее на вид выгодные его стороны.' Vasil'ko Petrov, 'Antrakty. Besedy o teatre' [Entr'actes. Conversations about the Theatre], *Muzykal'nyi i teatral'nyi vestnik*, 28 December 1858, 604–5; reproduced in Il'icheva, *Neizvestnyi Petipa*, 306.

112. 'Он сочинил несколько прелестных па [...] которые особенно замечательны тем, что идут к характеру каждой из этих танцовщиц. Это доказывает в молодом хореографе большой толк, знание дела и умение пользоваться находящимися в руках его средствами.' 'Benefis' g. Petipa', *Sankt-Peterburgskie vedomosti*, 21 December 1858, reproduced in *Peterburgskii balet tri veka, 1851–1900*, ed. Boglacheva, 70, and, with different references, in Il'icheva, *Neizvestnyi Petipa*, 307.

113. Elizaveta Surits, *Balet moskovskogo Bol'shogo teatra vo vtoroi polovine XIX veka*, 253 and 280.

114. 'Это скорее большой дивертисмент, составленный из разнообразных па и танцев, классических и характерных, нежели балет в настоящем его значении, так как в нем почти нет сюжета.' 'Vnutrennie novosti [Domestic News]. Peterburgskaia khronika'. *Golos*, 21 April 1870, quoted in *Peterburgskii balet. Tri veka. 1851–1900*, ed. Boglacheva, 149.

115. *Peterburgskii balet. Tri veka. 1851–1900*, ed. Boglacheva, 71; Boglacheva also reprints a detailed review by Mavrikii Rappaport, 'Teatral'naia letopis'' [Theatre Chronicle], *Teatral'nyi i muzykal'nyi vestnik*, 1859. See also: Skal'kovskii, *Balet: Ego istoriia i mesto v riadu iziashchnykh iskusstv*, 233–34; Pleshcheev, *Nash balet*, 236 and 243; and Il'icheva, *Neizvestnyi Petipa*, 308–9.

116. It has not been possible to establish if the music used *the* theme by Paganini or another one.

117. '[От этой изящной композиции, остающейся и поныне хореографическим] шедевром, повеяло чем-то новым, поэтичным, изящным.' Pleshcheev, *Nash balet*, 243.

118. 'В особенности удачен "Pas de cerises", в котором опять нас восхищала госпожа Петипа.' M[avrikii] Rappaport, 'Benefis' g-zhi Petipa', *Teatral'nyi i muzykal'nyi vestnik*, 3 May 1859, 164; quoted by Ia. Gurova, 'Parizhskii rynok' [Parisian Market], in *Baletmeister Marius Petipa*, ed. Fedorchenko, 9–12 (9). As suggested earlier, this *pas* was possibly an adaptation of a similar *scène dansante* choreographed by Perrot for insertion in Jean Petipa's 1849 *Lida, the Swiss Milkmaid*.

This study uses Ia. Gurova's description of the libretto.

119. Ia. Gurova, 'Parizhskii rynok', in *Baletmeister Marius Petipa*, ed. Fedorchenko, 10.

120. 'Peterburgskaia letopis'' [Petersburg Chronicle], *Sankt-Peterburgskie vedomosti*, 3 May 1859, 414.

121. 'Свое умение двигать довольно значительными кордебалетными массами.' M. Rappaport, 'Benefis' g-zhi Petipa', *Teatral'nyi i muzykal'nyi vestnik*, 3 May 1859, 164; quoted by Gurova, '*Parizhskii rynok*', in *Baletmeister Marius Petipa*, ed. Fedorchenko, 11.

122. 'Которые трудно танцевать лучше ее.' 'Peterburgskaia letopis'', *Sankt-Peterburgskie vedomosti*, 3 May 1859, 414.

123. '[Петипа обладает] несомненными хореографическими способностями.' Ibid.

124. 'M. Rappaport, *Teatral'nyi i muzykal'nyi vestnik*, 10 May 1859, 178; quoted by Ia. Gurova, '*Parizhskii rynok*', in *Baletmeister Marius Petipa*, ed. Fedorchenko, 12.

125. Matil'da Kshesinskaia describes dancing Petipa's *Camargo* while pregnant and adjusting the choreography so that she didn't appear in profile (*Dancing in Petersburg*, 86–87).

126. Alisa Sveshnikova, *Peterburgskie sezony Artura Saint-Leona*, 94–95; Arthur Saint-Léon, *Letters from a Ballet Master: The Correspondence of Arthur Saint-Léon*, ed. Guest, 10–11. A ballet in two-acts, *Saltarello*, was premiered in Lisbon on 29 October 1854. Saint-Léon had already danced, composed the music, and played the violin for an earlier work, *Tartini the Violinist* (Tartini il Violinista) which he created at La Fenice, Venice, on 29 February 1848 and revived in Paris in 1849 as *The Devil's Violin* (Le Violon du Diable).

127. Sergei Khudekov, *Istoriia tantsev*, vol. 4, 70.

128. Il'icheva's *Neizvestnyi Petipa* has provided much material for this analysis of *The Blue Dahlia*, 337–44. I have also used the published libretto, *Golubaia Georgina. Fantasticheskii balet v dvukh deistviiax* [The Blue Dahlia. A Fantastic Ballet in Two Acts] (St Petersburg, 1865).

129. Il'icheva, *Neizvestnyi Petipa*, 337–38.

130. Ibid., 341.

131. T. A. Stukolkin, 'Vospominaniia artista Imperatorskikh teatrov', in *Artist*, 46 (February 1895), 117–25 (122); 'Творчество и обилие фантазии […] преобла дает поэтичность содержания.' 'R[appaport] M[avrikii]', 'Teatral'naia letopis'', *Muzykal'nyi i teatral'nyi vestnik*, 17 April 1860, 120; reproduced in Il'icheva, *Neizvestnyi Petipa*, 343–44.

132. '[Выказался] и творческий талант, и воображение молодого хореографа. Танцы и группы отличаются свежестью вымысла, изяществом, разнообразием. Цветы, и в особенности олицетворенная георгина, играют главную роль в балете. Для нее балетмейстер придумал новые па, аттитюды, и позы, которые так и просятся под карандаш художника.' 'Teatral'nye novosti' [Theatre News], *Severnaia pchela*, 19 April 1860, 346; also reproduced in Il'icheva, *Neizvestnyi Petipa*, 343.

133. RGIA, *fond* 497, *op.* 5, *ed. khr.* 2467, *l.* 129.

134. S. Boglachev and I. Boglacheva, 'Mariia Sergeevna Surovshchikova-Petipa', in *Baletmeister Marius Petipa*, ed. Fedorchenko, 296.

135. Petipa, *Russian Ballet Master*, 36. Sergei Konaev's evidence is collected from local newspapers and shows that the Petipas visited Riga and Berlin March–May 1863 (*Marius Petipa. 'Memuary' i dokumenty*, 158–67).

136. Konaev has not been able to trace a minister called the duke de Morny (ibid.,169–70); however, the letters drafted by René Lordereau for Petipa included one to a count de Morny (see below). For the dates of the performances at the Paris Opera, see ibid., 172–73.

137. René Lordereau detailed his help to Petipa in a letter which was published in *Le Figaro*, 2 June 1861, 4, but is vague about his precise contribution to *Le Marché des Innocents*; the letter is reproduced by Konaev (*Marius Petipa. 'Memuary' i dokumenty*, 170–72) and the newspaper is available online (www.gallica.org). My thanks equally to Pascale Melani for the information in her unpublished paper 'The Paris[ian] Market', presented 8 June 2018 at the conference 'Marius Petipa's Ballet Empire: From Rise to Decline' in Moscow 6–8 June 2018.

    As already stated in this book's 'Overture', the Marché des Innocents was a well-known market in Paris.

138. About Lucien Petipa's contribution to the ballet see Romain Feist, 'Lucien, l'autre Petipa' [Lucien, the other Petipa] in 'De la France à la Russie, Marius Petipa', ed. Melani, 83–91 (87). See also Isnardon, *Le Théâtre de la Monnaie depuis sa fondation jusqu'à nos jours*, 532.

139. Guest, *The Ballet of the Second Empire*, 168–69.

140. Guest, *Jules Perrot*, 320.

141. S. Boglachev and I. Boglacheva, 'Mariia Sergeevna Surovshchikova-Petipa', in *Baletmeister Marius Petipa*, ed. Fedorchenko, 298. The programme's description is based on what Petipa lists in his memoirs (40).

142. 'Madame Petipa est le prototype du joli, du mignon. […] Son nez légèrement retroussé, ses dents blanches dans des lèvres roses donnent à sa physionomie quelque chose d'étrange, de sauvage, de tartare, auquel ajoutent encore ses cheveux d'un brun roux, dont les ondes offrent, çà et là, des reflets d'incendie. On n'a pas idée de l'emportement de sa danse.' Jules Le Sire, 'Revue dramatique', *Revue des races latines*, 28 (September–October 1861), 556–71 (558).

143. Louis Lemercier de Neuville, *Les Figures du temps: Notices biographiques: Marie Petipa*; Pierre Fiorentino, *Marie Petipa*.

144. *Annales de la propriété industrielle, artistique, et littéraire* [Annals of Industrial, Artistic and Literary Property], ed. by J. Pataille, vol. 7 (1861), 288 and 447. (There is an error in the date given for the litigation, 29 March 1861, since the poster for the ballet had not yet been displayed.) The *Figaro* of 2 June 1861, which contains the letter from Lordereau cited earlier, also has a report of the court proceedings (3), as has 'Courrier du Palais' [Bulletin from the Law Courts], *Le Monde illustré* [The Illustrated World], 8 June 1861, 366.

145. Guest, *Jules Perrot*, 321–22.

146. *Revue des grands procès contemporains. Tome VI. Année 1888* [Review of Important Contemporary Lawsuits], 272–74. This volume reprints the submissions of both prosecuting and defence lawyers and is therefore an excellent account of the *Perrot v Petipa* lawsuit (271–77).

147. Ibid., 274–77.

148. Ibid., 277. Petipa's account in his memoirs seems less than honest, stating that Perrot's name was on the poster (*Russian Ballet Master*, 39–41 and 42, n. 4). Unfortunately, the original poster is missing from the Paris archives; even so, Konaev (*Marius Petipa.'Memuary' i dokumenty*, 174–75) affirms that Perrot is absent from the names in the Opera's internal 'Journal de régie' [stage management journal], as well as in the announcements of *Le Ménestrel* (28 July 1861, 274) and *L'Orchestre* (7 August 1861, 4).

149. For example, performances on 9 and 12 August of *Robert le Diable* earned 4,593 and 5,559 francs respectively, while a similar opera and ballet mixed bill including *The Parisian Market* on 7 August earned 4,593 francs (Bibliothèque national de France, département Bibliothèque-musée de l'Opéra, RE-13, available online www.ark:/12148/btv1b53028374d).

   Eighteen thousand francs is the amount stated in *Russian Ballet Master*, which is translated from the 1906 published Russian version. Petipa's original manuscript in French gives the figure of 8,000, as reproduced by Konaev in *Marius Petipa. 'Memuary' i dokumenty*, 74 and 81.

150. *Russian Ballet Master*, 41. Petipa says this observation was written by the journalist Fiorentino, but no trace has been found (Konaev commentary, *Marius Petipa.'Memuary' i dokumenty*, 178–79).

151. Petipa claims that Feliks Kshesinskii performed the mazurka at the 1861 benefit in Paris, along with the 'Cosmopolite' pas (*Russian Ballet Master*, 40). However, Konaev's researches have led him to conclude that the mazurka with Kshesinskii was performed in Paris only in 1862 (*Marius Petipa. 'Memuary' i dokumenty*, 176).

152. S. Boglachev and I. Boglacheva, 'Mariia Sergeevna Surovshchikova-Petipa', in *Baletmeister Marius Petipa*, ed. Fedorchenko, 301–2.

153. Ibid., 299.

154. Ibid., 299–300; Vazem, *Zapiski baleriny*, 42–43.

155. The photo is reproduced in Boglacheva, *Artisty Sankt-Peterburgskogo Imperatorskogo baleta*, 106.

156. Petipa, *Russian Ballet Master*, 49; Khudekov, *Istoriia tanstev*, vol. 4, 72.

157. '[Розати еще более пополнела] и почти не поднималась от полу, исполняя только очень коротенькие вариации, которыми не могла удовлетворить любителей искусства.' Khudekov, *Istoriia tanstev*, vol. 4, 71.

158. '[Это следует приписать не силе ее таланта, а] невидимо поддерживавшей ее влиятельной руке.' Ibid., 72.

159. Petipa, *Russian Ballet Master*, 49.

160. Ibid., 49–50; N.A. Vasil'eva, 'Doch' Faraona' [The Pharaoh's Daughter], in *Baletmeister Marius Petipa*, ed. Fedorchenko, 12–25 (13). The essay by Vasil'eva has been a great help.

161. As always, there are exceptions: for example, Jean Aumer's *Les Amours d'Antoine et Cléopatre* in 1808.

162. *Materialy po istorii russkogo baleta*, ed. Borisoglebskii, vol. 1, 216.

163. Konaev's commentary, *Marius Petipa. 'Memuary' i dokumenty*, 188.

164. Petipa, *Russian Ballet Master*, 50–53.

165. The summary (supplemented with other material) and page references of the libretto are from the published original: *Doch' Faraona* (St Petersburg, 1862). The libretto is also reproduced in translation in Wiley, *A Century of Russian Ballet*, 221–33.

166. Libretto, Prologue, 3–9.

167. It was customary at that time for several designers to work on a big ballet, each designated one or more scenes.

168. Libretto, Act I, Scene 1, 10–14.

169. Vasil'eva, 'Doch' Faraona', in *Baletmeister Marius Petipa*, ed. Fedorchenko, 17.

170. Libretto, Act I, Scene 2, 15–19.

171. Vasil'eva, 'Doch' Faraona', in *Baletmeister Marius Petipa*, ed. Fedorchenko, 19–20; Fedor Lopukhov, *Khoreograficheskie otkrovennosti*, 61–64.

172. Vasil'eva, 'Doch' Faraona', in *Baletmeister Marius Petipa*, ed. Fedorchenko, 21; M. R[appaport], 'Doch' Faraona', *Syn otechestva*, 20 January 1862, 138–39 (139).

173. Vasil'eva, 'Doch' Faraona', in *Baletmeister Marius Petipa*, ed. Fedorchenko, 20.

174. Ibid., 20–21; Khudekov, *Istoriia tantsev*, vol. 4, 98–99.

175. *Peterburgskaia gazeta*, 24 October 1885; quoted by Vasil'eva, 'Doch' Faraona', in *Baletmeister Marius Petipa*, ed. Fedorchenko, 21.

176. Libretto, Act II, Scene 1, 20–23.

177. More properly *fellahi*, an Egyptian country dance.

178. Libretto, Act II, Scene 2, 23–25.

179. Lacotte's version reproduced the production details and libretto, but not the choreography.

180. '[Не забудем и г-жу Кошеву, явившуюся] прелестной китайкой (Конь-го).' *Syn otechestva*, 20 January 1862, 139. For the Huang He river, the poster gives both a cyrillic (Конь-го) and a Latin version (Keiang-ho).

181. Vasil'eva, 'Doch' Faraona', in *Baletmeister Marius Petipa*, ed. Fedorchenko, 22–23.

182. Libretto, Act III, 26–32.

183. Vasil'eva, 'Doch' Faraona', in *Baletmeister Marius Petipa*, ed. Fedorchenko, 23.

184. *Syn otechestva*, 20 January 1862, 139.

185. Khudekov, *Istoriia tantsev*, vol. 4, 74.

186. 'Просидеть пять почти часов [в созерцании всей рассказанной истории], даже при львах и обезьянах, немного утомительно. При некотором сокращении роскошное и драгоценное представление будет больше

нравиться.' 'Doch' Faraona', *Sankt-Peterburgskie vedomosti*, 21 January 1862; reprinted in *Peterburgskii balet. Tri veka. 1851–1900*, ed. Boglacheva, 91.

187. 'Votre ouvrage est un énorme succès artistique, et un énorme succès de [*sic*] la caisse. On s'arrache les billets trois jours d'avance.' Letter from Rosati to Saint-Georges, 6 February 1862; reproduced in Khudekov, *Istoriia tantsev*, vol. 4, 73.

188. '[В выполнении его заметны:] уверенность кисти, знание, вкус в соединении с изяществом, он сразу выказал свои блистательные способности, как хореограф, и заметно, что принадлежит к школе Перро, что ставив новый балет, был под его влиянием, хотя в его группах и танцах много оригинальности и характера.' *Syn otechestva*, 20 January 1862, 138.

189. 'Тут на нем сказалось несомненное влияние его предшественника Перро. Он смело, и конечно, не сознавая этого, следовал по направле нию, указанному Перро в его произведениях. Сильные драматические сцены, с вполне понятной, яркой пантомимой, иллюстрированной выразительными, содержательными танцами, делали балет настолько интересным, что несмотря на продолжительность его (от 7 час. до 12 час.), публика до конца не покидала зрительной залы.' Khudekov, *Istoriia tantsev*, vol. 4, 73.

190. T. A. Stukolkin, 'Vospominaniia artista imperatorskikh teatrov' (Part 2), *Artist*, 46 (1895), 121.

191. Khudekov, *Istoriia tantsev*, vol. 4, 72.

192. Vasil'eva says seven times, 'Doch' Faraona', in *Baletmeister Marius Petipa*, ed. Fedorchenko, 24; Khudekov, eight in *Istoriia tantsev*, vol. 4, 75.

193. '[Г-жа Петипа] произвела [в ней роль] такой фурор, что балет выдержал 27 представлений кряду в течение зимы; театр всегда был полон'. Vol'f, *Khronika peterburgskikh teatrov s kontsa 1826 do nachala 1881*, Part 3, 118.

194. Khudekov, 'The First Performance of the Ballet *The Pharaoh's Daughter*', translated in Wiley, *A Century of Russian Ballet*, 236.

195. Ibid., 237.

196. Vasil'eva, 'Doch' Faraona', in *Baletmeister Marius Petipa*, ed. Fedorchenko, 24.

197. RGIA, *fond* 497, *op.* 5, *ed. khr.* 2467, *l.* 137, 140, 148, and 159–60.

CHAPTER 5

1. 'Приезд в Россию Сен-Леона в 1859 году несколько изменил положение Петипа. Новый руководитель петербургского балета, постоянно находясь в разъездах и ставя спектакли в Петербурге, в Москве и в других городах Европы, благосклонно относился к балетмейстерским опытам молодого постановщика, тем более что ни в какой мере не считал его конкурентом, а помощник был ему необходим.' Iurii Bakhrushin, *Istoriia russkogo baleta*, 161. Actually, as previously stated, Petipa was not so young, and Saint-Léon was three years younger.

2. V. I. Zarubin, *Bol'shoi teatr. Pervye postanovki baletov na russkoi stsene 1825–1997*, 316–21 and 347. See also the account in Elizaveta Surits, *Balet moskovskogo Bol'shogo teatra vo vtoroi polovine XIX veka*.

3. Saint-Léon, *Letters from a Ballet Master*, ed. Ivor Guest, 9–13 (Guest's Introduction).

4. *The Times*, 28 April 1843; quoted in Saint-Léon, *Letters from a Ballet Master*, ed. Guest, 13 (Introduction).

5. Ibid., Guest, 14–17 (Introduction).

6. Ibid., 17 and 20–21.

7. Ibid., 23, and undated letter from Saint-Léon to Charles Formelle in the same volume, 53–54. According to Guest, this letter was attached to another letter from Formelle to Andrei Saburov (126, n. 1). Perhaps this is how Saburov became aware of Saint-Léon as a possible replacement for Perrot.

8. S. Boglachev and I. Boglacheva, 'Mariia Sergeevna Surovshchikova-Petipa', in *Baletmeister Marius Petipa*, ed. Fedorchenko, 303.

9. *Materialy po istorii russkogo baleta*, ed. Borisoglebskii, vol. 1, 369.

10. Alisa Sveshnikova, *Peterburgskie sezony Artura Saint-Léon*, 70.

11. *Materialy po istorii russkogo baleta*, ed. Borisoglebskii, vol. 1, 373.

12. Irina Boglacheva, *Artisty sankt-peterburgskogo imperatorskogo baleta*, 145–48. The chapter 'Marfa Nikolaevna Murav'eva. Materialy k biografii' [Materials for a Biography] has been invaluable (140–83).

13. '[Ее лицо с длинным носом напоминало] спугнутую с ветки птицу с длинным клювом'. Khudekov, *Istoriia tantsev*, vol. 4, 79.

14. Boglacheva, *Artisty sankt-peterburgskogo imperatorskogo baleta*, 150.

15. Gautier, reviewing Murav'eva in *Néméa* at the Paris Opera, *Le Moniteur universel*, 18 July 1864; translated in *Gautier on Dance*, ed. Guest, 305.

16. 'Муравьева восхищала всю залу своими правильными танцами, но никого не пленяла […] М. С. Петипа [не поражала своими танцами, а] очаровывала публику настолько, что чудный образ ее надолго запечатлелся в воображен ии зрителя.' Sergei Khudekov, 'Peterburgskii balet vo vremia postanovki *Kon'ka-Gorbunka*', *Peterburgskaia gazeta*, Part 1, 14 January 1896, 5.

17. 'Benefis' g-zhi Murav'evoï', *Sovremennoe slovo*, 8 December 1862, 934; quoted by Boglacheva, *Artisty sankt-peterburgskogo imperatorskogo baleta*, 154.

18. S. Boglachev and I. Boglacheva, 'Mariia Sergeevna Surovshchikova-Petipa', in *Baletmeister Marius Petipa*, ed. Fedorchenko, 306.

19. Bartlett, *Chekhov*, 86.

20. 'В городе было много "бешеных денег", и это отразилось на всех сторонах общественной жизни и, конечно, на театре.' Vazem, *Zapiski baleriny*, 189.

21. Boglacheva, *Artisty sankt-peterburgskogo imperatorskogo baleta*, 155.

22. S. Boglachev and I. Boglacheva, 'Mariia Sergeevna Surovshchikova-Petipa', in *Baletmeister Marius Petipa*, ed. Fedorchenko, 300.

23. Khudekov, 'Peterburgskii balet vo vremia postanovki *Kon'ka-Gorbunka*' (Part 2), *Peterburgskaia gazeta*, 21 January 1896, 5.

24. 'Il n'applaudira pas en levant ses gants blancs au-dessus de sa tête, comme les beaux des loges infernales […] il ne jettera pas de couronne à la cantatrice en vogue, parce que toute démarche qui attire sur vous l'attention de beaucoup de gens assemblés est toujours de mauvais goût'. Théophile Gautier, 'Le Parfait Gentleman', in *La Peau de tigre*, 325.

25. Khudekov, 'Peterburgskii balet vo vremia postanovki *Kon'ka-Gorbunka*', *Peterburgskaia gazeta* (Part 1), 14 January 1896, 5.

26. Vazem, *Zapiski baleriny*, 191–92.

27. Letter from Saint-Léon to Madame Dominique, 18 November 1865, in Saint-Léon, *Letters from a Ballet Master*, ed. Guest, 64–66 (66).

28. Krasovskaia, *Russkii baletnyi teatr vtoroi poloviny XIX veka*, 134. See also note 84 for chapter 3.

29. Khudekov, 'Peterburgskii balet vo vremia postanovki *Kon'ka-Gorbunka*' (Part 2), *Peterburgskaia gazeta*, 21 January 1896, 5.

30. Letter from Saint-Léon to Émile Perrin, 23 December 1865, in Saint-Léon, *Letters from a Ballet Master*, ed. Guest, 127, n. 1. Khudekov writes that it was Saint-Léon who alerted Perrin to Murav'eva (*Istoriia tantsev*, vol. 3, 299; quoted in Boglacheva, *Artisty sankt-peterburgskogo imperatorskogo baleta*, 159). However, Saint-Léon's letter to Perrin on 20 February 1863 implies that he was not involved, at least not directly (Saint-Léon, *Letters from a Ballet Master*, 54–55).

31. Boglacheva, *Artisty sankt-peterburgskogo imperatorskogo baleta*, 159; S. Boglachev and I. Boglacheva, 'Mariia Sergeevna Surovshchikova-Petipa', in *Baletmeister Marius Petipa*, ed. Fedorchenko, 308.

32. Gautier reviewing Léontine Beaugrand in *Diavolina* at the Paris Opera in *Le Moniteur universel*, 5 December 1864, translated in *Gautier on Dance*, ed. by Guest, 307.

33. Boglacheva, *Artisty sankt-peterburgskogo imperatorskogo baleta*, 160.

34. Ibid., 162–63, and Konaev's commentary, *Marius Petipa. 'Memuary' i dokumenty*, 179–80. Boglacheva gives the date 26 April for Murav'eva's debut, Konaev, 6 May.

35. Boglacheva, *Artisty sankt-peterburgskogo imperatorskogo baleta*, 164.

36. Petipa's claim that he and his wife watched a performance of Murav'eva's *Giselle* (*Russian Ballet Master*, 74) is disputed by Konaev who believes they watched *Diavolina* instead (*Marius Petipa.'Memuary' i dokumenty*, 180).

37. See chapter 4 and Konaev's commentary, *Marius Petipa. 'Memuary' i dokumenty*, 158–67.

38. Ibid.; S. Boglachev and I. Boglacheva, 'Mariia Sergeevna Surovshchikova-Petipa', in *Baletmeister Marius Petipa*, ed. Fedorchenko, 309; Petipa, *Russian Ballet Master*, 36–37.

    As Konaev shows (*Marius Petipa. 'Memuary' i dokumenty*, 164–65), Petipa's further claim that it was impossible for any talented ballerina to appear at the Berlin Opera because Paul Taglioni, the ballet master, kept the stage competition-free for his daughter, can't be true. Mariia's extra performances after the king's intervention necessitated pushing back the schedule of another guest ballerina, Claudina Cucchi, who had to wait until 12 May before she could start. (Petipa also mixes up Filippo and Paul Taglioni, wrongly stating that Filippo, Paul and Marie's father, was the Berlin ballet master.)

Sadly, this book does not include the photograph of Mariia Petipa holding her shoe. It can be found in Boglacheva, *Artisty sankt-peterburgskogo imperatorskogo baleta*, 119.

39. Sveshnikova, *Peterburgskie sezony Artura Sen-Léona (1859–1870)*, 280–81.

40. Boglacheva, *Artisty sankt-peterburgskogo imperatorskogo baleta*, 179.

41. 'Восторг всеобщий возбуждала/Ты с каждым новым своим па/ […] Ты гордость нашего балета.' S. Boglachev and I. Boglacheva, 'Mariia Sergeevna Surovshchikova-Petipa', in *Baletmeister Marius Petipa*, ed. Fedorchenko, 310.

42. Taken from the published libretto, quoted by Marina Il'icheva, *Neizvestnyi Petipa*, 403–4.

43. Il'icheva, *Neizvestnyi Petipa*, 407.

44. 'Сорок тысяч! Сорок тысяч!/Стоил новый наш балет!/Балетмейстера бы высечь,/Чтобы помнил сорок лет!' Quoted by S. Boglachev and I. Boglacheva, 'Mariia Sergeevna Surovshchikova-Petipa', in *Baletmeister Marius Petipa*, ed. Fedorchenko, 310.

45. 'Peterburgskii balet', *Russkaia stsena*, February 1865, 59; quoted by Il'icheva, *Neizvestnyi Petipa*, 409.

46. 'Мастер своего дела'. M. R[appaport], 'Teatral'naia letopis'' [Theatre Chronicle], *Syn otechestva*, 14 December 1863, 2355–57 (2357).

47. 'Он отличается, стараясь всегда верно схватить в них местный колорит.' Ibid., 2357.

48. Il'icheva, *Neizvestnyi Petipa*, 403.

49. M. R[appaport], 'Teatral'naia letopis'', *Syn otechestva*, 14 December 1863, 2357; Khudekov, 'Peterburgskii balet vo vremia postanovki *Kon'ka-Gorbunka*' (Part 2), *Peterburgskaia gazeta*, 21 January 1896, 5.

50. 'Содержания нелепее балета *Ливанской красавицы*, трудно и придумать'. Vsednevnaia zhizn' [Everyday Life], *Golos*, 15 December 1863, No. 333, 1318.

51. Krasovksaia, *Russkii baletnyi teatr vtoroi poloviny XIX veka*, 309.

52. 'Передать сладострастное выражение лица, […] невозможно!' M. R[appaport], 'Teatral'naia letopis'', *Syn otechestva*, 14 December 1863, 2357.

53. Ibid., 2355.

54. '[Танец с кинжалом в "Дочери Фараона" и "La charmeuse" в "Ливанской красавице"] приводили публику в какой-то бешеный экстаз.' Khudekov, 'Peterburgskii balet vo vremia postanovki *Kon'ka-Gorbunka*' (Part 1), *Peterburgskaia gazeta*, 14 January 1896, 5.

55. 'Без ущерба грации, пластики и выразительности'. 'A. P-ch' [Aleksandr Ushakov], 'Baletnaia khronika', *Russkaia stsena*, 1865, No. 1, 101–3; quoted by

S. Boglachev and I. Boglacheva, 'Mariia Sergeevna Surovshchikova-Petipa', in *Baletmeister Marius Petipa*, ed. Fedorchenko, , 313.

56. Ibid., 311 and 314–15.

57. Ibid., 312.

58. Khudekov, *Istoriia tantsev*, vol. 4, 70; Khudekov, 'Peterburgskii balet vo vremia postanovki *Kon'ka-Gorbunka*' (Part 1), *Peterburgskaia gazeta*, 14 January 1896, 5.

59. 'Он встряхнет, бывало, своими длинными черными волосами и как-то особенно, сверху ударит всем смычком по струнам, чтобы быстрым темпом исполнить мазурку. Скрипка делалась в его руках оживленным существом. [...] Едва касаясь подмостков, знаменитая Муравьева неслась по сцене. [...] Затем быстро поднялась на пуанты, на мгновение застыла, замерла ... чтобы перейти сначала в тихий темп Камаринской и все *crescendo*, учащая темп, заканчивала "пляску" широким размахом руки и низким, русским в пояс поклоном.' Khudekov, 'Peterburgskii balet vo vremia postanovki *Kon'ka-Gorbunka*' (Part 2), *Peterburgskaia gazeta*, 21 January 1896, 5.

60. 'Во время "Мужичка" тысяча патриотических сердец билась столь громко, что, клянусь, заглушала оркестр.' 'Zametki' [Notes], *Sankt-Peterburgskie vedomosti*, 23 January 1866, 2; quoted by S. Boglachev and I. Boglacheva, 'Mariia Sergeevna Surovshchikova-Petipa', in *Baletmeister Marius Petipa*, ed. Fedorchenko, 316.

61. 'Изучил основательно все оттенки русской, не театральной, но действительно народной пляски'. *Russkaia stsena*, no. 2, 1865, 222; quoted by Il'icheva, *Neizvestnyi Petipa*, 417.

62. 'Все [...] Было верно: на шляпе цветы,/Удаль русская в каждом размахе.../Не артистка—волшебница ты!/Ничего не видали вовеки/Мы сходней: настоящий мужик!' Nikolai Nekrasov 'Balet' (1865), http://libverse.ru/nekrasov/balet.html, lines 302–8.

   'Ты мила, ты воздушно легка,/Так танцуй же ты *Деву Дуная*,/Но в покое оставь мужика! Ibid., lines 324–26.

   La Fille du Danube (the original title) was created by Filippo Taglioni in 1836.

63. For a detailed analysis of the relationship between Petipa and Saint-Léon, see Sveshnikova, 'Sen-Leon i Petipa: K postanovke problemy', in *Baletmeister Marius Petipa*, ed. Fedorchenko, 261–66.

64. Letter to Charles Nuitter, 4 November (French style) 1866, in Saint-Léon, *Letters from a Ballet Master*, ed. Guest, 86–87 (87). Saint-Léon's *The Wallachian Bride, or The Golden Braid* (Valakhskaia nevesta, ili Zolotaia kosa) was premiered in Paris at the Théâtre-Italien as *La Fidanzata valacca* in 1865 and staged in St Petersburg on 11 November 1866 at a private performance in the Hermitage Theatre, before being transferred to the Bolshoi, with Mariia Petipa as the bride and Aleksei Bogdanov as the bridegroom.

65. Letter to Charles Nuitter, 11 October 1866, in Saint-Léon, *Letters from a Ballet Master*, ed. Guest, 83–84 (83).

66. Letter to Count Aleksandr Borkh, 15 June 1866, in ibid., 74–76 (75–76). Guest identifies Saint-Léon's recommendation as Théodore Guerinot, who worked at the Moscow Bolshoi 1834–1845 (132–33, n. 5). But Théodore Chion, professionally known as Théodore and the producer of many ballets by Saint-Léon and Perrot, fits Saint-Léon's description more closely. This is also the same Théodore who staged Petipa's *A Marriage during the Regency* (see chapter 4).

67. Letter to Charles Nuitter, 29 November 1869, in ibid., 114–16 (115).

68. 'Придет в голову мазурка в балете, где действуют краснокожие—ставь мазурку!' Khudekov, 'Peterburgskii balet vo vremia postanovki *Kon'ka-Gorbunka*' (Part 2), *Peterburgskaia gazeta*, 21 January 1896, 5.

69. 'Она плыла точно лебедь, помахивая платочком. [Это была солистка, которая] порожала всех своей чудной, манящей улыбкой.' Ibid.

70. Ibid.

71. Letter from Saint-Léon to Charles Nuitter, 10 September 1866, in Saint-Léon, *Letters from a Ballet Master*, ed. Guest, 78–80 (79).

72. 'Основательность этих выводов оставляем, конечно, на совести балетмейстера, прослужившего на русской сцене больше шестидесяти лет и ни разу не пробовавшего развернуть свои творческие силы в широких рамках русского сказочного мира'. Khudekov, *Istoriia tantsev*, vol. 4, 152–53.

73. 'Зачем же так настойчиво запускать руку все в один и тот же чужой карман, когда и в своем обретаются недурные ресурсы.' 'Svoĭ [One of Us], 'Benefis' baletmeistera M. I. Petipa', *Birzhevye vedomosti*, 10 December 1896, 3.

74. German Larosh, 'Muzykal'noe pis'mo iz Peterburga' [Music Bulletin from Petersburg], *Moskovskie vedomosti*, 17 January 1890, 3–4 (3).

75. Michele Carafa's opera (1825) and Jean Aumer's ballet (1829) *La Belle au bois dormant* at the Paris Opera were based on Perrault and perhaps inspired Vsevolozhskii's own choice of subject. Petipa's written plan, containing the scenario and musical indications, states that Act IV shows 'the esplanade of the chateau of Versailles' (*l'esplanade du château de Versailles*).

Petipa's plan is preserved in GTsTM *fond* 205. Wiley in *Tchaikovsky's Ballets* calls it 'The Ballet Master's Plan' and it is his reproduction in the original French (359–70) that is used for this book, although several other reproductions do exist. Wiley also reproduces and translates the published libretto for *The Sleeping Beauty*, 327–33, and Petipa's 'Instructions to Tchaikovsky', 354–59. He does the same for *The Nutcracker*: 'The Ballet Master's Plan', also preserved in GTsTM (*Tchaikovsky's Ballets*, 376–82); the published libretto (333–37); and the 'Instructions to Tchaikovsky' (371–76). The 'Instructions to Tchaikovsky' for both ballets are archived in the State Memorial Musical Museum—P. I. Tchaikovsky Reserve (Gosudarstvennyi memorial'nyi muzykal'nyi muzei—zapovednik P. I. Chaikovskii) and included (in Russian) in *Marius Petipa. Materialy, vospominaniia, stat'i*, ed. Nekhendzi, 129–44. Wiley uses these Russian versions, translated into English, for his own book.

76. Some Western writers have argued that *The Sleeping Beauty* might have a further significance in the realm of informal diplomacy, helping to further the cause of the Franco-Russian rapprochment of 1891–1894. For a detailed exposition of the debate see Tim Scholl, *Sleeping Beauty: A Legend in Progress*, 31–33; and Damien Mahlet, who applies the argument to both *The Sleeping Beauty* and *The Nutcracker* in 'The First *Nutcracker*, the Enchantment of International Relations, and the Franco-Russian Alliance', *Dance Research*, 34/2 (Winter 2016), 131–35.

77. Alexandre [Aleksandr] Benois, *Reminiscences of the Russian Ballet*, 47–48.

78. Letter from Saint-Léon to Émile Perrin, 23 December 1865, in Saint-Léon, *Letters from a Ballet Master*, ed. Guest, 131, n. 8.

79. Boglacheva, *Artisty sankt-peterburgskogo imperatorskogo baleta*, 179–83.

80. Letter from Saint-Léon to Perrin, 16 November 1865, in Saint-Léon, *Letters from a Ballet Master*, ed. Guest, 62–64 (64).

81. For a detailed account of *Florida*, see N. Kotova, '*Florida*', in *Baletmeister Marius Petipa*, ed. Fedorchenko, 25–32.

82. M. R[appaport], 'Teatral'naia letopis'', *Syn otechestva*, 22 January 1866, 147–48 (148).

83. '[Балет страдает этим] embarras de richesses [...] балет похож на альбом, в котором г-жа Петипа является в самых разнообразных видах. [...] [Недостаток содержания] производит в зрителе некоторое утомление.' 'Otmetki' [Notes], *Golos*, 22 January 1866, 3.

84. S. Boglachev and I. Boglacheva, 'Mariia Sergeevna Surovshchikova-Petipa', in *Baletmeister Marius Petipa*, ed. Fedorchenko, 316.

85. Guest, *Jules Perrot*, 349.

86. Saint-Léon, *Letters from a Ballet Master*, ed. Guest, 29 (Introduction) and letter from Saint-Léon to Perrin, 16 November 1865, 62–64 (63).

87. Letter from Saint-Léon to Madame Dominique, 18 November 1865, in ibid., 64–66 (64–65).

88. Letter from Saint-Léon to Perrin, 16 November 1865, in ibid., 62–64 (63).

89. 'Я считаю, что Гранцева была лучшей из виденных мною балерин.' 'Teatral', '55 let v balete' [Fifty-five Years in Ballet], *Peterburgskaia gazeta*, 1 May 1902, 4.

90. 'Бедняжка так безвременно умерла, из-за какого-то прыщика. Его неудачно срезали, вследствие чего образовалось заражение крови.' (Ibid.) Actually, Grantzow had a rash on her calf which an unqualified practitioner treated without taking proper precautions. Blood poisoning set in and in a desperate but futile attempt to save her life the doctors amputated her leg. Ivor Guest, *The Ballet of the Second Empire*, 233.

91. *Marius Petipa. Materialy, vospominaniia, stat'i*, ed. Nekhendzi, names the composer as Pugni (379), in contradiction to *Peterburgskii balet. Tri veka. 1851–1900*, ed. Boglacheva, which names Mendelssohn (122). Most likely, it was Mendelssohn, with some modifications by Pugni.

92. S. Boglachev and I. Boglacheva, 'Mariia Sergeevna Surovshchikova-Petipa', in *Baletmeister Marius Petipa*, ed. Fedorchenko, 317.

93. See, for example, Kraskovskaia, *Russkii baletnyi teatr vtoroi poloviny XIX veka*, 135.

94. 'Жалоба

В продолжении десятилетней моей супружеской жизни не проходило в буквальном смысле слова недели, чтобы муж мой, Мариус Иванов Петипа, не подвергал бы меня жестоким побоям, не оставшимся без последствий для моего и без того слабого здоровья.

'К такому обращению мужа с моей стороны не было подано ни малейшего повода. Зная его раздражительный и ревнивый до бешенства характер, я тщательно избегала всего того, что могло бы возбудить в нем не только чувство ревности, но даже досады, понимая, что под влиянием этих чувств человек, забывая о последствиях, делается способным на совершение прест упного деяния. С этой целью я отрешилась от всяких знакомств не только с лицами, не имеющими ничего со мною общего по роду моих занятий, но даже и с артистами театров; безмолвствовала перед ним, когда он рвал, за кулисами, поднесенные мне публикой букеты, сопровождая это выражени ями, неудобными для письменного заявления; никогда и ни в чем серьезно не прекословила ему, если замечала, что он не в хорошем настроении; словом—не задумывалась ни перед чем, лишь бы только успокоить его подозрительность, в которой предполагала причину его жестокости со мною. Но все было напрасно! Обращение его со мною делалось день ото дня жестче, побои стали повторяться все чаще и чаще и даже с большей против прежнего жестокостью. Таким образом, положение мое было невыносимо, но по чувству жены и матери я не решала сделать посредником между мною и мужем судебную власть и, быть может, не скоро обратилась бы к ней, если не происшествие 13 ноября, переполнившее меру моего терпения. В этот день, когда я возвращалась в карете из театра с горничной девушкой, муж мой, нагнав карету, остановил ее, вытащил из нее служанку, сел на ее место, схватил меня за горло и начал давить и плевать мне в лицо. Последнего оскор бления я не могла перенести и, с решимостью искать защиты перед Законом от жестокостей мужа, немедленно оставила его и поселилась у своей матери, у которой живу и поныне. В течение этих трех месяцев я старалась заставить мужа одуматься и изменить его обращение со мною, если не для меня, то для детей, на воспитание которых выходки отца не могут не иметь гибельного влияния; но убедившись, что подействовать на него гуманным образом— путем убеждения—невозможно, обращаюсь к Вашему Высокоблагородию с жалобой на моего мужа, прося произвести о поступках его формальное следствие.

'Опасаясь утомить Ваше внимание отдельными перечислениями каждого из поступков мужа—так как они, повторяясь беспрерывно в течение десяти лет, составляют слишком длинную вереницу и при том не отличаются один от другого характером,—то я считаю достаточным сказать только, в чем именно они заключались. Желая разделаться со мною за какую-нибудь вину, созданную его воображением, он хватал меня за руку, тащил в спальню, запирал ее на ключ и принимался бить меня, в большинстве случаев до тех пор, пока я не впадала в бесчувственное состояние, в каком находили меня, входившие в спальню по уходу из нее мужа, горничные девушки—Елена Соколова, Ольга Андреева, и прачка Соломонида Смирнова. Впоследствии времени муж перестал стесняться присутствием детей и прислуги и производил кулачные расправы в их присутствии, что может подтвердить упомянутая уже прачка Соломонида Смирнова.

'О происшествии 13 ноября прошлого года могут подтвердить: горничная девушка София Линдштрем, кучер Иван Аверин, и чиновник Аполлон Афан асьевич Гринев, привлеченный к месту происшествия моим криком в карете.

'Кроме указанных мною свидетелей, считаю нелишним упомянуть еще о двух, которым, при посещении нашего дома, не раз приходилось удерживать мужа от драки со мною—это Иван Фребелиус и его супруга Елизавета Яковлевна.' TsGIA, *fond.* 487, *op.* 1, *d.* 348, *ll.* 7–8.

95. Leonid Perov, 'Kriminal'noe *pa-de-de*', *Sankt-Peterburgskie vedomosti*, 9 February 2002, 8. See also Igor Stupnikov, 'Letter from St Petersburg: Mariinsky Triumph and a Petipa Scandal', *The Dancing Times*, July 2002, 45.

96. TsGIA, *fond.* 487, *op.* 1, *d.* 348, *l.* 13–14.

97. RGIA, *fond* 497, *op.* 5, *ed. khr.* 2467, *l.* 208 (overleaf).

98. S. Boglachev and I. Boglacheva, 'Mariia Sergeevna Surovshchikova-Petipa', in *Baletmeister Marius Petipa*, ed. Fedorchenko, 318–19.

99. A year earlier a curious bulletin appeared in the French newspaper *Le Petit Journal*: 'A dancer, Madame Petipa, who has enjoyed much success in Paris and is actually performing in St Petersburg, has won a prize of 75,000 roubles (300,000 francs) in the latest draw of the Russian state lottery.' 'Petites nouvelles' [Snippets], *Le Petit Journal*, 30 January 1868, 3. ('Une danseuse, que l'on a applaudie longtemps à Paris, Mme Petipa, actuellement au théâtre de Saint-Pétersbourg, a gagné le lot de 75,000 roubles [300,000 fr] au dernier tirage des obligations du crédit foncier russe'.) If Petipa's annual salary of 7,000 roubles is used as a measure, 75,000 was certainly a considerable sum. *Golos* (5 January 1868, 2) also reported that the winner was an unnamed dancer with a large popular following who had recently suffered illness. Although Mariia Petipa fits the bill, Praskovia Lebedeva (who, it should be remembered, had been injured in the eye) is more likely, since Mariia wrote to the directorate asking for financial help on 14 May 1868, having exceeded the three-months' absence with pay allowed by her contract. RGIA, *fond* 497, *op.* 2, *ed. khr.* 14655, *l.* 77–78.

100. See earlier in this chapter and Letter to Count Aleksandr Borkh, 15 June 1866, in Saint-Léon, *Letters from a Ballet Master*, ed. Guest, 74–76 (75).

101. RGIA, *fond 497, op. 5, ed. khr. 2467, l. 198–201.*

102. See earlier in this chapter and Letter to Charles Nuitter, 29 November, 1869, in Saint-Léon, *Letters from a Ballet Master*, ed. Guest, 115.

103. Wiley, *Tchaikovsky's Ballets*, 32.

104. S. Boglachev and I. Boglacheva, 'Mariia Sergeevna Surovshchikova-Petipa', in *Baletmeister Marius Petipa*, ed. Fedorchenko, 321.

105. РГИА, *fond 497, op. 5, ed. khr. 2467, l. 272.*

106. S. Boglachev and I. Boglacheva, 'Mariia Sergeevna Surovshchikova-Petipa', in *Baletmeister Marius Petipa*, ed. Fedorchenko, 325.

107. For a detailed biography of Marie Petipa see the chapter 'Mariia Mariusovna Petipa: Shtrikhi k portretu' [Brushstrokes for a Portrait], in Boglacheva, *Artisty Sankt-Peterburgskogo imperatorskogo baleta XIX vek*, 202–32.

108. 'Там она проявляла совершенно разительное для танцовщицы непоним ание сущности задаваемых па. Когда мы все пыхтели от напряжения при трудных, сложных темпах, она, не разобрав в чем дело, только удивлялась нашим потугам. По ее словам ей ничего не было трудно. Сама же она делала совсем не те движения, которые задавались преподавателем.' Vazem, *Zapiski baleriny*, 107.

109. Petipa, it will be remembered, took over the senior boys' class at the school after his father's death in 1855.

110. Khudekov, *Istoriia tantsev*, vol. 4, 135–36.

111. Boglacheva, *Artisty sankt-peterburgskogo imperatorskogo baleta*, 203.

112. Vazem, *Zapiski baleriny*, 108.

113. *Peterburgskii balet. Tri veka. 1851–1900*, ed. Boglacheva, 177–78.

114. 'Когда Мари появилась на сцене, ее красота вызвала общий взрыв восхищения в зрительном зале. […] Она ничего еще не успела спросить его, как услыхала от него: "Mais elle est si belle." Он был поражен ее успехом, он был побежден.' Vera Petipa, *Moia sem'ia*, RGALI, *fond 1945, op. 1, ed. khr. 66, l. 20.*

115. 'Если в техническом отношении молодая дебютантка и не достигла еще крайних пределов совершенства, доступного только вполне сформировавшимся хореографическим знаменитостям, то это—не более, как дело времени.' 'Pervoe vystuplenie M. M. Petipa [M[arie] Petipa's First Performance], *Golos*, 14 January 1874; reprinted in *Peterburgskii balet. Tri veka. 1851–1900*, ed. Boglacheva, 180.

116. Pleshcheev, *Nash balet*, 299.

117. '[Никак не мог] найти талии партнерши, чтобы ее поддержать. [Танцевальной техники Мария Петипа совсем не знала и] плела ногами что придется. [Кроме того,] она постоянно все путала, забывая постановку танца. [Поэтому] танцевать с ней было делом довольно тяжелым.' Shiriaev, *Peterburgskii balet*, 84.

118. Alexandre [Aleksandr] Benois, *Memoirs*, 138. Contrary to what Benois says, Petipa did sometimes put Marie into classical roles.

119. 'Как характерная танцовщица Мария Мариусовна, на мой взгляд, никакой выдающейся величины не представляла, хотя и блистала на этом амплуа не один десяток лет. Она больше размахивала руками и топталась на месте, чем выделывала те или другие па. […] В сценической судьбе Петипа решающую роль всегда играло балетмейстерство ее отца, умышленно не дававшего хода другим танцовщицам, которые в этой области могли бы явиться соперни цами его дочери. Однако у широкой публики Петипа имела всегда очень шумный успех. Такова была сила чар этой хорошенькой женщины.' Vazem, *Zapiski baleriny*, 109.

120. Fedor Lopukhov, *Khoreograficheskie otkrovennosti*, 91; Shiriaev, *Peterburgskii balet*, 84.

121. Khudekov, *Istoriia tantsev*, vol. 4, 136.

122. Alexandre Benois, *Reminiscences of the Russian Ballet*, 55; 'B', 'Teatral'noe ekho', *Peterburgskaia gazeta*, 25 October 1896; reprinted *Russkaia baletnaia kritika vtoroi poloviny XIX veka*, ed. Petrov, 281–82.

123. *Peterburgskaia gazeta*, 16 January 1895; quoted in Wiley, *The Life and Ballets of Lev Ivanov*, 175.

124. 'Ее амплуа характерной танцовщицы не давало ей возможности создания п олноценных и углубленных образов в стиле балетной классики.' Vera Petipa, *Moia sem'ia*, RGALI, *fond* 1945, *op.* 1, *ed. khr.* 66, *l.* 21.

125. Boglacheva, Artisty sankt-peterburgskogo imperatorskogo baleta, 210.

126. Ibid., 211, referring to 'Debiut M. M. Petipa v *Baiaderke*', *Minuta*, 22 October 1882, 6; see also Pleshcheev, *Nash balet*, 236.

127. Boglacheva, *Artisty sankt-peterburgskogo imperatorskogo baleta*, 221.

128. Lopukhov wrote that he made the solo for Lubov' Egorova in a performance at the Krasnosel'skii Theatre, and this was later danced by Elizaveta Gerdt (Pavel's daughter) at the Mariinskii. See Fedor Lopukhov, *Khoreographicheskie otkrovennosti*, 91–93; see also Makhar Vaziev, Sergei Vikharev, and Pavel Gershenzon, 'A Sleeping Beauty', *Ballet Review* (Spring 1999), 15–21 (19–21).

129. Bronislava Nizhinskaia [Nijinska], *Early Memoirs*, 115.

130. See 'The Ballet Master's Plan', in Wiley, *Tchaikovsky's Ballets*, 360; see also Petipa's earlier 'Instructions to Tchaikovsky', also reprinted by Wiley, 354–59 (354).

131. See Doug Fullington, 'The Sleeping Beauty Reconstructed', *Ballet Review* (Summer 2000), 79–89 (82); and Vaziev, Vikharev, and Gershenzon, 'A Sleeping Beauty', *Ballet Review* (Spring 1999), 19–21. Despite being supplemented by drawings, Lopukhov's own published description of his solo is too vague to offer conclusive evidence either way (*Khoreographicheskie otkrovennosti*, 92–96). There exists an English translation (without the drawings) of the relevant section in Lopukhov's book: Fedor [Fydor] Lopukhov, 'Annals of *The Sleeping Beauty*', trans. Debra Goldman, *Ballet Review*, 5/4 (1975–1976), 21–35.

132. 'Nos Echos', *Le Journal*, 8 June 1893, 1; 'Propos de coulisses' [Backstage News], *Gil Blas*, 6 June 1893, 3.

133. 'Propos de coulisses', *Gil Blas*, 5 November 1902, 3–4; 'Courrier des théâtres', *Figaro*, 3 August 1904, 4.

134. *Peterburgskii balet. Tri veka. 1851–1900*, ed. Boglacheva, 359.

135. Marie Petipa quotes this in her letter (5 June 1899) to her father while in Budapest (GTsTM, *fond* 205, *ed. khr.* 39). The Cossack victory is presumably a reference to the Hungarian uprising of 1849 in which Nicholas I came to the aid of the Hapsburgs.

136. *Peterburgskii balet. Tri veka. 1851–1900*, ed. Boglacheva, 322–23, 329, and 347.

137. 'Она отличалась от всех костюмом, прической, вообще законченной фигурой […] [она] танцевала с большим увлечением, чем немало оживила балет.' Vladimir Teliakovskii, diary entry 16 September 1901, *Dnevniki Direktora Imperatorskikh teatrov. 1901–1903*, 58.

138. 'Большой живот […] отвратительная […] оживленное лицо и сверкающие глаза были особенно противны'. Teliakovskii, diary entry 20 February 1905, *Dnevniki Direktora Imperatorskikh teatrov. 1903–1906*, 422.

139. Boglacheva, *Artisty sankt-peterburgskogo imperatorskogo baleta*, 224; '–ov', 'Beseda o balete u M. M. Petipa' [A Conversation about Ballet with M[arie] Petipa], *Peterburgskaia gazeta*, 20 January 1896; reprinted in *Russkaia baletnaia kritika vtoroi poloviny XIX veka*, ed. Petrov, 243–45.

140. Mikhail Fokin [Michel Fokine], *Fokine: Memoirs of a Ballet Master*, 92.

141. Boglacheva, *Artisty sankt-peterburgskogo imperatorskogo baleta*, 224 and 228.

142. Vera Petipa, *Moia sem'ia*, RGALI, *fond* 1945, *op.* 1, *ed. khr.* 66, *l.* 20.

143. *Materialy po istorii russkogo baleta*, ed. Borisoglebskii, vol. 1, 280.

144. Boglacheva, *Artisty sankt-peterburgskogo imperatorskogo baleta*, 230.

145. Ibid., 231–32.

CHAPTER 6

1. 'Художественный жанр, культивировавшийся Петипа, пришелся петербургской публике гораздо более по вкусу, чем тот, который насаждал Сен-Леон. В описываемую эпоху главной заботой Петипа было давать балеты *большого спектакля*, с занимательным, порой увлекательным драматическим сюжетом и блестящей мизансценой. На последнюю он ловко умел испрашивать у дирекции весьма значительные денежные средства.' Vazem, *Zapiski baleriny*, 63.

2. Marina Frolova-Walker, 'Grand Opera in Russia: Fragments of an Unwritten History', in *The Cambridge Companion to Grand Opera*, 344–67 (346).

3. George Balanchine and Francis Mason, '*Harlequinade*', in *Balanchine's Festival of Ballet*, vol. 1, 290–91.

4. The information about Gusev's *Harlequinade* comes from a talk given by Alexei Ratmanskii at the conference, 'Marius Petipa's Ballet Empire: From Rise to Decline', held in Moscow 6–8 June 2018. Ratmanskii also argued that Balanchine's 1973 version does, by reference to the Stepanov notation, contain Petipa elements.

5. A year earlier than the widely publicized Mariinskii reconstruction of *The Awakening of Flora*, there was reportedly another for the West Australian Ballet by Ashkat Galiamov.

6. *The Seasons* score has since been used by many other choreographers.

7. I have in mind, for example, the ballet producer Iurii Burlaka's interval comments on 9 October 2011 during a live cinema transmission by the Bolshoi Ballet; they were performing the 2009 reconstruction by Vasilii Medvedev and himself of Petipa's 1898 production of *Esmeralda*. See also Marian Smith and Doug Fullington, '*Giselle*'s Seattle Revival', *Dancing Times*, June 2011, 31.

8. 'Вообще, Перро можно скорей назвать балетным драматургом, чем хореографом.' Vazem, *Zapiski baleriny*, 53.

9. '[Перро, который,] прежде всего, искал «сюжета», стараясь, чтобы балет был цельным, осмысленным драматическим произведением, где все артисты могли бы блеснуть и танцами, и мимикою.' Sergei Khudekov, 'Peterburgskii balet vo vremia postanovki *Kon'ka-Gorbunka*' (Part 1), *Petersburgskaia gazeta*, 14 January 1896, 5.

10. Sylvie Jacq-Mioche, 'Ombres et flamboiements du ballet romantique à Paris', in *De la France à la Russie, Marius Petipa*, ed. Melani, 23–39 (29–30).

11. Pleshcheev, *Nash balet*, 258.

12. 'никогда не считал его мастером создать что-либо цельное, художественное. По-видимому, сознавая это, Сен-Леон и выбирал всегда сюжеты, лишенные содержания, где балерине негде было показать и развернуть свой мимический талант. Во всех сочиненных им балетах пантомима и сюжет—эта душа каждого цельного хореографического произведения—всегда отсутствовала. Его балеты—простые дивертисменты, с рядом танцев, органически мало связанных с действием. У него танцуют не в силу необходимости, а просто вызываемые по щучьему велению.' Sergei Khudekov, 'Peterburgskii balet vo vremia postanovki *Kon'ka-Gorbunka*' (Part 1), *Petersburgskaia gazeta*, 14 January 1896, 5.

13. 'По своему хореграфическому содержанию балеты Петипа были, в сущности, так же дивертисментны, как и балеты Сен-Леона, но только здесь дивертисмент был крепче сшит сюжетной нитью.' Vazem, *Zapiski baleriny*, 67.

14. *The Diaries of Marius Petipa*, 77.

15. *Sankt-Peterburgskie vedomosti*, 17 February 1849; reprinted in Guest, *Jules Perrot*, 233.

16. '[Он] не умел распоряжаться массами. [...] Все его «morceaux d'ensemble» безжизненны и лишены колорита.' Khudekov, 'Peterburgskii balet vo vremia postanovki *Kon'ka-Gorbunka*', *Petersburgskaia gazeta* (Part 1), 14 January 1896, 5.

17. '[С другой же стороны, Сен Леон] умел сочинять те правильные ритмические движения, которые на балетном языке называются классическими танцами-вариациями. Солистки говорили, что им всегда ловко танцевать сочиненные этим балетмейстером вариации.' Ibid.

18. Ann Hutchinson Guest's reconstruction of the pas de six from *La Vivandière* entered the repertoires of several companies including the Joffrey Ballet; Pierre Lacotte's, the repertoire of the Mariinsky.

19. Iu. Slonimskii, 'Marius Petipa', *Dance Index*, 6 (May–June 1947), 138.

20. See Tim Scholl's persuasive analysis in *From Petipa to Balanchine*, 6.

21. See 'The Ballet Master's Plan', in Wiley, *Tchaikovsky's Ballets*, 364.

22. Ibid., 367.

23. Vazem, *Zapiski baleriny*, 58.

24. Fleur-des-Champs was the heroine's original name; Russian productions named her (like the ballet) the 'Maid of the Danube'.

25. The details of the libretto for *La Fille du Danube* are taken from Cyril Beaumont, *The Complete Book of Ballets*, 120–25.

26. Vazem, *Zapiski baleriny*, 172; Sergei Khudekov, *Istoriia tantsev*, vol. 4, 119. The review that provoked Petipa's ire was: 'B', 'Benefis' g. Gerdt. Teatral'noe ekho', *Peterburskaia gazeta*, 4 December 1900, 3. Petipa's letter, and the sharp responses from Khudekov and Pleshcheev (whose book Petipa also attacks), were published as 'Pis'mo v redaktsiiu' [Letter to the Editor], *Peterburgskaia gazeta*, 7 December 1900, 4.

27. See the list of opera dances compiled by Petipa in *Russian Ballet Master*, 103; see also Konaev's edition of the memoirs, *Marius Petipa. 'Memuary' i dokumenty*, 118. Zina Richard made her Paris debut in another opera, *Il Trovatore*, in 1857; further research is needed to decide whether Petipa is misremembering the date or the actual event.

    Auber's *Le Dieu et la bayadère* was brought to St Petersburg in 1834 with dances by Titus and the title *The Bayadère in Love* (Vliublennaia baiaderka); three years later, when Marie Taglioni came, she danced the part of the bayadère. Khudekov, born in 1837, would have been seventeen at the time of the 1854 revival with choreography by Perrot. See Sokolov-Kaminskii, '*Baiaderka. Istoki siuzheta–i ne tol'ko*' [*Bayadère*. The Origins of the Plot—and Not Only'], in *Baletmeister Marius Petipa*, ed. Fedorchenko, 83; and *Peterburgskii balet. Tri veka. 1851–1900*, ed. Boglacheva, 36.

28. The libretto for *Sacountala* is included in Cyril Beaumont, *The Complete Book of Ballets*, 447–52.

29. Vazem, *Zapiski baleriny*, 169. Wiley cites forty-eight dancers from the Stepanov notation score, which records the scene as it was performed at the ballet's revival on 3 December 1900 (*Tchaikovsky's Ballets*, 21). The 1877 premiere's poster confirms a total of sixty-four (actually sixty-five, but maybe the extra was an understudy). This is the number in the Kirov (Mariinskii) production by Vakhtang

Chabukiani and Vladimir Ponomarev, broadcast on Soviet television in 1979 and available on DVD. According to Scholl (quoting Vadim Gaevskii), Petipa reduced the number to thirty-two when the company moved to the much shallower Mariinskii stage in 1887 (*From Petipa to Balanchine*, 138). Today's Royal Ballet production has twenty-four bayadères.

30. Tamara Karsavina, 'Romantika i volshebstvo tantsa' [The Romance and Magic of Dance], in *Marius Petipa. Materialy, vospominaniia, stat'i*, ed. Nekhendzi, 303–13 (312–13). This article is a translated reprint of a lecture Karsavina gave at the Royal Ballet School on 19 May 1965 (the English original is lost) combined with extracts from several articles published in the *Dancing Times*.

31. Strange as it may seem to modern eyes, Fedor Lopukhov sees echoes of Indian dance in the corps de ballet's port de bras during the closing moments of the scene, when they lie on the ground, half-encircling the ballerina (*Writings on Ballet and Music*, 178).

32. 'Teatr i muzyka. Benefis' g-zhi Vazem', *Novoe vremia*, 9 January 1877, 3.

33. 'Сюжет дал г. Мариусу Петипа полную возможность развернуть его богатую фантазию, применить к делу мастерское уменье, распоряжаться громадными кордебалетными массами.' *Golos*, 26 January 1877, 3.

34. The Lotus Dance, together with the final scene, is now absent from many modern productions; see later in this chapter. Karsavina's remark about the length of voile is in Karsavina, 'Romantika i volshebstvo tantsa', in *Marius Petipa. Materialy, vospominaniia, stat'i*, ed. Nekhendzi, 313.

35. 'Вообще, "царство теней"—полная вкуса и настроения хореографическая картина, лучшая во всем балете.' 'V. S[vetlov]', 'Teatr i muzyka' *Rossiia*, 23 October 1901, 3; '[реальный образ танцовщицы] производить впечатлен ие волшебной грезы, чуть намеченной в туманном блеске лунных лучей.' V. Svetlov, 'Balet Baiaderka', *Birzhevye vedomosti*, 20 September 1907, 4.

36. 'Teatral'noe ekho', *Peterburgskaia gazeta*, 25 January 1877, 2.

37. *Sankt-Peterburgskie vedomosti*, 19 December 1872, 1–2; Vazem, *Zapiski baleriny*, 183.

38. 'B.' [K. Skal'kovskii], 'Balet Kal'kabrino', *Novoe vremia*, 15 February 1891, 3.

39. 'A[leksandr] U[shakov]', 'Novyi balet', *Golos*, 19 October, 1868, 1; Anastasia Bagadaeva, 'Tsar' Kandavl', in *Baletmeister Marius Petipa*, ed. Fedorchenko, 32–45 (39).

40. 'Instructions to Tchaikovsky' and 'The Ballet Master's Plan', in Wiley, *Tchaikovsky's Ballets*, 356 and 363.

41. See 'Tsar' Kandavl', in *Marius Petipa: Materiali, vospominaniia, stat'i*, 155–66. Petipa's reproduced drawings 1–5 are wrongly identified as belonging to *King Candaules*. The mistake, which originated in the classification at GTsTM, was first identified by Wiley; however, changing the classification would have been complicated, so it was decided to leave the drawings in the *King Candaules* file (*fond* 205, *ed. khr.* 599–613 [601–5]).

42. Tamara Karsavina, 'Romantika i volshebstvo tantsa', in *Marius Petipa. Materialy, vospominaniia, stat'i*, ed. Nekhendzi, 309–10.

43. Alexei Ratmansky's staging was for both the Zurich and La Scala companies.

44. Alexandra Danilova, *Choura*, 33–34; quoted by Scholl, *From Petipa to Balanchine*, 9.

45. '[Но самое замечательное место в лидийском ballabile, был] общий финал коды, в которой все участвующие в па исполняют каждый свое соло, а все вместе взятые образуют удивительный ensemble, поразительное сочетание темпов. Это совершенно новый для балета эффект à la Мейербер, chef d'oeuvre, который даст новое движение хореографическому искусству.' 'A. U[shakov]', 'Novyi balet' [A New Ballet], *Golos*, 19 October 1868, 1.

46. 'B[ezobrazov]', 'Teatral'noe ekho. Balet *Tsar' Kandavl*', *Peterburgskaia gazeta*, 25 November 1891.

47. 'Балетные либретто теперь вовсе не заключают в себе драмы, [назначенной для сценического воспроизведения,] а пишутся, кажется, только для того, чтобы в них декораторы и машинисты могли найти темы и поводы для новых декораций, полетов, превращений, а балетмейстеры—канву, по которой можно бы было разместить готовые уже и составленные вне всякой связи с со держанием балета танцы.' A. N. Bazhenov, *Sochineniia i perevody* [Compositions and Translations], vol. 1 (Moscow, 1869), 382.

48. 'Целый батальон солдат, весь кордебалет и вся театральная школа согнаны на сцену.' 'Odin iz zritelei' [One of the Spectators], 'Po povodu benefisa g-zhi Lebedevoi' [Concerning Miss Lebedeva's Benefit Performance], *Sovremennaia letopis'*, Moscow, no. 41, November 1864, 11; quoted by Surits, *Balet moskovskogo Bol'shogo teatra vo vtoroi polovine XIX veka*, 87.

49. '[Они] […] блестят разнообразием и причудливостью фигур […] соврем енные балетмейстеры употребляют все, чтобы только занять глаз зрителя танцем, который сам по себе не может ничего сказать ни уму, ни душе его. С этой целью они дают в руки танцоров и танцовщиц то ярко-цветные шарфы, то высокие, прикрывающие человека тропические листья, то бубны, то факелы; ставят на головы танцоров корзины с цветами, а самих их заставляют подниматься и спускаться по ступеням нарочно устроенных для того табуретов, придумывают трудные, эффектные положения, составляют замысловатые фигуры, симметричными рядами сводят и разводят танцующих. Изо всего этого выходит действительно нечто очень приятное на первый взгляд, приковывающее глаз, но все это имеет характер того пересыпания пестрых камешков в калейдоскопе, которое беспрестанно изменяет их положение и дает совершенно новые фигуры, чрезвычайно с имметрично расположенные.' A. N. Bazhenov, *Sochineniia i perevody*, vol. 1, 383; also quoted by Surits, *Balet moskovskogo Bol'shogo teatra*, 87–88.

50. Ibid., 88.

51. Letter to Charles Nuitter, 29 November 1869, in Saint-Léon, *Letters from a Ballet Master*, ed. Guest, 114–16 (116).

52. A. Volynskii, *Kniga likovanii*, 217–22.

53. Tamara Karsavina, *Theatre Street*, 147.

54. Lisa C. Arkin and Marian Smith, 'National Dance in the Romantic Ballet', in *Rethinking the Sylph: New Perspectives on the Romantic Ballet*, 20.

55. Damien Mahiet, 'The First *Nutcracker*, the Enchantment of International Relations, and the Franco-Russian Alliance', *Dance Research*, 34/2 (Winter 2016), 122. See also Marie-Claude Canova-Green, 'Dance and Ritual: The *Ballet des nations* at the court of Louis XIII', *Renaissance Studies*, 9/4 (1995), 395.

56. Mary Clarke and Clement Crisp, *Ballet*, 43.

57. 'The Ballet Master's Plan', in Wiley, *Tchaikovsky's Ballets*, 369.

58. See Wiley, *Tchaikovsky's Ballets*, 188, 305 (n. 116), 358, 370, 407, and 410. It was the reviewer of *Novosti i birzhevaia gazeta* who criticized the juxtaposition of the sarabande and mazurka (5 January 1890, 3), quoted by Wiley (188). My thanks to Doug Fullington for reminding me of Wiley's information. See also Damien Mahiet, 'The First *Nutcracker*, the Enchantment of International Relations, and the Franco-Russian Alliance', 122–23.

    Rudolf Nureyev, in his 1975 staging for London Festival (now English National) Ballet, introduced the sarabande at the beginning of Act III and presented it, to great effect, with the tropes of a *ballet de cour*.

59. Vazem, *Zapiski baleriny*, 162; Pleshcheev, *Nash balet*, 298. See also I. Borisova's detailed essay, '*Bandity*', in *Baletmeister Marius Petipa*, ed. Fedorchenko, 69–75. Vazem's judgement of the narrative indicates either an admirable objectivity on her part, or a lingering grudge, since the librettist, according to Khudekov, was her first husband, the balletomane and critic Apollon Grinev (Khudekov, *Istoriia tantsev*, vol. 4, 106).

60. 'Peterburgskie zametki' [Petersburg Notes], *Syn otechestva*, 29 January 1875, 2.

61. Borisova, '*Bandity*', 73–74.

62. Vazem, *Zapiski baleriny*, 162–63.

63. 'Приверженец балетной классики, Петипа шел к характерному танцу от нее же, а не от народных плясок.' Shiriaev, *Peterburgskii balet*, 62.

64. See the audience reaction to Petipa's *Star of Granada* (chapter 4 of this book).

65. GTsTM, *fond* 205, *ed. khr.* 726, 730, and 746–47.

66. Surits, 'Moskovskaia redaktsiia baleta *Don Kikhot*', in *Baletmeister Marius Petipa*, ed. Fedorchenko, 45–54 (49–50). The bullfighters' dance was also an echo of Mazilier's *en travesti* 'Pas des toréadors', in *Paquita* (Sylvie Jacq-Mioche, 'Ombres et flamboiements du ballet romantique à Paris', in 'De la France à la Russie', ed. Melani, 34).

67. Preface by M. Frangopulo (ed.), in Shiriaev, *Peterburgskii balet*, 13; Shiriaev, ibid., 86–89.

68. Preface by M. Frangopulo (ed.), in ibid., 15–16.

69. *The Talisman*, published libretto, St Petersburg, 1889, 40; for the ballet's revival in 1909 some of the names of the principal characters were changed and Ella became Niriti.

70. *Kal'kabrino*, published libretto, St Petersburg, 1891, 16.

71. Natalia Makarova's production for American Ballet Theatre (1980) and the Royal Ballet (1989) has a final, if inauthentic, act and apotheosis, while Sergei Vikharev's reconstruction for the Mariinskii Ballet (2001) reproduced the originals, using the Stepanov notations. The premiere of Aleksei Ratmanskii's production (4 November 2018) comes too late for this book.

72. Khudekov, *Istoriia tantsev*, vol. 4, 88–89; see also 'X', [K. Skal'kovskii], 'Fel'eton' [Feuilleton], *Novoe vremiia*, 25 October 1868, 1.

73. 'Царь Кандавл заслуживает [еще] внимания как художественное целое, не имеющее ни малейшего сходства с прежними хореографическими произведениями, лишеными осмысленности действия. [...] на сцене пре обладает не любовь [...] а самую видную роль в интриге играют другие человеческие страсти: мщение и жажда славы.' 'X' [Skal'kovskii], 'Fel'eton', *Novoe vremia*, 25 October 1868, 1.

74. This synopsis is based on an 1875 Moscow edition of the published libretto.

75. A. Bagadaeva, 'Tsar' Kandavle', 36, quoting *Sankt-Peterburgskie vedomosti*, 17 November 1868.

76. Ibid., 41–42.

77. 'Tremblement de terre avec pétards, comme dans Herculaneum'. GTsTM, *fond 205, ed. khr.* 612.

78. Bagadaeva, 'Tsar' Kandavle', 42–43.

79. 'A. U[shakov]', 'Novyi balet', *Golos*, 19 October 1868, 1.

80. 'Большой похвалы заслуживает наш талантливый балетмейстер г-н Петипа, ставивший этот колоссальный балет, имевший большой и вполне заслуже нный успех. Все танцы поставлены [...] с видимым желанием осмыслить их, придать каждому из них известный характер и сюжет [...] [все танцы составляют каждый в отдельности] небольшую хореографическую поэму'. 'X' [Skal'kovskii], 'Fel'eton', *Novoe vremia*, 25 October 1868, 1.

81. ' "Не беспокой, Иванов," сказал он ему своим ломаным языком, "в последний акт у тебя будет большой мимический сцен." [Дорепетировали до этого последнего акта.] Оказалось, что вся эта большая сцена Гигеса заключалась в том, что он выходил и садился на трон, откуда смотрел на дивертисмент. Мы долго потешались над этим эпизодом. ...' Vazem, *Zapiski baleriny*, 69.

82. 'Стоя на пальцах левой ноги, она делала, между прочим, без всякой опоры пять медленных туров, а правой ногой в то же время делала баттеманы.' 'B[ezobrazov]', 'Teatral'noe ekho', *Peterburgskaia Gazeta*, 25 November 1891; reprinted in *Russkaia baletnaia kritika vtoroi poloviny XIX veka*, ed. Petrov, 191–15 (193). *Golos* reported eight turns, not five ('Peterburgskaia khronika', *Golos*, 2 September 1869, 2).

83. See, for example, 'X' [Skal'kovskii], 'Fel'eton', *Novoe vremia*, 25 October 1868, 1.

84. '[Ценность его заключалась не в запутанном, порой непонятном сюжете], а в массовых и воинских танцах, поставленных с большим искусством'. Lopukhov, 'Tsar' Kandavl', in *Marius Petipa. Materialy, vospominaniia, stat'i*, ed. Nekhendzi, 155. Nikolai Soliannikov, 'Glava russkogo baleta' [The Head of Russian Ballet], in ibid., 259–66 (261–62).

85. 'Кандвал неоднократно появлялся в репертуаре, но обыкновенно не надолго: публика явно его не любила, да и сам Петипа называл этот балет "грехом своей молодости".' Vazem, *Zapiski baleriny*, 69. And yet Petipa, in an interview in 1903, listed *King Candaules* as one of the 'good ballets' ('Star[yi] Baletoman' [Old Balletomane], Teatral'noe ekho. Balet', *Peterburgskaia gazeta*, 1 January 1903). But maybe he was also speaking with a canny eye to publicity, since *King Candaules* was being prepared for a revival.

86. '[Мимические сцены] буквально заполняли весь балет. […] Сен-Жорж собрал здесь множество мелодраматических эффектов, но на публику балет навевал одну тоску.' Vazem, *Zapiski baleriny*, 68.

87. 'Вовсе не эстетично и, откровенно говоря, даже уродливо.' Ibid., 86. '[Она была] лишена всякой женственности.' Ibid., 84.

88. Letter to Charles Nuitter, 29 November 1869, in Saint-Léon, *Letters from a Ballet Master*, ed. Guest, 114–16 (116).

89. ' "Да, мадам, я знай, что это па ошень не красив," отвечал Петипа, "но если ви не будь это дансовайт, все артист подумай, что ви не можь, … Я советую дансовайт".' Vazem, *Zapiski baleriny*, 164.

90. Ibid.

91. 'B', 'Teatral'noe ekho. Balet *Tsar' Kandavl*', *Peterburgskaia gazeta*, 25 November 1891; 'A. U[shakov]', 'Novyi balet. Tsar' Kandavl', *Golos*, 19 October 1868, 1.

92. In the 1920s, the subject of Candaules, the despot, and Gyges, the noble shepherd, was seen as having socialist-dramatic potential. The ballet's return to St Petersburg was discussed in 1920; in 1925 it was staged in a revised production after Petipa, with the title *Kandavl*, by Leonid Leont'ev.

93. Surits, *Balet moskovskogo Bol'shogo teatra vo vtoroi polovine XIX veka*, 91–92 and 283–89; Vasilii Fedorov, *Repertuar Bol'shogo teatra SSSR 1776–1955*.

94. Surits, *Balet moskovskogo Bol'shogo teatra vo vtoroi polovine XIX veka*, 92.

95. According to the premieres and revivals listed by Surits, Minkus's earliest compositions at the Moscow Bolshoi were as follows: the entre'acte music between Acts I and II of *Météora* (the rest of the score was by Pugni and the Portuguese violinist Francisco dos Santos Pinto); the music for Blasis's four-act *Two Days in Venice* (*Dva dnia v Venetsii*); and a redaction of Adam's score for Blasis's version of Mazilier's *Orpheus* (*Orfa*). All these were in the same year (1862), followed by the music for Saint-Léon's *The Flame of Love, or the Salamander* (*Plamia liubvi, ili Salamandra*) in 1863. See *Balet moskovskogo Bol'shogo teatra vo vtoroi polovine XIX veka*, 251–78 (255–56).

96. Surits, 'Moskovskaia redaktsiia baleta *Don Kikhot*', in *Baletmeister Marius Petipa*, ed. by Fedorchenko, 45–54; Elena Dem'ianovich, 'Peterburgskaia redaktsiia baleta *Don Kikhot*', in ibid., 54–61. See also Surits, *Balet moskovskogo Bol'shogo teatra vo vtoroi polovine XIX veka*, 92–100.

97. Surits, 'Moskovskaia redaktsiia baleta Don Kikhot', in *Baletmeister Marius Petipa*, ed. by Fedorchenko, 49; Surits, *Balet moskovskogo Bol'shogo teatra vo vtoroi polovine XIX veka*, 94.

98. 'Moskovskii fel'eton', *Novoe vremia*, 20 December 1869, 3. Surits records performances up to 1872, but notes that Fedorov in *Repertuar Bol'shogo teatra SSSR 1776–1955* also lists performances in 1873. See Surits, *Balet moskovskogo Bol'shogo teatra vo vtoroi polovine XIX veka*, 283–85, and Fedorov, 341. V. Zarubin includes 1873 in *Bol'shoi teatr. Pervye postanovki baletov na russkoi stsene 1825–1997*, 45, and, contrariwise, describes the ballet as having a phenomenal success.

99. Surits, 'Moskovskaia redaktsiia baleta *Don Kikhot*', in *Baletmeister Marius Petipa*, ed. by Fedorchenko, 53, and *Balet moskovskogo Bol'shogo teatra vo vtoroi polovine XIX veka*, 98–99; also email from Surits, 2 April 2017.

100. *Vseobshchaia gazeta*, 16 December 1869, 1–2 (1).

101. 'Moskovskii fel'eton', *Novoe vremia*, 20 December, 1869, 3.

102. Surits, 'Moskovskaia redaktsiia baleta *Don Kikhot*', in *Baletmeister Marius Petipa*, ed. by Fedorchenko, 52, and *Balet moskovskogo Bol'shogo teatra vo vtoroi polovine XIX veka*, 98. The memoirs are: K. F. Val'tz, *65 let v teatre* (Leningrad: Academia, 1928).

103. Figures quoted by Surits, 'Moskovskaia redaktsiia baleta *Don Kikhot*', in *Baletmeister Marius Petipa*, ed. by Fedorchenko, 53, and *Balet moskovskogo Bol'shogo teatra vo vtoroi polovine XIX veka*, 99.

104. Roslavleva, *Era of the Russian Ballet*, 97.

105. Dem'ianovich, 'Peterburgskaia redaktsiia baleta *Don Kikhot*', in *Baletmeister Marius Petipa*, ed. by Fedorchenko, 60–61.

106. 'Дон Кихот—не шуточный балет, как многие предполагали, а серьезно-драматический', 'Teatral'nye novosti', *Novosti*, 11 November 1871, 2.

107. Surits, 'Moskovskaia redaktsiia baleta *Don Kikhot*', in *Baletmeister Marius Petipa*, ed. Fedorchenko, 53–54, and *Balet moskovskogo Bol'shogo teatra vo vtoroi polovine XIX veka*, 98.

108. Dem'ianovich, 'Peterburgskaia redaktsiia baleta *Don Kikhot*', in *Baletmeister Marius Petipa*, ed. Fedorchenko, 55.

109. 'Ничего из этого понять было нельзя'. *Peterburgskii listok*, 14 November 1871, 2–3 (2).

110. 'Teatral'nye novosti' [Theatre News], *Novosti*, 11 November 1871, 2–3 (3); 'Peterburgskii listok' [Petersburg Bulletin], *Vechernaia gazeta*, 16 November 1871, 1.

111. Surits, 'Moskovskaia redaktsiia baleta Don Kikhot', in *Baletmeister Marius Petipa*, ed. Fedorchenko, 53, and *Balet moskovskogo Bol'shogo teatra vo vtoroi polovine XIX veka*, 99.

112. August Bournonville, *My Theatre Life*, 581–82.

113. Ibid., 582.

114. Saint-Léon, *Letters from a Ballet Master*, ed. Guest, 34 (introduction by Guest).

115. Ibid., 115 and 141 (n. 2).

116. Ibid., 34 (introduction by Guest).

117. *Materialy po istorii russkogo baleta*, ed. Borisoglebskii, vol. 1, 375.

CHAPTER 7

1. Marius Petipa, *Russian Ballet Master*, 60.

2. 'Дама очень грубая и невоздержная на язык, частенько на репетициях ссорилась со своим мужем, причем подчас осыпала его самой площадной бранью.' Vazem, *Zapiski baleriny*, 76.

3. 'В доме Петипа, чтоб уйти от греха, все подчинялись ее грозной воле. Если пробовали сопротивляться,—разгорался неистовый скандал.' Elizaveta Gerdt, 'Chto vspomnilos' [What Is Remembered], *Marius Petipa. Materialy, vospominaniia, stat'i*, ed. Nekhendzi, 236–38 (236–37).

4. '[Мне лично всегда импонировало] это яркое, темпераментное семейство, живое, обаятельное, пусть несправедливое, но всегда занятное, шумное и интересное. Мариус Петипа, на моей памяти, был, по контрасту со всеми, самым тихим и спокойным в семье.' Ibid., 237.

5. Отец—очень подвижный, углубленный в свою работу, пунктуальный, весь в своем искусстве, которое он боготворил, без которого тосковал во время отдыха. Мама—очень живая, непосредственная, пунктуальности никакой, вся в настроениях, вне времени, очень рассеянная и с большим юмором. Их разговор часто вызывал у нас, детей, дружный смех—так они были противоположны, но это не помешало им прожить вместе много лет и любить друг друга. Мать вносила в нашу нервную и напряженную театральную атмосферу струю освежающей непосредственности и увлекательного юмора.' Vera Petipa, *Moia sem'ia*, RGALI, *fond* 1945, *op.* 1, *ed. khr.* 66, *l.* 5.

6. Legat, The Story of the Russian School, 34.

7. Mikhail Ivanov, 'Marius Ivanovich Petipa', *Novoe vremia*, 12 July 1910, translated in Wiley, *A Century of Russian Ballet*, 350–56 (353).

8. '[Он] заводил романы с кем придется—от светских дам до театральных портних—и чрезвычайно гордился своими любовными успехами.' Vazem, *Zapiski baleriny*, 76.

9. Vera Petipa, *Moia sem'ia*, RGALI, *fond* 1945, *op.* 1, *ed. khr.* 66, *l.* 13–15. She doesn't specify which jubilee.

10. RGIA, *fond* 497, *op.* 5, *ed. khr.* 2467, *l.* 273–74.

11. 'Общим у сына с отцом было много, особенно—деликатное отношение к людям и жизнерадостное восприятие жизни.' Vera Petipa, *Moia sem'ia*, RGALI, *fond* 1945, *op.* 1, *ed. khr.* 66, *l.* 17.

12. According to Petipa's file at RGIA, his youngest son's official name was Marii, a Russian version, it would seem, of Marius (RGIA, *fond* 497, *op.* 5, *ed. khr.* 2467, *l.* 294). Vera Petipa calls her brother Marii (*Moia sem'ia*, 28–29); Petipa in his diaries calls him Marius, prompting the editor Lynn Garafola to write Marius II, to differentiate him from the other, older Marius Mariusovich.

13. S. Durylin gives another version of the same anecdote, locating it in Odessa, but dating it as the 1908–1909 season when Petipa was still alive. The play was *Henry of Navarre* and Marii's brother Viktor was performing, as was Nikolai Radin. Petipa, who was in the audience, laughed louder than anyone else. But Viktor, whose monologue was sabotaged, was furious. S. Durylin, *N. M. Radin*, 20–21.

14. Vera Petipa, *Moia sem'ia*, RGALI, *fond* 1945, *op.* 1, *ed. khr.* 66, *l.* 17–19, 26, and 28–29.

15. Ibid., *l.*10.

16. Petipa, diary entries 27 February and 6 May 1904, *The Diaries of Marius Petipa*, 46 and 51.

17. 'Большое горе выпало на долю нашей семьи. Еще и сейчас я помню скорбь моих родителей, когда умерла вторая их дочь Евгения, надежда моего отца: он находил ее очень способной. Она умерла от саркомы, ножка была ампутирована.' Vera Petipa, *Moia sem'ia*, RGALI, *fond* 1945, *op.* 1, *ed. khr.* 66, *l.* 21.

18. 'Она, безусловно, обладала большими способностями к танцу, и были все данные к тому, что из нее выработается незаурядная классическая солистка, а может быть балерина, с мягким, легким танцем.' Vazem, *Zapiski baleriny*, 212.

19. Vera Petipa mistakenly says that Liubov' danced the title role of *The Awakening of Flora, Moia sem'ia*, *l.* 21.

20. 'что жизнь имеет свои непреложные законы'. Ibid., *l.* 22.

21. Ibid., *l.* 10–11, 16.

22. Ibid., *l.* 13.

23. 'Она была мила, приятна, очень начитана, и беседовать с ней было весьма интересно.' S. Grigor'ev, 'Реплика' [Riposte], in *Marius Petipa. Materialy, vospominaniia, stat'i*, ed. Nekhendzi, 238–29.

24. Diary entry 2 May 1903, *The Diaries of Marius Petipa*, 15.

25. 'чтобы занять положение, достойное дочери моего отца'. Vera Petipa, *Moia sem'ia*, RGALI, *fond* 1945, *op.* 1, *ed. khr.* 66, *l.* 29.

26. Petipa, *The Diaries of Marius Petipa*, ed. Lynn Garafola, 8 (editorial note). See also entries 25 September 1903 and 8 September 1904, 20 and 53–54 (54).

27. Diary entries 21 April 1904 and 26 October 1903, *The Diaries of Marius Petipa*, 23 and 50. Even Teliakovskii singled out Vera for praise in his own diary entry for 2 May 1903 (*Dnevniki Direktora Imperatorskikh teatrov 1901–1903*, 473).

28. Entries for 22 and 25 September 1904, *The Diaries of Marius Petipa*, 54–55.

29. The information about Liubov' Petipa's visit (with only her mother) to Milan in 1899 was supplied by Valentina Bonelli, whose paper 'In the summer of 1899, in Milan' was presented at the conference, 'Marius Petipa's Ballet Empire: From Rise to Decline' in Moscow 6–8 June 2018.

30. In his diary for 6 October 1907 Teliakovskii records that Vera and Nadezhda Petipa came to see him. Nadezhda asked for permission to extend her summer vacation on grounds of illness; Vera announced her departure from the company, because of her tuberculosis (*Dnevniki Direktora Imperatorskikh teatrov 1906–1909*, 264–65). The directorate behaved well towards Vera, offering her the possibility of remaining in the ballet company (and presumably receiving a salary) while simultaneously attending the school's drama course, after which she would be transferred to the Aleksandrinskii troupe. However, pressured by her anxious parents, she turned this option down (Vera Petipa, *Moia sem'ia*, RGALI, *fond* 1945, *op.* 1, *ed. khr.* 66, *l.* 30).

31. Diary entries 9 May and editorial note, 14 and 16–17 June, 1 and 10 July 1907, *The Diaries of Marius Petipa*, 77–79.

32. Vera Petipa, *Moia sem'ia*, RGALI, *fond* 1945, *op.* 1, *ed. khr.* 66, *l.* 30–32.

33. Letter to Charles Nuitter, 19 September 1867, in *Saint-Léon, Letters from a Ballet Master*, ed. Guest, 105–16 (106).

34. GTsTM *fond* 205, *ed. khr.* 98–109 and 112–16.

35. Ibid., *ed. khr.* 612; Petipa, *Russian Ballet Master*, 76–77.

36. Shiriaev, *Peterburgskii balet*, 46.

37. Petipa's instructions to Minkus for *Mlada* are in GTsTM, *fond* 205, *ed. khr.* 245–46.

38. For details about the 'Ballet Master's Plans' and 'Instructions to Tchaikovsky' see note 75 in chapter 5.

    Wiley analyses the variable precision of Petipa's instructions and Chaikovskii's responses: neither was scrupulous, the inference being that they must have had fairly frequent meetings to discuss details and changes (*Tchaikovsky's Ballets*, 110–11). This is corroborated by Vera Petipa's account, outlined later in this chapter.

39. *Marius Petipa. Materialy, vospominaniia, stat'i*, ed. Nekhendzi, 129; Wiley, *Tchaikovsky's Ballets*, 354.

40. *Marius Petipa. Materialy, vospominaniia, stat'i*, ed. Nekhendzi, 132; Wiley, *Tchaikovsky's Ballets*, 356.

41. 'При всех достоинствах музыки Петипа был связан ею и работать над *Спящей* ему было трудно. В этом он признавался и мне.' Shiriaev, *Peterburgskii balet*, 45–46.

42. Ibid.

43. Vera Petipa, *Moia sem'ia*, RGALI, *fond* 1945, *op.* 1, *ed. khr.* 66, *l.* 9–10.

44. Wiley, *Tchaikovsky's Ballets*, 161.

45. A. Pleshcheev, *Moe vremia* (Paris, 1939), 147; translated and quoted in Wiley, *Tchaikovsky's Ballets*, 160.

46. 'Петр Ильич незаметно, украдкой бросал взгляд в мою сторону, видимо, давая мне оценку как артистке. Судя по выражению его слегка улыбающегося лица, он был мною доволен. [...] Заканчивая разговор, Петр Ильич сделал несколько шагов по направлению ко мне со свойственной ему манерой—небольшим наклоном корпуса. Подойдя ближе, он стал задавать мне разные вопросы, по привычке перемешивая русскую и французскую речь и играя своим пенсне. Когда Петр Ильич закончил свои вопросы, на которые я отвечала робко и сдержанно, М. Петипа, думая что я не понимаю по-французски, стал пояснять мне на ломаном русско-французском диалекте, о чем идет речь. В "переводе" это значило, что в балете *Спящая красавица* я должна буду танцевать "маленькую кошку, как хочет Чайковский.' This passage is from Mariia Anderson, *Vospominaniia o P. I. Chaikovskom* [Reminiscences about P. I. Chaikovskii] and is available online http://www.tchaikov.ru/memuar123.html, accessed 14 August 2015; the same passage is also reproduced and translated in Wiley, *Tchaikovsky's Ballets*, 158–59.

47. 'Monsieur Glazounoff ne veut pas changer une seule note, ni dans la variation de Mlle Legnani, et non plus, une petite coupure dans le galop. C'est terrible de composer le ballet avec un compositeur qui d'avance a vendu et fait imprimer le ballet.' Petipa's copy of his undated 1897 letter to an unknown correspondent, GTsTM, *fond* 205, *ed. khr.* 22. The same letter is included in *Marius Petipa. Materialy, vospominaniia, stat'i*, ed. Nekhendzi, with the estimated date of September–October 1897 (124).

48. 'Я указываю, во-первых, темп. Во-вторых, Петипа уже стар и забывает многое, что говорил мне раньше; у нас постоянно столкновения, которые благодаря моему присутствию кончаются довольно благополучно. Не будь меня, все ставилось бы невпопад. Петипа бы сердился, на что имеет право, так как его торопят, и наделали бы мне таких купюр, что мне сделалось бы все не мило.' Letter to Mitrofan Beliaev, end of 1897, reprinted in *A. K. Glazunov. Pis'ma, stat'i, vospominaniia* (Moscow: Gosudarstvennoe muzykal'noe izdatel'stvo, 1958), 200–201 (200). The letter is also translated into French in André Lischke, 'Un Chef-d'oeuvre *fin de siècle*', 'De la France à la Russie, Marius Petipa', ed. Melani, 223–34 (231–32).

49. 'Chaque jour je répète deux fois et suis très occupé jusqu'à 2 heures du matin à écrire les détails qu'il faut pour les spectacles à L'Hermitage.' GTsTM, *fond* 205, *ed. khr.* 22. Petipa's reference to the Hermitage suggests he was already planning the short ballets staged there in early 1900.

50. 'Как правило, Петипа прорабатывал всю постановку нового балета дома, куда он обыкновенно вызывал к себе пианиста и скрипача. Заставляя их по многу раз играть отдельные отрывки музыки, он планировал постановку на столе, пользуясь, особенно для массовых танцев и групп, небольшими

куколками из папье-маше. Они передвигались балетмейстером в самых разнообразных комбинациях, которые он самым детальным образом списывал, отмечая нулями женщин, крестиками—мужчин, а разные перемещения—стрелками, черточками, линиями, значение которых было известно ему одному. Таким образом Петипа графически воссоздавал всю свою будущую постановку.' Shiriaev, *Peterburgskii balet*, 59.

51. Reproduced with a commentary by Lopukhov in *Marius Petipa: Materialy, vospominaniia, stat'i*, 166–69.

52. Shiriaev, *Peterburgskii balet*, 60–61.

53. 'Он ставил в течение сезона не менее двух больших балетных спектаклей, не считая одноактных балетов и отдельных танцев.' Vazem, *Zapiski baleriny*, 74.

54. 'Балетмейстер никогда не был уверен в удаче своих постановок, хотя и разрабатывал их у себя дома, и сплошь и рядом менял их в процессе репетирования. Отсюда вытекало очень большое число репетиций, гораздо большее, чем их требовалось у Сен-Леона. На репетициях Петипа часто суетился и нервничал, и эта нервность невольно передавалась и артистам.' Vazem, *Zapiski baleriny*, 64.

55. Letter to Charles Nuitter, 19 September 1867, in *Saint-Léon, Letters from a Ballet Master*, ed. Guest, 105–6 (106).

56. RGIA, *fond* 497, *op.* 5, *ed. khr.* 2467, *l.* 183.

57. 'В обращении с труппой Петипа был расчетлив до наглости. Если с отдельными артистами он бывал всегда вежлив и любезен, часто расточая им комплименты с чисто французской приторностью (надо учесть, что среди моих товарок по сцене были особы, имевшие "друзей" среди великих князей и разных власть имущих лиц, от которых всецело зависела карьера балетмейстера),—то с "мелкой сошкой" он разговаривал безапелляционным тоном командира, часто не стесняясь в выражениях. "Послюшь, ma belle,"— таково было любимое обращение Петипа к корифейкам и кордебалетчицам. "Ти дансуй, как мой кухар" (кухарка),—слышалось на репетициях и т.п.

'Болезненно–самолюбивый, Петипа весьма ревниво оберегал свой балетмейстерский авторитет и очень не любил, чтобы ему перечили. Он очень раздражался, если артисты критиковали его постановки. Второстепенные силы, разумеется, всегда покорно молчали, но с первыми сюжетами у него нередко происходили стычки. Меня он недолюбливал за то, что я ему часто перечила, хотя всегда ценил как артистку. Впрочем, надо отдать ему справедливость, что после разных споров, если он воочию убеждался в своей неправоте, он последнюю был готов всегда признать. Я перетанцевала очень много балетов Петипа и всегда встречала с его стороны полное удовлетворение моей работой и благодарность. Петипа много содействовал моей карьере, ставя для меня выигрышные номера, и я, скажу без бахвальства, также немало помогла успеху его постановок своим участием. Во всяком случае, художественные результаты нашего сотрудничества получались самые положительные.' Vazem, *Zapiski baleriny*, 75.

58. 'На склоне лет редко выходил из себя.' Nikolai Soliannikov, 'Glava russkogo baleta' [The Head of Russian Ballet], in *Marius Petipa. Materialy, vospominaniia, stat'i*, ed. Nekhendzi, 259–66 (260).

59. 'Несмотря на преклонный возраст, показывал сам изумительно, насыщенно, образно, в то же время не глушил индивидуальности актера, а предоставлял ему инициативу и был чрезвычайно доволен, когда тому удавалось по заданной балетмейстером канве расшить новые узоры.' Ibid., 260.

60. Liubov' Egorova, 'Na Repetitsiï [At Rehearsal], in *Marius Petipa. Materialy, vospominaniia, stat'i*, ed. Nekhendzi, 239–40 (239).

61. 'Петипа вел себя с достоинством, граничащим с заносчивостью, но это было *tenue* человека, знающего себе цену и уважающего искусство. Если в обращении с артистами проглядывала некоторая надменность, то он не гнул спины и перед начальством. Правда, Петипа не был борцом, шел на компр омиссы и с царедворческой дипломатичностью избегал конфликтов. "C'est la vie," говорил он с легкой усмешкой. [...] И все же, несмотря на крайнюю осторожность и умение маневрировать в мире придворно-театральных интриг, Петипа во время работы оставался только художником.' Soliannikov, 'Glava russkogo baleta', in *Marius Petipa. Materialy, vospominaniia, stat'i*, ed. Nekhendzi, 260.

62. 'С уходом Сен-Леона с нашей сцены навсегда пропали все упоминавшиеся выше мелкие "бисерные" *pa*, требовавшие от танцовщицы настоящей фил игранной работы. Вариации сочинения Петипа были однообразными, я бы сказала, "грубее" сен-леоновских.' Vazem, *Zapiski baleriny*, 64.

63. 'Les jambes qui enlacent le corps de l'homme, le corps de la danseuse au dessus de la tête de l'homme, le tambourin à la main.' *Marius Petipa. Materialy, vospominaniia, stat'i*, ed. Nekhendzi, 166–69 (167). I. Borisova, '*Bandity*', in *Marius Petipa Baletmeister*, ed. Fedorchenko, brings attention to these drawings (71–72).

64. 'Учили нас и поддержке, но самой примитивной, сводившейся к держанию партнерши за талию на двойных турах в адажио. В то время еще не знали взлетов танцовщиц при помощи кавалера. Специальный класс поддержки [...] был заведен в более позднее время, незадолго до моего выпуска из училища.' Shiriaev, *Peterburgskii balet*, 29–30.

65. Vazem, *Zapiski baleriny*, 207; Shiriaev, *Peterburgskii balet*, 33; Legat, *The Story of the Russian School*, 67.

66. Karsavina, *Theatre Street*, 116; Shiriaev, *Peterburgskii balet*, 28–29.

67. Legat, *The Story of the Russian School*, 31–33.

68. Nizhinskaia [Nijinska], *Early Memoirs*, 114.

69. Roslavleva, *Era of the Russian Ballet*, 111.

70. Karsavina, *Theatre Street*, 116.

71. Legat, *The Story of the Russian School*, 39.

72. *The Dying Swan* (originally *The Swan*) can be found on YouTube; *Torch Dance* is in the Archives Françaises du Film, Centre National de Cinématographie.

73. 'Он неоднократно повторял артистам: "Танцевать ногами—это ничто, а уметь распоряжаться руками—это все в искусстве, представляющем собой стройную движущуюся пластику." Khudekov, *Istoriia tantsev*, vol. 4, 151.

74. 'Отец не отрицал большого значения техники для достижения виртуозности, но и не ставил технику краеугольным камнем. Его артистическое кредо закл ючалось в том, что артист балета должен совмещать в себе, помимо техники как обязательное условие артистичности, сознание образа в гармонии с музыкой и способность его передать через мимику лица, пластичность и выразительность движений.' Vera Petipa, *Moia sem'ia*, RGALI, *fond* 1945, *op.* 1, *ed. khr.* 66, *l.* 8.

75. *Peterburgskaia gazeta*, 2 December 1896, 2, and 2 May 1907, 4–5.

76. Legat, *The Story of the Russian School*, 35 and 37.

77. 'Он не чувствовал музыки, ее ритма; поэтому часто сочиненные им танцы ок азывались крайне неудобными для исполнения, и солистам приходилось или просить его изменить постановку или "контрабандой" переставлять самим свои номера.' Vazem, *Zapiski baleriny*, 64. Vazem's account is contradicted by an anecdote from Liubov' Egorova in which she remembers an occasion when Anna Pavlova made slight changes to a variation she found difficult: 'After the variation, a deathly silence ensued. Petipa said nothing for a long time. Then he suddenly spoke: "*Ma belle*, tomorrow you will dance the variation I composed. This is not by me. Understood? Let us continue." Pavlova burst into tears.' ('После вариации наступила мертвая тишина. Петипа долго молчал. Потом вдруг: "*Ma belle завтра ты danseras la variation que j'ai reglée. C'est pas moi. Compris? Plus loin!*" Павлова ударилась в слезы.') 'Na repetitsii', in *Marius Petipa. Materialy, vospominaniia, stat'i*, ed. Nekhendzi, 239–40 (240).

78. Lopukhov, *Writings on Ballet and Music*, ed. Stephanie Jordan.

79. 'С балеринами Петипа работал всегда отдельно. Перед тем как поставить тот или иной сольный танец, балетмейстер тщательно изучал все наиболее типичные черты и особенности дарования балерины, с которой ему предстояло работать. Изучал не для того, чтобы приспособить танец к индивидуальности и способностям балерины, а для того, чтобы в танце возможно полнее раскрыть и выявить их. И если музыка какой-либо вариации не соответствовала средствам исполнительницы, он заменял ее другим вставным номером, пусть даже в ущерб музыкальной цельности спектакля, но не в ущерб успеху балерины.' Shiriaev, *Peterburgskii balet*, 61–62. About modifying a score: such an approach, prevalent in the nineteenth century, might not impress concert-hall composers, but there have even been twentieth-century choreographers, such as Balanchine and Paul Taylor, who have defended musical disrespect in the interests of the choreographic outcome.

80. 'Бывало так, что покажет балерине новое движение, она бьется, бьется, ничего не выходит; тогда он переставлял па.' A. Shiriaev, 'Riadom Petipa' [Alongside Petipa], in *Marius Petipa. Materialy, vospominaniia, stat'i*, ed. Nekhendzi, 266–72 (267)

81. Petipa, *Russian Ballet Master*, 86.

82. *Tchaikovsky's Ballets*, 360. In the original designs 'Miettes qui tombent' wore a tutu appliqued with mice, which is a nice detail.

83. '[Petipa est toujours l'artiste bien digne, vraiment, de la mode dont il jouit,] et capable de dissiper les préventions du public contre les danses masculines, préventions malheureusement trop justifiées, mais que le talent peut venir à bout de détruire.' *Le Courrier des théâtres*, 30 July 1843; quoted by Sylvie Jacq-Mioche, 'Ombres et flamboiements du ballet romantique à Paris', in 'De La France à la Russie, Marius Petipa', ed. Melani, 34.

84. '[Saint-Léon aussi fut très applaudi: cela tint à ce que] depuis très longtemps l'on n'a pas vu de danseur proprement dit en France; la défaveur où la danse masculine était tombée faisait extrêmement réduire dans les ballets la partie chorégraphique confiée aux hommes. Petipa lui-même, acteur élégant, mime plein de feu et de passion, semblait demander grâce pour sa danse, pour son feu, en se dévouant complètement à l'effet de sa partenaire. Depuis la retraite de Perrot, Saint-Léon est le seul homme qui ait osé faire à l'Opéra de la danse pour la danse, et il a surpris un succès.' Théophile Gautier, *La Presse*, 23 October 1848; quoted by ibid.

85. 'Un point est à noter ici: c'est l'importance des rôles d'hommes, dans les ballets. Les hommes sont aussi bien 'étoiles' que les femmes; il n'est que juste de dire, au reste, qu'ils dansent à merveille.' Paul Ginisty, '*Gil Blas* à Moscou', *Gil Blas*, 6 June 1883, 2.

86. Bénédicte Jarrasse, 'Être et/ou ne pas être? Le danseur dans le ballet impérial' [To Be and/or Not to Be? The Dancer in the Imperial Ballet], in 'De La France à la Russie, Marius Petipa', ed. Melani, 237–52 (246–47). The Bournonville letter (n. 30) is dated 2 May 1874 and quoted by Jarrasse from Vera Krasovskaia's entry 'Marius Petipa', in the *International Encylopedia of Dance*, ed. Selma Jeanne Cohen, vol. 5, 153.

87. 'Его дарование светило ровным светом, без вспышек.' Vazem, *Zapiski baleriny*, 117.

88. Wiley, *The Life and Ballets of Lev Ivanov*, 33.

89. Bagadaeva, 'Tsar' Kandavl', in *Baletmeister Marius Petipa*, ed. Fedorchenko, 42. It will be remembered that, in fact, Ivanov had little to do as Gyges (see chapter 6).

90. 'А г. Гердт 1-й, [по-прежнему,] легкостью и отчетливостью своих танцев, вызывал громкие рукоплескания.' *Golos*, 26 January 1877, 2–3 (2).

91. Roslavleva, *Era of the Russian Ballet*, 108–9.

92. 'В театральной школе моим преподавателем танцев, а также и по классу мимики, был П. А. Гердт. Я помню, как исключительно четки и выразительны

были его жест, мимика лица, поворот головы, движение спины, плеч, что доступно только большому художнику.' Vera Petipa, *Moia sem'ia*, RGALI, *fond* 1945, *op.* 1, *ed. khr.* 66, *l.* 11.

93. '[В балете *Спящая красавица* совместные выступления Гердта с балериной в adagio] отличались скульптурным рисунком и ловкостью партнера, а его небольшие танцевальные выступления, благодаря своему изяществу всегда сопровождались аплодисментами.' Ibid., 8.

94. 'N. B.' [Bezobrazov], 'Teatr i muzyka', *Sankt-Peterburgskie vedomosti*, 15 February 1891; reprinted in *Russkaia baletnaia kritika vtoroi poloviny XIX veka*, ed. Petrov, 183–85 (185). The libretto suggests that Kal'kabrino was, unlike Prince Désiré, a highly dramatic role.

95. Wiley, *The Life and Ballets of Lev Ivanov*, 39; Jarrasse, 'Être et/ou ne pas être? Le danseur dans le Ballet impérial', in 'De La France à la Russie, Marius Petipa', ed. Melani, 247.

96. 'K. S[kal'kovskii]', 'Teatr i muzyka', *Novoe vremia*, 9 January 1879, 3.

97. 'Петипа при постановке балетов вообще не любил терять время на прохожд ение мимических сцен с мужчинами, отдавая все свое внимание балеринам. Дав общую схему роли, он предоставлял разрабатывать ее артистам самостоятельно, по мере их сил и уменья. Поэтому я, как и многие другие, взял себе за правило писать свои роли в тетрадке.' Shiriaev, *Peterburgskii balet*, 57.

98. Vazem, *Zapiski baleriny*, 82–83. The information about the Moscow *Tril'by* also comes from Surits, *Balet moskovskogo Bol'shogo teatra vo vtoroi polovine XIX veka*, 100–102.

99. E. Krivenok, 'Tril'by', in *Baletmeister Marius Petipa*, ed. Fedorchenko, 61–68 (65); Vazem, *Zapiski baleriny*, 156–57.

100. Khudekov, *Istoriia tantsev*, vol. 4, 103.

101. [K. Skal'kovskii], 'Benefis' g-zhi Vazem. Novyi balet *Babochka*' [Vazem's Benefit. The New Ballet *The Butterfly*], *Sankt-Peterburgskie vedomosti*, 8 January 1874, 2; reprinted in K. A. Skal'kovskii, *Stat'i o balete 1868–1905*, 38–41. Also, see Vazem, *Zapiski baleriny*, 161–62.

102. Roslavleva, *Era of the Russian Ballet*, 103; Vazem, *Zapiski baleriny*, 159–60.

103. For a detailed account of *The Daughter of the Snows*, see Elizaveta Shmakova, '*Doch' snegov*', in *Baletmeister Marius Petipa*, ed. Fedorchenko, 108–15.

104. K.S[kal'kovskii], 'Teatr i muzyka', 'Novyi balet', *Novoe vremia*, 9 January, 1879, 3.

105. 'Letopis' iskusstv, teatra i muzyki', *Vsemirnaia illiustratsiia*, 532 (1879), 235–28; quoted by Shmakova in '*Doch' snegov*', in *Baletmeister Marius Petipa*, ed. Fedorchenko, 108.

106. *Golos*, 9 January 1879, 3.

107. Vazem, *Zapiski baleriny*, 73.

108. Petipa, *Russian Ballet Master*, 56.

109. 'Он относился к числу дешевых. [...] Конец балета также вышел как будто скомканным.' Baletoman [K. Skal'kovskii], *Balet, ego istoriia i mesto v riadu iziashchnykh iskusstv*, 266.

110. K.S[kal'kovskii], 'Teatr i muzyka', 'Novyi balet', *Novoe vremia*, 9 January, 1879, 3. *Les Enfants du Capitain Grant* was a stage version of Verne's novel of the same name, published in English as *In Search of the Castaways*.

111. Vazem, *Zapiski baleriny*, 146.

112. 'Я ему заметила, что такие темпы здесь совершенно не согласуются ни с музыкой, ни с костюмом. Какие, в самом деле, можно делать кабриоли в широких штанах? Балетмейстер по обыкновению заспорил. [...] [пляска будет носить характер] хореографического монолога, обращенного баядеркой к ее возлюбленному Солору. [...] Я, не стесняясь, забракова ла постановку. [...] [Он наскоро поставил мне что-то другое, еще менее удачное. [Я ему снова] спокойно [возразила, что танцевать этого не буду.] Тут он совсем вышел из себя и в сердцах закричал: "Я не понимай, что вам нужно дансовайт? Ви то не можь, другой не можь! ... Какой ви talent (талант), если ви нитшего не можь?" [...] Я, ни слова не говоря [...] У него, как видно, творческая фантазия совсем иссякла. Торопясь с окончанием постановки, он мне заявил: "Если ви ничего другой дансовайт не можь, делайте то же, что делает мадам Горшнеков." [...] "Как хошь, как хошь," отвечал Петипа [...] Балетмейстер, как бы желая снять с себя ответственность за свое pas d'action, твердил артистам: "Я не знай, что мадам Вазем будет дансовайт, она никогда не дансуй на репетиц." [...] Внутри меня кипело [...] Хотелось проучить зазнавшегося француза [...] буквально вылетела на сцену, перескочив даже через головы стоявших на коленях в группе танцовщиц. [...] "Мадам, прости, я—дурак. . .".' Vazem, *Zapiski baleriny*, 166–68.

113. Khudekov, *Istoriia tantsev*, vol. 4, 106.

114. Ibid., 172–73.

115. Pleshcheev, *Nash balet*, 320.

116. Ibid., 318 and 397–98.

117. Iurii Burlaka's 2008 staging for the Bolshoi Ballet of the grand pas under the title 'Grand pas from *Paquita*' claims greater authenticity than previous revivals. In 2001 Pierre Lacotte re-created the whole ballet for the Paris Opera Ballet.

118. Vazem, *Zapiski baleriny*, 173–74.

119. At that time dancers of the Imperial Theatres were expected to retire after twenty years, counting from their sixteenth birthday, although a few exceptions were made, especially for male dancers, among them Gol'ts, Johansson, and Kshesinskii.

120. '*que l'Europe nous envie*'. K. S[kal'kovskii], 'Teatr i muzyka', 'Novyi balet', *Novoe vremia*, 9 January 1879, 3.

121. Vazem, *Zapiski baleriny*, 92.

122. Ibid., 72.

123. Slonimskii, 'Marius Petipa', 110–11.

124. For an account of this ballet see Evgeniia Mikhailova, '*Roksana, krasa chernogorii*', in *Baletmeister Marius Petipa*, ed. Fedorchenko, 99–108.

125. Hariot, Lady Dufferin, *My Russian and Turkish Journals* (London: John Murray, 1916), 13. The author adds a mention of Marie Petipa: 'the beauty of the *corps dramatique* is called *Petit pas*, which I thought was a nickname, but it is her real name.'

126. Aleksandr Benois, *Reminiscences of the Russian Ballet*, 50–51; Skal'kovskii, *V teatral'nom mire*, 243.

127. 'В конце 80-х гг., когда балет еще не был искушен бесконечной беготней на носках целого ряда заезжих итальянских балерин, танцам на пуантах не п ридавалось такого первенствующего значения, как потом.' Vazem, *Zapiski baleriny*, 207.

128. Pictures reproduced in Judith Chazin-Bennahum, *The Lure of Perfection*, 190 and 192.

129. Author's conversation with the nineteenth-century ballet specialist and chore-ographer Pierre Lacotte in 1997; see chapter 3 and Vazem, *Zapiski baleriny*, 87; Théophile Gautier, *La Peau de Tigre* (Paris: Michel Lévy, 1866), 335–36.

130. Perhaps the most obvious illustration of point technique as an emblem of sta-bility and virtuosity is the 'Rose Adagio' of *The Sleeping Beauty*.

131. See Iuliia Iakovleva's detailed analysis of the ballet: '*Mlada*', in *Baletmeister Marius Petipa*, ed. Fedorchenko, 119–47. For more about Wagner in Russia, see also Rosamund Bartlett, *Wagner and Russia*.

132. The following synposis is taken from the published libretto (St Petersburg, 1879).

133. Iakovleva, '*Mlada*', in *Baletmeister Marius Petipa*, ed. Fedorchenko, 125–26.

134. GTsTM, *fond 205, ed. khr.* 239–94.

135. For *La Bayadère*'s other sources, see chapter 6.

136. *Golos*, 5 January 1880, 3; *Vsemirnaia illiustratsiia*, no. 571, 1879, 498, and no. 583, 1880, 215.

137. Iakovleva, '*Mlada*', in *Baletmeister Marius Petipa*, ed. Fedorchenko, 131.

138. See chapter 6.

139. Iakovleva, '*Mlada*', in *Baletmeister Marius Petipa*, ed. Fedorchenko, 140. The play of light and shade is apparent in Degas's 1876 painting 'Ballet Scene from Meyerbeer's Opera *Robert le Diable*', which shows, from the perspective of the orchestra pit, the 'Dance of the Nuns' on the Paris Opera stage. This was the scene, choreographed by Filippo Taglioni for the opera's premiere in 1831, that launched part of the Romantic aesthetic in ballet.

140. Iakovleva '*Mlada*', in *Baletmeister Marius Petipa*, ed. Fedorchenko, 133–34.

141. 'Новый балет—это пространный дивертисмент, состоящий из характерных и классических танцев и групп.' *Sufler*, 6 December 1879, no. 16, 7.

142. *Vsemirnaia illiustratsiia*, 1880, no. 583, 215.

143. 'Одна долина недурна, если бы не прорвалось небо и не виднелись, в течение целого акта, из прорехи газовые рожки с мелькающим газом.' *Sufler*, 6 December 1879, 7.

144. *Sufler*, 6 December 1879, 7; Iakovleva, '*Mlada*', in *Baletmeister Marius Petipa*, ed. Fedorchenko, 134–35.

145. *Teatr i iskusstvo*, 27 April 1897, 325.

146. Aleksandr Benois in *Reminiscences of the Russian Ballet* thought that *The Sleeping Beauty* had a *Gesamtkunstwerk* dimension because of Ivan Vsevolozhskiĭ's role in coordinating all the different components of music, narrative, design, and choreography (131). However, a few pages before (126) he offers another perspective: 'It [*The Sleeping Beauty*] is a *ballet à grand spectacle* similar to *La Fille du Pharaon*, *Koniok Gorbunok* or *Le Talisman*. Its author Vsevolozhskiĭ never intended to try any new experiments or present a new formula of ballet.'

147. 'Чем богаче постановка, тем больше и сборы.' *Sankt-Peterburgskii vedomosti*, 4 December 1879; quoted by Iakovleva, '*Mlada*', in *Baletmeister Marius Petipa*, ed. Fedorchenko, 126.

148. Riasanovsky and Steinberg, *A History of Russia*, 355–57.

149. Paul Ginisty, *Gil Blas*, 6 June 1883, 2. See also *Gil Blas*, 2 June 1883, 2, for a summary of the ballet's libretto. C. W. Beaumont's *Complete Book of Ballets* also has the libretto and cast list, 522–24.

150. Pleshcheev, *Nash balet*, 329. Pleshcheev also reproduces the full cast list (330–31).

151. 'A travers toute cette mythologie, les allusions sont, on le voit, faciles à comprendre.' Paul Ginisty, *Gil Blas*, 2 June 1883, 2. See also Richard S. Wortman, *Scenarios of Power*, vol. 2, 226.

152. Riasanovsky and Steinberg, *A History of Russia*, 364.

153. Ibid., 363.

CHAPTER 8

1. 'На нашей балетной сцене наклонность балета к феерии не могла обнаружиться особенно резко и проявиться в несимпатичных новшествах. При неограниченности ресурсов дирекции театров, богатство, фееричность постановки у нас существовала для балета издавна; затем, ставя балет-феерию, дирекция не была в необходимости сводить на нет хореографическую часть балета. Есть еще одна симпатичная сторона, проявившаяся в последнее время на нашей балетной сцене и способствующая ее оживлению. Это то, что дирекция отдает должное значению музыки в балете. Поручая писать балетные партитуры нашим выдающимся композиторам, дирекция успела уже дать несколько прекрасных партитур балетной музыки, с такою

жемчужиною во главе, как музыка Чайковского в *Спящей красавице*.' 'Ia. D.', 'Teatr i muzyka. Balet.', *Sankt-Peterburgskie vedomosti*, 7 December 1893; reprinted in *Russkaia baletnaia kritika vtoroi poloviny XIX veka*, ed. Petrov, 211–12 (211).

2. Pleshcheev, *Nash balet*, 320.

3. As previously listed, the Alexandrinskii was for Russian drama, the Mikhailovskii for French and German drama and operetta. (In Moscow, the Bolshoi presented opera and ballet, and the Malyi, drama.)

4. After 1882 the Maly (*Malyi*) was leased to a succession of impresarios and presented ballet, vaudeville, *féeries*, and operettas.

5. 'Надо было удивляться терпению и выносливости русских «вечеровых» солдатиков, которые, за незначительную плату, проводили почти шесть часов кряду по колено в воде, передвигая [разные] машины.' 'Peterburgskii balet vo vremia postanovki *Kon'ka-Gorbunka*', *Peterburgskaia gazeta*, Part 1, 14 January 1896, 5.

6. Teliakovskii, *Vospominaniia*, 29.

7. Ianina Gurova, *Ivan Aleksandrovich Vsevolozhskii i ego znachenie v istorii russkogo muzykal'nogo teatra*, 113.

8. See Arkady Ostrovsky [Arkadii Ostrovskii], 'Imperial and Private Theatres 1882–1905', in *A History of Russian Theatre*, eds. Robert Leach and Victor Borovsky, 218–53 (218–19).

9. Frame, *School for Citizens*, 87.

10. Frame, *The St Petersburg Imperial Theatres*, 39.

11. Pleshcheev, *Nash balet*, 319–20.

12. A. Sokolov, *Teatral'nyi al'manakh na 1875*, 193; see also 'Peterburgskie zametki', *Syn otechestva*, 28 January 1876, 2.

13. Wiley, *A Century of Russian Ballet*, 291–92.

14. Vazem, *Zapiski baleriny*, 142–44.

15. Ibid., 74–75.

16. 'Прошло то время, когда балерины делали сборы.' 'Teatral'noe ekho', *Peterburgskaia gazeta*, 20 January 1882, 3.

17. Skal'kovskii, *V teatral'nom mire*, 118–21; Shiriaev, *Peterburgskii balet*, 34.

18. 'Говорили, [правда,] что публика охладела, потому что балет не в моде. Но это несправедливо; танцы такое искусство, которое всегда будет нравиться, ибо оно в натуре человека. Уверяли ведь, будто и итальянская опера не в моде, когда она была плоха и ее не посещали, но стоило пригласить Патти, Нильсон, Мазини—и опера вошла в моду. [...] С балетом та же история; мода на него всегда была в Петербурге, когда танцевали Тальони, Эльслер, Гризи, Гранцева, Муравьева и т.п.; когда же танцевали посредственности, то и в 40-х, и в 50-х годах балет был совершенно пуст. [...]

   'Заверение же, будто балерин нет в Европе, хотя и подкреплялось командировкой балетмейстера, было также нелепо. [...] Отличных италья нских танцовщиц, далеко превосходивших своей техникой русских балерин последнего времени, было несколько, а Милан готовил постоянно новых.' Skal'kovskii, *V teatral'nom mire*, 120–21.

19. Gurova, *Ivan Aleksandrovich Vsevolozhskii*, 79–86.

20. Ibid., 152–58.

21. 'Это был настоящий барин, со вкусами европейца и хитростью дипломата.' Teliakovskii, *Vospaminaniia*, 30–31.

22. Petipa, *Russian Ballet Master*, 58.

23. 'Он все время должен был считаться с желаниями императорской фамилии и в течение восемнадцати лет своего директорства лавировать между тем, что он сам признавал полезным для театрального дела, и бесконечными просьбами и даже требованиями, сыпавшимися на него со всех сторон.' Quoted by Gurova, *Ivan Aleksandrovich Vsevolozhskii*, 135.

24. 'Курьезно, что судьба поставила его во главе оперного дела именно тогда, когда любимая его итальянская опера с итальянскими выдающимися артистами прекратила свое существование […] [русская опера стала] все более и более завоевывать симпатии публики. […] [Чайковский,] музыка которого нравилась всем как музыка мелодичная. […] Он, как директор и бывший дипломат, избегал это говорить.' Teliakovskii, *Vospaminaniia*, 30.

25. Gurova, *Ivan Aleksandrovich Vsevolozhskii*, 89–90.

26. Wiley, *The Life and Ballets of Lev Ivanov*, 31.

27. Pleshcheev, *Nash balet*, 320; Wiley, *Tchaikovsky's Ballets*, 96–102; Frame, *The St Petersburg Imperial Theatres*, 38; Gurova, *Ivan Aleksandrovich Vsevolozhskii*, 116–18.

28. *Materialy po istorii russkogo baleta*, ed. Borisoglebskii, vol. 1, 282–85.

29. My thanks to Olga Panteleeva for clarifying the question of opera training at the conservatoire.

30. Skal'kovskii, *V teatral'nom mire*, 225.

31. See Pleshcheev, *Nash balet*, 325; 'Kronika', *Golos*, 4 September 1882, 3.

32. Teliakovskii, *Vospominaniia*, 29. See also Frame, *The St Petersburg Imperial Theatres*, 38.

33. Gurova, *Ivan Aleksandrovich Vsevolozhskii*, 123–24.

34. Elizabeth Souritz, 'Moscow vs Peterburg. The Ballet Master Alexis [Aleksei] Bogdanov and Others', keynote lecture at the International Symposium of Russian Ballet, Harriman Institute, 12–13 October 2007, 6–9, http://harriman.columbia.edu/event/international-symposium-russian-ballet; Teliakovskii, *Vospominaniia*, 144–45.

35. Khudekov, *Istoriia tantsev*, vol. 4, 148 (footnote). Khudekov also writes that Petipa was subjected to the machinations of enemies during the 1880s, to the extent that a decision was almost taken not to renew his contract until members of the highest echelons (the emperor? Vorontsov-Dashkov?) intervened (148–49). Another enigma is three drafts of a letter of resignation, written by

Petipa, dated 20 December 1886, and found in the manuscript section of St Petersburg's Russian National Library (*Rossiiskaia natsional'naia biblioteka*). The drafts vary in language and intensity of anger and would seem to be addressed to Vsevolozhskii. Are they connected to Khudekov's claim of company intrigues? Or was Petipa angered by one of Vsevolozhskii's reforms? Or by Zucchi's insistence on appearing in the mediocre ballet *Brahma* and her suggestion that either Giovanni Marzagora or Achille Coppini stage it? (In the event it was Cecchetti who staged it for Zucchi's benefit performance on 17 January 1888.) See Nataliia Dunaeva, 'Un Mystérieux autographe de Marius Petipa' [Petipa's Mysterious Letter], in 'De la France à la Russie, Marius Petipa', ed. Melani, 123–33.

36. 'К сожалению, хореографические произведения г. Петипа, сочиненные в это время, были слабее его прежних, подобных произведений. От нашего почтенного балетмейстера требовали слишком много; тем более, что для балетмейстера недостаточно сочинить балет, он должен его разучить и поставить и затем следить за всеми представлениями—труд громадный. Не считая нового балета, танцев к *Нерону*, занимавших целый акт, и отдельных па для разных опер, г. Петипа пришлось сочинить в один сезон еще большие танцы к операм *Ричарду III* и *Пчилемоны и Бавкиде*.' Skal'kovskii, *V teatral'nom mire*, 227–28.

37. The Russian title for *La Fille mal gardée* translates as *A Vain Precaution*.

38. Petipa, *Russian Ballet Master*, 57–58.

39. Skal'kovskii, 'Benefis' Zucchi v balete *Prikaz korolia*', *Novoe vremia*, 16 February 1886, 4; reprinted in Skal'kovskii, *Stat'i o balete*, 224–27 (225).

40. Shiriaev, *Peterburgskii balet*, 73.

41. A. U[shakov], 'Novyi balet', *Golos*, 19 October 1868, 1; *Russkie vedomosti*, 8 December 1891, quoted by Bagadaeva, 'Tsar' Kandavl', in *Baletmeister Marius Petipa*, ed. Fedorchenko, 35.

42. Exhibition catalogue for *Excelsior* exhibition (20 November 2001–3 March 2002) at the Palais Garner, Paris, linked to the La Scala ballet company's revival of *Excelsior* which was premiered in Paris in January 2002.

43. This footage, filmed by Luca Comerio, was displayed in the Ballets Russes exhibition at the Victoria and Albert Museum in 2010–2011.

44. The Eden-Théâtre closed in 1894 and today the Théâtre de l'Athenée stands there, a much smaller theatre built on the space belonging to just the Eden-Théâtre's foyer.

45. This was a permutation of the European custom of presenting ballet in a double bill with opera or as part of a music hall's programme.

46. Ivor Guest, *The Divine Virginia: A Biography of Virginia Zucchi*, 38–41.

47. Tim Scholl, *Sleeping Beauty, a Legend in Progress*, 22.

48. Arkady Ostrovsky 'Imperial and Private Theatres', in *A History of Russian Theatre*, eds. Robert Leach and Victor Borovsky, 222; Krasovskaia, *Russkii baletnyi teatr vtoroi poloviny XIX veka*, 361.

49. Alexandre Benois, *Reminiscences of the Russian Ballet*, 77.

50. Krasovskaia, *Russkii baletnyi teatr vtoroi poloviny XIX veka*, 361–62.

51. Guest, *The Divine Virginia*, 55–59. *The Voyage to the Moon* was still being staged in the summer of 1910 (*Obozrenie teatrov*, 4 July 1910, no. 1106, 8–9).

52. Iurii Alianskii, *Uveselitel'nye zavedeniia starogo Peterburga*, 192–93; *Peterburgskii balet. Tri veka. 1851–1900*, ed. Boglacheva, 261 and 379–80.

53. 'Если эти влюбленные не бросались в Большую Невку, то только из боязни быть вытащенными самим г. Лентовским, который, закутавшись в испанский плащ, плавал часто, ради удовольствия, в ресторан Фелисьена, напоминая морского льва из Зоологического сада.' Pleshcheev, *Nash balet*, 344.

54. Skal'kovskii, 'Feeria *Puteshestvie na lunu*' [The *Féerie Voyage to the Moon*], *Novoe vremia*, 8 June 1885, 2–3, reprinted in Skal'kovskii, *Stat'i o balete*, 175–79; Guest, *The Divine Virginia*, 57 and 59.

55. Alexandre Benois, *Memoirs*, 142–13.

56. Guest, *The Divine Virginia*, 68.

57. 'Наше сонное казенное балетное царство, со времени отъезда Гранцовой пр ебывавшее в коснении и сумевшее за выходом в отставку лучших солисток и отсутствием новых талантов мало-помалу разогнать публику и обратиться в небольшой кружок папенек, дочек, тетенек.' Skal'kovskii, 'Ital'ianskie baleriny Giuri i Zucchi v opere-balete *Aréthuse*' [The Italian ballerinas Giuri and Zucchi in the opera-ballet *Aréthuse*], *Novoe vremia*, 20 July 1885, reprinted in Skal'kovskii, *Stat'i o balete*, 179–81 (180). In fact, Sokolova left the following year.

58. 'Первая мимистка в Европе'. (Ibid., 181.)

59. Khudekov, *Istoriia tantsev*, vol. 4, 122.

60. '[Не лишняя она была бы и для того, чтобы заставить поработать вне рутины] нашего балетмейстера, [не лишенного дарования, но] состарившегося и без должного стимула опустившегося. [...] Нравиться публике, [как известно], давно составляет величайшее преступление в глазах театральных людей [...] как решит он [Всеволожский] головоломную задачу иметь балет без балерин.' Skal'kovskii, 'Ital'ianskie baleriny Giuri i Zucchi v opere-balete *Aréthuse*', *Novoe vremia*, 20 July 1885, 2–3, reprinted in Skal'kovskii, *Stat'i o balete*, 181.

61. '[Точно также не по сердцу было и балетмейстеру Петипа приглашение этой] разнузданной, [по его словам,] итальянки виртуозки, которая и в Париже не могла добиться приглашения в *Grand Opéra*.' Khudekov, *Istoriia tantsev*, vol. 4, 121.

62. Guest, *The Divine Virigina*, 72–73.

63. Benois, *Reminiscences of the Russian Ballet*, 97.

64. Olga Racster, *The Master of the Russian Ballet: The Memoirs of Cav. Enrico Cecchetti*, 135.

65. Benois, *Reminiscences of the Russian Ballet*, 97.

66. 'N. B' [Bezobrazov], 'Balet. Iubileinyi spektakl' g-na Gerdta' [Gerdt's Jubilee Performance], *Sankt-Peterburgskie vedomosti*, 17 December 1885; reprinted in *Peterburgskii balet. Tri veka. 1851–1900*, ed. Boglacheva, 246.

67. Benois, *Reminiscences of the Russian Ballet*, 90.

68. Guest, *The Divine Virginia*, 86–87.

69. Letters in GTsTM, *fond* 205, *ed. khr.* 17, 35–37.

70. Guest, *The Divine Viriginia*, 110; Pleshcheev, *Nash balet*, 379; Surits, *Balet moskovskogo bol'shogo teatra vo vtoroi polovine XIX veka*, 243.

71. Giovanna Limido and Adelina Rossi only ever appeared on St Petersburg's commercial stages.

72. Shiriaev, *Peterburgskii balet*, 50–51.

73. Skal'kovskii, *V teatral'nom mire*, 210. All the sources consulted agree that Legnani was the first ballerina to perform thirty-two *fouettés*, except for Khudekov who remembers twenty-eight (*Istoriia tantsev*, vol. 4, 134).

74. Presumably as *maîtresse de ballet* in St Petersburg, Beretta was required to coach and teach. See Claudia Celi's entry for Beretta in *The International Encyclopedia of Dance*, ed. Selma Jeanne Cohen, vol. 1, 427. About the visits to Beretta in Milan, see also Shiriaev, *Peterburgskii balet*, 4; Tamara Karsavina (details in the next note); and the letter from Pierina Legnani advising Petipa about hotels near Beretta's studio for the visit of his daughter Liubov' (5 April 1899, GTsTM, *fond* 205, *ed. khr.* 35).

75. Tamara Karsavina, *Theatre Street*, 166–67.

76. Shiriaev, *Peterburgskii balet*, 52.

77. 'При первом взгляде на него никто бы не сказал, что это—балетный танцовщик-солист: немолодой, неважно сложенный, коренастый, с виду даже неуклюжий. Однако в танце все эти дефекты совершенно исчезали. Чекетти показал нам ярко выраженное искусство гротескового танцовщика, исполнителя темпов, которые нашим артистам и не снились [...] у нас была принята только строго-классическая, французская школа мужского танца. Главный его представитель и высший образец—премьер П.А. Гердт покорял мягкостью, изяществом движений, но был чужд виртуозности; в его танцах не было и намека тур-де-форса. По Гердту равнялись и другие наши танцовщики–солисты.

'Чекетти привез к нам из Италии ряд эффектных и трудных, почти акробатических танцевальных движений. "Коньками" его были бесконечн ые большие пируэты, во время которых он, не останавливаясь, переходил с позы ноги, вынутой вбок на 90˚ (*développé*), на аттитюд и заканчивал вращение в арабеске. Впрочем, иногда он возвращался в конце пируэта к первоначальной позе. [...]

'Большие пируэты [...]. Он сыпал ими, как из рога изобилия. Его можно было назвать "царем пируэта." Помнится, однажды в балете *Весталка*, заканчивая пируэтами свою вариацию, он поскользнулся и упал. Публика заплодировала и требовала повторения. Рассердившись на свою неловкость, Чекетти, бисируя вариацию, сделал в начале ее два–три прыжка и сразу же перешел на пируэты, варьируя их на разные лады, то *à la seconde*, то на аттитюд, то на арабеск и т.п. На этот раз он сделал в общей сложности до ста пируэтов!' Shiriaev, *Peterburgskii balet*, 39–41.

78. *Materialy po istorii russkogo baleta*, ed. Borisoglebskii, vol. 2, 38–39.

79. Shiriaev, *Peterburgskii balet*, 29.

80. 'Учащимся прививались: мягкость, плавность, грациозность движений, холодный, скульптурно-законченный стиль исполнения. Изучавшиеся темпы были самые простые: assemblés, прыжки, développés, круги, ronds de jambe, антраша, кабриоли, мелкие бризэ. Туры в воздухе допускались только в виде исключения—для отдельных танцовщиков, обнаруживших особую к ним способность. Так, эти туры делал мой однокашник Платон Карсавин (отец известной балерины Тамары Карсавиной), очень сильный танцовщик, который прекрасно делал и пируэты—мягко, спокойно, плавно.' Shiriaev, ibid.

81. Guest, *The Divine Viriginia*, 111.

82. Krasovskaia, *Russkii baletnyi teatr vtoroi poloviny XIX veka*, 596.

83. 'В', 'Teatral'noe ekho', *Peterburgskaia gazeta*, 25 November 1891; reprinted in *Russkaia baletnaia kritika vtoroi poloviny XIX veka*, ed. Petrov, 191–95 (193).

84. Krasovskaia, *Russkii baletnyi teatr vtoroi poloviny XIX veka*, 591; Shiriaev, *Peterburgskii balet*, 73; Benois, *Reminiscences of the Russian Ballet*, 130.

85. Shiriaev, *Peterburgskii balet*, 42; Nizhinskaia [Nijinska], *Early Memoirs*, 221.

86. This is preserved, along with other footage filmed by Shiriaev, on *Zapozdavshaia prem'era: A Belated Premiere* (DVD: Kinokompaniia Miris, 2003). The same DVD contains the solo 'Le Petit Corsaire', which Petipa created for his first wife (see note 84 for chapter 3), and versions using animated puppets of *Harlequinade* and of the Hindu drumming dance from *La Bayadère*. Shiriaev became interested in film and the potential of animation, devoting much time and energy to it. His suggestion of filming the Imperial Ballet's dancers in their roles was very regrettably turned down by Teliakovsky.

87. 'Петипа, сидевший во время спектакля обыкновенно в первой левой кулисе, поворачивал обыкновенно свой стул спиной к сцене, чтобы не видеть, как я сломаю себе ногу. [...] Однако старый балетмейстер оказался прозорливым. Гастролируя в 1912 году в Лондоне, я в этой пляске действительно сломал себе малую берцовую кость и пролежал полтора месяца в Чэрингкроссовском госпитале.' Shiriaev, *Peterburgskii balet*, 67.

88. Nizhinskaia [Nijinska], *Early Memoirs*, 139.

89. Ibid., 162.

90. Ibid., 137 and 156–57.

91. '[Он зарекомендовал себя, как всегда,] редким кавалером для танцовщиц, а ведь последних поддерживать при современной технике необходимо и нелегко.' 'А. P[okhvisnev]', 'Teatral'noe ekho', *Peterburgskaia gazeta*, 23 October 1895; reprinted in *Russkaia baletnaia kritika vtoroi poloviny XIX veka*, ed. Petrov, 221–23 (222).

92. Shiriaev, *Peterburgskii balet*, 29–30.

93. Vazem, *Zapiski baleriny*, 67.

94. Shiriaev, *Peterburgskii balet*, 61.

95. See, for example, 'Bukva' [Ippolit Vasilevskii], 'Peterburgskie nabroski' [Petersburg Sketches], *Russkie vedomosti*, 26 February 1886, 2–3 (3); Skal'kovskii, 'Benefis' Zucchi v balete *Prikaz korolia'*, *Novoe vremia*, 16 February 1886, 4, reprinted in K. A. Skal'kovskii, *Stat'i o balete*, 224–27 (225); M. N., 'Balet *Prikaz korolia'*, *Syn otechestva*, 17 November 1887, 3.

96. Benois, *Reminiscences of the Russian Ballet*, 93.

97. Guest, *The Divine Virginia*, 88.

98. 'Когда ее стали упрекать в чрезвычайной угловатости и резкости танца, то она посредством усиленных упражений старалась избавиться от этих характерных недостатков миланской школы. И действительно труды ее увенчались успехом. В свое исполнение она внесла большую мягкость, округлость и эластичность, то есть, те свойства, которые вообще присущи представительницам русской школы. Технически совершенный танец ее много выиграл благодаря тому, что она внимательно присмотрелась к изящным русским балеринам, не дозволявшим себе никаких антихудожественных уклонений от классических заветов хореографии.' Khudekov, *Istoriia tantsev*, vol. 4, 129.

99. 'Движения были плавны, округленны и вполне женственны; никогда не нарушали они общей гармонии ее симпатичной фигуры. [...] [П. Леньяни можно назвать] хореографическим хронометром.' Ibid., 132–34 (133).

100. Krasovskaia, *Russkii baletnyi teatr vtoroi poloviny XIX veka*, 612–14.

101. 'Ни один присутствующий в театре геолог не объяснил бы причины его внезапного появления. [...] [Огромная сцена—] сплошное море огня'. 'Bukva' [Ippolit Vasilevskii], 'Peterburgskie nabroski', *Russkie vedomosti*, 26 February 1886, 2–3 (2).

102. Skal'kovskii, 'Volshebnye piliuli', *Novoe vremia*, 11 February 1886, 3; reprinted in Skal'kovskii, *Stat'i o balete*, 222–24 (223).

103. 'Bukva' [Ippolit Vasilevskii], 'Peterburgskie nabroski', *Russkie vedomosti*, 26 February 1886, 2–3 (3); Krasovskaia, *Russkii baletnyi teat vtoroi poloviny XIX veka*, 367–68; Roslavleva, *Era of the Russian Ballet*, 114–15; the catalogue for the exhibition *Dva veka Petipa* [Two Centuries of Petipa] at GTsTM, 6 March–10 June 2018, has a photograph of Zinaida Frolova as the spinning top and reproduces the costume design along with Petipa's working notes (27).

104. *Teatral'nyj mirok*, 15 February 1886, 1.

105. '[Г. Мариус Петипа]—один из лучших и талантливейших хореографов и балетмейстеров в Европе.' *Golos*, 28 September, 2; '[Бенефис талантливейшего и бесспорно лучшего балетмейстера в Европе [Мариуса Петипа].' 'Teatral'noe ekho', *Peterburgskaia gazeta*, 20 January 1882, 3.

106. 'Весталка оказалась больше самого большого из наших балетов—*Дочери фараона*'. 'Veto', 'Novyi balet', *Novosti i birzhevaia gazeta*, 18 February 1888, 3.

107. Ianna Gurova in *Ivan Aleksandrovich Vsevolozhskii* writes that *The Vestal* was advertised as a *ballet-féerie* (293), but this is contradicted by all other sources and by the poster in the GTsTM's *Vestal* papers (*fond* 205, *ed. khr.* 128). Although the last item bears Petipa's written comment 'this poster is wrong' (*cette affiche n'est point juste*), in what way is unclear. However, perhaps it is futile to try fully to understand labels. The reason for announcing *The Sleeping Beauty*, *The Nutcracker*, and *Bluebeard* as *ballet-féeries* but *Cinderella* and *The Magic Mirror* as *ballets fantastiques* was perhaps clear to audiences at the time, but is a mystery to this author.

108. Letter from Saint-Léon to Charles Nuitter, 1 December 1866, in Saint-Léon, *Letters from a Ballet Master*, ed. Guest, 97–98.

109. Simon Morrison, *Bolshoi Confidential*, 152.

110. 'N', 'Farewell Benefit of L. Minkus', *Novosti i birzhevaia gazeta*, 11 November 1886, 3; quoted and translated by Wiley, *Tchaikovsky's Ballets*, 7.

111. Wiley, *Tchaikovsky's Ballets*, 38 and 23.

112. 'Personal Reminiscences of R. E. Drigo', Part 1, *Dancing Times*, May 1982, 578.

113. Wiley specifies in *The Life and Ballets of Lev Ivanov* that the published libretto has only Ivanov's name on the title page; however, in the working notes for his memoirs Petipa repeatedly included the ballet in lists of his works, while reviewers of the premiere all named Petipa as being involved in the staging (101–2).

114. Pleshcheev, *Nash balet*, 377, and Skal'kovskii, *V teatral'nom mire*, 167; the other brief quotes are taken from Wiley's translated round-up of reviews in *The Life and Ballets of Lev Ivanov*, 105.

115. Skal'kovskii, *V teatral'nom mire*, 237–38.

116. Mikhail Ivanov, 'Marius Ivanovich Petipa', *Novoe vremia*, 12 July 1910; translated in Wiley, *A Century of Russian Ballet*, 350–56 (350).

117. Elena Bobrova, '*Vestalka*', in *Baletmeister Marius Petipa*, ed. Fedorchenko, 175–92 (178). Bobrova's essay is an invaluably detailed analysis of the ballet. See also Wiley, *A Century of Russian Ballet*, 323–49.

118. Skal'kovskii, *V teatral'nom mire*, 141.

119. Mikhail Ivanov, 'Marius Ivanovich Petipa', 354.

120. Ibid.

121. Quoted by Wiley, *Tchaikovsky's Ballets*, 54.

122. Ibid., 55 and 59–62; Morrison, *Bolshoi Confidential*, 176. Zarubin includes Hansen's 1880 production but not his 1882 one (*Bol'shoi teatr. Pervye postanovki baletov na russkoi stsene 1825–1997*, 74).

123. Elizabeth Souritz, 'Moscow vs Peterburg. The Ballet Master Alexis Bogdanov and Others', keynote lecture at the International Symposium of Russian Ballet, Harriman Institute, 12–13 October 2007, 13, http://harriman.columbia.edu/event/international-symposium-russian-ballet; Krasovskaia, *Russkii baletnyi teatr vtoroi poloviny XIX veka*, 606–8.

The manager of the Moscow theatres at that time was Pavel Pchelnikov and he defended Bogdanov against his critics; however, during 1886–1888 Pchelnikov's authority was subordinate to the chairman of the Moscow board of censors Apollon Maikov who, like Ostrovskii, disapproved of Bogdanov (Morrison, *Bolshoi Confidential*, 443).

124. 'Balet *Vestalka*', *Nuvellist*, April 1888, 3–5.

125. Dismayed by Wenzel Reisinger's choreography in *Ariadne* (1875), Sobeshchanskaia had run to Petipa for dances for herself and the accompanying corps de ballet, which she then mounted on the Moscow stage (Surits, *Balet moskovskogo Bol'shogo teatra vo vtoroi polovine XIX veka*, 109–10).

126. This was for the ballet's fourth performance, when Sobeshchanskaia took over the role of Odette-Odile from its creator Polina (Pelageia) Karpakova. (About the casting of Karpakova, not the starrier Sobeshchanskaia, for the ballet's premiere, see Morrison, *Bolshoi Confidential*, 172, and Wiley, *Tchaikovsky's Ballets*, 46–47.) The new pas de deux replaced the pas d'action of the ballroom scene (no. 19 in the 1877 published score), but after some time it was dropped. Its music was then rediscovered in the Bolshoi archives in the early 1950s and found its way back into Bourmeister's 1953 version of *Swan Lake*, staged by the ballet of the Stanislavsky and Nemirovich-Danchenko Theatre and later by the Paris Opera Ballet. It was also used by Balanchine in 1960 for his *Tchaikovsky Pas de Deux*. See also Wiley, *Tchaikovsky's Ballets*, 58–59, and Simon Morrison, *Bolshoi Confidential*, 175–76.

127. Tim Scholl points to the closely similar opinions offered about Chaikovskii's score by the *Nuvellist* writer and by Ivanov in *Novoe vremia* (*Sleeping Beauty*, 6). His suspicion that they might be one and the same person is confirmed by *Ezhegodnik Imperatorskikh teatrov 1891–1892*, which names Ivanov as the editor of *Nuvellist* (420–21).

128. '[Музыка…] при всем своем изяществе, легкости и мелодичности, отличается серьезным отношением автора к своему делу.' *Nuvellist*, April 1888, 5.

129. 'Справедливость наших замечаний удостоверяется и тем, что в операх мы наоборот находим массу превосходной балетной музыки. Почему? Потому что балетмейстеры не осмеливаются в этих случаях налагать свою руку на музыку; так как балетных номеров в опере мало, то они решаются даже порою несколько отступить от традиции, шевельнуть воображением, если оно есть у них.' Ibid., 4.

130. As already detailed (Chapter 5, n. 91), *Peterburgskii balet. Tri veka 1851–1900*, ed. Boglacheva, attributes the music for *Titania* to Mendelssohn (122). Other sources list Pugni as composer, although it seems likely that Pugni was simply the music's arranger. All sources, however, are agreed that the music for the subsequent *Midsummer Night's Dream* was by Mendelssohn and Minkus.

131. About *The Adventures of Peleus* see, for example, 'Peterburgskie zametki', *Syn otechestva*, 28 January 1876, 2; 'Khronika', *Golos*, 11 (enthusiastic) and 20

January 1876, 2. Garafola names it as incorporating music by Delibes (*The Diaries of Marius Petipa*, 84); among the other sources some mention Delibes, others only Minkus.

132. 'J'ai fait tout ce que j'ai pu pour que M. Minkus compose la musique de notre ballet. Hélas! J'ai échoué de ce côte là! Celui qui composera la musique, tu dois le connaître, c'est un homme nommé M. Ivanoff, qui écrit dans le Nouveau Temps. J'ai fait sa connaissance, c'est un homme charmant et très doux. Comme compositeur je le crois capable. La musique qu'il a composé est très mélodieuse. Enfin, espérons!' (GTsTM, *fond* 205, *ed. khr.* 20).

133. Wiley, *The Life and Ballets of Lev Ivanov*, 92–111. However, Drigo in his memoirs categorizes both Fitinhof-Schell's score and Ivanov's *Vestal* as the first attempts to create a new kind of ballet music. See 'Personal Reminiscences of R. E. Drigo', Part 1, *Dancing Times*, May 1982, 578. See also earlier in this chapter and n.112.

134. Wiley draws attention to how Petipa, ever the 'borrower', recycled key elements and characters from *The Haarlem Tulip* into later ballets. For example, the benevolent Fairy of the Enchanted Field seems to be a precursor of the Lilac Fairy in *The Sleeping Beauty*, the fairy godmother in *Cinderella*, and the White Lady in *Raymonda* (*The Life and Ballets of Lev Ivanov*, 104).

135. 'B' [K. Skal'kovskii], *Novoe vremia*, 6 October 1887, 3, and *Peteterburgskaia gazeta*, 6 October 1887, 3 (both newspapers quoted by Wiley, *The Life and Ballets of Lev Ivanov*, 98 and 100). Also Skal'kovskii, *V teatral'nom mire*, 166; Pleshcheev, *Nash balet*, 378.

136. See the photo in ibid., 370.

137. GTsTM, *fond* 205, *ed. khr.* 70–128; the surviving notes for *The Vestal* are particularly extensive. See also Skal'kovskii, *V teatral'nom mire*, 177.

138. *La Vestale* was subsequently made into a ballet by Salvatore Vigano at La Scala in 1818; the opera was famously revived in 1954 at La Scala, directed by Luchino Visconti and starring Maria Callas.

139. Published libretto: *Vestalka* (St. Petersburg: Eduard Goppe, 1888).

140. Bobrova, 'Vestalka', in *Baletmeister Marius Petipa*, ed. Fedorchenko, 185.

141. 'B. N'. [Bezobrazov], 'Balet *Vestalka*', *Sankt-Peterburgskie vedomosti*, 19 February 1888, 3.

142. 'Ma fille est trop nue, costume pas assez drapé.' GTsTM, *fond* 205, *ed. khr.* 73.

143. Mikhail Ivanov, 'Marius Ivanovich Petipa', 352.

144. '[Thalie] une couronne de lierre sur la tête, un masque et une plume dans les mains, elle est suivie d'un petit singe—symbole d'imitation. [...] [Terpsichore] sur la tête une parure de plumes de différentes couleurs; un tambourin dans la main.' GTsTM, *fond* 205, *ed. khr.* 72.

145. Ibid., *ed. khr.* 73.

146. The Parnassus scene has parallels with the Balanchine-Stravinsky *Apollo* (1928) for the Ballets Russes; and yet Balanchine was born in 1904, when

this ballet had already disappeared. It is possible that Diagilev, as a student in St Petersburg, did see *The Vestal*, but Vera Stravinsky was adamant that both the scenario and staging were exclusively Stravinsky's. See *Stravinsky and Balanchine* (Yale University Press: New Haven and London, 2002), 85. Stravinsky was a young boy during the ballet's lifetime, so it seems likely that the parallels are coincidental.

147. Skal'kovskii, *V teatral'nom mire*, 176.

148. 'Новый балет—произведение безусловно выдающееся, талантливое и гран диозное. […] Неистощимая фантазия балетмейстера г. М. Петипа [и его творчество проявились в новом балете во всем своем блеске].' *Syn otechestva*, 18 February 1888, 3.

149. *Syn otechestva*, 19 February 1888, 3–4 (3); 'B. N.' [Bezobrazov], 'Balet *Vestalka*', *Sankt-Peterburgskie vedomosti*, 19 February 1888, 3. 'Появление муз […] было такой роскошной, живописной картиной, что вызвало бурные аплодисменты.' 'Vl. Kh-N', 'Teatr i muzyka', *Birzhevye vedomosti*, 19 February 1888, 2.

150. 'Vl. Kh-N', 'Teatr i muzyka', *Birzhevye vedomosti*, 23 February 1888, 3.

151. 'Balet *Vestalka*', *Sankt-Peterburgskie vedomosti*, 19 February 1888, 3.

152. See also Skal'kovskii, *V teatral'nom mire*, 175.

153. Mikhail Ivanov, 'Marius Ivanovich Petipa', 351.

154. Extracts from this correspondence are reproduced by Gurova, *Ivan Aleksandrovich Vsevolozhskii*, 291–93.

155. 'Balet *Vestalka*', *Nuvellist*, April 1888, 5.

156. 'Это нечто невозможное, как музыка для балета. Это какой-то хаос всевозможных звуков, без ритма, и можно только удивляться, как наши танцовщицы умудрились танцевать под такую музыку. […] Есть, впрочем, в *Весталке* несколько прелестных музыкальных номеров, но они сочинены не г. Ивановым, а капельмейстером, г. Дриго. На этих номерах публика отдыхала.' 'B.N.' [Bezobrazov], 'Balet *Vestalka*', *Sankt-Peterburgskie vedomosti*, 19 February 1888, 3.

157. 'Нападавшие на эту музыку балетоманы совсем не принимали в расчет, что самостоятельный композитор не мог ограничиться польками и вальсами, да еще там, где преобладает драматический элемент. Содержательность *Весталки* требовала несколько удалиться от традиционных балетных приемов, благодаря которым плачут и терзаются под звуки вальса, а умирают под аккомпанемент барабана … Г–н Иванов пошел по самостоятельной дороге, не угождая балетоманам, и написал музыку, которая, по мнению одного музыканта, имела тот недостаток, что слишком хороша для балета.' Pleshcheev, *Nash balet*, 391.

158. 'Сознаюсь, что после таких балетных композиторов, как Пуни и Минкус, с их незатейливой мелодикой и четкой ритмикой, нам, артистам, было не легко свыкаться с музыкой Иванова. Сложная партитура была трудна для

танцев и заставила немало поработать и балетмейстера, и артистов.' Shiriaev, *Peterburgskii balet*, 43.

159. Mikhail Ivanov, 'Marius Ivanovich Petipa', 354.

160. Pleshcheev, *Nash balet*, 381.

161. Skal'kovskii, *V teatral'nom mire*, 173–74 and 176; Pleshcheev, *Nash balet*, 391.

162. Ibid., 380.

163. 'Роль эта сильно мимическая и имеет полные драматизма места, в которых г—жа Корнальба была весьма слаба [...]. Зато танцевала балерина прекрасно, как всегда щеголяя своей элевацией, чистотой отделки [разных *pas]* и силой носка.' *Syn otechestva*, 19 February 1888, 3.

164. *Syn otechestva*, 18 February 1888, 3.

165. Wiley, *The Life and Ballets of Lev Ivanov*, 109.

166. Guest, *The Divine Virginia*, 119; Benois, *Reminiscences of the Russian Ballet*, 94.

167. Wiley, *The Life and Ballets of Lev Ivanov*, 108–9.

168. My thanks to Lidia Ader from the Rimskii-Korsakov apartment museum for her analysis of Ivanov's score.

169. 'Но что следовало бы действительно изменить в *Весталке* от начала до конца—это музыку, сочиненную г. Ивановым. Она погубит *Весталку*, и с ней балет долго не проживет.' 'N. B.' [Bezobrazov], 'Teatr i muzyka. Benefis' g. Petipa', *Sankt-Peterburgskie vedomosti*, 23 February 1888, 3.

170. M. A. Ryleeva, *'Talisman'*, in *Baletmeister Marius Petipa*, ed. Fedorchenko, 193. This essay has been a useful source of information.

171. Pleshcheev, *Nash balet*, 399.

172. 'Teatr i muzyka', *Birzhevye vedomosti*, 31 January 1889, 2.

173. Pleshcheev, *Nash balet*, 401; Benois, *Reminiscences of the Russian Ballet*, 121–22.

174. Walter Zidaric, 'Riccardo Drigo, le dernier héritier de la tradition musicale italienne en Russie à l'époque de Marius Petipa' [R. D., the Last Representative of the Tradition of Italian Music in Russia], 'De la France à la Russie, Marius Petipa', ed. Melani, 213–22 (219–20).

175. Khudekov, *Istoriia tantsev*, vol. 4, 159.

176. 'Итальянский акробатизм, шумно ворвавшийся в наш балет, вместо отпора, вполне естественного, был встречен г. Петипа приветливо и поощрительно.' 'Svoï', *Birzhevye vedomosti*, 8 December 1896, 3.

177. 'В юбилейном празднестве М. И. Петипа, представляющем апофеоз его п олувековой балетмейстерской деятельности, было бы вполне естествен но встретить нечто выдающееся, составляющее квинтэссенцию красот творчества, которых местами не лишены и слабейшие произведения его. Но, увы, первый сигнал к разочарованию был подан афишей, возвещавшей, что "будет представлено" балет-феерия *Синяя борода*. [...] Тем грустнее это, что юбиляр, с успехом дебютировавший у нас превосходным балетом *Пахитой*, полвека спустя выступает с детищем мало приличествующим образцовой сцене. [...] Балеты-феерии дают понятие о мозаике, блещущей яркостью

красок, но не дающей художественных рисунков, освещенных ясностью мысли.' 'Svoĭ', 'Benefis' M. I Petipa', *Birzhevye vedomosti*, 10 December 1896, 3.

178. [' "– Развивается балет или падает?"

' "– За границей безусловно падает, у нас пока еще нет."]

' "– Чем-же вы объясняете падение за границей?"

' "– Главным образом тем, что там постепенно уклоняются от настоящего, серьезного искусства, переход в танцах в какие-то клоунские упражнения. ... Балет—серьезное искусство, в котором глаз [unreadable] пластика и красота, а не всевозможные прыжки, бессмысленное кружение и поднимание ног выше головы. Это не искусство, а—повторяю вам еще раз—клоунада."

' "– Иначе—итальянская школа?"

' "– Да ... эта развращает публику, отвлекая ее от серьезных балетов и приучая к феериям, которые вводят на балетную сцену такие господа, как например Манзотти, написавший феерию—да, да, не балет, а феерию—*Эксельсиор*. В Париже уже перестали ставить большие балеты и довольствуются одними маленькими. ... Там балет падает—безусловно падает. А поддержать его некому. [...] Искусство занимается танцами или грубого, неприличного характера, или акробатическими упражнениями."

' "– В Петербурге этого нет?"

' "– Пока нет. ... Я считаю петербургский балет первым в мире именно потому, что в нем сохранилось то серьезное искусство, которое утрачено за границей. ... Петербургский балет не падает и не будет падать до тех пор, пока в него не проникнет увлечение итальянской школой." ' 'V. P.', *Peterburgskaia gazeta*, 2 December 1896, 2.

179. Wiley, *The Life and Ballets of Lev Ivanov*, 106.

180. See, for instance, 'Ia. D.', 'Teatr i muzyka', *Sankt-Peterburgskie vedomosti*, 7 December 1893; reprinted in *Russkaia baletnaia kritika vtoroi poloviny XIX veka*, ed. Petrov, 211–12 (211).

181. Tamara Karsavina, 'Origins of the Russian Ballet', in *Dancing Times*, September 1966, 622–24 and 636 (624 and 636).

182. 'B', 'Teatral'noe ekho', *Peterburgskaia gazeta*, 9 December 1896, 3; 'Z' [Skal'kovskii], 'Teatr i Muzyka', *Novoe vremia*, 10 December 1896, 3–4; 'Teatral'noe ekho', *Peterburgskaia gazeta*, 10 December 1896, 4.

183. 'B', 'Teatral'noe ekho', *Peterburgskaia gazeta*, 17 February 1898; reprinted in *Russkaia baletnaia kritika vtoroi poloviny XIX veka*, ed. Petrov, 308–10 (310). The purpose of these trips was also for Petipa to acquaint himself with new productions, as stated in directorate memos concerning travels in March 1888 (to Italy and Austria) and March 1891 (for two months). See RGIA, *fond* 497, *op.* 5, *ed. khr.* 2467, *l.* 301 and 304. Pleshcheev also writes about a much earlier trip, in 1884, when Vazem's retirement was being felt in both the repertoire

and the box office, so that the question of inviting foreign ballerinas turned from idle discussion into action. Petipa went to Paris with the ballet troupe's supervisor Aleksandr Frolov and their choice fell on the Paris Opera's Rosita Mauri. However, nothing came of it because her fee was too high (*Nash balet*, 339).

184. 'Teatral'noe ekho', *Peterburgskaia gazeta*, 23 April 1898, 4.

CHAPTER 9

1. From Skal'kovskii's review of *The Sleeping Beauty* in *Novoe vremia*, 5 January 1890, which is translated in Wiley, *A Century of Russian Ballet*, 373–76 (375). Other quotations from Skal'kovskii in this chapter are taken from *V teatral'nom mire* which reproduces the *Novoe vremia* review, but omits this particular comment.

2. Vsevolozhskii's contributions as librettist and designer were rarely acknowledged on posters and programmes; these examples are taken from Ianina Gurova's list in *Ivan Aleksandrovich Vsevolozhskii*, 367–82.

3. Evgeni Ponomarev, 'I. A. Vsevolozhskii', *Ezhegodnik Imperatorskikh teatrov 1899–1900*, Part 1, 25–32 (32).

4. Some sources give Peterhof as the location for the private performance.

5. A phoenix is normally a species of moth.

6. 'Какой апломб, какая сила, легкость и уверенность!' 'Teatral'nyi kur'er', *Peterburgskii listok*, 27 October 1889, 3.

7. Ibid.

8. Ibid.

9. 'Если мы дадим *Сон в летнюю ночь*, то мы спасены. Сознаюсь, что это громадный труд, но я обращаюсь к мужественному военачальнику, сделавшему уже множество кампаний и командующему великолепной армией.' Undated letter quoted by Khudekov, *Istoriia tantsev*, vol. 4, 156.

10. Wiley, *Tchaikovsky's Ballets*, 102.

11. Ibid., 102–4. Letter quoted by Wiley, 104.

12. 'Я боюсь, если закажу музыку Визентини, будет шум и гвалт по всему Петербургу, тем более, что второй балет он не стал бы писать даром.' Quoted by Gurova from Vsevolozhskii's letter, 27 July 1888, to his assistant Vladimir Pogozhev, *Ivan Aleksandrovich Vsevolozhskii*, 238–39 (239).

13. 'Перенести действо в земли мавров, т.е. Испанию, но, во-первых, повторяет ся *Зорайя*, а, во-вторых, уничтожается прелесть и наивность Перро.' Quoted in ibid. from another letter to Pogozhev (no date given), 239.

14. Wiley, *Tchaikovsky's Ballets*, 108.

15. The request was made to Vsevolozhskii and repeated in a letter dated 1 October 1888 from Chaikovskii to Pogozhev; see Wiley, *Tchaikovsky's Ballets*, 108–9.

16. Benois, *Reminiscences of the Russian Ballet*, 121.

17. Pleshcheev says she was twenty-two when she died, but the dates (1869-1889) show she was twenty (*Nash balet*, 404–5).

18. 'Teatral'noe ekho', *Peterburgskaia gazeta*, 14 February 1889, 3.

19. Skal'kovskii, *V teatral'nom mire*, 160–61 and 195.

20. Ibid., 198.

21. Benois, *Reminiscences of the Russian Ballet*, 128–29.

22. Skal'kovskii, *V teatral'nom mire*, 196–97; see also Benois, *Reminiscences of the Russian Ballet*, 131.

23. Ibid., 132. It was in this revival that Lopukhov's new prologue variation for the Lilac Fairy was inserted.

24. 'Bukva' [Ippolit Vasilevskii], 'Novyi balet *Spiashchaia krasavitsa*' [The new ballet *Sleeping Beauty*], *Russkie vedomosti*, 14 January 1890, 2.

25. Skal'kovskii, *V teatral'nom mire*, 196.

26. 'Сказки Перро представляют собой хороший материал для внешнего зрелища в силу поэтичности их описаний, но внутреннее их содержание, по своей нес ложности, простоте и детской наивности, не может дать пищи фантазии, нео бходимой для сочинения программы большого балета того типа, к которому наша публика привыкла [...]. Если же балет будет только зрелище, пестрый калейдоскоп костюмов и декораций, то никакая роскошь постановки не выкупит его пустоты, бессодержательности и той скуки, которая неминуемо к концу овладеет всяким "взрослым", не говоря уже об эстетически развитом зрителе.' 'N' [Dmitrii Koroviakov], *Novosti i birzhevaia gazeta*, 5 January 1890; reprinted in *Russkaia baletnaia kritika vtoroi poloviny XIX veka*, ed. Petrov, 181.

27. German Larosh, 'Muzykal'noe pis'mo iz Peterburga' [Letter about Music from Petersburg], *Moskovskie vedomosti*, 17 January 1890, 3–4. See also chapter 5.

28. 'Apollon, en costume de Louis XIV, éclairé par le soleil'. Wiley, *Tchaikovsky's Ballets*, 370. The young Louis XIV first danced the part of The Sun-Apollo in the 1653 court spectacle *Le Ballet royal de la nuit*; this fixed his image as the Sun King, and he would subsequently appear in the same role in other court spectacles. The tableau described is based on Sergei Vikharev's 1999 reconstruction of *The Sleeping* Beauty for the Mariinsky.

29. Balanchine wrote that the 'Jewels' dances in the ballet's final act represent the mineral world, just as the fairy-tale cameos refer to the animal and human world. See his essay 'Vyshe vsekh masterov' [The Greatest Master of All], in *Marius Petipa. Materialy, vospominaniia, stat'i*, ed. Nekhendzi, 280. A further possible allegorical touch can be found in Act I where Aurora's four suitors are summoned from the four corners of the world, to form a grouping with Aurora, the dawn of life, at the centre.

30. Wiley, *Tchaikovsky's Ballets*, 107–8; Vsevolozhskii's words are from an undated letter quoted in ibid., 103.

31. Ibid., 108.

32. Skal'kovskii, *V teatral'nom mire*, 197.

33. 'Местный колорит французский, а *стыл* русский'. Larosh, 'Muzykal'noe pis'mo iz Peterburga', *Moskovskie vedomosti*, 4.

34. '[*Спящую красавицу* надо считать] одним из удачнейших произведений ее даровитого композитора.' *Nuvellist*, no. 2, 1890, 3–5 (5).

35. '[Это обстоятельство, в связи с музыкой Чайковского, имеющей вполне достойного исполнителя в лице балетного оркестра, руководимого музыкально образованным капельмейстером г–ном Дриго, обеспечивает *Спящей красавице* солидный успех еще на долгое время. Танцовщицы, выросшие] на банальной музыке заурядных балетных композиторов, [сроднились с характером музыки Чайковского, и теперь *Спящая красавица* идет во всех отношениях на славу.]' 'N. B' [Bezobrazov], *Sankt-Peterburgskie vedomosti*, 5 October 1890; reprinted in *Russkaia baletnaia kritika vtoroi poloviny XIX veka*, ed. Petrov, 181–83 (182).

36. '*Спящая красавица или торжество швейного искусства*.' Skal'kovskii, *V teatral'nom mire*, 197–98.

37. Benois, *Reminiscences of the Russian Ballet*, 126.

38. Ibid., 131. Benois's *Gesamtkunstwerk* argument is disputed in Chapter 7.

39. Ibid., 133.

40. Letter from Petipa to Chaikovskii about this plan, dated 22 March 1890 and reproduced in *Marius Petipa. Materialy, vospominaniia, stat'i*, ed. Nekhendzi, 119–20. The company tour headed by Marie Petipa, it will be remembered, came later, in 1899.

41. 'Иностранная публика знакомится все больше с произведениями П. И. Чайковского. Нынешней зимой в Милане в театре La Scala ставится впервые балет "Спящая красавица" П. И. Чайковского. Балетмейстер La Scala г. Сарракко вчера прибыл в Петербург и повидался с нашим балетмейстером г. Петипа. Г. Сарракко воспользуется здесь указаниями нашего балетмейстера. Танцевать в "Спящей красавице" будет г-жа Брианца. Несомненно, поэтичный балет с прелестной музыкой Чайковского понравится итальянцам.' 'Teatral'noe ekho', *Peterburgskaia gazeta*, 10 September 1895, 4.

42. 'Балет очень подходил к хореографическим возможностям Брианцы. В нем все было подогнано к ней, [...]; смуглая брюнетка с черными глазами, она действительно выглядела здесь какой-то чертовкой.' Shiriaev, *Peterburgskii balet*, 46–47.

43. 'Двойных туров в танцах балерины такое обилие, что удивляешься, как у нее голова не закружилась.' 'N. B.' [Nikolai Bezobrazov], 'Teatr i muzyka', *Sankt-Peterburgskie vedomosti*, 15 February 1891, reprinted in *Russkaia baletnaia kritika vtoroi poloviny XIX veka*, ed. Petrov, 183–85 (185) See also, for example, 'B'. [Skal'kovskii], 'Balet Kal'kabrino', *Novoe vremia*, 15 February 1891, 3, and 'S. Kh.' (Khudekov), 'Teatral'noe ekho', *Peterburgskaia gazeta*, 19 February 1891, 3. As always, though, Khudekov railed against the emphasis on technique to the detriment of meaning.

44. 'B' [Skal'kovskii], 'Balet Kal'kabrino', *Novoe vremia*, 15 February 1891, 3; 'Pl' [Pleshcheev], 'Teatral'noe ekho', *Peterburgskaia gazeta*, 15 February 1891, 3.

45. For an analysis of the ballet, see Sergei Iuzenkov, '*Kal'kabrino*', in *Baletmeister Marius Petipa*, ed. Fedorchenko, 207–17.

46. 'Один из грандиознейших балетов "доброго старого времени".' 'B' [Skal'kovskii], 'Teatral'noe ekho', *Peterburgskaia gazeta*, 25 November 1891, reprinted in *Russkaia baletnaia kritika vtoroi poloviny XIX veka*, ed. Petrov, 191–95 (191).

47. See, for example, 'B', 'Teatral'noe ekho', *Peterburgskaia gazeta*, 11 January 1893, reprinted in *Russkaia baletnaia kritika vtoroi poloviny XIX veka*, ed. Petrov, 205–7 (205).

48. Pleshcheev, *Nash balet*, 436 and 439.

49. Skal'kovskii, *V Teatral'nom mire*, 203.

50. Ibid., 213; *Peterburgskii balet. Tri veka. 1851–1900*, ed. Boglacheva, 333.

51. Debra Hickenlooper Sowell, 'Brianza, Carlotta', in *The International Encyclopedia of Dance*, ed. Selma Jeanne Cohen, vol. 1, 540–41 (540).

52. Wiley, *Tchaikovsky's Ballets*, 197; *The Life and Ballets of Lev Ivanov*, 132–33; Benois, *Reminscences of the Russian Ballet*, 133.

53. Wiley, *Tchaikovsky's Ballets*, 197.

54. Children often appeared in Petipa's ballets—not in leading roles, but in dances. It gave them important stage experience, and they never failed to conquer audiences.

    About the Sugar Plum Fairy: her French name, *la Fée Dragée*, refers to the traditional sugar-coated almonds called *dragées*. About her cavalier: the Russian translation of Petipa's instructions to Chaikovskii, published in *Marius Petipa. Materialy, vospominaniia, stat'i*, ed. Nekhendzi, 137–44, gives his name as Prince Barley Syrup, *orshad* in Russian (144); Wiley's English translation of the same text calls him Prince Coqueluche (*Tchaikovsky's Ballets*, 376), about which see note 58 below.

55. Wiley, *Tchaikovsky's Ballets*, 198.

56. Wiley, 'On Meaning in *Nutcracker*', *Dance Research*, 3/1 (1984), 12–18.

57. Fedor Lopukhov, 'Baletmeisterskie eksplikatsii' [A Ballet Master's Analysis], in *Marius Petipa. Materialy, vospominaniia, stat'i*, ed. Nekhendzi, 153–224 (206–9).

58. The lyrics of 'Bon voyage Monsieur Dumollet', composed in 1809 by Marc-Antoine Désaugiers, could be read as having a subtext connected with the French Revolution.

    The song inspired a children's novel, *Le Voyage de M. Dumollet*, by Albert Robida, in which the hero travels on a donkey whose name, Coqueluchon, is derived from *coqueluche*, French for whooping cough, the sound reminiscent of a donkey. So maybe this is the source for Prince Coqueluche—or maybe not, since *coqueluche* has another meaning, designating someone who is particularly admired or loved.

59. See also Damien Mahiet who posits a political reading for *The Nutcracker* in the light of the Franco-Russian rapprochment of the 1890s: 'The First *Nutcracker*, the Enchantment of International Relations, and the Franco-Russian Alliance', *Dance Research*, 34/2 (Winter 2016), 119–49. Another writer is Margaret Fleming-Markarian, *The Original Nutcracker Ballet—A Hidden Allegory* (Fleming-Markarian, 2014).

60. Skal'kovskii, 'Teatr i muzyka', *Novosti i birzhevaia gazeta*, 8 December 1892, 3.

61. 'Балетный сезон начинается заболеваниями. Первый балетмейстер М. Петипа болен довольно серьезно.' 'Teatral'noe ekho', *Peterburgskaia gazeta*, 26 August 1892, 3. 'Здоровье балетмейстера г. М. Петипа до сих пор еще настолько слабо, что врачи не позволяют ему выходить из квартиры.' 'Teatral'noe ekho', 9 September 1892, *Peterburgskaia gazeta*, 3.

62. *Birzhevye vedomosti*, 29 September 1892, 3; quoted in Wiley, *Tchaikovsky's Ballets*, 200.

63. Chaikovskii's resulting letter, dated 13 March 1891, is quoted in ibid., 195–96; see also 306–7, n. 11.

64. There is confusion about the date of creation of *The Fairy Tale*: Lynn Garafola's list in *The Diaries of Marius Petipa* says 4 April 1891 (89), as does *Marius Petipa. Materialy, vospominaniia, stat'i*, ed. Nekhendzi (384), but the more recent *Peterburgskii balet. Tri veka. 1851–1900*, ed. Boglacheva, says 10 February 1892.

65. '[Отец присутствовал при операции.] Пережитые им страдания вызвали у него нервное заболевание.' Vera Petipa, *Moia sem'ia*, RGALI, *fond* 1945, *op.* 1, *ed. khr.* 66, *l.* 21.

66. RGIA, *fond* 497, *op.* 5, *ed. khr.* 2467, *l.* 328–29.

67. This information has been gratefully received from the dermatologist Dr C. M. E. Rowland Payne.

68. RGIA, *fond* 497, *op.* 5, *ed. khr.* 2467, 328–29.

69. Khudekov, *Istoriia tantsev*, vol. 4, 172; Wiley, *Tchaikovsky's Ballets*, 308–9, 371–76, and 376–82; Petipa, *Russian Ballet Master*, 85.

70. *Birzhevye vedomosti*, 29 September 1892, 3; quoted by Wiley, *Tchaikovsky's Ballets*, 200.

71. *Novosti i birzhevaia gazeta*, 8 December, 1892, 3; reprinted in Skal'kovskii, *Stat'i o balete 1868–1905*, 281–84 (282–83) and in *Russkaia baletnaia kritika vtoroi poloviny XIX veka*, ed. Petrov, 200–203 (201–2).

72. 'Для танцовщиц в нем весьма мало, для искусства—ровно ничего, а для художественной судьбы нашего балета—это еще одна ступенька книзу.' Ibid., 284 and 203.

73. Quoted in Wiley, *Tchaikovsky's Ballets*, 221.

74. Wiley, *Tchaikovsky's Ballets*, 221; and 'B', 'Teatral'noe ekho', *Peterburgskaia gazeta*, 7 December 1892; reprinted in *Russkaia baletnaia kritika vtoroi poloviny XIX veka*, ed. Petrov, 196–99 (197 and 199).

75. V. Baskin, 'Shchelkunchik', *Peterburgskaia gazeta*, 9 December, 1892; reprinted in *Russkaia baletnaia kritika vtoroi poloviny XIX veka*, ed. Petrov, 203–5.

76. Khudekov, *Istoriia tantsev*, vol. 4, 132.

77. Apparently the trick was achieved by means of a small concealed platform that travelled along a rail. See Wiley, *Tchaikovsky's Ballets*, 219. There exists a photograph of the couple performing the sequence.

78. Khudekov, *Istoriia tantsev*, vol. 4, 132; Vladimir Soliannikov, unpublished 'Vospominaniia' [Memoirs]; quoted and translated in Wiley, *Tchaikovsky's Ballets*, 204.

79. '[Я никогда не рассчитывал быть ни режиссером, ни балетмейстером,] зная свой слишком добрый и слабый характер; [...] [Должность режиссера] весьма беспокойная [...] [хотя быть балетмейстером тоже не особенно покойно, но все же лучше.' Lev Ivanov, 'Moi vospominaniia' [My Reminiscences], *Sovetskii balet* (January–February 1987), 39–43 (42). This edition of *Sovetskii balet* provides the full text of Ivanov's manuscript memoirs, preserved in GMTMI. Parts were also published in *Peterburgskaia gazeta*, 13 December 1901. A translation of the memoirs is in Wiley, *The Life and Ballets of Lev Ivanov*, 5–20.

80. '[Это был] удивительно скромный, нетребовательный, бесхарактерный, очень хороший, незлобивый, хотя подчас и вспыльчивый человек.' Vazem, *Zapiski baleriny*, 118.

81. Pleshcheev, *Novoe vremia*, 13 December 1901; quoted by Wiley, *The Life and Ballets of Lev Ivanov*, 68.

82. Ibid., 47.

83. Kshesinskaia [Kschessinska], *Dancing in Petersburg*, 23–24.

84. Vazem, *Zapiski baleriny*, 118.

85. Ibid., 118–20.

86. Wiley, *Tchaikovsky's Ballets*, 201, quoting Shiriaev, *Peterburgskii balet. Vospominaniia*, 48.

87. Wiley, *The Life and Ballets of Lev Ivanov*, 89–90.

88. Roslavleva, *Era of the Russian Ballet*, 128–30.

89. Different sources give different dates for Cecchetti's appointment. Borisoglebskii in *Materialy po istorii russkogo baleta* says 1890 (vol. 2, 39) and the first *Ezhegodnik Imperatorskikh teatrov*, which covers the 1890–1891 season, lists him as a ballet master (58) without giving the start date. The Imperial Theatre archives at RGIA (*fond* 497) should shed further light.

90. Roslavleva, *Era of the Russian Ballet*, 128.

91. 'Отличный знаток балетного дела и классического танца в частности, Иванов нередко ставил отдельные танцевальные номера и даже балеты для спектаклей Театрального училища, а также и для большой сцены, особенно, когда был режиссером балетной труппы. Однако в этом направлении Петипа ему большого хода не давал, не желая создавать себе соперника. Впоследствии Иванов занимал в Петербурге должность второго

балетмейстера, но и на этом посту ему не удалось в полной мере проявить свой несомненный талант хореографа.' Vazem, *Zapiski baleriny*, 117–18.

Others claiming Ivanov was unjustly treated by the directorate and Petipa include: Vladimir Teliakovskii, in *Vospominaniia*, 150, and in an infamous interview he gave to *Peterburgskaia gazeta*, 11 September 1905, 3; Borisoglebskii in *Materialy po istorii russkogo baleta*, vol. 1, 192; and lines in Lev Ivanov's manuscript memoirs, *Moi vospominaniia* (1899), added to the final page by his widow: 'He bore much injustice from Petipa Marius and contracted heart disease from stress.' See the translated memoirs in Wiley, *The Life and Ballets of Lev Ivanov*, 5–20 (20).

92. Wiley, *The Life and Ballets of Lev Ivanov*, 50–51.

93. Tamara Karsavina, 'La Fille mal gardée at the Mariinsky', in *La Fille mal gardée*, ed. Ivor Guest, 25–29 (27).

94. Wiley, *The Life and Ballets of Lev Ivanov*, 51.

95. Petipa, *Russian Ballet Master*, 85–86.

96. 'Петипа относился к Иванову с большим уважением, и об этом мне лично говорили и П. Гердт, и Н. Легат, и А. Ширяев, да и многие другие. Слухи о недружелюбии Петипа к Иванову распускали враги и завистники как Петипа, так и Иванова, и я становлюсь здесь на защиту большого мастера от подмастерьев. Мастеров—увы!—всегда было гораздо меньше, чем подмастерьев, которые занимаются не столько творчеством, сколько саморекламой. [...] Если бы великий мастер был жив, я посоветовал бы ему свою фамилию Пети-па изменить на Гран-па, что было бы правильно.' Fedor Lopukhov, *Xoreograficheskie otkrovennosti*, 65.

97. Wiley, *The Life and Ballets of Lev Ivanov*, 53 and 89–90.

98. 'Лев Иванов, по совету Петипа, готовил свои постановки дома, но, по природе очень ленивый, часто все же приходил в театр неподготовленным. Тогда он охотно позволял отдельным артистам не только переделывать кое-что [...], но и ставить самим целые танцы. Он, казалось, подчас был даже рад, что кто-то пришел помочь ему. Скромный и необычайно добрый по натуре, Иванов вообще не любил о себе говоритъ, никогда не хлопотал о себе и ничего не добивался для себя лично.

'Но зато, бывало, Иванов блеснет такой оригинальностью построения и движения, так ярко поставит, что прямо удивляешься, откуда это у него взялось.' Shiriaev, *Peterburgskii balet*, 63.

99. Karsavina, 'La Fille mal gardée at the Mariinksy', in *La Fille mal gardée*, ed. Ivor Guest, 28–29; also quoted in Wiley, *The Life and Ballets of Lev Ivanov*, 53–54.

100. 'Хотя я не обладаю таким талантом, как г. Петипа, но все же ставлю балеты не хуже многих других балетмейстеров.' Ivanov, 'Moi vospominaniia', in *Sovetskii balet*, 42.

101. 'Tantsovshchitsa v ogne' [Dancer on Fire], *Peterburgskaia gazeta*, 4 December 1893; reprinted in *Peterburgskii balet. Tri veka. 1851–1900*, ed. Boglacheva, 313.

102. On 20 September 1892 Perrot's *Naiad and the Fisherman* and on 11 October 1892 Mazilier's *Paquita* were revived, both in Petipa's stagings, but it is not clear how much Petipa was involved.

103. Petipa applied for both himself and his children by Liubov' Savitskaia, since by Russian law the children took their father's nationality, but their mother's religion (RGIA, *fond 497, op. 5, ed. khr.* 2467, *l.* 319–20). However, Russian nationality was initially refused for his children (*l.* 326–27), so it was just Petipa who took the oath (*l.* 334–35). Permission was granted to the children in 1899 (*Peterburgskii balet. Tri veka. 1851–1900*, ed. Boglacheva, 366).

104. Skal'kovskii, *V teatral'nom mire*, 209.

105. Sergei Konaev and Pavel Gershenzon, 'Commenti a *Raymonda*', in *Raymonda*, the programme booklet for the production staged by the Ballet of La Scala, Milan in 2011 (113–26 [113]). See also Wiley, *The Life and Ballets of Lev Ivanov*, 158, about Pashkova.

106. Ibid., 161–62.

107. Ibid., 164–65.

108. Skal'kovskii, *V teatral'nom mire*, 210.

109. Pleshcheev, *Nash balet*, 471.

110. 'Teatral'noe ekho', *Peterburgskaia gazeta*, 3 March 1894, reprinted in *Russkaia baletnaia kritika vtoroi poloviny XIX veka*, ed. Petrov, 219.

111. Wiley, *The Life and Ballets of Lev Ivanov*, 165–66.

112. *Peterburgskaia gazeta*, 25 July 1894, 3, reprinted and translated in ibid., 168. The same review credits the dances to both Ivanov and Petipa, but 'chiefly to M. I. Petipa' which prompted Petipa once again to take up his pen for a letter. He wrote: 'The libretto of this ballet was put together by Mr Ivanov and me together, the arrangement of the dances and mise-en-scène belongs exclusively to me; Mr Ivanov took no part in it.' (Программа этого балета составлена была г. Л. И. Ивановым и мной вместе, постановка же танцев и mise-en-scène принадлежит исключительно мне; г. же Иванов в ней никакого участия не принимал.) 'Teatral'noe ekho', *Peterburgskaia gazeta*, 27 July 1894, 3; also translated in Wiley, *The Life and Ballets of Lev Ivanov*, 168. Wiley argues that there is no reason to disbelieve Petipa's claim (167–68).

113. Wiley, *The Life and Ballets of Lev Ivanov*, 169.

114. Quoted in Wiley, *Tchaikovsky's Ballets*, 243. See also Roslavleva, *Era of the Russian Ballet*, 131–32. August Berger's version in Prague subsequently received a further eight performances (*Tchaikovsky's Ballets*, 243).

115. See Wiley, *Tchaikovsky's Ballets*, 244–45; Roslavleva, *Era of the Russian Ballet*, 132; Petipa, *Russian Ballet Master*, 62 and 64–65, n. 7.

116. Petipa's notes are reproduced with a commentary in Fedor Lopukhov, 'Baletmeisterskie eksplikatsii', in *Marius Petipa. Materialy, vospominaniia, stat'i*, ed. Nekhendzi, 153–224 (215–24). Lopukhov shows that Ivanov's patterns differed from those planned by Petipa.

117. Wiley, *Tchaikovsky's Ballets*, 245–46; Roslavleva, *Era of the Russian Ballet*, 133.

118. Wiley, *Tchaikovsky's Ballets*, 245.

119. Ibid., 246–47.

120. [Bezobrazov], *Peterburgskaia gazeta*, 18 February 1894, 3, quoted in Wiley, *The Life and Ballets of Lev Ivanov*, 171–72 (171).

121. Roslavleva, *The Era of Russian Ballet*, 80–81; Morrison, *Bolshoi Confidential*, 167–68; Wiley, *Tchaikovsky's Ballets*, 32–33 and 37–39.

122. Quoted in ibid., 248; see also 33–34, 248–49, 321–27, 337–41. Modest's version was itself further revised by the directorate and the format modified from four to three acts, with Acts I and II now recast as Act I, Scenes 1 and 2.

123. Quoted in ibid., 249; also see *The Memoirs of R. E. Drigo*, Part 2, *The Dancing Times*, June 1982, 661.

124. Wiley, *Tchaikovsky's Ballets*, 255–56.

125. Ibid., 244–45. The 'dramatically jarring change of key' is my subjective observation as an ordinary listener. A more detailed—and reliable—analysis of Chaikovskii's score and Drigo's adaptation can be found in Wiley's book.

126. 'Le second tableau est composé', quoted in Wiley, *The Life and Ballets of Lev Ivanov*, 174, and taken from the GTsTM, *fond* 205, *ed. khr.* 231; also reprinted in *Marius Petipa. Materialy, vospominaniia, stat'i*, ed. Nekhendzi, 212.

127. Shiriaev, *Peterburgskii balet. Vospominaniia*, 64; Pleshcheev, *Nash balet*, 486.

128. Wiley, *Tchaikovsky's Ballets*, 261.

129. These observations are based on present-day productions which include modifications and on Wiley's account which uses the ballet's notation score (probably written 1906–1907) and other sources (*Tchaikovsky's Ballets*, 259–69).

130. Ibid., 269.

131. *Novoe vremia*, 16 January 1895, 3, and 'Veteran', *Novosti i birzhevaia gazeta*, 17 January 1895, 3, both quoted in ibid., 269 and 263.

132. [Bezobrazov], *Peterburgskaia gazeta*, 16 January 1895, 3, quoted in ibid., 266; Coryne Hall, *Imperial Dancer: Mathilde Kschessinska and the Romanovs*, 47.

133. *Novosti i birzhevaia gazeta*, 17 January 1895, 3; [Bezobrazov], *Peterburgskaia gazeta*, 18 February 1894, 3; and *Novosti i birzhevaia gazeta*, 6 April 1901, 3. All quoted in Wiley, *Tchaikovsky's Ballets*, 263–64, and *The Life and Ballets of Lev Ivanov*, 171–72.

134. Wiley, *Tchaikovsky's Ballets*, 258.

135. Wiley, *The Life and Ballets of Lev Ivanov*, 169.

136. Boglacheva, *Artisty Sankt-Peterburgskogo imperatorskogo baleta. XIX vek*, 219–20.

137. Wiley, *The Life and Ballets of Lev Ivanov*, 188–89, 193–95, and 197–98.

138. Ibid., 63–66.

139. 'au maître de ballet—poète, grand artist, souvenir de reconnaissance à jamais'. 'B', 'Teatral'noe ekho', *Peterburgskaia gazeta*, 9 December 1896, 3.

140. 'Z', 'Teatr i Muzyka', *Novoe vremia*, 10 December 1896, 3–4.

141. '[Мне кажется,] ежели она упадет со второго этажа, то смело встанет на носки и не покачнется.' 'Beseda o balete u M. M. Petipa', *Peterburgskaia gazeta*,

20 January 1896, reprinted in *Russkaia baletnaia kritika vtoroi poloviny XIX veka*, ed. Petrov, 243–45 (245).

142. *Peterburgskii balet. Tri veka. 1851–1900*, ed. Boglacheva, 334.

143. Shiriaev, *Peterburgskii balet*, 53. Cecchetti would teach the girls' class up to 1901: see Nizhinskaia [Nijinska], *Early Memoirs*, 119 and 134.

144. 'B-v', 'Balet', *Teatral'nyj mirok*, no. 39, 1892, reprinted in *Peterburgskii balet. Tri veka. 1851–1900*, ed. Boglacheva, 307.

145. Shiriaev, *Peterburgskii balet*, 54–55. Also *Peterburgskaia gazeta*, 10 November 1897, 3, quoted in Wiley, *The Life and Ballets of Lev Ivanov*, 198.

146. Elvira Roné, *Olga Preobrazhenskaya*, 46.

147. Ibid., 26.

148. 'У него училось немало наших лучших классических танцовщиц. Он закалял их ноги, придавая им своим экзерсисом ту силу мускулов, которой отличался сам. Ему многим обязана в развитии своего дарования и Анна Павлова— величайшая балерина двух десятилетий XX века. Высокий подъем ног мешал Павловой твердо стоять на носках. Французская школа ее учителя Гердта мало уделяла внимания этой стороне балетной подготовки. В начале своей карьеры Павлова так плохо справлялась с "пуантами", что однажды, вертясь в финале вариации, не удержалась на ногах и села на осветительную будку. Занятия с Чекетти устранили эти недочеты ее искусства и создали ей настоящий "стальной носок".' Shiriaev, *Peterburgskii balet*, 42–43.

149. Elvira Roné, *Olga Preobrazhenskaya*, 32–33.

150. Kshesinskaia [Kschessinska], *Dancing in Petersburg*, 35.

151. Ibid., 45.

152. 'Почти каждый выход г-жи Кшесинской 2-й сопровождался опустошением петербургских цветочных магазинов. Ей подносились не корзины, а целые клумбы цветов.' 'В', 'Teatral'noe ekho', *Peterburgskaia gazeta*, 3 March 1894, reprinted in *Russkaia baletnaia kritika vtoroi poloviny XIX veka*, ed. Petrov, 218–21 (219).

153. Kshesinskaia [Kschessinska], *Dancing in Petersburg*, 28–29.

154. Ibid., 43.

155. Coryne Hall, *Imperial Dancer*, 37–44.

156. Kshesinskaia [Kschessinska], *Dancing in Petersburg*, 50–51.

157. Ibid., 57–58; Coryne Hall, *Imperial Dancer*, 51–52; Richard S. Wortman, *Scenarios of Power: Myth and Ceremony in Russian Monarchy*, vol. 2, 357–58. In what was an augur of the calamitous destiny of the new regime, the most memorable event during the coronation festivities was a tragedy: the massacre of more than a thousand ordinary Russians on Khodynskoe Field, gathered for a people's feast in honour of the new tsar. The near-total absence of crowd control and the surge of more than half a million people towards the booths providing food and souvenir mugs resulted in people crushed underfoot or pushed into the field's open ditches and pits (Wortman, vol. 2, 358–63).

158. Coryne Hall, *Imperial Dancer*, 45–46.

159. Ibid., 81.

160. Ibid., 137–39.

161. Ibid., 71–72, quoting Alexandra Danilova, *Choura*, 38.

162. Rudolf Nureev [Nureyev] staged several versions during his lifetime, notably one for the Paris Opera Ballet in 1983, and Sergei Vikharev's reconstruction for the company of the La Scala, Milan, was premiered on 11 October 2011.

163. 'Si vous êtes reposé après vos tribulations de Moscou, ne vous sentiez-vous pas capable de recevoir M. Glazounoff pour lui donner vos indications au sujet du ballet qu'il aurait à composer en vue de la saison 1897/8. Je voudrais qu'il ait plus de temps pour méditer sa musique. Au dernier dîner au palais du Kremlin, l'orchestre de l'Empereur a executé une [illegible] de sa composition qui m'a ravi. C'est du Delibes doublé de Tchaikovsky. Décidémment, c'est l'homme désiré pour nous composer des ballets.' GTsTM, *fond* 205, *ed. khr.* 28.

164. 'О музыке г–на Глазунова, скажем со своей стороны только, что своим гран диозным успехом *Раймонда* обязана в весьма значительной степени музыка льной партитуре г–на Глазунова. Музыка красива, блещет богатством оркес тровки и необыкновенной сочностью. Музыка *Раймонды* по большей части "дансантна", что после тех партитур, под которые заставляли танцевать нашу образцовую балетную труппу, конечно должно цениться.' 'В', 'Teatral'noe ekho', *Peterburgskaia gazeta*, 8 January 1898, 4; reprinted in *Russkaia baletnaia kritika vtoroi poloviny XIX veka*, ed. Petrov, 302–3.

165. 'V. B.' [V. Baskin], 'Teatral'noe ekho', *Peterburgskaia gazeta*, 13 January 1898; reprinted in *Russkaia baletnaia kritika vtoroi poloviny XIX veka*, ed. Petrov, 303–5 (304).

166. 'Несмотря на почти полную бессодержательность и скудость его сюжета, г. Глазунов, тем не менее, сумел внести в него много фантазии, вкуса, колорита, красивой, оживленной музыки, ритмического разнообразия и интереса, инструментовав его звучно и эффектно.' 'V. Ladov' [Frolov], 'Teatral'nyi kur'er', *Peterburgskii listok*, 8 January 1898, 4.

167. The 'Pas classique hongrois' with the *palotás* has, over the decades, appeared as *Raymonda Act III* in the repertoires of the Royal Ballet and Birmingham Royal Ballet. In Sergei Vikharev's 2011 reconstruction at La Scala the troubador's solo from Act I, Scene 2 was transferred to the 'Pas classique hongrois' for Jean de Brienne.

168. Roslavleva, *Era of the Russian Ballet*, 122.

169. Krasovskaia, *Russkii baletnyi teatr vtoroi poloviny XIX veka*, 412.

170. 'Г. Петипа в первый раз дал общую вариацию для четырех танцовщиков. На других европейских сценах это немыслимо, потому что нигде не найдется четырех первых танцовщиков, да еще таких, как гг. Легат 1-й и 3-й, Кякшт и Горский.' Pleshcheev, *Nash balet*, 538.

171. As performed in modern productions, the dance for the male pages in the Prologue of *The Sleeping Beauty* might be considered a precursor of this pas de quatre, given that it also contains spectacular jumps. However, according to the information generously provided by Douglas Fullington, only its ground plan exists in the Stepanov notation, made around 1903, not the steps. So beyond the probability that there was a dance in the original 1890 version, it is impossible to establish whether today's version is authentic. Pleshcheev, who saw the original *Sleeping Beauty*, singles out *Raymonda*'s pas de quatre as trailblazing, not *The Sleeping Beauty*'s.

172. 'Vous me désespérez. Enfin, si cela ne vous dit rien, tendez moi une perche pour un ballet Criméen.' GTsTM, *fond* 205, *ed. khr.* 38.

173. The ballet's subject is advertised on the posters as 'borrowed from a knightly legend'. About the revisions, see the letters from Vsevolozhskii to Petipa (22 October 1895), from Petipa to Vsevolozhskii (18 June 1896) and from Petipa to Glazunov (19 June 1896). GTsTM, *fond* 205, *ed. khr.* 14 and 26.

174. Vikharev's La Scala staging in 2011 omits Abderrakhman's entry in Act I, Scene 1, on the grounds that it was a last-minute addition to the original and disrupts the musical structure. However, the reason for the introduction of Abderrakhman at this point could well be that, without it, spectators would be confused by his later appearance in the ballet's dream sequence, not knowing who he was. See the published programme for the Scala production, 118–19.

175. *Cour d'amour* (Court of Love): a festival of troubadour poetry and romantic debate. *Cour d'amour* was also the title of a *ballet à grand spectacle* in 1884 at the Théâtre-Eden and an *opéra-comique* at the Théâtre des Bouffes-du-Nord in 1885.

176. Skal'kovskii, *V teatral'nom mire*, 218.

177. GTsTM, *fond* 205, *ed. khr.* 470.

178. Teliakovskii, *Vospominaniia*, 35.

179. Prince Sergei Volkonskii [Serge Wolkonsky], *My Reminiscences*, vol. 2, 70–71.

180. Teliakovskii, *Vospominaniia*, 35–36.

181. Petipa, *Russian Ballet Master*, 60.

182. Teliakovskii, *Vospominaniia*, 31.

183. Benois, *Reminiscences of the Russian Ballet*, 126 and 131.

184. Sergei Konaev and Pavel Gershenzon, 'Commenti a *Raymonda*', in *Raymonda* programme booklet, 119.

185. 'Художник был более чем посредственный и вкус имел дилетантский.' Teliakovskii, *Vospaminaniia*, 31. To this writer's eyes the hectic colours and shapes of the costumes in the Mariinsky Ballet's 1999 reconstruction of *The Sleeping Beauty* support Teliakovsky's view.

186. 'Балет давно завоевал себе на западе почти равные права с другими отраслями сценического искусства, а у нас в Петербурге он занимает даже

исключительное положение и пользуется таким вниманием со стороны дирекции Императорских театров, такими заботами, какими, к сожалению, не пользуется и опера. Объяснение этому найти очень легко: почти все высокоторжественные спектакли, по традициям, составляются из балетных представлений, а потому балет наш отличается роскошью постановки, блеском и художественностью. Вот почему дирекция так заботливо относится к этой отрасли искусства, не жалеет средств на постановку и обстановку балетных спектаклей, держит для одной петербургской сцены трех балетмейстеров, организовала специальную школу для подготовки новых артистов и, кроме того, приглашает иностранных балерин.' 'Neskol'ko slov o peterburgskom balete' [A Few Words about the Petersburg Ballet], *Teatral*, Book 33, no. 83, 1896, 106–11 (106–7).
187. Mikhail Ivanov, 'Marius Ivanovich Petipa', 351.

CHAPTER 10

1. 'На меня страшно зол за то, что его вышибаю я из грязной его колеи.' Vladimir Teliakovskii, *Dnevniki Direktora Imperatorskhikh teatrov 1901–1903*, 363.
2. 'Он тщательно проверял актера, прежде чем поручить ему ту или иную партию. Если актеру она сразу не удавалась, не отнимал роль, пока актер не сыграет несколько спектаклей. [...]

    'Внешне Петипа скорее напоминал сановника, чем актера. Особенно в парадных случаях, когда надевал все ордена и медали. Походка у него была своеобразная: мелкие пажки и неподвижный корпус. [...]

    'Всегда подтянутый, привыкший властвовать, он крепко держал балетный коллектив в своих руках. Многоголосая топла артистов балета мгновенно стихала, когда мимо нее не спеша проходил маститый балетмейстер. Легким кивком отвечал на приветствия молодых артистов; рукопожатием Петипа жаловал в редких случаях. Строгая дисциплина, которую требовал и которой добивался Петипа, конечно, играла немалую роль в общей слаженн ости спектакля и в становлении сплоченного балетного коллектива.' Nikolai Soliannikov, 'Glava russkogo baleta', in *Marius Petipa. Materialy, vospominaniia, stat'i*, ed. Nekhendzi, 259–66 (260).
3. '[С. М. Волконский,] энергично принявшийся за реформирование всех частей своего управления. Особенное внимание обратил он на балет, который, по его мнению, [в художественном отношении] сильно отстал от других искусств и требовал обновления.' Shiriaev, *Peterburgskii balet*, 67.
4. The first issues, vol. 1, nos. 1 and 2, were published together on 10 November 1898, although they were dated January 1899 (Richard Buckle, *Diaghilev*, 41).
5. S. Grover, 'The World of Art Movement in Russia', *Russian Review*, 32/1 (1973), 34, cited in Orlando Figes, *Natasha's Dance*, 211.
6. Ibid., 202–3; Rosamund Bartlett, *Wagner and Russia*, 65–67, 79–81.

7. Krasovskaia, *Russkii baletnyi teatr vtoroi poloviny XIX veka*, 416; Petipa, *Russian Ballet Master*, 66.

8. Benois, *Reminiscences of the Russian Ballet*, 205.

9. Gurova, *Ivan Aleksandrovich Vsevolozhsky*, 256–57, quoting both RGIA, *fond 407, op. 14, ed. khr. 12, l. 7*, and 'N. B.' [Bezobrazov], 'Itogi baletnogo sezona [The Results of the Ballet Season]. Teatral'noe ekho', *Peterburgskaia gazeta*, 27 February 1900; Wiley, *Tchaikovsky's Ballets*, 102, quoting Dnevniki P. I. Chaikovskogo (Moscow and Petrograd, 1923), 110. Aleksandr Gorskii choreographed a version of *Salammbô* for the Moscow stage in 1910.

10. Benois, *Reminiscences of the Russian Ballet*, 140; 'N. B.' [Bezobrazov], 'Benefis' P. Legnani', *Peterburgskaia gazeta*, 24 January 1900, 4; 'Z' [Skal'kovskii], 'Teatr i muzyka', *Novoe vremia*, 14 April 1900, 4.

11. The libretti for *The Seasons* and for *The Trial of Damis* (called *Ruses d'amour*) are reproduced in Beaumont, *The Complete Book of Ballets*, 558–61.

12. Krasovskaia, *Russkii baletnyi teatr vtoroi poloviny XIX veka*, 417–18.

13. Petipa, *Russian Ballet Master*, 66; see also Shiriaev, *Peterburgskii balet*, 67.

14. Volkonskii [Wolkonsky], *My Reminiscences*, vol. 2, 69.

15. Teliakovskii, *Vospominaniia*, 37.

16. Volkonskii [Wolkonsky], *My Reminiscences*, vol. 2, 71.

17. Benois, *Reminiscences of the Russian Ballet*, 207.

18. Ibid., 205–6.

19. As early as 1881, Vazem had inserted the pizzicato solo from Sylvia into Zoraiia. See Vazem, *Zapiski baleriny*, 173.

20. Benois, *Reminiscences of the Russian Ballet*, 213–17.

21. Ivanov was then asked to stage Sylvia and by October 1901 he had almost finished Act I. It was at this point, however, that he fell terminally ill. Gerdt, required to take over, proved out of his depth and turned to Shiriaev for help. The result, premiered on 2 December 1901, was, despite the music, a damp squib (Wiley, *The Life and Ballets of Lev Ivanov*, 207–8).

22. Volkonskii [Wolkonsky], *My Reminiscences*, vol. 2, 94.

23. 'Раз один наивный человек меня спросил: "Да что же это, наконец? В Александринском театре—Савина, в Мариинском—Кшесинская распоряжается, а вы кто же?"

    'Я отвечал: "Директор".' Teliakovskii, *Vospominaniia*, 153.

24. *The Diaries of Marius Petipa*, 25.

25. 'Вот перед выходом этого репертуара в дирекцию являлся главный режиссер балета Аистов. Он был такой большой и солидный мужчина, говорил громко и басом: "Кшесинская прислала мне сказать, что тогда-то она будет танцевать такой-то балет, о чем и считаю долгом поставить ваше превосходительство в известность."

    '"Что же, хорошо," отвечал директор. "Пускай танцует. А я думал было дать балет другой, и такой-то танцовщице. ... Ну, все равно, я повременю, отложим до следующего раза".' Teliakovskii, *Vospominaniia*, 153–54.

26. Ibid., 153.
27. 'Khronika teatra i iskusstva', *Teatr i iskusstvo*, no. 42, 1899, reprinted in *Peterburgskii balet. Tri veka. 1851–1900*, ed. Boglacheva, 359–60.
28. Kshesinskaia [Kschessinska], *Dancing in Petersburg*, 71–72.
29. Volkonskii [Wolkonsky], *My Reminiscences*, vol. 2, 95–103 and 107–10; Kshesinskaia [Kschessinska], *Dancing in Petersburg*, 81–82.
30. V. Svetlov, *Rossiia*, 28 September 1901, quoted in *Peterburgskii balet. Tri veka. 1901–1950*, ed. N. Zozulina and V. Mironova, 23. Teliakovskii reports that Kshesinskaia was booed at Bekefi's benefit performance, diary entry 21 November 1901, *Dnevniki Direktora Imperatorskikh teatrov 1901–1903*, 108–9.
31. Teliakovskii, diary entry 4 October 1901, ibid., 71–72 (72).
32. Teliakovskii, diary entry 13 October 1901, ibid., 80–81 (81); see also the interview 'Balet. M. I. Petipa', *Peterburgskaia gazeta*, 1 January 1903, 4, where Petipa says she is the best of the contemporary ballerinas.
33. '[Эта настоящая балерина] высшей школы с необыкновенной грацией и с большим талантом мимики.' Teliakovskii, diary entry 28 October 1901, *Dnevniki Direktora Imperatorskikh teatrov 1901–1903*, 91.
34. Teliakovskii diary entry 4 November 1901, ibid., 96.
35. Teliakovskii, diary entries 21 and 23 November 1901, ibid., 108–9 (108) and 110–11 (111).
36. Frame, *The St Petersburg Imperial Theatres*, 28.
37. Shiriaev, *Peterburgskii balet*, 70–71.
38. Benois, *Reminiscences of the Russian Ballet*, 220.
39. D. Zolotnitskii, 'Ob avtore etoi knigi' ('About the Author of this Book'), preface in Teliakovskii, *Vospominaniia*, 5–16 (6).
40. Teliakovskii, *Vospominaniia*, 39.
41. Ibid., 144–45.
42. Ibid., 165.
43. Benois, *Reminiscences of the Russian Ballet*, 197–98; Lynn Garafola, *Diaghilev's Ballets Russes*, 15.
44. Teliakovskii, *Vospominaniia*, 162. Volkonskii's attempts in Petersburg to introduce new designers came a little later.
45. After a brief career at the Mariinskii, Chaliapin only attracted attention after joining the Private Opera Company in 1896. His return to the imperial stage, first in Moscow, then St Petersburg, contributed to the Private Opera's collapse (Zolotnitskii's preface in Teliakovskii, *Vospominaniia*, 7–8).
46. However, Sergei Konaev's commentary in *Marius Petipa. 'Memuary' i dokumenty* (212) records the Moscow dancer Ol'ga Nekrasova's claim, in her memoirs, that Gorskii's notation of the ballet was stolen during the very first rehearsal.
47. Teliakovskii, *Vospominaniia*, 147.
48. Ibid., 146–47. Teliakovskii names Nikolai Dosekin as the third designer, but other sources, including *Ezhegodnik Imperatorskikh teatrov*, give Nikolai Klodt.
49. D. Zolotnitskii's preface in Teliakovskii, *Vospominaniia*, 7.

50. Teliakovskii, *Vospominaniia*, 148.

51. Roslavleva, *Era of the Russian Ballet*, 159. However, this is not to suggest that Petipa's own action group scenes were expressionless. Vera Petipa remembers how her father instructed the children, when Aurora faints in *The Sleeping Beauty*, to take part in the general manifestation of grief (Vera Petipa, *Moia sem'ia*, RGALI, *fond* 1945, *op.* 1, *ed. khr.* 66, *l.* 11). The difference must be that Petipa kept everything within a geometrically ordered, classical stylisation.

52. Benois, *Reminiscences of the Russian Ballet*, 222.

53. Roslavleva, *Era of the Russian Ballet*, 159.

54. Teliakovskii, *Vospominaniia*, 148.

55. Petipa, *Russian Ballet Master*, 78. Actually, Petipa's assertion that Gorskii had not staged a work of his own before going to Moscow is not quite correct: on 11 April 1899 he created *Clorinda*, a one-act ballet for the school.

56. Ibid., 78. Petipa, as reported by *Peterburgskaia gazeta*, 5 September 1905, was thinking of taking court action over Gorskii's *Pharaoh's Daughter*, but seems subsequently to have been advised against it or at least changed his mind. There is, of course, some irony in all this, considering Petipa's own run-in with legal action in Paris, but the injury here was on a bigger scale. See also about Gorskii's *Don Quixote* further on in this chapter.

57. Teliakovskii, *Vospominaniia*, 150–51.

58. Spencer Golub, 'The Silver Age, 1905–1917', in *A History of Russian Theatre*, 278–301 (281); Jean Benedetti, 'Stanislavsky and the Moscow Art Theatre 1898–1938', in ibid., 254–77 (263–64).

59. Arkady Ostrovsky, 'Imperial and Private Theatres, 1882–1905', in ibid., 218–53 (234).

60. Teliakovskii, *Vospominaniia*, 151–52.

61. 'Когда я говорил, что в театре хорошо и достойно, но скучно, мне отвечали: "Как скучно, когда до вас было весело? Чего вам недостает? В озобновите Орлеанскую деву Шиллера, Кориолана Шекспира, Руслана и Людмилу Глинки, наконец, Фиделио Бетховена или балеты Весталку, Зорайю или Царя Кандавла—и будет весело. Ведь это все образцовые, испытанные произведения".' *Teliakovskii*, *Vospominaniia*, 165–66.

62. Ibid., 166–68.

63. Ibid., 166.

64. 'Иван Александрович Всеволожский носится с Петипа как с писаной торбой.' Teliakovskii, diary entry 23 January 1902, *Dnevniki Direktora Imperatorskikh teatrov 1901–1903*, 156–57 (157).

65. '[Иванов, не занимаясь совершенно балетом,] тем не менее продолжает заниматься составлением либретто балетов в надежде, конечно, что может быть, какое-нибудь и пригодится Дирекции, и тогда он получит отдельную плату. Обирание казны—[отсутствие работы и бесцеремонность получения даром содержания—вообще практикуется здесь в самом широком размере,

при этом тот же] Иванов имеет нахальство жаловаться на слабое здоровье Ширяева—помощника.' Teliakovskii, diary entry 5 November 1901, in ibid., 96–97 (97).

66. Teliakovskii, diary entry 26 February 1902, in ibid., 192–93 (193).

67. 'Старый, злой старик, взяточник, нахальный француз, за пятьдесят лет не выучившийся в России на русские деньги говорить по-русски, чувствует инстинктивно все то презрение, которое я к нему питаю. Имея раздутую и ни на чем не основанную репутацию гениального балетмейстера, он чувствует, что в лице меня встретил Директора, не поддающегося обману его обаяния, и этого он не может простить. [...] Он отстаивает с пеной у рта свою позицию, и его злой язык в беззубом рте, похожий на змеиное жало, всякий день на сцене старается меня дискредитировать. Балет боится его—его взяток и его обаяния—и молчит. Но, конечно, видят, как у него из рук валится дело. Довольно взять список балетов, поставленных Петипа, чтобы убедиться, что почти все из них провалились и не оставили следа в репертуаре. Все, что идет и хорошо, принадлежит Перро и С. Жоржу и С. Леону. Петипа лишь удачны, и то не по постановке, а по успеху, балеты, поддержанные музыкой Чайковского.' Ibid., diary entry 22 November 1902, 358. My thanks to Pascale Melani, 'Les Coulisses du ballet: Petipa contre Teliakovskii' [Backstage at the Ballet: Petipa against Teliakovskii], in 'De la France à la Russie, Marius Petipa', ed. Melani, 263–83 (263–64), for bringing this passage to my attention.

68. For example, Teliakovskii, diary entries 9 September 1901, 3 November 1902, and 27 January 1903, *Dnevniki Direktora Imperatorskikh teatrov 1901–1903*, 52, 340, and 413.

69. Teliakovskii, diary entries 27 October 1903, 10 April 1905, *Dnevniki Direktora Imperatorskikh teatrov 1903–1906*, 57–58 and 459.

70. Teliakovskii, *Vospominaniia*, 149.

71. Petipa, *Russian Ballet Master*, 91.

72. 'Мне, по моему положению помощника балетмейстера, приходилось более, чем кому-нибудь другому из балетной труппы, быть невольным свидетелем всех перипетий этой систематической травли выдающегося балетмейстера.' Shiriaev, *Peterburgskii balet*, 71.

73. Petipa, *Russian Ballet Master*, 67–68.

74. Teliakovskii, diary entry 12 September 1901, *Dnevniki Direktora Imperatorskikh teatrov. 1901–1903*, 55.

75. Teliakovskii, *Vospominaniia*, 438.

76. Moreover copyright in ballet was made all the more complicated by the fact that copyright laws varied from country to country. But copyright is a big subject, far beyond the scope of this book. Guesswork suggests that when a ballet was transferred from, say, the Paris Opera to St Petersburg, the money paid—to the Paris Opera or to the ballet's creators—depended on the various contracts that had been drawn up.

77. 'Талантливый балетмейстер, возобновляя прежние балеты, будет сочинять танцы в соответствии с собственной фантазией, своим талантом и вкусами публики своего времени и не станет терять свое время и труд, копируя то, что было сделано другими в стародавние времена.' Marius Petipa, 'Otzyv o knige V. I. Stepanova' [A Response to Stepanov's Book], in *Marius Petipa: Materialy, vospominaniia, stat'i*, 121. Petipa's letter was addressed to a committee set up to examine the viability of the Stepanov Notation. Following the committee's findings, the system was added to the school curriculum.

78. From all this, it would seem that the ballets created by Petipa were deemed to belong to the Imperial Theatres.

79. Teatral, '55 let v balete', *Peterburgskaia gazeta*, 1 May 1902, 4.

80. 'Staryi baletoman', 'Teatral'noe ekho', *Peterburgskaia gazeta*, 22 January 1902, 2–3 (2).

81. Teliakovskii, diary entry 12 September 1901, *Dnevniki Direktora Imperatorskikh teatrov 1901–1903* 55.

82. Teliakovskii, diary entry 29 March 1902, ibid., 217.

83. John Percival, 'Don Quixote', *Dance Now*, 6/2 (Summer 1997), 2–7 (6).

84. '[Печать и рецензенты,] конечно, настроены против, руководимые жидами и желанием всегда ругать все, что сколько-нибудь выдается над общим уровнем.' Teliakovskii, diary entry 20 January 1902, *Dnevniki Direktora Imperatorskikh teatrov 1901–1903*, 154. Teliakovskii's anti-semitism, a widespread fact of nineteenth-century Russia (and elsewhere), also appears on other pages of his diaries.

85. 'Это свет мешает тьме, царящей во всей театральной атмосфере.' Teliakovskii, diary entry 20 January 1902, ibid., 155.

86. Teliakovskii, diary entry 1 May 1902, ibid., 240.

87. Teliakovskii, *Vospominaniia*, 150.

88. Percival, 'Don Quixote', 6.

89. However, Liubov' Egorova, who joined the company in 1898, remembers, like Soliannikov, 'an iron discipline' in Petipa's own rehearsals: 'When he entered the rehearsal room, everybody stood up, even the ballerinas.' 'дисциплина была железная. Когда он входил в репетиционный зал, все вставали, не исключая балерин.' Liubov' Egorova, 'Na Repetitsii', in *Marius Petipa. Materialy, vospominaniia, stat'i*, ed. Nekhendzi, 239–40 (239).

90. Teliakovskii, diary entry 12 September 1901, *Dnevniki Direktora Imperatorskikh teatrov 1901–1903*, 51.

91. Quoted in *Materialy po istorii russkogo baleta*, ed. Borisoglebskii, vol. 1, 285–86. Mikhail Fokin has a slightly different take: when he graduated into the company, he became depressed at not having influential relatives or acquaintances to get him noticed. Later, he realized this was in fact a stroke of luck, because it made him work harder and when he was eventually noticed he had become a better artist (*Fokine: Memoirs of a Ballet Master*, 43).

92. Teliakovskii, diary entries 17 and 27 December 1901, *Dnevniki Direktora Imperatorskikh teatrov 1901–1903*, 129 and 136. Pascale Melani writes in detail about the question of bribes: 'Les coulisses du ballet: Petipa contre Teliakovskiï', in 'De la France à la Russie, Marius Petipa', ed. Melani, 263–83.

93. Teliakovskii, diary entry 7 September 1902, *Dnevniki Direktora Imperatorskikh teatrov 1901–1903*, 281.

94. See, for example, Teliakovskii, diary entry 22 January 1902, ibid., 155–56 (156). For a different picture of General Nikolai Bezobrazov and the 'very nice and kind' Vasil'eva, see Benois, *Reminiscences of the Russian Ballet*, 259–60 and 283.

95. Diary entry 12 September 1903, *The Diaries of Marius Petipa*, 19.

96. Vazem, *Zapiski baleriny*, 75–76.

97. Petipa, *Russian Ballet Master*, 79; Teliakovskii, diary entries 20 and 22 January 1903, *Dnevniki Direktora Imperatorskikh teatrov 1901–1903*, 411 and 412–13 (413).

98. Teliakovskii, diary entry 22 January 1903, ibid., 412–13 (413).

99. Diary entries 13 and 14 April 1903, and 20 February 1905, *The Diaries of Marius Petipa*, 14 and 66.

100. Teliakovskii, diary entries 3 October and 1 November 1903, *Dnevniki Direktora Imperatorskikh teatrov 1903–1906*, 38–40 (39) and 62–63 (62).

101. Teliakovskii, diary entry 4 June–5 July 1908, *Dnevniki Direktora Imperatorskikh teatrov 1906–1909*, 458–66 (459); Melani, 'Les coulisses du ballet: Petipa contre Teliakovskiï', in 'De la France à la Russie, Marius Petipa', ed. Pascale Melani, 269.

102. Melani points to two diary entries years later when Teliakovskii discovers that his Moscow protégé Gorskii had long been demanding enormous payments in exchange for roles and promotions; he had, in this way, been almost doubling his yearly salary to fund an expensive way of life. See ibid., 273, n. 33, and Teliakovskii, diary entries 22 January and 24 February 1908, *Dnevniki Direktora Imperatorskikh teatrov 1906–1909*, vol. 4, 364–66 (365) and 392–93 (392).

103. See, for example, Teliakovskii, diary entries 8 May and 21 June 1902, *Dnevniki Direktora Imperatorskikh teatrov 1901–1903*, 245 and 255–56 (256).

104. 'Она не преподавательница, а зараза, которая все время мутит балет.' Teliakovskii, diary entry 25 April 1904, *Dnevniki Direktora Imperatorskikh teatrov 1903–1906*, 223–24 (224).

105. Diary entry 9 February 1903, *The Diaries of Marius Petipa*, 7.

106. Roland John Wiley, *A Century of Russian Ballet*, 406; 'Teatral'noe ekho. Benefis' M. I. Petipa', *Peterburgskaia gazeta*, 10 February 1903, 3.

107. Teliakovskii, diary entry 19 November 1901, *Dnevniki Direktora Imperatorskikh teatrov 1901–1903*, 106–7 (107).

108. Veronika Kulagina, 'Poslednii balet Petipa *Volshebnoe zerkalo*' [Petipa's Last Ballet, *The Magic Mirror*], in *Baletmeister Marius Petipa*, ed. Fedorchenko, 242–43. This essay has provided much useful information.

109. Her involvement is inferred by Petipa (*Russian Ballet Master*, 81). It is also inferred by the shouting, during the premiere, of one elderly balletomane, 'Get rid of Gurlia and Teliakovskii! They will ruin the theatre with their novelties!' Teliakovskii reports this in the 'Baletomany' section of his memoirs (*Vospominaniia*, 441) and the same passage is translated and printed in Wiley, *A Century of Russian Ballet*, 418–20 (419). See also Konaev's commentary in *Marius Petipa. 'Memuary' i dokumenty*, 194, which quotes the description given by the Teliakovskiis' son, Vsevolod, of how Golovin and Gurlia worked collaboratively on the costume designs.

110. 'Я сказал, что не могу его освободить от постановки Волшебного зеркала. Нельзя быть балетмейстером, получать 9000 р. жалованья и в течение 2-х лет отказываться от постановки балетов. Прошлый год он отказался от Сильвии (которую неудачно поставил Гердт), потом от Волшебного зеркала. Волшебное зеркало отложили на год, теперь пришло время его ставить, и он старается под тем или другим предлогом уйти. Конечно, дело тут гораздо проще. Петипа по старости выжил из ума и не может вообще ничего ставить вновь. [...] Но подать в отставку не желает, и вот причина этих отговорок.' Teliakovskii, diary entry 14 October 1902, *Dnevniki Direktora Imperatorskikh teatrov 1901–1903*, 320–21. See also Teliakovskii, *Vospominaniia*, 436.

111. For example, Teliakovskii, diary entries 3 and 7 November and 16 December 1902, Teliakovskii, *Dnevniki Direktora Imperatorskikh teatrov 1901–1903*, 340–41 (341), 344–45, and 380.

112. 'Теперь, кажется, дело налаживается, все, кроме последнего акта, поставлено и есть несколько красивых танцев.' Teliakovskii, diary entry 23 December 1902, ibid., 385–86 (386).

113. 'Петипа продолжает быть невыносимым [...], всем недоволен и ругает весь кордебалет и начальство. Перемены все продолжаются. Появляются все новые и новые танцы. Просто не знаю, когда успеют сшить костюмы.' Teliakovskii, diary entry 3 January 1902, ibid., 393–94 (394).

114. Diary entries 3 January to 9 February 1903, *The Diaries of Marius Petipa*, 2–7.

115. Teliakovskii, diary entry 29 January 1903, *Dnevniki Direktora Imperatorskikh teatrov 1901–1903*, 240–41 (241); see also diary entry 29 January 1903, *The Diaries of Marius Petipa*, 5. In his memoirs, Petipa gives a different reason for his refusal: 'I did not agree, taking the view that all the tickets had been sold, and it was impossible to treat the public so unceremoniously.' Petipa, *Russian Ballet Master*, 81.

116. Teliakvoskii, in his memoirs, mistakenly says Nadezhda Petipa (Petipa 2) was the stepmother queen, when in fact she was the nurse (Teliakovskii, *Vospominaniia*, 440).

117. Teliakovskii, diary entry 8 February 1903, *Dnevniki Direktora Imperatorskikh teatrov 1901–1903*, 432–33 (432).

118. Diary entry 8 February 1903, *The Diaries of Marius Petipa*, 7.

119. 'Teatral', '55 let v balete', *Peterburskaia gazeta*, 1 May 1902, 4.

120. Teliakovskii, diary entry 8 February 1903, *Dnevniki Direktora Imperatorskikh teatrov 1901–1903*, 432–33 (432). Apparently, the patched-up mirror cracked again at the premiere and more mercury spilled out, provoking further laughter in the already unruly audience (Teliakovskii, *Vospominaniia*, 440).

121. Ibid., 440–41.

122. Kulagina, 'Poslednii balet Petipa *Volshebnoe zerkalo*', in *Baletmeister Marius Petipa*, ed. Fedorchenko, 254.

123. 'Агитация, которую всю зиму вел Петипа, сделала свое дело, и балет, несмотря на громадные усилия Дирекции, провалился. Правда, музыка скучновата и очень вымучена. Поставлен балет Петипа не очень удачно, декорации Головина некоторые не совсем дописаны, костюмы—часть взята из Москвы из Лебединого озера и, конечно, не давали полной красивой картины. Тем не менее было много удачного и красивого. Но публика, то есть балетоманы, агитацией Петипа, Безобразова, Лаппы и других была подготовлена к выражению протеста, и когда открылась картина гномов, то в зале раздался с левой стороны смех довольно наглый, даже Великий Князь Владимир Александрович высунулся из ложи, чтобы посмотреть, кто шумит. После этого акта в коридорах публика страшно критиковала балет.' Teliakovskii, diary entry 9 February 1903, *Dnevniki Direktora Imperatorskikh teatrov 1901–1903*, 433. Vladimir Lappa-Starzhenetskii had been Teliakovskii's assistant, until Teliakovskii fired him on 18 July 1902 (ibid., 259–60).

124. Benois, *Reminiscences of the Russian Ballet*, 222–23.

125. The following synopsis is taken from the published libretto (St Petersburg, 1903), but it is also translated in Wiley, *A Century of Russian Ballet*, 408–16.

126. 'N. N.', 'Teatral'noe ekho. Benefis' M. I. Petipa', *Peterburgskaia gazeta*, 10 February 1903, 3; 'Sigma' and 'A', 'Teatr i muzyka', *Novoe vremia*, 11 February 1903, 4; V. Kulagina, 'Poslednii balet Petipa *Volshebnoe zerkalo*', in *Baletmeister Marius Petipa*, ed. Fedorchenko, 248–49; *Ezhegodnik Imperatorskikh teatrov 1903–1904*, Part 1, 115–16; *Ezhegodnik Imperatorskikh teatrov 1904–1905*, Part 1, 202–3 (about the Moscow production, libretto by Petipa and Vsevolozhskii, staging by Gorskii).

127. Kulagina, 'Poslednii balet Petipa *Volshebnoe zerkalo*', in *Baletmeister Marius Petipa*, ed. Fedorchenko, 250.

128. *Novoe vremia*, 11 February 1903, 4; V. Kulagina, 'Poslednii balet Petipa *Volshebnoe zerkalo*', in *Baletmeister Marius Petipa*, ed. Fedorchenko, 250; Nizhinskaia [Nijinska], *Early Memoirs*, 117. (Nizhinskaia, also a student, appeared in a later episode of the ballet, as one of the everlasting flowers around the Princess's coffin.)

129. V. Kulagina, 'Poslednii balet Petipa *Volshebnoe zerkalo*', in *Baletmeister Marius Petipa*, ed. Fedorchenko, 251; *Ezhegodnik Imperatorskikh teatrov 1904–1905*, Part 1, 204.

130. *Fokine: Memoirs of a Ballet Master*, 32–33. Nikolai Legat also became famous as a teacher.

131. Immortelles were also a type of burial wreaths, popular in France.

132. Fedor [Theodore] Kozlov, after graduating from the Moscow theatre school, spent a 'polishing' year at the Petersburg school and danced at the Mariinskii from 1901 to 1904 (See also diary entry 11 October 1904, *The Diaries of Marius Petipa*, 56). He then worked in Moscow and took part in the Ballets Russes season of 1909. He ended up in the United States and eventually settled as a teacher in Los Angeles where his pupils included Agnes de Mille. There is footage of him dancing with his wife Aleksandra Baldina, https://www.youtube.com/watch?v=AbhqQniMKdg.

   Veronika Kulagina quotes *Peterburgskaia listka* (11 February 1903) about Kozlov's unfortunate costume ('Poslednii balet Petipa *Volshebnoe zerkalo*', in *Baletmeister Marius Petipa*, ed. Fedorchenko, 254).

133. This is the order of the Act IV dances as given on the poster for the premiere and differs from the account in *Ezhegodnik Imperatorskikh teatrov 1903–1904*, Part 1, 117. Perhaps the yearbook reflects the changes made for subsequent performances. See also Kulagina, 'Poslednii balet Petipa *Volshebnoe zerkalo*', 253–54.

134. *The Diaries of Marius Petipa*, 18.

135. Petipa's diaries as reprinted in *Marius Petipa. Materialy, vospominaniia, stat'i*, ed. Nekhendzi, 68–112 (88.) The Garafola edition, although more complete, does not contain the entries for 27 and 28 December 1903.

136. *Novoe vremia*, 30 December 1903, 5; 'Никуда не годным и бездарным произведением.' 'V. B.', *Peterburgskaia gazeta*, 8 January 1904, 4.

137. Diary entry 8 January 1904, *The Diaries of Marius Petipa*, 29.

138. *Ezhegodnik Imperatorskikh teatrov 1904–1905*, Part 1, 202–9. The description of the final act, for example, lists the same order of dances as the St Petersburg poster, except the classical pas de trois becomes a Tyrolean dance for three dancers, not the lead couple, and the coda is described as a csardas (207 and 209).

139. RGIA, *fond 497, op. 5, ed. khr. 2467, l. 428–29*; diary entry 18 February 1903, *The Diaries of Marius Petipa*, 8.

140. Diary entry 19 February 1902, ibid.; Petipa, *Russian Ballet Master*, 68. About Teliakovsky's role in the terms of Petipa's retirement, see Konaev's commentary in *Marius Petipa. 'Memuary' i dokumenty*, 196–97. Konaev found the evidence in RGIA, *fond 497, op. 5, ed. khr. 2467, l.424*, a page which I overlooked.

141. RGIA, *fond 497, op. 5, ed. khr. 2467, l. 431*.

142. The ballets were: *Le Corsaire*, *The Pharaoh's Daughter*, *The Trial of Damis*, *La Bayadère* [The Kingdom of Shades], *King Candaules*, *Giselle*, *The Awakening of Flora*, *Raymonda*, *The Halt of the Cavalry*, *Harlequinade*, *The Whims of the Butterfly*, *Swan Lake*, and *The Little Humpbacked Horse*.

143. Diary entry 11 November 1903, *The Diaries of Marius Petipa*, 25. In the event, this plan was modified: the corps de ballet benefit became the occasion (on 28 December 1903) when the revised production of *The Magic Mirror* was premiered (*Ezhegodnik Imperatorskikh teatrov 1903–1904*, Part 2, 20).

144. Diary entry 25 March 1904, *The Diaries of Marius Petipa*, 48.

145. Vera Petipa, *Moia sem'ia*, RGALI, *fond* 1945, *op.* 1, *ed. khr.* 66, *l.* 16.

146. Diary entry 12 December 1903, *The Diaries of Marius Petipa*, 28.

147. Melani, 'Les coulisses du ballet: Petipa contre Teliakovskii', in 'De la France à la Russie, Marius Petipa', ed. Melani, 270, states that Petipa owned a small house in Crimea. However, as late as the summer of 1904 he was paying 125 roubles per month for lodgings in Gurzuf, the resort near Yalta, and in the summer of 1907 took the same lodgings with the same rent (Petipa, diary entries 15 May 1904 and 11 June and 10 July 1907, *The Diaries of Marius Petipa*, 52 and 77–79). Local legend does talk of a small house with a garden in Gurzuf in his very last years, but it was rented. See Nataliia Makarukhina, *Gurzuf. Pervaia zhemchuzhina iuzhnogo berega Kryma*, 207. I am grateful to Lena Vitenberg and her husband for going on holiday to Gurzuf and acquainting me with the book of their friend Natalia Makarukhina.

148. Diary entry 24 February 1903, *The Diaries of Marius Petipa*, 9.

149. Diary entries 27 June and 15 July 1904, *Journal du maître de ballet des Théâtres Impériaux Marius Petipa*, ed. Pascale Melani, 143 and 147.

150. Diary entries 19 March and 15 May 1903, *The Diaries of Marius Petipa*, ed. Garafola, 12 and 17.

151. Diary entry 16 April and 17 October 1903, ibid., 14 and 22.

152. Shiriaev, *Peterburgskii balet*, 75–76; *Fokine: Memoirs of a Ballet Master*, 115; Benois, *Reminiscences of the Russian Ballet*, 247.

153. Teliakovskii, *Vospominaniia*, 157.

154. Petipa, *Russian Ballet Master*, 69–70. Even Teliakovskii, in his memoirs, recognizes Krupenskii's self-importance and taste for gossip and intrigue. Krupenskii was also afraid of women. Artists played tricks on him and one young opera singer, as a bet, set out to embarrass him. She made some absurd request and, when he refused, said in a loud voice that others could hear: 'Are you really trying to pretend, Sasha, that you don't live with me?' Teliakovskii, *Vospominaniia*, 157.

    However, as often, testimonies contradict each other. Teliakovskii also records that at one time the rumour flew round that Krupenskii, fed up, was going to leave, whereupon the corps de ballet and soloists signed a petition begging him to stay (Teliakovskii, diary entry 8 January 1904, *Dnevniki Direktora Imperatorskikh teatrov 1903–1906*, 127–30 (129)).

155. Diary entries for the year 1903 in *The Diaries of Marius Petipa* for the following: 9 March (about *Romance of the Rosebud*); 1, 10, 22, and 31 March, 9 April (*King Candaules*); and 13 April (*Sleeping Beauty*), 10–13 and 14.

156. Teliakovskii diary entry 23 April 1903, *Dnevniki Direktora Imperatorskikh teatrov 1901–1903*, 468.

157. Vazem, *Zapiski baleriny*, 76. At this point there seem to have been additional committee members: Petipa names Preobrazhenskaia, his daughter Marie, and the Legat brothers. His argument against the committee's purpose to assign roles—that 'they will always divide the pie between themselves'—seems sound (*Russian Ballet Master*, 69). But casting is never immune from personal tastes and biases, as demonstrated by Petipa himself. Even so, the delimitation of his power is evident in his letter to the directorate, dated 25 February 1884, in which he requests an extension for a year or two of Mariia Kuzmina's service. She is, he writes, his best coryphée, invaluable as an understudy, knows all the dances so that she is able to teach them to replacements, and, in addition, she remains svelte and young-looking (RGIA, *fond* 497, *op.* 5, *ed. kh.* 2467, *l.* 284).

158. Teliakovskii, diary entries 27 September and 4 October 1903, *Dnevniki Direktora Imperatorskikh teatrov 1903–1906*, 32–33 and 40; an editorial note for the 4 October entry suggests that maybe Vsevolozhskii had persuaded Petipa to attend the committee when it was first founded (737). See also diary entries 25, 27, and 29 September, 13 October 1903, *The Diaries of Marius Petipa*, 20 and 22.

159. Diary entries 13, 14, and 30 October 1903, ibid., 22 and 24; Teliakovskii, diary entry 13 October 1903, *Dnevniki Direktora Imperatorskikh teatrov 1903–1906*, 46–47 (46).

160. Diary entries 1 October and 7 November 1904, *The Diaries of Marius Petipa*, 55 and 57. See also entries 22 September and 6 December 1904, 54 and 60.

161. For example, diary entries 14 and 17 January and 7 September 1904, *The Diaries of Marius Petipa*, 30 and 53.

162. About Nikolai Sergeev, see this book's Overture and *Materialy po istorii russkogo baleta*, ed. Borisoglebskii, vol. 2, 76–79 (76).

163. Diary entry 30 September 1903, *The Diaries of Marius Petipa*, 21; Shiriaev, *Peterburgskii balet*, 76–77; Teliakovskii, *Vospominaniia*, 156.

164. 'Рамольный старик, всю жизнь лгавший, преклонявшийся и льстивший великим.' Teliakovskii, diary entry 27 October 1903, *Dnevniki Direktora Imperatorskikh teatrov 1903–1906*, 57–58 (58). 'Его мозг, сердце, понимание— все застыло уже несколько лет.' Teliakovskii, diary entry 14 May 1903, *Dnevniki Direktora Imperatorskikh teatrov 1901–1903*, 480–82 (481–82).

165. 'Три кучки песка'. Ibid., 481.

166. 'Боже мой, какая это лубочная работа с претензиями на художество, рисунки эти годны, скорее, для […] открытой сцены Зоологического сада. […] только его дилетантское художество спасет театр.' Teliakovskii, diary entry 13 August 1903, 496–97 (497).

167. This is preserved in GMTMI.

168. Lepidopterists might point out that Vsevolozhskii was mistaken: sphinxes are a species of moth.

The old butterfly was added after the typewritten libretto, but included in Vsevolozhskii's costume designs.

169. Petipa, *Russian Ballet Master*, 78.

170. 'Не может Всеволожский, как бывший Дирецкор, не знать и не понимать, что в Эрмитажном спектакле участвовать для артиста большая честь. Раз Кшесинская прима-балерина, она и должна участвовать.' Teliakovskii, diary entry 31 October 1903, *Dnevniki Direktora Imperatorskikh teatrov 1903–1906*, 61–62.

171. Ibid., 62.

172. Teliakovskii, diary entry 3 December 1903, ibid., 93–94 (94). See also diary entry 5 December 1903, ibid., 96.

173. Teliakovskii, diary entry 7 January 1904, ibid., 126–27 (126).

174. 'Так будет удобнее.' Teliakovskii, diary entry 9 January 1904, ibid., 130–31 (130).

175. Diary entry 9 January 1904, *The Diaries of Marius Petipa*, 29–30.

176. *Peterburgskii balet. Tri veka. 1901–1950*, ed. N. Zozulina and V. Mironova, 232 and 265–66. However, Drigo writes that the production conditions in 1919 were very unfavourable ('Personal Reminiscences of R. E. Drigo', Part 2, *Dancing Times*, June 1982, 662). My thanks again to Elena Fedosova at GMTMI for her inspired help, especially concerning Aleksandr Chekrygin.

177. Diary entry 13 January 1904, *The Diaries of Marius Petipa*, 30; see also detailed account in Teliakovskii, diary entry 8 January 1904, *Dnevniki Direktora Imperatorskikh teatrov 1903–1906*, 127–30 (129).

178. Diary entries 7 and 27 February, 11 and 16 March 1904, *The Diaries of Marius Petipa*, 45–47.

179. The ballets are: *The Sleeping Beauty, The Little Humpbacked Horse, Paquita, Le Corsaire, The Magic Mirror, Coppélia, La Fille mal gardée, Awakening of Flora, The Travelling Dancer*, and *Masquerade* (*divertissement* for Preobrazhenskaia's benefit).

180. Diary entry 15 April 1904, *The Diaries of Marius Petipa*, 50.

181. Diary entries 10 March and 7 and 8 April 1904, ibid., 47 and 49.

182. Diary entries 14, 15, 16, and 17 April 1904, ibid., 50.

183. Diary entry 23 April 1904, ibid., 50.

184. Diary entry 18 May 1904 and editorial note, ibid., 52.

185. Diary entry 23 August 1904; ibid., 52–52. 'Yesterday, I began to write my memoirs.' Diary entry 21 September 1904, ibid., 54.

186. Diary entry 22 September 1904, ibid., 54.

187. Diary entry 25 October 1904, ibid., 57. It was encored at its performance on 27 November (diary entry 28 November 1904, ibid., 59).

188. Diary entries 5 March, 1, 2, and 27 November, and 3 December 1904, ibid., 47, 57, and 59–60.

189. It has been difficult to find any hard facts about Cecchetti; the dates of his removal as second ballet master and departure from the company are taken from

the staff lists in *Ezhegodnik Imperatoriskikh teatrov 1895–1896, 1896–1897* and *1902–1903*.

190. Benois, *Reminiscences of the Russian Ballet*, 228–31.

191. Teliakovskii, *Vospominaniia*, 157–58.

192. See chapter 6 and Tamara Karsavina, *Theatre Street*, 145–46.

193. Diary entries 19 September (with footnote) and 7 October 1905, *The Diaries of Marius Petipa*, 71–72; Roslavleva, *Era of the Russian Ballet*, 170–71.

194. Diary entry 31 August 1903, *The Diaries of Marius Petipa*, 18.

195. Shiriaev, *Peterburgskii balet*, 80.

196. Ibid., 81; Petipa, *Russian Ballet Master*, 70–71.

197. 'Однако директор и слушать не хотел о том, чтобы на афише стояло имя Петипа. [Скрепя сердце, мне пришлось подчиниться и сочинить новую лезгинку,] гораздо менее интересную, чем старая.' Shiriaev, *Peterburgskii balet*, 81.

198. Diary entry 4 December 1904, *The Diaries of Marius Petipa*, 60; Teliakovskii describes Shiriaev's *lezginka* in the same way (4 December 1904, *Dnevniki Direktora Imperatorskikh teatrov 1903–1906*, 345–46 (346).

199. Petipa, *Russian Ballet Master*, 71–72.

200. Shiriaev, *Peterburgskii balet*, 23–24, 82–83. Teliakovskii records the incident slightly earlier on 18 December 1904 (*Dnevniki Direktora Imperatorskikh teatrov 1903–1906*, 357).

201. In accordance with what Shiriaev writes, *Ezhegodnik Imperatorskikh teatrov 1904–1905* gives the date of his departure from the post of second ballet master as 1 March 1905, after less than two years, and from the company as 12 May 1905, after twenty years. The date of Nikolai Legat's appointment is listed in *Ezhegodnik Imperatorskikh teatrov 1905–1906*. Shiriaev later returned to the Mariinsky company and school in 1906 and 1918–1921 to teach the national-dance system he had developed in 1891. The task of staging *The Talisman* went to Nikolai Legat, with poor results.

202. 'Почтенный, незаменимый М. И. Петипа [как известно, уже давно устранен от театра] [...] Сезон начинается при довольно исключительных, прямо небывалых обстоятельствах: без балетмейстера! [...] Но разве записки могут заменить балетмейстера?' 'Teatral', 'K segodniashemu otkrytiiu baleta' [The Opening of the Ballet Season], *Peterburgskaia gazeta*, 4 September 1905, 4.

203. Although Petipa remained officially in his post until his death, in practical terms, by the time of the article, he was no longer there.

204. 'Чем объясняется отставка в балете г. Петипа, и действительно ли балет остался без балетмейстера?'

'Без балетмейстера мы, правду говоря, уже давно. М. И. Петипа слишком стар для того, чтобы оставаться на своем месте, ему за 80 лет.

'За последние годы ему стала изменять память и дело доходило до того, что вчера он приказывал делать одно, а сегодня, забыв о том, что говорил вчера, велел делать совсем другое.

'Тем, что у нас не находится, к сожалению, заместителя г–ну Петипа, мы обязаны этим ему же: г. Петипа не мог слышать о каком-нибудь претенденте на его должность и чуть замечал, что какой-нибудь молодой артист обнаруживает задатки будущего балетмейстера, старался отстранять его от дела. Таким образом, пришлось убрать из Петербурга и перенести в Москву г. Горского, ученика г. Петипа, подававшего большие надежды.' 'Beseda s direktorom Imperatorskikh teatrov' [Interview with the Director of the Imperial Theatres], *Peterburgskaia gazeta*, 11 September 1905, 3. In his diary Teliakovskii claims his words were distorted by the journalist (11 September 1905, *Dnevniki Direktora Imperatorskikh teatrov 1901–1903*, 509–10), but it is difficult to see how, especially since he makes similar accusations earlier (23 January 1902, ibid., 156–57).

205. 'Действительно, я отстранен от руководства петербургского балета, но не потому, что стал стар, утратил понимание и вкус, а потому, что за всю свою долгую службу привык работать самостоятельно, подчиняясь лишь т ребованиям искусства, а не капризам гг. чиновников, вмешивающихся во все и распоряжающихся не только распределением ролей, но и постановк ой балетов.' Marius Petipa, 'Pis'mo v redaktsiiu' [Letter to the Editor], *Novoe vremia*, 17 September 1905, 13. See also diary entries 11–12 September 1905, *The Diaries of Marius Petipa*, 70. Petipa's independence had always been relative: as previously suggested, he was never entirely free to do as he wanted. However, a director like Vsevolozhskii had a diplomat's way of steering Petipa towards a given goal, using persuasion rather than demand.

206. '[Я думаю, что] за все время существования Дирекции [это] первый случай подобного нахальства.' Teliakovskii, diary entry 17 September 1905, *Dnevniki Direktora Imperatorskikh teatrov 1903–1906*, 512.

207. Sergei Diagilev, *Rus'*, 15 September 1905, quoted in Teliakovskii, diary entry 16 September endnote (n. 2), *Dnevniki Direktora Imperatorskikh teatrov 1903–1906*, 821–22; Iurii Beliaiev, *Novoe vremia*, 15 September 1905, quoted in *The Diaries of Marius Petipa*, editorial footnote, 70. '[Нельзя не указать на одну] весьма положительную заслугу [нынешнего директора: это его принцип] давать ход молодым артистическим силам.' Valerian Svetlov, 'Novoe v balete' [New in Ballet], *Slovo*, 30 December 1905, quoted in *Peterburgskii balet. Tri veka. 1901–1950*, ed. Zozulina and Mironova, 74. See also the editorial in *Teatr i iskusstvo*, no. 38, 1905, 599, parts of which are also reproduced in an endnote for Teliakovskii's diary entry 18 September 1904 (n. 4), 822–23.

208. Petipa, *Russian Ballet Master*, 75.

209. Teliakovskii, *Vospominaniia*, 149. Zolotnitskii's editorial notes in the same book refute this and other attacks made on Petipa (nos. 52–55, 457–58).

210. *Fokine: Memoirs of a Ballet Master*, 71–72 and 87–90.

211. Diary entry 10 April 1905, *The Diaries of Marius Petipa*, 67–68 (68).

212. Diary entry 1 May 1903, ibid., 15.

213. *Fokine: Memoirs of a Ballet Master*, 92. Petipa's message in this book is actually given as 'Dear colleague, delighted by your work'. ('Cher confrère, enchanté de votre composition'.) The longer version comes from the Russian edition in *Protiv techeniia: Vospominaniia baletmeistera. Stat'i, pis'ma*, ed. Iu. Slonimskii (Leningrad: Iskusstvo, 1962), 166; Lillian Moore gives the original French in her note in Petipa's memoirs: 'Cher camarade, enchanté de votre composition, continuez et vous serez un grand maître de ballet.' Petipa, *Russian Ballet Master*, 82–86 (86), no. 6.

214. 'Эта балетная труппа, опечаленная отсутствием в театре Петипа, [...] просит его вернуться в театр и занять подобающее место, ибо без него балетное искусство стало падать.' Teliakovskii, diary entry 19 November 1904, *Dnevniki Direktora Imperatorskikh teatrov 1903–1906*, 328–29.

215. Diary entry, 21 December 1904, *The Diaries of Marius Petipa*, 61.

216. Diary entry 9 January 1905 and editorial note, ibid., 63; Riasanovsky and Steinberg, *A History of Russia*, 380.

217. Diary entries 10, 11, and 12 January 1905, *The Diaries of Marius Petipa*, 63–64.

218. Diary entry, 15 October 1905, ibid., 72; Teliakovskii, diary entry 15 October 1905, *Dnevniki Direktora Imperatorskikh teatrov 1903–1906*, 533–35 (533–34).

219. Teliakovskii, diary entries 16 and 17 October 1905, ibid., 535–38. See also Karsavina, *Theatre Street*, 185–89.

220. Ibid., 189–90.

221. Legat, *The Story of the Russian School*, 66.

222. 'Он был вчера очень нервный, ходил в толпе на улице, кричал, и чтобы его успокоить, вечером повели в Михайловский театр; вернувшись домой, Петипа хотела его не выпускать и заперла в комнату, где он бритвой перерезал себе сонную артерию и истек кровью. Когда приехал доктор, то мог только констатировать смерть.' Teliakovskii, diary entry 19 October 1905, *Dnevniki Direktora Imperatorskikh teatrov 1903–1906*, 540–42 (540).

223. Diary entry 19 October 1905, *The Diaries of Marius Petipa*, 73; Petipa, *Russian Ballet Master*, 56.

224. Teliakovskii, *Vospominaniia*, 262.

225. Teliakovskii, diary entry 21 October 1905, *Dnevniki Direktora Imperatorskikh teatrov 1903–1906*, 543–44 (543); diary entries 15 and 29 October 1905, *The Diaries of Marius Petipa*, 72–73. Karsavina's account makes no mention of the Petipa family as being supporters of the agitation.

226. Teliakovskii, diary entry 31 October 1905, *Dnevniki Direktora Imperatorskikh teatrov 1903–1906*, 550–51 (551).

227. Teliakovskii, *Vospominaniia*, 278–92; editorial note to diary entry 23 November 1905, *The Diaries of Marius Petipa*, 74–75.

228. 'Словом, дирекции инчего не оставалось делать, кроме уборки театров и передачи денег [образовавшейся так называемой "балетной] комиссии.' Teliakovskii, *Vospominaniia*, 282. See also diary entry 15 December 1905 and

editorial note, *The Diaries of Marius Petipa*, 75–76; and Teliakovskii, diary entry 17 December 1905, *Dnevniki Direktora Imperatorskikh teatrov 1903–1906*, 594–95 (594).

229. According to Roslavleva, Mikhailov entered St Petersburg University in 1906, graduating with outstanding marks and eventually becoming a Doctor of Law in Paris. She further writes that another prominent dissident dancer Petr Presniakov was also dismissed (*Era of the Russian Ballet*, 168).

230. Teliakovskii, diary entry 10 January 1906, *Dnevniki Direktora Imperatorskikh teatrov 1903–1906*, 615–16 (616).

231. Teliakovskii makes this assertion about Pavlova's earnings (diary entry 19 November 1904, ibid., 328–29 [329]) With his usual prudish suspiciousness, he also claims she had several lovers on the go: 'the yid Rafalovich, Dandré, Vintulov, and others'.

232. Kshesinskaia had made her case to Teliakovskii in the same letter (defending her brother) from Cannes. See Teliakovskii, *Vospominaniia*, 286–87.

233. Teliakovskii, ibid., 287–88.

234. Diary entries 4 and 7 January 1905, *The Diaries of Marius Petipa*, 62–63.

235. Diary entries 18 and 20 February 1905, ibid., 66. The unexplained absence of Petipa's name provoked indignation in *Peterburgskii dnevnik teatrala* [Theatregoer's Petersburg Diary], which also reported that members of the audience became confused, wondering if this was another, different ballet. See editorial note to the 20 February 1905 diary entry; see also *Peterburgskii dnevnik teatrala*, 27 February 1905, quoted in *Peterburgskii balet. Tri veka. 1901–1950*, ed. N. Zozulina and V. Mironova, 69.

236. Petipa, *Memoirs of a Ballet Master*, 87.

237. Diary entry 1 March 1905, *The Diaries of Marius Petipa*, 67.

238. Diary entries 18 August and 5 December 1905, ibid., 69 and 75.

239. Diary entries 23 and 29 September 1905, ibid., 71.

240. 'Ninov', 'Balet po sluchaiu iubileia A. K. Glazunov' [The Ballet on the Occasion of Glazunov's Jubilee], *Teatr i iskusstvo*, no. 5, 4 February 1907, 79–80; V[alerian] Svetlov, 'Baletnyi spektakl' po sluchaiu 25-letnei kompozitorskoi deiatel'nosti A. K. Glazunova', [Ballet Performance on the Occasion of the Twenty-five-year Jubilee of Glazunov's Musical Career], *Birzhevye vedomosti*, 29 January 1907, reprinted in *Peterburgskii balet. Tri veka. 1901–1950*, ed. N. Zozulina and V. Mironova, 89.

241. 'Неужели дирекция не даст [юбиляр] бенефиса за столько лет службы? [...] Дирекция по-прежнему не церемонится с М. И. Петипа.' '60-letyi iubilei M. I. Petipa', *Peterburgskaia gazeta*, 7 March 1907, 5.

242. 'Teatral', '60 let stsenicheskoi deiatel'nosti' [Sixty Years of a Stage Career], *Peterburgskaia gazeta*, 2 May 1907, 4–5 (5); 'Iubilei M. I. Petipa', *Birzhevye vedomosti*, 29 May 1907, 3. The fact that Petipa arrived in Russia on 30 May 1847, not 24 May, has been explained earlier, in Overture.

243. 'Это не победа русского балета, а торжество рекламы XX века. Когда я слышу о "победе русского балета за границей" моя душа плачет. [...] Все, что я берег и лелеял многие годы, переживает агонию.' *Teatr i iskusstvo*, 1910, no. 28, 533.

244. Ibid., 529 and 531.

245. I am indebted to Makbal Musina for discovering Petipa's original burial place.

246. '[Я помню] его трепетную руку, направлявшую меня к выходу на сцену, когда я, смутившись и оробев, заколебалась перед темной впадиной зрительного зала и подалась назад. В годы юности, когда я в первый раз выступала перед публикой, как артистка, в балете Арлекинада, я никогда не могу забыть волнение отца и благославляющий шепот за кулисами. Когда я заболела в Ялте и лежала в тяжелом состоянии туберкулеза, отец, рядом с хлопотавшей около меня матери, стоял как-то сразу состарившись и, не зная, чем помочь мне, шептал нежные слова, гладил по голове и заглядывал в глаза, предлагал читать мне—много, много читать.

    'Наконец, последнее горестное воспоминание—его смерть в Гурзуфе, когда мы все столпились у его кровати и слабо слышится мое имя, а холодеющие пальцы сжимают мою руку.' Vera Petipa, *Moia sem'ia*, RGALI, *fond* 1945, *op.* 1, *ed. khr.* 66, *l.* 32–33.

APOTHEOSIS

1. 'В последнее время, когда пошла по всей линии искусства переоценка художественных ценностей, когда изменились в многом взгляды на искусство, когда проявились новые в нем веяния, балеты Петипа, конечно, отошли на второй план. Но заслуга Петипа ничуть не умалилась, она останется вечной в летописях русской хореографии, заслужившей ныне всемирную славу и всеобщее признание.' Valerian Svetlov, *Sovremennyi balet*, 65.

2. '[Хореграфия,] подобно архитектуре, основана на красоте и гармоничности линий.' 'Teatral', '60 let stsenicheskoi deiatel'nosti' [60 Years of Theatre Work], *Peterburgskaia gazeta*, 2 May 1907, 4–5 (4).

3. Teliakovskii reports that at the time of *The Magic Mirror* Petipa said to Korovin he was an old man and maybe wrong, but he could not understand Golovin's designs for *The Magic Mirror*. See Teliakovskii, diary entry 10 February 1903, *Dnevniki Direktora Imperatorskikh teatrov 1901–1903*, 433–35 (434).

4. '[Я] не могу примириться с современными "гротесками" и "тур-де-форсами." [...] Я нахожу, что это—неизящно.' 'Teatral', '55 let v balete' [55 Years in Ballet], *Peterburgskaia gazeta*, 1 May 1902, 4.

5. Khudekov, *Istoriia tantsev*, vol. 4, 152.

6. Sergei Diagilev, letter to *Peterburgskaia gazeta*, 1 January 1904, translated and reprinted by Wiley in *A Century of Russian Ballet*, 420–21.

7. 'Балет императорских театров стал мне чуждым […] я живу словно на другой планете. […] [Кордебалет старался] не отражая никаких нюансов музыки, только под щелканье пальцев Сергеева, отбивавшего такты.' Bronislava Nizhinskaia [Nijinska], 'Petipa pobedil' [Petipa Victorious], in *Marius Petipa. Materialy, vospominaniia, stat'i,* ed. Nekhendzi, 315–19 (317 and 316–17).

8. Ibid., 317-18; 'Я прониклась глубоким уважением к Петипа, к его гениальной хореографии.' Ibid., 318.

9. Benois, *Reminiscences of the Russian Ballet,* 127.

10. 'Конечно, этот триумф, это победное шествие русской хореографии по городам Нового и Старого Света есть ближайший результат кипучей и талантливой деятельности Дягилева, Фокина и блестящей плеяды их единомышленников—артистов и художников. Но это именно *результат,* результат той могучей творческой работы, которую в течение многих десятков лет вынес на плечах гений старого балета—Петипа.' Valerian Svetlov, *Sovremennyi balet,* 47.

11. Roland John Wiley, 'Dances from Russia: An Introduction to the Sergeev Collection', 94–112 (106–7).

12. Just as the classes of Caterina Beretta in Milan had sharpened the techniques of Russian ballerinas, so promising dancers of the Royal Ballet, such as Margot Fonteyn, Pamela May, and June Brae, used to make regular pilgrimages to Paris in the summer vacation to study with Kshesinskaia, Preobrazhenskaia, Trefilova, and Egorova, who were living there.

13. Quoted by Roslavleva, *Era of the Russian Ballet,* 191.

14. In 1935 GATOB became the Kirov Opera and Ballet, or more accurately Leningradskii teatr opery i baleta imeni S. M. Kirova [Leningrad Academic Theatre for Opera and Ballet named after S. M. Kirov]; and in 1991 it reverted to being the Opera and Ballet of the Mariinskii Theatre.

15. Diary entries 5 September 1904 and 27 February 1905, *The Diaries of Marius Petipa,* 53 and 66.

Bibliography

PRIMARY SOURCES

Writings by the Petipa Family and Their (Near) Contemporaries

ACKERMAN, GALIA, and LORRAIN, PIERRE (eds.), *Marius Petipa: Mémoires* (Arles, Paris: Actes Sud, 1990).

BALETOMAN [KONSTANTIN SKAL'KOVSKII], *Balet: Ego istoriia i mesto v riadu iziashchnykh iskusstv* [Ballet: Its History and Place in the Fine Arts] (St Petersburg, 1882).

BENOIS, ALEXANDRE [ALEKSANDR], *Memoirs*, trans. Moura Budberg (London: Chatto & Windus, 1960); repr. (London: Columbus Books, 1988).

—— *Reminiscences of the Russian Ballet*, trans. Mary Britnieva (London: Putnam, 1941).

BOURNONVILLE, AUGUST, *My Theatre Life*, trans. Patricia N. McAndrew (London: Adam & Charles Black, 1979).

CUSTINE, MARQUIS DE, *Lettres de Russie: La Russie en 1839*, ed. Pierre Nora (Paris: Gallimard, 1975).

DANILOVA, ALEXANDRA, *Choura* (New York: Knopf, 1986); repr. (New York: Fromm, 1988).

DICEY, EDWARD, *A Month in Russia during the Marriage of the Czarevitch* (London, 1867).

DRIGO, RICCARDO, *Personal Reminiscences of R. E. Drigo*, trans. and ed. Roland John Wiley; publ. as 'Memoirs of R. E. Drigo', *Dancing Times* (May 1982), 577–78; (June 1982), 661–62.

DUFFERIN, LADY HARIOT, *My Russian and Turkish Journals* (London: John Murray, 1916).

DURYLIN, S., *N. M. Radin* (Moscow, Leningrad: Iskusstvo, 1941).

FIORENTINO, P. A., *Marie Petipa* (Paris, 1862).

FOKINE, MICHEL [MIKHAIL FOKIN], *Fokine: Memoirs of a Ballet Master*, ed. Anatole Chujoy, trans. Vitale Fokine (London: Constable & Company, 1961).

GAUTIER, THÉOPHILE, *Gautier on Dance*, ed. and trans. Ivor Guest (London: Dance Books, 1986).

—— *La Peau de tigre* [Tiger Skin] (Paris: Michel Lévy, 1866).

—— *Voyage en Russie* (Paris, 1866); repr. (Paris, Geneva: Slatkine Reprints, 1979).

GLAZUNOV, ALEKSANDR, *A. K. Glazunov. Pis'ma, stat'i, vospominaniia* [Letters, Articles, Reminiscences], ed. Mariia Ganina (Moscow: Gosudarstvennoe muzykal'noe izdatel'stvo, 1958).

GLUSHKOVSKII, ADAM, *Vospominaniia baletmeistera* [Reminiscences of a Ballet Master], ed. Petr Gusev (Leningrad, Moscow, 1940).

HORMIGÓN, LAURA, *Marius Petipa en España 1844–1847* (n.p.: Danzarte Ballet, 2010).

IGNATENKO, A. (ed.), *Marius Petipa* (St Petersburg: Soiuz khudozhnikov, 2003).

IVANOV, LEV, 'Moi vospominaniia' [My Reminiscences]. *Sovetskii balet* 32 (January–February 1987), 39–43. (The original, dated 2 February 1899, is in GMTMI. It is also translated by Wiley in *The Life and Ballets of Lev Ivanov*, 5–20.)

IVANOV, MIKHAIL, 'Marius Ivanovich Petipa', *Novoe vremia* (12 July 1910). (The version used is the translation in Wiley, *A Century of Russian Ballet*, 350–56.)

KARATYGIN, PETR, *Zapiski* [Memories] (St Petersburg, 1880); repr. (St Petersburg: Azbuka, 2011).

Karsavina, Tamara, '*La Fille mal gardée* at the Mariinsky', in Ivor Guest (ed.), *La Fille mal gardée* (London: The Dancing Times Limited, 1960), 25–29.

—— *Theatre Street* (London: W. Heinemann, 1930); repr. (London: Dance Books, 1981).

KELLY, LAURENCE (ed.), *Moscow: A Traveller's Companion* (London: Constable and Co., 1983); repr. (London: Robinson, 2004).

KHUDEKOV, SERGEI, 'The First Performance of the Ballet *The Pharaoh's Daughter*', in *Peterburgskaiagazeta* (15 October 1898). (This book uses the translation in Wiley, *A Century of Russian Ballet*, 234–37.)

—— *Istoriia tantsev* [A History of Dancing], 4 vols. (St Petersburg: Peterburgskaiag azeta, 1913–1918).

—— 'Peterburgskii balet vo vremia postanovki *Kon'ka-Gorbunka*' [The Petersburg Ballet at the Time of the Staging of *The Little Humpbacked Horse*], in *Peterburgskaia gazeta* (14 January 1896; part 1) and (21 January 1896; part 2). (Both parts are translated in Wiley, *A Century of Russian Ballet*, 250–75.)

KSCHESSINSKA, MATHILDE [MATIL'DA KSHESINSKAIA], *Dancing in Petersburg*, trans. Arnold Haskell (London: Gollancz, 1960); repr. (Alton: Dance Books, 2005).

LEGAT, NICOLAS [NIKOLAI], *Ballets Russes: Memoirs of Nicolas Legat*, trans. Paul Dukes (London: Methuen, 1939).

LEMERCIER DE NEUVILLE, L., *Les Figures du temps: Notices biographiques: Marie Petipa* [Notable People: Biographical Notes] (Paris: A. Bourdilliat, 1861).

LOPUKHOV, FYDOR [FEDOR]. 'Annals of *The Sleeping Beauty*', trans. Debra Goldman, *Ballet Review*, 5/4 (1975–76), 21–35.

—— *Khoreograficheskie otkrovennosti* [Choreographic Revelations] (Moscow: Iskusstvo, 1972).

—— *Writings on Ballet and Music*, ed. Stephanie Jordan, trans. Dorinda Offord (Madison: University of Wisconsin Press, 2002).

MÉRIMÉE, PROSPER, *Lettres de Prosper Mérimée à la Comtesse de Montijo*, 2 vols. (Paris, 1930).

NATAROVA, ANNA, 'Iz vospominanii artistki A. P. Natarovoĭ [From the Reminiscences of the Artist A. P. Natarova], *Istoricheskii vestnik* [Historical Messenger] (October 1903), 25–44; (November 1903), 420–42; (December 1903), 778–803. (Extracts are translated in Wiley, *A Century of Russian Ballet*, 135–69.)

NEKHENDZI, ANNA, et al. (eds.), *Marius Petipa. Materialy, vospominaniia, stat'i* [Marius Petipa: Documents, Reminiscences, Articles] (Leningrad: Iskusstvo, 1971).

NIJINSKA [NIZHINSKAIA], BRONISLAVA, *Early Memoirs*, trans. and ed. Irina Nijinska and Jean Rawlinson (New York: Holt, Rinehart, and Winston, 1981); repr. (Durham and London: Duke University Press, 1992).

PANAEVA, AVDOT'IA, *Vospominaniia* [Reminiscences] (Moscow: Zakharov, 2002). (Originally published in *Istoricheskii vestni*, 1889).

PETIPA, MARIUS, *The Diaries of Marius Petipa*, ed. Lynn Garafola (Pennington, NJ: Studies in Dance History, Spring 1992).

—— *Journal du maître de ballet des Théâtres Impériaux*, ed. Pascale Melani (Moscow: RGALI; Pessac: MSHA, 2017).

—— *Marius Petipa.'Memuary' i dokumenty*, ed. Sergei Konaev (Moscow: GTsTM; RGALI; Navona, 2018).

—— *Memuary Mariusa Petipa, solista ego Imperatorskogo Velichestva i baletmeistera Imperatorskikh teatrov* [The Memoirs of Marius Petipa, Soloist of his Imperial Majesty and Ballet Master of the Imperial Theatres] (St Petersburg: 'Trud', 1906); repr. (St Petersburg: Predpriiatie S.-Peterb. soiuza khudozhnikov, 1996).

—— *Russian Ballet Master: The Memoirs of Marius Petipa*, ed. Lillian Moore, trans. Helen Whittaker (New York: Macmillan, 1958).

PETIPA, VERA, *Moia sem'ia: Petipa v zhizni i iskusstve* [My Family: Petipa in Life and Art]. Undated typescript is in RGALI, *fond* 1945, *ed. khr.* 66, *l.* 1–33. Also abridged as 'Nasha sem'ia' ('Our Family') in Nekhendzi (ed.), *Marius Petipa: Materialy, vospominaniia, stat'i*.

PETROV, OLEG (ed.), *Russkaia baletnaia kritika kontsa XVIII–pervoi poloviny XIX veka* [Russian Ballet Criticism: The End of the Eighteenth–First Half of the Nineteenth Century] (Moscow: Iskusstvo, 1982).

—— *Russkaia baletnaia kritika: vtoroi poloviny XIX veka: Peterburg* [Russian Ballet Criticism: The Second Half of the Nineteenth Century: Petersburg] (Ekaterinburg: Sfera, 1995).

PLESHCHEEV, ALEKSANDR, M. I. Petipa (1847–1907). K 60-letiiu ego khoreograficheskoi deiatel'nosti v Peterburge' [For the 60th Anniversary of his Choreographic Work in Petersburg] (St Petersburg, 1907), also published in *Istoricheskii vestnik* (May 1907), 561–68.

—— *Nash balet* [Our Ballet] (St Petersburg, 1896); repr. (St Petersburg: Planetamu zyki, 2009).

SAINT-LÉON, ARTHUR, *Letters from a Ballet Master: The Correspondence of Arthur Saint-Léon*, ed. Ivor Guest (London: Dance Books, 1981).

SHIRIAEV, ALEKSANDR, *Peterburgskii balet. Iz vospominanii artista Mariinskogo teatra.* [The Petersburg Ballet. From the Reminiscences of an Artist of the Mariinsky Theatre], ed. Iurii Slonimskii (Leningrad: VTO, 1941) (This hard-to-find book is in the National Library of Russia in St Petersburg (I used a photocopy); however, it has been reprinted (in full?) in *Kinovedcheskie zapiski* [Notes on Film Studies], 67, 2004, 61–101).

SKAL'KOVSKII, KONSTANTIN [BALETOMAN], *Balet: Ego istoriia i mesto v riadu iziashchnykh iskusstv* [Ballet: Its History and Place in the Fine Arts] (St Petersburg, 1882).

—— *Stat'i o balete 1868–1905* [Articles about Ballet], ed. Igor Stupnikov and Olga Fedorchenko (St Petersburg: Chistyi list, 2012).

—— *V teatral'nom mire: Nabliudeniia, vospominaniia, i rassuzhdeniia* [In the Theatrical World: Observations, Reminiscences, and Debates] (St Peterburg, 1899).

SOKOLOV, A., 'Teatral'nye vospominaniia' [Theatre Reminiscences], *Novoe slovo*, 3–5 (1894).

STUKOLKIN, T. A., 'Vospominaniia artista Imperatorskikh teatrov' [Reminiscences of an Artist of the Imperial Theatres], *Artist*, 45 (January 1895), 126–33; 46 (February 1895), 117–25. (Also translated in Wiley, *A Century of Russian Ballet*, 108–34.)

SVETLOV, VALERIAN, *Sovremennyi balet* [Contemporary Ballet] (St Petersburg, 1911); rep. (St Petersburg: Planeta Muzyki, 2009).

TELIAKOVSKII, VLADIMIR, *Dnevniki Direktora Imperatoriskikh teatrov* [Diaries of the Director of the Imperial Theatres], 4 vols. (Moscow: Artist. Rezhisser. Teatr, 1998–2011).

—— *Vospominaniia* [Reminiscences] (Leningrad and Moscow: Iskusstvo, 1965). (Extracts are translated by Nina Dimitrievich in *Dance Research* 8/1 [Spring 1990], 37–46; 9/1 [Spring 1991], 26–39.)

VALERA, JUAN, *Correspondencia, 1847–1857*, 2 vols. (Madrid: Impr. Alemana, 1913).

VAZEM, EKATERINA, *Zapiski baleriny Sankt-Peterburgskogo Bol'shogo teatra* [Memoirs of a Ballerina of the St Petersburg Bolshoi Theatre] (Leningrad, Moscow: Iskusstvo, 1937). (Extracts are translated by Nina Dimitrievich in *Dance Research*; 3/2 [Summer 1985], 3–22; 4/1 [Spring 1986], 3–28; 5/1 [Spring 1987], 21–41; and 6/2 [Autumn 1988], 30–47.)

VOLYNSKII, A., *Kniga likovanii. Azbuka klassicheskogo tantsa* [The Book of Exultations. An Alphabet of Classical Dance] (Leningrad, 1925); repr. (St Petersburg: Planeta Muzyki, 2008).

—— *Stat'i o balete* [Articles about Ballet] (St Petersburg: Giperion, 2002).

WOLKONSKY, PRINCE SERGE [PRINCE SERGEI VOLKONSKII], *My Reminiscences*, trans. A. E.Chamot, 2 vols. (London: Hutchinson Guest, 1924).

RUSSIAN NEWSPAPERS AND JOURNALS

Birzhevye vedomosti [Stockbrokers' Gazette]

Golos [The Voice]

Istoricheskii vestnik [Historical Messenger]

Journal de St. Pétersbourg [St Petersburg Newspaper]

Literaturnaia gazeta [Literary Gazette]

Muzykal'nyi i teatral'nyi vestnik [Musical and Theatrical Herald]

Novoe slovo [New Word]

Novoe vremia [New Times]

Novosti [News]

Novosti i birzhevaia gazeta [News and Stockbrokers' Gazette]

Nuvellist [News Writer]

Obozrenie teatrov [Review of Theatres]

Panteon [Pantheon]

Panteon i repertuar russkoi stseny [Pantheon and Repertoire of the Russian Stage]

Peterburgskaia gazeta [Petersburg Gazette]

Peterburgskii listok [Petersburg Bulletin]

Sankt-Peterburgskie vedomosti [St Petersburg Gazette]

Severnaia pchela [Northern Bee]

Sovremennaia letopis' [Contemporary Chronicle]

Sovremennoe slovo [The Modern Word]

Sufler [The Prompter]

Syn otechestva [Son of the Homeland]

Teatr i iskusstvo [Theatre and Art]

Teatral [The Theatregoer]

Teatral'nyi mirok [Theatrical World]

Vechernaia gazeta [Evening Gazette]

Vsemirnaia illiustratsiia [Illustrated World]

Vseobshchaia gazeta [Universal Gazette]

ANNALS AND ALMANACS

St Petersburg and Moscow

BOGLACHEVA, IRINA (ed.), *Peterburgskii balet. Tri veka. Khronika. Tom II. 1801–1850* [The Petersburg Ballet. Three Centuries. Chronicle] (St Petersburg: Akademia russkogo baleta imeni A. Ia. Vaganova, 2014).

—— *Peterburgskii balet. Tri veka. Khronika. Tom III. 1851–1900* (St Petersburg: Akademia russkogo baleta imeni A. Ia. Vaganova, 2015).

Ezhegodnik Imperatorskikh teatrov [The Yearbook of Imperial Theatres] (St Petersburg, 1890–1915).

Fedorov, Vasilii, *Repertuar Bol'shogo teatra SSSR 1776–1955*, 2 vols. (New York: Norman Ross Publishing, 2001).

Sokolov, A., *Teatral'nyi al'manakh na 1875* [Theatrical Almanac for 1875] (St Petersburg, 1875).

Vol'f, A., *Khronika peterburgskikh teatrov s kontsa 1826 do nachala 1881* [Chronicle of the Petersburg Theatres from the End of 1826 to the Beginning of 1881], 3 parts (St Petersburg, 1877–1884).

Zarubin, V. I., *Bol'shoi teatr. Pervye postanovki baletov na russkoi stsene 1825–1997* [The Bol'shoi Theatre. The First Productions of Ballets on the Russian Stage] (Moscow: Ellis Luck, 1998).

Zozulina, Nataliia (ed.), *Peterburgskii balet. Tri veka. Khronika. Tom 1. XVIII vek* (St Petersburg: Akademia russkogo baleta imeni A. Ia. Vaganova, 2014).

Zozulina, Nataliia, and Mironova, V. (eds.), *Peterburgskii balet. Tri veka. Xronika. Tom IV. 1901–1950* (St Petersburg: Akademia russkogo baleta imeni A. Ia. Vaganova, 2015).

—— *Peterburgskii balet. Tri veka. Xronika. Tom V. 1951–1975* (St Petersburg: Akademia russkogo baleta imeni A. Ia. Vaganova, 2016).

—— *Peterburgskii balet. Tri veka. Xronika. Tom VI. 1976–2000* (St Petersburg: Akademia russkogo baleta imeni A. Ia. Vaganova, 2017).

Brussels

Almanach des spectacles pour l'an 1822 [Almanac of Stage Productions for the Year 1822] (Paris: J-N Barba, 1822).

Almanach royal de la Cour, des Provinces méridoniales, et de la Ville du Bruxelles [Royal Almanac of the Court, of the Southern Provinces, and of the City of Brussels], 15 vols., 1816–1830 (Brussels: Adolphe Stapleaux); consulted online: https://books.google.co.uk/.

Almanach théâtral, ou Résumé des représentations données sur le Théâtre royal de Bruxelles [Theatre Almanac, or a Summary of the Performances Given at the Theatre Royal of Brussels], *16 May 1824* (Bruxelles: Gambier, 1825).

Paris

Annales de la propriété industrielle, artistique, et littéraire [Annals of Industrial, Artistic and Literary Property], ed. J. Pataille, vol. 7 (Paris, 1861).

Revue des grands procès contemporains. Tome VI. Année 1888 [Review of Important Contemporary Trials] (Paris: Chevalier-Marescq et cie, 1888).

New York

Odell, George, *Annals of the New York Stage*, vol. 4 (1834–1843) (New York: Columbia University Press, 1928).

SECONDARY SOURCES

ALIANSKII, IURII, *Uveselitel'nye zavedeniia starogo Peterburga* [Places for Leisure in Old Petersburg] (St Petersburg: Avrora, 2003).

ARKIN, LISA. C., and SMITH, MARIAN, 'National Dance in the Romantic Ballet', in Lynn Garafola (ed.), *Rethinking the Sylph: New Perspectives on the Romantic Ballet* (Hanover and London: Wesleyan University Press, 1997), 11–68.

BAKHRUSHIN, IURII, *Istoriia russkogo baleta* [History of Russian Ballet] (Moscow: Prosveshchenie, 1977).

BALANCHINE, GEORGE, and MASON, FRANCIS, *Balanchine's Festival of Ballet*, 2 vols. (New York: Doubleday, 1954); British edition (London: W. H. Allen, 1978).

BARTLETT, ROSAMUND, *Wagner and Russia* (Cambridge: Cambridge University Press, 1995).

—— *Chekhov: Scenes from a Life* (London: Simon & Schuster, 2004; repr., 2005).

BEAUMONT, CYRIL W., *The Ballet Called 'Giselle'* (London: C. W. Beaumont, 1944).

—— *The Ballet Called 'Swan Lake'* (New York: Dance Horizons, 1982).

—— *Complete Book of Ballets: A Guide to the Principal Ballets of the Nineteenth and Twentieth Centuries* (London: Putnam, 1937; rev. ed., 1949).

—— *A History of Ballet in Russia (1613–1881)* (London: C. W. Beaumont, 1930).

BELOVA, E. P., and others (eds.), *Russkii balet: Entsiklopediia* [Russian Ballet: Encylopaedia] (Moscow: Soglasie, 1997).

BOGLACHEVA, IRINA, *Artisty Sankt-Peterburgskogo baleta. XIX Vek* [Artists of the St Petersburg Ballet. XIX Century] (St Petersburg: Chistyi list, 2015).

BORISOGLEBSKII, MIKHAIL (ed.), *Materialy po istorii russkogo baleta* [Materials relating to the History of Russian Ballet], 2 vols. (Leningrad: Leningrad State Choreographic School, 1939).

BUCKLE, RICHARD, *Diaghilev* (London: Weidenfeld and Nicolson, 1979); repr. (London: Hamish Hamilton, 1984).

BURGESS, M. A. S., 'The Early Theatre,' in Robert Auty and Dimitri Obolensky (eds.), *An Introduction to Russian Language and Literature*, vol. 2, *Companion to Russian Studies* (Cambridge: Cambridge University Press, 1977), 231–46.

BURLAKA, IURII, and LEONOVA, MARINA (eds.), *Balety M. I. Petipa v Moskve* (Moscow: Progress-traditsiia, 2018).

CANOVA-GREEN, MARIE-CLAUDE, 'Dance and Ritual: The *Ballet des nations* at the Court of Louis XIII', *Renaissance Studies*, 9/4 (1995), 395–403.

CHAZIN-BENNAHUM, JUDITH, *The Lure of Perfection* (New York and London: Routledge, 2005).

CLARKE, MARY, and CRISP, CLEMENT, *Ballet* (London: A. and C. Black, 1973; repr. 1978).

COHEN, SELMA JEANNE (ed.), *International Encyclopedia of Dance*, 6 vols. (Oxford and New York: Oxford University Press, 1998; paperback repr. 2004).

CRAINE, DEBRA, and MACKRELL, JUDITH (eds.), *Oxford Dictionary of Dance* (Oxford: Oxford University Press, 2000).

DETCHEVERRY, ARNAUD, *Histoires des théâtres de Bordeaux depuis leur origine dans cette ville jusqu'à nos jours* [The Histories of Theatres in Bordeaux from Their Beginnings in this City up to the Present Day] (Bordeaux, 1890).

DURYLIN, S., *N. M. Radin* (Moscow, Leningrad: Iskusstvo, 1941).

EGLEVSKY, ANDRÉ, and GREGORY, JOHN (eds.), *Heritage of a Ballet Master: Nicolas Legat* (London: Dance Books, 1978).

FABER, FRÉDÉRIC, *Histoire du théâtre français en Belgique*, 5 vols. (Paris and Brussels, 1878–1880).

FEDORCHENKO, OL'GA, SMIRNOV, IU., and FOMKIN, A. (eds.), *Baletmeister Marius Petipa. Stat'i, issledovaniia, razmyshleniia* [The Ballet Master Marius Petipa: Articles, Investigations, Reflections] (Vladimir: Foliant, 2006).

FIGES, ORLANDO, *Natasha's Dance* (London: Penguin Books, 2003).

FRAME, MURRAY, *The St. Petersburg Imperial Theaters: Stage and State in Revolutionary Russia, 1900–1920* (Jefferson, NC, and London: McFarland & Company, 2000; repr. 2009).

—— *School for Citizens: Theatre and Civil Society in Imperial Russia* (New Haven and London: Yale University Press, 2006).

FROLOVA-WALKER, MARINA, 'Grand Opera in Russia: Fragments of an Unwritten History', in David Charlton (ed.), *The Cambridge Companion to Grand Opera* (Cambridge: Cambridge University Press, 2003), 344–67.

—— *Russian Music and Nationalism: From Glinka to Stalin* (New Haven and London: Yale University Press, 2007).

GAEVSKII, VADIM, *Dom Petipa* [The House of Petipa] (Moscow: Artist. Rezhisser. Teatr, 2000).

GARAFOLA, LYNN, *Diaghilev's Ballets Russes* (New York, Oxford: Oxford University Press, 1989).

GUEST, IVOR, *The Ballet of the Second Empire*; 3rd ed. (London: Pitman Publishing, 1974).

—— *The Divine Virginia: A Biography of Virginia Zucchi* (New York: Marcel Dekker Inc., 1977).

—— *Fanny Elssler* (London: A&C Black, 1970).

—— (ed.), *La Fille mal gardée* (London: The Dancing Times, 1960).

—— *Jules Perrot: Master of the Romantic Ballet* (London: Dance Books, 1984).

—— *The Romantic Ballet in Paris*; rev. ed. (Alton: Dance Books, 2008).

GUROVA, IANINA, *Ivan Aleksandrovich Vsevolozhkii i ego znachenie v istorii russkogo muzykal'nogo teatra* [Ivan Alexandrovich Vsevolozhsky and His Significance in the History of Russian Lyric Theatre] (St Petersburg, 2015).

HALL, CORYNE, *Imperial Dancer: Mathilde Kschessinska and the Romanovs* (Stroud, UK: Sutton Publishing, 2005).

HOMANS, JENNIFER, *Apollo's Angels* (London: Granta, 2010).

IAKOVLEV, M., *Baletmeister Marius Petipa* (Leningrad: P. P. Soikin, 1924).

IAKOVLEVA, IULIIA, *Sozdateli i zriteli. Russkie balety epokhi shedevrov* [Creators and Spectators. Russian Ballets in the Era of Masterpieces] (Moscow: Novoe literaturnoe obozrenie, 2017).

IL'ICHEVA, MARINA, *Neizvestnyi Petipa* [The Unknown Petipa] (St Petersburg: Kompozitor, 2015).

ISNARDON, JACQUES, *Le Théâtre de la Monnaie depuis sa fondation jusqu'à nos jours* [The Monnaie Theatre from Its Foundation up to the Present Day] (Brussels: Schott, 1890).

IVANOV, I., and IVANOV, K., *Marius Ivanovich Petipa 1822–1922: K stoletiiu dnia rozhdeniia* [Marius Petipa […]: For the Centenary of His Birth] (Petrograd, 1922).

KANT, MARION (ed.), *The Cambridge Companion to Ballet* (Cambridge: Cambridge University Press, 2007).

KELLY, LAURENCE (ed.), *Moscow: A Traveller's Companion* (London: Constable and Co., 1983); repr. (London: Robinson, 2004).

KOEGLER, HORST (ed.), *The Concise Oxford Dictionary of Ballet*, 2nd ed. (Oxford and New York: Oxford University Press, 1987).

KRASOVSKAIA, VERA, 'Marius Petipa and *The Sleeping Beauty*', trans. Cynthia Read, *Dance Perspectives*, 49 (Spring 1972).

—— *Russkii baletnyi teatr ot vozniknoveniia do serediny XIX veka* [Russian Ballet Theatre from the Beginning to the Middle of the Nineteenth Century] (Leningrad and Moscow: Iskusstvo, 1958); repr. (St Petersburg: Planeta muzyki, 2008).

—— *Russkii baletnyi teatr vtoroi poloviny XIX veka* [Russian Ballet Theatre of the Second Half of the Nineteenth Century] (Leningrad and Moscow: Iskusstvo, 1963); repr. (St Petersburg: Planeta muzyki, 2008).

KUZOVLEVA, TATIANA, 'Inostrantsy i formirovanie russkogo baletnogo teatr' ['Foreigners and the Formation of Russian Ballet Theatre'], in G. A. Lapkina (ed.), *Teatral'nyi Peterburg: Interkul'turnaia model'* [Theatrical Petersburg: An Intercultural Model] (St Petersburg: Sankt-Peterburgskaia gosudarstvennaia akademiia teatral'nogo iskusstva, 2002), 32–44.

LATREYTE, JEAN, *Le Grand Théâtre de Bordeaux: Des scènes dans la pierre* [The Grand Theatre of Bordeaux: Stages in Stone] (Bordeaux, 1977).

LEACH, ROBERT, and BOROVSKY, VICTOR (eds.), *A History of Russian Theatre* (Cambridge: Cambridge University Press, 1999).

LESHKOV, DENIS, *Marius Petipa (1822–1910): K stoletiiu ego rozhdeniia* [Marius Petipa 1822–1910: For the Centenary of His Birth] (Petrograd, 1922).

MAHLET, DAMIEN, 'The First *Nutcracker*, the Enchantment of International Relations, and the Franco-Russian Alliance', *Dance Research*, 34/2 (Winter 2016), 119–49.

MAKARUKHINA, NATALIA, *Gurzuf: Pervaia zhemchuzhina iuzhnogo berega Kryma* [Gurzuf: The Pearl of the Southern Coast of Crimea] (Simferopol: Business Inform, 2010).

Melani, Pascale (ed.), 'De la France à la Russie, Marius Petipa' [From France to Russia], *Slavica Occitania* 43 (2016).

Moore, Lillian, *Echoes of American Ballet: A Collection of Seventeen Articles*, ed. Ivor Guest (New York: Dance Horizons, 1976).

—— 'The Petipa Family in Europe and America', *Dance Index*, 1/5 (May 1942), 72–84.

Morrison, Simon, *Bolshoi Confidential: Secrets of the Russian Ballet from the Rule of the Tsars to Today* (London: 4th Estate, 2016).

Percival, John, 'Don Quixote', *Dance Now*, 6/2 (Summer 1997), 2–7.

—— *The World of Diaghilev* (London: Studio Vista, 1971).

Poesio, Giannandrea (ed.), *To and by Enrico Cecchetti* (Novi Ligure: Edizioni Joker, 2010).

Racster, Olga, *The Master of the Russian Ballet: The Memoirs of Cav. Enrico Cecchetti* (London: Hutchinson, 1922).

Raymonda Programme Booklet (Milano: Edizione del Teatro alla Scala, 2011).

Riasanovsky, Nicholas, *Nicholas I and Official Nationality in Russian, 1825–1855* (Berkeley and Los Angeles: University of California Press, 1959).

——, and Steinberg, Mark D., *A History of Russia* (New York and Oxford: Oxford University Press, 2005).

Rogger, Hans, *National Consciousness in Eighteenth-Century Russia* (Cambridge, MA, 1960).

Roné, Elvira, *Olga Preobrazhenskaya*, trans. and ed. Fernau Hall (New York and Basel: Marcel Dekker, 1978).

Roslavleva, Natalia, *Era of the Russian Ballet 1770–1965* (London: Victor Gollancz, 1966).

Scholl, Tim, *From Petipa to Balanchine* (London and New York: Routledge, 1994).

—— *'Sleeping Beauty', a Legend in Progress* (New Haven and London: Yale University Press, 2004).

Slonimskii, Iu., 'Marius Petipa', trans. Anatole Chujoy, *Dance Index*, 6 (May–June 1947), 100–142.

Smith, Douglas, *The Pearl* (New Haven and London: Yale University Press, 2009).

Smith, Marian, *Ballet and Opera in the Age of Giselle* (Princeton and Oxford: Princeton University Press, 2000).

—— (ed.), *La Sylphide: Paris 1832 and Beyond* (Alton: Dance Books, 2012).

——, and Fullington, Doug, 'Giselle's Seattle Revival', *Dancing Times* (June 2011), 30–33.

Souritz, Elizabeth, *Balet moskovskogo Bol'shogo teatra vo vtoroi polovine XIX veka* [The Ballet of the Moscow Bolshoi Theatre in the Second Half of the Nineteenth Century] (Moscow: Muzizdat, 2012).

—— 'Moscow v Petersburg: The Ballet Master Alexis Bogdanov and Others', Paper at the International Symposium of Russian Ballet, Harriman Institute, New York, 2007.

——, and BELOVA, E. (eds.), *Baletmeister A. A. Gorskii. Materialy. Vospominaniia. Stat'i* [Ballet Master A. A. Gorskii. Documents. Reminiscences. Articles] (St Petersburg: Dmitrii Bulanin, 2000).

SVESHNIKOVA, ALISA, *Peterburgskie sezony Artura Sen-Léona (1859–70)* [The Petersburg Seasons of Arthur Saint-Léon] (St Petersburg: Baltiiskie Sezony, 2008).

SWIFT, MARY GRACE, *A Loftier Flight: The Life and Accomplishments of Charles-Louis Didelot, Balletmaster* (Middletown, CT: Wesleyan University Press; London: Pitman Publishing, 1974).

VAN AELBROUCK, JEAN-PHILIPPE, *Dictionnaire des danseurs à Bruxelles de 1600 à 1830* (Liège: Pierre Mardaga, 1994).

VOLKOV, SOLOMON, *St Petersburg: A Cultural History*, trans. Antonina W. Bouis; 2nd ed. (New York: Simon & Schuster, 1997).

WELLES, JACQUES D', *Le Grand Théâtre de Bordeaux: Naissance et vie d'un chef-d'oeuvre* [The Grand Theatre of Bordeaux: Birth and Life of a Masterpiece] (Bordeaux: Delmas, 1949).

WILEY, ROLAND JOHN, *A Century of Russian Ballet: Documents and Eye Witness Accounts, 1810–1910* (Oxford: Clarendon Press, 1990); repr. (Alton: Dance Books, 2007).

—— 'A Context for Petipa', Dance Research: The Journal of the Society for Dance Research, 21 (Summer 2003), 42–52.

—— 'Dances from Russia: An Introduction to the Sergeyev Collection', *Harvard Library Bulletin*, 24 (January 1976).

—— *The Life and Ballets of Lev Ivanov* (Oxford: Clarendon Press, 1997).

—— 'On Meaning in *Nutcracker*', *Dance Research*, 3/1 (1984), 12–18.

—— *Tchaikovsky's Ballets: Swan Lake, Sleeping Beauty, Nutcracker* (Oxford: Clarendon Press, 1985; repr. 2003).

WORTMAN, RICHARD S., *Scenarios of Power: Myth and Ceremony in Russian Monarchy*, 2 vols. (Princeton: Princeton University Press, 1999).

Index

All titles refer to ballets, unless otherwise indicated. Where possible, the date of a ballet's Russian premiere is given as well as the date of its creation. I have also tried to give the dates of Jean Petipa's versions of existing ballets.

Dates, however, are not included for Marius Petipa's work, since they are detailed in the List of Works.

There are no entries for the endnotes, although in an ideal world they would have been included. However, the appended List of Works is included, but only for references to ballets (not operas), ballet masters, dancers, composers and, occasionally, librettists.